AUGUSTUS

EDINBURGH READINGS ON THE ANCIENT WORLD

GENERAL EDITORS
Michele George, *McMaster University*
Thomas Harrison, *University of Liverpool*

ADVISORY EDITORS
Paul Cartledge, *University of Cambridge*
Richard Saller, *Stanford University*

This series introduces English-speaking students to central themes in the history of the ancient world and to the range of scholarly approaches to those themes, within and across disciplines. Each volume, edited and introduced by a leading specialist, contains a selection of the most important work, including a significant proportion of translated material. The editor also provides a guide to the history of modern scholarship on the subject. Passages in ancient languages are translated; technical terms, ancient and modern, are explained.

PUBLISHED

Sparta
Edited by Michael Whitby

Sex and Difference in Ancient Greece and Rome
Edited by Mark Golden and Peter Toohey

Greeks and Barbarians
Edited by Thomas Harrison

The Ancient Economy
Edited by Walter Scheidel and Sitta von Reden

Roman Religion
Edited by Clifford Ando

Athenian Democracy
Edited by P. J. Rhodes

The Athenian Empire
Edited by Polly Low

Augustus
Edited by Jonathan Edmondson

Greek Athletics
Edited by Jason König

AUGUSTUS

Edited by
Jonathan Edmondson

EDINBURGH UNIVERSITY PRESS

© in this edition Edinburgh University Press, 2009, 2014
© in the individual contributions is retained by the authors

Edinburgh University Press Ltd
The Tun – Holyrood Road, 12(2f) Jackson's Entry,
Edinburgh EH8 8PJ

www.euppublishing.com

First published in hardback by Edinburgh University Press 2009

Typeset in Sabon
by Norman Tilley Graphics Ltd, Northampton

A CIP record for this book is available from the British Library

ISBN 978 0 7486 1594 0 (hardback)
ISBN 978 0 7486 1595 7 (paperback)
ISBN 978 0 7486 9538 6 (epub)

The right of the contributors
to be identified as authors of this work
has been asserted in accordance with the
Copyright, Designs and Patents Act 1988,
and the Copyright and Related Rights
Regulations 2003 (SI No. 2498).

Published with the support of the Edinburgh University
Scholarly Publishing Initiatives Fund.

Contents

Illustrations	vii
Acknowledgments	xii
Note to the Reader	xiv
Abbreviations	xvi
Map of the Roman Empire, c. AD 14	xxx

Introduction: Approaching the Age of Augustus 1

PART I THE *NOVUS STATUS*: FROM *III VIR REI PUBLICAE CONSTITUENDAE* TO *PRINCEPS*

Introduction to Part I 33

1. Imperator Caesar: A Study in Nomenclature 40
   Ronald Syme

2. Triumvirate and Principate 60
   Fergus Millar

3. The Powers of Augustus 90
   Jean-Louis Ferrary, trans. Jonathan Edmondson

4. Augustus, War and Peace 137
   J. W. Rich

5. Livia and the Womanhood of Rome 165
   Nicholas Purcell

PART II *RES PUBLICA RESTITUTA*

Introduction to Part II 197

6. The Political Significance of Augustus' Military Reforms 203
   Kurt A. Raaflaub

7	The Administrative Reforms of Augustus: Pragmatism or Systematic Planning? *Werner Eck, trans. Claus Nader*	229
8	Family and Inheritance in the Augustan Marriage Laws *Andrew Wallace-Hadrill*	250
9	To Honour the *Princeps* and Venerate the Gods: Public Cult, Neighbourhood Cults, and Imperial Cult in Augustan Rome *John Scheid, trans. Jonathan Edmondson*	275

PART III IMAGES OF POWER AND THE POWER OF IMAGES

	Introduction to Part III	303
10	Monuments of the Battle of Actium: Propaganda and Response *Tonio Hölscher, trans. Claus Nader*	310
11	*Meretrix regina*: Augustan Cleopatras *Maria Wyke*	334
12	Cybele, Virgil and Augustus *T. P. Wiseman*	381
13	Livy, Augustus, and the Forum Augustum *T. J. Luce*	399

PART IV THE IMPACT OF AUGUSTUS IN THE ROMAN PROVINCES

	Introduction to Part IV	419
14	Colonia Augusta Emerita, Capital of Lusitania *Walter Trillmich, trans. Claus Nader*	427
15	The Cities of the Greek World under Augustus *Glen Bowersock*	468
	Chronology	483
	Glossary	494
	Guide to Further Reading	503
	Bibliography	509
	Index	531

Illustrations

Map of the Roman Empire, *c.* AD 14	xxx
Fig. 3.1 Aureus of Octavian, 28 BC. Obverse: Head of Octavian, with laurel wreath. IMP. CAESAR DIVI F. COS. VI. Reverse: Octavian, sitting on *sella curulis*, with a scroll in his r. hand. LEGES ET IVRA P R RESTITVIT ("He restored the laws and rights of the Roman people"). British Museum, London. (Photo © Trustees of the British Museum)	92
Fig. 9.1 Map of cult places in and near Rome. 1. Periphery; 2. Urban centre	283
Figs 10.1 and 10.2 Frieze with naval trophies and priestly emblems, Rome. Musei Capitolini, Rome. (Photo: DAI-Rome, neg. 31.657-658)	315
Fig. 10.3 Frieze from the Temple of the Deified Iulius, Rome. Antiquario forense, Rome. (Photo: DAI-Rome, neg. 63.1230)	316
Figs 10.4 and 10.5 Sections from the frieze of the Temple of Apollo *in circo* (Apollo Sosianus), Rome. Centrale Montemartini, Musei Capitolini, Rome. (Photo: DAI-Rome, neg. 71.45 and 60.1252)	320
Fig. 10.6 Neo-Attic relief with Victory and a trophy. Museo Nazionale delle Terme, Rome. (Photo: museum)	321
Fig. 10.7 Neo-Attic relief with Victory, a trophy, and a warrior. Musée du Louvre, Paris. (Photo: M. Chuzeville, Paris)	322
Fig. 10.8 Terracotta roof-tile with naval trophy. Akademisches Kunstmuseum, Bonn. (Photo: J. Schubert, Archäologisches Institut und Akademisches Kunstmuseum, Universität Bonn, neg. 07-2307)	325
Fig. 10.9 Terracotta roof-tile with Victory and Capricorns. Private collection, Heidelberg. (Photo: H. Vögele, Heidelberg)	326

Fig. 10.10 Sardonyx cameo with Neptune/Octavian on a chariot drawn by sea-horses. Museum of Fine Arts, Boston. (Photo: museum)   327

Fig. 10.11 Cameo with Augustus in a *quadriga* drawn by Tritons. Kunsthistorisches Museum, Vienna. (Photo: museum)   328

Fig. 10.12 Gemstone with Neptune/Octavian. Kestner Museum, Hannover. (Photo: museum)   329

Fig. 10.13 Arretine vase with Apollo and Victory. Museum of Fine Arts, Boston. (Photo: museum)   330

Fig. 10.14 Oil-lamp with Victory on a globe. Vindonissa Museum, Brugg (Switzerland). (Photo: after A. Leibundgut, *Die römischen Lampen in der Schweiz*, Berne: Francke, 1977, fig. 23.3)   331

Fig. 10.15 Oil-lamp with Victory and *clipeus virtutis* (shield of virtue). Carthage: Musée de Carthage. (Photo: after T. Hölscher, *Victoria romana*, Mainz: P. von Zabern, 1967, pl. 13.2)   332

Fig. 11.1 Cleopatra's bronze coinage from Cyprus, dated *c.* 47–30 BC. British Museum, London. (Photo © The Trustees of the British Museum)   340

Fig. 11.2 Silver denarius of Antony, dated *c.* 32 BC. British Museum, London. (Photo © The Trustees of the British Museum)   352

Fig. 11.3 Coin issued to celebrate the Actian victory. British Museum, London. (Photo © The Trustees of the British Museum)   363

Fig. 11.4 Coin issued in celebration of the capture of Egypt, dated *c.* 28–27 BC. British Museum, London. (Photo © The Trustees of the British Museum)   364

Fig. 11.5 Coin issued in celebration of Julius Caesar's Gallic victories, dated *c.* 48 BC. British Museum, London. (Photo © The Trustees of the British Museum)   366

Fig. 11.6 Coin marking Julius Caesar's victories in Gaul, dated *c.* 48 BC. British Museum, London. (Photo © The Trustees of the British Museum)   367

Fig. 11.7 Statue of Augustus from Prima Porta, detail of cuirass. Vatican Museums. (Photo: Alinari/Art Resource NY: ART 130614)   369

Fig. 11.8 Detail of breastplate of statue of Augustus from Prima Porta. Vatican Museums. (Photo: DAI-Rome neg. 37.744)   370

Fig. 12.1 Sketch-map of central Rome and the western corner of the Palatine in the time of Augustus (T. P. Wiseman)   391

Fig. 12.2 The Gemma Augustea. Kunsthistorisches Museum, Vienna. (Photo: museum)   396

Fig. 13.1 View of the Forum Augustum, Rome, with the Temple of Mars Ultor and part of the exedra of the portico on the south-east side. (Photo: J. Edmondson)   400

Fig. 13.2 Plan of the Forum Augustum, with a proposed reconstruction of its sculptural programme. (After P. Zanker, *Forum Augustum*. Tübingen, c. 1968.)   401

Fig. 14.1 1 [= Taf. 22.1]. Silver denarius, issued by P. Carisius (*BMC* I no. 279 & plate 5.3). British Museum, London. (Photo © The Trustees of the British Museum); 2 [= Taf. 22.2]. Silver denarius, issued by P. Carisius (*BMC* I no. 280 & plate 5.4). British Museum, London. (Photo © The Trustees of the British Museum); 3 [= Taf. 22.3]. Silver denarius issued by P. Carisius (*BMC* I no. 286 & plate 5.7). British Museum, London. (Photo © The Trustees of the British Museum); 4 [= Taf. 22.4]. Silver denarius issued by P. Carisius (*BMC* I no. 287 & plate 5.8). British Museum, London. (Photo © The Trustees of the British Museum); 5 [= Taf. 22.5]. Silver quinarius issued by P. Carisius (*BMC* I no. 295 & plate 5.14). British Museum, London. (Photo © The Trustees of the British Museum); 6 [= Taf. 22.6]. Silver denarius issued by P. Carisius (*BMC* I no. 288 & plate 5.9). British Museum, London. (Photo © The Trustees of the British Museum)   430

7 [= Taf. 22.7]. Silver denarius issued by Octavian, c. 29–28 BC. Obv. Octavian; rev. Venus (*BMC* I no. 599 & plate 14.16). British Museum, London. (Photo © The Trustees of the British Museum); 8 [= Taf. 22.8]. Silver denarius issued by Octavian, c. 29–28 BC. Obv. Octavian; rev. Victory (*BMC* I no. 602 & plate 14.18). British Museum, London. (Photo © The Trustees of the British Museum); 9 [= Taf. 22.9]. Silver denarius issued by Octavian, c. 29–28 BC. Obv. Octavian; rev. Pax (*BMC* I no. 605 & plate 15.2). British Museum, London. (Photo © The Trustees of the British Museum); 10 [= Taf. 22.10]. Silver denarius issued by Octavian,c. 29–28 BC. Obv. head of Mars; rev. shield with *sidus Iulium* (*BMC* I no. 644 & Plate 15.18). British Museum, London. (Photo © The Trustees of the British Museum); 11 [= Taf. 22.11].

Gold aureus issued by Octavian. Obv. head of Diana; rev. naval trophy on a prow within a tetrastyle temple (*BMC* I no. 643 & plate 15.14). British Museum, London. (Photo © The Trustees of the British Museum);

12 [= Taf. 22.12]. Silver denarius issued byOctavian. Obv. head of Apollo; rev. priest with oxen ploughing *sulcus primigenius* (*BMC* I no. 638 = plate 15.17). British Museum, London. (Photo © The Trustees of the British Museum)   432

13 [= Taf. 22.13]. Bronze *as* issued by local mint at Emerita, after 2 BC. (*RPC* I, Emerita, no. 6). British Museum, London. (Photo © The Trustees of the British Museum);

14 [= Taf. 22.14]. Bronze *as* issued by local mint at Emerita, after 2 BC. (*RPC* I, Emerita, no. 11). British Museum, London. (Photo © The Trustees of the British Museum)   433

Fig. 14.2a–b Plans of Emerita (courtesy of the Consorcio de la Ciudad Monumental de Mérida)   434, 435

Fig. 14.3 [= Taf. 5h] Bridge over the river Anas (Guadiana). (Photo: G. Fittschen-Badura)   436

Fig. 14.4a [= Taf. 8a] Orchestra of the theatre, Emerita. Dedicatory inscription set up by M. Agrippa over the *aditus maximus*, 16 BC. (Photo: J. Edmondson)   440

Fig. 14.4b [= Taf. 23e] Theatre, Emerita: north entrance to the orchestra with the remains of a dedicatory inscription set up by Agrippa, 16–15 BC. (Photo: G. Fittschen-Badura)   440

Fig. 14.5a–b (= Taf. 23f–g] Amphitheatre, Emerita: dedicatory inscriptions set up by Augustus, 8/7 BC. (Photos: (a) J. Edmondson; (b) G. Fittschen-Badura)   441

Fig. 14.6a [= Taf. 24a] So-called "Temple of Diana," Emerita. (Photo: G. Fittschen-Badura)   442

Fig. 14.6b [= Taf. 24b] Detail of the corner of the "rostra" in front of the "Temple of Diana." (Photo: J. Edmondson)   442

Fig. 14.7a–b [= Taf. 24c] Colossal statues of an emperor found near the "Temple of Diana." Museo Arqueológico Provincial, Sevilla. (Photo: DAI-Madrid: P. Witte); Museo Nacional de Arte Romano, Mérida. (Photo: museum, M. de la Barrera)   443

Fig. 14.8a–c [replacing Taf. 25a–f] *Clipei* with heads of Jupiter Ammon and Medusa from the "marble forum." Museo Nacional de Arte Romano, Mérida. (Photos: museum, M. de la Barrera)   451

Fig. 14.9a [= Taf. 26c], 9b–c [replacing Taf. 26d] Caryatids

from the "marble forum." Museo Nacional de Arte
Romano, Mérida. (Photos: museum, M. de la Barrera)   454

Fig. 14.10 [= Fig. 77] Reconstruction of Caryatid from the
"marble forum." (Line-drawing: U. Städtler)   455

Fig. 14.11 [= Taf. 28c] Statue of a man ("Agrippa" statue)
from the "marble forum." Museo Nacional de Arte
Romano, Mérida. (Photo: G. Fittschen-Badura)   457

Fig. 14.12 Reconstruction of the statue-group of Aeneas
(centre), Ascanius (left) and Anchises (right) from the
"marble forum." (Photo: courtesy of Museo Nacional de
Arte Romano, Mérida, based on a drawing by W. Trillmich,
U. Städtler, and T. Nogales Basarrate)   458

Fig. 14.13a [= Taf. 28b] Togate statue from the "marble
forum." Museo Nacional de Arte Romano, Mérida.
(Photo: J. Edmondson)   459

Fig. 14.13b [= Taf. 28a] Togate statue probably belonging
to the "marble forum." Museo Nacional de Arte Romano,
Mérida. (Photo: museum)   459

Fig. 14.14a–b [= Taf. 48a–b] Cuirassed statues decorated
with trophy-carrying centaurs from the theatre. Museo
Nacional de Arte Romano, Mérida. (Photos:
G. Fittschen-Badura)   462

Fig. 14.15a [= Taf. 29a] Male limestone portrait (originally
stuccoed?) from Emerita. Museo Nacional de Arte
Romano, Mérida. (Photo: G. Fittschen-Badura)   463

Fig. 14.15b [= Taf. 29b] Male marble portrait, Emerita.
Museo Nacional de Arte Romano, Mérida. (Photo:
G. Fittschen-Badura)   463

Acknowledgments

For permission to reprint the essays in this volume, I should like to thank the following: Fergus Millar (Chapters 1 and 2); Franz Steiner Verlag (Chapter 1); the Society for the Promotion of Roman Studies and the University of North Carolina Press (Chapter 2); Jean-Louis Ferrary and the Centre Gustave Glotz (Chapter 3); John Rich, Lukas de Blois, and E. J. Brill Publishers (Chapter 4); Nicholas Purcell (Chapter 5); the Cambridge Philological Society (Chapters 5 and 8); Kurt Raaflaub and Archaeopress (Chapter 6); Werner Eck and Friedrich Reinhardt Verlag (Chapter 7); Andrew Wallace-Hadrill (Chapter 8); John Scheid and Presses universitaires de Rennes (Chapter 9); Tonio Hölscher and Akademie Verlag (Chapter 10); Maria Wyke and Gerald Duckworth & Co. Ltd (Chapter 11); Peter Wiseman and Cambridge University Press (Chapter 12); T. J. Luce and the University of California Press (Chapter 13); Walter Trillmich and the Bayerische Akademie der Wissenschaften (Chapter 14); and Glen Bowersock and Oxford University Press (Chapter 15).

For photographs and permission to reproduce images, I am very grateful to the Musei Vaticani, the Musei Capitolini, the Soprintendenza per i Beni Archeologici di Roma, the Musée du Louvre, the Kestner Museum (Hannover), the Institut für Kunstgeschichte und Archäologie of the Rheinische Friedrich-Wilhelms-Universität Bonn, the Vindonissa Museum, the Kunsthistorisches Museum (Vienna), the Museo Nacional de Arte Romano (Mérida) and its Director Dr J. M. Álvarez Martínez, the Consorcio de la Ciudad Monumental de Mérida and its Research Director, Dr P. Mateos Cruz, the Delegación Provincial de Cultura of the Junta de Andalucía and the Museo Arqueológico Provincial de Sevilla, the British Museum, the Museum of Fine Arts (Boston), Art Resource (New York), and the Rome and Madrid departments of the Deutsches Archäologisches Institut.

I should also like to thank Donna Bilak, who so expertly drew the map of the Roman Empire. I am extremely grateful to Claus Nader for his translations of the articles by W. Eck, T. Hölscher, and W. Trillmich, and to him, William Den Hollander, Tommaso Leoni, and Meggie MacDonald for various kinds of assistance in the preparation of this volume. Clifford Ando, Christer Bruun, Michele George, Ben Kelly, and James Rives generously provided very useful comments on the introductory material, and I am very grateful for the collegiality and cooperation shown by Jean-Louis Ferrary, Werner Eck, John Scheid, Tonio Hölscher, and Walter Trillmich during the process of revising the translations of their chapters. I should like to thank Michele George and Tom Harrison for inviting me to contribute this volume to the Edinburgh Readings on the Ancient World series and for their patience over the time it has taken to bring it to completion.

For Edinburgh University Press Fiona Sewell edited the manuscript with great skill and efficiency, while James Dale, John Davey, Carol Macdonald, Máiréad McElligott, and Esmé Watson have all been extremely helpful and encouraging throughout the preparation and production of the volume. Finally, I should like to thank my family for their patience and support during the writing and editing of this work. We have all lived with Augustus for far longer than we ever imagined.

Note to the Reader

The articles and excerpts from books that are to be found in this volume were originally published in a wide variety of journals, collections of essays, and books, and some of them (for instance, Chapters 2, 6, 7, and 11) have been published in more than one version. For the sake of clarity, the more obscure abbreviations have been modified to bring them more into line with those used in the other chapters, but according to the editorial principles of the series, the essays have been left as far as possible in their original format, which will explain the eclectic styles used in the citation of the ancient evidence and the scholarly literature.

Again in line with the aims of the series, all quotations from Latin and Greek have been translated into English and placed within square brackets. Unless otherwise stated, all translations are my own. In a number of cases quotations in the original languages have been eliminated and replaced with an English translation of the quotation, and in certain articles some of the footnotes have been eliminated or abbreviated to keep the volume within reasonable bounds. During consultation with the authors regarding the translation of their articles, Jean-Louis Ferrary and Werner Eck have made a number of slight modifications to the original texts, while Nicholas Purcell and Walter Trillmich have added brief postscripts. As editor, I have tacitly corrected a few small typographical and other errors that I have noticed in the original versions.

Explanatory glosses for some of the less familiar technical terms have been provided within square brackets. A number of the most important terms are explained in the Glossary that appears at the end of the volume. For the reader's convenience, full lists of abbreviations of all ancient texts, modern collections, books, and journals, and Roman *praenomina* (first names) have been provided on pp. xvi–xxviii.

The final bibliography contains works referred to by the editor.

In Chapter 14 (by W. Trillmich) a number of the many illustrations that appeared in the original German version of this chapter have had to be omitted. This has been done in full consultation and cooperation with the author. In this instance, a few new images replace those used in the original version, to take account of some important discoveries made since the article was first published in 1990. I have also added photographs of the important new aureus of Octavian from 28 BC in Chapter 3 (by J.-L. Ferrary) and of the Forum Augustum in Rome in Chapter 13 (by T. J. Luce).

Abbreviations

1 ANCIENT AUTHORS, TEXTS, AND CORPORA

Anth. Pal.	*Anthologia Palatina* (*The Palatine Anthology*)
App.	Appian
BC; *B. Civ.*	*Bella Civilia* (*Civil Wars*)
Hist.	*Historiae* (*Histories*)
Illyr.	*Illyrica* (*Illyrian Affairs*)
Arist.	Aristotle
Pol.	*Politica* (*Politics*)
Aristides	Aristides
Orat.	*Orationes* (*Orations*)
Arnob.	Arnobius
Adv. nat.	*Adversus nationes* (*Against the Nations*)
Ascon.	Asconius
Mil.	Commentary on Cicero, *Pro Milone*
Aug. (see *RG*)	Augustus
August.	Augustine
De civ.	*De civitate Dei* (*The City of God*)
Aul. Gell.	Aulus Gellius
NA; *Noct. Att.*	*Noctes Atticae* (*Attic Nights*)
Aurelius Victor	Aurelius Victor
Epit.	*Epitome de Caesaribus* (*Epitome of the Caesars*)
Caes.	Caesar
BC	*Bellum Civile* (*The Civil War*)
BG	*Bellum Gallicum* (*The Gallic War*)
Cassiod.	Cassiodorus
Chron. min.	*Chronica minora*
Catull.	Catullus

Cic.	Cicero
ad Att.; *Att.*	*Epistulae ad Atticum* (*Letters to Atticus*)
ad Brut.	*Epistulae ad Brutum* (*Letters to Brutus*)
ad Fam.; *Fam.*	*Epistulae ad Familiares* (*Letters to his Friends*)
Balb.	*Pro Balbo* (*In Defence of Balbus*)
Cat.	*In Catilinam* (*Against Catiline*)
De imp. Cn. Pomp.	*De imperio Cn. Pompeii* (*On the Command of Pompey*)
De leg.	*De legibus* (*On Laws*)
De or.	*De oratore* (*On Oratory*)
De senec.	*De senectute* (*On Old Age*)
Dom.	*De domo sua* (*On his House*)
Flacc.; *pro Flacc.*	*Pro Flacco* (*In defence of Flaccus*)
Har. resp.	*De haruspicum responso* (*On the Response of the Haruspices*)
Mur.	*Pro Murena* (*In Defence of Murena*)
Off.	*De Officiis* (*On Duties*)
Phil.	*Orationes Philippicae* (*Philippic Orations*)
Pis.	*In Pisonem* (*Against Piso*)
Pro Rab. Post.	*Pro Rabirio Postumo* (*In Defence of Rabirius Postumus*)
Prov. cons.	*De provinciis consularibus* (*On the Consular Provinces*)
Sest.	*Pro Sestio* (*In Defence of Sestius*)
Verr.	*In Verrem* (*Against Verres*)
CIL	*Corpus Inscriptionum Latinarum* (1863–)
Cooley	M. G. L. Cooley, ed., *The Age of Augustus* (LACTOR 17) (2003)
Cyrene Edicts	F. de Visscher, *Les édits d'Auguste découverts à Cyrène* (1940)
Dig.	*Digesta* (*Digest* of Justinian)
Dio	Cassius Dio
Diod. Sic.	Diodorus Siculus
Dion. Hal.	Dionysius of Halicarnassus
Ant. Rom.	*Antiquitates Romanae* (*Roman Antiquities*)
Dio Prus.	Dio of Prusa (Dio Chrysostom)
Or.	*Orationes* (*Orations*)
EJ; EJ²	V. Ehrenberg and A. H. M. Jones, eds, *Documents Illustrating the Reigns of*

	Augustus and Tiberius (2nd edn, 1955; expanded version, 1976)
Eur.	Euripides
Bacch.	Bacchae
Eutr.	Eutropius
FGrH	F. Jacoby, ed., Die Fragmente der griechischen Historiker (1923–)
FIRA	S. Riccobono et al., eds, Fontes Iuris Romani AnteIustiniani (1941)
Firm. Mat.	Firmicus Maternus
De errore	De errore profanarum religionum (On the Error of the Pagan Religions)
Frag. Vat.	Fragmentum Vaticanum (Vatican Fragment)
Frontin.	Frontinus
Aq.	De Aquaeductu urbis Romae (On the Water Supply of the City of Rome)
Str.	Strategemata (Stratagems)
Gaius	Gaius
Inst.	Institutiones (Institutes)
Gellius	Aulus Gellius
NA	Noctes Atticae (Attic Nights)
Gran. Licin.	Granius Licinianus
Hdt.	Herodotus
Herod.	Herodas
Hes.	Hesiod
Theog.	Theogonia (Theogony)
Hor.	Horace
Carm.	Carmina (Odes)
Carm. Saec.	Carmen Saeculare (Secular Hymn)
Epist.	Epistulae (Letters)
Ep.; Epod.	Epodi (Epodes)
Sat.	Satirae or Sermones (Satires)
I. Alexandreia Troas	M. Ricl, ed., The Inscriptions of Alexandreia Troas (1997)
IG	Inscriptiones Graecae (1873–)
IGLS	L. Jalabert, R. Mouterde, et al., eds, Inscriptions grecques et latines de la Syrie (1929–)
IGR; IGRR	R. Cagnat, ed., Inscriptiones Graecae ad Res Romanas Pertinentes (1906–1927)
I. Kyme	H. Engelmann, ed., Die Inschriften von Kyme (1976)

ILLRP	A. Degrassi, ed., *Inscriptiones Latinae Liberae Rei Publicae* vol. 1^2 (1965), vol. 2 (1963)
ILS	H. Dessau, ed., *Inscriptiones Latinae Selectae* (1892–1916)
Inscr. It.	*Inscriptiones Italiae* (1931–)
IRT	J. Reynolds and J. B. Ward-Perkins, eds, *The Inscriptions of Roman Tripolitania* (1952)
Jer.	Jerome
adv. Jov.	*Adversus Jovinianum* (*Against Jovinianus*)
Ep.	*Epistulae* (*Letters*)
Jos.	Josephus
AJ; Ant.	*Antiquitates Judaicae* (*Antiquities of the Jews*)
BJ	*Bellum Judaicum* (*The Jewish War*)
Just.	Justinus
Juv.	Juvenal
Sat.	*Satirae* (*Satires*)
LACTOR	London Association of Classical Teachers – Original Records
Liv.	Livy
Per.	*Periochae* (*Summaries*)
Lucr.	Lucretius
Lydus	(John) Lydus (John the Lydian)
De mens.	*De mensibus* (*On the Months*)
Macr.	Macrobius
Sat.	*Saturnalia*
Malcovati, ORF	H. Malcovati, ed., *Oratorum Romanorum Fragmenta* (2nd edn, 1955; 4th edn, 1967)
Menand.	Menander
Theoph.	*Theophoroumene* (*The Girl Possessed*)
Milet i,2	T. Wiegand, ed., *Milet: Ergebnisse der Ausgrabungen und Untersuchungen seit dem Jahre 1899*, I.2. *Das Rathaus von Milet* (1908)
OCT	Oxford Classical Texts
OGIS	W. Dittenberger, ed., *Orientis Graeci Inscriptiones Selectae* (1903–1905)
Ov.	Ovid
Ars am.	*Ars amatoria* (*The Art of Love*)
Fast.	*Fasti* (*The Calendar*)
Met.	*Metamorphoses*

Pont.	*Epistulae ex Ponto* (Letter from Pontus)
Rem. am.	*Remedia amoris* (Remedies for Love)
Tr.; *Trist.*	*Tristia* (Sorrows)
Ox. Pap.	*Oxyrhynchus Papyri* (1898–)
Pan. Lat.	*XII Panegyrici Latini* (XII Latin Panegyrics)
Paus.	Pausanias
P. Berol.	*Berlin Papyri*
Pind.	Pindar
Pyth.	*Pythian Odes*
P. Köln	*Köln Papyri*
PL	*Patrologia Latina*
Plin.	Pliny (the Elder)
HN; *Nat.*; *NH*	*Naturalis Historia* (Natural History)
Plin.	Pliny (the Younger)
Ep.	*Epistulae* (Letters)
Pan.	*Panegyricus* (Panegyric of Trajan)
Plut.	Plutarch
Aem.	*Aemilius Paulus*
Ant.; *Life of Ant.*	*Antonius*
Caes.	*Caesar*
Cam.	*Camillus*
Cic.	*Cicero*
Coriolan.	*Coriolanus*
Fab.	*Fabius Maximus*
Mar.	*Marius*
Marc.	*Marcellus*
Quaest. Conv.	*Quaestiones Conviviales* (Questions at Dinner)
Sull.	*Sulla*
Polyb.	Polybius
P. Osl.	*Papyri Osloenses* (1925–1936)
P. Oxyrh.	*Oxyrhynchus Papyri* (1898–)
Prop.	Propertius
Quint.	Quintilian
Inst. Orat.	*Institutio Oratoria* (Institutes of Oratory)
RDGE	R. K. Sherk, ed., *Roman Documents from the Greek East* (1969)
RG; RGDA	*Res Gestae Divi Augusti* (Accomplishments of the Divine Augustus)
Sall.	Sallust
Cat.	*Bellum Catilinae* (The Catilinarian War) or *De Catilinae coniuratione* (The

	Catilinarian Conspiracy)
Sardis vii	W. H. Buckler and D. M. Robinson, eds, *Sardis VII: Greek and Latin Inscriptions I* (1932)
SB	F. Preisigke et al., *Sammelbuch griechischen Urkunden aus Ägypten* (1915–)
Schol. Veron.	Scholia Veronensia
Aen.	*Aeneid*
SEG	*Supplementum Epigraphicum Graecum* (1923–)
Sen.	Seneca (the Elder)
Controv.	*Controversiae* (*Controversies*)
Suas.	*Suasoriae* (*Persuasions*)
Sen.	Seneca (the Younger)
Clem.	*De clementia* (*On Clemency*)
De benef.	*De beneficiis* (*On Favours*)
Dial.	*Dialogi* (*Dialogues*)
Ep.	*Epistulae* (*Letters*)
Marc.	*Consolatio ad Marciam* (*Consolation to Marcia*)
QN; Q.Nat.	*Quaestiones Naturales* (*Natural Questions*)
Serv.	Servius
ad Aen.	*Commentarius in Vergilii Aeneidos* (*Commentary on Virgil's* Aeneid)
ad Georg.	*Commentarius in Vergilii Georgicon* (*Commentary on Virgil's* Georgics)
SHA	Scriptores Historiae Augustae (The Augustan History)
Alex. Sev.	*Alexander Severus; Severus Alexander*
Aurel.	*Aurelian*
Heliog.	*Heliogabalus*
Sept. Sev.	*Septimius Severus*
Sherk, *RE*	R. K. Sherk, ed. and trans., *The Roman Empire: Augustus to Hadrian* (Translated Documents of Greece and Rome 6) (1988)
Sherk, *RGE*	R. K. Sherk, ed. and trans., *Rome and the Greek East to the Death of Augustus* (Translated Documents of Greece and Rome 4) (1984)
Sherk, *Roman Documents*	R. K. Sherk, ed., *Roman Documents from the Greek East* (1969)

SIG³	W. Dittenberger, ed., *Sylloge Inscriptionum Graecarum* (3rd edn) (1915–1924)
Sil. It.	Silius Italicus
Sozomen	Sozomen
Hist. Eccl.	*Historia ecclesiastica*
Steph. Byz.	Stephanus Byzantius or Byzantinus
Suet.	Suetonius
Aug.; *Div. Aug.*	*Augustus*; *Divus Augustus* (Deified Augustus)
Caes.; *Div. Jul.*; *Iul.*	*Caesar*; *Divus Julius* (Deified Julius); *Julius*
Calig.	*Caligula*
Claud.	*Claudius*
Dom.	*Domitian*
Tib.	*Tiberius*
Vit.	*Vitellius*
Tac.	Tacitus
Agr.	*Agricola*
Ann.	*Annales* (*Annals*)
Dial.	*Dialogus de oratoribus* (*Dialogue on Orators*)
Hist.	*Historiae* (*Histories*)
Theoc.	Theocritus
Id.	*Idylls*
Thuc.	Thucydides
Tib.	Tibullus
Tit. Ulp.	*Tituli ex corpore Ulpiani* (*Extracts from the Works of Ulpian*)
Ulpian	Ulpian
ad edict.	*Ad Edictum* (*On the Edict*)
Val. Max.	Valerius Maximus
Varro	Varro
ap. Non.	*apud Nonium* (i.e., quoted by Nonius Marcellus)
Ling. lat.	*De lingua Latina* (*On the Latin Language*)
Men.	*Saturae Menippeae* (*Menippean Satires*)
Vell.; Vell. Pat.	Velleius Paterculus
Verg.; Virg.	Virgil
Aen.	*Aeneid*
Ecl.	*Eclogae* (*Eclogues*)
G.; *Georg.*	*Georgica* (*Georgics*)

Vir. Ill. De viris illustribus (*On Famous Men*)
Vitr. Vitruvius

2 JOURNALS, MONOGRAPHS, AND WORKS OF REFERENCE

AA *Archäologischer Anzeiger*
Abh. Ak. Wiss. Göttingen, Phil.-hist. Kl. *Abhandlungen der Akademie der Wissenschaften, Göttingen, Philosophisch-historische Klasse*
Abh. Bayer. Ak. Wiss., Phil.-hist. Kl., N.F. *Abhandlungen der Bayerischen Akademie der Wissenschaften, Philosophisch-historische Klasse, Neue Folge*
Abh. Preuss. Ak. Wiss., Phil.-hist. Kl. *Abhandlungen der Preussischen Akademie der Wissenschaften, Philosophisch-historische Klasse*
Abh. Säch. Ak. Wiss., Phil.-hist. Kl. *Abhandlungen der Sächsischen Akademie der Wissenschaften, Philosophisch-historische Klasse*
ActaInstRomNorvegiae *Acta ad archaeologiam et artium historiam pertinentia*, Institutum Romanum Norvegiae
AE *L'Année Épigraphique* (1888–)
AEspA *Archivo Español de Arqueología*
AF *Alter Folge*
AJA *American Journal of Archaeology*
AJAH *American Journal of Ancient History*
AJP; *AJPh* *American Journal of Philology*
Alvarez Martínez, *Puente* J. M. Alvarez Martínez, *El puente romano de Mérida*, Monografías Emeritenses 1 (1983)
ANRW *Aufstieg und Niedergang der römischen Welt* (1972–)
Ant. Class. *L'Antiquité classique*
BAR British Archaeological Reports
BCH *Bulletin de Correspondance Hellénique*
BCom *Bullettino della Commissione Archeologica Comunale di Roma*
BEFAR Bibliothèque des Écoles françaises d'Athènes et de Rome
BGU *Berliner griechische Urkunden* (*Ägyptische Urkunden aus den Königlichen* [later

	Staatlichen] Museen zu Berlin)
BICS	Bulletin of the Institute of Classical Studies
BIDR	Bullettino dell'Istituto di Diritto Romano
Bimilenario	Augusta Emerita: Actas del simposio internacional conmemorativo del Bimilenario de Mérida 1975 (1976)
BMC I	H. Mattingly, Coins of the Roman Empire in the British Museum I. Augustus to Vitellius (1923)
BMC Phoenicia	G. F. Hill, A Catalogue of the Greek Coins in the British Museum. 26. Phoenicia (1910)
BMC Ptolemies	R. S. Poole, A Catalogue of Greek Coins in the British Museum. 6. The Ptolemies, Kings of Egypt (1883)
BMCR	Bryn Mawr Classical Review
BMCRE	H. Mattingly et al., Coins of the Roman Empire in the British Museum (1923–)
BMCRR	H. A. Grueber, Coins of the Roman Republic in the British Museum (1910; rev. edn 1970)
Bowersock, Aug.	G. W. Bowersock, Augustus and the Greek World (1965)
CAH	Cambridge Ancient History (1st edn 1923–1939; 2nd edn 1961–)
CCGG	Cahiers du Centre Gustave Glotz
CEFR	Collection de l'École française de Rome
Ciudades superpuestas	Arqueología de las ciudades modernas superpuestas a las antiguas (Coloquio Internacional, Zaragoza 1983) (1985)
CJ	Classical Journal
Class. Phil.	Classical Philology
CommHumLit	Commentationes Humanarum Litterarum
Conf. Int. Ritratto Romano	Conferenza internazionale sul ritratto romano
CongrNacArqueología	Congreso Nacional de Arqueología
CP	Classical Philology
CQ	Classical Quarterly
CR	Classical Review
CRAI	Comptes rendus de l'Académie des Inscriptions et Belles-lettres
CSCA	California Studies in Classical Antiquity
CW	Classical World

Daremberg–Saglio	C. Daremberg and E. Saglio, eds, *Dictionnaire des antiquités grecques et romaines d'après les textes et les monuments* (1877–1919)
Diz. Epigr.	E. de Ruggiero, *Dizionario epigrafico di antichità romana* (1886–)
Eck, *Italien*	W. Eck, *Die staatliche Organisation Italiens in der Hohen Kaiserzeit* (1979)
Eck, *Verwaltung*	W. Eck, *Die Verwaltung des römischen Reiches in der Hohen Kaiserzeit* (1995)
EE	*Ephemeris Epigraphica* (1872–1913)
EMC/CV	*Echos du monde classique/Classical Views*
EPRO	*Études préliminaires aux religions orientales dans l'empire romain*
EREP	A. García y Bellido, *Esculturas romanas de España y Portugal* (1949)
G&R	*Greece and Rome*
Gesch. d. röm. Lit.	*Geschichte der römischen Literatur*
Giard I	J.-B. Giard, *Bibliothèque Nationale. Catalogue des monnaies de l'empire romain I: Auguste* (1976)
Hesp.	*Hesperia*
Hist.	*Historia*
Histor. Zeitschr.	*Historische Zeitschrift*
HN	*Historia Numorum*
HSCP	*Harvard Studies in Classical Philology*
JdI	*Jahrbuch des deutschen archäologischen Instituts*
J. Fam. Hist.	*Journal of Family History*
JHS	*Journal of Hellenic Studies*
Jones, CERP	A. H. M. Jones, *Cities of the Eastern Roman Provinces* (1971)
Jones, GC	A. H. M. Jones, *The Greek City* (1940)
JRA	*Journal of Roman Archaeology*
JRS	*Journal of Roman Studies*
Kienast, *Augustus*	D. Kienast, *Augustus: Princeps und Monarch* (1982; 3rd edn, 1999)
LCM	*Liverpool Classical Monthly*
LF	*Listy filologické*
LIMC	*Lexicon Iconographicum Mythologiae Classicae* (1981–1997)
LTUR	E. M. Steinby, ed., *Lexicon Topographicum*

	Urbis Romae (1993–2000)
MAAR	*Memoirs of the American Academy in Rome*
MEFRA	*Mélanges d'archéologie et d'histoire de l'École française de Rome*
MemJuntaSupExcav	Memorias de la Junta Superior de Excavaciones y Antigüedades
MemMusAProvinc	*Memorias de los Museos Arqueológicos Provinciales*
MM	*Madrider Mitteilungen*
Mommsen, *Staatsrecht*	T. Mommsen, *Römisches Staatsrecht*, 3 vols (3rd edn, 1887–1888)
Mommsen, *Stafrecht*	T. Mommsen, *Römisches Stafrecht* (1899)
MRR	T. R. S. Broughton, *The Magistrates of the Roman Republic*, 3 vols (1951–1986)
Mus. Helv.	*Museum Helveticum*
Nash	E. Nash, *A Pictorial Dictionary of Ancient Rome*, 2 vols (2nd edn, 1968)
NC; *Num. Chron.*	Numismatic Chronicle
Num. Zeitschr.	*Numismatische Zeitschrift*
PAAR	Papers and Monographs of the American Academy at Rome
PBSR	*Papers of the British School at Rome*
PCPhS; PCPS	*Proceedings of the Cambridge Philological Society*
Pflaum, *Procurateurs*	H.-G. Pflaum, *Les procurateurs équestres sous le Haut-Empire romain* (1950)
Platner–Ashby	S. B. Platner and T. Ashby, *A Topographical Dictionary of Ancient Rome* (1929)
PLLS	*Papers of the Liverpool Latin Seminar*
Proc. Brit. Acad.	*Proceedings of the British Academy*
PVS	*Proceedings of the Virgil Society*
P.W.; P–W	A. Pauly, G. Wissowa, and W. Kroll, eds, *Realencyclopädie der classischen Altertumswissenschaft* (1893–)
RA	*Revue archéologique*
RE	A. Pauly, G. Wissowa, and W. Kroll, eds, *Realencyclopädie der classischen Altertumswissenschaft* (1893–)
REG	*Revue des études grecques*
REL	*Revue des études latines*
Rev. Arch.	*Revue archéologique*

RevArchBiblMus	*Revista de archivos, bibliotecas y museos*
Rev. Hist.	*Revue historique*
Rev. hist. droit	*Revue historique de droit français et étranger*
Rev. intern. des droits de l'ant.; RIDA	*Revue internationale des droits de l'antiquité*
RFIC	*Rivista di filologia e di istruzione classica*
RhMus	*Rheinisches Museum für Philologie*
RIC	*Roman Imperial Coinage* (1923–)
Richmond	I. A. Richmond, "The first years of Emerita Augusta," *Archaeological Journal* 87, 1930, 98–116
RIDA	*Revue internationale des droits de l'antiquité*
RivFil	*Rivista di filologia e di istruzione classica*
RM	*Mitteilungen des deutschen archäologischen Instituts: Römische Abteilung*
RPC	*Roman Provincial Coinage* (1992–)
RPh	*Revue philologique*
RRC	M. H. Crawford, *Roman Republican Coinage* (1974)
RSA	*Rivista storica dell'antichità*
SBer	Sitzungsberichte der Wissenschaftlichen Gesellschaft an der J. W. Goethe-Universität Frankfurt
Script. Class. Isr.; SCI	*Scripta Classica Israelica*
SEHRE^2	M. Rostovtzeff, *The Social and Economic History of the Roman Empire* (2nd edn, rev. P. M. Fraser) (1957)
Stadtbild	W. Trillmich and P. Zanker, eds, *Stadtbild und Ideologie: Die Monumentalisierung hispanischer Städte zwischen Republik und Kaiserzeit*. Abhandlungen der Bayerischen Akademie der Wissenschaften, Philosophisch-historische Klasse, Neue Folge, Heft 103 (1990)
TAPA	*Transactions of the American Philological Association*
Vives	A. Vives y Escudero, *La moneda hispánica* IV (1926)
ZPE	*Zeitschrift für Papyrologie und Epigraphik*
ZRGG	*Zeitschrift für Religions- und Geistesgeschichte*

ZSS *Zeitschrift der Savigny-Stifung für Rechtsgeschichte. Romanistische Abteilung*

3 ROMAN *PRAENOMINA* (FIRST NAMES)

A.	Aulus	P.	Publius
Ap.	Appius	Q.	Quintus
C.	Gaius	Ser.	Servius
Cn.	Gnaeus	Sex.	Sextus
D.	Decimus	Sp.	Spurius
L.	Lucius	T.	Titus
M.	Marcus	Ti.	Tiberius
M'.	Manius	V.	Vibius
N.	Numerius		

To Caroline, Katie and Christopher
Filiabus, Filio Optumis

Map of the Roman Empire, c. AD 14

Introduction:
Approaching the Age of Augustus

I

Few would seriously question the claim that the age of the first Roman emperor Augustus was "one of the pivotal periods of western history, if not world history."[1] The man who was granted the name "Augustus" by the Roman senate on 16 January 27 BC was born C. Octavius on 23 September 63 BC to a prominent local family from the town of Velitrae (modern Velletri), some 30 km south-east of Rome. By the time of his birth, his father had already embarked on a successful political career at Rome. He was elected praetor for 61 BC and then went out to govern the province of Macedonia as proconsul in 60–59, but died on his way back from his province before being able to stand for the consulship, the highest and most prestigious of the annual magistracies of the Roman state. Fifteen years later in 44 BC the young Octavius was vaulted to prominence, when at the age of 18 he was named principal heir to the property of Julius Caesar, his great-uncle on his mother Atia's side. As Caesar's heir and posthumously adopted son, he took his adoptive father's name, as was customary, becoming C. Iulius C.f. Caesar Octavianus (hence "Octavian"), and was immediately embroiled in the political turmoil that erupted in the wake of the dictator's murder on the Ides of March.[2] From that moment onwards until his own death on 19 August AD 14, just over a month short of his seventy-seventh birthday, the man we know as Augustus played a central role in a crucial period of the history of Rome and its Empire.

During his long period in power the Roman political landscape

---

[1] Galinsky 2005b: 1.
[2] Following Caesar's deification early in 42 BC the young man became *Divi f(ilius)* ("son of the Deified") rather than *C(ai) f(ilius)* ("son of Gaius"). He preferred to avoid the use of "Octavianus," to emphasise his link to Caesar. By 38 BC at the latest he had dropped the dictator's *praenomen* and *nomen* to become "Imperator Caesar Divi f.," to which the *cognomen* "Augustus" was added in 27 BC. For a penetrating evaluation of these shifts in his nomenclature, see Syme 1958a (= Chapter 1, below); note also Rubincam 1992.

was radically transformed as what was in effect a monarchy came to coexist alongside the traditional Republican magistracies and organs of government: "an absolute monarchy distinguished by the form of a commonwealth," as Gibbon characterised it. There was also a significant increase in the sheer territorial extent of the Roman Empire, while the system employed for administering Rome's provinces was substantially modified. Furthermore, a whole new ideology or mythology developed that emphasised the birth of an entirely new order throughout the Roman world and celebrated the widespread return of peace and prosperity.

Augustus' personal achievements were manifold and wide-ranging. Granted a series of extraordinary powers and offices from 43 BC onwards, sometimes in response to his blatant threats of armed force, he eventually emerged victorious from the complex series of bloody civil wars that followed Caesar's death.[3] The early third-century historian Cassius Dio rightly saw his victory at the battle of Actium on 2 September 31 BC as a crucial turning-point in Roman history (51.1.1): "On that day for the first time Caesar held total power all by himself; as a result, the calculation of the years of his monarchy are reckoned from that very day." As the sole surviving figure able to command a consensus of support from among all competing groups in Roman society and as the acknowledged leading citizen (*princeps*), he set about restoring the Roman state (the *res publica Romana*), in the process establishing – by means of a series of ongoing experiments and negotiations with key elements in the Roman state (especially the senatorial order, the army, and the Roman people) – a lasting constitutional system that historians soon came to classify as the "Principate" (*principatus*).[4]

A cornerstone of Augustus' programme of restoration was his determination to reassert traditional Roman values and morality, not

---

[3] Fundamental on this is Syme 1939; Carter 1970; Millar 1973 (= Chapter 2, below) and 2000; Bleicken 1990; Pelling 1996; Osgood 2006.

[4] On the political history of the Augustan age: Syme 1939, 1958a (= Chapter 1, below), and 1986: 439–454 ("The Apologia for the Principate"); Jones 1951 and 1955; Brunt 1961a, 1982 (in English despite its title), and 1984; Eder 1990; Ferrary 2001 (= Chapter 3, below). Balanced overviews in Jones 1970; Crook 1996a and 1996b; Kienast 1982; Eck 1998 = 2003: esp. chs 3–8, and 2008; Gruen 2005; Richardson 2012. The term *principatus* already appears quite frequently in Velleius Paterculus' history, written under Tiberius: e.g. 2.89.6: *principatus eius* (sc. *Augusti*) ("his (i.e., Augustus') Principate"; 2.124.2: *soli huic* (sc. *Tiberio*) *contigit paene diutius recusare principatum quam, ut occuparent eum, alii armis pugnaverunt* ("he (i.e., Tiberius) is the only man who has happened to refuse the Principate for almost a longer time than others have taken up arms to acquire it"); 2.129.1: *quasi universa principatus Ti. Caesaris forma* ("a sort of general outline of the Principate of Tiberius Caesar"); cf. Sen., *Clem.* 1.1.6: *tuus* (sc. *Neronis*) *principatus* ("your (i.e., Nero's) Principate"); 1.9.1: *a principatu suo* (sc. *Augusti*) "from his (i.e., Augustus') Principate onwards").

least since moral decline and an associated neglect of religion were seen by contemporaries as major causes of the fall of the Republic. This led him personally to introduce laws (*leges Iuliae*) that aimed to regulate marriage, adultery, and sexual conduct more tightly than hitherto.[5] Religious revival was also central to his mission. He repaired many temples in Rome and its environs and by a mixture of his own personal example and conscious religious reform he sought to re-establish traditional respect for the gods and piety at all levels of Roman society. His careful handling of requests from around the Empire to establish cults to his own divinity during his lifetime reveals his nuanced attitude towards religion and the care he took to avoid too extreme a position.[6] The city of Rome was dramatically refurbished and reorganised; many dilapidated public buildings were repaired, steps were taken to improve urban living conditions, not least with regard to the administration of Rome's aqueducts and the grain supply, but, most of all, the city was embellished with a series of new monuments and monumental complexes, all laden with symbolic meaning. With no little justification Augustus was able to boast that he had found Rome a city of brick, but left it a city of gleaming marble (Suet. *Aug.* 28.3).[7]

At the same time as he was restoring the Roman state at home, Augustus launched a series of military campaigns overseas to pacify regions that had tenaciously remained outside Rome's direct sphere of influence: in particular in northern Spain, the Alpine region, the Balkans, and Germany. His armies extended Roman control to the Danube and by 9 BC had won victories in Germany to the east of the Rhine as far as the river Elbe. Other campaigns – for example, those in Egypt and Arabia – solidified Roman control of areas that had supported his political rivals during the civil wars. In other parts of the East he employed vigorous diplomacy to ensure peace in Asia Minor, Syria, and Judaea.[8] As commander-in-chief of a reformed

---

[5] Last 1934; Treggiari 1996; Raditsa 1980; Galinsky 1981; on the marriage laws, Brunt 1971b: 558–566 and Wallace-Hadrill 1981 (= Chapter 8, below); Treggiari 1991: 60–80 (marriage), 277–298 (sexual relations); Cohen 1991 (adultery); Williams 1962 (on the resonances of the legislation in contemporary poetry). For immorality as an explanation for the fall of the Republic, see Edwards 1993: 34–62; Wallace-Hadrill 1982.

[6] See Beard et al. 1998: 167–210; Price 1984; Fishwick 1987: 73–149; more briefly Scheid 2001 (= Chapter 9, below) and 2005.

[7] The best overall synthesis is Zanker 1987 (Engl. trans. Zanker 1988); see also Galinsky 1996: 141–224; Favro 1996; Haselberger et al. 2002; Haselberger 2007; more briefly, Wallace-Hadrill 1993: esp. ch. 4, "Golden Rome."

[8] On military expansion under Augustus, Syme 1934 (which, despite its title, also includes discussion of Spain and Africa); Brunt 1990b and 1990c; Kienast 1982: 274–310; Gruen 1985, 1990, and 1996; Rich 2003 (= Chapter 4, below); Eck 2003: 93–104 (ch. 12), updated in 2007: 123–136 (ch. 13); Wells 1972.

Roman army, he was able to claim the credit and glory for the achievements of the commanders he had appointed as his deputies (*legati*). His evolving titulature reflected these ongoing military successes, as further salutations as *Imperator*, traditionally granted to Roman commanders after important victories, were added to his titles.[9] His military triumphs did not always involve campaigning. A key diplomatic settlement in 20 BC saw the return of the Roman military standards that had been lost to the Parthians in 53 BC and this was represented to the Roman people as another military triumph. There were setbacks, of course, not least the series of revolts in Germania, Pannonia, and Dalmatia from AD 4 to 9, culminating in the shattering defeat of the army of P. Quinctilius Varus in Germania in the *saltus Teutoburgiensis* (now identified in the area around Kalkriese near Osnabrück).[10] But these setbacks should not detract from the significant military successes of Augustus' principate. As a result of them, peace was re-established across a vastly enlarged Roman Empire after many years of instability.

Under Augustus significant changes occurred too in the organisation of Rome's expanded Empire. A number of new provinces were created, some provincial boundaries were redrawn, and colonies of veteran soldiers were founded in both the West and the East: in Spain, Gaul, Africa, Sicily, Macedonia, Achaea, Asia, Pisidia, and Syria. Control of the majority of provinces was invested in the *princeps* himself, who determined whom to send as his deputies (*legati Augusti*) to govern each province. In the most potentially troublesome areas – in Germany along the Rhine, in Dalmatia, Pannonia and Moesia, in Syria and Egypt, in northern Spain, and (to a lesser degree) in Africa – military garrisons of legions and auxiliary troops were established to secure a lasting Roman peace. In a return to the practice that had prevailed under the Republic, the Senate and People of Rome (*SPQR*: *senatus populusque Romanus*) were given back control, in name at least, of certain of the more quiescent provinces: Sicily, Baetica in southern Spain, Narbonese Gaul, Macedonia, Achaea, Asia, Bithynia and Pontus, Crete and Cyrenaica, Cyprus, and Africa; but in practice the emperor could intervene in these

---

[9] *Imp(erator) I* on 16 April 43 BC, *Imp. II* before 15 March 40, *Imp. III* probably in September/October 40, *Imp. IV* in August 36, *Imp. V* perhaps in 33, *Imp. VI* on 2 September 31, *Imp. VII* in August 30, *Imp. VIII* in 25, *Imp. IX* perhaps 12 May 20, *Imp. X* in 15 or 14, *Imp. XI* in 12, *Imp. XII* in 11, *Imp. XIII* in 10 or 9, *Imp. XIV* early summer 8, *Imp. XV* in AD 2 or 3, *Imp. XVI* in AD 6, *Imp. XVII* in AD 7, *Imp. XVIII* in AD 8, *Imp. XIX* perhaps on 3 August AD 9, *Imp. XX* in AD 11, *Imp. XXI* in AD 13. See further Kienast 2004: 66; Barnes 1974; Syme 1979.

[10] For the site of Varus' defeat, see now Schlüter 1999.

regions too if he saw fit. Members of Augustus' own household (the emperor's freedmen, assisted by his own slaves) were active in all the provinces, administering the emperor's estates and possessions. Everywhere somewhat more regular procedures were put in place to organise periodic local censuses and regulate taxation. Even if it was impossible to eradicate all abuses of power by Roman officials, at least there was some regularisation of what had often previously been left very much up to the man on the spot, the senatorial ex-magistrate appointed to govern an overseas *provincia*.[11]

This whole process of transformation, restoration, and reorganisation owed not a little to good fortune, in particular to the fact that Augustus remained in power for forty-five years following his victory at the battle of Actium in 31 BC, the longest period in power of any *princeps* in Roman history. He also lived a charmed life, contrary to most expectations, since he was frequently ill as a younger man. In particular in 23 BC he was so close to death that he handed his signet-ring to M. Agrippa and lists of the armed forces and public revenues to one of the consuls, Cn. Calpurnius Piso (Dio 53.30.2; for his illnesses, cf. Suet. *Aug.* 81). It is difficult to imagine precisely what might have happened had he died in 23, but a return to civil war is by no means out of the question. From then onwards the need to designate an heir to his vast property and political influence became a major priority, with the main focuses of his dynastic attentions first his son-in-law M. Agrippa (from 23 until the latter's death in 12 BC), then his stepson and son-in-law Tiberius (from 12 until Tiberius' withdrawal to Rhodes in 6 BC), then his grandsons, adopted as his sons in 17, Gaius and Lucius Caesar (until their untimely deaths in AD 4 and 2 respectively), and finally once again Tiberius, whom he eventually adopted as his son in AD 4.[12]

Our main surviving sources for the period 44 BC–AD 14 place the spotlight very much on Augustus. The laconic account of his "Achievements and Expenditures" that Augustus himself prepared to be set up after his death outside his mausoleum in Rome, but which was soon put on display in the Roman provinces too – the *Res Gestae et Impensae Divi Augusti* – not surprisingly emphasises his own personal role in engendering the changes that took place and

---

[11] On changes in the system of provincial administration, see Lintott 1993: 111–128; Richardson 1976; Brunt 1961b; Bowman 1996; Eck 1986 (revised in Eck 1995: 83–102 = Chapter 7, below). On the allocation of provinces, there is much of value in Ferrary 2001 (= Chapter 3, below); note also Millar 1966; Eck 1997b. For military garrisons, Keppie 1996: esp. 376–387.

[12] For Agrippa, see esp. Roddaz 1984; for Tiberius and Gaius and Lucius Caesar, Hurlet 1997: esp. 79–162, 415–484; Levick 1972, 1975, and 1976; Bowersock 1984.

establishing the new status quo.¹³ Three literary accounts also focus very much on Augustus: the biographies by Nicolaus of Damascus and Suetonius – the former concentrating on the life of the young Octavian, written probably during the later 20s BC, the latter composed a century after Augustus' death and detailing his entire life and career – and Tacitus' brief but hostile sketch of Augustus' reign with which the historian opens his *Annales* (1.1–5, 9–10), a year-by-year narrative of the principates of Tiberius, Caligula, Claudius, and Nero, covering the period AD 14 to 68, also written in the early second century AD. Similarly in the early third century, Cassius Dio, who compiled a vast annalistic history of Rome from its foundation to his own day, not only identified the reign of Augustus as a pivotal moment in Roman history, as we have already seen (above, p. 2), but also focused his narrative primarily on Augustus, even attempting to reconstruct his supposed motivations for particular political and military actions.¹⁴ Not surprisingly in such accounts, the role played by other key individuals and elements within the Roman state tended to get downplayed. In explaining the changes that occurred, such sources arguably give too much credit to the first *princeps*.

Some of the transformations were the culmination of long-term processes that were already in motion well before Augustus assumed power. From the second half of the second century BC onwards the Republican system of government, designed to meet the needs of a small city-state with a relatively circumscribed territory, was proving inadequate to the task of governing a Mediterranean-wide Empire. Increasing wealth acquired by the Roman elite through overseas conquest had created much wider economic divergences between the richest and poorest Romans, fuelling the flames of internecine strife. It was also allowing the wealthiest Romans, especially those who led armies on increasingly long military campaigns, to dominate the political landscape in a way that was an anathema to the traditions and the spirit of the Republican system, whereby the senate, as a

---

¹³ The text is customarily referred to as the *Res Gestae*, but the heading explicitly states that it is "a copy of the achievements of the Deified Augustus by which he brought the world under the power (*imperium*) of the Roman people and of the expenses which he incurred for the state and the Roman people." For authoritative editions, see Gagé 1935; Volkmann 1942; Riccobono 1945; and esp. Scheid 2007. For useful editions of the text with English translation and commentary, see Brunt and Moore 1967 (Latin text only); Cooley 2009 (Latin and Greek versions). For other English translations, see Sherk, *RE* no. 26; Cooley 2003: 23–35; Eck 2003: 134–152 = 2007: 172–190 (by S. A. Takács); A. E. Cooley is currently preparing another new edition, with English translation and commentary. For studies, note Yavetz 1984; Ramage 1987; Ridley 2003.

¹⁴ For Nicolaus of Damascus see the edition, with English translation, of Bellemore 1984; for Suetonius' life, see Carter 1982; for Dio's account of Augustus, see Rich 1989 and 1990; Reinhold and Swan 1990; Swan 2004. For Tacitus' and Dio's views on Augustus, Gabba 1984.

collective body of aristocrats who provided advice to the magistrates in office on the best course of action, had held informal control over the political process and where there had previously been a high degree of cohesion among members of the elite, who collectively shared responsibility for the governance of the Roman state. During the first century BC, however, the richest members of the Roman elite were increasingly able, and willing, to use their wealth to subvert the regular functioning of the Republic's political institutions by engaging in direct or, more often, indirect bribery at elections or by recruiting armed support when civil war flared up between competing oligarchs. The growing tolerance of violence as a political tool did not help matters, while the need to keep Roman armies in the field for longer and longer campaigns encouraged the establishment of closer bonds between soldiers and their generals, which had a further destabilising effect on the political process. Even though certain elements of this explanatory paradigm accounting for the so-called "fall of the Roman Republic" have been challenged in some of the recent scholarship, it remains clear that a gradual, long-term transformation of the Roman political system was already under way well before the young Octavian, later Augustus, entered the political arena in 44 BC.[15] On this view, some of the changes that occurred during his period in power may be legitimately treated as the continuation of processes whose origins can be traced back long before his birth. In other words, any history of the age of Augustus needs to confront the classic historiographical problem of evaluating the relative importance of long-term trends, the impact of single events, and the direct influence of a clearly powerful political leader. The ancient sources, as we have seen, arguably overemphasise Augustus' personal role in bringing about change. Their picture needs to be balanced by an objective weighing of other factors. Such a process provides one of the ongoing fascinations of studying this crucial period of Roman history.

Another challenge, and a point of enduring historical interest, is the fact that Augustus became such an emblematic figure for later rulers. All subsequent Roman emperors, for example, took the name "Augustus," which quickly developed into one of the standard imperial titles. Furthermore, their actions were often implicitly or

---

[15] The classic analysis (in English) of the complex set of factors that led to what historians have termed the "fall of the Republic" remains Brunt 1988 (a full elaboration of the brief sketch offered in Brunt 1971a); see also Gabba 1973; Crawford 1978; Hopkins 1978: 1–98. For a thoughtful recent assessment of Brunt's analytical scheme, see Morstein-Marx and Rosenstein 2006. For a set of reflections on the social and political implications of the change from Republic to Principate in Rome, Italy, and the Mediterranean at large, see Ando 2011.

explicitly compared to those of the first *princeps*, who as a result became a sort of touchstone by which later emperors were judged.[16] In addition, Augustus' influence extended far beyond the confines of Roman history. A number of later rulers in a variety of European states during the Renaissance and the modern age adopted Augustus as their model, seeking to imitate his style of rule in the hope of enhancing their authority in the process. This arguably reached its most extreme form in the career of the Italian Fascist leader, Benito Mussolini, who ruled first as Prime Minister and then Leader of the State from 1922 to 1943 and then as head of the Italian Social Republic from 1943 to 1945. As a result, some historical treatments of Augustus have been coloured by the use to which his example and style of rule were put by these later European leaders, as we shall explore in greater detail below (pp. 17–19).

The age of Augustus also continues to attract historians because no consensus has been reached on how best to explain all aspects of his rule despite the voluminous scholarly literature on the period and on the man. Agreement has proved impossible not least because of the difficulties posed by the main ancient sources. As we have seen, with the exception of Nicolaus of Damascus' biography, the most important were composed some time after Augustus' death and their accounts were written with the benefit of hindsight and in full awareness of the later evolution of the system of the Principate. So it is sometimes difficult to peel away the layers that owe more to later developments than to the realities of the Augustan age. Augustus' Principate is best seen as a period of ongoing experimentation as the *princeps* tested out what would prove palatable to the other key groups in Roman society.[17] Moreover, precisely how we should interpret certain ambiguous statements in Dio and other sources regarding the complex constitutional changes that took place after the battle of Actium has given rise to often widely divergent interpretations of them and continues to fuel intense debate and controversy among historians.[18]

New discoveries, especially of inscriptions and archaeological material, whether resulting from careful excavation of sites or through more casual finds, continue to add to our knowledge of Augustus and his age, but at the same time often throw up further interpretative problems and add fresh levels of complexity to the

---

[16] For this in Cassius Dio, see Edmondson 1992: 49–54.
[17] For a good example of this in the area of administration, see Eck 1986 (revised in Eck 1995: 83–102 = Chapter 7, below).
[18] See Ferrary 2001 (= Chapter 3, below).

discussion. This means that interpretations of the history of the Augustan age constantly need to be modified, usually in minor ways, but occasionally to a much more significant degree. For instance, in the nineteenth and early years of the twentieth century fragments of a Greek version of Augustus' *Res Gestae* were discovered at Apollonia (modern Uluborlu) in Pisidia and of a Latin version at Pisidian Antioch (near modern Yalvaç). These allowed crucial gaps in the bilingual text long since known from Ancyra (Ankara) in Galatia, where it had been discovered in 1555 inscribed on the walls of the Temple of Roma and Augustus, to be restored with greater security. The Latin text from Antioch, for instance, revealed that Theodor Mommsen's restoration of a crucial chapter of the document was seriously erroneous. Relying on the surviving Greek text from Ancyra, Mommsen had restored section 34.3 of the Latin version to read *post id tempus dignitate omnibus praestiti* ("from that time onwards I excelled everyone in rank/dignity"), but the discovery of the Latin text at Antioch showed that this had to be disregarded in favour of the reading *post id tempus auctoritate omnibus praestiti* ("from this time onwards I excelled everyone in authority"). The revised text thus underlined the central importance of the concept of *auctoritas* to Augustus' political position.[19] Another new fragment of the *Res Gestae* from Antioch, first published in 2005, invalidates another of Mommsen's textual restorations. It is now clear that the text of the very important section 34.1 did not read *per consensum universorum potitus rerum omnium rem publicam ex mea potestate in senatus populique Romani arbitrium transtuli* ("when with universal consent I had gained complete control of affairs, I transferred the republic from my power to the control of the senate and people of Rome"), but rather *per consensum universorum potens rerum omnium ...* ("being in possession of complete power with universal consent ...").[20] These small textual changes to key sections of this major document, made possible by fresh discoveries, have a significant effect on how we interpret Augustus' self-presentation of his political position.

Other new documents have proved just as enlightening. A dossier of important inscriptions from Aphrodisias in Caria (in south-west Turkey), inscribed on the wall of one of the entrances to the theatre,

---

[19] For the original text from Ancyra, see Mommsen 1865; for the new texts from Pisidia, Ramsay and von Premerstein 1927. For more recent editions of this key document, see above, n. 13.

[20] For the new fragment from Antioch, see Drew-Bear and Scheid 2005, integrated into the new edition of the text in Scheid 2007.

published in 1982, but partially known since the early 1970s, allowed Octavian's constitutional position in the 30s BC to be reexamined in a fresh light.[21] A fragmentary papyrus containing a Greek translation of the eulogy Augustus delivered at M. Agrippa's funeral enhanced our understanding of the latter's powers at the time of his death in 12 BC, but also opened up fresh areas of controversy.[22] Five edicts from Cyrene (in modern Libya), dating to 7/6 and 4 BC, first published in 1927, provided totally new information about the handling of legal disputes in the provinces and showed that Augustus had no qualms about intervening directly in a province that was nominally under the control of the senate and people of Rome, i.e., one of the "proconsular" or "public" provinces.[23] Most recently, if the bronze plaque found in northern Spain on which they were inscribed is indeed genuine, the edicts of Augustus issued at Narbo on 14 and 15 February 15 BC regulating the settlements, territories, and fiscal responsibilities of various peoples in north-west Spain in the wake of the Roman victory in the Cantabrian-Asturian wars, first published in 1999, provide in their preamble the first known case of Augustus using the term *proconsul* in addition to his tribunician power to describe his constitutional position.[24]

Newly discovered coin issues can also throw fresh light on the Augustan principate: for instance, the aureus issued in 28 BC and acquired by the British Museum in 1995 (illustrated below, Chapter 3, Fig. 3.1) that shows on its reverse Octavian sitting on a magistrate's stool (*sella curulis*) holding a scroll in his right hand, with the legend LEGES ET IVRA P R RESTITVIT ("He restored the laws and rights of the Roman people"). This confirms Dio's narrative in which the supposed "restoration of the Republic" took place gradually over the two years 28 and 27 BC and not just in 27 BC, as scholars have sometimes assumed.[25]

As for archaeological evidence, the monumental *Ara Pacis*

---

[21] Reynolds 1982: nos. 6, 7, 8, 10, 11, 12, already exploited prior to their full publication by Millar 1973 (= Chapter 2, below).

[22] P. Köln 10 = EJ² 366; trans. Sherk, RE, no. 12 = Cooley no. T14, with Koenen 1970; for discussion, see Ferrary 2001: 135–141 (= Chapter 3, below, pp. 114–121).

[23] For the five edicts, see De Visscher 1940 = SEG IX 8 = EJ² 311; trans. Sherk, RGE, no. 102 = Sherk, RE, no. 13 = Cooley nos M60 and M78; discussed further in Ferrary 2001: 137–138 (= Chapter 3, below, pp. 117–118).

[24] AE 1999, 915 = 2000, 760; trans. Cooley no. M27; Alföldy 2000; for doubts as to its authenticity, see Le Roux 2001; Richardson 2002; briefly discussed by Ferrary 2001: 116, n. 62 (= Chapter 3, below, p. 99, n. 33).

[25] See Rich and Williams 1999. For the restoration *leges et iura p(opuli) R(omani) restituit* rather than *leges et iura p(opulo) R(omano) restituit*, as proposed by Rich and Williams, see Mantovani 2008, also drawing attention to a second example of the aureus that has formed part of the Blackburn Museum's coin collection since 1946.

Augustae (the "Altar of Augustan Peace"), decreed by the senate on 4 July 13 BC and dedicated on 30 January 9 BC in the Campus Martius just to the west of the Via Flaminia, the main road leading north out of Rome, provides great insight into the official ideology of the Augustan regime. Particularly important are the sculpted relief panels, which on its west side show Mars at the Lupercal watching over Romulus and Remus (though only parts of the figure of Mars survive) and Aeneas sacrificing to the Penates, and on its east side feature the goddess Roma and a goddess whose identity is disputed at the centre of a scene of superabundant fertility. The long friezes on its north and south sides depict the imperial family, the priestly colleges, and the senate engaged in a ritual procession.[26] But even here problems of identification complicate matters and continue to fuel debate about how some parts of the monument should be interpreted. Is the goddess on the left-hand panel on the east façade Tellus ("Mother Earth"), Venus, or Ceres, or a personification of Italy or of Pax ("Peace")?[27] Even the traditional identification of the male figure sacrificing on the right-hand panel on the west side as Aeneas has recently been challenged.[28]

In the same area of Rome, archaeological probes conducted between 1979 and 1981 located elements of the monumental sundial (*horologium*) erected by Augustus in the Campus Martius in 10 BC and discussed by Pliny the Elder (*NH* 36.72–73), allowing its complex relationship to the *Ara Pacis* to be worked out in close detail, or so it appeared at first. The sundial's pointer (*gnomon*), an Egyptian obelisk, it was argued, cast its shadow in a straight line right up against the entrance to the altar only on the afternoon of the autumn equinox, 23 September, Augustus' birthday, while the obelisk was aligned with Augustus' mausoleum north-north-west of the sundial rather than along the north–south meridian line that was laid out as part of the sundial. This all suggested in very dramatic terms that cosmic symbolism played a major role in the layout of these three monuments and hence contributed to the public construction of Augustus' image. The monuments conveyed the subliminal message that the heavenly bodies were somehow in accord with the conception, birth, and eventual death of the *princeps*. This interpretation was enthusiastically championed in many studies of Augustus during the 1980s and 1990s, but it has now been shown that the

---

[26] On the *Ara Pacis*, Moretti 1948; Toynbee 1953 and 1961; Simon 1967; Elsner 1991; Kleiner 1992: 90–99; Galinsky 1996: 141–155; Rossini 2006.
[27] Note, for example, Zanker 1988: 172–183; Galinsky 1992; Spaeth 1994.
[28] Rehak 2001 and 2006: 115–120.

mathematical calculations that underpinned the conclusions about the length of the shadow cast by the sundial on Augustus' birthday are seriously erroneous, and what in fact had been revealed by excavation were parts not of Augustus' *horologium* but of Domitian's later reconstruction of it.[29]

Nevertheless, it still remains the case that the sundial, altar, and mausoleum were planned as an interrelated group of monuments with symbolic resonance. The mausoleum was planned perhaps as early as 32 BC as a pointed response to M. Antonius' wishes to be buried in Egypt alongside Cleopatra, and completed by 28 BC (Suet. *Aug.* 100.4).[30] The Egyptian obelisk that formed part of the *horologium* commemorated the annexation of Egypt as a province of the Roman people, as its dedicatory inscription proclaimed.[31] This annexation had marked the end of the civil wars, just as the *Ara Pacis* celebrated the bringing of peace to the West. In addition, the sundial was one of the first monuments erected by Augustus after he had become *pontifex maximus* in 12 BC, one of whose responsibilities it was to ensure that the calendar was functioning correctly. The mausoleum and the *Ara Pacis* also emphasised Augustus' dynastic concerns, inscribing his family very much into the suburban landscape. The former was designed as the final resting-place for Augustus and his extended family, with M. Claudius Marcellus, Augustus' nephew and son-in-law, the first to have had his ashes laid to rest there after his untimely death in 23. The latter was dedicated on his wife Livia's birthday (30 January) and, as we have noted, prominently displayed down its long south side the extended Augustan family in religious procession.[32]

Archaeological discoveries made outside Rome can also be important for changing our understanding of the history of the Augustan age. Archaeological work to the east of the river Rhine in

---

[29] Buchner 1976, 1980, and 1982; enshrined in *LTUR* III 35–37 and championed in (e.g.) Wallace-Hadrill 1993: 94–96; Eck 2003: 122–123 = 2007: 160–161. In general on the importance of cosmic ideology in Augustan Rome, see Barton 1995; Schmid 2005. For the mathematical errors in Buchner's reconstruction, see Schütz 1990; for the Domitianic monument and a general reevaluation, Heslin 2007; see also Rehak 2006: 62–95 (ch. 4).

[30] See Zanker 1988: 72–77; Rehak 2006: 35–58; more fully, von Hesberg and Panciera 1994.

[31] *CIL* VI 701–702 = *ILS* 91 = EJ² 14; trans. Cooley no. K35: *Imp(erator) Caesar divi f(ilius) / Augustus / pontifex maximus / im(perator) XII co(n)s(ul) XI trib(unicia) pot(estate) XIV / Aegupto in potestatem / populi Romani redacta / Soli donum dedit* ("Imperator Caesar Augustus, son of the Deified One, *pontifex maximus*, (saluted as) *imperator* 12 times, consul 11 times, in his 14th year of tribunician power (i.e., between 26 June 10 and 25 June 9 BC), with Egypt now reduced into the power of the Roman people, dedicated (this) as a gift to the Sun").

[32] For the friezes on the *Ara Pacis*, Kleiner 1978; Koeppel 1987 and 1988; Zanker 1988: 118–125.

Germany, for example, has uncovered a series of Roman forts and, most importantly, a town that was developed in the Augustan period on the site of a former marching-camp at Waldgirmes near Wetzlar in the Lahn valley. In its forum stood a gilt bronze equestrian statue of Augustus. These discoveries confirm the statements of Velleius Paterculus (2.97.4) and Dio (56.18.1), hitherto given little credence by historians, that Augustus was founding cities in German territory east of the Rhine and engaged in the process of making it into a new province until the plan was abandoned following the crushing defeat in AD 9 of his army, led by P. Quinctilius Varus, in the *saltus Teutoburgiensis*.[33]

As for Augustan ideology, excavations in north-western Greece at Nikopolis ("Victory City"), the settlement founded by Augustus near the site of the naval battle of Actium as a memorial to his great victory, have proved very revealing. In a series of excavations beginning in 1913 archaeologists uncovered part of the central victory monument, constructed above the city on the site of Octavian's camp on the eve of the crucial battle. The monument comprised a terraced platform to the façade of which were affixed the bronze rams taken from the ships of M. Antonius' and Cleopatra's defeated fleet along with a monumental Latin inscription, only partially preserved but probably consecrating the monument to Neptune and Mars (cf. Suet. *Aug.* 18.2). More recently, more than 21,000 fragments have been discovered of a sculpted frieze that decorated the altar or pedestal that stood in the centre of this terraced platform. On it were depicted ships, a possible Amazonomachy, military trophies, and not least Augustus riding in a triumphal procession, accompanied by many leading Romans and non-Romans. When fully published, this promises to be the next major addition to our understanding of the public image of the first *princeps*. Most intriguing of all is the fact that Augustus has two children (a boy and a girl) with him in the triumphal chariot (*quadriga*). Are these perhaps the children of M. Antonius and Cleopatra, Alexander Helios and Cleopatra Selene, shown clemency by the victor and now visibly under his protection?[34] Or are they Julia and Drusus, Augustus' daughter and stepson, born in 39 and 38 BC respectively?[35] Problems of interpretation once again

---

[33] For Waldgirmes, see von Schnurbein 2003.
[34] For the victory monument, see Murray and Petsas 1989; for a preliminary report of the new finds (and a well-illustrated summary of the earlier discoveries), see Zachos 2003. I am most grateful to Susan Walker and William Murray for discussing with me these very important new finds prior to their full publication.
[35] As suggested by Beard 2007: 224–225.

intrude, not least since on closer examination the portrait-busts look too mature in years to represent children. Are they perhaps in fact busts of Antonius and Cleopatra being paraded in the triumph? Their publication will allow the debate about their full significance to begin in earnest.

As a result of such ongoing discoveries, our understanding of the age of Augustus is constantly developing, never static. New finds have the potential to overturn long-cherished views and can often lead to further controversies that prevent any completely satisfying synthesis being reached. The combined effect of many of these factors may be seen in the manner in which modern scholarship on Augustus and his age has evolved since the later nineteenth century.

II

Modern historical research on Augustus began, as did so much else of importance in Roman history, with Theodor Mommsen (1817–1903). His *Römische Geschichte* ("Roman History"), for which he was awarded the Nobel Prize for Literature in 1902, never reached the age of Augustus. After bringing the third volume to a close with an account of the battle of Thapsus of 46 BC, Mommsen laid the work aside in favour of other projects. However, in his later *Römisches Staatsrecht* ("Roman Constitutional Law"), the first parts of which were published in 1871, but later revised for the definitive third edition of 1887–1888, he analysed in detail the constitutional powers upon which the political position of the Roman emperor rested. In this account, he elaborated his theory of a supposed "dyarchy" to describe what he saw as a crucial sharing of power between the *princeps* and the senate that lay at the heart of the Augustan political system.[36]

The last years of the nineteenth and the first decade of the twentieth century saw the first comprehensive histories of the reign of Augustus. The most detailed was that of Viktor Gardthausen (1843–1925) in his *Augustus und seine Zeit* ("Augustus and his Age"), which appeared between 1891 and 1904, amounting in the end to two massive volumes equipped with copious footnotes and bibliography. In the same period two biographically oriented works in English by John B. Firth (1868–1943) and Evelyn S. Shuckburgh (1843–1906) were published, the former proudly claiming to be the

---

[36] On Mommsen, see the recent biography of Rebenich 2002; more briefly and with specific reference to Augustus, Linderski 1990.

first biography of Augustus in English, but the latter more influential, as its string of reprints attests.[37] The sober critical method and straightforward narrative style of Gardthausen were taken up in English by T. Rice Holmes (1855–1933) in his *The Architect of the Roman Empire*, published in two volumes in 1928 and 1931 as a follow-up to his well-received book *The Roman Republic and the Founder of the Empire* (1923), which had focused on the career of Julius Caesar.

Although Mommsen's theory of a "dyarchy" between *princeps* and senate was not widely shared by later historians (it finds no place, for instance, in Gardthausen's substantial work), his overall approach, firmly grounded in the study of Augustus' constitutional position, proved highly influential and to this day continues to make an important contribution to our understanding of the Augustan Principate.[38] In Germany the work in particular of Eduard Meyer (1855–1930) developed Mommsen's approach based on constitutional law, even accepting his model of a "dyarchy," while in Italy Emilio Betti (1890–1968), a distinguished jurist and legal theorist, between 1913 and 1915 produced important studies on the crisis of the Republican constitution and on the foundation of the Principate, in which he reacted sharply to what he saw as Mommsen's overschematic analysis.[39] Meyer's work was in turn taken up most influentially in the English-speaking world by Hugh Last (1894–1957), Camden Professor of Ancient History at Oxford from 1936 to 1949. He had been taught by T. Rice Holmes when a pupil at St Paul's School in London and came to develop a "reverence for the achievements of nineteenth-century German historians" to the exclusion of other types of approach. While Last himself was not the most prolific of scholars, his lectures on Roman constitutional history at Oxford were clearly influential.[40] One of Last's early students was the American Mason Hammond (1903–2002), who went on to a long and influential career at Harvard. He quickly published his Oxford doctoral thesis, *The Augustan Principate in Theory and Practice*

---

[37] Gardthausen 1891–1904; Firth 1902; Shuckburgh 1903.

[38] See, in particular, Ferrary 2001 (= Chapter 3, below); Lacey 1996 (a collection of his articles). For arguments that Mommsen's theory of a "dyarchy" has been misunderstood by his critics, see Winterling 2005.

[39] Meyer 1903 and 1918; on Meyer, see Stahlmann 1988. Betti 1982 [orig. publ. 1913–1915]: esp. 497–584; on Betti, note Gabba's introduction to the 1982 edition of his works (Betti 1982) and Badian 1986.

[40] See the enlightening entry on him by P. M. Fraser in the digital *Oxford Dictionary of National Biography* (www.oxforddnb.com), from which the quotation about Last's reverence for German scholarship is taken. Last's two main contributions on Augustus' constitutional position were published towards the end of his career: Last 1947 and 1951.

during the Julio-Claudian Period, in 1933, dedicating it to Last. In an appendix he prepared for an updated edition of this work in 1968, Hammond made explicit his intellectual debt to Mommsen and Meyer.[41] Another much-read, and many times reprinted, study of Augustus by the politician and novelist John Buchan (Lord Tweedsmuir, 1875–1940) was written when he was governor-general of Canada from 1935 to 1940 and dedicated to the Canadian prime minister William Lyon McKenzie King on its publication in 1937. This work also benefited from the comments of Last on an initial draft.[42]

In this same period the first edition of volume X of the *Cambridge Ancient History* had appeared in 1934, providing a sensible narrative and interpretative overview of Augustus' rise to power and Principate.[43] W. W. Tarn (1869–1958) and M. P. Charlesworth (1895–1950) contributed the narrative of events from 44 to 27 BC (chs iii–iv) and Sir Henry Stuart Jones (1867–1939), formerly Camden Professor at Oxford, treated the constitutional position of the *princeps* and the role of the senate and the Roman people in the Augustan regime (chs v–vi), while F. E. Adcock (1886–1968), professor of ancient history at Cambridge, contributed a concluding assessment of Augustus' achievement (ch. xviii). Last wrote on the social policy of Augustus (ch. xiv), while two younger scholars who were to play a leading role in the study of ancient history in the next fifty years, Arnaldo Momigliano (1908–1987) and Ronald Syme (1903–1989), contributed chapters on Herod of Judaea and the northern frontiers of the Empire respectively (chs xi–xii).

Hugh Last's influence on the study of Augustan Rome in England in the 1930s was also significant in a negative sense, in that his dogged preference for constitutional history stimulated his younger Oxford colleague Ronald Syme to approach the subject from an entirely different perspective in his classic work *The Roman Revolution*, first published on 7 September 1939 just two weeks after the

---

[41] Hammond 1968: 383: "New approaches have supplemented rather than replaced Mommsen's constitutional and legal interpretation, which *The Augustan Principate* primarily follows."

[42] See Buchan 1937: v. The Latin phrase *immensa Romanae pacis majestas* ("the immense majesty of the Roman peace") appears on the title page, a plaintive cry, perhaps, as war with Germany loomed and as Buchan was already shoring up Canadian support and negotiating with US president F. D. Roosevelt for backing should war break out. On Buchan, see the detailed entry by H. C. G. Matthew in the *Oxford Dictionary of National Biography* (www.oxforddnb.com). For discussion on Buchan I am also much indebted to Jonathan Scott Perry (University of South Florida), who is currently preparing a monograph on work published on Augustus during the 1930s.

[43] Cook et al. 1934.

outbreak of World War II. Syme, in many ways an outsider to the traditions of ancient history at Oxford (and not just because of his New Zealand origins), firmly rejected Mommsen's – and hence Last's – approach based on constitutional law in favour of one grounded in prosopography, i.e., the study of individuals, families, and family connections, a method developed in particular by a group of German historians in the 1920s and 1930s, principally Friedrich Münzer (1868–1942), Edmund Groag (1873–1945), and Arthur Stein (1871–1950). All three had prepared numerous entries on members of the Roman aristocracy for the standard German encyclopedia of classical antiquity, Pauly-Wissowa's *Realencyclopädie*, and for the important research tool *Prosopographia Imperii Romani* ("Prosopography of the Roman Empire"). Their work had demonstrated the value of the prosopographical method and Syme acknowledged his debt to all three scholars in the preface to *The Roman Revolution*. Münzer's monograph on the politics of the Roman Republic and early Empire was particularly influential.[44] Syme also singled out the writings of the distinguished "gentleman scholar" W. W. Tarn on Antony and Cleopatra – as we have seen, Tarn had contributed the narrative chapters on the triumviral period for the *Cambridge Ancient History* – and of Anton von Premerstein (1869–1936), from whose monograph *Vom Werden und Wesen des Prinzipats* ("On the Origins and Nature of the Principate"), published posthumously in 1937, Syme derived much benefit, especially in its characterisation of the position of the *princeps* as party leader.[45]

For his mode of analysis Syme chose vivid narrative, again in patent contradistinction to the drier structural expositions of the constitutional historians who had preceded him. And, as many have noted, Syme's preference for a Tacitean style of prose betrays an analytical affinity with the Roman annalist, who had opened his account of Augustus' Julio-Claudian successors with a scathingly critical retrospective of the first *princeps* (*Ann.* 1.1–5, 9–10). But Syme did not compose his gripping narrative of Augustus' rise and the transformation of the Roman state just to score methodological points on how best to write about the Roman past. More than any other work of Roman history written in English in the twentieth century, *The Roman Revolution* was composed very much against

---

[44] On Syme's indebtedness to their prosopographical methods, see Syme 1939: viii; Galsterer 1990; Linderski 1990; for Syme's debt to Münzer 1920, see Millar 1981: 146. For enlightening general assessments of Syme, see Millar 1981; Alföldy 1993; Bowersock 1994; and Millar's contribution on Syme in the digital *Oxford Dictionary of National Biography* (www.oxforddnb.com).
[45] Syme 1939: viii.

the backdrop of the turbulent political events that were taking place in Europe during the 1920s and 1930s. The rise of Fascism in Italy, Germany, and Spain, as well as the promulgation of a supposed "Constitution" of the Soviet Union in 1936 at a time when Stalin's dictatorial position was becoming ever more firmly entrenched, made the story of Rome's transformation from a citizen-Republic to a centrifocal autocracy particularly compelling and instructive. Syme's depiction of Augustus as a ruthless faction leader proved a bracingly refreshing antidote to the largely pro-Augustan accounts that had been produced in the years leading up to World War II. For Syme was by no means alone in viewing the Roman past through a contemporary lens.

In Germany Hitler's rise had coloured historical interpretations of the first Roman emperor in that country too, with many scholars casting Augustus as a prototype "Führer".[46] In Italy the use (or abuse) to which Benito Mussolini ("Il Duce") put Augustus as a model for his own political regime made the contemporary relevance of Syme's analysis of Augustus strikingly obvious. What is more, 1937 was the two thousandth anniversary of Augustus' birth. Not only did this lead to the publication of an unprecedented spate of historical works on Augustus throughout the scholarly world,[47] but it also presented Mussolini with an unparalleled opportunity to display to his own Italian subjects and the world beyond the glory that was Augustan Rome. A focal point was the famous exhibition, the "Mostra Augustea della Romanità" ("Augustan Exhibition of Romanness"), which opened in 1937 on Augustus' birthday, 23 September, and remained on display for precisely one year. Leading Italian historians contributed to a commemorative volume, *Augustus: Studi in occasione del bimillenario augusteo* ("Studies on the occasion of the two thousandth anniversary of Augustus' birth"), published in 1938 by the major national academy, the Reale Accademia Nazionale dei Lincei, which covered such key topics as the Augustan constitution, Augustan legislation, imperial jurisprudence, territorial and financial administration, Augustus' military reforms (by A. Momigliano), religion, literature, art, coinage, and

---

[46] This is most apparent in the work of Rehrmann 1937, but note also Weber 1936; Siber 1940. For a series of studies on nineteenth- and twentieth-century Italian and German historical scholarship on Caesar and Augustus, see Christ and Gabba 1989.

[47] Note, among others, in English Baker 1937; Buchan 1937; Allen 1937; in German the works cited in n. 46; also Hönn 1937; Kornemann 1936; and, slightly later, Birkenfeld 1944; in French the important series of articles by Gagé (1930a, 1930b, 1931, 1932, 1936); also Homo 1935; Piganiol 1937; in Italian De Martino 1936; Ciccotti 1938. In Italy M. A. Levi's 1933 monograph *Ottaviano capoparte* ("Octavian Party-Leader") clearly owed much to contemporary politics.

public works, as well as providing a general assessment of the Augustan Principate.[48] In addition, in February 1937 Mussolini's Council of Ministers had passed a decree instructing that work should resume on excavating and reassembling the surviving fragments of that most Augustan of monuments from the city of Rome, the *Ara Pacis*. The work was completed at feverish pace just in time to allow Mussolini to inaugurate the restored altar on the final day of the bimillenary celebrations.[49]

In the face of such political and scholarly developments, *The Roman Revolution*, with chapters given such evocative titles as "The First March on Rome" (ch. ix), "The Second March on Rome" (ch. xiii), "Dux" (ch. xxi), "The Party of Augustus" (ch. xxiv), and "The National Programme" (ch. xxix), sought to lay bare the evils of despotism and a totalitarian state. Syme's work did not provide a comprehensive account of Augustus' reign in the style of Gardthausen; that was not its intent. But a number of potentially fruitful topics not treated in it were quickly pointed out in a detailed review by Arnaldo Momigliano, who was later to contribute an insightful introduction to an Italian translation of Syme's book.[50] Sceptical of the value of the prosopographical approach, Momigliano questioned whether Syme's emphasis on Augustus as a successful faction leader was a sufficient explanation for the emergence of the Augustan Principate, since it ignored the spiritual and material needs of the individuals who supported him. He also thought that Syme should have placed more weight on Italian municipal society as a model for what was to be replicated in the provinces and on the importance of Augustus' reforms of the Roman army to the success of the Augustan system. As we have seen, Momigliano had contributed the chapter on these military reforms to the bimillenary volume on Augustus when still Professor of Roman History in Turin, but had been stripped of his chair soon thereafter because he was Jewish. In 1938 he had sought refuge in Oxford, where his arrival was facilitated by Hugh Last, who was developing a striking antipathy towards Syme. This did not go unreciprocated and was exacerbated when Syme succeeded Last as Camden Professor of Ancient History in 1949, which required him to take up residence in Brasenose College, of which Last had just become the principal. A series of

---

[48] On Roman history in Mussolini's Italy, see the illuminating treatment in Perry 2006: 89–190; Cagnetta 1976 (focusing in particular on studies of Augustus).

[49] For the *Ara Pacis* project, see most recently Rossini 2006: 14–21, 116–117, with several archival photographs of the difficult excavations and the inauguration of the reassembled monument.

[50] Momigliano 1940 and 1962.

profound disagreements with Last soured Syme's life in Brasenose until failing health forced Last to resign in 1956.[51]

The period from the immediate post-war years to the early 1980s saw a number of important specialist studies and useful syntheses, but no significant changes in perspective. The fact that Augustus had been used so much as a model by Fascist leaders meant that after the fall of their regimes scholarly interest in the first *princeps* declined from the heady heights of the 1930s. In the English-speaking world the influence of Syme's *Roman Revolution* was far-reaching, achieving a dominance without much precedent in classical scholarship. New editions of monographs first published prior to World War II appeared, but for the most part the post-war years were marked by a series of important articles on institutional aspects of the Augustan principate by scholars such as A. H. M. Jones (1904–1970), successively Professor of Ancient History at the University of London from 1946 to 1951 and then at Cambridge from 1951 until his death, E. Togo Salmon (1905–1988), who taught Roman history at McMaster University in Canada from 1930 until his retirement in 1973, and not least Last himself, whose articles on Augustus' *imperium maius* and tribunician power appeared in 1947 and 1951 respectively.[52] In the same period in Italy M. A. Levi (1902–1998) completed the second volume of his detailed history of Augustus, while in Switzerland Jean Béranger (1903–1988) produced a series of important studies on Augustan political ideology. In 1949 the Soviet scholar Nicolai Mashkin (1900–1950) published a detailed Marxist interpretation of Augustus, casting him in the guise of a military dictator, a work which was translated into German in 1954 and into Italian in 1956.[53]

From the 1950s to the early 1980s, a steady flow of general assessments of Augustus' Principate appeared alongside further specialised studies.[54] Some of the most important work was produced in the form of detailed papers by Syme's successors as Camden Professor of Ancient History at Oxford: Peter Brunt (1917–2005) and Fergus Millar (1935–), who held the Camden chair from 1970 to 1982 and

---

[51] For a detailed discussion, see Bowersock 1994.
[52] Jones 1951, 1955, 1960b; Salmon 1956; Last 1947 and 1951; note also Chilver 1950.
[53] Levi 1951; Béranger 1953 and 1958; Mashkin 1949; note also Paribeni 1950; Tibiletti 1953; Wickert 1954 (with much discussion of Augustus).
[54] Among broad syntheses, note, for example, Grimal 1955; Vittinghoff 1959; Rowell 1962; Laugier et al. 1967; Earl 1968; Jones 1970; André 1974; Bengston 1981; Kienast 1982 (2nd edn, 1992; 3rd edn, 1999); Levi 1986 (a reworking of Levi 1933 and 1951). For more specialised studies, see Sattler 1960; Bowersock 1965 (from which Chapter 15, below, is taken); Carter 1970; Judge 1974; Syme 1986. Note also Schmitthenner 1969 and Binder 1987, important collections of reprinted essays, translated into German.

from 1984 to 2002 respectively. Brunt, who had begun research for his (unfinished) doctorate at Oxford under Hugh Last in the years immediately following World War II, deployed his considerable powers of logic and formidably wide learning to undermine several long-cherished views in a series of closely argued articles that fundamentally altered our understanding of the factors that led to the breakdown of the Republic and the establishment of the Principate. Most significantly, he argued that patronage and family connections were less crucial in determining the practice of late Republican politics than Münzer and Syme, among others, had maintained; he rightly insisted on exploring a whole nexus of social and economic causes of the violence and civil strife that led eventually to the principate of Augustus; and his analysis focused just as much on the proletariat as on the Roman nobility.[55] In addition, he produced revisionist studies on a series of issues relating to Augustus' political position, arguing that both the senate and the people still exercised a greater degree of influence in Augustan Rome than Syme had allowed. Brunt also probed the nature of Augustan imperialism, basing his interpretation in the main on the testimony of contemporary Augustan authors.[56]

Fergus Millar, one of Syme's few doctoral students, provided a very different appraisal of the rise of Augustus and the nature of the Augustan regime from that of his DPhil supervisor. He maintained that the Roman people were much more influential in the political process both in the middle and late Republic and in the Augustan age than scholars have usually been willing to admit. So in an article published in 1973 he argued, against his former supervisor, that the young Octavian gained much of his authority and power thanks to a series of constitutional votes taken by the Roman people; the young Caesar was not simply a faction leader whose position was based on the armed support of the clients he had inherited from his adoptive father and on his political connections, as Syme had argued.[57] Similarly in two more recent articles, Millar has continued to advocate the crucial importance of the Roman people during

---

[55] Brunt 1988, a series of detailed essays expanding on Brunt 1971a. For the demographic framework, Brunt 1971b.

[56] For elections under Augustus, see Brunt 1961a; for the senate, Brunt 1984; Augustan imperialism: Brunt 1963 and 1978, revised in Brunt 1990a: 96–109 (ch. 5) and 288–323 (ch. 14) respectively, and for some modifications in his viewpoint, Brunt 1990c. On Brunt, see the sympathetic obituaries published in the *Independent* on 25 November 2005 (by M. Griffin) and in the *Guardian* of 28 November 2005 (by O. Murray, describing him as "the last of the English positivists").

[57] Millar 1973 = 2002: 241–270 (= Chapter 2, below).

the early Principate, in the process mildly criticising Brunt for his emphasis on the role of the senate in the Augustan regime.[58] Throughout, Millar has also advocated the need to look at the impact of Augustus throughout the Roman world in preference to the often Romanocentric analyses of the first *princeps*.[59] During this same period various sourcebooks on the Augustan age were produced for teaching purposes,[60] and several important volumes of collected essays based on conferences appeared, not least those that celebrated Syme's eightieth birthday in 1983 and marked the fiftieth anniversary of the publication of *The Roman Revolution* in 1989.[61]

By this date, however, there were already signs of an important shift in how scholars chose to approach Augustus and his age. This involved integrating more closely the literature and, especially, the art and monumental architecture of the period into historical accounts of Augustus' Principate. The twentieth century had seen voluminous scholarship on the literary output of the Augustan age, and earlier historical accounts of Augustus often had sections on this material, but these usually stood alone, almost as appendices, rather than being closely interwoven into the political analysis.[62] A partial exception was Syme, who had discussed the role of the poets and other writers in his *Roman Revolution* in examining the "national programme" and the "organisation of opinion," but he had almost entirely omitted reference to the monuments and statues that so radically transformed the physical landscape of Rome and the towns of Italy and the provinces during the age of Augustus.[63] Two major

---

[58] Millar 1988a = 2002: 350–359; cf. Brunt 1984; Millar 1993 = 2002: 321–349, a study of how the Augustan regime was viewed by "Augustan" authors such as Valerius Maximus, Velleius Paterculus, and (especially) Ovid as opposed to by "triumviral" authors such as Virgil, Horace, Propertius, and Livy, has a section on "Emperor and Roman People" (1993: 10–13 = 2002: 338–343).

[59] Millar 1966, 1984a, and 1984b.

[60] Ehrenberg and Jones 1949 (2nd edn 1955; reprint with addenda, 1976); Étienne 1970 (in French); Reinhold 1978; Chisholm and Ferguson 1981; more recently, Bringmann and Schäfer 2002 (in German); Cooley 2003.

[61] Millar and Segal 1984; Raaflaub and Toher 1990. Note also *Rivoluzione romana* 1982; Winkes 1985.

[62] For surveys of the scholarship on Augustan literature, see Kenney 1982: 297–494; Conte 1994: 247–397; Galinsky 1996: 225–287; Albrecht 1997: 1.639–891; for the social background of literary production, Fantham 1996: esp. 55–101 ("Augustan Literary Culture") and 102–125 ("Un-Augustan Activities"). As for the treatment of literature in historical works, the first edition of volume X of *The Cambridge Ancient History*, published in 1934, has two discrete chapters (chs. xvi and xvii) by T. R. Glover and E. Strong on the literature and art, respectively, of the Augustan age. By comparison, in the second edition published in 1996, J. A. Crook has a section on "ideology" in his assessment of Augustus' achievement that integrates the evidence of public monuments and literature (Crook 1996b: 133–140). Note also the essays in Binder 1988.

[63] Syme 1939: 440–475. For the use of Augustan poetry as evidence for Augustan foreign

exhibitions, in London and Berlin, framed the emergence of this new paradigm.

At the British Museum the Roman art historian Susan Walker and numismatist Andrew Burnett jointly curated an exhibition on "The Image of Augustus," which opened in 1981. Although its catalogue and handbook were relatively modest, the exhibition signalled – in particular to an English-speaking audience – the historical value of analysing closely the many sculpted portraits of Augustus, public monuments, and coin images produced during his reign.[64] The more ambitious Berlin exhibition, held in 1988 in the context of the quinquennial conference of the Associazione Internazionale di Archeologia Classica (AIAC; International Association of Classical Archaeology) and to help celebrate Berlin's year as European City of Culture, brought together the very best archaeologists and art historians working on the Augustan age from Germany, Italy, and France to survey the most important recent archaeological work and to demonstrate in detail the far-reaching impact of the visual image of the first *princeps*.[65]

Central to both these exhibitions was the work of the distinguished German art historian Paul Zanker (1937–), Professor of Classical Archaeology at the Ludwig-Maximilians-Universität in Munich, who had for many years been working on Roman portraiture and the monumental architecture of Augustan Rome.[66] In 1987 he produced a masterly synthesis of Augustan architecture, public monuments, portraiture, sculpture, coinage, and "Kleinkunst" (small finds such as jewellery, lamps, pottery, even knife-handles and cake-moulds) to argue the compelling case that under Augustus there developed a whole new "visual language," which contributed in a major way towards consolidating his authority as *princeps* throughout the Roman world and helped facilitate social and cultural renewal after civil war. Delivered first as the Jerome lectures at the American Academy in Rome and at the University of Michigan in 1983–1984 and published not just in German but very quickly in an English translation too, Zanker's work had an immediate, international impact.[67]

To be fair, Zanker was not operating in isolation. A number of

policy, see Meyer 1961 (to be read with Brunt 1963 = 1990b); as evidence for the contemporary moral climate, Williams 1962.

[64] Walker and Burnett 1981a and 1981b.
[65] Hofter et al. 1988.
[66] For example, Zanker 1968, 1972, 1973; Vierneisel and Zanker 1979; Fittschen and Zanker 1985.
[67] Note the important review-discussion of Wallace-Hadrill 1989.

other archaeologists and art historians – for instance, Erika Simon and Tonio Hölscher in Germany, Filippo Coarelli and Eugenio La Rocca in Italy, and Pierre Gros in France – had laid much of the groundwork that made Zanker's broad synthesis possible. Indeed just a year before Zanker's major work appeared, Erika Simon, who had been producing important studies on individual Augustan monuments since the late 1950s, published her own wide-ranging synopsis of Augustan artistic culture.[68] But Zanker's work made the monuments and art of Augustan Rome integral to the historical analysis of the period. Its original German title *Augustus und die Macht der Bilder* ("Augustus and the Power of Images") implicitly attributes more agency to Augustus than the rather more neutral title chosen for the English translation: *The Power of Images in the Age of Augustus*. The subtle difference between these two titles brings us back once again, in microcosm, to one of the most difficult and central questions that any historian studying the Augustan age has to confront: how dominant was Augustus himself in shaping general developments during his own Principate?

Zanker's book stimulated a major new wave of work on Augustus that explored the ideological impact of the new visual communicative system on the cities of Italy and the provinces in all sorts of media.[69] Its influence is clear in more general works too, such as Karl Galinsky's wide-ranging analysis of Augustan culture, the balanced assessment of Augustus by John Crook in the second edition of the *Cambridge Ancient History*, and Werner Eck's succinct history of the age of Augustus.[70] It also suggested new ways to interpret the literature of the period, allowing substantial progress to be made in moving beyond the rather tired question of whether it was pro- or anti-Augustan.[71] The poetry is crucial for our historical understand-

---

[68] Simon 1986. For her earlier work, for example, on the Prima Porta statue of Augustus, see Simon 1957 and 1991 (in fact completed in 1983); on the *Ara Pacis*: Simon 1967. Also crucial were Gros 1976; Hölscher 1984 and 1985 (= Chapter 10, below); La Rocca 1987; Coarelli 1985: esp. 237–257 (on Augustus' obliteration of monuments in the Roman Forum that too vividly recalled his violent triumviral past). On Augustan coinage, Kraft 1969; Wallace-Hadrill 1986; Trillmich 1988. For a collection of republished essays, including some of those just cited, Binder 1991.

[69] Architecture: Trillmich and Zanker 1990 (from which Chapter 14, below, is taken); Favro 1996; Spannagel 1999 (with the review of Rich 2002); Rehak 2006; Haselberger 2007. Portraiture: Boschung 1993; Smith 1996; Rose 1997. For public inscriptions as monuments, especially the *Res Gestae*, see Elsner 1996. "Kleinkunst": Kuttner 1995. More generally: MacMullen 2000; Strothmann 2000; Boschung 2003; Koortbojian 2006; Navarro Caballero and Roddaz 2006; and note the direct allusion to Zanker's work in the titles of Hölscher 2000, Barceló 2002, and Schmid 2005.

[70] Galinsky 1996; Crook 1996a and 1996b; Eck 1998 = 2003 (2nd edn, 2007); note also Wallace-Hadrill 1993 and 2000.

[71] For this, note, in particular, Kennedy 1992; P. White 1993 and 2005; Barchiesi 1994 (Engl.

ing of Augustus, since it constitutes our only primary evidence for the contemporary written discourse that developed in Augustan Rome, to be set alongside the "visual language" of the art and monuments.

In more or less the same period, the leading French historian Claude Nicolet (1930–2010), Professor of Ancient History at the Sorbonne (Université de Paris I), produced a stimulatingly original work in which he explored how the representation and control of space played a crucial role in the politics and administrative practices of the Augustan age.[72] Again the original French title, *L'inventaire du monde: géographie et politique aux origines de l'Empire romain*, is more evocative than the rather prosaic one devised for its English translation, *Space, Geography, and Politics in the Early Roman Empire*. The term "l'inventaire du monde" conveys the sense of the creation of an administrative inventory of the world, but also of its geographical discovery. In exploring how Augustus harnessed geographical knowledge to bolster his image as world conqueror and to control and organise the space and peoples that now made up the vastly increased Roman Empire, Nicolet underlined the importance of transformations in Roman knowledge and of new ways of conceptualising the known world to the success of the Augustan regime. This in turn has led to further work on Roman concepts of space, administrative practices, and the importance of record-keeping and archiving to the process of governing an Empire, which are now seen to have been less rudimentary than was once simply assumed to be the case.[73]

Zanker's and Nicolet's work has also served as a catalyst for further research on the cultural transformations that took place under Augustus, and the work here of Andrew Wallace-Hadrill (1951–), Professor of Classics at the University of Reading and from

---

trans. 1997); Gurval 1995; Griffin 1984. A number of key collections of essays from the 1980s and 1990s explored the relationship between literature and power in Augustan Rome: Woodman and West 1984 (including Wiseman 1984 = Chapter 12, below); Raaflaub and Toher 1990 (including Luce 1990 = Chapter 13, below); Powell 1992 (including Wyke 1992, revised at Wyke 2002: 196–243 = Chapter 11, below); Habinek and Schiesaro 1997; and note the special issue of the journal *Klio* (67.1, 1985), publishing the papers (including Hölscher 1985 = Chapter 10, below) from a conference on the culture of the Augustan age held at the Universität Jena in June 1982.

[72] Nicolet 1988 = 1991, with the important review article of Purcell 1990. Relevant also here are Nicolet's earlier important studies of the propertied classes under Augustus: Nicolet 1976 and 1984.

[73] See in particular Nicolet 1994; Moatti 1998; Ando 2000; for a specific case study on the province of Egypt, Rathbone 1993; cf. the much less sophisticated picture sketched in Garnsey and Saller 1987: 20–40 ("Government without Bureaucracy"). For a parallel exploration of Roman concepts of time and their impact on Rome's imperial subjects, see Feeney 2007; Severy 2007.

1996 until 2009 Director of the British School at Rome, has been particularly influential. Since the mid-1980s he has probed the literary texts and cultural history of the Augustan age to trace the fundamental shifts in mentality that took place in this crucial period of Roman history. For Wallace-Hadrill it was in seizing control of the production of knowledge of what it meant to be Roman from the Roman aristocracy, by encouraging the growth of professionals who made advances in fields as diverse as geography, medicine, astrology, rhetoric, law, philosophy, morality, and literature, that Augustus ensured that this cultural revolution very much bolstered his own influence and authority within the Roman state.[74]

The introduction of new ways of studying Augustan Rome by scholars such as Zanker, Nicolet, and Wallace-Hadrill does not mean that more traditional approaches are no longer valid. Studies of Augustus' constitutional position, for example, still have the potential to produce significant advances in our understanding of the period.[75] Other members of the *domus Augusta* are also now gaining more attention, with Zanker's influence clear in the more recent and best of these works.[76] And narrative histories, interpretative synopses, and even popular histories of the age of Augustus, of varying length and quality, continue to appear with some frequency in a variety of languages.[77] The need for fresh syntheses may be in part explained by the new evidence for Augustus' principate that continues to appear. But it is just as much the result of the centrality of the period as a fulcrum of Roman history. For historians of both Republican and imperial Rome, Augustus and the political, social, economic, and cultural transformations that occurred during his period in power require continuing attention, as scholars continue to engage in ongoing debate.

---

[74] Wallace-Hadrill 1987, 1997, 2005; for a full articulation, Wallace-Hadrill 2008.

[75] Lacey 1996 (a collection of his articles); Ferrary 2001 (= Chapter 3, below); Cotton and Yakobson 2002.

[76] On Agrippa, see Roddaz 1984; on Livia, Purcell 1986 (= Chapter 5, below, a pathbreaking analytical study) and now Bartman 1999; Barrett 2002; on Augustus' daughter Julia, Fantham 2006. On the *domus Augusta* more generally, Corbier 1995; Moreau 2005. For two recent monographs exploring the importance of family and the domestic to Augustus, note Severy 2003; Milnor 2005.

[77] Gabba 1991; Shotter 1991 (2nd edn, 2005); Néraudau 1996; Cardoso 1996; Southern 1998; Fraschetti 1990 and 1998; Bleicken 1998; Eck 1998 = 2003 (with a 2nd Engl. edn published in 2007); a third edition of Kienast 1982 appeared in 1999; Thomsen 2001; Renucci 2003; Mellor 2006. Popular histories: Holland 2004; Everitt 2006. Historical novel: Massie 1986. The success of the joint BBC–HBO–RAI television series *Rome*, first shown in 2005, illustrates the enduring fascination of the story of the fall of the Republic and Augustus' rise to power for non-specialist audiences.

III

Given the voluminous literature that has accrued in many languages on Augustus and his age, it has proved a very difficult task to provide even a taste of the many complex issues and debates that have exercised scholars over the years. But in line with the stated aims of the series, this volume makes a modest attempt to introduce readers to a selection of the most important work on the age of Augustus. After much reflection, I have decided to restrict these selections to scholarship published in the last fifty years, even though, as this Introduction has already made clear, much crucial work on the subject appeared in the latter part of the nineteenth and the first half of the twentieth centuries. The selection was made with the aim of providing readers with as wide a range of scholarly approaches as possible on what are, in my view, some of the key topics that historians need to confront when studying Augustus. Five of the chapters have been translated from French and German, since so much of the fundamental scholarship has been produced in languages other than English. (It is a matter of some regret that limits of space prevented the inclusion of a sample of the rich Italian scholarship on the topic.) In making the selection, I have decided not to include extracts from three important monographs on Augustus: Syme's *The Roman Revolution*, Zanker's *The Power of Images in the Age of Augustus*, or Nicolet's *L'inventaire du monde*. Students will need to read those works in their entirety. In addition, I have not, as a general rule, reproduced essays from four of the most important recent collections of essays on Augustus: (1) *Caesar Augustus: Seven Aspects* (eds F. Millar and E. Segal, 1984), the papers from the conference held at Oxford to mark Syme's eightieth birthday; (2) *Between Republic and Empire: Interpretations of Augustus and his Principate* (eds K. Raaflaub and M. Toher, 1990); (3) the proceedings of the Fondation Hardt conference on "The Roman Revolution after Ronald Syme" (ed. A. Giovannini, 2000) (these last two resulting from conferences celebrating the fiftieth and sixtieth anniversaries respectively of the publication of *The Roman Revolution*); or (4) the recent valuable *Cambridge Companion to the Age of Augustus* (ed. K. Galinsky, 2005).[78]

The volume begins by focusing on the political history of Augustus' rise to power and the establishment of the "new state of

---

[78] An exception is the inclusion of T. J. Luce's essay on "Livy, Augustus, and the Forum Augustum" (= Chapter 13, below) from Raaflaub and Toher 1990: 123–138, since there is nothing comparable on this key topic.

affairs" (the *novus status*), to borrow Suetonius' term (*Aug.* 28.2), in the years following his victory at the battle of Actium: Part I, "The *novus status*: From *IIIvir rei publicae constituendae* to *princeps*." Part II, "*Res publica restituta*," then moves to consider some of the most important reforms of Roman institutions and society that took place during Augustus' principate. Part III, "Images of Power and the Power of Images," draws together four studies that use the monumental architecture, art, coins, and literature of the Augustan age to explore key elements of Augustan ideology. The final section, Part IV, "The Impact of Augustus in the Roman Provinces," comprises two case studies, one a general assessment of Augustus' impact on the cities of the Greek world, the other a more specific investigation of Augusta Emerita (modern Mérida in Spain), an Augustan colony founded for retired veteran soldiers in 25 BC These two contributions underline the need to focus not just on the city of Rome and Italy, but on the provinces too, since the latter experienced major transformations in the period from 44 BC to AD 14 in terms of their internal political organisation, their relationship to the imperial power of Rome, their social and cultural fabric, and, in many cases, their physical landscapes as well. In examining the impact of the Augustan changes in provincial contexts, we can enhance our understanding of the nature of the transformations that were taking place at the centre of power.

The articles in this volume marshal a range of analytical strategies and a variety of types of evidence to make their case. Syme, for instance, in Chapter 1 uses the shifts in nomenclature of the man we refer to as "Augustus" as a means of evaluating the nature of the broader political changes that were taking place at Rome in the period from 44 BC to AD 14. In Chapter 2 Millar examines a large selection of documentary evidence, in particular inscriptions, to argue for a radically different interpretation of Octavian's constitutional position in the triumviral period from that of the faction leader with little respect for legality so memorably developed by Syme in *The Roman Revolution*. Andrew Wallace-Hadrill combines social, legal, and political analysis in Chapter 8. In Chapter 10 Hölscher uses a wide variety of types of iconographic evidence to probe the importance of the battle of Actium in the official ideology of the Augustan regime and public memory in Rome, Italy, and the provinces. It is literary and artistic representations of Cleopatra VII of Egypt in the Augustan period that form the focal point of Maria Wyke's analysis in Chapter 11.

In making this inevitably personal selection, it has been necessary to pass over a huge amount of important scholarship on Augustus. It would have been useful, for instance, to include something on the role of the senate in the Augustan regime or a sample of the scholarly literature on the political opposition to Augustus as he sought to build consensus for the *novus status*.[79] In Part IV, rather than singling out the cities of the Greek East and a single Roman colony in Spain for special treatment, it would have been just as valuable to have explored Roman Gaul or North Africa or Augustan Athens.[80] But a volume such as this can only do so much; it cannot hope to be comprehensive. If it helps to introduce readers to some of the crucial questions, if it assists them to become more familiar with some of the wide range of historical sources and approaches that can be applied to tackling these questions, and if it stimulates them into evaluating critically and challenging previous views and into asking new questions, then it will have served a useful purpose.

---

[79] For the role of the senate, see Brunt 1984; Talbert 1984. For political opposition, Atkinson 1960; Stockton 1965; Bosworth 1972 (arguing that C. Asinius Pollio was not quite such an independent Republican spirit as Syme had claimed: e.g. Syme 1939: 320: "Pollio ... was preserved as a kind of privileged nuisance"); Badian 1982; Gabba 1984: esp. 79–85; Raaflaub and Samons 1990; Rohr Vio 2000.

[80] For instance, Gros 1987 on the colony at Arelate (Arles); Bénabou 1976 on Augustus' construction of a new order in North Africa; Walker 1997 on the physical transformation of the urban landscape of Augustan Athens.

PART I

The novus status: *from* III vir rei publicae constituendae *to* princeps

Introduction to Part I:
The novus status: *from* III vir rei publicae constituendae *to* princeps

The political history of the rise to power of the man who in 27 BC was granted the name "Augustus" and the establishment of the new regime that historians have come to term the "Principate" form the focus of Part I of this volume. The nature of Octavian's power-base following his adoption as Julius Caesar's heir in 44 BC, the complex shifts in political alliances and loyalties that took place during the period of the Triumvirate, the reasons for Octavian's eventual victory in the civil wars against M. Antonius and Cleopatra, and the nature of the "new state of affairs" – the *novus status*, as Suetonius (*Aug.* 28.2) termed it – that took shape at Rome following Octavian's victory have all exercised scholars since the mid-nineteenth century, if not earlier, as the general Introduction to this volume has made clear. In scholarship in the English-speaking world, the work of Sir Ronald Syme has been predominant on these topics, and on many more besides. *The Roman Revolution*, first published in 1939, provides not only a gripping narrative of the events of the period 44 BC to AD 14, but, even more importantly, a challenging interpretation of them that stresses the naked opportunism and the brutal and often illegal methods of "young Caesar." All those interested in this key period of history will profit from reading *The Roman Revolution* in its entirety; for that reason, no excerpts from it have been presented in this volume. Instead, this first Part opens with one of Syme's best articles, published, in 1958, almost twenty years after his path-breaking book; it provides an illustration of his distinctive qualities and methods as a historian.

"Imperator Caesar: A Study in Nomenclature" (Chapter 1) begins with a series of reflections upon Roman styles of nomenclature, hardly promising material for Roman political history, one might at first suppose.[1] However, from such technical details Syme brilliantly weaves an argument that demonstrates just how revealing the changes in name of the man who began life in 63 BC as C. Octavius are for our understanding of the political history of the period from 44 BC to AD 14. "Young Caesar" was by no means the only Roman aristocrat in the spoilingly competitive politics of the late Republic and triumviral age to use names for political purposes (compare Cn. Pompeius "Magnus," Pompey "the Great"), but his appropriation of the military salutation "Imperator" ("Commander") for use as his *praenomen* in 40 BC was, in Syme's view, "exorbitant, far outdistancing any predecessor or competitor." Once Octavian's supremacy was incontestably established following his victory at the battle of Actium, the emphasis switched with the award of the *cognomen* "Augustus" in January 27; he now became the "august one," the "venerable one," the "one worthy of honour." The needs of the pious restorer of the *res publica* were given precedence over the military exigencies of the triumviral age. In short, this detailed onomastic analysis reveals much about Syme's general interpretation of the evolving political position of Octavian, the later Augustus.[2]

The second chapter, "Triumvirate and Principate," is by Fergus Millar, who from 1984 until his retirement in 2002 was Camden Professor of Ancient History at Oxford. One of the few doctoral students taken on by Syme during his own tenure of the Camden Chair from 1949 to 1970, Millar offered this study, on its first appearance in 1973, as a tribute to Syme. However, as readers will quickly see, it presents a radically different picture of Octavian's position during the triumviral period from the one drawn so vividly by Syme. In contrast to the revolutionary young leader who paid little attention to legality, Millar stresses that Octavian's position was in fact based on a series of laws passed in the popular assemblies at Rome. Although its controversial thesis has not won universal acceptance, the article demonstrates the potential of new discoveries, in this case the important dossier of inscriptions discovered at Aphrodisias in the province of Asia, for reopening a question and forcing us to rethink long-held views. In it, Millar makes a conscious attempt to apply the methods of *The Roman Revolution* and to develop its conclusions further, but, in so doing, places a rather differ-

---

[1] But for further works that illustrate the value of onomastics for political, social, and cultural history, see Duval 1977; Salway 1994; and a whole series of works by three gener-ations of Finnish scholars: e.g. Kajanto 1965; Solin 1982 and 1996; Salomies 1987 and 1992; Kajava 1994; Bruun 2003.

[2] For Syme's further reflections towards the end of his career, see Syme 1986: 439–454.

ent emphasis not just on the politics of the triumviral age, when, he argues, the institutions of the *res publica* remained much more active than Syme had presumed, but also on the changes that culminated in the "settlement" of 28 to 27 BC "restoring the *res publica*." Throughout, Millar pays careful attention to the precise wording of the pronouncements of Imperator Caesar in the 30s BC as evidence for the emergence of monarchy at Rome. (Here, as elsewhere, he does not eschew the use of the term "monarchy" to describe Augustus' position, since he believes, as did the historian Cassius Dio in the early third century, that this is precisely what Augustus' rule ushered in at Rome.)[3]

The third chapter, "The Powers of Augustus," presents the mature reflections of one of France's leading Roman historians, Jean-Louis Ferrary, on a question that is central to our understanding of the Augustan Principate. What precisely was the legal and constitutional basis for Augustus' political position?[4] During his distinguished career at the Sorbonne and the École Pratique des Hautes Études in Paris, Ferrary's work has focused on Rome's political and intellectual relations with the Greek world, especially in the later Republic, on Roman political institutions, on Roman law and legislation, and on the history of ideas and political theory at Rome. He is also one of France's leading specialists in the epigraphy of the Roman period, and was elected a member of the Académie des Inscriptions et Belles Lettres in 2005, one of France's highest academic honours. Many of Ferrary's scholarly interests and strengths are revealed in his masterly article on Augustus' powers, first published in French in 2001.[5] It provides an unusually wide-ranging yet detailed sense of the history of the question, engaging with the views of scholars working in a variety of intellectual traditions as far back as Mommsen. It is remarkable not just for its sheer thoroughness, but also for the fairness of the argument, as Ferrary gives his predecessors due credit for advancing the question, as he builds on their work, though never afraid to show where their interpretations were in his view erroneous. As a result, Ferrary's article will provide readers with a very useful road-map of evolving scholarly views on, and approaches to, the central question of the evolving powers of the first *princeps*.

---

[3] See also Millar 1984a.
[4] Previous important discussions on this topic include De Francisci 1938; Jones 1951 and 1960b; Lacey 1996 (a collection of his articles); Giovannini 1999; Girardet 2000; note also Cotton and Yakobson 2002.
[5] For another, shorter article tackling some of the same issues, see Ferrary 2003. For a sample of some of his earlier work, note Ferrary 1977–1979, 1984, and 1988.

However, it also makes a strikingly original case that has shifted the terms of the debate. It was, Ferrary argues, the governance of Rome's provinces that formed the focal point of the various powers granted Augustus in 27 and which were then modified and renewed in 23, 18, and at various intervals for the rest of his life. This naturally entails detailed treatment of his *imperium* (literally, his "power to command"), which was to become in time defined as "power greater than" (*imperium maius quam*) that held by other holders of *imperium*, and his tribunician power (*tribunicia potestas*). But Ferrary also discusses Augustus' censorial powers, his powers of jurisdiction, the extent of his control over the election of state magistrates, as well as the consular privileges he enjoyed while resident in the city of Rome even after he had resigned the consulate in 23. Since some of these powers were eventually bestowed upon his most important political assistants, such as Agrippa and then Tiberius, Ferrary's discussion also sheds much light on the manner in which Augustus relied on "co-rulers" during his Principate and on the whole question of the succession. The article adopts a clear diachronic approach, tracing the gradual evolution and development of Augustus' powers, as the *novus status* became, step by step, more entrenched and Augustus' position (his *statio*) within that new state of affairs became ever more clearly defined during his long period of political supremacy.[6]

Discussion of Augustus' powers raises the question of the nature of the relationship between the *princeps* and the senate, and ideally it would have been useful to include here one of the main contributions on this topic: for instance, P. A. Brunt's 1984 article, "The Role of the Senate in the Augustan Regime."[7] Limits of space unfortunately did not permit this, but it is vital to take to heart the central thesis of that article, namely that our ancient sources tend to focus, arguably to an excessive degree, on the figure of Augustus and do not necessarily give due coverage to other historical actors or organs of the Roman state, not least the senate, that still played an important role in the political system known as the Principate. This is not to advocate a return to Mommsen's over-schematic view of a "dyarchy" between *princeps* and senate, but the senate's significance should not

---

[6] Augustus himself referred to his *statio* in a letter sent to his grandson/adopted son Gaius Caesar in AD 1, quoted by Aulus Gellius (*NA* 15.7.3), already assuming that it was heritable: he hoped that Gaius and his brother Lucius were flourishing, behaving in a manly fashion, and preparing to succeed to his position (*statio*).

[7] Brunt 1984; note also Talbert 1984 and, on senatorial self-representation under Augustus, Eck 1984.

be underplayed. Its continued centrality under Augustus, along with some of the evidence and arguments deployed by Brunt, is explored further by Werner Eck in his article on "The Administrative Reforms of Augustus" (Chapter 7, below).

The *imperium* that Augustus was granted, first and foremost, recognised him as the supreme commander-in-chief of Rome's armed forces. Thus the military history of the age of Augustus must feature prominently in any assessment of his Principate. It is no exaggeration to say that, despite the revolts in Illyricum and Pannonia and serious setbacks in Germania in the final decade of his life, more territory was brought firmly under Roman control during his reign than under any of his successors as emperor. Conquest and imperial control were thus central to his success as *princeps*. As Anchises reminds his son Aeneas at a key moment of Virgil's *Aeneid*, "Remember, Roman, to exercise your power to rule over nations (these will be your skills), to impose tradition upon peace, to spare those subjected, and to wage war to subdue totally those who disrespect you."[8] Not surprisingly, success in war and foreign conquest loomed large in the manner in which Augustus was represented to his contemporaries in Rome, Italy, and the territories of the vastly expanded Roman Empire, as John Rich, Professor of Ancient History at the University of Nottingham, points out in his wide-ranging article, "Augustus, War and Peace" (Chapter 4), originally written for a colloquium, held in 2002, on the representation and perception of Roman imperial power. In addition to his historical commentary on Cassius Dio's narrative of the "Augustan settlement," Rich has produced a series of important articles on Augustan Rome.[9] In this contribution, he starts by examining the ways in which military victories and their important corollary, pacification, were dominant themes in representations of Augustus in a variety of visual media and in the literature of Augustan Rome. (The influence of Zanker's work on the "power of images" and Nicolet's on the importance of geographical knowledge and the lack thereof for Augustan imperialism is clearly apparent here: see further Part III, below.) In particular, Rich registers a discrepancy between the actual achievements of foreign conquest and the manner in which these were presented and perceived at the centre of power. This leads him to examine a key problem of historical interpretation: whether we should view Augustus' imperial policies as basically defensive in aim, as was Syme's view, or as favouring

---

[8] Virg. *Aen.* 6.851–853: *tu regere imperio populos, Romane, memento / (hae tibi erunt artes), pacique imponere morem, / parcere subiectis et debellare superbos.*
[9] On Dio, Rich 1990; cf. 1989. Other key articles: Rich 1996, 1998; Rich and Williams 1999.

unlimited expansion, as Brunt argued in a classic review-article first published in 1963, subsequently revised and expanded.[10] Rich argues that no monolithic policy objective (whether defensive or aggressive) remained in force throughout Augustus' Principate and convincingly makes the case that his foreign policy evolved over the course of his long period in power. In particular, shifts in policy, notes Rich, can often be closely connected to Augustus' dynastic needs, as he sought to groom a preferred successor by allowing him to win military glory in the service of the *princeps*. As in Ferrary's and Eck's chapters (Chapters 3 and 7 respectively), it is the shifts in Augustus' policies over time as he responded to changing needs that receive the attention here they deserve but often fail to attract.

Another relative oversight in previous studies of Augustus' Principate, at least until recently, was the important public, even political, role played by his second wife, Livia Drusilla, whom Augustus married in 38 BC after abruptly divorcing his first wife Scribonia, who had just given birth to their daughter Julia. In 1986 Nicholas Purcell, since 2011 Camden Professor of Ancient History at the University of Oxford and a leading Roman social, economic, and cultural historian with wide-ranging and eclectic scholarly tastes,[11] successfully resuscitated interest in the *princeps femina* (the "leading female") of Augustan Rome, as she was described in a contemporary eulogy of her younger son Drusus. Purcell was not interested in writing a biography of Livia, which would, he rightly claimed, be the "preserve of speculation or historical fiction,"[12] but instead argued that as the leading matron (*matrona*; i.e., married woman) in Roman society she served as a focal point and example for all Roman married women, who were in this way encouraged to fulfil a significant public function in the restored *res publica*. To uncover Livia's fundamental position in the *novus status*, one needs to peel away the layers of hostility that have portrayed her, in Roman and more recent times, as a scheming stepmother, whose intense stepmotherly hatreds (*novercalia odia*) constitute such a dominant leitmotif in historical accounts of the Augustan and Julio-Claudian

---

[10] Syme 1934: esp. 351–354; Brunt 1963, 1978, 1990b; cf. 1990c. In turn, this stems from the more general debate about the nature of Roman imperialism, on which see Badian 1968; Harris 1979; North 1981; Sherwin-White 1984; Gruen 1984; Mattingly 1997; Champion 2004.

[11] For some of his key work in Roman economic history, note esp. Horden and Purcell 2000; in economic/cultural history, Purcell 1985; for leisure, note Purcell 1995 (on dicing); for further contributions on the Augustan period, note Purcell 1996a, 1996b, and 2005.

[12] For a more recent, and partly successful, attempt, see Barrett 2002. In the field of historical fiction, Robert Graves' portrait of Livia in his 1934 novel *I, Claudius* has not been bettered. For the juridical and social position of Livia, see now Frei-Stolba 1998.

periods from Tacitus onwards. Rather, Purcell argues, Roman matrons with Livia at their head were to be a key constituent part of the body politic, an *ordo*, at the level of both the Roman state and the local municipality. The accolades, titles, and public monuments erected in her honour around the Empire are testimony to the weight of her authority.

While Purcell's rather defensive apology for the fact that he, a male scholar, should be writing women's history appears somewhat quaint twenty years later, now that women's history is firmly established in the mainstream of historical scholarship and is terrain that no longer needs to be barricaded as the sole preserve of female, or feminist, scholars, his article was pathbreaking in placing Livia and the matrons of Rome at the very centre of our picture of Roman public life under Augustus. Furthermore, his main conclusions received dramatic confirmation in 1996 with the publication of the *senatus consultum* of AD 20 concerning Cn. Piso senior, the man who committed suicide after being accused of murdering Tiberius' adopted son Germanicus in 19. This document confirms not only Tacitus' claim (*Ann.* 3.15, 17) that Piso's wife Plancina was spared from the charges laid against her thanks to the intervention of Livia, but also Purcell's analysis of Livia's prominent public position within the Roman state, as the following statement so fulsomely reveals:

> The senate believes that to Iulia Aug(usta) (i.e., Livia), who has served the *res publica* superlatively not only in giving birth to our Princeps but also through her many great favours (*beneficia*) towards men of every rank, and who rightly and deservedly could have supreme influence in what she asked from the senate, but who used that influence sparingly, ... support and indulgence should be accorded and has decided that the punishment of Plancina should be waived.[13]

---

[13] Eck et al. 1996, Copy A (from Irni), lines 115–120; translated by Griffin 1997: 250–253. The Latin text here is: *senatum arbitrari ... Iuliae Aug(ustae) optume de r(e) p(ublica) meritae non partu tantum modo principis nostri, sed etiam multis magnisq(ue) erga cuiusq(ue) ordinis homines beneficis, quae cum iure meritoq(ue) plurumum posse<t> in eo quod a senatu petere deberet, parcissume uteretur eo ... suffragandum indulgendumq(ue) esse remittiq(ue) poenam Plancinae placere.*

1 *Imperator Caesar:*
A Study in Nomenclature†

RONALD SYME

Each and every Roman citizen must possess at the very least a *praenomen* and a *nomen*, to constitute, along with the filiation and the tribe, his official designation; and the *praenomen*, duly abbreviated, continues to figure in any formulation that requires a man's *état civil* [civil status], from public documents down to funerary inscriptions. Otherwise, apart from its use in domestic or familiar intercourse, the *praenomen* tends to be suppressed in the last age of the Roman Republic. Various fashions can be detected as they grow and spread. A well known person may be referred to by one of his other names only, *nomen* or *cognomen*, thus 'Pompeius' and 'Caesar'. Especially notable and destined finally to prevail in serious prose is the practice of designating a man by two names, the *nomen gentilicium* [name of the *gens*, i.e., family name] and the *cognomen*, as in 'Asinius Pollio'. Significant variations, almost categories, can be registered, according to the type of literature or the social status of the individual. The same holds for a further innovation, that inversion which places the *cognomen* before the *gentilicium*, as in 'Balbus Cornelius'. It begins with persons of low degree, and gradually ascends the social scale. Cicero never permits himself to refer to contemporary members of the *nobilitas* [nobility] in this manner.

Not but what the *praenomen*, ostensibly a trivial item of nomenclature, exhibits powers of resistance, precisely among the *nobiles* [nobles]. The proper and choice fashion of designating those exalted personages, in formal or honorific address, seems to be by *praenomen* (abbreviated) and *cognomen*. Thus 'L. Sulla', 'P. Scipio', 'C. Caesar', 'M. Metellus'. The name of the *gens* being omitted in this formulation, that of the family or branch takes its place and is elevated into the rank and status of a *nomen*. So much so that the

† Originally published in *Historia* 7 (1958), 172–188.

filiation, which normally follows the *nomen* and precedes the *cognomen*, will conform to the change of function, with M. Caecilius Q. f. Metellus being styled on his coins 'M. Metellus Q. f.'.¹ Here 'Metellus' is patently doing duty as a *nomen*. An instructive extension of this procedure is furnished by the name 'M. Piso M. f. Frugi'.² This man's father, the consul M. Pupius Piso, was a Calpurnius Piso by birth, adopted by a certain M. Pupius. The son, it appears, was eager to suppress the undecorative *nomen* 'Pupius', and emphasize his noble lineage. Technically not a member of the *gens Calpurnia*, he could not call himself 'Calpurnius', but he took the ancestral cognomen 'Piso' and converted it into a *nomen*.³

Predilection for the aristocratic *cognomen* is in no way enigmatic. The *gentilicia* of the *nobiles* forfeit much of their distinctiveness through being transmitted to clients and freedmen and consequently vulgarised. There came to be myriads of Cornelii, most notorious the freedmen of L. Sulla the Dictator. The address by *praenomen* and *cognomen* is therefore proper to the *nobilitas*. Cicero never applies the form 'L. Balbus' to L. Cornelius Balbus, an alien who derived his name 'Cornelius' from his patron, one of the Cornelii Lentuli.

Moreover, certain *praenomina*, restricted almost wholly to the aristocracy, or rather to its primordial nucleus, the patriciate, are quite anomalous. 'Servius' belongs all but exclusively to the Sulpicii, 'Appius' to the one branch of the Claudii, the Claudii Pulchri. Such peculiar *praenomina* make mock of all rules. So closely is 'Servius' associated with the *gens Sulpicia* that, to take an extreme example, Tacitus can employ it as though it were a *gentilicium* and write 'post Iulios Claudios Servios' ['after the Iulii, Claudii and Servii'].⁴ And 'Appius' instead of 'Claudius' was attached to a road or an aqueduct: 'via Appia' and 'aqua Appia.' Cicero refers to the consul of 54 B.C. as 'Appius' without the marked and perhaps excessive familiarity which the use of a *praenomen* would normally imply.⁵ This, it is true, is in letters, not in public pronouncements or in serious prose. Livy, however, writing history, will name an historic Claudius simply as 'Appius'.⁶ Finally, not only does 'Appius' oppose a certain resistance

---

¹ E. A. Sydenham, *The Coinage of the Roman Republic* (1952), 719.
² Sydenham 824 ff.
³ Though this man (praetor 44 B.C.) may have taken that further step, for he (not his parent) may be the 'M. Calpurnius M. f. Piso Frugi [pr(aetor)]' of *CIL I²*. 745.
⁴ *Hist.* II. 48. 2.
⁵ e.g. *Ad fam.* I. 9. 4: 'me cum Caesare et cum Appio esse in gratia' ['that I am on good terms with Caesar and Appius'].
⁶ III. 36. 1.

to abbreviation or stand by itself: unlike the normal *praenomen*, it is not transmitted to freedmen.⁷

Paradoxically but not inexplicably, the revolutionary age enhances the pride and the ambition of the *nobiles*, and the first dynasty to rule at Rome is patrician, the line of the Julii and Claudii. Sulla, Caesar and Augustus all made conspicuous efforts to bring back the patriciate to a rank of leadership in the *nobilitas*. One sign of exorbitant personal claims is the choice of abnormal *praenomina*. As is fitting, Sulla the Dictator opens the roll. Taking 'Felix' as his own *cognomen*, he transmutes it and gives it to his son as a *praenomen* in the shape of 'Faustus'; and Faustus Sulla with appropriate bravado inscribes the 'Faustus', standing alone, on his coins.⁸ Then after an interval L. Aemilius Paullus, the second son of that Aemilius who raised civil war to overthrow the Dictator's ordinances, transfers his *cognomen* to his own son, who is called Paullus Aemilius Lepidus (*cos. suff.* 34 B.C.). A Valerius (*suff.* 29 B.C.) brings back the ancient name 'Potitus'; and before long two Fabii publicise an ancestry that is both Aemilian and Scipionic by the *praenomina* 'Paullus' and 'Africanus' (the consuls of 11 and 10 B.C. respectively). To the same generation as the Fabii belongs a plebeian *nobilis*, but of dynastic family, Iullus Antonius (*cos.* 10 B.C.), the younger son of the Triumvir. The choice of the name 'Iullus', which belonged in old time to the Julii, shows how Marcus Antonius advertised 'pietas' ['dutiful respect'] towards his dead friend and leader, Caesar the Dictator: Iullus Antonius was born about 43 B.C. Contemporary to within a few years are the two heirs of the Claudii Nerones, the stepsons of Augustus. Both bear a name ancient in the family, 'Nero', which, like 'Appius', is of Sabine origin. But whereas the elder conforms to established practice and is simply Ti. Claudius Nero, the younger has the name as a *praenomen* and is called Nero Claudius Drusus.⁹

That a *cognomen* should be taken and exploited as a *praenomen* is not so outrageous an operation as it might on the surface appear. Denoting originally a person as a person, the *cognomen* is by its nature akin to the *praenomen*. Reference has already been made to the frequent practice of dropping the *praenomen* and inverting the other two names. In the order *cognomen* and *gentilicium*, as in 'Balbus Cornelius', it may not be altogether fanciful to suppose that the displaced *cognomen* has something of the force and function of

---

⁷ Hence 'P. Clodius Ap. l. Eros' ['P(ublius) Clodius Eros, freedman of Ap(pius)'] (*CIL* I.² 1282).
⁸ Sydenham, 879 ff.
⁹ His original *praenomen* had been 'Decimus' (Suetonius, *Divus Claudius* I. 1).

a *praenomen*: the inversion is not at all arbitrary. Cicero, it has been observed, does not apply this license to the names of persons of consequence. It is, however, only fair to mention that the two young *nobiles* who completed the monumental gate which Ap. Claudius Pulcher (*cos*. 54 B.C.) dedicated at Eleusis do not disdain to call themselves 'Pulcher Claudius' and 'Rex Marcius'.[10]

Two significant fashions in the nomenclature of the *nobiles* have now been adverted upon, viz., a predilection for the type 'C. Caesar', with consequent neglect of the *gentilicium*, and a taste for fancy *praenomina*. Both are illustrated by the sons of Cn. Pompeius Magnus. The elder, who fell at Munda, uses the form 'Cn. Magnus'.[11] The younger maintains the family cause for a decade against the heirs to Caesar's power; and, having likewise adopted the paternal *cognomen*, goes on to exhibit startling combinations and permutations. It is not always easy to date them, but one case happens to be authenticated with welcome precision. In a speech delivered before the Roman Senate on the first day of January, 43 B.C., Cicero refers to him as 'Sextus Pompeius Gnaei filius Magnus' ['Sextus Pompeius Magnus, son of Gnaeus'];[12] before the end of March he occurs in the draft of a *senatus consultum* as 'Magnus Pompeius Gnaei filius'.[13] Therefore 'Magnus' has moved into the place of a *praenomen*.

Other and further devices were already, it seems, being played upon. 'Pietas' was familiar as the badge of the Metelli: it was plagiarised by their allies and adopted as the battle cry of the Pompeian loyalists at Munda.[14] Sextus, the surviving brother, affected 'Pius' as a *cognomen*. Fleeing at first to Lacetania in Hispania Citerior, he returned before long to Ulterior and raised war against the Caesarian generals, engaging first C. Carrinas, then Asinius Pollio.[15] The signal defeat of Pollio may without discomfort be assigned to the spring or early summer of 44 B.C. Hence presumably Sextus' imperatorial acclamation. Certain of his Spanish coins can therefore be assigned to the interval between this event and his assumption of the title of 'praefectus classis et orae maritimae' ['prefect of the fleet and sea-coast'], which office was voted to him in the next year by the Senate after the Battle of Mutina (April, 43 B.C.).[16] Brass coins struck

[10] *ILS* 4041.
[11] Sydenham 1035 ff.
[12] *Phil*. V. 41.
[13] *Phil*. XIII. 50, cf. 8; 'Magnum Pompeium, clarissimum adulescentem' ['Magnus Pompeius, most illustrious youth'].
[14] Appian, *BC* II. 104.
[15] Appian, *BC* IV. 83 f.; Dio XLV. 10.
[16] Dio XLVI. 40. 3; Velleius II. 73. 2.

by Eppius, one of his legates in Spain, represent his name as 'Magnus Pius' – that is, *praenomen* and *cognomen*.[17] But there are also certain mysterious *denarii*, struck, it appears, at the town of Salacia, on which he figures as 'Sextus Magnus Pius'.[18] In terms of strict nomenclature, these words can be interpreted as *praenomen*, *gentilicium* and *cognomen*. That is to say, in this instance, 'Magnus' has been promoted to the rank of a family name. It may seem far-fetched as an explanation – but there was soon to be a Caesarian parallel.

His position legalised with the rank of a commander of the seas, the young adventurer moved closer to Italy, and by the end of the year 43 B.C. he had established himself in Sicily, which island he occupied and held until his defeat in 36 B.C. The coins which Sextus struck as 'praef. clas. et orae merit.', uniformly show his name as 'Magnus Pius'.[19] The onomatological function of those two words is demonstrated and confirmed by a dedication set up by one of his legates at Lilybaeum – 'Mag. Pompeio Mag. f. Pio'.[20] The process thus becomes clear. The young Pompeius has discarded the praenomen 'Sextus' long ago; and the experiment with 'Magnus' as a *gentilicium*, as exemplified in the Spanish *denarii* showing 'Sextus Magnus Pius', has not been repeated. Though the old family name has not been altogether lost sight of, as witness the inscription from Lilybaeum, the nomenclature 'Magnus Pius' is preferred, in the style of *praenomen* + *cognomen*. As 'Cn. Magnus', the elder of the sons of Magnus is unexceptionable: the younger, 'Magnus Pius', is revolutionary and foretells the monarchy.

There was another pretender, Caesar's heir, whose ambition outstripped Pompeius and the sons of Pompeius. C. Julius Caesar (for so he chose to be known, spurning the 'Octavianus' that would have perpetuated the memory of his real parentage) was able to parade as 'Divi filius' ['son of the Deified One'] as soon as the Senate and People consecrated his adoptive father early in 42 B.C.[21] A few years later

---

[17] Sydenham 1045.
[18] Sydenham 1041 ff. Six types (two of them without 'Pius'). Grueber, *BMCRR* II, p. 370 f., registered three. On these coins see further H. Bahrfeldt, *Num. Zeitschr.* XXIX (1897), 50 f.; L. Laffranchi, *Rivista italiana di numismatica* XXV (1912), 511 ff.; M. Grant, *From Imperium to Auctoritas* (1946), 22 f.; 409. It should be noted that the town is 'Salacia cognominata urbs imperatoria' ['Salacia with the surname Imperial City'] (Pliny, *NH* IV. 116). Its coins have 'Imp. Sal.' and 'Imp. Salac.' on the reverse (Vives y Escudero, *La moneda hispánica* III [1924], 26).
[19] Sydenham 1344 ff.
[20] *ILS* 8891 (Lilybaeum).
[21] Dio XLVII. 18. 3. It is notable and important, however, that 'Divi f.' cannot be attested on his coins before 38 B.C., cf. K. Kraft, *Jahrbuch für Numismatik und Geldgeschichte* III/IV (1952/3), 69.

he discards the *gentilicium* of the Julii and the *praenomen* as well, and bursts into official nomenclature with a portentous and flamboyant *praenomen* as 'Imp. Caesar'.

Aristocratic preference for the *cognomen* has already been observed; and a *cognomen* could be given the function of a *gentilicium*. In one case, indeed, the transmutation was thorough and official. In 59 B.C., if not earlier, M. Junius Brutus, adopting the name of a maternal kinsman, became a Servilius Caepio in the strange style of 'Q. Caepio Brutus'.[22] Closely parallel is the case, already quoted, of M. Piso Frugi. Like 'Piso' and 'Caepio', 'Caesar' is henceforth converted into a *gentilicium*. The more striking phenomenon, however, is the use of 'Imperator' as a man's first and individual name.

For this style the earliest unequivocal and contemporary evidence is provided by coins struck by Agrippa, consul designate, when commanding in Gaul: that is to say, in 38 B.C.[23] Is this a new and sudden thing, is there a discernible line of development, a precedent even?

If there were an exact precedent, the problem would be simple. And such a precedent is alleged. Cassius Dio states that in 45 B.C. the Senate voted to Caesar the Dictator the title of 'imperator' as a proper name.[24] Dio is explicit. It was, he says, something distinct alike from the traditional imperatorial salutation and from the designation of a commander in possession of *imperium*; it was precisely the title of imperial power borne by the Emperor in his own day. Further, the title was to pass to the sons and to the descendants of Caesar. Dio also reverts to this grant under the year 29 B.C., after he has spread himself at some length on the speeches of Agrippa and Maecenas: he affirms that Octavianus now adopted the hereditary title that had been conferred upon Caesar.[25] Moreover, Suetonius also records the bestowal of the *praenomen imperatoris* [the first name 'Imperator', i.e., commander] on the Dictator.[26] These passages in Dio and in Suetonius have been the occasion of perpetual argumentation. It may be said at once that no other author, contemporary or subsequent, is aware of this momentous innovation; that no coin

---

[22] The 'Q. Caepio hic Brutus' ['this Q(uintus) Caepio Brutus'] of *Ad Att.* II. 24. 3 finds confirmation later in Cicero's draft of the *senatus consultum* in February of 43, 'Q. Caepio Brutus pro consule' ['acting as consul, i.e., proconsul'] (*Phil.* X. 26). Cf. Sydenham 1287 ff.
[23] Sydenham 1329; 1331.
[24] Dio XLIII. 44. 2 ff.
[25] Dio LII. 41. 3.
[26] *Divus Julius* 76. 1. It is difficult to argue that Suetonius and Dio do not mean the same thing. Dio's phrase ὥσπερ τι κύριον ['as a kind of proper name'] must not be neglected.

exists, or inscription, attesting 'Imperator Caesar' as the nomenclature of Caesar the Dictator.[27]

Such are the facts. There is anachronism in Dio's view of the original function of the *praenomen* 'Imp.' There are other anachronisms and anticipations in his account of the prerogatives of the Dictator. The hereditary *praenomen* is matched by hereditary transmission of the office of *pontifex maximus*.[28] There is also the permission accorded to Caesar to offer the *spolia opima* [lit. the 'rich spoils', i.e., those taken from an enemy leader], even though he had not killed an enemy leader with his own hands.[29] That is grotesque – the *spolia opima*, forgotten for centuries, did not emerge into Roman politics until 29 or 28 B.C. when the inopportune claim of an ambitious proconsul caused Octavianus no little embarrassment.[30]

There is no Caesarian precedent for the *praenomen* of Caesar's heir. Nor is there a Pompeian precedent: there is nothing abnormal in Sextus Pompeius' use of the imperatorial acclamation after his name. It has been suggested, it is true, that on one of the surviving specimens of his Spanish *denarii* (belonging to 44/3 B.C.), the legend 'Imp. Sex. Magnus' both could and should be read.[31] If this were conceded, 'imp.' still does not function as substitute for a *praenomen*, as in 'Imp. Caesar', but is merely prefixed to the *praenomen*. At the most, admitting the suggestion, a sporadic deviation has been detected, patently of no subsequent influence on the nomenclature of Sextus Pompeius, or of anybody else.[32]

A different approach to the problem is indicated. The retention of 'imp.' after a general's name might appear to give it something of the function of a *cognomen*; and a *cognomen* can be transferred and used as a *praenomen*.

The Republican general, acclaimed after victory by his troops, has the right to carry 'imp.' with him until he enters the City again, to keep the title for the day of his triumph only, if the celebration be

---

[27] cf. D. McFayden, *The History of the Title Imperator under the Roman Empire* (Chicago, 1920), 11 ff. Scholars are naturally reluctant to throw over the evidence of Dio, and various attempts are made to utilise it. See, for example, A. v. Premerstein, *Vom Werden und Wesen des Prinzipats*, Abh. Bayer. Ak. Wiss. Philos.-hist. Kl., N.F. 15 (1937), 245 ff.; A. Alföldi, *Studien über Caesars Monarchie* (Lund, 1953), 28 ff.; K. Kraft, *Jahrbuch für Numismatik und Geldgeschichte* III/IV (1952/3), 64 ff.
[28] Dio XLIV. 3. 3.
[29] Dio XLIV. 5. 3.
[30] Dio LI. 24. 4, cf. H. Dessau, *Hermes* XLI (1906), 142 ff.; E. Groag, P-W XIII. 283 ff.
[31] M. Grant, op. cit. 22 f.; 409. Accepted by Alföldi, op. cit. 30.
[32] Indeed, 'Imp.' may not belong at all before the 'Sex. Magnus', cf. K. Kraft, op. cit. 68. The coin in question is Sydenham 1043 (reproduced on pl. 27) = *BMCRR* II, p. 371, 94 (pl. CI, 12).

approved by the Senate, otherwise to forfeit it at once. It might happen that an *imperator*, thwarted by the 'calumnia inimicorum' ['malicious charge of his personal enemies'] and condemned to wait for a long time and perhaps in vain, would linger for months or for years outside the sacred precinct, tenacious of his imperatorial acclamation and the laurelled *fasces*. The advent of the civil war surprised a retiring proconsul of Cilicia, M. Tullius M. f. Cicero imp., still in possession of the *imperium* and all the paraphernalia, and thus technically available for high command. The experience of other wars and other ages shows military men not eager to relinquish the titles and aura of authority when the office has lapsed. Pompeius Magnus had earned three acclamations and three triumphs; hence three periods in his career amounting to a fair sum of years, in which he had borne the title as of right until a triumph supervened and abolished it. Victory and the prestige of victory had abode with Magnus from his earliest enterprises. For Magnus, or for others, there must have been a temptation to overstep the proprieties and assume that the appellation still adhered to his name, befitting Rome's greatest soldier. Furthermore, in this age a second or a third salutation is not necessarily indicated by a numerical symbol. A dedication set up at Auximum in 52 B.C., nine years from his last triumph, styles him 'Cn. Pompeius Cn. f. Magnus imp.'.[33] The dedication is an official act of the colony of Auximum, in the region Picenum which the Pompeii dominated. This being so, it is not inconceivable that other documents showing Pompeius as 'imp.' also belong to periods in his career when he had no legal right to the appellation. Nor, to take a later instance, is it surprising to find that a 'vir triumphalis' [a man who had celebrated a triumph] of the Triumviral period, Ap. Claudius Pulcher (*cos*. 38 B.C.), keeps 'imp.' after his triumph – and after his death. It has remained a part of his title and honours, like 'cos.'[34]

The behaviour of Caesar might have been expected to furnish useful guidance – Caesar's aspirations to tyrannical power as well as to military glory are commonly detected at a quite early stage in his career, and transgressions against the spirit and the letter of the Roman constitution are taken as a matter of course. Yet Caesar the proconsul of Gaul seems wholly indifferent to the imperatorial salutation, not bothering to assume one until quite late in his conquest of

---

[33] *ILS* 877.
[34] *ILS* 890.

Gaul – at least none is recorded in his *Commentaries*.³⁵ The honour had indeed been sadly debased of recent years, if the last three proconsuls of Cilicia were worth it, L. Lentulus, Ap. Pulcher and M. Tullius Cicero; and Caesar himself in the narrative of the Civil Wars makes an ironical comment about the cheap and paltry distinction arrogated to himself by Metellus Scipio.³⁶ Caesar bears his Gallic acclamation till his triumph in 46 B.C., though he has entered the city in the meantime – and then before long there is another acclamation and a triumph celebrated from Spain (October, 45 B.C.). In strict propriety he should now have given it up. Precisely what happened is not clear: Cassius Dio, as has been stated, records a decreee of the Senate after the triumph to the effect that Caesar should be permitted to retain the title 'imp.'. But, as Dio understands and expounds the matter, this is the *praenomen imperatoris*, and Dio is manifestly in error. It is not certain that all the honours voted to the Dictator in the last months of his life were in fact adopted by him. If the right to retain 'imp.' was both offered and accepted, and that could be argued, it comes to very little. The legend 'Caesar imp.' occurs on the coins of three out of the four masters of the Roman mint in 44 B.C. Alternatives are 'Caesar dict. quart.' ['dict(ator) for the fourth time'], changing to 'Caesar dict. perpetuo' ['dict(ator) for life'], and 'Caesar parens patriae' ['father of the fatherland'] (posthumous).³⁷ The title thus has no exclusive significance. It is absent from the Dictator's official nomenclature on the *Fasti Consulares* [official list of consuls].

To return to Caesar's heir. His first acclamation had been registered in the War of Mutina, in April, 43 B.C. The date and occasion of the second has not been established, while the third is recorded for the first time on Agrippa's coins of 38 B.C. The evidence does not permit any significant deductions about his employment of 'imp.' after his name between the first salutation and the third. Now, however, the *praenomen* 'imp.' emerges. The *denarius* carries the legend 'Imp. Caesar Divi Iuli f.', but on the *aureus* the formula is peculiar – 'Imp.

---

³⁵ The inscription at Issa in Dalmatia, recording a deputation sent to Aquileia, has ἐπὶ Γαίου Ἰουλί[ου] Καί[σαρος] / αὐτοκράτορος ['in the presence of Gaius Iulius Cae[sar], imperator'] (*Bull. dalm.* XXXI. [1908], 101 [= *RDGE* 24, tr. Sherk, *RGE* no. 76]). But this is perhaps irrelevant because of the common use of αὐτοκράτωρ to describe a Roman holder of *imperium* (cf. below).

³⁶ *BC* III. 31. 1: 'detrimentis quibusdam circa montem Amanum acceptis imperatorem se appellaverat' ['after sustaining some setbacks around Mt Amanus, he had himself saluted as "imperator"'].

³⁷ These coins have naturally excited much interested – and controversy. Cf. A. Alföldi, op. cit. 1 ff.; K. Kraft, op. cit. 7 ff.; C. M. Kraay, *Num. Chron.*⁶ XIV (1955), 18 ff. (criticising Alföldi's chronological arrangement). Kraay present the attractive view that coins with 'Caesar imp.' are contemporaneous with the others, but from a different mint – and to be explained by the imminent campaigns of the Dictator. [See now *RRC* 480.]

Divi Iuli f. ter.'³⁸ That is to say, the 'imp.' in the notation of the third acclamation is thrown into the position of the *praenomen*. On the face of things this style might seem to demonstrate beyond doubt that the *praenomen* 'Imp.' derives from the imperatorial salutation.

At the same time, it must be admitted that this explanation may not carry the whole truth. Even if the line of derivation seems clear, the full force and validity of the *praenomen* in the titulature 'Imp. Caesar' may be of another kind. Prepossession with the imperatorial salutation should not be allowed to obscure a wider use, or uses, of the word 'imperator'. It can denote the magistrate or pro-magistrate holding *imperium*; and further, in normal or traditional prose usage, a general or commander. Laxity, impropriety or confusion is only to be expected in the revolutionary age – 'non mos, non ius' ['no custom, no law']. And there was respectable precedent for 'imperator' as a convenient and attractive title.

When a magistrate or pro-magistrate had been hailed as 'imperator', a certain incompatibility seems to have been felt between that name and the titles of his authority, consul or proconsul, praetor or propraetor. They tend not to occur in conjunction, and the more splendid name prevails. Thus as early as 180 a propraetor in Spain in an edict describes himself as 'L. Aemilius L. f. imperator'.³⁹ The title cannot fail to have appealed to the Roman general, expressing as it did the prestige of victory and the claim to victory's crown, the triumph at Rome; and to the provincial, in the western lands and even more in the eastern, it conveyed the fact of a power that was regal and military in a clearer and simpler fashion than did 'consul' and 'proconsul'. Translated into Greek, 'imperator' is αὐτοκράτωρ; and αὐτοκράτωρ, by extension, can render the Roman titles of magistracy or pro-magistracy.⁴⁰ The historian Josephus quotes an edict pronounced by the proconsul P. Dolabella at Ephesus early in 43 B.C. Dolabella is styled (in Greek) 'autokrator'.⁴¹ Now it might even be doubted whether P. Dolabella had by this time recorded an imperatorial salutation. In his journey from Rome Dolabella, it is true, had had a brush with insurgent Republicans in Macedonia, and he had dispossessed Trebonius the proconsul of Asia. But those incipient stages of civil war should have provided no occasion or excuse for him to be acclaimed as 'imperator'.

---

³⁸ Sydenham 1331 and 1329 respectively.
³⁹ *ILS* 15. For subsequent instances, A. Rosenberg, P-W IX. 1141 f. A good instance is the milestone from Pont-de-reiles (in the Aude): 'Cn. Domitius Cn. f. / Ahenobarbus / imperator / XX' (*AE* 1952, 38).
⁴⁰ cf. A. Rosenberg, P-W IX. 1142; E. J. Bickermann, *Class. Phil.* XLII (1947), 138 f.
⁴¹ *AJ* XIV. 225.

In the Civil Wars, Caesarian and Triumviral, generals of all parties freely added 'imp.' to their names: a notable exception is the constitutionalist M. Porcius Cato.[42] Not all of them could properly assert a right to legal authority; and it is fair to suppose that 'imp.' could derive not so much from a victory as from an act of usurpation, that it could represent not merely a claim to a triumph one day as a title of authority and command. Thus, for all that one can tell, Sex. Pompeius might have taken the title 'imp.' when he raised the Pompeian standard in Hispania Citerior (45/4 B.C.), and not when he defeated a Caesarian general subsequently in Hispania Ulterior (spring or early summer of 44 B.C.).

There was no limit to usurpations of title or prerogative. The dynasts set men of equestrian rank in command of armies of Roman legions and conceded them the appropriate honours. Thus Octavianus' marshal, the notorious Salvidienus Rufus, is 'imp.' as early as 40 B.C.[43] After a time, when the Triumvirs felt their authority was stronger, or desired to advertise a return to settled government, restrictions might be imposed. In 36 B.C. Octavianus forbade the wearing of the purple cloak by commanders not of senatorial status;[44] and Cornelius Gallus the Roman knight, bold and ostentatious though he be, does not dare to usurp the title 'imp.' for his exploits in the invasion of Egypt, when he commanded a whole army coming from Cyrenaica and captured Paraetonium (30 B.C.).

Finally, the plain and simple meaning of 'leader' or 'commander'. That sense is old in the Latin language, being in no way an innovation created by the revolutionary epoch of the great *imperatores*, the extensive *imperia* and the monarchic dynasts. It will be enough to cite Plautus in support, 'deinde utrique imperatores in medium exeunt' ['then both commanders went out into the middle (sc. of the battlefield)'];[45] Lucretius has 'induperatorem classis' ['commander of the fleet'];[46] and Sallust is not irrelevant, describing the institution of the consulate in language that is deliberately archaic and non-technical – 'annua imperia binosque imperatores sibi fecere' ['they instituted annual commands and two commanders'].[47] Official titulature may exercise only a slight influence on linguistic developments. A notable parallel can be discovered in the ways in which the Greek East came to employ 'autokrator', 'Kaisar', 'basileus' as desig-

---

[42] Sydenham 1052 ff., where he is 'pro pr.'
[43] Sydenham 1326.
[44] Dio XLIX. 16. 1.
[45] *Amphitryo* 223 (I.i.71).
[46] V. 1227.
[47] *Cat.* 6. 7.

nations for the Roman Emperor.[48] Similarly 'hegemon' possessed its own independent validity as a descriptive term, and would have retained it, even if 'hegemon' had not been adopted by Augustus as an official rendering of 'princeps'. When Strabo uses the word he is not just translating a Latin title into Greek.[49]

The wider connotations of 'imperator' being admitted, it will appear plausible that the *praenomen* 'Imperator' embodies and advertises the peculiar claim of Octavianus to be the military leader *par excellence*. The poet Catullus had acclaimed C. Caesar the proconsul of Gaul as 'imperator unice' ['unparalleled commander'].[50] What was irony in Catullus now became with Caesar's heir an item of official nomenclature – 'Imp. Caesar, Divi f.'

If the year was 38 B.C., the date is singularly felicitous. Octavianus made an elaborate attempt to invade the island of Sicily: he was easily defeated by Pompeius, and a tempest destroyed the remnants of his fleet. The contrast between official propaganda and known facts is not seldom to be observed in the career of Octavianus.

The young Caesar stood in sore need of prestige, comfort and advertisement. The Caesarian leaders made much of their loyalty to the Dictator, emulating in passionate resolve to avenge him. Devotion to the virtue of 'pietas' was precluded from full flower and recognition, for the young Pompeius had annexed 'Pius' long ago as part of his name. Nor was there any distinction left in the mere retention of an imperatorial salutation. Salvidienus had had it, though not a senator, the upstart admiral Laronius was to take it twice.[51] Agrippa, the modest and faithful marshal, victorious in Gaul this year, not only declined the triumph that would have emphasized his leader's discomfiture but also singled himself out from lesser men by refusing ever after to bear the vulgar distinction of 'imp.' after his name.[52] What was good enough for Laronius or for a mere aristocrat like Appius Claudius Pulcher, was not good enough for Marcus Agrippa.

It has been conjectured that no other than Agrippa first hit upon the device of publicising the young Caesar as the unique *imperator*; and it may have been his own salutation in Gaul that was surrendered

---

[48] cf. A. Wifstrand, ΔΡΑΓΜΑ *Martino P. Nilsson ... dedicatum* (1939), 529 ff.

[49] Strabo VI. 288; VII. 314; XVII. 840.

[50] Catullus 29. 11, cf. 54. 7. Compare later Cicero, *Pro Ligario* 3.7: 'cum ipse imperator in toto imperio populi Romani unus esset' ['although he himself was the only true commander in the whole of the empire of the Roman people'].

[51] *CIL* X. 8041^{18} (Vibo, on a tile).

[52] It occurs, however, on *ILS* 8897 (Ephesus) and on the original dedication of the Maison Carrée at Nemausus (*CRAI* 1919, 332).

to the leader's titulature, there to figure as 'imp. III'. Agrippa had been playing tricks with his own name. In 38 B.C. if not earlier he is 'M. Agrippa', having dropped the *gentilicium* 'Vipsanius'.

If the new Caesarian *praenomen* is in effect something more than a transferred imperatorial salutation, Sextus Pompeius turns out to be strikingly relevant. Caesar's heir needed every weapon for the contest, and propaganda not least when his generalship proved defective. From 44 or 43 B.C. onwards the young Pompeius had been asserting 'Magnus' as his *praenomen*. 'Imperator' looks like a Caesarian counterblast and overbid against the Pompeian emblem.[53] No longer 'C. Iulius Caesar' or 'C. Caesar', the Caesarian leader is now 'Imp. Caesar'. That style represents precisely *praenomen* and *nomen*. Similarly, the 'Divus' in 'Divus Iulius' might be interpreted as a *praenomen*, designating that individual Julius who happens to have become a god. And there will be no reason to quarrel with Tacitus for his practice of emphasising the personality of Caesar the Dictator by means of the form 'Dictator Caesar'.

The reason for giving importance to these terms is not to assert to the utmost a pedantry of onomatological study. Doctrines of the gravest moment in Roman public law are concerned. Should 'Imp.' as a part of Octavianus' name be regarded as possessing any legal force? Now it has been seen that 'imp.' not only commemorates a salutation but can be retained after a general's name as a kind of title; it may also have been understood as a claim to exercise authority, especially when borne by commanders whose status was dubious or usurped, like the sons of Pompeius, or the Republican admiral Cn. Domitius Ahenobarbus.[54] One might cite as an extreme instance Labienus, styling himself 'Parthicus imp.'[55]

Even if this be conceded, it does not follow that, as some believe, the *praenomen* 'Imperator' in Octavianus' nomenclature is actually a title of competence, signifying the possession of *imperium*, even of an *imperium maius*.[56] Nobody can prove that opinion. The facts exhibit 'Imp. Caesar' as a name constructed on the model of 'Faustus Sulla' or 'Magnus Pius'. The events of the year 38 B.C. provide a strong presumption that 'Imperator' is a retort to 'Magnus'. Regarded as a personal name, 'Imp.' is exorbitant, far outdistancing any predecessor or competitor. So is Caesar's heir.

---

[53] Given 'Magnus Pompeius' in 43 (*Phil.* XIII. 50), the facts are clear. The notion that Sex. Pompeius imitated Octavian (M. Grant, op. cit. 23; 415 f.) is erroneous.
[54] Sydenham 1176 ff.
[55] Sydenham 1356.
[56] As has been urged by M. Grant, op. cit. 415 ff.

'Imp.' is a name of power, precise yet mystical, a monopolisation of the glory of the *triumphator*, but it is not a title of authority.

The next modification of the Caesarian name comes neither after the victory of Actium nor after the fall of Alexandria: it commemorates the return of normal government, as proclaimed in the month of January, 27 B.C. A grateful Senate duly votes to Caesar a *cognomen* of more than mortal amplitude. He now has three names: 'Imperator Caesar Augustus' in his complete and official designation. It occurs on the consular *Fasti*, on dedications which the ruler makes or receives, on edicts he pronounces. And in this fashion does the historian Livy entitle him in a reference to the closing of the Temple of Janus, solemn and almost epigraphical in its conception – 'post bellum Actiacum ab imperatore Caesare Augusto pace terra marique parta' ['after the Actian war when peace was born on land and sea through the efforts of Imperator ('Commander') Caesar Augustus'].[57]

But it was not customary save in official documents to refer to a Roman by the sum total of his *tria nomina* ['three names']; and the new *cognomen* at once adds to the permissible variations in the formula with two names. The following brief observations may be made about prose usage, conjectural because of the scantiness of contemporary prose evidence. 'Imperator Caesar' is used in his dedication by Vitruvius, writing, or completing, his work on architecture soon after 27 B.C.:[58] Vitruvius was an old officer. 'Imperator Augustus' seems not to be found. The form is parallel to 'Magnus Pius'. Perhaps the collocation of two such highly individual and peculiar names as the *praenomen* 'Imperator' and the personal *cognomen* 'Augustus' was not aesthetically satisfying.[59] 'Caesar Augustus' on the other hand, *nomen* and *cognomen*, would conform to the fashion that had been growing up in the previous generation. 'Caesar Augustus' may be described as normal prose order. Inversion had also been becoming more respectable in the nomenclature of *nobiles*, as witness 'Rex Marcius'. The inverted form 'Augustus Caesar' throws the word 'Augustus' into sharp relief. It occurs in the other two references of Livy.[60] *Cognomina*, it has been shown, are in origin and

[57] I. 19. 3.
[58] Vitruvius I praef. 1: 'cum divina tua mens et numen, Imperator Caesar, imperio potiretur orbis terrarum' ['when your divine mind and divine power, Imperator ('Commander') Caesar, gained power over the whole world'], etc. Otherwise he is 'Caesar' (seven times), but 'aedes Augusti' ['Temple of Augustus'] occurs (V. 1. 7).
[59] Observe, however, some coin issues, BMCRE I, 17 ff., 51 ff., etc.
[60] IV. 20. 7; XXVIII. 12. 12.

nature akin to *praenomina*. The name 'Augustus' is peculiar to 'Imp. Caesar', it can be taken very much as a *praenomen*. That order, 'Augustus Caesar', even occurs sporadically on inscriptions where an especial emphasis seemed fitting or desirable.[61]

Imperfect though it is, the evidence appears to indicate a certain recession of 'Imperator'. That was only to be expected. 'Imp.' is in fact a *praenomen*, and the remarkable new *cognomen* introduces the forms 'Caesar Augustus' and 'Augustus Caesar', in conformity with the observed tendency of Roman usage to affect two names. Moreover, the *praenomen* 'Imp.', assumed in civil war during the contest against Magnus Pompeius Pius, is redolent of the age of the despots. Emphasis now falling upon peace and 'normal conditions', the military propaganda of the government abates. The glory of Romulus, much advertised after Actium, is allowed to fade into the background. Actium itself is transcended by the achievements of the new régime of constitutional government, 'libertas et principatus' ['freedom and the Principate, i.e., rule of the *princeps* (first citizen)'].

As published on coins after 27 B.C., the ruler's titulature eschews the *praenomen* for the most part. That avoidance can tell something about official propaganda, nothing about public law.[62] Not only are 'Caesar' and 'Augustus' of use, alone or together, but new titles, 'trib(unicia) pot(estate)' ['with tribunician power'], 'pontifex maximus' and 'pater patriae' in turn become available and permit many variations.

From the inception of the Triumvirate to the last day of December, 33 B.C., the official competence of Octavianus reposed upon the title 'III vir r(ei) p(ublicae) c(onstituendae)' ['triumvir for the ordering of the Republic'].[63] Throughout the year 32 B.C. he holds no office. During the years 31–28 B.C. his only link with the *res publica* is the consulate, which gives legal cover, in so far as it can be given, to a paramount *imperium* not different from that of the Triumvir;[64] and from the first constitutional settlement to the second, from 27 B.C. to 23 B.C., the consulate is likewise the sole title of authority that appears in the titulature of Caesar Augustus, although his *imperium* embraces the better part of the Empire.

Since 'Imp.' is not even a title, still less a title of competence, but

---

[61] e.g. *ILS* 110 (Pola); 139 l. 11 (Pisae); 915 (Histonium).

[62] Grant (op. cit. 417 ff.) argues that the recession of 'Imp.' is to be explained by the abandonment of government by *imperium maius*.

[63] That is, assuming that (whatever the legal term of the *Lex Titia* as renewed in 37) Octavian resigned triumviral powers at the beginning of 32 B.C.

[64] As Tacitus firmly and neatly indicates, 'posito triumviri nomine consulem se ferens' ['putting aside the name of Triumvir, he presented himself as consul'] (*Ann.* I. 2. 1).

precisely a part of the ruler's name, its presence or absence cannot be taken as evidence about changes in the character of Augustus' *imperium*, in 27 B.C. or at any other time. It had not in fact been uniformly employed before 27 B.C. To some scholars it has been a distressing fact that the *imperium* should not be indicated either in the name or in the titulature of Caesar Augustus. Yet it is a fact. Similarly, the *Res Gestae Divi Augusti* ['The Accomplishments of the Deified Augustus'] do not reveal the vast *provincia* voted in 27 B.C. and carrying with it command over almost all the armed forces of the Republic, or the modification of the *imperium* in 23 B.C. which extended it to cover the public provinces in the form of *imperium maius*. After that date the ruler could (and, be it said, should) have born 'pro cos.' on his titulature.

One cannot but suspect that preoccupation with the law and the constitution has led to a certain neglect of patent facts about nomenclature. The *praenomen* 'Imp.' has more weight and splendour than an ordinary name, as Pinarius Scarpus, Antonius' general in the Cyrenaica, showed when he commemorated his surrender by the legend 'Imp. Caesari Scarpus imp.'[65] None the less, and even though it may embody a claim to power as well as prestige, it has no legal force, no constitutional significance: it is a *praenomen* in rank and function. So closely does it adhere to Caesar Augustus that it is not transmitted to his son by adoption and successor, Ti. Caesar.[66] Many years were to pass before the *praenomen* 'Imperator' became what Cassius Dio fancied it was from the beginning, the title of the imperial office.[67]

'Augustus' goes even further than 'Imp.' as a name, it is almost superhuman; yet 'Augustus' is not a title of competence but precisely a *cognomen*, and as such subject to inversion in the emphatic form 'Augustus Caesar'. Indeed 'Augustus' was felt to be so peculiar to Caesar Augustus that Ti. Caesar, so it is recorded, did not employ it more often than he could help.[68]

In short, Caesar Augustus, the ruler of Rome, exalts himself above all rivals or forerunners in the choice of names as of titles. By contrast, Caesar the Dictator is modest and sober, Marcus Antonius the Triumvir an arrant traditionalist, without even the advertisement of a *cognomen*. Yet Caesar Augustus, in nomenclature as in his deal-

---

[65] Sydenham 1282 ff.
[66] It occurs sporadically, e.g. *ILS* 151; *IRT* 329.
[67] For the stages and variations, cf. A. Rosenberg, P-W IX. 1149 f. The first ruler to bear 'Imp. Caes.' as a regular title is Vespasian.
[68] Suetonius, *Tib.* 26. 2 (exaggerated).

ings with the *res publica*, exhibits ostensible obedience to the rules, and thereby discloses his essential enormity. The thing is monstrous. He even has *tria nomina*, precisely 'Imperator Caesar Augustus'.

As has been demonstrated, in certain branches of the Roman *nobilitas* the *cognomina* tend to pass into *nomina*. 'Caesar' goes the whole way, and the 'Iulius' is discarded, not merely in current use but in official record. 'Caesar' is a *gentilicium* in the form 'Imp. Caesar', and so it continues in the names of Augustus' adopted sons, first, from 17 B.C., C. Caesar and L. Caesar, then, from A.D. 4, Ti. Caesar. At the same time, however, the old name of the Julii is not entirely obscured. It is transmitted to freedmen and to persons granted the Roman citizenship; it is retained by the princesses of the Julian line; and, as the dynastic names reveal on the arch at Ticinum (erected in A.D. 7/8),[69] it emerges in the next male generation of the 'domus regnatrix' ['ruling house']: the sons of Ti. Caesar, the one of his body, the other adopted, are styled 'Drusus Iulius Caesar' and 'Germanicus Iulius Caesar' respectively, and the two sons of Germanicus are also 'Iulii'. Another prince, Agrippa's posthumous son, also belonged now to the *gens Iulia*; but Agrippa Julius Caesar, having been relegated, is not allowed a place on the Ticinum arch.

What Marcus Agrippa himself did with his name is highly instructive. According to the elder Seneca, he deliberately discarded the *gentilicium* 'Vipsanius' because it patently revealed his humble origin.[70] Of the flavour of the name 'Vipsanius' there is no doubt. It had never been known before. There was no Vipsanius even among the municipal adherents of C. Marius or among the Roman knights and financiers of the generation following, let alone in the Senate. The motive assigned by Seneca is sometimes called into question. Needlessly. Octavianus' other marshal of the early days, Salvidienus, seems to have felt a little unhappy about a non-Latin *gentilicium*, and even to have modified its form – at least his coins of 40 B.C. style him 'Q. Salvius imp. cos. desig.' ['imperator, consul designate'].[71] Therefore M. Vipsanius Agrippa is exalted to M. Agrippa. The proud plebeian not only emulates the nobles by employing his *cognomen* as a *gentilicium*, he imposes it, exclusively. 'M. Agrippa' is parallel to 'Imp. Caesar.'

The *gentilicium* of a noble house, being transferable to freedmen and aliens, might approximate by its very vulgarisation to the ignobility of a patently plebeian name like 'Vipsanius'. And so, with

---

[69] ILS 107.
[70] Seneca, *Controv.* II. 4. 13. It emerges with females and freedmen.
[71] Sydenham 1326.

the rise of the Julii, 'Iulius' goes the way of 'Cornelius'. The Roman knight L. Julius Vestinus, the friend of Claudius Caesar, had a senatorial son, the consul of 65: he drops the 'Julius' and calls himself 'M. Vestinus Atticus'. A common and indistinctive *gentilicium* will elsewhere be inferred where the sources omit it. Thus the enigmatic M. Primus, proconsul of Macedonia in 23 B.C., if his name has been correctly transmitted, is certainly not a *nobilis*, with such a *cognomen*.[72] Conjecture is safer with A. Atticus, an equestrian officer who fell at the Battle of the Mons Graupius: he was probably a Julius Atticus.[73] Finally, M. Aper, the low born orator from Gaul, from a 'civitas minime favorabilis' ['a least favourable community'], who plays a leading part in the *Dialogus* of Tacitus, is a surely Julius or a Flavius.[74]

Those examples illustrate and support Seneca's comment on 'Vipsanius'. Agrippa usually got his way. No surviving coins or inscriptions transgress his interdict. The nomenclature of his youngest son (commonly known as Agrippa Postumus) will demonstrate to the full that 'Agrippa' has become a *nomen*; and a further permutation emerges, precisely parallel to the charges enforced upon 'Magnus' by the son of Pompeius Magnus. The infant, before receiving a *praenomen*, carries 'Agrippa' as a *gentilicium*, being 'Pup. Agrippa M. f.';[75] and the boys similarly is 'M. Agrippa M. f.' in 5 B.C.[76] Then, in A.D. 4, he passes into the Julian House, being adopted by Augustus, and the appropriate form of nomenclature ensues, 'Agrippa Iulius Caesar'.[77] The stages are clearly discernible by which 'Agrippa' moves from *cognomen* to *gentilicium*, but reverts to a *praenomen*: such indeed it had been in ancient days.

The tendency of the Roman *praenomen* to lose importance in the last age of the Republic is contradicted only among the *nobiles*; and the practices of the *nobiles* foreshadow the triumphant anomalies of the Caesarian dynasty.

An eccentric *praenomen* like 'Appius' or 'Faustus' can stand by itself. It is therefore not surprising to find that Tacitus employs

---

[72] Dio LIV. 3. 2.

[73] Tacitus, *Agr.* 37. 6. Observe the procurator M. Julius Atticus (*CIL* XII. 1854: Vienna), or Julius Atticus, the writer on viticulture, of whom Agricola's father was 'velut discipulus' ['his pupil, as it were'] (Columella I. 1. 14).

[74] His 'civitas', *Dial.* 7. 1. The item 'Iulius Aper' occurs in the nomenclature of the polyonymous consul of 169 (*ILS* 1104), grandson of Q. Pompeius Falco (*suff.* 108). But observe the senator Flavius Aper (Pliny, *Epp.* V. 13. 5), who looks like an ex-consul, and who is presumably the parent of M. Flavius Aper (*cos.* 130).

[75] *ILS* 141.

[76] *ILS* 142.

[77] *CIL* X. 405.

'Appius' and 'Mamercus' in this fashion.[78] The *praenomina* of princes suitably usurp this distinction. The milder form of the license is when the context, by an indication of relationship, allows the family name to be understood, or when the name 'Caesar' has previously been mentioned. Thus a prose writer like Velleius Paterculus proceeds to speak of 'Gaius' barely; and in Tacitus 'Tiberius' is almost without exception the sole appellation for the Emperor Ti. Caesar.

There is a futher consequence touching orthography. Peculiar *praenomina* tend to resist abbreviation. In the early Empire as in the late Republic, 'Gaius', 'Lucius' and 'Marcus' are the commonest of all *praenomina*. If they belong, however, to members of the ruling house, they acquire distinction and relief, and so may be written out in full. Thus on the *Res Gestae*: 'filios meos, quos iuvenes mihi eripuit fortuna, Gaium et Lucium Caesares' ['my sons, whom Fortune snatched away from me when they were still young, Gaius and Lucius Caesar'].[79] Moreover, the common practice of referring to a man by two names only (whether he has two, three, or more) may sometimes, in serious prose, have permitted the writing out in full of the *praenomen*, for emphasis or for variety. This is another, and a larger question. An examination of Tacitus' practice might reveal, not just the whims of transcribers, but devices of orthography expressing stylistic preferences.[80]

To conclude. In spite of the tricks and permutations, the house of the Caesars submits after all to rules of nomenclature. The man of destiny himself, the 'Divi Filius' ['Son of the Deified One'], though portentous and unexampled, is not unexplained: as 'Imp. Caesar Augustus' he owns to 'tria nomina'. The founder of the monarchy at Rome proclaimed that he had restored the 'res publica'. And, truly enough, the fabric is there, 'senatus leges magistratus' ['senate, laws, magistrates'], and the names, 'eadem magistratuum vocabula' ['the same titles for the magistracies']. The genuine and unbroken continuity belongs elsewhere; it is exhibited in the development of dynastic politics, and even in the small matter of nomenclature. The Julii, the dominant faction of the *nobilitas*, are now known as the

---

[78] *Dial.* 21. 7: 'inter Menenios et Appios' ['among men like Menenius (Agrippa) and Appius (Claudius Caecus)']; *Ann.* III. 66. 1: 'Mamercus antiqua exempla iaciens' ['Mamercus tossing in some ancient precedents'].

[79] *RG* 14.

[80] cf. R. Syme, *JRS* XXXVIII (1948), 124 f. Some editors have insisted on abbreviating *praenomina* (both normal and abnormal) which the *Codex Mediceus* gives in full.

'Caesares'. Caesar the Dictator disdained to emulate Sulla Felix and Pompeius Magnus by adopting an ostentatious cognomen. Caesar's restraint is impressive. His heir goes far beyond 'Felix' and 'Magnus'. He refurbishes the whole name, in every single member, transmuting 'C. Julius C. f. Caesar' ['Gaius Julius Caesar, son of Gaius'] into 'Imp. Caesar Divi f. Augustus' ['Imp(erator = 'Commander') Caesar Augustus, son of the Deified One'].

The fortune of Caesar and of Caesar's heir was miraculous. Other claimants there were in the *nobilitas*, of ancient fame and pretension, and Fate might have ordained it otherwise. The last Scipio of any consequence in Roman history is that P. Scipio who was adopted by Metellus Pius and who contributed the double prestige of Scipiones and Metelli to the Pompeian alliance when he gave his daughter Cornelia to Pompeius Magnus in 52 B.C. Metellus Scipio raised proud assertion of family tradition and of military glory, not always adequate, but commemorated for all time by his dying utterance on the stricken field in Africa, 'imperator se bene habet' ['the imperator ('commander') is doing fine'].[81] On coins he so disposes his titulature as to throw 'Scipio imp.' into relief and emphasis.[82] If the power had gone in the end to one of his line, Rome might have known as her ruler not 'Imp. Caesar Augustus', but 'Imp. Scipio Pius.'[83]

---

[81] Livy, *Per.* CXIV.
[82] Sydenham 1046 ff.
[83] The above is the text of a lecture delivered in the University of Heidelberg in 1952. Annotation has deliberately been kept to a minimum.

2 Triumvirate and Principate†*

FERGUS MILLAR

INTRODUCTION

More than thirty years after its publication *The Roman Revolution* still stands unrivalled, not as the "definitive" account of the emergence of a monarch from the ruins of the Republic but as something far more than that, the demonstration of a new method in the presentation of historical change. The aspect of this method which has found most imitation is, of course, prosopography; and it is indeed essential to it. But far more important is the use made of contemporary literature to mirror events, and to analyse and define the concepts and the terms in which the events were seen by those who lived through them.

It is the common characteristic, perhaps even the definition, of great works of history that they invite imitation and offer a challenge, not just to apply their methods and standards to other areas, but to pursue their own conclusions further. The present chapter is gratefully offered as an attempt to portray with a different emphasis some aspects of the establishment of Octavian as a monarch, first by demonstrating the extent to which the institutions of the *res publica* remained active in the Triumviral period, and secondly by redefining the change which culminated in 27 B.C., precisely by asking again in

---

† Originally published in the *Journal of Roman Studies* 63 (1973), 50–67; revised in F. Millar, *The Roman Republic and the Augustan Revolution* (eds. H. M. Cotton and G. M. Rogers) (Rome, the Greek World, and the East 1), Chapel Hill and London: University of North Carolina Press, 2002, pp. 241–270 (chapter 10).

* An earlier version of this chapter was given at a research seminar in Berkeley in the autumn of 1968, and part of a more recent version at the Scuola Normale Superiore at Pisa in January 1973. It is offered here first and foremost as a tribute to Sir Ronald Syme; secondly as an attempt to make some preliminary remarks about the unpublished Triumviral documents from the excavations by Professor Kenan Erim at Aphrodisias, which Miss J. M. Reynolds has very kindly allowed me to use; and thirdly as the last of a series of preliminary studies towards a book to be called *The Emperor in the Roman World*. I am most grateful for critical comment (and general disagreement) to Professors E. Badian and G. W. Bowersock in Harvard and A. D. Momigliano and E. Gabba in Pisa, and to Miss Reynolds for generous advice and assistance. [The note has been left as it stood in 1973. *The Emperor in the Roman World* was published in 1977, and J. M. Reynolds, *Aphrodisias and Rome* was published in 1982.]

what terms it and the "new order" (*novus status*) which emerged from it were seen by contemporaries.

Monarchy is an infinitely complex phenomenon, in each case unique to the particular society from which it springs. The complexity is only increased when it emerges from a centuries-old aristocratic republic whose web of customs, rights, and traditions is dignified by moderns with the title of a constitution; and further when it immediately involves the direct relationship of the monarch to a vast range of regions and communities of varying cultures and political characters. This is the essential new factor, foreshadowed by Pompey during his command in the East, and briefly in Rome by Caesar as dictator. Moreover it allows us to simplify, and to focus a large part of the discussion on a single criterion of monarchy, the issuing by the monarch of pronouncements which are themselves treated by his subjects as effective legal acts. It is all-important to stress the difference between these and pronouncements which either complete some collective legal process, or merely promise that such a process will take place. Among such effective pronouncements the personal judicial verdicts of the monarch have a particular significance. Considerations such as these will be vital in determining the relevance of the Triumviral period to the emergence of monarchy, and the nature of the change completed in 27 B.C.

THE TRIUMVIRATE AND THE *RES PUBLICA*

Nobody, then or since, could dispute that the Triumviral period was profoundly marked by violence, illegality, and the arbitrary exercise of power. This view was openly expressed at the time by the jurist Cascellius, who refused to give a legal formula in respect of properties granted by the Triumvirs, "considering all of their grants outside the realm of law".[1] Even Octavian himself admitted this, abolishing (whatever that may mean) all that had been done unlawfully and unjustly up to his sixth consultate in 28 B.C.[2] None the less, if we rely too uncritically on the famous, but also typically emotive, rhetorical, and imprecise, phrase of Tacitus which introduces his reference to this "abolition" – "and then continuous discord for twenty years, no custom, no law" (*exim continua per viginti annos discordia, non mos, non ius*)[3] – we shall miss important features of the Triumviral situation.

[1] Val. Max. 6, 2, 12.
[2] Dio 53, 2, 5; cf. Tac., *Ann.* 3, 28, 3.
[3] Tac., *Ann.* 3, 28, 1.

It is necessary to emphasise first how little can be confidently deduced from the brief accounts we have of the establishment of the Triumvirate, which in this respect resemble the accounts of the "settlement" of 27.[4] Moreover the evidence we have relates partly to the pact of Bononia and partly to the Lex Titia itself. In spite of a very useful discussion,[5] it is necessary to review the main points here.

For the actual powers of the Triumvirs, none of our earliest sources – Livy as represented in the *Epitome*, Augustus himself in the *Res Gestae*, and Velleius Paterculus – gives any help.[6] Nor does the opening narrative section of Suetonius' *Divus Augustus* (12–13) or his later references (27, 96), or the descriptions of the pact and the proscriptions in Plutarch's *Cicero* (46) and *Antonius* (19–20), or in Florus (2, 15). So it is important to emphasise that the narrative sources on which we depend for our conception of the formation of the Triumvirate and the powers of its members are essentially Appian and Dio. From Appian (*BC* 4, 2/4–7, on the pact of Bononia) we learn that their power was to be equal to that of the consuls and to last for five years. They were "to appoint" the city magistrates at once for each of the next five years. They were to divide the governorships of provinces and "have" the different regions separately. Nothing is said about how the government of the provinces would actually work, except (in 3/9) that Lepidus was to be consul for the following year, to remain in Rome and to govern Spain through others. When Appian (in 4, 7/27) comes to describe the passing of the tribunician Lex Titia itself he repeats only the detail that their power was to be consular and for five years.

Dio, describing Bononia (46, 55, 3–4), mentions the five-year term, the right to give offices (*archai*) and honours (*timai*), and the division of the provinces; he does, however, add some sort of definition of their powers – "they should manage all public business, whether or not they made any communication about it to the people and the Senate." He adds, still describing Bononia, that they agreed on executions of their enemies (46, 56, 1). When mentioning their subsequent actions in Rome he makes only a passing allusion to the Lex Titia – "the measures which they had dictated and forced through assumed the name of law" (47, 2, 2). It is thus evident that our major sources for these events are not only remote from them in time but lacking in

---

[4] For the direct evidence on the provincial aspects of the settlement of 27, see F. Millar, *JRS* 56 (1966): 156–57 (= *The Roman Republic and the Augustan Revolution* (2002), 270–73).
[5] V. Fadinger, *Die Begründung des Prinzipats: quellenkritische und staatsrechtliche Untersuchungen zu Cassius Dio und der Parallelüberlieferung* (Diss. Munich, 1969), esp. 31–83.
[6] See Livy, *Per.* 120; *Res Gestae* 1, 7; Vell. Pat. 2, 69.

clarity. Only the *Epitome* of Livy tells us formally that the Lex Titia gave a legal basis to the proscriptions; only Aulus Gellius (14, 7, 5) records that the Triumvirs had "the right to convene the senate"; and only the *Fasti Colotiani*[7] give us the terminal date of the five-year period of the Triumvirate – "[M. A]emilius, *M. Antonius* [erased], Imp. Caesar, triumvirs for the ordering of the *res publica*, from the fifth day before the Kalends of December to the day before the sixth Kalends of January following." These *Fasti*, which the erased name of Antonius show to have been inscribed before September 30 B.C., thus make clear that the Triumvirate was due to expire on December 31, 38 B.C.

What remains quite obscure is what effects the appointment of triumvirs for the ordering of the *res publica* – *triumviri rei publicae constituendae* – was expected to have on the assemblies, the Senate, and the annual magistracies. Least obscurity attaches to the question of elections and of appointments to provincial commands, which are explicitly stated to have been within the powers of the Triumvirs. But was *every* annual magistracy in the period filled by Triumviral appointment? And, if so, did this mean that the centuriate and the tribal assemblies actually ceased to meet for electoral purposes until 27 B.C.? Or might they have met to elect formally lists of candidates put forward by the Triumvirs? A number of important articles on the elections under Augustus ignore the problems of the Triumviral period.[8] Only the valuable study of R. Frei-Stolba traces the fortunes of the elections from the Republic through the Caesarian and Triumviral periods, to the Empire.[9] There is of course abundant evidence to show arbitrary use of the power of appointment by the Triumvirs, including gross affronts to Republican custom in certain years. At the end of 43 they appointed two suffect consuls, one of them a praetor in office, who was replaced by one of the aediles; and five days before the end of the year they sent the praetors off to provinces, and appointed replacements.[10] In 42 Dio speaks of them as appointing the city magistrates for several years in advance.[11] In 40 suffect consuls and praetors were again appointed right at the end

---

[7] A. Degrassi, *Inscriptiones Italiae* XIII, 1: *Fasti Consulares* (1947), 273–74.

[8] A. H. M. Jones, "The Elections under Augustus," *JRS* 45 (1955): 9 = *Studies in Roman Government and Law* (1960), 27; P. A. Brunt, "The Lex Valeria Cornelia," *JRS* 51 (1961): 71; B. M. Levick, "Imperial Control of the Elections under the Early Principate," *Historia* 16 (1967): 207.

[9] R. Frei-Stolba, *Untersuchungen zu den Wahlen in der römischen Kaiserzeit* (1967). On the period from 42 to 28 B.C., see pp. 80–86.

[10] Dio 47, 15, 2–3.

[11] Dio 47, 19, 4.

of the year, and an aedile to replace one who died on the last day of December.[12] In 39 Triumvirs are recorded as making appointments to magistracies several years ahead and to the consulate for eight years, subsequently making additions and subtractions to the list. Dio carefully emphasises that it was at this point that the arbitrary appointment of suffect consuls became regular, and underlines the continuity with established imperial practice.[13] Similarly, when agreement was temporarily reached with Sextus Pompeius in the same year, its terms included praetorships, tribunates, and priesthoods for his followers, and a consulate and the position of *haruspex* (diviner) for himself (he was deposed from both in 37).[14] The following year saw the culmination of the period of disturbance of the republican magistracies.[15] Sixty-seven praetors were appointed in the course of the years, and a boy was made quaestor.[16] Under the next year Dio notes continual multiplication of office-holders, and gives the reason, namely that the offices were valued not for themselves but as the necessary preliminary to provincial commands.[17]

In the following years such irregularities were greatly reduced,[18] though suffect consulates continued (Octavian abandoning his consulate in 33 on the first day).[19] The suffect consulate in 30, for which, as Plutarch says, Octavian "chose" Cicero's son as his colleague,[20] ended the systematic use of suffect consulates for several decades. The abandonment of this practice was surely intended as a sign of approaching normality.

The extensive powers of appointment exercised by the Triumvirs naturally led to the distribution of appointments as favours, and to requests for them from interested parties. So Plutarch mentions that Octavia after her rejection by Antonius continued to assist men sent by him "in quest of office or on other business" to obtain their requests from Octavian (*Ant.* 54); while Aelian has the incident of a runaway slave who was given the praetorship by Antonius, and was recognized by his former master while "he was sitting on a tribunal and dispensing justice in the Roman Forum."[21] If we can trust a

---

[12] Dio 48, 32, 1 and 3.

[13] Dio 48, 35, 1–3. Under 31 B.C. Dio duly notes that the arrangement of eight years before had been that Octavian and Antonius should be consuls, 50, 10, 1.

[14] Dio 48, 36, 4; 54, 6.

[15] I am indebted to Professor Badian for emphasising to me the importance of indicating the extent to which Triumviral irregularities increased or decreased in the course of time.

[16] Dio 48, 43, 2.

[17] Dio 48, 53, 1–3.

[18] One may note a couple of suffect praetors in 33, Dio 49, 43, 7.

[19] Appian, *Illyrica* 28/80; Dio 49, 43, 6.

[20] Plut., *Cic.* 49.

[21] Aelian, *Apospasmata* 66. Cf. *Dig.* 1, 14, 3.

curious anecdote in Dio,[22] the right of patronage was extended even beyond the Triumvirs; for he records that Statilius Taurus was rewarded by the people for completing his theatre in 30 B.C. and celebrating the event with a gladiatorial show, by being granted the right to select one of the praetors each year.

None the less, there remain a few indications that the ritual of the elections continued, and even that some places were filled by election. Dio mentions that there were no aediles in 36 B.C. for lack of candidates.[23] In the proscriptions, according to Appian, one praetor was killed holding an assembly in the Forum, and another fled while canvassing the voters for the quaetorship for his son. In this case the son revealed his father's hiding place, and was rewarded by the Triumvirs with both his father's property and an aedileship.[24] The first part of the latter story is confirmed by Valerius Maximus.[25] Similarly, according to Plutarch (*Cic.* 49), it was when Antonius was conducting an assembly in December 43 that Cicero's head and hands were brought to him. One story in Appian (*BC* 4, 41/173) records that the people elected a man as aedile in this period.

But although appointment by patronage was clearly normal, the theory that the republican magistrates, once in office, should exercise their traditional functions persisted throughout the period. When the soldiers imposed an agreement on Octavian and L. Antonius at Teanum in 41 B.C., one of its conditions was that the consuls should exercise their traditional powers (*ta patria*) without hindrance from the Triumvirs.[26] Similarly, when Octavian's fortunes turned in 36, "he allowed the annual magistrates to administer a great part of the *res publica* in the traditional ways."[27] While these references clearly indicate that full normality was not actually achieved, it is none the less important to stress the extent to which the traditional duties of the magistrates in fact continued. Sacrifices were carried out,[28] games and festivals conducted,[29] and public buildings constructed and dedicated.[30] As is clear from an anecdote in Appian (*BC* 4, 41/173) and

---

[22] Dio 51, 23, 1.
[23] Dio 49, 16, 2.
[24] *BC* 4, 17–18/68–70.
[25] Val. Max. 9, 11, 6.
[26] Appian, *BC* 5, 20/79.
[27] Appian, *BC* 5, 132/548.
[28] Dio 51, 21, 1–2 (Valerius Potitus, suffect consul of 29).
[29] Dio 48, 32, 4; Vell. Pat. 2, 79, 6, M. Titius "giving games in the theatre of Pompey," presumably as suffect consul in 31; Dio 48, 20, 2, Agrippa as praetor in 40 giving the *ludi Apollinares*.
[30] Dio 49, 42, 2, Aemilius Lepidus Paullus, suffect consul of 34, dedicating the Basilica Aemilia; 49, 45, 1–5, Agrippa's building programme as aedile in 33.

Dio (48, 53, 4), office in Rome continued to demand substantial expenditure. Both the continuation of routine business and its subjection to violent interference are illustrated by Suetonius' story (*Div. Aug.* 27) of a praetor dragged from his tribunal by Octavian's soldiers.

Much more important, however, are the indications that substantial matters were still put through by the consuls. Twice under the year 42, Appian represents Antonius as getting the consul Munatius Plancus to have a safe-conduct voted for someone.[31] Ten years later, as is notorious, the consuls Sosius and Domitius Ahenobarbus resolutely opposed Octavian, and refused his demands for publication of Antonius' Donations of Alexandria;[32] Sosius would have taken direct action against Octavian but for the veto of the tribune Nonius Balbus.[33] Two years after that, it was Cicero's son who, as suffect consul of 30, read the news of the death of Antonius to the people.[34] At about this time, after the conspiracy of the younger Lepidus, a puzzling passage of Appian (*BC* 4, 50/218–19) shows a consul on his tribunal and with his lictors accepting a "pledge" (*vadimonium*) from Lepidus' mother for her appearance before Octavian.

More important that these scattered examples of consular or magisterial action is the evidence of votes by the Senate, or by the Senate and people. First, a number of laws, or popular votes. From 42 we have the Lex Munatia Aemilia enabling the Triumvirs to make grants of citizenship (see no. 5 in the next section), the law for the deification of Julius Caesar, "whom the Senate and the Roman People assigned a place among the Gods" (*ILS* 72, Aesernia);[35] and perhaps a Lex Rufrena.[36] From 40 (?) we have the important tribunician law, the Lex Falcidia.[37] From the mid 30s onwards various honours were voted to Octavian, some abortively;[38] but more significant is the fact that Antonius continued to wish to have his eastern dispositions ratified in Rome (Dio 49, 41, 4). Whether the renewal of the Triumvirate in 37 was ratified, even retrospectively, remains in doubt. In *BC* 5, 93/398, Appian says that they renewed it "no longer asking

---

[31] Appian, *BC* 4, 37/158; 45/193.
[32] Dio 49, 41, 4.
[33] Dio 50, 2, 3.
[34] Appian, *BC* 4, 51/221.
[35] See also Dio 47, 18–19, and Triumviral Documents (below, pp. 69–70), no. 6.
[36] *ILS* 73 "To the deified Julius by order of the Roman people. It was ordered in the Lex Rufrena"; cf. *ILS* 73a. See *Diz. Epig.*, s.v. "lex," 730–1; Degrassi, *ILLRP* I², 409.
[37] Dio 48, 33, 5 etc. *Diz. Epig.*, s.v. "lex" 731–2. See Broughton, *MRR* II, 372.
[38] Appian, *BC* 5, 131/543; Dio 49, 15, 5–6; 51, 19–20.

for the assent of the people" but in *Illyrica* 28/80 that the people ratified it. However, in 30 B.C. the Senate and People certainly passed a Lex Saenia allowing Octavian to create patricians,[39] and voted the privilege to Statilius Taurus mentioned above.

The Senate acting without the people in substantive matters appears even more frequently. In 41, according to Florus (2, 16) the senators declared L. Antonius a public enemy. In 40 they condemned Salvidienus Rufus to death, voted the "care" (*cura*) of the city to the Triumvirs,[40] and ratified the grant of the kingdom of Judaea to Herod.[41] In 39 they ratified all the official acts of the Triumvirs down to that time.[42] More traditional functions continued as well; in 37, on the advice of the *pontifices*, the Senate ordered the removal of the bones of a man whom the populace had honoured with burial on the Campus Martius.[43]

Then, ignoring various votes in favour of Octavian,[44] we may note that the Senate declared Antonius a public enemy, presumably in 30 – and that one senator voted against.[45] It was apparently subsequently to this that they voted to take down the image of Antonius and cancel the honours voted to him (Plut., *Cic.* 49); and in 29 to close the close the gates of the temple of Janus (*RG* 13; Dio 51, 20, 4).

Nobody would argue that the formal exercise of their traditional functions by the Senate and People demonstrates the continuance of the free play of politics. But the evidence does seem to indicate that the institutions of the *res publica* themselves persisted through the Triumviral period. Moreover the Triumvirs not only, as we shall see (texts to nn. 103–4), made repeated promises to restore effective power to the republican institutions, but showed considerable concern to have their actions formally approved and ratified by the traditional organs of the state. This intermingling of the exercise of individual power and of the role and influence of the republican institutions comes out very clearly in the now extensive dossier of Triumviral documents.

---

[39] *RG* 8; Tac., *Ann.* 11, 25, cf. Dio 52, 42, 5. For other possible laws of this period, see G. Rotondi, *Leges publicae populi Romani* (1912), 435–41.
[40] Dio 48, 33, 2–3.
[41] Josephus, *Ant.* 14, 14, 4–5 (384–89). For the date and circumstances, see now E. Schürer, *The History of the Jewish People in the Age of Jesus Christ*, ed. G. Vermes and F. Millar, I (1973), 281.
[42] Dio 48, 34, 1.
[43] Dio 48, 53, 5–6.
[44] E.g. Appian, *BC* 5, 130/538, 541; Dio 49, 43, 6; 45, 1; Appian, *Illyrica* 28/83.
[45] Appian, *BC* 4, 45/193.

TRIUMVIRAL DOCUMENTS

The documents containing official decisions from the Triumviral period come entirely from the Greek East. In this context it will be sufficient to note their essential contents and their relevance to the way in which decisions were made. To illustrate a certain progression of form and attitude they will be given in chronological order.

1. Letters of Antonius to Hyrcanus and the *ethnos* of the Jewish people, 42/1 B.C. Jos., *Ant.* 14, 12, 3 (306–13).
2. Letter of Antonius to Tyre, 42/1 B.C. Jos., *Ant.* 14,12,4 (314–18).
3. Letter of Antonius to Tyre enclosing his edict (διάταγμα). 42/1 B.C. Jos., *Ant.* 14, 12, 5 (319–22).

Josephus notes that similar letters were sent to Sidon, Antioch, and Arados (14, 12, 6 [323]), but does not quote them. The letters which he does quote were evoked by an embassy to Antonius at Ephesus some time after Philippi, which brought a gold crown and asked for the freeing of Jewish prisoners taken in the period of Cassius' domination, and the restoration of lost territories. Antonius accepted these claims at once. In his letter to Hyrcanus he refers to a previous embassy to himself in Rome, discourses extravagantly on Philippi, and orders the release of the captives, the maintenance of grants previously granted by himself and Dolabella (proconsul of Syria in 43 B.C.), and the restoration of lands taken by the Tyrians. Writing to Tyre he emphasises that his opponents at Philippi had not been appointed to their provinces by the Senate, orders restoration, and offers them the opportunity of presenting their case before him when he reaches their vicinity. In the second letter he orders the inscription in a prominent place of a general edict referring to the illegal seizure of Syria by Cassius and the losses suffered by the Jews. Here he uses his full titulature, "Marcus Antonius, *imperator*, one of three men in charge of the *res publica*, said." It is to be noted that the issue is brought forward, as so often, by an embassy from an interested party, that the decisions on it are taken directly and individually by the Triumvir concerned, but that some reference is made to the legality of his position.

4. Letter of Antonius to the provincial council (*koinon*) of Asia on the rights of the world-wide association of victorious athletes in sacred games who had won crowns. (?) 41 B.C. *SB* 4224; R. K. Sherk, *Roman Documents from the Greek East* (1969), no. 57; trans. Sherk, *RGE*, no. 85.

Antonius refers to two embassies, a previous one when M. Antonius Artemidorus, "my friend and trainer," and the eponymous priest of the association, Charopinus of Ephesus, had approached him in Ephesus and requested the maintenance of its privileges; and a second by Artemidorus asking permission to have the privileges inscribed on a bronze tablet. This letter, preserved on papyrus, is addressed to the provincial council presumably for information and as further protection for the rights of the association. The pre-existing role and importance of the provincial council is now clear from a document from Aphrodisias showing that earlier in the century it had sent an embassy to Rome to protest against the excesses of the publicans.[46]

5. A grant (*decretum*?) of citizenship by Octavian (or the Triumvirs?) to Seleucus of Rhosus, (?) 41 B.C. *IGLS* III, no. 718, ii; Sherk, *Roman Documents*, no. 58, ii; trans. Sherk, *RGE*, no. 86.

The document is much mutilated, and there is ample room for doubt about both its correct designation and its date. What is significant in this context is that it refers (l. 10) to a Lex Munatia Aemilia, evidently passed by the consuls of 42 B.C., Munatius Plancus and Aemilius Lepidus, in accordance with which the grant is made. There is no indication of date, but it is probably early, as the donor appears as "Caesar Imperator" – Καῖσαρ αὐτοκράτωρ. "Imperator" does not yet appear as a *praenomen*, which it came to do from 38, or possibly 40, B.C.[47] On the other hand, the verb given in line 11 is in the plural, "gave," which has suggested to some that an original which referred to a grant by two or three of the Triumvirs has been tampered with before being inscribed several years later. The aftermath of Philippi remains a reasonable, but not in the least a certain, context for the original grant. More important for our purposes is its justification in terms of a law, its formal and detailed character, and its references (ll. 68–71) to the rights of embassy to the Senate, and to Roman magistrates and promagistrates, and to fines payable to the Roman people.

6. (?) Greek translation of a law establishing ceremonies in honour of the deified Julius Caesar? 41 B.C.? *Forschungen in Ephesos* IV, 3 (1951), 280, no. 24; see now M. Crawford, ed., *Roman Statutes* I–II (1996), no. 35.

---

[46] First published by K. Erim, *PBSR* 37 (1969): 92–95; see T. Drew-Bear, *ZPE* 8 (1971): 285–88, and for a full discussion his "Deux décrets hellénistiques d'Asie Mineure," *BCH* 46 (1972): 435, on pp. 443–71; now, J. M. Reynolds, *Aphrodisias and Rome* (1982), no. 5.
[47] See R. Syme, "Imperator Caesar, a Study in Nomenclature," *Historia* 7 (1958): 172 = *Roman Papers* I (1979), 361 [= Chapter 1, above]; R. Combès, *Imperator* (1966), 132–35.

The first words (*thelete, keleuete*) translate "velitis, iubeatis" ("May you wish and command"), the terminology of a law,[48] and the expression "the deified Julius" is likely not to have been used until after the vote of divine honours in 42 B.C. (Dio 48, 18–19). Whether the reference to Marcus Antonius relates in any way to his presence in Ephesus in 41 B.C.[49] must remain a matter of speculation.

7. A decree of the senate in response to an embassy, probably from Panamara, Caria. 39 B.C. Sherk, *Roman Documents*, no. 27.

The document is formally dated to August in the consulship of L. Marcius Censorinus and Gaius Calvisius. All that emerges is that a large Greek embassy, probably, but not necessarily, from Panamara itself, made some request which Censorinus put to the Senate, and which was evidently received favourably.

8. Part of a decree of the Senate relating to Plarasa-Aphrodisias, 39 B.C. J. M. Reynolds, *Aphrodisias and Rome* (1982), no. 8 (henceforward *Aphrodisias*).

The decree is dated to the consulship of 39, L. Marcius Censorinus and Gaius Calvisius, and it confirms grants of rights and privileges, including freedom and immunity, to the city, and to the sanctuary (*temenos*) of Aphrodite there, made by Divus Julius, Octavian, and Antonius. Among the provisions are some for the reception of future embassies from the city coming before the Senate. Compare no. 12.

9. Edict of the Triumvirs. 39 B.C.? or soon after. *Aphrodisias*, no. 7.

The document contains the last part (about thirty letters) of each of twelve lines of an edict by two of the Triumvirs. There is no formal indication of date, but the succeeding lines contain references to a war and its effects, which is likely to be the Parthian invasion of 39 B.C., although it may refer also to oppression by Brutus and Cassius.

10. Letter of Octavian to Ephesus, promoted by an embassy from Plarasa-Aphrodisias, 38 B.C.? *Aphrodisias*, no. 12.

Octavian appears with the *praenomen* "Imperator," which suggests a year not earlier than 38, or possibly 40, B.C., and his letter is concerned with restoration after the war of Labienus, which suggests not later than 38. The sufferings of Plarasa-Aphrodisias were

---

[48] Mommsen, *Staatsrecht* III, 312, n. 2. S. Weinstock, *Divus Julius* (1972), 402, suggests, surely wrongly, that this is a letter from the Senate.

[49] Weinstock (n. 48).

detailed to Octavian, he says, by an ambassador, Solon, son of Demetrius, the same man who appears in no. 12. The most striking feature of the letter is that Octavian writes that he has given *entolai* to his colleague Antonius to repair the damage; but this may translate *mandata*, in the sense of a commission, and hence be less dramatic than it at first appears. The letter comes to Ephesus because it has been reported to Octavian that a gold statue of Eros dedicated by Divus Julius, having been looted from Aphrodisias, has been dedicated to Artemis of Ephesus. They are firmly warned to restore it. There is no reference to the institutions of the *res publica*.

11. Letter of Octavian to Stephanus concerning Aphrodisias (and letter of Stephanus to Aphrodisias). 38 B.C.? *Aphrodisias*, nos. 10 and 11.

Octavian instructs someone called Stephanus to protect Plarasa-Aphrodisias, whose interests he has at heart above all other cities in Asia, in the absence of Antonius (this will hardly help to date the letter, for the Antonius was only rarely in the province of Asia). The first line adds to the evidence on an interesting figure discussed in some typically illuminating pages by L. Robert,[50] and proves conclusively his view that Zoilus belongs in this period and not in the second century A.D. The documents are notable for Octavian's attachment to Aphrodisias, and the cult of Venus-Aphrodite, which he had inherited from Julius Caesar; he writes that he has "taken" for himself this one city from all Asia. The date will again be about 38 B.C., for Stephanus in his letter refers to the handing-over of free men and slaves and also a gold crown after the war of Labienus.

12. Letter of Octavian to Aphrodisias. 39–34 (39/8?) B.C. Sherk, *Roman Documents*, no. 28A; *Aphrodisias*, no. 6.

This letter to Aphrodisias from a Triumvir whose name is missing was earlier supposed, as in Sherk, *Roman Documents*, to be from Antonius, solely because Asia formed part of "his" territory. But its contents, and the comparison with no. 13, ought to have made it clear that it was from Octavian, even before the discovery of the Aphrodisias dossier. Octavian, as it certainly is, writes in response to a request brought by their ambassador, Solon, son of Demetrius (the same man as in no. 10), for copies of the documents granting them privileges (ll. 22–31). The careful distinction between the different forms of Roman official acts, *decretum* (?), *senatus consultum*,

---

[50] L. Robert, "Inscriptions d'Aphrodisias," *Ant. Class.* 35 (1966): 401–32.

iusiurandum, and *lex*, and the reference to the public archives (in the *aerarium*),[51] emphasises again the extent to which the Triumvirs, at least formally, operated within the framework of the *res publica*. The possible limits of the date are indicated by Octavian's titulature as it survives: "consul designate for the second and third time," so between 39 and 34 B.C. If this were the same journey on the part of Demetrius as that which produced no. 10, the document would date to the first year or so of the period.

13. Letter of Octavian to Rhosus, Syria. 36–34 B.C. *IGLS* III, no. 718; Sherk, *Roman Documents*, no. 58, i; trans. Sherk, *RGE*, no. 86.

This is a covering letter ordering the filing in the public archives of Rhosus of no. 5 (nos. 16 and 17, which are inscribed on the same stone, were written later than this). Octavian surprisingly omits the title *triumvir rei publicae constituendae*, but is Imperator IV (from 36 B.C.) and consul designate for the second and third time, so 39–34 B.C. The date is therefore 36–34 B.C. He writes "What is written below has been excerpted from a pillar on the Capitol at Rome, and [I ask that it should be] filed in your public records." Copies are also to be sent for registration to Tarsus, Antioch, and Seleucia. The letter is evidence that Octavian's relations with cities in the Greek East were not confined to the special case of Aphrodisias; and, along with nos. 5–7, that Greek cities other than Aphrodisias continued to be in active contact with the institutions of the *res publica* in Rome.

14. Edict of Octavian on the privileges of veterans. 38–33 B.C.?, *BGU* II, no. 628; *CIL* XVI, p. 145. no. 10; Riccobono, *FIRA*² I, no. 56; Cavenaille, *Corpus Papyrorum Latinarum*, no. 103; S. Daris, *Documenti per la storia dell'esercito romano in Egitto* (1964), no. 100.

The edict is quoted in a Latin papyrus of the first century A.D., itself evidently part of a report of legal proceedings. It begins "Imp. Caesar [d]ivi filius trium[v]ir rei publicae consultor(?)" – or "consul ter" (= consul for the third time) or "consul iter." (= consul for the second time) or "constit(uendae) iter(um)" (= to reorganize for the second time) – "said," which seems to suggest a date between 38 and 33. The extremely legalistic terms of the document are noticeable, including for instance a provision for veterans to be enrolled in a certain tribe for the census and for voting purposes.

---

[51] See F. Millar, *JRS* 54 (1964): 34–35 (= *Government, Society, and Culture in the Roman Empire* (2003), chapter 4); cf. M. W. Frederiksen, "The Republican Municipal Laws: Errors and Drafts," *JRS* 55 (1965): 183, on pp. 184–87.

It will be convenient to complete the dossier with three "post-Triumviral" documents. It is to be emphasised that in all three the titulature of Octavian mentions no public office other than the consulate.

15. Letter of Octavian to Mylasa, Caria, in response to an embassy. 31 B.C. (or 32?). Sherk, *Roman Documents*, no. 60.

Octavian writes to Mylasa as "appointed as consul for the third time." The titulature is puzzling, and the presence of the particle "and" after the word consul perhaps suggests that something has been omitted – he was Imperator V before Actium and VI after it. The expression *may* mean, as it is normally taken, that he was simply consul for the third time, that is, in 31. But might it not be a document of late 32, when (perhaps) his only official position was that of consul designate for the third time? The letter refers to two successive embassies which the Mylasans had sent to report their sufferings and losses in the war. On either of these datings this must refer to the preliminaries of the war of Actium.[52]

16. Letter of Octavian to Rhosus, in response to an embassy. 31 B.C. *IGLS* III, no. 718; Sherk, *Roman Documents*, no. 58, iii; trans. Sherk, *RGE*, no. 86.

Octavian writes as Imperator VI (after Actium), consul for the third time (31 B.C.) and "designated (consul) for the fourth time" (for 30), so in the last four months of 31. He mentions that the embassy from Rhosus met him in Ephesus and offered a crown and various honours (Dio indeed refers to his brief visit to Asia before his return to Italy in the middle of the winter of 31/0).[53] He undertakes to do the people of Rhosus further services when he comes to Syria, through which he did subsequently pass in 30 B.C.; and he testifies most emphatically to the constant intercessions which Seleucus, who was one of the ambassadors, had made on behalf of his city.

17. Letter of Octavian to Rhosus, recommending Seleucus. 30 B.C. *IGLS* III, no. 718; Sherk, *Roman Documents*, no. 58, iv; trans. Sherk, *RGE*, no. 86.

Octavian writes as consul for the fourth time, but is apparently not yet designated as consul for 29. He refers again to the services of

---

[52] For comparative evidence, see Magie, *Roman Rule in Asia Minor* (1950), 439-40 and notes. If, however, the titulature has been seriously abbreviated, it remains possible that Octavian wrote as consul designate for the second and third time, i.e., in 39-34, and that these embassies too referred to the war of Labienus.

[53] Dio 51, 4, 1-3.

Seleucus as naval commander, and to his immunity, Roman citizenship, and other privileges. He continues in a very significant manner: "I recommend this man to you. For such men render one's benevolence more ready towards their native cities as well. On the assumption therefore that I will gladly do for you whatever is possible for the sake of Seleucus, have confidence, and send to me on whatever matter you wish." Octavian writes as a monarch. If in 30 B.C. he expected or intended any future diminution of his effective power to confer benefits, there is no sign of it here. On the contrary he confidently expects, and even invites, petitions for benefits, which will be addressed to himself personally. It is here, rather than in the documents of the Triumvirate proper, with their recurrent formalism and repeated references to the institutions of the *res publica*, that a pattern appears in which decisions will be made by the untrammelled will and judgement of an individual.

It is striking how exactly these two letters match the assumptions of Virgil in the *Georgics*, which, according to the *Vita* by Donatus (27/91–95), were read to Augustus at Atella in 29: "... while great Caesar thunders to the deep-flowing Euphrates and, as victor in war, gives out rights, among the willing peoples and prepares for himself the road to Olympus" (4, 560–62).

TRIUMVIRAL FUNCTIONS AND THE EMERGENCE OF PERSONAL JURISDICTION

As we have seen, the only attested formal definition of the Triumvirs' power in relation to the Republican magistrates is that it was to be consular. What the powers of a Triumvir were in Rome therefore remains unclear; and the obscurity is increased by the fact, which Dio carefully notes, that the successive divisions of territory between them never included Rome and Italy. For, as he says with the rather undervalued acerbity with which he records the emergence of monarchy, they were supposed to be striving not to gain Italy but on its behalf.[54] One respect in which they were clearly distinguishable from the consuls while in Italy did emerge in 41 B.C.: the Triumvirs had a praetorian cohort, but the consuls did not.[55] The rest of the apparatus of Triumviral office seems, however, to have been very similar to that of the consuls. An anecdote in Appian shows them seated on the tribunal in the Forum (*BC* 4, 37/157). As we have seen, they were

---

[54] Dio 48, 2, 1.
[55] Appian, *BC* 5, 21/82. Cf. Sen., *Ep.* 114, 6, the seal being obtained from Maecenas "when he performed the tasks of the absent Caesar." For further evidence, see M. Durry, *Les cohortes prétoriennes* (1938), 76–77; A. Passerini, *Le coorti pretorie* (1939), 30–33.

granted the right to convene the Senate; when in 32 B.C. Octavian summoned the Senate and sat on the consuls' bench (Dio 50, 2, 5), and later continued to summon and address it when the consuls had fled (50, 3, 2), it is to be presumed that he was exercising a triumviral right, whether formally lapsed or not. Like other magistrates, they could also issue pronouncements as edicts, of which we have seen some examples among the documents listed above. Such was presumably the proclamation quoted by Appian, in which the Triumvirs announced the prescriptions: as given, it begins with the conventional terminology of an edict: "they say."[56]

However, it was an inevitable product of the situation that embassies, petitioners, and perhaps ordinary litigants should address themselves directly to the Triumvirs, or to one or two of them, and thereby tend to isolate them from the environment of Republican institutions, and to create a monarchical situation in which decisions were made by individual pronouncement. We have already seen a number of instances of embassies to one or other of them, and the literary sources offer more.[57] Individual petitioners took the same course. Perhaps the best illustration of the working of government in the period is provided by the so-called *Laudatio Turiae*.[58] The husband of the unnamed matron records that he was restored from exile "by the favour and judgement of the absent Caesar Augustus" ("beneficio et i[ud]icio apsentis Caesaris Augusti") (the document was inscribed after 27 B.C.), but that in his absence actual permission for his return had to be sought from Lepidus – "when seeking my restitution, you petitioned the then present colleague, Lepidus, and lay on the ground at his feet." In the face of abuse and physical assault the matron (apparently) managed to quote Octavian's edict of restitution. Similarly, another priceless and undervalued contemporary source, Cornelius Nepos, in the *Life of Atticus*, records that Atticus' daughter was married to Agrippa, with Antonius acting as mediator "although he might have increased his possessions through his influence, so far was he [Atticus] from a lust for money that he only used that influence in begging for the removal of his friends' dangers or inconveniences" (12, 2). Against this background there is surely no difficulty in accepting that Virgil in the *First Eclogue* (42–5) is referring to a successful petition to Octavian:

---

[56] Appian, *BC* 4, 8–11/34–44. It is not clear what was the form of the pronouncement quoted in 4, 38/159, by which Messala was removed from the list of the proscribed. But the term "edict of proscription," applying to an individual, is attested in Seneca, *De clementia* 1, 9, 5.

[57] Plut., *Ant.* 24; Jos., *Ant.* 14, 12, 2 (301); Appian, *BC* 4, 47/201; 5, 52/216.

[58] *CIL* VI, 1527 = *ILS* 8393: M. Durry, *Eloge funèbre d'une matrone romaine (éloge dite de Turia)* (1950), II, lines 21–28.

Here, Meliboeus, I am that youth for whom our altars smoke twice six days and years. Here he was the first to give my plea an answer ("hic mihi responsum primus dedit ille petenti"): "Feed, swains, your oxen as of old; rear your bulls."

A major public episode was the petition of the married women (*matronae*) to the Triumvirs over an imposition of a tax, recorded by Valerius Maximus (8, 3, 3) and Appian (*BC* 4, 32–4/136–46): since none of the men would offer their advocacy, Hortensia, the daughter of Hortensius, "pleaded the women's cause before the Triumvirs firmly and successfully: imitating her father's eloquence, she obtained the remission of the greater part of the money demanded from them." According to Appian the scene took place before the tribunal of the Triumvirs in the Forum, and they first had the women driven off by their lictors, and then announced a reduction in the tax on the next day.

It is not an accident that the episode concerns the demand for a benefaction which is granted by the simple pronouncement of the Triumvirs, or that in describing the petition Valerius Maximus resorts to the typical vocabulary of the law court. For precisely one of the characteristics of monarchy is the blurring of the distinction between the issuing of decisions and giving of legal judgements by the holder, or holders, of power. As Mommsen notes,[59] Quintilian alludes to this development in just this period in discussing the occasions and functions of "pleas for mercy" (*deprecationes*) – "Pleas for mercy, which are not in any sense a method of actual defence, can rarely be used, and only before judges who are not limited to some precise form of verdict. Even those speeches delivered before Gaius Caesar and the Triumvirs on behalf of members of the opposite party, although they do employ such pleas for mercy, also make use of the ordinary methods of defence." He continues directly to the situation of speaking before the *princeps* – "But if when pleading before the *princeps* or any other person who has power either to acquit or condemn, it is incumbent on us to urge ..."[60]

Summary, semi-judicial procedures for disposing of enemies taken in the field are amply attested for the Triumviral period,[61] right down to Octavian's hearings in 31 and 30.[62] These are of course a crucially important instance of the arbitrary exercise of power in this period.

---

[59] *Strafrecht*, 144, n. 5.
[60] Quintilian, *Inst. Orat.* 5, 13, 5–6 (Loeb trans.).
[61] The evidence is collected and discussed only, so far as I know, by H. Volkmann, *Zur Rechtsprechung im Principat des Augustus*² (1969), 11–50.
[62] Val. Max. 1, 7, 7; Plut., *Ant.* 72; Dio 51, 2, 4–6; 51, 16, 1.

But in the long term, for the fundamental transformation of the Roman state, the development of a routine personal jurisdiction by the holder of individual power is of much greater importance. The complexities of this development, which can be roughly described as the introduction into the city of Rome of the system of "investigation" (*cognitio*)[63] by a republican provincial governor, cannot be discussed here. But it must be emphasised that we have excellent evidence, which seems to be neglected both in books on Julius Caesar[64] and in those on the legal procedure of the late Republic,[65] that Caesar as dictator exercised a routine personal jurisdiction in Rome – "he administered justice most conscientiously and most severely," as Suetonius records (*Div. Jul.* 43). The generalization is confirmed by two anecdotes. Valerius Maximus (6, 2, 11) tells a story of Galba, "who dared to accost the deified Caesar in this manner when the latter, his victories accomplished, was dispensing justice in the forum." From the same period, after Munda, Seneca (*De benef.* 5, 24) records an incident when a veteran of Caesar's army was engaged in a case before him which concerned nothing more than a dispute between himself and his neighbour. It is clear that the fact that the man was a veteran was *not* the reason why the case came to Caesar. For it is only in the middle of the proceedings that he succeeds in establishing his identity as such, and hence his claim to a benefaction. Caesar is described as "angry because diverted in the middle of the investigation by this old story." So the procedure was that of *cognitio*, and the point at issue an entirely insignificant matter. (Whether it was a civil or a criminal case is not entirely clear.)

Whether it results from the limited nature of our sources or not, it is a fact which has not yet received its due emphasis that there is very little evidence for a routine personal jurisdiction by the Triumvirs in minor, non-political matters, and none at all for its exercise in Rome. The evidence of Triumviral jurisdiction other than over Roman political enemies in fact all relates to Antonius. Plutarch's *Life* records "that in his judicial decisions he was reasonable" (23),

---

[63] Not "cognitio extra ordinem," an expression which, as indicated in *JRS* 58 (1968): 222, is a grammatical monstrosity, since "extra ordinem" (out of order) is an adverbial phrase, which can qualify various verbs including "cognoscere" (to investigate), but is not found as an adjectival phrase. The modern use of the pseudo-concept "cognitio extra ordinem," even in the titles of books – some are listed in M. Kaser, *Das römische Zivilprozessrecht* (1966), 339 – is a classic instance of the process of nominalization brilliantly discussed by D. Daube, *Roman Law: Linguistic, Social and Philosophical Aspects* (1960), chap. 1.

[64] No trace of the question in the excellent work of M. Gelzer, *Caesar: Politician and Statesman* (1968).

[65] Even A. H. J. Greenidge, *The Legal Procedure of Cicero's Time* (1901), contains no discussion of the jurisdiction of Caesar as dictator.

and that he often gave judgement "seated on a tribunal" to tetrarchs and kings (58). An example, illustrating the confusion between judgement and political decision, will be the accusations against Hyrcanus and Herod[66] which preceded the steps which produced documents 1–3. We have two specific instances of cases before Antonius: Lachares, the father of Eurycles, was beheaded by him for robbery (Plut., *Ant.* 67); and Boethus of Tarsos was accused before him of peculation, but evidently acquitted (Strabo 674). That jurisdiction was part of his normal routine seems clear from Appian's description (*BC* V, 76/324) of his emergence from his Athenian holiday over the winter of 39/8 B.C.: standards, guards, and officers were seen at his door, embassies were received, and cases decided.

As regards Octavian, by contrast, who was of course based in Rome, we have no concrete instances of routine jurisdiction, and no general references to the issue until we reach the notoriously puzzling reference in Dio (51, 19, 6–7) to a vote in 30 B.C. which allowed him, among other things: "to administer justice on appeal." It is not necessary to discuss the peculiarities of this report, or whether the right was actually accepted by Octavian at this time, and, if so, how it relates to the later exercise of jurisdiction by the *Princeps*. It is important to stress instead what has sometimes been denied[67] – that a routine jurisdiction was subsequently exercised by Augustus himself, not just in the provinces,[68] or on appeal,[69] but in Rome and Italy and as the court of first instance, and in both civil and criminal cases.[70] The routine nature of the work is clear from Suetonius: "he himself gave jurisdiction assiduously and on occasion into the night, and if he were physically too weak would do so with his litter placed on the tribunal, or even lying down at home" (33); "of his country retreats he particularly frequented Tibur, where he very often gave jurisdiction, even in the porticoes of the temple of Hercules" (72).

In this important respect therefore the Triumvirate, so far as our evidence goes, may perhaps mark if anything a slight step back in the development of a monarchic institution which was already known before, in the dictatorship of Caesar, and which was to come into full effect in the principate of Augustus.

---

[66] Jos., *Ant.* 14, 12, 2 (302–3).
[67] E.g., by J. Bleicken, *Senatsgericht und Kaisergericht* (1962), 72–73.
[68] One may list by way of illustration Livy, *Epit.* 134 (I presume that "he held assizes in Narbo" must refer to Augustus' jurisdiction in 27); Seneca, *Controv.* 10 *praef(atio)* [preface] 14; from "senatorial" provinces, Jos., *BJ* 1, 26, 4 (531); Suet., *Div. Aug.* 93.
[69] Suet., *Div. Aug.* 33.
[70] Criminal: Val. Max. 9, 15, 2; Ovid, *Tristia* 2, 127ff.; Dio 54, 15, 4; 55, 7, 2; 56, 23, 2–3; 24. 7; Seneca, *QN* 1, 16, 1; Suet., *Div. Aug.* 24; 33; 45, 1; *Dig.* 48, 24, 1; Strabo 670. Civil: Val. Max. 7, 7, 3 and 4; 9, 15, *ext(erna)* [external] 1; Suet., *Div. Aug.* 97; *Dig.* 8, 3, 35.

THE "RESTORATION OF THE REPUBLIC"

Nothing said thus far is claimed to prove that the period of the Triumvirate was not one where violence and illegality played a crucial role. But the discussion will, it may be hoped, have emphasised that the Triumvirate was an institution which was created by a form of law, and which was superimposed on, but did not replace, the institutions of the *res publica*. In consequence, it exhibited many of the ambiguities in the exercise of authority, and many of the compromises between individual power and traditional institutions which characterise the Principate itself. Moreover, the existence of suspicions and rivalries between the Triumvirs caused them, in the search for political support, to pay repeated lip service to the Senate and the Roman people. Not only did the *res publica* survive, if much weakened, but the "Augustan" revival might be considered to have begun in the later thirties, with the building programme of Agrippa as aedile in 33; and its characteristic archaism is already visible in the use of the Fetial rite to declare war in 32.[71] When Atticus died on the last day of March 32 B.C., and was buried "escorted by all men of substance and by very large crowds of the common people,"[72] the outward appearance of Roman life must have been much as it had always been. It is against this background that we can come back to the two central questions. What really changed in the development from Triumvirate to Principate? And, more important even than the facts of constitutional change, what did men think and say had happened, and how did they characterise the "new order" in which they lived?

As is notorious, our evidence does not serve to resolve unambiguously the question of when the Triumviral powers came to an end, either in strict theory or in practice.[73] All that we can say for certain is that from 31 onwards, indeed until his assumption of the tribunician power in 23, the only actual office or power which the titulature of Octavian/Augustus reveals is that of consul. In this formal and outward aspect the only change in 27 was the appearance of the cognomen "Augustus."

There were of course more substantial changes, but their character and significance still require re-examination against the Triumviral background. In 28 Dio records that Octavian shared the *fasces*

---

[71] Dio 50, 4, 5.
[72] Nepos, *Atticus* 22, 3–4 (N. Horsfall's trans.).
[73] For discussions, see Fadinger (n. 5), chap. 2; K. E. Petzold, "Die Bedeutung des Jahres 32 für die Entstehung des Principats," *Historia* 18 (1969): 334; E. Gabba, "La data finale del secondo Triumvirato," *RFIC* 98 (1970): 3.

with Agrippa and his colleague in the consulate,[74] a gesture evidently intended as a symbol of normality, but one whose significance we cannot interpret for lack of evidence from the preceding period. In the same year, as we have noted (see text to n. 2), he abolished the illegal acts of the Triumvirate and, at the end of it, took the customary oath of a consul leaving office.[75] Tacitus indeed appears to couple with this abolition, and to place in this year, the substantial steps which created the Principate – "Finally Caesar Augustus, when consul for the sixth time, secure in his power, abolished what he had decreed as triumvir and gave us the laws by which we enjoy peace and the rule of a Princeps."[76] As so often with Tacitus, we cannot discern precisely to what he is referring. Augustus himself (*RG* 34) speaks of his sixth and seventh consulates. Dio, however, clearly relates the essential change to the "settlement" of 27.

Of the changes which now took place, those affecting the government of the provinces at least are reasonably clear.[77] The Triumvirs had been empowered to appoint all provincial governors, and we have adequate evidence of their doing so,[78] and of Octavian continuing to do likewise between Actium and 27.[79] But it should be noted that the republican title proconsul (*pro consule*) had not been abandoned,[80] though *legatus pro praetore* (legate with praetorian rank), first attested in the seventies B.C.,[81] is found also, though in Sicily under Sextus Pompeius.[82] More significantly, these proconsuls, although they were the appointees of, and in some sense subordinate to, the Triumvirs, continued to celebrate triumphs[83] (a fact which surprised Dio).[84] In 29 B.C., however, Octavian shared the triumph of Gaius Carrinas (Dio 51, 21, 6), and denied the deposition of the *spolia opima* (spoils removed from an enemy general by the Roman commander who had personally killed him in battle) to Licinius Crassus (Dio 51, 24, 4; cf. Livy 4, 20, 5–7). From 27 B.C. some

---

[74] Dio 53, 1, 1.
[75] Dio 53, 1, 1.
[76] Tac., *Ann.* 3, 28.
[77] Cf. *JRS* 56 (1966), 156–57 (= *The Roman Republic and the Augustan Revolution* (2002), chapter 11).
[78] E.g., Appian, *BC* 5, 129/537; 132/549; Dio 48, 22, 1.
[79] E.g., Appian, *BC* 4, 38/161; Dio 51, 23, 2 (cf. Dio 51, 17, 1, Cornelius Gallus left in charge of Egypt).
[80] E.g., Degrassi, *ILLRP*² I, 433; cf. Broughton, *MRR* II, 369, n. 1; and my n. 83. Documentary evidence for the titles borne by governors is however extremely sparse throughout the Triumviral period.
[81] *ILS* 37 = Degrassi, *ILLRP*² I, 372.
[82] Degrassi, *ILLRP*² I, 426.
[83] The evidence on triumphs between 43 and 28 B.C. is admirably collected by A. Degrassi, *Fasti Consulares et Triumphales, Inscriptiones Italiae* XIII, 1 (1947), 567–70.
[84] Dio 48, 42, 4.

provincial governors continued to have the title proconsul, and appointment by lot was now restored in their case.⁸⁵ But the governors of most of the major military provinces lost this title in favour of *legatus*, and continued to be appointed by Augustus; how soon the full title, "legatus Augusti pro praetore" (a legate of Augustus with praetorian rank), came into regular use is curiously difficult to determine;⁸⁶ but "leg. Augusti" appears on coins of P. Carisius in Lusitania in the mid 20s B.C.,⁸⁷ and "leg. imp. Caesaris Aug." (*ILS* 929) is used of Articuleius Regulus, governor there in the period A.D. 2–14. The change was thus far from being unambiguously a step in the direction of republicanism; our evidence provides only a single uncertain instance from the Republic of a legate using his commander's name in his title.⁸⁸ Moreover, while proconsuls continued for a few years, down to 19 B.C., to celebrate triumphs, no legate appointed by Augustus ever did, or could.

The notion that these two methods of appointment and two forms of titulature reflected a fundamental division of political and administrative responsibility between Princeps and Senate is an illusion.⁸⁹ Nor can we tell what formal description was applied to Augustus' position in relation to the imperial provinces. It may be that he was formally proconsul of these provinces while concurrently holding the consulship (Pompey had already been proconsul of Spain – Caes. *BG* 6, 1, 2 – when elected consul in 52 while continuing his command; cf. Vell. Pat. 2, 48, 1); but no document gives Augustus or any other emperor the *title* of proconsul until the reign of Trajan.⁹⁰ It may be, alternatively, that some formula employing the term "proconsular *imperium*" (*imperium proconsulare*), or a similar expression, was devised; but for that we have no evidence at this stage. It remains entirely open to suggest that the provincial aspects of the settlement of 27 amount, on Augustus' side, simply and solely to the right to appoint legates as governors of most of the major military provinces.

---

⁸⁵ Dio 53, 11, 2.
⁸⁶ I owe this essential point to Professor Badian. The documentary evidence is still very poor for this period. In Hispania Citerior, however, it is clear that "legatus pro praetore" was normal – see G. Alföldy, *Fasti Hispanienses* (1969): 3–13 – though Paullus Fabius Maximus, c. 3/2 B.C., uses "legat. Caesaris" (p. 9). "[Legatus pro] pr. Augusti Caesaris in [Illyrico]" is used of M. Vinicius, there 10/9 or some years later; see A. Dobo, *Die Verwaltung der römischen Provinz Pannonien* (1968), 16–18. Milestones from Galatia of 6 B.C. have "Commodus Aquila, his *legatus propraetore* being charge" (*curante Com. Aquila leg. suo pro pr.*); see R. K. Sherk, *The Legates of Galatia* (1951), 24.
⁸⁷ Alföldy (n. 86), 131.
⁸⁸ See J. M. Reynolds, "Cyrenaica, Pompey and Cn. Cornelius Lentulus Marcellinus," *JRS* 52 (1962): 99–100, no. 7 = *ILLRP*² I, 1234.
⁸⁹ See Millar (n. 77).
⁹⁰ Mommsen (n. 48), 2, 778.

As regards the city magistracies, our evidence tends to suggest that the *form* of republican elections had continued through the Triumviral period (see text to nn. 23–39). If that is correct, and it is not certain, then when Dio asserts (53, 21, 6–7) that electoral assemblies began to meet again from 27 onwards, we may take this as a reference to the recommencement of genuine competition for election, which is clearly attested for the Augustan period; the competition was limited in practice, but not formally, by imperial recommendation (*commendatio*).[91] (None the less, our sources do in certain instances speak of Augustus "offering" or "giving" the consulate to a man.[92]) As regards the holders of the city magistracies, no change was made in their powers in 27, for no formal change had been made in the Triumviral period.

Thus the changes which culminated in 27 were of a fairly limited kind, and not all of them clearly tended towards a revived Republic. But that brings us to our central question: now that we have seen the extent to which the institutions of the *res publica* survived through the Triumviral period, what evidence have we to justify the normal view that 27 saw either a real or a proclaimed "Restoration of the Republic"?[93]

The question involves acute problems as to what terms are used in our sources to describe the change of 27 or the state of affairs resulting from it, and what these terms meant at different periods. When if ever, for instance, was *res publica* used to mean "the Republic" in our sense? It surely has something like that meaning in one passage of Tacitus, referring to the year A.D. 14: "how many were left who had seen the Republic with their own eyes?"[94] But did it have the same meaning in the 20s B.C.? Already in 29 B.C. the Senate and People of Rome had made a dedication to Octavian "the *res publica* having been preserved" (*re publica conservata*).[95] More important perhaps is a passage from the third book of Livy, written precisely in the two years after 27 B.C.[96] Here Livy describes the Senate's reaction to a determined and patriotic speech by L. Quinctius Cincinnatus, consul in 460 B.C.: "the uplifted senators believed that the *res publica*

---

[91] See works cited in n. 8.
[92] Tac., *Ann.* 2, 43 (Calpurnius Piso); 3, 75 (Ateius Capito); Seneca, *De Clementia*, 1, 9, 12 (L. Cinna); *Dig.* 1, 2, 2, 47 (Antistius Labeo).
[93] The following argument returns, in greatly expanded form, to some points briefly made in *CR*, n.s., 18 (1968): 265–66.
[94] Tac., *Ann.* 1, 3, 7.
[95] *CIL* VI, 873; *ILS* 81.
[96] R. M. Ogilvie, *A Commentary on Livy Books 1–5* (1965), 2.

had been restored."⁹⁷ "Res publica" here means "the state" or "the condition of public affairs," and certainly cannot mean anything like "the Republic."

This passage also serves to emphasise that, even if it were the case that contemporary sources consistently used "res publica restituta" of the change completed in 27, this is not likely to have meant that "the Republic was restored." In fact it is remarkable, firstly, how little reflection the event has in contemporary literature – nothing in Virgil, Horace or Propertius echoes it – and, secondly, how varied are the expressions used in those literary and documentary sources which do refer to it. The expression "res publica restituta" is used almost certainly in the *Laudatio Turiae* (text to n. 58), ii, 25, "the world having been pacified, [and] the *res publica* restored"; and possibly in the *Fasti Praenestini* for January 12:⁹⁸

> [The Senate decreed] that an oak crown should be fixed above the door to Caesar Augustus' house [because he restored the *res publica*] to the Roman people.

It must be emphasised that these two cases are the *only* ones in which the expression is used, or may be used. In Ovid, *Fasti*, under 13 January, a quite different formulation appears (1, 589-90): "all the provinces have been restored to our people, and your grandfather was called by the name Augustus." Alternatively, coins of 28/7 B.C. have "vindicator of the liberty of the Roman people" (*Libertatis p.R. vindex*).⁹⁹ What might be taken as a reference to the restoration of political liberty is in fact more precisely a reference to the end of the civil war; the reverse of the coins has "peace" (*pax*), and the *Fasti* note on August 1 "since on this day Imperator Caesar son of the deified Julius delivered the *res publica* from terrible danger."¹⁰⁰

Our most general statement comes from the loyalist Velleius; in describing the general settlement of affairs after the end of the civil wars he echoes in part the words of Cicero addressing Julius Caesar in *Pro Marcello* 23: "It is for you alone [to do], Gaius Caesar, ... the courts must be re-established, credit must be called back, licentiousness must be curbed, population growth must be encouraged; all that has become disintegrated and dissipated must be bound by severe laws." Velleius' version is more detailed and ornate: "The civil wars

---

⁹⁷ Livy 3, 20, 1.
⁹⁸ *CIL* I² p. 231; Degrassi, *Inscr. It.* XIII, 2 (1963), 112-13.
⁹⁹ *RIC* I, Augustus no. 10; C. H. V. Sutherland, *Coinage in Roman Imperial Policy, 31 B.C.–A.D. 68* (1951), 31; C. H. V. Sutherland, N. Olcay, and K. E. Merrington, *The Cistophori of Augustus* (1970), 89-90.
¹⁰⁰ Degrassi, *Inscr. It.* XIII, 2 (1963), 191 (*Fasti Amiternini*); cf. pp. 31, 135.

were ended after twenty years, foreign wars suppressed, peace restored, the frenzy of arms everywhere lulled to rest; validity was restored to the laws, authority to the courts, and dignity to the Senate; the power of the magistrates was reduced to its former limits, with the sole exception that two were added to the eight existing praetors. The old traditional form (*forma*) of the *res publica* was restored."[101] We could reasonably paraphrase this passage as "Augustus restored the *res publica*," but not as "Augustus restored the Republic." The reference to the raising of the number of praetors from eight to ten shows how precise and restricted is the meaning of "the form of the *res publica*" in this context.

Our most valuable source for these events would have been Livy. But while his preface refers to the closing of the gates of Janus in 29 (1, 19, 3), it happens not to refer to the political settlement which followed. However, insofar as we may judge by the *Epitome* 134, when he came to the settlement he described it in neutral terms: "Gaius Caesar, when everything had been put in order, and all the provinces brought within a definite framework, also received the *cognomen* Augustus." It is unnecessary and pointless to go on to list the references in later authors to the settlement of affairs at this time, for our concern is essentially with how it was described and thought of by contemporaries. But we may note the two well-known passages in which Tacitus characterises the development of Octavian from triumvir to princeps:

> *Ann.* 1, 2: After he laid down the name of triumvir, he conducted himself as consul, and as content with (having) the tribunician power with which to protect the plebs.
> *Ann.* 3, 28: Finally Caesar Augustus, when consul for the sixth time (28 B.C.), secure in his power, abolished what he had decreed as triumvir and gave us laws by which we enjoy peace and the rule of a *Princeps*.

In both of these passages Tacitus alludes to, rather than describes, features of Augustus' position in the 20s B.C. Neither reflects any knowledge of a claim that the Republic had been restored. In fact the only statement in our sources which can be interpreted as making a claim of that sort comes from Augustus himself in *Res Gestae* 34. However well known, his words still need reconsideration:

> In my sixth (28) and seventh (27) consulships, after I had extinguished the flames of the civil wars, and had gained control of all things by universal consent, I transferred the *res publica* from my own power [*potestas*] to the discretion [*arbitrium*] of the Senate and the Roman people. For this worthy

---

[101] Vell. Pat. 2, 89, 3–4

act of mine I was named Augustus. ... After this time I stood above everyone else by virtue of my *auctoritas*, but I did not have any more power than the other colleagues serving in office with me.

Augustus' words are carefully chosen: except for the consulates of 27–23, 5, and 2 B.C. he never held any republican magistracy after January 27. What he says can only be absolved of actual falsehood by being understood to mean, in the strictest sense, that as consul he had no powers greater than those of his successive colleagues. But at all times he held other powers which they did not, in the initial period specifically the right to appoint legates to govern his provinces (see text to nn. 86–88); and after 23 B.C. his occasional consulates were essentially irrelevant to his position.

So we have to be cautious in considering the words he uses to describe the events of 28 and 27. He conspicuously fails to claim any constitutional basis for his power up to that point. But what he does claim is that he transferred the *res publica* to the *arbitrium* of the Senate and the Roman people. We cannot, in interpreting this, disregard the view of our only narrative source for these events, Cassius Dio, who considered that the offer of resignation of his powers made by Octavian in January 27 B.C. was a charade which was deliberately intended to, and immediately did, result in a formal continuation of his control of the state.[102] The word "discretion" (*arbitrium*), again, can refer to a historical fact if it alludes to Octavian's offer and the subsequent vote of Senate and People in January 27 B.C.; but if it carries an implication of a continued political freedom lasting beyond that point, that is another matter.

To Dio, of course, there never was any such event as the restoration of the Republic; for he, like Appian (*Hist.*, *praef.* 14/60), regarded Actium as the moment when monarchy returned to the Roman world.[103] It should, however, be noted that he, Appian, and Suetonius all refer to proposals or promises, made at various times by Octavian and Antonius, which would have amounted to "restoring the Republic." The form of words used is almost always that of *giving back* power:

> 36 B.C. Appian, *BC* 5, 132/548: "Caesar ... said that he would give back the whole *res publica*, if Antonius came back from Parthia."
> 34 B.C. Dio 49, 41, 6: "Now while Antonius was engaged as described, he had the effrontery to write to the Senate that he wished to give up his

---

[102] Dio 53, 2, 6–12, 3.
[103] Dio 51, 1, 1–2.

office and put the whole administration of the state into the hands of this body and of the people."

32 B.C. Dio 50, 7, 1: "Antonius ... promised that that within two months after his victory he would relinquish his office and restore to the Senate and people all its authority."

30 B.C. Suetonius, *Div. Aug.* 28: "Twice Augustus thought of giving back the *res publica*: immediately after the fall of Antonius, when he remembered that Antonius had often accused him of being the one obstacle to such a change; and again when he could not shake off an exhausting illness. He then actually summoned the magistrates and the Senate to his house and gave them a financial account of the state of the empire."

29 B.C. Dio 52, 1, 1: "After this they [the Romans] reverted to what was, strictly speaking, a monarchy, although Caesar planned to lay down his arms and to entrust the management of the state to the Senate and to the people."

The last passage serves only as an introduction to the debate of Agrippa and Maecenas, and need not be taken as evidence of an intention by Octavian specifically in 29 to restore power to Senate and People. It should be noted that the earlier passages all refer to unfulfilled public promises from the Triumviral period, and that of Suetonius to an unfulfilled private intention. Suetonius gives no hint of an awareness that it had ever been claimed that the event in question had actually occurred.

However, since men writing in the established Empire could hardly have doubted that they were living under a monarchy, it might reasonably be objected that this has coloured their view of the crucial transitional period. So we may come finally to the essential question – how did the matter seem to contemporaries? First we may note the remarkable frankness with which Cornelius Nepos, writing some time after the death of Atticus at the end of March 32, and apparently after the death of Antonius, characterises the ambitions of the two Triumvirs – "when each of them desired to be the first man [*princeps*] not only in Rome but also in the entire world."[104] This passage was probably written before January 27. But the preface of Vitruvius' *De architectura* is another matter, for it seems certain that it was written after January 27, and not later than 23 B.C.[105] The tone of his address to Augustus in his preface is therefore of primary importance for assessing the conceptions which obtained in Rome in the 20s:

---

[104] Nepos, *Atticus* 20, 5.

[105] Vitr. 5, 1, 7, referring to a "temple of Augustus" (*aedes Augusti*) at Fanum, ought to be conclusive, but it has sometimes been suggested on general historical grounds that the expression is impossible in Italy at this date. But other indications show that the work was complete by 23 or 22 B.C.: Schanz-Hosius, *Gesch. d. röm. Lit.*⁴ II (1935), 387–88; cf.

When your divine mind and power, Imperator Caesar, put the whole world under its command, your citizens gloried in your triumph and victory: for all their enemies were crushed by your invincible courage and all mankind obeyed your bidding. The Roman people and Senate, liberated from fear, has been guided by your bountiful thoughts and counsels. ... When I observed that you cared not only about the common life of all men and the constitution of the state, but also about the provision of suitable public buildings ... Since, however, it was the heavenly counsel to commit him [Julius Caesar] to the regions of immortality and transfer imperial control to your power.

The passage contains no precise allusions to the current constitutional position. But its unabashed acceptance of the personal dominance of Augustus is unmistakable. Moreover, and this is the essential point, its obsequious flatteries could certainly be disregarded and considered as of no historical significance *if* they had been written under any conditions *except* those supposed by modern scholars, namely a recently proclaimed "restoration of the Republic." Had such a thing been proclaimed, Vitruvius' words would have been grossly undiplomatic – and would not have been written.

The same considerations apply, with rather less force, to a number of passages in Horace and Ovid. None is very precise or significant in itself, and most are less close in time to 27 B.C. than the preface of Vitruvius, but all are incompatible with the hypothesis that Augustus had proclaimed a restoration of the Republic:

Horace, *Odes* 1, 12, 49–52: "O father and guardian of the human race, thou son of Saturn, to thee by fate has been entrusted the charge of mighty Caesar; mayst thou be lord of all, with Caesar next in power ..." and later (58) "second to thee alone shall he with justice rule the broad earth."

Horace, *Odes* 3, 14, 14–16: "Neither civil strife nor death by violence will I fear, while Caesar holds the earth."

Horace, *Odes* 4, 5, 1–2: "Sprung from the blessed gods, best guardian of the race of Romulus, too long already art thou absent"; cf. 4, 15, 17: "while Caesar guards the state."

Ovid, *Fasti* 1, 531–32: "In the line of Augustus the guardianship of the fatherland shall abide: it is decreed that his house shall hold the reins of Empire."

Ovid, *Fasti* 2, 138–42: "All that exists beneath the canopy of Jove is Caesar's own. ... Thine was a rule of force: under Caesar it is the laws that reign. Thou didst the name of master bear: he bears the name of *princeps*."

Ovid, *Tristia* 4, 4, 13–16: "Even the father of his country [*pater patriae*] – and what can be more like the behaviour of a fellow citizen? – submits to frequent mention in my verse, nor can he prevent it, for Caesar is the *res publica*, and of the common good I too have a share."

A. Boethius, "Vitruvius and the Roman Architecture of His Age," ΔΡΑΓΜΑ *M.P. Nilsson dedicatum* (1939), 114.

Nothing much needs be claimed for these well-known passages, except that they reveal a perfectly open recognition of the control of the Roman state by one man. With the exception of one of the passages of Ovid (*Fasti* 2, 138–42), none betrays the slightest anxiety to cloak this domination in constitutional forms. Even more emphatic is Horace in *Epistulae* 2, 1, 1–4:

> While you sustain so many and so heavy tasks alone, protect the life of Italy with arms, and adorn it with good customs, reform it by laws, I would be committing a sin against the public interest if by a prolonged discourse I were to interrupt your urgent concerns, Caesar.

Augustus himself objected to being acclaimed publicly as "master" (*dominus*),[106] refused the dictatorship in 22 B.C.,[107] and at the end of his life claimed, somewhat disingenuously as we have seen, to have excelled others only in authority (*auctoritas*). But he too had no hesitation in recognising the facts of his position. In a letter to his grandson Gaius he wrote, "But I pray to the Gods that whatever time is left to me I may pass with you safe and well, with the *res publica* in a flourishing condition, while you are playing the men and preparing to succeed to my position [*statio mea*]."[108] "Res publica" here means just what it does in a letter of Ateius Capito, who died in A.D. 22, referring to the love of liberty which possessed his great rival Antistius Labeo. "But an excessive and mad love of liberty possessed the man, to such a degree that, although the deified Augustus was then *princeps* and in control of the *res publica* [*rem publicam obtinebat*], he looked upon nothing as lawful, and accepted nothing, unless he had found it ordered and sanctioned by the old Roman law."[109]

Labeo thus saw the principate of Augustus in a light not entirely different from that in which Cascellius had seen the Triumvirate. Moreover, even the complaisant Capito regarded the principate as a state of affairs in which Augustus was "in control of the *res publica*." That the *res publica* had been duly "restored" – *restituta* – by Augustus he would surely have agreed; but he clearly did not suppose that it had ever been given back – *reddita*.

The regimes of Julius Caesar, of the Triumvirs, and of Augustus all had to adjust themselves in differing ways to the *res publica* of Rome and its institutions, whose tenacity in survival was to be one of the

---

[106] Suet., *Div. Aug.* 53.
[107] *RG* 5; Vell. Pat. 2, 89; Suet., *Div. Aug.* 52; Dio 54, 1, 3–4.
[108] Aul. Gell., *NA* 15, 7, 3 = E. Malcovati, *Imperatoris Caesaris Augusti Operum Fragmenta*[5] (1969), *Ep(istulae)* [*Letters*] XXII (Loeb trans.).
[109] Aul. Gell., *NA* 13, 12, 1–2 (based on Loeb trans.).

most remarkable features of imperial history. The temporary nature of the Triumvirate, its very lack of definition, and the competition for political support between its three, and then two, holders, caused it to be, if anything, more dependent on the Republican institutions than were the regimes of Caesar and of Augustus which preceded and followed it. The victory of Actium, the death of Antonius, and the stabilisation of affairs in Rome all marked steps towards, not away from, the establishment of a monarchy; and no good evidence suggests that anybody at the time claimed, or supposed, otherwise.

3 The Powers of Augustus[†]

JEAN-LOUIS FERRARY
translated by Jonathan Edmondson

1 THE SETTLEMENT OF 27 AND THE LAWS ON THE PROVINCES

In *Römisches Staatsrecht* Mommsen argued that it was by means of proconsular *imperium* that Augustus in 27, even though consul, gained control of the imperial provinces and the legions stationed there. This theory was linked to Mommsen's hypothesis that an important reform of Sulla's had completely dissociated the senior magistracies and promagistracies. Senior magistrates were henceforth restricted, Mommsen argued, to duties in the city of Rome, where they exercised *imperium domi* ["power of command at home"], while promagistrates gained a monopoly in governing provinces. On this view the Pompeian law of 52 completed the process of dissociation by instituting a five-year interval between a magistracy and promagistracy. In 27 the return to the normal functioning of the institutions of the Roman state entailed a revival of the reform initiated by Sulla and Pompey. Hence it was not by virtue of consular *imperium* that Augustus retained control of the Gauls, the Spains, Syria, and Egypt, but rather by proconsular *imperium*.[1]

This thesis still has its adherents, even in some of the recent scholarly literature.[2] But as early as 1888 it was contested by Kromayer and Pelham, who argued that Augustus governed the imperial provinces by means of his consular *imperium*.[3] The most important

---

[†] Originally published in French as "À propos des pouvoirs d'Auguste," *Cahiers du Centre G. Glotz* 12 (2001), 101–154. [Editor's note: I would like to thank the author for his generous cooperation in the abridgement and translation of his article.]

[1] Mommsen 1887–1888, II: 845 (Augustus' proconsular *imperium* in 27); I: 57 and II: 94–95 (Sulla's reform); II: 241–242 (Pompeian law of 52).

[2] Thus Kienast 1982 = 1999: 87; Castritius 1982: 38–40; Bleicken 1978, I: 27–29; 1990: 88; 1998: 326. On the other hand, the thesis of an "unspecified *imperium*," of which Siber and De Francisci were the last great proponents, seems now to be totally abandoned.

[3] Kromayer 1888: 32–34; Pelham 1888 (repr. 1911; I shall use the pagination of this reprinted version in what follows).

critique of Mommsen's view was that of Pelham, since he questioned the very existence of the Sullan reform that Mommsen had postulated, and Pelham was to exercise a lasting influence on scholarship on the late Republic and the powers of Augustus in the English-speaking world.[4] Mommsen's analysis has now been criticised on new grounds by A. Giovannini and K. M. Girardet.[5] Both of these scholars, however, remain to a certain degree prisoners of Mommsen's explanatory system in the sense that they continue to search for the date of a fundamental reform that supposedly stripped the consulate of its military *imperium*. In 1983 Giovannini concluded that this did not occur under either Sulla or Pompey, but only under Augustus in the year 27. Girardet, to whose position Giovannini has now partially moved, thinks that this took place no earlier than in 23, more probably in 19 or 18.[6]

In my view this all poses the wrong question and leads to an imprecise interpretation of both the *lex Pompeia* and the Augustan reforms. In this paper I shall demonstrate that, first, there never was a law expressly stripping consular *imperium* of its military component, but only laws, passed in 52 and 27, that dealt with the method used each year for the allocation of the provinces, including consular provinces; and, second, provinces assigned to consuls for five or ten years, which occurred for the first time in 59 to benefit Julius Caesar, were allocated in such an extraordinary fashion that this prevents them being considered consular provinces in the traditional sense of the term, since they were abnormal both in the method of their conferral and in their duration and because they were almost never subject to the normal rule of collegiality. The discussion has hitherto focused incorrectly on the evolution of consular *imperium*; it needs to be reoriented, it seems to me, to concentrate instead on the problem of the provinces and the way in which they were conferred.

(a) Pompey's and Caesar's laws on the provinces

[*In the opening section of his article (here omitted) Ferrary discusses Sulla's supposed reforms of the senior magistracies and argues in support of Giovannini's view that Sulla never tried to strip consuls of*

---

[4] For the Republic after Sulla, Balsdon 1939; for the powers of 27, Hammond 1933: 29–30; Jones 1951 (repr. 1960, 5; I shall use the pagination of this reprinted version here); Brunt 1962; Badian 1986: 81–84.

[5] Giovannini 1983; Girardet 1990, 1992b, and 2000.

[6] Giovannini 1999. But, in contrast with Girardet, he continues to date to 27 the reorganisation of the proconsular provinces described by Cassius Dio at 53.14.2.

Fig. 3.1. Aureus of Octavian, 28 BC, with the legend on the reverse *LEGES ET IVRA P(opuli) R(omani) RESTITVIT* ("He restored the laws and rights of the Roman people")

their military imperium. *Provinces continued to be allocated by the senate. The* lex Pompeia *of 52 introduced a gap of five years between the holding of a magistracy and promagistracy, and this applied to consular as well as praetorian provinces. Caesar, however, at some point between 46 and 44 had a new law on the provinces passed, which invalidated Pompey's law. During Caesar's dictatorship former consuls and occasionally private individuals were sent out to govern provinces. From 43 to 28 provinces were assigned by the triumvirs according to the terms of the* lex Titia *and then later by Octavian himself.*]

(b) *The laws on the provinces of 27*

The publication of an *aureus* of 28 with the legend *LEGES ET IVRA P(opuli) R(omani) RESTITVIT* ["He restored the laws and rights of the Roman people": see Fig. 3.1] has allowed us to gain a better understanding of the gradual nature of the *restitutio rei publicae* ["restoration of the State"], which took place, as Augustus himself stated (*RG* 34), over the two years 28 and 27. The final stage of this process concerned the particularly delicate problem of the provinces and, an issue very much connected with that, command of the legions.[7]

Elected consul without a break from 31 onwards and re-elected for

---

[7] Rich and Williams 1999. [For the new interpretation of the coin legend, in place of the previously proposed *leges et iura p(opulo) R(omano) restituit* ("he restored their laws and rights to the Roman people"), see Mantovani 2008.]

27 with Agrippa as his colleague after the *comitiorum pristinum ius* ["long-standing right of elections"] had been re-established (Suet. *Aug.* 40.4), Augustus possessed consular *imperium* and had no need for any new *imperium* to be conferred on him to govern by means of his chosen legates [*legati*] the provinces entrusted to him and to command the troops stationed there. We have already argued that Mommsen's theory that from Sulla onwards *imperium* was split into *imperium consulare domi* ["consular *imperium* at home"] and *imperium proconsulare militiae* ["proconsular *imperium* in the military sphere"] should be rejected. There is no reason to retroject to the Augustan period, and more particularly to 27, a formula, *imperium proconsulare*, which appears for the first time during the reign of Tiberius in a passage of Valerius Maximus concerning the governors of the province of Asia in the 60s BC and is attested only from Tacitus onwards to denote one of the powers of the *princeps* or his "co-rulers" as well as the power of proconsuls in the proconsular provinces.[8] There can be no doubt, therefore, that Augustus was called upon to govern his provinces by virtue of the consular *imperium* he already possessed when they were entrusted to him. But as he received his provinces for ten years and since it could not be assumed that he would continue to hold the consulship throughout this ten-year period, the *senatus consultum* that was adopted and the law by which it was doubtless ratified[9] must have envisaged that he would govern them "as consul or as proconsul" (*consule prove consule*).

That one should think in terms of a *lex de provincia* and not a *lex*

---

[8] Val. Max. 6.9.7 (T. Aufidius, proconsul of Asia in 67 or 66) and 8.1.*amb*.2 (P. Cornelius Dolabella, proconsul of Asia in 68); Tac. *Ann*. 1.14.3 (Germanicus in 14); 12.41.2 and 13.21.7 (Nero in 51). Regarding the *imperium* of governors of proconsular provinces: *Ann*. 1.76.4; 3.58.4; 12.59.2; 13.52.1. For convenience, I shall speak of "proconsular provinces" and "imperial provinces," even though I realise that in official terms all, including Egypt, were *provinciae populi Romani* ("provinces of the Roman people"). It is better to avoid the traditional, but imprecise, term "senatorial provinces": see Millar 1989.

[9] Dio 53.12.1 talks of an act of the assembly conferring the power on Augustus, but he gives the impression that the division of the provinces was only conducted this way at a later time thanks to a concession by the *princeps*, who did not wish to appear to be depriving the Roman people of its power. For Dio, the events of 27 in fact came down to the establishment of a monarchy, hidden behind a theatrical show of Republicanism. The existence of a law can be upheld, even if its content was not what Dio claimed. Two decisive arguments lead to this conclusion: on the one hand, the Republican precedents going back to the *lex Gabinia* and *lex Vatinia*; on the other, the laws regarding "co-rulers" (the law of 13 regarding Tiberius, known thanks to Vell. Pat. 2.121.1 and Suet. *Tib*. 21.1; the laws regarding Agrippa and Germanicus, revealed quite recently in the *laudatio* of Agrippa and the s.c. on Cn. Piso senior). It is true that in these last three cases there was a grant of *imperium* at the same time as that of a *provincia*. But, as I am going to try to show, the provinces conferred on Augustus in 27 were not a simple proconsular province, which the senate was able to grant, but an "extraordinary" province, which, according to tradition, required ratification by the assembly.

de imperio has been noted already for some time, in particular by certain historians in the English-speaking world, working in the tradition of Pelham.[10] But it is almost as seriously imprecise, in my opinion, to talk of a *provincia consularis* ["consular province"]. This error has been carried to extreme lengths in the works of Lacey, when he supposes that Octavian's *relatio* ["motion"] on 13 January 27 was simply a traditional *relatio de provinciis consularibus* ["motion on the consular provinces"],[11] and further when he imagines that Agrippa received as his province a *praefectura classis et orae maritimae* ["prefecture of the fleet and sea-coast"], for which there is not a shred of evidence in any of our sources.[12] The designation "consular province" is found in other studies too,[13] but this seems to me to misrepresent the real situation. It makes sense only in the context of the regular conferment of a province on the two consuls during their term in office and then, after the *lex Pompeia* of 52 (and again, as we shall see, after a law of 27), in the context of the regular grant of a province to two men of consular rank for a year, eventually renewable under the terms of the *lex Pompeia* and the *lex Iulia Caesaris*. The provinces allocated Augustus in 27 (it is significant that these are never designated globally as his *provincia*, in the singular)[14] do not correspond to these criteria, but, as has generally been recognised elsewhere, fit into the tradition of the extraordinary commands of the final years of the Republic, which could be bestowed upon a *privatus* ["private citizen"] granted consular *imperium* for a specific purpose, as occurred in the case of Pompey by means of the *lex Gabinia* in 67 and the *lex Manilia* in 66, or upon a consul currently in office, as happened in 59 with Caesar thanks to the *lex Vatinia* or in 55 with Pompey and Crassus by means of the *lex Trebonia*.

The expression "consular province" seems to me just as inappropriate in these last two cases as in the two former ones, even if, in the case of the *lex Trebonia*, a form of consular collegiality was involved;

---

[10] See, for example, Brunt 1977: 96–97.

[11] Lacey 1996: 77–99; *contra* Rich and Williams 1999: 203 n. 98. B. van Groningen (1926: 8) had already reduced the events of 27 to the simple grant by the Senate of a consular province, from which he deduced that a law would not have been necessary. On the grounds that it did not require a law, Dettenhofer 2000: 78 argues that the division of the provinces did lie within the power of the senate.

[12] Lacey 1996: 117–131, which Girardet (2000: 218) is tempted to follow, but note the objections raised by Hurlet 1998: 453–454.

[13] For example, Jones 1970: 46; Badian 1982: 25 n. 18; Girardet 2000: 191; in this same direction, Crook 1996: 78; Birley 2000: 725. This theory goes back in fact to Pelham 1888 = 1911: 68 (on this point quite relevant objections were raised by Hardy 1893: 62) and Kromayer 1888: 33.

[14] As noted by Millar 1966: 156.

for in terms of their method of conferment, duration, and geographical extent these commands were not regular consular provinces, but belong in the same category as the commands conferred upon Pompey in 67 and 66. The extraordinary nature of the conferment of Augustus' provinces in 27, freed as it was from the rules of collegiality and tenure for a single year, has long been emphasised, and it has contributed to Siber's unfortunate idea that Pompey in 67 and Augustus in 27 possessed a "namenlose Imperium" ["unspecified *imperium*"].[15] Neither Pompey's nor Augustus' *imperium* was unspecified; it was consular *imperium*. It is their *provincia* that could, with greater justification, be termed "unspecified" in the sense that it did not fall within the categories of either a consular or a praetorian province.

The law of 27 on Augustus' provinces was in some regards completed by the reorganisation of the governance of proconsular provinces, which must have been the subject of another law,[16] very probably adopted the same year or shortly afterwards, re-establishing a five-year interval between the holding of a senior magistracy and a provincial governorship, as well as restricting the tenure of a proconsulship to a single year. Cassius Dio provides some information about the regulation of 27 in his general remarks on developments in the administration of proconsular and imperial provinces. In overall terms it is possible to isolate what Dio considered went back to Augustus himself and, despite certain anachronisms, the historian comes out reasonably well from this difficult discussion.[17] It is sometimes regarded as uncertain whether the rules concerning the sending of men of consular or praetorian rank to the proconsular provinces for a one-year term date back to 27.[18] However, as Rich correctly notes,[19] it must have been in 27 that, once *sortitio* ["the use of the ballot"] had been reintroduced for determining provinces, rules were laid down according to which governors would henceforth be sent to the provinces restored to the senate and people. Since

---

[15] Siber 1933: 9–10; 1940: 25–31; 1944; 1952: 276–279.

[16] One must in fact envisage two separate measures, even if one thinks that they were adopted almost simultaneously. The passing of a hotchpotch measure that regulated the regular annual grant of the consular and praetorian provinces and at the same time granted an extraordinary province for ten years would not have been good politics; the adoption of two distinct but complementary laws could benefit from the precedent of 52.

[17] Dio 53.13.2–15.6, with the comments of Rich 1990: 143 *ad loc.*

[18] See the sensible comments of Syme 1946: 154 and Brunt 1984: 431, but esp. Girardet 1990 and 1992a (followed by Dettenhofer 2000: 134–135): it was only in about 18 that Augustus re-established the rule of requiring a gap of five years between the holding of the praetorship or consulship and the proconsular governorship of a province.

[19] Rich 1990: 144.

the lists (*fasti*) of provincial governors, incomplete though they are, are sufficient to show that governors were not sent out during their magistracy or soon thereafter, we must accept that from 27 onwards an interval was prescribed between holding a magistracy and a provincial governorship. As Rich also notes, that could only have happened by means of a new law, since the Augustan regulations, though largely based on those of the *lex Pompeia* of 52, did not reproduce them in identical fashion.[20]

To these arguments, which seem to me to be decisive, I would like to add a few further comments. First, one cannot suppose, as has often been the case,[21] that the *lex Pompeia* was simply reactivated: i.e., to imagine in effect that Augustus' aim was simply to bring to an end the hiatus caused by the *lex Titia*. It would not have been the *lex Pompeia* that would have had to have been reactivated, but the *lex Iulia*, if it had totally replaced the *lex Pompeia*, or, if there had been just a partial abrogation (*derogatio*) of the latter, then the *lex Iulia* and those parts of the *lex Pompeia* that had not been repealed. Indeed the system put into effect under Augustus does not appear to have reproduced Caesar's system in identical fashion, however poorly understood the latter may be.[22] One must, therefore, suppose that a new law was passed, and the most likely occasion for the passage of such a law was when the practice was re-established whereby proconsular provinces were once again to be governed by former magistrates designated under senatorial control.

The objection raised against this hypothesis, which is at the same time the most logical one and the one that fits best the text of Cassius Dio, is in fact based on a rather questionable interpretation of the law. I accept Girardet's view that a reform stripping the consulate of

---

[20] Rich and Williams 1999: 204. A notable difference from the *lex Pompeia* was that governors of praetorian rank left as proconsuls and not as propraetors: perhaps Augustus took over this point from the *lex Iulia*.

[21] Thus Syme 1946: 154; Jones 1951 = 1960: 5; Lacey 1996: 95.

[22] In relation to the *lex Iulia*, the main differences seem to have been the re-establishment of an obligatory gap between magistracy and provincial promagistracy and the one-year limit for the provincial governorships of men of both consular and praetorian rank. The known cases of consular proconsuls whose terms were extended once or even twice during the reign of Augustus are clearly exceptions, which were authorised by the senate on the advice of the *princeps*. If they were not, the specification "*proconsul* twice," clearly *honoris causa*, would not be found in inscriptions. The parallel proposed by Giovannini (1999: 99–100) between the imperial provinces of 27 and the consular provinces of 52, which could be governed by magistrates during their term in office, and between the proconsular provinces of 27 and the praetorian provinces of 52, which could only be governed by former magistrates, seems to me unacceptable. Even if a *legatus Augusti pro praetore* could be a consul during his term in office (which did not occur at the start of the Principate, but at the earliest under the Flavians: see Syme 1958b), the main point, which should not be overlooked, is that he was governing a province not in his capacity as consul, but as the emperor's legate.

military *imperium* would have been inconceivable in 27. But such a reform must never have been officially introduced, no more in 23 or 19 than in 52 or 27. On the other hand, there is no difficulty in my opinion in dating to the year 27 a law that was limited to reinforcing the main points of the *lex Pompeia* on provincial governance, with one clause specifying that this in no way affected the law that had just conferred on Augustus control of the Gauls, the Germanies, Syria, and Egypt. As with Pompey in 52, but to an even greater degree, Augustus found himself granted an exorbitant position, but there was no fundamental juridical contradiction in it, since his provinces were not entrusted to him as consular provinces and since, on the other hand, the consuls had not been expressly stripped of military *imperium*, even if in practice, with the exception of Augustus, they no longer had the opportunity to exercise it.

The two laws of 27 on the provinces formed an important element both of the *restitutio rei publicae* ["restoration of the State"] and of the pre-eminence of the *princeps* within the *res publica restituta* ["restored State"]. On the one hand, one group of provinces and legions was handed over to proconsuls, who were granted control of them after holding senior magistracies and according to a procedure that had Republican precedents. As regards the other provinces, they remained in the hands of the *princeps*, but after a two-stage conferment (first by the senate and then by the Roman people) and for a limited duration, even though this was double the five-year period that had applied in the case of extraordinary commands during the Republic. On the other hand, the overwhelming superiority of the provinces and, most of all, the legions that he continued to control and also the length of time for which he was appointed, in stark contrast to the strictly annual term that was re-established for governors of proconsular provinces, protected the *princeps* against any risk that a stronger competitor might emerge, while at the same time the grant of the *cognomen* "Augustus" sanctified and consolidated his *auctoritas* ["authority"] still further.

There is no need to suppose that he received anything more, and Premerstein's thesis that he was officially invested by the senate and people with a *cura et tutela rei publicae universa* ["universal guardianship and protectorship of the State"] has rightly been rejected, even by those who have broadly accepted the part of his work devoted to the social foundations of Augustus' power.[23] A

---

[23] Premerstein 1937: 117–133. *Contra*, note esp. Andersen 1938: 56–57; Syme 1939: 313; Siber 1940: 20–24; Béranger 1953: 203–206, 256–277; De Martino 1962, IV: 1, 256–259 (2nd edn, 1974: 289–292); most recently, Dettenhofer 2000, 74–77.

noticeably pared down version of Premerstein's hypothesis has nonetheless been taken up by Liebeschuetz,[24] and Rich has pared it down still further.[25] Any attempt to return even partially to Premerstein's position is, I am afraid, bound to fail and can only lead to further ambiguities. For Liebeschuetz, a decision of the senate and people conferred on Augustus a general kind of responsibility, an authority (*auctoritas*) similar to that enjoyed by the senate under the Republic, set him up as an *auctor publici consilii* ["authoritative source of public advice"] or something of the sort, or at least ratified the fact that Augustus had agreed to accept this responsibility, to play this role, before the senate gave him indications of its gratitude, in particular by doubling the pay of his praetorian guard. This would then explain how Tiberius in AD 14, although he already possessed *imperium* and *tribunicia potestas* ["tribunician power"], still had to receive control over the empire in an explicit manner. Such a hypothesis would be acceptable only if it were reduced in the end to an attempt to reconstruct the contents of a senatorial decree,[26] but in this case the attack on Syme with which Liebeschuetz's article opens[27] would be pointless, since Syme did not exclude the possibility of such contents.[28] On the other hand, it remains unacceptable if it returns in essence to Premerstein's thesis; that is, if it argues for the existence of a fundamental element of imperial power that was more important than *imperium* and *tribunicia potestas*. In its interpretation of the nature of the *auctoritas* with which the *princeps* was invested by the senate and people, it goes further still than Premerstein, it seems to me, in making his *auctoritas* subject to legal definition.[29]

Rich's variant on this line of argument no more avoids its difficulties or ambiguities. What is the meaning of an "informal primacy" accepted for ten years at the same time as the provinces?[30] How could

---

[24] Liebeschuetz 1986, esp. 346 n. 4.

[25] Rich 1990: 140. Note also Turpin 1994: the idea that in January 27 a *senatus consultum* and a law conferred full powers on Augustus before a chronological limit had been imposed on his powers and before he had handed back some of the provinces rests on a totally incorrect interpretation of both *RG* 34 and Dio 53.12.1.

[26] Thus Liebeschuetz 1986: 350, supposing that "the resolution began with a full description of the responsibility that Augustus had agreed to accept (whereas Imp. Caesar has ...) and then continued outlining the vote of pay for the guard and other honours" and that the measure of the senate and people "stated, or at least assumed, that the *princeps* would continue indefinitely as *auctor publici consilii*, or something of that kind."

[27] Liebeschuetz 1986: 345–346.

[28] Syme 1946: 154.

[29] Premerstein (1937: 176–225) did not seek to trace the institutional foundations of Augustus' *auctoritas* to the *cura et tutela* or to a series of senatorial decrees. It is in the work of De Francisci (1941: 40–41; 1948: 263) that the *cura et tutela* becomes the institutional expression of Augustus' *auctoritas*.

[30] Rich 1990: 140; Rich and Williams 1999: 211–212.

anything that was "informal" be limited in time? The passages of Cassius Dio and Strabo that have been invoked since Premerstein as the basis for this view[31] do more than associate directly the division of the provinces and the *hegemonia* ["supremacy"] or *prostasia* ["primacy"] they attribute to Augustus; they give us quite simply their interpretation of this division, and that is clearly why Dio presents the renewals of Augustus' provincial powers throughout his principate as renewals of his *hegemonia*, of his *prostasia*.[32]

2 THE REDEFINITION OF AUGUSTUS' POWERS FROM HIS RESIGNATION OF THE CONSULSHIP IN 23 TO THE RENEWAL OF HIS PROVINCIAL POWERS IN 18

Augustus' resignation of the consulship in June 23 required a redefinition of his powers, with further additions in 22 and especially in 19. It is helpful, I believe, to treat as a whole the period leading up to the year 19 and even up to the first renewal in 18 of the provincial powers received in 27.

(a) The consequences of Augustus' resignation of the consulship and the institution of tribunicia potestas

By resigning the consulship, Augustus did not lose control of the provinces he had received in 27 for ten years, and they did not need to be conferred upon him afresh. Nor did he in any way lose his consular *imperium*. Taking care to be at Alba, outside the *pomerium*, at the moment of his resignation, he retained his *imperium* so long as he did not re-enter the city of Rome (while waiting to be freed from the obligation to remain outside the *pomerium*), but now he only held it *pro consule* ("as though consul").[33] It is often said that his consular *imperium* was automatically transformed into proconsular *imperium*,[34] and Cassius Dio indeed talks of his "proconsular power" (ἀρχὴ ἀνθύπατος).[35] But this was not, as we have stated, the

---

[31] Dio 53.12.1; Strabo 17.3.25, C 840.
[32] Dio 54.12.4–5; 55.6.1, 12.3; 56.28.1, 39.6.
[33] Augustus described himself as *pro co(n)s(ule)* in an edict of 15 BC issued at Narbonne, which has recently come to light thanks to the discovery of a bronze plaque in Spain (*AE* 1999, 915 = 2000, 760; tr. Cooley no. M27). On this text, see Costabile and Licandro 2000, esp. 197–235; Alföldy 2000, esp. 193–194. These articles reveal that there is a danger that the new document will be interpreted as proving that Augustus possessed *imperium proconsulare* from 23 onwards.
[34] Thus M. Gelzer in a letter of 1954 cited by Wickert 1954: 2277; Badian 1974: 163 n. 16; Eck 1998: 54–55 (= 2003: 56–58 = 2007: 64–66).
[35] Dio 53.32.5.

Republican practice whereby a consul became proconsul once his magistracy had ended, but retained his consular *imperium*. It is very probable that the new phrase *imperium proconsulare*, attested for the first time in a work completed during the reign of Tiberius, appeared only gradually, when after 23 (except on those rare occasions when the *princeps* or a co-ruler invested with *imperium* over the provinces held the consulship) the same person no longer exercised consular *imperium* "at home" (*domi*) and "in the military sphere" (*militiae*) at the same time. Since henceforth the latter was held only by proconsuls, it might have appeared useful to give it the new designation of *proconsulare imperium* informally at first, then officially. Therefore, it will be sensible not to anticipate this usage in any way, when we consider that, for example, in the *Res Gestae*, *imperium consulare* would necessarily already have had the limited meaning of *imperium consulare domi* in implicit opposition to the term *imperium proconsulare*.

It is, nevertheless, the case that with the loss of the consulship Augustus had also lost the right to exercise consular *imperium* at home (*domi*). Not being satisfied with the situation that Pompey had experienced after 55, when he had remained at the gates of Rome while his Spanish provinces were governed by legates, Augustus had himself invested with a new power and privileges that partially compensated him for this loss. Dio informs us that in 23 Augustus received the right to be tribune for life and to propose a *relatio* ["motion"] in the senate at each meeting, even when he was not consul; the right to hold proconsular power once and for all, in the sense that he would not have to lay it down and then renew it every time he crossed the *pomerium*; and finally a power greater than that of those who governed each province throughout the Empire;[36] in 22 he received the right to summon a meeting of the senate whenever he wanted;[37] and finally in 19 a *cura morum* ["oversight of morals"] and censorial power for five years, as well as consular power for life, in the sense that from then onwards he would always be preceded in public by twelve lictors carrying *fasces* and would sit on a curule stool between the two consuls.[38] All of these pieces of information have stirred up debate and all pose problems, but a certain number of points now appear to be accepted, and it would be helpful to comment briefly on each one.

First, it was certainly only in 23 that Augustus was invested with

[36] Dio 53.32.5.
[37] Dio 54.3.3.
[38] Dio 54.10.5.

tribunicia potestas on an annual basis, but automatically renewed and ongoing.[39] This was a considerable novelty, even if Octavian's possession of tribunician sacrosanctity from 36 onwards and perhaps also the *ius auxilii* ["right to come to the aid of his fellow-citizens"] from 30 onwards had helped to make it conceivable and then acceptable. Its initial purpose seems to me to be perfectly clear.[40] The loss of *imperium* at home was very inconvenient in that it deprived Augustus of the *ius agendi cum plebe* ["right to conduct business with the people"] and the *ius agendi cum senatu* ["right to conduct business with the senate"]. Indeed the possibility of a close collaboration between *princeps* and senate was a fundamental principle of the functioning of the *res publica restituta* ["restored State"], and it was not sufficient that the *princeps* could act through a supportive magistrate to summon meetings of the senate and place an item of business on the agenda. The grant of tribunician power (which included the *ius agendi cum senatu* and *ius agendi cum plebe*) responded to this need, no matter how imperfectly, and it is significant that from 23 onwards it was felt necessary to give the *princeps* a *ius agendi cum senatu* that was superior to that of the tribunes. Granting him a special *ius relationis* ["right to make a motion"], even when he had not summoned the senate into session, in part compensated for the fact that the tribunes' *ius agendi* was not as great as that of the consuls.[41] It is no less significant that his *ius agendi cum senatu* seems to have been reinforced from the following year onwards.[42] It

---

[39] The unfortunate formulation of Dio 53.32.5 (δήμαρχον διὰ βίου: "tribune for life") is corrected in the following paragraph by the use of the phrase ἐξουσία δημαρχική ("tribunician power"). Mommsen (since the second edition of his *Staatsrecht*, 1877, II: 836–837) makes Augustus' tribunician power date back to 36. The correct chronology (sacrosanctity in 36, tribunician power in 23) was established by Kromayer 1888: 38–43. Lacey (1985) is not convincing when he supposes that *tribunicia potestas* was conferred on Octavian in 30, but remained dormant until its reactivation in 23 after his resignation of the consulship and his refusal of the senate's offer of the tribunate for life.

[40] Tribunician power indeed allowed Augustus to appear as the defender of the plebs, but that does not mean that it was conceived as a latent menace against the old nobility: see Rich 1990: 169. On the other hand, Lacey 1979 has clearly demonstrated that dating by means of his tribunician power only came into use gradually.

[41] Dio's text at 53.32.5 ("the senate voted him the privilege of bringing before each meeting of the senate a motion on whatever subject he wanted at whatever time, even when he was not consul") does not exactly describe what modern scholars have called the *ius primae relationis* ["the right of making the first motion"]. Cf. Andersen 1938: 29; Strack 1939: 374–375.

[42] Why was there a further increase in his powers in 22 and what precisely did this involve, since tribunician power already contained the right to summon the senate? The historicity of a new privilege granted in 22 has been called into question, since Dio claims that it was conferred to compensate Augustus for his intervention during the trial of M. Primus and scholars have often wanted to date the trial of Primus and the conspiracy of Murena back to the year 23 (Fluss 1934: 708–709; Stockton 1965; Jameson 1969; Bleicken 1990: 94, 99 n. 272; 1998: 345, 728). But this questioning of Dio's chronology is probably unjustified: see Atkinson 1960a; Swan 1967; Weinrib 1968: 49–51; Badian 1982: 19–23, 28–31; Rich 1990: 174–175; Crook 1996:

is undeniably the case that in practical terms Augustus willingly left the business of drawing up the senate's agenda on important matters of which he was the true instigator to the consuls.[43] But it is also the case that after 17 Augustus very often refused to have laws voted into effect by means of his own *tribunicia potestas*, preferring to allow the consuls to appear as if they were initiating legislation.[44] These formal concessions could not conceal the precautions he had taken to acquire a right to transact business (*ius agendi*) both with the senate and with the people that was superior to that of all the magistrates. One might even say that it was the guarantee of this superiority that permitted him, over time, to use this power only in a restricted fashion.

On the other hand, there was a clear link, it seems to me, between Augustus' grant of *tribunicia potestas* and the fact that he was now liberated from the ban on crossing the *pomerium* on pain of losing his proconsular *imperium*.[45] Even if the *princeps*' tribunician power

---

84. Syme, who did not hesitate to date the conspiracy to 23 in *The Roman Revolution* (1939: 333–334), is much much circumspect in *The Augustan Aristocracy* (1986: 388–390). On the other hand, Augustus' intervention at the trial of Primus could in fact only satisfy the senate, by refuting the allegations according to which he felt justified in giving orders to a proconsul, secretly and without the knowledge of the senate. The exact nature of the new privilege granted in 22 remains to be identified. The only hypothesis that has been proposed on this topic goes back to Pelham (1888 = 1911: 77–78): Augustus took precedence over all the other magistrates, including the consuls, in summoning the senate. But it must be admitted that this would have been a pretty meagre advantage, the need for which would have been unclear in 22, when Augustus was about to leave on a long journey around the eastern provinces. For his part, Magdelain (1947: 64) thought in terms of the right to summon the senate outside fixed sessions. But what should one understand by that, before the institution of *senatus legitimi* ["statutory meetings of the senate"] on a fixed date following Augustus' regulation of 9 BC (Suet. *Aug.* 35.3; Dio 55.3.1–2)? Chapters 2 and 3 of the *lex de imperio Vespasiani* only provide indirect evidence for the measures of 23 and 22, since the latter must have been redefined or made more specific at least once, under Augustus, on the occasion of the ruling of 9. I wonder whether the privilege of 22 ought to be related to Augustus' imminent departure; perhaps he was granted the right to summon the senate and for it to deal with a question in his absence by reference to his motion (*relatio*).

[43] For sensible remarks in this direction, see Jones 1951 = 1960: 10, referring to the senatorial decrees of 17 BC on the Secular Games, 11 BC on the aqueducts, and 4 BC on the new extortion procedures.

[44] For example, the *lex Quinctia* (AD 9), *lex Fufia Caninia* (2 BC), *lex Aelia Sentia* (AD 4), and *lex Papia Poppaea* (AD 9).

[45] The *imperium* mentioned by Dio at 53.32.5 allowed Augustus to continue to govern his provinces. Dio points out that he would possess it "once and for all" and so would not have to lay it down and then take it up again each time he crossed the *pomerium*. In the third edition of his *Staatsrecht* (II: 794 n. 1 and 1087), Mommsen unfortunately allowed himself to be convinced that Dio was really talking about an ongoing *imperium* and he argued that Augustus accumulated two types of *imperia proconsularia*, one supposedly granted him for periods of five or ten years allowing him to govern the imperial provinces, the other allegedly granted for life and covering the entire Empire. This was a considerable step backwards, which significantly helped to bolster theories that two or three accumulated *imperia* were conferred on Augustus. Kromayer (1919: 428), Kahrstedt (1938: 20), and Kolbe (1931: 55) interpreted Dio's text correctly, as Mommsen had done up until the second edition (1877) of *Staatsrecht*, II: 770 n. It is true that there was a lacuna in the measure of 23. In Republican Rome, a magistrate's

did not require him to remain, like the tribunes, permanently inside the city or within one mile's radius of the *pomerium*,⁴⁶ it would have been unthinkable in retrospect if he could not exercise it within the city. Freeing him from the *pomerium* regulation allowed Augustus to exercise his tribunician power within the *pomerium* and also to control his provinces from Rome, but it did not give him back the *imperium* at home (*domi*) that he had lost when he resigned his consulate.⁴⁷ To compensate him for this loss, as we have seen, another solution was adopted in 23: the grant of tribunician power bolstered by the *ius agendi cum senatu*.

(b) The measures of 19

How then should one interpret the measures of 19, which seem to return at least in part to the question of Augustus' resignation of the consulate in 23? Should their significance be minimised, in the sense that Augustus only received the insignia of consular power at Rome

---

imperium had a fixed term, whereas a promagistrate's did not. Except perhaps in the few years when the *lex Pompeia* of 52 was in force, a promagistrate could remain in charge of his province until his successor arrived, and even after he had left his province, he still held *imperium*, which he lost only at the moment when he crossed the *pomerium*. It is this limit that the reform of 23 abolished with regard to the *princeps*, without taking care to introduce or define a new legal limit. The consequence of this lacuna could become apparent only if a *princeps* neglected to have his powers renewed, as Tiberius did in AD 23 rather than in 24, when his powers that had been renewed in 13 expired. It was only then that it became clear that his *imperium* no longer had a legal limit and continued, therefore, to remain in force, while the provinces that had been conferred on him remained his, since the senate did not try to send proconsuls there to relieve his propraetorian legates of their responsibilities. It was clearly a consequence of the measure of 23 BC, but a consequence that I do not think Augustus anticipated and which even ran contrary to the way in which Augustus interpreted this measure.

⁴⁶ I prefer to use this expression rather than talk in general terms, as is often the case with other scholars, of the geographical limits from which the *princeps'* tribunician powers were liberated. For tribunes, their function of coming to the aid of their fellow citizens required them to remain within the first milestone of Rome and explains why they were not permitted to be away from the city for a whole day. Augustus was released from the ban on crossing the *pomerium* and from that on absenting himself from the city: the combination of his proconsulship and his tribunician power required this double privilege. But during the Republic tribunes were permitted in exceptional circumstances to leave Rome to carry out their official functions, while preserving their sacrosanctity (Livy 9.36.14; 9.29.20; cf. Mommsen 1887–1888, II: 292). When Tiberius used his tribunician power while on Rhodes (Suet. *Tib.* 11.3), this was to take penal action for what he considered an attack on his sacrosanctity (Strack 1939: 377–378). On the other hand, the "right to conduct business with the plebs" and the "right to conduct business with the senate" were exercised at Rome, since it was the only place where the senate and the Roman plebs could legitimately hold meetings, but their sphere of application was unlimited, and tribunes could propose measures that dealt with the entire Empire, as well as relations with foreign peoples and kingdoms. The problem of the geographical limit of Augustus' *tribunicia potestas* only makes sense, it seems to me, with regard to his coming to the aid of his fellow-citizens (*auxilium*), and it may be compared to the search for the institutional origins of his jurisdiction, in particular the "appeal to Caesar" (*provocatio ad Caesarem*).

⁴⁷ I cannot subscribe to Bleicken's view (1998: 730) that "after he was granted the privilege whereby he did not have to lay down his proconsular *imperium* when he crossed the *pomerium*, the conferral of an *imperium consulare* became superfluous."

itself – twelve lictors carrying *fasces* and the right to sit on a curule stool between the consuls?[48] Or should we argue that this was when he truly received consular power for life?[49] Or again, in line with the subtle variants proposed by Jones, Brunt, Girardet, and Cotton and Yakobson, should we admit that his consular *imperium* was declared equal to that which the consuls exercised at Rome and which he continued to enjoy for the governance of his provinces and that he was granted the right to exercise this *imperium* without the slightest territorial limitation – hence in Italy and even at Rome?[50]

There is greater force, to be sure, in not introducing the theory of an accumulation of *imperia*. In Augustus' case, as in Pompey's before him,[51] it is only a construction of modern scholars who refuse to distinguish *imperium* from the functions, eventually multifaceted, that could be conferred on its holder. The solutions proposed by Jones and Brunt satisfy the demands of "constitutional law," but suffer, it seems to me (especially that of Jones), from other quite serious objections. Brunt admits that Augustus did not keep nor recover all the powers of the consuls either in 23 or in 19.[52] Thus he was never seen presiding at the consular and praetorian elections or proposing laws in the assemblies of the Roman people (i.e., in the *comitia tributa* or *comitia centuriata*). If Augustus had recovered *imperium domi* in 19 or if, having only partially lost it in 23, he had recovered it fully in 19, what purpose did the grant of tribunician power serve? But, most of all, why did his tribunician power, instead of declining in importance after 19, see its importance increase in the following years, and why did it become, to use the famous phrase of Tacitus (*Ann*. 3.56.1), the *summi fastigii vocabulum* [literally the "title of highest pinnacle"; i.e., the title designating the most important office]? Why in 18 were the Julian laws proposed by virtue of his *tribunicia potestas*, not his *imperium consulare*? Why was Agrippa promoted to "co-rulership" by being granted *tribunicia potestas*?

One should start from the only case where we are certain that Augustus exercised consular *imperium* in the domestic sphere

---

[48] This is the opinion of Mommsen, Kromayer, Pelham, De Martino (from 1936 onwards), Premerstein, Wickert (from 1941–1942), Castritius (1982: 44 n. 67, 52), and Bleicken (since 1990: 100–103).

[49] This is the opinion, in particular, of Abele, Betti, De Francisci (from 1930), Béranger, Kienast, and Eck.

[50] Jones 1951 = 1960: 13–15; 1970: 59–60; Brunt 1962: 73; Girardet 1990: 120; Cotton and Yakobson 2002.

[51] For Pompey, see Ridley 1983 and previously Gelzer 1943: 43 = 1963: 188.

[52] Brunt 1962: 71; 1977: 96 n. 9.

(*domi*). Augustus himself states in the *Res Gestae* (8.2-4) that he conducted the census on three occasions: in 28 with Agrippa "in his sixth consulship," in 8 BC alone *consulari cum imperio* ["with consular *imperium*"], and in AD 14 with Tiberius, again *consulari cum imperio*. Scholars have asked whether this *consulare imperium* was the one he was granted for life in 19 or an exceptional power granted on two occasions for the holding of the census, which risks interpretations that, once again, imply an accumulation of *imperia*. The text of the *Res Gestae*, in my view, does no more than note carefully that in these three cases Augustus was either consul or at least exercising consular *imperium*. Indeed in the absence of censors, consuls had in the past been granted censorial powers: this occurred in 75, not for the census but for the *locatio* of the *vectigalia* ["the leasing of state contracts," which included the rights to collect state taxes], and the consuls were assigned this task expressly by means of a *senatus consultum* ratified by the assembly.[53] Although Augustus does not state this in his *Res Gestae*, a similar procedure must have been used for the first of the three censuses he held, since the Fasti ["Calendar"] from Venusia (Venosa) state that he and Agrippa "carried out the *lustrum* [census cycle] thanks to their censorial power" (*censoria potes(tate) lustrum fecer(unt)*).[54] After the failure of the two censors who had been elected in 22, tradition demanded that censorial functions devolve upon the consuls. But the trick lay in persuading people that Augustus could be granted the functions of a censor without him holding the consulship, since he was at that moment in Rome and he was holding consular *imperium*. In the *Res Gestae* Augustus does not say that he proceeded to the ceremony of completing the census "thanks to his (or a) consular *imperium*," but rather "when he was holding consular *imperium*," which allowed him to be granted the functions of a censor.[55] As Pelham suggested,

---

[53] Cic. *II Verr*. 3.18–19.

[54] *Inscr. It*. 13, 1, p. 259. It is impossible to agree with Mommsen (1887–1888, II: 337 n. 1) that this information is incorrect, with Augustus and Agrippa carrying out the census as consuls and the *censoria potestas* indicated in the Fasti from Venosa as an "additional attribute of the superior magistracy ... conforming to the system in force in the municipalities." The evidence of the Venosa Fasti has been rehabilitated by Premerstein 1937: 160 and Siber 1940: 46: Augustus in the *RG* does not say that he carried out the census with Agrippa as consul, but "in his sixth consulship," which in no way prevents him being granted censorial powers.

[55] *RG* 8.3: *consulari cum imperio lustrum solus feci* ("I performed a *lustrum* with consular *imperium* without a colleague"). Hardy 1893: 64 glimpsed the importance that should be attached to the preposition *cum*, but he based his interpretation mainly on the Greek version of the text, concentrating on the difference between a power specially granted and a permanent power. For the phrase *cum imperio*, cf. Cic. *Mur*. 89; *Att*. 6.4.1; Caes. *BC* 1.31.2. The ablative can be used on its own to give the same sense when an adjective qualifies *imperio*: Cic. *Pis*. 38; cf. Livy 26.29.4 and Pliny *Ep*. 7.27.2; Cic. *Flacc*. 85; cf. *Sest*. 128. I have found no other

this *imperium consulare* must simply have been the one he had retained in 23 to govern his provinces.⁵⁶

This does not mean that I am going back on what I have previously argued, namely that Augustus did not recover the right to exercise *imperium consulare* at home (*domi*) either in 23 or in 19. To compensate him for the loss of this right, the choice was made in 23 to grant him *tribunicia potestas*, even at the price of furnishing him with exceptional privileges (which were not otherwise those of any magistrate, not even the consul) with regard to the *ius agendi cum senatu*. This decision, I repeat, was not challenged in 19; on the contrary, it was confirmed in 18. But there were some functions that could not be grafted onto the *tribunicia potestas*, in particular the functions of a censor. It was by taking advantage of the ambiguity of the situation created in 23 that Augustus, without possessing *imperium* "at home," had been liberated from the regulations concerning the *pomerium*. Contrary to the view put forward by certain scholars, the year 19 did not put an end to this ambiguity.⁵⁷ On the contrary, it reinforced it by permitting Augustus to enjoy in Rome the outward signs of consular *imperium*. This was deliberately exploited when he was granted censorial powers at any moment he wanted on the pretext that they were being bestowed upon him thanks to his consular *imperium*. That could have happened for the first time in 19, even if there was not a full census, but it only actually occurred in 18, when there was a review of the senate (*lectio senatus*). According to Dio, Augustus received censorial powers in 19 for a period of five years, which normally separated two *lustra*; but these censorial powers must have lapsed after the completion of the review of the senate (*lectio senatus*).⁵⁸ If my interpretation of chapter 8 of the *Res*

---

example of the type of expression *consulari cum imperio aliquid facere*; it was perhaps to avoid any ambiguity that Augustus included the preposition despite the presence of the adjective *consulari*.

⁵⁶ Pelham 1888 = 1911: 68–69. This interpretation probably allows us to understand better the striking text of Dio 55.13.5, according to which in AD 4 Augustus "assumed proconsular *imperium*" to conduct a census, which was in reality a review of the senate (*lectio senatus*): cf. Blumenthal 1909.

⁵⁷ Lacey 1996: 110 n. 28, 151.

⁵⁸ The grant in 19 of *censoria potestas* to conduct the review that took place in 18 (Dio 54.13–14) is accepted by Jones 1960 and Grenade 1961: 313–335 (along with the rather fragile idea that it was renewed from 13 onwards), but rejected by Astin 1963. All of these scholars, however, have a rather different conception of the relationship between *consulare imperium* and *censoria potestas* than the one I am proposing here. As for the three powers which Dio claimed were conferred on Augustus in 19 and accepted by him, only the "guardianship of morals" (*cura morum*) for five years was, in my view, rejected, and the same goes for that conferred in 12 according to Dio 54.30.1 (but Augustus dates his refusal of this to 11 at *RG* 6.1). The thesis of Parsi Magdalain 1964, that in 19 and in 11 Augustus was invested with a "guardianship of the laws and morals" of which *censoria potestas* was just one element,

Gestae is correct, Augustus' *imperium* was not, strictly speaking, extended in 19, but rather he was granted censorial powers, probably by means of a *senatus consultum* confirmed by a law, for a limited period under the rubric of this *imperium*.

One is justified, therefore, in asking whether further powers were conferred on Augustus on the grounds that he possessed consular *imperium*, even if one is reduced here to mere hypotheses and probabilities. Several of these stem from the fact that in many respects the year 19 marked a clear watershed. This was the year in which a triumph was celebrated for the last time by a person who was not a member of the imperial family, L. Cornelius Balbus, proconsul of Africa, while it was also in 19 that Agrippa declined the triumph that he had been decreed by the senate. Thus Frédéric Hurlet has developed the interesting hypothesis that in 19 Augustus may also have received the ongoing right to hold the auspices, which would have permitted him, when faced with private citizens (*privati*) sent out as proconsuls with *imperium*, to be assured of a monopoly of these same auspices.[59] It was also in the year 19 that the mint at Rome resumed issuing gold and silver coinage, whereas bronze issues must have recommenced from 23 onwards. It has been argued that the powers conferred on Augustus in 19 included the right to issue gold and silver coinage at Rome rather than just at provincial mints, a view that raises several points of controversy, including the status of the *III viri monetales* and the significance of the letters *SC* on the bronze coinage.[60] But the most important and most complex problems regarding the nature of the powers of 19 concern, without doubt, the role of the *princeps* in organising elections and in jurisdiction (both direct jurisdiction and appeals).[61] On these two particularly delicate matters, I shall limit myself here to just a few observations.

---

cannot be reconciled, it seems to me, with *RG* 6.1 (the evidence of which cannot simply be rejected, as it was by Hampl 1978: 206–208, on the grounds that in 14 only a few elderly senators and legal specialists would have remembered what took place in 19, 18, or 11). I think that Dio's error, at least regarding 19, stemmed from the fact that he believed that the *cura morum* and *censoria potestas* could be linked.

[59] Hurlet 2001.
[60] Burnett 1977, esp. 60–62; Crawford 1985: 256–262.
[61] Jones 1951 = 1960: 14 also includes among the privileges linked to the consular power that Augustus regained in 19 the right to command the praetorian cohorts in Italy, to levy troops in Italy, and to nominate an urban prefect (*praefectus urbi*). The first two must be privileges granted in 23 at the same time as he was freed from the *pomerium* regulation (Piganiol 1937: 154–155 noted that recruitment went back to 23; the right to levy troops in Italy without the need to gain the prior approval of the senate went back as far as 27 according to Brunt 1974: 162–170). As for the supervisory role granted to T. Statilius Taurus when Augustus once again left Rome in 16, it must have been an informal measure and not the nomination of a *praefectus urbi* (Dio 54.19.6; cf. Rich 1990: 196–197).

Scholars have wanted to establish a direct link between the problems that bedevilled the consular elections in 21 and 19 and the measures of 19. Their aim, or at least one of their envisaged aims, was to give Augustus the power to control elections by drawing up a list of candidates invited to stand for office.[62] It should be noted, however, that the problem of undesirable candidates only arose in 19, when M. Egnatius Rufus wished to be elected consul in open disregard of the *lex annalis* ["the law regulating the age at which individuals could hold state magistracies"] (Dio 54.10.1-2, filling out Vell. 2.92.4). The troubles of 21 had been provoked by political intrigue (Dio 54.6.2-3), and a Julian law on electoral bribery (*lex Iulia de ambitu*) was passed to deal with such problems from the year 18 onwards (Dio 54.16.1). In these two cases, it is in the end clear that Augustus' absence from Rome, following so soon upon his resignation from the consulship after an uninterrupted sequence of nine such magistracies, was a serious destabilising factor. In 21, as in 19, one of the two consulships had been reserved for him at the time of the elections, and after Augustus had sent notice of his refusal of the position, the other consul, who had entered office alone, had to proceed to hold an election to appoint his consular colleague. The simple fact of Augustus' return to Rome (where he remained until 16) put an end to such anomalies, and his appearance in Rome surrounded by the consular insignia must have had the advantage, among other things, of calming the doubts or worries of the urban plebs. Nothing allows us to conclude on the other hand that after 19 Augustus presided over the elections or that he even legally had the power to control candidacies. His intervention in electoral matters was conducted essentially by means, *suffragatio* ["support for candidates"] and *commendatio* ["recommendation of candidates"], that were in no way related to his consular power. His *auctoritas* is a sufficient explanation for the fact that candidates decided to inform the *princeps* of their intention to stand for office, to ensure themselves if not of his support, then at least of his consent.[63] Here again one should not suppose that this was the result of any consular power that he held. In any case nothing allows us to place as early as 19 a strengthening of his control of the elections, which is in reality attested only much later; this had to wait for the *lex Valeria Cornelia*

---

[62] Jones 1951 = 1960: 14; Frei-Stolba 1967: 106–113; Pani 1974: 44–45; Kienast 1982 = 1999: 201; Eck 1998: 57 = 2003, 60 = 2007: 68–69.
[63] A practice that was not a legal obligation during Tiberius' reign: Tac. *Ann.* 1.81.3.

of AD 5, which established a "determining assembly."⁶⁴ The surviving sources on the praetorian elections of 14, which were prepared by Augustus before his death, are difficult to interpret and can only be used to discuss the functioning of the electoral assemblies in the final years of the reign.⁶⁵

The emergence of the *princeps'* jurisdiction and the identification of its origins are problems still more complex and disputed. To a greater degree than Siber,⁶⁶ it was A. H. M. Jones who placed particular importance on the *imperium* granted Augustus in 19 in this area: according to Jones this was the direct source of the *princeps'* civil jurisdiction in the first instance and the indirect source of his criminal jurisdiction in the first instance, thanks to a judiciary law that granted the consuls and holders of consular *imperium* the "carrying out of public jurisdiction" (*publici iudicii exercitio*), allowing them to hear cases on capital charges without infringing the laws on appeal (*provocatio*) or the *lex Sempronia*.⁶⁷ The great weakness of this hypothesis, it seems to me, is that the consuls had for a long time surrendered the exercise of civil jurisdiction to the praetors,⁶⁸ and for about a century they had ceased to hear capital suits at Rome. Other lines of approach may permit us to uncover the origins of the *princeps'* jurisdiction.

A *senatus consultum* of 30, perhaps confirmed by a plebiscite, might have allowed Octavian to take matters into his own hands at the request of one of the parties, but its exact nature remains disputed, as well as the use he made of it.⁶⁹ The fact that from 27 onwards one group of provinces was governed by legates of Augustus inevitably introduced the possibility of appealing a legate's decision to the *princeps*, and this appeal process must have become common. Finally, as Brunt correctly saw,⁷⁰ the judiciary powers of the *princeps* were one of the areas where his *imperium* and *auctoritas* were

---

⁶⁴ Tibiletti (esp. 1953) was wrong to deduce from *RG* 14.1 that a determining assembly was already in existence in 6 BC and might even have dated back to 27. For a refutation of this view, see Jones 1955.

⁶⁵ Vell. Pat. 2.124.3–4; Tac. *Ann.* 1.14.4; on the meaning of the term *nominare*, see Levick 1967; Astin 1969.

⁶⁶ Siber (1933: 5–6) had viewed the *imperium* of 19 as the source of the *princeps'* civil jurisdiction in Italy, and he was followed by De Francisci 1938: 93. But Siber went back on this view from 1937 onwards, only then attributing to the *imperium* granted in 19 the right of the *princeps* to examine a case of high treason in front of the senate: Siber 1937: 451–454; 1940: 49–53; 1952: 289.

⁶⁷ Jones 1954; 1970: 126; 1972: 93; Crook 1996: 123.

⁶⁸ See however Jones 1954 = 1960: 73–74, 83–84; Millar 1977: 519–520 (but the relegation of Lamia by Gabinius in 58 was more an act of *coercitio*).

⁶⁹ Dio 51.19.7.

⁷⁰ Brunt 1962: 72.

inextricably linked: not that *auctoritas* could have constituted the foundation of the *princeps'* jurisdiction, but it allowed him to extract all profit possible from the powers that had been conferred on him, and even to develop from them a practice that surpassed their original definition and aim, without anyone claiming to be opposed to it. The exercise of *imperium* nevertheless formed the most likely basis of the *princeps'* jurisdiction in the first instance and of its development. But the objection based on the consuls' lack of competence in judicial matters in the late Republic leads me rather to think that the *princeps* did not exercise in competition with the consuls a jurisdictional capacity which all holders of *imperium* possessed, which would be a new development, not least inside the *pomerium*. Rather, the model for it is to be sought in the evolution of the jurisdiction of provincial governors. Jurisdiction is perhaps the first area in which the ambiguity of the *imperium* of the *princeps* favoured a kind of "provincialisation" of Italy and Rome. A similar phenomenon can be identified, it seems to me, with regards to relations between the *princeps* and proconsuls and the problem of what is traditionally known as *imperium maius* ["greater *imperium*"].

(c) *The problem of* imperium maius quam

There is one final aspect of the powers granted Augustus in 23 according to Dio that I have not yet discussed; namely that he held throughout the Empire a power greater than that of all those who governed a province.[71] Similarly Dio indicates that in 13 Agrippa received power greater than that of the various governors outside Italy.[72] The view that this privilege of 23 did not increase Augustus' power, but only allowed him to retain, in relation to the governors of proconsular provinces, the *imperium maius* (the "greater *imperium*") that his status as consul had conferred on him from 27 onwards is one that goes back to Kromayer and Pelham.[73] On the other hand, McFayden was the first to question whether Augustus would have allowed himself to be granted permanent *imperium maius* in 23; Grant then reinforced this idea; but they both remained isolated in their views.[74] However, since the 1980s doubts have

---

[71] Dio 53.32.5.
[72] Dio 54.28.1.
[73] Kromayer 1888: 33–34; Pelham 1888 = 1911: 72–73.
[74] McFayden 1921. The Cyrene edicts, first published in 1927, invalidated McFayden's doubts, and his later analysis (McFayden 1928) was not convincing: see Grant 1946: 424–453 and 1949. It was in reaction to Grant that Last proposed his famous theory of two types of *imperium maius* (Last 1947), which, I am afraid, did more to cloud the issue than help resolve

grown whether Augustus was granted power officially greater than that of the proconsuls,[75] and this has culminated in Girardet's study of *imperium maius* covering the entire period from the *lex Gabinia* to Germanicus' mission.[76] Although I support Girardet's analysis on a number of important points, there are others, no less important, where it is impossible to follow his views. It is on these points of disagreement that I am forced to concentrate, but these disagreements should not conceal the fact that the discussion that follows owes much to his work.

There did not exist, as one might believe from reading the work of modern scholars, a type of superior power called *imperium maius*. As the *senatus consultum de Cn. Pisone patre* ["the senatorial decree concerning Cn. Piso senior"] has now confirmed, a greater form of *imperium* only existed in relation to another form of *imperium*; i.e., when the *imperium* of X was recognised as greater than (*maius quam*) that of Y. But what precisely does this mean? When was the need felt, in particular, to establish a hierarchy among holders of the same type of *imperium* (consular *imperium* and later proconsular *imperium*, once this notion developed)? Originally this occurred only when circumstances, in particular military operations, demanded that two holders of the same type of *imperium* operate in the same geographical area and when it was desirable to establish precisely which of the two could impose his authority on the other to prevent any risk of conflict between them. Such a practice only developed gradually, and not without difficulties.

In 105 the Roman defeat at Arausio at the hands of the Cimbri was due in part to the fact that the consul Cn. Mallius did not have the power to give orders to the proconsul Cn. Servilius Caepio and as a result the necessary unity of command was lacking.[77] The *lex Gabinia* of 67 conferred on Pompey command of the war against the pirates and power extending fifty miles inland from every sea-coast; this law only specified that he enjoyed an *imperium* equal to that of the relevant provincial governor.[78] That was insufficient to avoid conflicts with the consul C. Calpurnius Piso and with Q. Caecilius Metellus, a former consul entrusted with the war against the

---

it (cf. De Martino 1962: 126–128, 143–147, 163 = 1974: 143–145, 163–167, 184–185; Staveley 1963: 472).

[75] Bleicken 1962: 149–151; 1978, I: 37–39; Castritius 1982: 40–42; Scheid in Jacques and Scheid 1990: 19; Ameling 1994; Hurlet 1997: 277–303.

[76] Girardet 2000. (I am grateful to the author for letting me read this article in advance of its publication.)

[77] Gran. Licin. 33.6–7; Dio, fr. 91; cf. Staveley 1963: 478.

[78] Vell. Pat. 2.31.2 (probably more precise than Tac. *Ann.* 15.25.7).

Cretans. The *lex Manilia* of 66, which similarly conferred on Pompey command in the war against Mithridates, nevertheless did not introduce any modifications in this area. Since Pompey saw himself granted the provinces of Cilicia and Bithynia, his new command could have led to conflict only with the governor of Asia. Girardet incorrectly believed that the Romans took steps to avoid this risk by sending out governors with praetorian *imperium* to Asia until Pompey's return.[79] As I have shown elsewhere, inscriptions from Claros and Magnesia-on-the-Meander do not permit any doubt that L. Valerius Flaccus was proconsul when he governed Asia in 62.[80] The solution imagined by Girardet does not seem to be necessary, since there was little risk that Pompey would have experienced the same kind of difficulties with governors of praetorian rank (even if they had been granted consular *imperium*) that the consul Piso and Metellus of consular rank had caused him earlier.

Nevertheless, when he was entrusted with the task of supervising Rome's grain supply in 57, besides the consular law that was passed, a tribunician project was conceived which Pompey would have preferred and which would have granted him significant military forces, an almost discretionary power in financial matters, and an *imperium* superior to that of the provincial governors.[81] Cicero was upset at the tribune's impudence (and Pompey's as well), without otherwise placing much emphasis on the clause of the law dealing with Pompey's *imperium*. But when Cicero wanted to confer on Cassius in February 43 not just the province of Syria but also command of the war against Dolabella, he proposed a *senatus consultum* in which it was specified that Cassius' *imperium* should be greater than that of the governors of the provinces in which he would be forced to intervene in conducting this war.[82] Cicero's advice was not followed, since the consul Pansa preferred that this mission be reserved for the consuls.[83] But command of the war against Dolabella and general control of overseas provinces were conferred upon Cassius (and Brutus) a little later after the battle of Mutina (Modena). Unfortunately, for this event we no longer have available any speech or letters of Cicero, but the information provided by Velleius on this subject is corroborated by Cassius Dio and should not, it seems, be rejected. It is extremely likely that this *senatus*

---

[79] Girardet 1991: 205; 1992a: 183.
[80] Ferrary 2000: no. 5.
[81] Cic. *Att.* 4.1.7.
[82] Cic. *Phil.* 11.30.
[83] Cic. *Fam.* 12.7.1; *ad Brut.* 2.4.2.

consultum incorporated the arrangements proposed by Cicero in his earlier motion in favour of Cassius.[84]

The refusal of the proconsul Caepio to collaborate with the consul Mallius in 105 weakens the theory (in support of which only very fragile arguments can be mustered) that a consul was invested with an *imperium* superior to that of a proconsul.[85] As Staveley has shown, the only superiority that a consul could have exercised was derived from his *auctoritas*. This situation was just as valid with regard to Augustus in the years 27 to 23, with the exception that for him the holding of the consulship was a rather minor element of his *auctoritas*, which was completely exceptional, even more so after the grant of the *cognomen* "Augustus" in 27.[86] The famous inscription from Kyme,[87] whose importance has been much disputed, does not appear to me to imply that Augustus' *imperium* was superior. It comprises two texts: the first is an edict of the consuls Augustus and Agrippa, dated to 27 by the appearance of the *cognomen* "Augustus,"[88] prescribing for the province of Asia, and perhaps for other overseas provinces too,[89] the restoration of public lands, sacred lands, and statues consecrated to divinities that had been subjected to looting and giving the provincial governors instructions on how to carry out this decision; the second text is a letter of the proconsul of Asia, responding favourably to the request of a sacred association (*thiasos*) of the city of Kyme, referring to the consular edict of 27 and describing it as "the order of Augustus Caesar" (*iussus Augusti Caesaris*). Even if the inscribing of this dossier should be attributed to the *thiasos* and not to the civic authorities, we are not entitled to

---

[84] Vell. Pat. 2.62.2 (with Woodman 1983: 132–134), 73.2; cf. Dio 46.40.3; 47.28.5, 29.6. The evidence of Appian (*BC* 3.63, 78) is weakened by chronological confusions. Girardet 2000, correctly noting the rejection of Cicero's motion in February, does not discuss the problem of the commands granted after the battle of Mutina. Conversely, it does not seem to me necessary to suppose (with Ehrenberg 1953a, esp. 133–135) that Brutus and Cassius received an *imperium* similar to that of a dictator.

[85] See the refutation of Staveley 1963: 472–428; also De Martino 1962: 118–119 = 1974: 134–135.

[86] Cf. Brunt 1974: 166 n. 17: the superiority of the consul over the proconsul "was at least obsolescent or obsolete in the late Republic; if Augustus could claim it in 27–23, we have an illustration of the way in which *auctoritas* fortified *imperium*."

[87] *RDGE* 61 = *I. Kyme* 17 (trans. Sherk 1984: no. 95 = Sherk 1988: no. 2).

[88] Crook 1962 points out a suggestion by J. Reynolds that the term "Sebastos" may be an anachronism introduced by the stonecutter and hence the edict may date to 28 before the restoration of the provinces. This hypothesis should only be retained if it were absolutely necessary (as is the case in *Aphrodisias and Rome*, no. 7, line 1, and perhaps no. 13, line 1) that the edict could not have taken this form in 27. I do not think that this is the case. On the contrary, the extension of the responsibilities of the two consuls to cover relations with the provinces makes greater sense in 27 than in 28.

[89] Depending on whether one translates a phrase in line 3 as "[...] of each city of the province" or "[...] of the city of each province."

suppose that the elements contained in it were not faithfully reproduced. Thus Atkinson's theory that the first text was in fact the despatch by the consuls of a *senatus consultum* with the omission of its entire heading (*praescriptio*) has rightly been rejected.[90] It is possible that the consuls may have consulted the senate before drafting their edict[91] and may have specified this in a letter to the proconsul(s) accompanying the text of the edict, which did not then need to be repeated in the dossier. But in the edict itself, addressed first and foremost to provincials, there is no mention of the role played by the senate. More remarkable still, whereas the edict had been issued by the two consuls, a proconsul of Asia shortly afterwards attributed it solely to Augustus and decided to have a text inscribed on the shrine restored to the *thiasos* giving the credit for the benefaction solely to Augustus (line 19): *Imp(erator) Caesar Deivei f(ilius) Augustus restituit* ["Imp(erator) Caesar Augustus, son of the Deified One, restored this"]. That has nothing to do with a hierarchy of *imperia*. We would be more justified in saying that it was the authority (*auctoritas*) of Augustus that eclipsed all other organs of Roman power, whether it be the senate, his colleague as consul, or the proconsul of Asia. The Kyme inscription, therefore, does not require us to suppose that a superior *imperium* had been conferred on Augustus in 23 because it would have been necessary to compensate him for a loss of power that resulted from his resignation of the consulship. Nor is such a view sufficient to invalidate the account of Cassius Dio, who presents this greater *imperium* as a new privilege, which Augustus did not enjoy before 23.

Two documents have recently come to light that enrich our information: in 1970 a fragment of a Greek translation of the eulogy (*laudatio*) delivered by Augustus at Agrippa's funeral, which on this point has unfortunately done nothing but increase our confusion;[92] in 1996 the *s.c. de Pisone patre*, the first official text in which the phrase *maius imperium (quam)* appears, in relation to Germanicus'

---

[90] Atkinson 1960b. The theory that the "order of Augustus Caesar" does not refer to the first text, but rather to a rescript of the *princeps* obtained by the *thiasos* and presented to the proconsul, is just as unacceptable; in this case, the dossier could not have failed to include the rescript. The same objection may be raised against Bleicken's suggestion (1990: 88 n. 247) that it concerns actions taken by Octavian before 27 when he was present in Asia.

[91] So Sherk 1969: 317–319; see also Charbonnel 1979; Kienast 1982 = 1999: 87 n. 32; Giovannini 1999: 101–105; Girardet 2000.

[92] *P. Köln* VI, no. 249, lines 7–11 (trans. Sherk 1984: no. 99 = Sherk 1988: no. 12, Cooley no. T14): "And into whatever provinces the Republic of the Romans should ever summon you, it had been sanctioned in a law that your power <was to be> not less than that of any (other) magistrate) in those (provinces)."

mission in the East in the year AD 17.[93] I shall start by discussing the latter text, an interpretation of which Girardet has recently proposed that I cannot accept.[94] According to Girardet, an *imperium* greater than that of the proconsuls was granted for the first time in AD 17, perhaps as a sort of compensation to mollify Germanicus after his recall from Germania, and it was this grant that required the clarification that Tiberius' *imperium* was nevertheless greater than that of Germanicus; on the latter's death in 19 Tiberius' *imperium* returned to what it had been in 17; in other words, it was the same as Augustus' without any specification that it was greater than other *imperia*. By such a process, it seems to me, Tiberius would have offended Germanicus as much as he would have honoured him, since the superiority of his own *imperium* would for the first time have been defined in relation to Germanicus'. But most of all a system such as this with a complex hierarchy of three grades of *imperium* could not have been created in 17 from scratch. It implies, in my view, that Tiberius' *imperium* was already greater than that of the proconsuls; a new intermediate level was now added to define Germanicus' status.

If the law of AD 17 provides a *terminus ante quem*, I do not think, on the other hand, that the funerary eulogy of Agrippa provides any *terminus* at all. The only certainty is that Augustus could not have expressed himself as he did if Agrippa's *imperium* had been defined in a manner comparable to that of Germanicus in 17. Besides, the key phrase in the funeral speech can be interpreted just as easily to mean that Agrippa received an *imperium* equal to Pompey's in 67 or that he shared with Augustus an *imperium* greater than that of the provincial governors. It limits the number of possible hypotheses, but it does not prove anything.

On the other hand, the clause in lines 7–9 of the *laudatio* "into whatever provinces the Republic of the Romans should ever summon you" (εἰς ἃς δήποτέ σε ὑπαρχείας τὰ κοινὰ τῶν Ῥωμαίων ἐφέλκοιτο, translating the Latin *et quascumque in provincias res publica Romana te adhiberet*) should be compared with that in

---

[93] Eck et al. 1996 = AE 1996, 885, lines 33–36; cf. CIL II²/5, 900, lines 27–29 (trans. Griffin 1997: 250–253): *ei proco(n)s(uli), de quo lex ad populum lata esset, ut in quamcumq(ue) provinciam venisset, maius ei imperium quam ei qui eam provinciam proco(n)s(ul) optineret esset, dum in omni re maius imperium Ti(berio) Caesari Aug(usto) quam Germanico Caesari esset*: "to a proconsul for whom a law had been passed by the people to the effect that in whatever province he entered he would have greater *imperium* than the person who was governing that province as proconsul, so long as in every matter Ti. Caesar Augustus would have greater *imperium* than Germanicus."
[94] Girardet 2000: 219–227.

Cicero's motion in favour of Cassius (*quamcumque in provinciam ... advenerit*) ["into whatever province he should enter"] and to the *s.c. de Pisone patre* regarding the law of 17 (*in quamcumque provinciam venisset*) ["into whatever province he had come"]: the superiority of the *imperium* is linked in each case to arrival in a province; its aim was to regulate power conflicts that might develop there; it was not, at least originally, an absolute superiority permitting orders to be issued directly from Rome. It seems to me that, from this point of view, the two new texts strengthen one of McFayden's hypotheses. If Augustus received an *imperium* greater than that of the proconsuls in 23, as Dio says he did, it was not to compensate him for resigning the consulship, but was granted in the context of his trip to Sicily and then the East from the years 22 to 19, which would require him to enter a number of proconsular provinces (Syria being the only province controlled by the *princeps*).[95] But the renewal of this privilege at a time when the *princeps* travelled less and less (especially in proconsular provinces)[96] and the fact that it was extended to Tiberius (in AD 13 at the latest) and probably to Agrippa previously could only alter its real significance, even if the original terminology was preserved. In the law of 17 the superiority granted Germanicus retained its original sense, but the specification "so long as in every matter Ti. Caesar Augustus should have greater *imperium* than Germanicus" is revealing of the manner in which the *princeps'* superiority had taken on a new meaning. Tiberius' superiority over Germanicus did not envisage the possibility that the two men might arrive in the same province;[97] it was an absolute superiority, exercised from Rome. As formulated, this restriction already anticipated in its entirety the texts of the classical jurists.[98] It seems to me, therefore, that Cassius Dio's information on the *imperium* of 23 is imprecise only in the sense that it interprets the privilege conferred on Augustus in the light of subsequent gradual developments.

[95] McFayden 1921:, 36–37 (a solution already sketched by Hardy 1893: 65). Rich (1990: 170) also notes that Augustus' future trip to the East must have led to "the immediate need for the provision" (see also Jones 1951 = 1960: 8; 1970: 55; Salmon 1956: 468–470; Grenade 1961: 214, 373). Girardet 2000 is led to suppose at the very least that during Augustus' trip to the East "a corresponding senatorial decree ... perhaps concerning the manner in which he [i.e., Augustus] was granted his province, administering it *pro magistratu / pro consule*, also introduced political measures regulating the proconsuls then in office as the need arose."

[96] On this point I must part company with McFayden (1921), who argued that in 23 it was a case of a "temporary grant," which Dio incorrectly thought to be permanent.

[97] It is clearly stated in the s.c. that Germanicus had been sent in place of Tiberius (lines 30–32).

[98] Dig. 1.16.8; 1.18.4 (Ulpian, *Edict* Book 39): *praeses provinciae maius imperium in ea provincia habet omnibus post principem* ("a provincial governor has greater *imperium* in that province than everyone except the *princeps*").

If the hypothesis that I am proposing is correct, Augustus received for the first time in 23 *imperium* that was greater than that of the governors of proconsular provinces, and it was formulated in such a way that it permitted him, if he found himself in those provinces, to take decisions that were also binding on the proconsuls. This privilege did not, therefore, initially give him by implication the right to take measures at Rome regarding the proconsular provinces. Between 27 and 23, as we have seen from the Kyme inscription, Augustus could have exercised such a right in his capacity as consul acting in collaboration with the senate, but also (if not more so) thanks to his *auctoritas*, which was recognised by the proconsuls. After 23 it was Augustus' tribunician power that replaced the consulship as the basis of his collaboration with the senate,[99] while his *auctoritas* remained, on the other hand, a key element in relations between the *princeps* and the proconsuls.

It is this that is attested in the Cyrene edicts. Apart from the *senatus consultum* of 4 BC, which introduced a streamlined procedure for extortion cases (*repetundae*), the four other documents, dated to 7/6 BC, are edicts of Augustus relating solely to the proconsular province of Cyrenaica; they were issued without any mention of previous consultation of the senate, even if the possibility was at some point envisaged that the edict might be amended if Augustus himself or the senate found a better solution,[100] and even though we do not possess here, as at Kyme, the accompanying letters that must have been sent to the proconsul and which might well have mentioned a consultation of the senate. Particularly striking is the combination of phraseology expressing a command and phraseology expressing a pressing piece of advice analogous to language that can already be found in *senatus consulta* of the Republican period.[101]

---

[99] The importance of *tribunicia potestas* as a means of collaboration between the *princeps* and the senate has been underlined, in particular, by Grant 1946: 446–453. I would not, however, go so far as Girardet 2000: 208 (in his analysis of the Cyrene decrees) to say that "in general when the Princeps refers to this *potestas*, one may assume a corresponding senatorial decree, even when we lack specific evidence in the sources and when the particular document appears linguistically to be a statement of intent on the part of Augustus (towards his provincial subjects)." *Tribunicia potestas* is mentioned in the first Cyrene edict, which was clearly not prefaced by any s.c. (see the following note). It also appears alongside the title *pro co(n)s(ule)* in an edict issued by Augustus at Narbonne in 15 BC concerning an imperial province (*AE* 1999, 915 = 2000, 760, on which see above n. 33); in this case one cannot postulate any prior consultation of the senate.
[100] Edict I (De Visscher 1940, trans. Sherk 1984: no. 102 = Sherk 1988: no. 13, Cooley no. M60), lines 13–14: "until the senate may decide about this or I myself might find some better solution."
[101] Edict I, lines 13–14: "the fair and appropriate course of action, it seems to me, would be for those who govern the province of Crete and Cyrenaica to take action"; cf. lines 35–36. For

Scholars have generally wanted to use the Cyrene edicts by putting the emphasis on one or other type of phrase and by deducing from this that Augustus might have or might not have held *imperium* greater than that of proconsuls. If one wants, as one must, to explain the edicts in their entirety, one needs to ask oneself whether this fluctuating phraseology in fact reflects an ambiguity over the juridical basis of these actions. Augustus was not formally entitled to issue edicts concerning the proconsular provinces from Rome at any moment or to require proconsuls to supervise their implementation. This is why he adopted a tone towards them that counted on their cooperation in the name of his own *auctoritas*. But at the same time the privilege granted in 23 and renewed from 18 onwards could lend itself to a broader interpretation, which would allow the *princeps* to take decisions regarding the proconsular provinces from Rome and without necessarily consulting the senate. This broader interpretation gradually resulted in the principle, formulated for the first time, as far as we know, in the law of AD 17, that the *imperium* of the *princeps* was greater than that of all the other proconsuls everywhere and in all matters.

We must now return to the delicate problem of Agrippa's *imperium*. Whereas the previous comments in the *laudatio* regarding his *tribunicia potestas* contain two precise consular dates relating to the years 18 and 13 BC, the sentence about his *imperium* is just as imprecise chronologically as it is distorted regarding its contents. It is not impossible that the two things are linked and that Augustus may have sought a form of language that in aggregate would fit different statuses at different dates. The phrase "it was enacted by law" (νό[μωι ἐ]κυρώθη) appears in the Greek version of the *Res Gestae* (10.1) to describe two measures that came into effect at different times: the sacrosanctity he obtained in 36 and the tribunician power he was granted in 23. Even so in his *laudatio* of Agrippa, Augustus could envisage three or four grants of *imperium* in 23, 20 (if there was a new grant on this occasion),[102] 18, and 13.[103] It seems to me scarcely probable that in 23 Agrippa would have been sent to the East – very probably as proconsul and not simply as a legate of

---

a comparison of such phraseology with that of early senatorial decrees, see De Visscher 1940: 47–48.

[102] In favour of a law of 23 conferring *imperium* on Agrippa for five years, see Hurlet 1997: 59–60, 309, 313–314.

[103] Girardet 2000: 218, following Lacey 1996: 117–131, thinks that this could date to as early as 27. Nothing in our sources supports such a view. Agrippa did not receive a province during his third consulship and there was no reason to define the *imperium* that he would have exercised during and after his magistracy.

the *princeps* – with an *imperium* greater than that of the governors of the proconsular provinces, for the simple reason that such a decision would have been taken prior to Augustus' resignation of the consulship and the privileges that he received shortly thereafter, including the greater *imperium*.[104] It is probably no coincidence that Agrippa used the free city of Mytilene as his headquarters; that is to say, a city that juridically speaking lay outside the province of Asia. It seems quite possible, on the other hand, that he was granted the capacity to intervene, whenever the need arose, by means of an equal *imperium* (an *imperium aequum*). In 20 and in 19 in the West Agrippa operated most of the time in imperial provinces, although he might also have had to intervene in Gallia Narbonensis, which from 22 onwards had been returned to the Roman people. It was the year 18 that marked a new and final stage in Agrippa's rise.

The situation was totally different from the one that prevailed in 23. Marcellus was now dead. Agrippa had become Augustus' son-in-law in 21 and the two sons that he had had with Julia, in 20 and in 17, were going to be adopted by Augustus in 17. In 18 he became Augustus' colleague in the *tribunicia potestas*, just as he was going to be his colleague as president of the Secular Games in 17.[105] As a result, it seems to me quite possible that in 18 Agrippa saw himself granted the same greater *imperium* than that of the proconsul in any province in which he was led to intervene at the same time as Augustus had this privilege renewed.[106] The same practical reason that had allowed Augustus to have himself granted this privilege in 23 was equally valid for Agrippa in 18, since he was now going to travel for a long period in the East, moving through all the provinces during a period of intensive activity there from 17 to 13. It is true that Cassius Dio is content to write that Augustus in 18 granted him (in fact, had him granted) powers practically equal to his own, including tribunician power,[107] and that he only mentions in his account of the year 13 an *imperium* greater than that of the

---

[104] I borrow this argument from Crook 1996: 85.
[105] *RG* 22.2. The opening, unfortunately damaged, of the s.c. on the Secular Games shows in any case that there was a link between the fact that Agrippa was Augustus' colleague in the *tribunicia potestas* and the fact that he was his colleague appointed to act on behalf of the board of *XV viri* for the celebration of the games: see *CIL* VI 32323, lines 52–53 (trans. Sherk, *RE* no. 11, Cooley no. L27g): "whereas the consul Gaius Silanus announced that the Secular Games would take place after sever[al years - - - with Imperator Caesar] Augustus and M. A[grip]pa holding tribunician power ..."
[106] For the modification of Agrippa's *imperium* in 18, see Reinhold 1933: 167–175; Roddaz 1984: 347–350 (slightly modified in Roddaz 1992: 207–210). *Contra* Hurlet 1997: 43–45, 64–65.
[107] Dio 54.12.4.

governors.[108] I see this as imprecise only in the sense that he places the emphasis at one moment on tribunician power, at another on *imperium*; there is nothing here that invalidates the hypothesis that I have just proposed. Finally in 13 there had to be a renewal of all the powers granted Agrippa as well as Augustus in 18, all the more so since Agrippa was being sent to Pannonia, and Illyricum remained a proconsular province until the year 11 BC.[109] Augustus' phraseology in the *laudatio* allows Agrippa's *imperium* to be defined in its entirety from the year 23 onwards as not being subject to that of anyone else. That was just as true for the period in which he had held *imperium* equal to that of governors of proconsular provinces as for when he held *imperium* that was greater; and it was equally true in the case of his relationship with Augustus from the year 18 onwards.

For the years 23 to 18, one may wonder whether the (probable) law which granted the *princeps* a series of privileges in 23 contained a clause of the type *quominus ... e(ius) h(ac) l(ege) n(ihil) r(ogatur)* ["whereby ... nothing of it is proposed by this law"], thus keeping intact the powers that had just been granted Agrippa in the same year, 23.[110] It was not strictly necessary, since Augustus and Agrippa never found themselves together in a proconsular province. But this hypothesis, which I have borrowed from Bringmann even if I disagree with him on other points of his interpretation of the *laudatio*,[111] seems to me a real possibility, for it was quite natural that the law of 23 on Augustus' powers would have specified whether or not it

---

[108] Dio 54.28.1 does not, strictly speaking, talk about an increase in Agrippa's *imperium*, but only says that Augustus enhanced Agrippa's position by renewing his powers, in particular his tribunician power; cf. Hurlet 1997: 74.

[109] Dio 54.34.4.

[110] The hypothesis that I am proposing is on this point totally opposed to that of Crook 1996: 86: "not the least importance of the new device was to function as a distinction, keeping Augustus' *imperium* one stage higher than the new *imperium* of Agrippa." This interpretation seems hardly compatible with the text of the *laudatio*, and I cannot believe that *imperium maius* was introduced to establish a hierarchy between the *princeps* and his co-ruler rather than between the *princeps* and proconsuls.

[111] According to Bringmann 1977: 221–227, the *laudatio* would not have spoken of law(s) granting Agrippa *imperium*, but only of a law exempting Agrippa from the *imperium maius* of Augustus (originally a clause of the law of 23 on Augustus' *imperium*, renewed in 18 and 13). This principle would have applied each time Agrippa received *imperium*. Bringmann has been followed in part by Ameling (1994: 9–16), who argues that the privilege granted Augustus as well as Agrippa in 23 was *imperium aequum* rather than *imperium maius* and that it was granted Agrippa on an ongoing basis. The idea shared by Bringmann and Ameling of a privilege unconnected with the grant of *imperium* and designed to come into operation "in situations of need" (Ameling 1994: 15 talks of "optional *imperium*") seems to me unacceptable. It requires us to interpret the sentence of the *laudatio funebris* as if it was describing in its entirety the contents of a law, whereas Augustus was simply singling out the most honorific features of one or more laws whose aim was without any doubt much more complex. See also the objections of Fraschetti 1990 and Hurlet 1997: 47–48.

involved a derogation of the law that had been passed a little earlier concerning Agrippa. If one supposes that Agrippa had received in 23 an *imperium* equal to that of the governors of the proconsular provinces that he would enter, that the law granting Augustus greater *imperium* soon afterwards included a clause specifying that it represented neither an abrogation nor a derogation of the law in favour of Agrippa, and that Agrippa received in 18 and 13 the same *imperium* as Augustus (i.e., greater than that of the proconsuls in the provinces he would be required to enter), I do not see how Augustus could have simply summarised all these privileges except by emphasising that in all the provinces to which the *res publica* had sent him Agrippa had by law been provided with an *imperium* than which no other was greater. These hypotheses obviously imply a clear difference in status between the relationship between Agrippa and Augustus and that between Germanicus and Tiberius, but this difference is striking if one compares the texts of the *laudatio* and the *s.c. de Pisone patre*. It can be explained in terms of a deterioration in relations between the *princeps* and his co-ruler,[112] but also, it seems to me, independently of personal issues, by a consolidation between 13 BC and AD 17 of the idea that the *princeps' imperium* was greater than that of everyone else throughout the Empire: a notion that was not asserted all of a sudden, but which developed naturally from the more restricted privilege he had been granted in 23.

(d) The importance of the year 18

The year 18 witnessed two important events.[113] The first was the renewal of Augustus' *imperium* and provincial powers. The provinces that were once again entrusted to him were the same as in 27, with the exception of Gallia Narbonensis and Cyprus, which had became proconsular provinces in 22.[114] His prorogued *imperium* remained consular *imperium*; it cannot yet have been designated officially as proconsular *imperium*. The renewal of 18 (very probably determined by a *senatus consultum* submitted to the assembly for ratification) must have covered all those powers and honours conferred on him since 23 that were not ongoing. In fact, although the importance under Augustus of ten- and five-year renewals has

---

[112] After the events in Germania in 14–16, Tiberius could feel the need "to cloak the actual hierarchical relationship [between himself and Germanicus] in legal terms as well" (Eck et al. 1996: 160).
[113] Dio 54.12.4–5.
[114] Dio 54.4.1.

quite rightly been emphasised,[115] one should not forget that certain powers were not covered by such renewals. This was the case with his *tribunicia potestas*, which was at the same time both annual and ongoing: Dio's evidence on this last point is confirmed by Augustus himself in the *Res Gestae*.[116] The complementary powers providing him the "right to conduct business with the senate" (*ius agendi cum senatu*), granted in 23 and in 22, must have been of this same ongoing nature.[117] The renewal in 18 must, therefore, have revived for another five years the privilege of being exempted from the regulation concerning the *pomerium*,[118] the superiority of Augustus' *imperium* over that of the proconsuls when he entered a proconsular province, and the possession of consular honours while in Rome. In this way powers that had been granted in several stages in 27, 23, and 19 were now combined into a single package.

The other important event of the year 18 was Agrippa's joint holding of tribunician power and *imperium* with Augustus. Independently of the superiority of Augustus' *auctoritas*, there was no real equality in terms of their powers: the notion of collegiality could be employed with regards to their *tribunicia potestas*,[119] but Augustus maintained his superiority since his tribunician power was ongoing, whereas Agrippa's was granted only for a five-year period. As regards his *imperium*, I have explained why it seems to me that in 18 Agrippa received the same privilege that Augustus possessed of superiority over the governors of proconsular provinces, but his *imperium* and the privileges related to it must have been limited to overseas provinces (*provinciae transmarinae*). It appears to me almost certain that Agrippa was also released from the rule governing the *pomerium* thanks to his tribunician power.[120] On the other hand, nothing allows us to suppose that Augustus shared the consular honours of 19 with Agrippa. In spite of everything, Agrippa's sharing the powers of the *princeps* was a considerable

---

[115] Credit for this goes back particularly to Pelham 1888 = 1911: 60–65; see also Piganiol 1937.

[116] Dio 53.32.5: διὰ βίου; *RG* 10.1: *quoad viverem* in the Latin text; διὰ βίου in the Greek.

[117] As regards the error of talking of the power of the consuls "for life" (Dio 54.10.5), it must be connected to the fact that Dio, while certainly mentioning the renewals of Augustus' powers, considered them a mask that struggled to conceal the fact that he possessed power for life (cf. 53.16.2: "with the result that by means of a succession of ten-year periods he came to hold sole power for life").

[118] I stated above (pp. 102–103) that this privilege was a necessary consequence of the grant of *tribunicia potestas*. It was also a feature of the exercise of *imperium*, subject to the same rhythm of renewal as the latter.

[119] *RG* 6.2. Note also the use of the word *collegium* (i.e., colleague in the tribunician power) in the so-called imperial Fasti from Brixia (Brescia): *Inscr. It.* X, 5, nos 95–100.

[120] This would have been from 23 onwards according to Hurlet 1997: 59–60, 313–314.

novelty and its significance ambiguous, for it tended to institutionalise and perpetuate the Principate at the same time as it blurred its monarchical character. The year 18 was an important stage, but it was only a stage. Augustus' powers must have increased still more with his election as *pontifex maximus* in 12 BC following the death of Lepidus, without taking into account the importance of the bestowal of the honorific title *pater patriae* in 2 BC. Most of all, Agrippa's death in 12 BC and the difficult problem of putting in place a dynastic succession without being able to advertise it publicly meant that after the crisis of 6 BC, when Tiberius withdrew to Rhodes just after he had been invested with *tribunicia potestas* for five years and *imperium* over the overseas provinces, the system that operated from 18 to 12 BC could be revived only in AD 4 after the deaths of Gaius and Lucius Caesar and the adoption of Tiberius.

Only occasional attempts have been made to explain the difficult problem of the date of the renewal: it occurred in 18 rather than in 17, which would have been the logical moment since the provinces conferred in January 27 had been conferred for ten years, but subsequent renewals took place with 18 as the point of departure. I shall mention just for the record the thesis of Grenade, who argued that the renewal in 18 would imply that Augustus had gained his powers over the provinces in 28, which must then simply have been modified in 27 by a reduction in the number of provinces directly entrusted to the *princeps*.[121] Much more persuasive is the hypothesis of Piganiol, who believed that he could explain the date 18 on the basis of the care which Augustus took in anticipating their expiry by making the people vote on laws the year before they were due to come into force on the following 1 January (i.e., to take effect on 1 January 17, 12, 7, etc.).[122] But is that sufficient to explain a renewal that Dio appears to date quite early in the year 18, during the summer at the latest, i.e., exactly five years after the grant of his powers in 23?[123] Hurlet has recently argued that Augustus advanced the renewal of his own powers to make this coincide with the renewal of those of Agrippa.[124] This does not seem to me fully convincing. It rests on the interesting

---

[121] Grenade 1961. This hypothesis, which finds no support in any source, has been unanimously rejected. The importance of the year 28 confirmed by the publication of the new *aureus* does not concern the governance of the provinces and does not authorise the hypothesis to be resuscitated: see Rich and Williams 1999: 197 n. 86.
[122] Piganiol 1937: 151.
[123] The renewal of Augustus' powers and the vote on those of Agrippa (Dio 54.12) are mentioned at the beginning of events of the years 18 before the *lectio senatus* (Dio 54.13–14) and the Julian laws (54.16).
[124] Hurlet 1997: 309.

but by no means proven hypothesis that in 23 Agrippa was granted *imperium* for five years, which he would first exercise in the East and then (after a change in just the title of his *provincia*) in the West.

If Piganiol's explanation is insufficient and as a result one needs to trace the origins of the renewal of 18 to a five-yearly cycle going back to 23, it seems to me that one should rather concentrate on the powers of Augustus himself. It cannot be a question of his provinces, granted for ten years in 27; or of his *imperium*, announced as lasting until January 17 and even beyond that, in so far as Augustus would not entertain any successor in his provinces; or finally of his exemption from the regulation concerning the *pomerium*, which was connected with his holding of *imperium* and the ongoing possession of *tribunicia potestas*. That leaves the superiority of his *imperium* to that of the proconsuls. As we have already pointed out, it must have been restricted at the start to cases where Augustus found himself in a province. It must also have been limited in time,[125] and I would not exclude the possibility that the duration envisaged in 23 was a five-year period, which had Republican precedents. Here can be found another element of the delicate compromise between Augustus and the nobility, which must have lain behind the measures of 23. The measures of 18 in turn represented another compromise, in the sense that the ten-year term established in 27 was replaced by a return to a five-year term, this time for all aspects of Augustus' *imperium*. It was not until 8 BC that Augustus returned to the ten-year system of 27. Such considerations lead to a certain overestimate of the importance of the measures of 23, without going so far as to suppose, as did Andersen, that the *imperium* granted in 27 was in 23 replaced purely and simply by a new *imperium* and that Dio, to emphasise the importance of the events of 27,[126] concealed the fact that the *imperium* renewed in 18 was in fact a renewal of that of 23 rather than that of 27.[127] Instead I would argue that the provinces granted for ten years in 27 involved an *imperium* that was the object of a certain number of modifications or additions in 23 and then again in 19, and the fact that some change or changes were made in 23 for a

---

[125] Augustus' powers are in effect either carefully limited to periods that were renewable or ongoing but automatically renewed each year. Anything relating to his *imperium* belonged in the first category, since Augustus had declined the offer of an "annual and perpetual consulship" (*RG* 5.3).

[126] This aspect of Dio's narrative has rightly been emphasised in the recent study of Rich and Williams 1999.

[127] Andersen 1938: 41–48. I do not agree with Andersen's interpretation of Dio's phraseology at 53.32.5, which leads him to suppose that Augustus in 23 accepted only for five years an *imperium* that the senate had proposed he should hold for life.

five-year term could help explain the renewal from the summer of 18 onwards of a conglomeration of powers that traced their origins back to the years 27, 23, and 19.

3 TIBERIUS AS "CO-RULER" AND HIS ACCESSION TO THE PRINCIPATE (AD 4–14)

On Agrippa's death in 12 BC Augustus' stepson Tiberius was sent to his posting in Pannonia as legate of Augustus. Tiberius married Julia the following year, as soon as the delays required by law permitted him to marry a pregnant widow, and he must have received in the same year an *imperium* that was his very own,[128] and which was renewed in 6 BC at the same time as he was granted *tribunicia potestas*. But shortly thereafter Tiberius retired to Rhodes. In 1 BC, when his *tribunicia potestas* expired, he once again became a *privatus* ["private citizen"]. The deaths of Gaius and Lucius Caesar, however, forced Augustus to turn once again to him, this time not just as his *adiutor imperii* ["assistant in power"], but also as his future successor. In AD 4 Augustus adopted Tiberius, just after the latter had adopted his own nephew Germanicus. This same year Tiberius received once again his own *imperium* and *tribunicia potestas*, both for five years. In 9 these powers were renewed for another five-year term. In 13, a year before their scheduled expiry but at the moment when Augustus' powers were renewed for the last time, Tiberius' were increased further.[129] A consular law gave him *imperium* equal to that of Augustus with respect to all the provinces and armies (i.e., a sharing of command over the imperial provinces and an *imperium* greater than that of the governors of all the proconsular provinces he might enter), as well as the right to initiate a census (i.e., a *censoria potestas*, which was grafted onto the consular

---

[128] Hurlet 1997: 87–89.
[129] Vell. Pat. 2.121.1; Suet. *Tib.* 21.1. The date of this law has been the subject of a long controversy, because Velleius seems to date it before Tiberius' triumph on 23 October AD 12 (2.121.2–3), but Suetonius' chronology seems more precise on this point, and it has generally been accepted (see, however, Woodman 1977: 211). The mention of a "legate of Imperator Caesar Augustus and Tiberius Caesar" in an Athenian inscription (*IG* II² 3233 = *Hesperia* 17, 1948, 41, no. 30 = EJ 81a; trans. Sherk, *RE*, no. 24e) would be evidence of a "joint-rule" if one could deduce from the text that there were joint legates of Augustus and Tiberius after the law of 13 (as argued by Oliver 1948: 436; Ehrenberg 1953b). But one cannot rule out the possibility that the man concerned was a legate first of Augustus, then of Tiberius, even though one might expect the title *theos Sebastos* (i.e., the Deified Augustus), if this were the case (cf. *CIL* III 1741 and *AE* 1914, 136: *leg. divi Augusti et Ti. Caesaris Augusti*); but the omission of *divus* after 14 is not unparalleled: see Orth 1978: 58; Raubitschek 1953: 330–331. Even before the law of 13, Tiberius was associated with Augustus in levying troops at Rome: see *AE* 1973, 501 = *I. Alexandreia Troas* no. 34 (trans. Sherk, *RE*, no. 21, Cooley no. N27); cf. Brunt 1974; Orth 1978: 57–60.

imperium of both Tiberius and Augustus, but which came to an end with the closing of the *lustrum*, before Augustus's death).

It is equally possible, but by no means certain, that from before 13 and following his victories in Pannonia Tiberius also enjoyed the same consular honours that Augustus had acquired in 19 BC.[130] His *tribunicia potestas* was also renewed in 13, but there is nothing in our sources to confirm Mommsen's theory that it then became ongoing,[131] nor do we have any indication that Tiberius had conferred upon him during Augustus' lifetime the special powers of the *ius agendi cum senatu* ["right to conduct business with the senate"], which Augustus had received in 23 and 22. On Augustus' death, Tiberius perhaps, therefore, lacked the consular honours on a permanent basis and probably lacked ongoing *tribunicia potestas* and its extension, the "right of conducting business with the senate"; he certainly was not *pontifex maximus*; and, among his honours, he lacked the *praenomen* "Imperator," the *cognomen* "Augustus," and the title *pater patriae* (but we do know that he turned down the *praenomen* "Imperator" and the title *pater patriae*, but inherited the *cognomen* "Augustus" in Augustus' will). It is, therefore, clear that there was not very much of importance left for Tiberius to receive and it is rather difficult to understand what took place in the senate after Augustus' death, since the principle of the succession would seem to have been resolved with the important sharing of powers that took place in the final year of Augustus' Principate. It should also be recognised that our sources on this point are particularly inadequate, Tacitus included. His narrative is the richest in detail, but it does not provide any precise account of the consuls' motion during the session held on 17 September.[132]

Some hypotheses can for sure be discarded. I have already stated that nothing, as far as I can see, allows us to believe that the main basis of the power of the *princeps* was, independently of his *imperium* and *tribunicia potestas*, the grant in 27 (by means of a senatorial decree and a law) of a *cura et tutela rei publicae* ("guardianship and protectorship of the Republic") or the function of being an *auctor consilii publici* ("source of public advice"), which

---

[130] During the winter of 9–10, he was to be seen sitting with Augustus between the consuls during a brief return to Rome at a ceremony marking his turning down of a triumph in the wake of Varus' disastrous defeat (Suet. *Tib.* 17.5). But it took place in the Saepta, and so outside the *pomerium*, and it was not a formal meeting of the senate. Most of all, it could have been an exceptional honour and not a permanent privilege.

[131] Mommsen 1887–1888, II: 1161–1162, followed by Schwartz 1945: 40.

[132] The interpretation of Tacitus' text is far from obvious; see the recent proposals of Griffin 1995 and Woodman 1998.

Tiberius would in turn receive in AD 14 according to the same procedure.¹³³ Since on Augustus' death Tiberius gave the watchword to the praetorian cohorts, wrote to the armies, and summoned the senate by virtue of his *tribunicia potestas*,¹³⁴ we can exclude the hypothesis that his powers, renewed in 13, came to an end on Augustus' death.¹³⁵ Such a view is based on the idea that a co-ruler's powers were only delegated powers, whereas Tiberius' *imperium* had been conferred upon him by means of a consular law and, as we know from the *laudatio* of Agrippa, the co-ruler's *tribunicia potestas* was also conferred by the people.¹³⁶

On the other hand, since Mamercus Scaurus remarked during the debate in the senate that Tiberius had not made use of his *tribunicia potestas* to intercede on the consuls' *relatio* ["motion"],¹³⁷ we can also exclude the hypothesis that Tiberius began by resigning the powers he held to have them granted to him afresh.¹³⁸ One cannot, therefore, claim that the *princeps'* powers would *de facto* become ongoing at the moment of such a re-investiture for the simple reason that Tiberius, by refusing to make a clear commitment, would have prevented them from being restored to him for a fixed length of time.¹³⁹ If the powers that Tiberius already possessed were neither cancelled by Augustus' death nor returned to the senate for it to dispose of them as it saw fit, they must have remained in force, unless they were explicitly replaced by ongoing powers.

Augustan precedent had made only the *tribunicia potestas* ongoing. It is probable, therefore, that Tiberius' tribunician power similarly became ongoing, if it had not been that already, and this

---

¹³³ See above pp. 97–98 for my discussion of Liebeschuetz 1986.

¹³⁴ Tac. *Ann.* 1.7.

¹³⁵ Similarly refuted is the theory of Castritius (1982: 32–33, 51–61) that Tiberius' *tribunicia potestas* remained in force on Augustus' death, while his *imperium* ended because it was defined in relation to that of Augustus.

¹³⁶ Badian 1980.

¹³⁷ Tac. *Ann.* 1.13.4, which does not imply only that Tiberius had tribunician power at the start of the session, as argued by Goodyear 1972: 174 n. 1. It seems just as inconceivable if Tiberius had handed over all his powers to the senate after the consuls had made their motion and before the debate began.

¹³⁸ As argued by Grenade 1961: 394–443; De Martino 1962 = 1974: 469. That there was no resignation and formal re-conferral does not prevent us supposing that a *senatus consultum* solemnly confirmed Tiberius' powers as well as Germanicus' *imperium*. This is how Tac. *Ann.* 1.14.3 should be interpreted: see Brunt 1974: 179–180; Syme 1977: 240–241; 1979; 320–321; Hurlet 1997: 172–173.

¹³⁹ For this, see Timpe 1962: 54–55. Brunt (1977: 97–98) notes that Suetonius (*Tib.* 24.3) claims to be citing Tiberius' actual words in reluctantly accepting imperial power: "until I reach the point where you consider it right to give me some rest in my old age." But such reservations did not prevent a s.c. or a law indicating a limit, which anyway fixed only a maximum limit in the same way that in 27 Augustus had received his powers for ten years in the hope of returning his provinces before this period came to an end (Dio 53.13.1).

was perhaps the only law that was then submitted to the assembly for ratification.[140] On the other hand, it seems to me very difficult to argue that Tiberius' *imperium* may also have been made ongoing in 14.[141] Such a break with Augustan precedent would totally contradict Tiberius' attitude in the weeks following Augustus' death. In fact, the evidence of Cassius Dio (or rather, unfortunately, his epitomator Xiphilinus) tells against the theory that there was a new investiture rendering Tiberius' *imperium* ongoing, explicitly or even only *de facto*. According to Dio, Tiberius, unlike Augustus, did not request his powers be renewed at the end of their ten-year limit.[142] Such an oversight, which needs to be placed in the context of an attempt, whether affected or genuine, not to continue in power after the death of his son Drusus in AD 23,[143] did not in the end have any practical effect. It was at that moment that it became quite clear that following the reform of 23 BC, which had liberated the *princeps* from the rule of the *pomerium*, his *imperium* no longer had any legal limit from the moment that the senate showed no inclination to reclaim the provinces that had been assigned to him and to send proconsuls there instead.

The problem of the "accession of Tiberius" seems to me, in general terms, to have been clearly appreciated by Levick: the subject of debate was not Tiberius' possession of *imperium* (hence the date of his *dies imperii* does not need to be discussed), but rather the implications of his exercise of that power. Tiberius tried, without much success, to redefine the role of the *princeps* and his relations with the senate.[144] It is indeed clear that the powers with which Tiberius was already invested were insufficient to prevent Augustus' death stirring up anxiety and debate.[145] By the powers that he had had conferred upon Agrippa and Tiberius, hadn't Augustus himself admitted that

---

[140] Tac. *Ann.* 1.46.1 seems to indicate that a law on Tiberius' powers had to be submitted for ratification in the assembly (Brunt 1977: 97). On the other hand, the phrase *patres et plebs*, frequently used to mean the senate and people, is not sufficient to prove that this ratification took the form of the plebiscite, as argued by Siber 1933: 18; 1940: 15.

[141] As argued by Syme 1958a, I: 411 n. 4; Kienast 1982 = 1999: 88 n. 32, 149 and n. 235 (for the theory, not supported in the sources, that this reform of the *princeps'* powers was in fact part of Augustus' political testament).

[142] Dio 57.24.1 (Xiphilinus; Dio's text is lost between 57.16.8 and 58.16.2), but Dio must have made this remark in his account of the year 24, since he later wrote (58.24.1) that the consuls of 34, L. Vitellius and Fabius Persicus, "celebrated the second *decennalia*" (i.e., ten-year period in power).

[143] Tac. *Ann.* 4.9.1.

[144] Levick 1976: 75–81; Syme 1974: 485–486.

[145] Woodman 1998 conveniently reminds us that memories of Tiberius' retirement to Rhodes in 6 BC could not have failed to haunt people's minds in AD 14 and to increase the ambiguity of some of his remarks.

the Principate was a responsibility too heavy for one person to bear alone? Shouldn't Tiberius also have thought of a way of sharing his power? Shouldn't he have promoted Germanicus to be a partner in the *tribunicia potestas*, even if he was just thirty years old? Or seek an *adiutor* ["assistant'] in the form of a man mature in experience, but whose position would have been threatening for the two young princes, Germanicus and Drusus, or on the other hand as uncomfortable and as unbearable as Tiberius' own position had been when he decided to withdraw to Rhodes? Tacitus' narrative, as distorted as it is in its prejudice against Tiberius and composed in the light of a century of experience of the Principate and its drift towards monarchy, clearly shows that this was indeed the hub of the problem.

The final years of Augustus' principate had seen a general strengthening of the powers of the *princeps* at the expense in particular of the senate. Tiberius quite clearly did not wish to perpetuate such a system, which above all would have benefited Germanicus; he preferred to return to a situation in which the senate would have had a more important role in the administration of the Empire without giving the impression that he was disowning Augustus. This is consistent with his overall policy at the start of his Principate. Nevertheless, because he could not make himself understood, or because the senators preferred not to understand him, the debate got bogged down. Tiberius went so far as to threaten to retire,[146] and the debate eventually ended through weariness without things getting settled as clearly as would have been desirable.[147] The principle that Tiberius had accepted the sort of role that Augustus had played could be considered established by the end of the senatorial meeting on 17 September. The *imperia* of Tiberius and Germanicus were solemnly confirmed. The additional measures could then be taken gradually,[148] and Tacitus, who had no interest in procedures in the assembly[149] and does not say a word, for instance, about Tiberius' election as *pontifex maximus*, would have passed over them in silence without the slightest difficulty.[150]

---

[146] Tac. *Ann.* 1.12.3.
[147] Tac. *Ann.* 1.13.6.
[148] Tiberius' election as *pontifex maximus* only took place six months later on 10 March 15, a date known to us from epigraphic sources. But there was no question that this would occur, since Augustus had been elected *pontifex maximus* in March 12 BC and this precedent established the normal date of priestly elections: Nero thus waited until March 55 to be elected *pontifex maximus*. See Scheid 1992: 228 and n. 18.
[149] Thus he does not mention the law of 17 on the *imperium* of Germanicus or the *lex Valeria Aurelia* of 20, restricting himself in both cases to the measures taken by the senate.
[150] The original French version of the article ends with a brief discussion (pp. 150–154) of the evidence of the so-called "Law on the *imperium* of Vespasian" (*CIL* VI 930 = *ILS* 244; trans.

WORKS CITED

Abele, T. A. 1907. *Der Senat unter Augustus* (Studien zur Geschichte und Kultur des Altertums I, 2). Paderborn.

Alföldy, G. 2000. "Das neue Edikt des Augustus aus El Bierzo in Hispanien," *ZPE* 131: 177–205.

Ameling, W. 1994. "Augustus und Agrippa. Bemerkungen zu P.Köln VI 249," *Chiron* 24: 1–28.

Andersen, H. A. 1938. *Cassius Dio und die Begründung des Principates*. Berlin.

Astin, A. E. 1963. "Augustus and *censoria potestas*," *Latomus* 22: 226–235.

Astin, A. E. 1969. "'Nominare' in Accounts of Elections in the Early Principate," *Latomus* 28: 863–874.

Atkinson, K. M. T. 1960a. "Constitutional and Legal Aspects of the Trial of Marcus Primus and Varro Murena," *Historia* 9: 440–473.

Atkinson, K. M. T. 1960b. "*Restitutio in integrum* and *iussum Augusti Caesaris* in an Inscription at Leyden," *RIDA* 7: 227–272.

Badian, E. 1974. "The Quaestorship of Tiberius Nero," *Mnemosyne* 27: 160–172.

Badian, E. 1980. "Notes on the *laudatio* of Agrippa," *CJ* 76: 97–107.

Badian, E. 1982. "'Crisis Theories' and the Beginning of the Principate," in G. Wirth, ed., *Romanitas – Christianitas. Festschrift für J. Straub*. Berlin and New York. 18–41.

Badian, E. 1986. "The Young Betti and the Practice of History," in G. Crifò, ed., *Costituzione romana e crisi della Repubblica. Atti del convegno su E. Betti (25–26 ottobre 1984)*. Naples. 73–96.

Balsdon, J. P. V. D. 1939. "Consular Provinces in the Late Republic," *JRS* 29: 58–65.

Béranger, J. 1953. *Recherches sur l'aspect idéologique du principat* (Schweizerische Beiträge zur Altertumswissenschaft 6). Basel.

Betti, E. 1915. *Il carattere giuridico del principato di Augusto*. Città di Castello (reprinted in *La crisi della repubblica e la genesi del principato in Roma*, ed. G. Crifò, intro. E. Gabba, Rome, 1982, 540–584).

Birley, A. R. 2000. "Q. Lucretius Vespillo (cos. ord. 19)," *Chiron* 30: 711–748.

Bleicken, J. 1962. *Senatsgericht und Kaisergericht. Eine Studie zur Entwicklung des Prozeßrecht im frühen Prinzipat* (Abh. Ak. Wiss. Göttingen, Phil.-hist. Kl. III, 53). Göttingen.

Sherk, *RE*, no. 82, Cooley no. H52) and the Acts of the Arval Brethren (Scheid 1998) for the process whereby the emperors from Caligula to Domitian were granted their powers. The evidence is inconclusive, but Ferrary argues that the system used to invest Tiberius in 14 perhaps set a precedent for ongoing tribunician power being granted by a law passed by the assembly, which would help to explain Dio's phraseology (53.32.6) in describing Augustus' grant of tribunician power in 23 BC: "as a result, both he and later emperors gained a legal right to use tribunician power as well as their other powers."

Bleicken, J. 1978. *Verfassungs- und Sozialgeschichte der römischen Kaiserreiches*. Paderborn.
Bleicken, J. 1990. *Zwischen Republik und Prinzipat. Zum Charakter des zweiten Triumvirats* (Abh. Ak. Wiss. Göttingen, Phil.-hist. Kl., 3.Folge, no. 185). Göttingen.
Bleicken, J. 1998. *Augustus. Eine Biographie*. Berlin.
Blumenthal, F. 1909. "Zur zensorischen Tätigkeit des Augustus," *Klio* 9: 493–500.
Bringmann, K. 1977. "Imperium proconsulare und Mitregenschaft im frühen Prinzipat," *Chiron* 7: 219–238.
Brunt, P. A. 1962. Review of Jones 1960. *CR* n.s. 12: 70–73.
Brunt, P. A. 1974. "C. Fabricius Tuscus and an Augustan Dilectus," *ZPE* 13: 161–185.
Brunt, P. A. 1977. "*Lex de imperio Vespasiani*," *JRS* 67: 95–116.
Brunt, P. A. 1984. "The Role of the Senate in the Augustan Regime," *CQ* n.s. 34: 423–444.
Burnett, A. M. 1977. "The Authority to Coin in the Late Republic and Early Empire," *NC* 137: 37–63.
Castritius, H. 1982. *Der römische Prinzipat als Republik*. Husum.
Charbonnel, N. 1979. "À propos de l'inscription de Kymé et des pouvoirs d'Auguste dans les provinces au lendemain du règlement de 27 av. n.è.," *RIDA* 26: 177–225.
Costabile, F. and Licandro, O. 2000. "*Tessera Paemeiobrigensis*. Un nuovo editto di Augusto dalla *Transduriana provincia* e l'*imperium proconsulare* del *princeps*," *Minima epigraphica et papyrologica* 3: 147–237.
Cotton, H. M. and Yakobson, A. 2002. "*Arcanum imperii*: The Powers of Augustus," in G. Clark and T. Rajak, eds, *Philosophy and Power in the Graeco-Roman World: Essays in Honour of Miriam Griffin*. Oxford. 193–209.
Crawford, M. H. 1985. *Coinage and Money under the Roman Republic*. London.
Crook, J. A. 1962. "An Augustan Inscription in the Rijksmuseum at Leyden (*S.E.G.* xviii, no. 555)," *PCPhS* 188: 23–29.
Crook, J. A. 1996. "Political History, 30 B.C. to A.D. 14," and "Augustus: Power, Authority, Achievement," in *CAH*² X: 70–146.
De Francisci, P. 1930. "La costituzione augustea," in *Studi in onore di Pietro Bonfante*. Milan. 13–43.
De Francisci, P. 1938. "La costituzione augustea," in *Augustus: studi in occasione del bimillenario augusteo*. Rome. 61–100.
De Francisci, P. 1941. *Genesi e struttura del principato augusteo* (Memorie della Reale Accademia d'Italia, Classe scienze morale e storiche), ser. 7, vol. 2, fasc. 1. Rome.
De Francisci, P. 1948. *Arcana imperii*, III. 1. Milan.
De Martino, F. 1936. *Lo stato di Augusto. Introduzione*. Naples.
De Martino, F. 1962. *Storia della costituzione romana*. Naples (2nd edn, 1974).

De Visscher, F. 1940. *Les édits d'Auguste découverts à Cyrène*. Louvain.

Dettenhofer, M. H. 2000. *Herrschaft und Widerstand im augusteichen Principat. Die Konkurrenz zwischen respublica und domus Augusta* (*Historia* Einzelschriften 140). Stuttgart.

Eck, W. 1998. *Augustus und seine Zeit*. Munich (English trans. Eck 2003).

Eck, W. 2003. *The Age of Augustus* (trans. D. L. Schneider). Oxford (2nd expanded edn, 2007).

Eck, W., Caballos Rufino, A., and Fernández Gómez, F. 1996. *Das Senatus Consultum de Cn. Pisone patre* (Vestigia 48). Munich.

Ehrenberg, V. 1953a. "*Imperium maius* in the Roman Republic," *AJPh* 74: 113–136.

Ehrenberg, V. 1953b. "*Legatus Augusti et Tiberii?*", in *Studies Presented to D. M. Robinson*, II. St Louis. 938–944 (reprinted in *Polis and Imperium*, Zurich and Stuttgart, 1965, 607–613).

Ferrary, J.-L. 2000. "Les inscriptions du sanctuaire de Claros en l'honneur de Romains," *BCH* 124: 331–376.

Fluss, M. 1934. "A. Terentius A.f. Varro Murena, cos. ord. 23 B.C.," *RE* VA: cols 706–710.

Fraschetti, A. 1990. "Augustus et la 'laudatio' di Agrippa,' in *Il Bimillenario di Agrippa*. Genova. 83–98.

Frei-Stolba, R. 1967. *Untersuchungen zu den Wahlen in der römischen Kaiserzeit*. Zurich.

Gelzer, M. 1943. *Das erste Consulat des Pompeius und die Übertragung der grossen Imperien* (Abh. Preuss. Ak. Wiss., Phil.-hist. Kl. 1). Berlin (reprinted in *Kleine Schriften*, II, Wiesbaden, 1963: 146–189).

Giovannini, A. 1983. *Consulare imperium*. Basel.

Giovannini, A. 1999. "Les pouvoirs d'Auguste de 27 à 23 av. J.-C. Une relecture de l'ordonnance de Kymè de l'an 27 (IK 5, no. 17)," *ZPE* 124: 95–105.

Girardet, K. M. 1990. "Die Entmachung des Konsulates im Übergang von der Republik zur Monarchie und die Rechtsgrundlagen des augusteischen Prinzipats," in *Pratum Saraviense. Festgabe für P. Steinmetz*. Stuttgart. 89–126.

Girardet, K. M. 1991. "Der Triumph des Pompeius im Jahre 61 v. Chr. – *ex Asia?*" *ZPE* 89: 201–215.

Girardet, K. M. 1992a. "*Imperium* und *provinciae* des Pompeius seit 67 v. Chr.," *CCGG* 3: 177–188.

Girardet, K. M. 1992b. "Zur Diskussion um das *imperium consulare militiae* im 1.Jh. v. Chr.," *CCGG* 3: 213–220.

Girardet, K. M. 2000. "*Imperium 'maius'*: politische und verfassungsrechtliche Aspekte. Versuch einer Klärung," in A. Giovannini, ed., *La révolution romaine après Ronald Syme: bilans et perspectives* (Entretiens de la Fondation Hardt 46). Vandœuvres. 167–227.

Goodyear, F. R. D., ed., 1972. *Tacitus*, Annals *1.1–54*. Cambridge.

Grant, M. 1946. *From Imperium to Auctoritas. A Historical Study of the*

Aes Coinage in the Roman Empire, 49 B.C.-A.D. 14. Cambridge.
Grant, M. 1949, "The Augustan Constitution," *G&R* 18: 97–112.
Grenade, P. 1961. *Essai sur les origines du Principat*. BEFAR 197. Paris.
Griffin, M. T. 1995. "Tacitus, Tiberius and the Principate," in I. Malkin and Z. Rubinsohn, eds, *Leaders and Masses in the Roman World. Studies in Honor of Zvi Yavetz*. Leiden. 37–43.
Griffin, M. T. 1997. "The Senate's Story," *JRS* 87: 249–263.
Groningen, B. A. van. 1926. "De Octaviani Caesaris ante principatum conditum imperio," *Mnemosyne* 54: 1–9.
Hammond, M. 1933. *The Augustan Principate in Theory and Practice during the Julio-Claudian Period*. Cambridge, MA (rev. edn, with additions, 1968).
Hampl, F. 1978. *Geschichte als kritische Wissenschaft*, III. Darmstadt.
Hardy, E. G. 1893. "*Imperium consulare* and *proconsulare*," *Journal of Philology* 21: 56–65.
Hurlet, F. 1997. *Les collègues du prince sous Auguste et Tibère: de la légalité républicaine à la légitimité dynastique* (CEFR 227). Rome.
Hurlet, F. 1998. Review of Lacey 1996. *Latomus* 57: 452–456.
Hurlet, F. 2001. "Les auspices d'Octavien/Auguste," *CCGG* 12: 155–180.
Jacques, F. and Scheid, J. 1990. *Rome et l'intégration de l'Empire (44 av. J.-C.–260 ap. J.-C.). 1. Les structures de l'empire romain*. Paris.
Jameson, S. 1969. "22 or 23?" *Historia* 18: 204–227.
Jones, A. H. M. 1951. "The *imperium* of Augustus," *JRS* 41: 112–119 (reprinted in Jones 1960: 3–17).
Jones, A. H. M. 1954. "Imperial and Senatorial Jurisdiction in the Early Principate," *Historia* 3: 464–488 (reprinted in Jones 1960: 69–98).
Jones, A. H. M. 1955. "The Elections under Augustus," *JRS* 45: 9–21 (reprinted in Jones 1960: 29–50).
Jones, A. H. M. 1960. *Studies in Roman Government and Law*. Oxford.
Jones, A. H. M. 1970. *Augustus*. London.
Jones, A. H. M. 1972. *The Criminal Courts of the Roman Republic and Principate*. Oxford.
Kahrstedt, U. 1938. Review of Premerstein 1937. *Göttingische Gelehrte Anzeigen* 200: 5–23.
Kienast, D. 1982. *Augustus. Prinzeps und Monarch*. Darmstadt (3rd edn, 1999).
Kolbe, W. 1931. "Von der Republik zur Monarchie," in *Aus Roms Zeitwende. Von Wesen und Wirken des augusteischen Geistes* (Das Erbe der Alten, II.20). Leipzig. 37–65.
Kromayer, J. 1888. *Der rechtliche Begründung des Prinzipats*. Marburg.
Kromayer, J. 1919. Review of O. Schulz, *Vom Prinzipat zum Dominat*, Paderborn, 1919. *Göttingische Gelehrte Anzeigen*: 419–435.
Lacey, W. K. 1979. "*Summi fastigii vocabulum*: The Story of a Title," *JRS* 69: 28–43 (reprinted in Lacey 1996: 154–168).
Lacey, W. K. 1985. "Augustus and the Senate: 23 B.C.," *Antichthon* 19:

55–67 (reprinted in Lacey 1996: 100–116).
Lacey, W. K. 1996. *Augustus and the Principate: The Evolution of the System*. Leeds.
Last, H. 1947. "*Imperium maius*: A Note," *JRS* 37: 157–164.
Levick, B. 1967. "Imperial Control of the Elections under the Early Principate: *commendatio*, *suffragatio* and *nominatio*," *Historia* 16: 207–230.
Levick, B. 1976. *Tiberius the Politician*. London (rev. edn, 1999).
Liebeschuetz, J. H. W. G. 1986. "The Settlement of 27 B.C.," in *Studies in Latin Literature and Roman History IV* (Collection *Latomus* 196). Brussels. 345–365.
Magdelain, A. 1947. *Auctoritas principis*. Paris.
Mantovani, D. 2008. "*Leges et iura p(opuli) R(omani) restituit*: principe e diritto in un aureo di Ottaviano," *Athenaeum* 96: 5–54.
McFayden, D. 1921. "The Princeps and the Senatorial Provinces," *CP* 16: 34–50.
McFayden, D. 1928. "The Newly Discovered Cyrenean Inscription and the Alleged *Imperium Maius Proconsulare* of Augustus," *CP* 23: 388–393.
Millar, F. 1966. "The Emperor, the Senate and the Provinces," *JRS* 56: 156–166 (reprinted in Millar 2002: 271–291).
Millar, F. 1977. *The Emperor in the Roman World*. London (rev. edn, with afterword, 1992).
Millar, F. 1989. "'Senatorial Provinces': An Institutional Ghost," *Ancient World* 20: 93–97 (reprinted in Millar 2002: 314–320).
Millar, F. 2002. *The Roman Republic and the Augustan Revolution* (eds H. M. Cotton and G. M. Rogers) (Rome, the Greek World, and the East 1). Chapel Hill and London.
Mommsen, T. 1887–1888. *Römisches Staatsrecht* (3rd edn). 3 vols. Leipzig.
Oliver, J. H. 1948. Review of E. Groag, *Die römischen Reichsbeamten von Achaia bis auf Diokletian* and E. Groag, *Die Reichsbeamten von Achaia in spätrömischer Zeit*. *AJPh* 69: 434–441.
Orth, W. 1978. "Zur Fabricius-Tuscus-Inschrift aus Alexandreia/Troas," *ZPE* 28: 57–60.
Pani, M. 1974. *Comitia e senato. Sulla trasformazione della procedura elettorale a Roma nell'età di Tiberio*. Bari.
Parsi Magdalain, B. 1964. "La *cura legum et morum*," *Revue d'histoire du droit* 42: 373–412.
Pelham, H. F. 1888. "The '*imperium*' of Augustus and his Successors," *Journal of Philology* 17: 27–52 (reprinted in *Essays on Roman History*, Oxford, 1911, 60–88).
Piganiol, A. 1937. "Les pouvoirs constitutionnels et le principat d'Auguste," *Journal des savants*: 150–166.
Premerstein, A. von 1937. *Vom Werden und Wesen des Prinzipats* (Abh. Bayer. Ak. Wiss., Phil.-hist. Kl., N.F. 15). Munich.
Raubitschek, A. E. 1953. "Two Notes on the *Fasti* of Achaia," in *Studies*

Presented to D. M. Robinson, II. St Louis. 330–333.

Reinhold, M. 1933. *Marcus Agrippa: A Biography*. New York.

Rich, J. W., ed. and trans., 1990. *Cassius Dio: The Augustan Settlement (Roman History 53–55.9)*. Warminster.

Rich, J. W. and Williams, J. H. C. 1999. "*Leges et iura p. R. restituit*: A New Aureus of Octavian and the Settlement of 28–27 B.C.," *NC* 159: 169–213.

Ridley, R. T. 1983. "Pompey's Commands in the 50s: How Cumulative?" *RhMus* 127: 136–148.

Roddaz, J.-M. 1984. *Marcus Agrippa* (BEFAR 253). Rome.

Roddaz, J.-M. 1992. "*Imperium*: nature et compétences à la fin de la République et au début de l'Empire," *CCGG* 3: 189–211.

Salmon, E. T. 1956. "The Evolution of Augustus' Principate," *Historia* 5: 456–478.

Scheid, J. 1992. "L'investiture impériale d'après les commentaires des Arvales," *CCGG* 3: 221–237.

Scheid, J. 1998. *Commentarii fratrum Arvalium qui supersunt: Les copies épigraphiques des protocoles annuels de la confrérie arvale (21 av.– 304 ap. J.-C.)*. Rome.

Schwartz, J. 1945. "Recherches sur les dernières années du règne d'Auguste (4–14)," *RPh* 71: 21–90.

Sherk, R. K. 1969. *Roman Documents from the Greek East*. Baltimore.

Sherk, R. K., trans. 1984. *Rome and the Greek East to the Death of Augustus* (Translated Documents of Greece & Rome 4). Cambridge.

Sherk, R. K., trans. 1988. *The Roman Empire: Augustus to Hadrian* (Translated Documents of Greece & Rome 6). Cambridge.

Siber, H. 1933. *Zur Entwicklung der römischen Prinzipatverfassung* (Abh. Säch. Ak. Wiss., Phil.-hist. Kl., 42.3). Leipzig.

Siber, H. 1937. Review of De Martino 1936. *ZSS* 57: 449–455.

Siber, H. 1940. *Das Führeramt des Augustus* (Abh. Säch. Ak. Wiss., Phil.-hist. Kl., 44.2). Leipzig.

Siber, H. 1944. "Zur Prinzipatverfassung," *ZSS* 64: 233–266.

Siber, H. 1952. *Römisches Verfassungsrecht in geschichtlicher Entwicklung*. Lahr.

Staveley, E. S. 1963. "The *fasces* and *imperium maius*," *Historia* 12: 458–484.

Stockton, D. L. 1965. "Primus and Murena," *Historia* 14: 18–40.

Strack, P. L. 1939. "Zur *tribunicia potestas* des Augustus," *Klio* 32: 358–381.

Swan, P. M. 1967. "The Consular *Fasti* of 23 B.C. and the Conspiracy of Varro Murena," *HSCP* 71: 235–247.

Syme, R. 1939. *The Roman Revolution*. Oxford.

Syme, R. 1946. Review of Siber 1940. *JRS* 36: 149–158 (reprinted in *Roman Papers* I, Oxford, 1979, 181–196).

Syme, R. 1958a. *Tacitus*. 2 vols. Oxford.

Syme, R. 1958b. "Consulates in Absence," *JRS* 48: 1–9 (reprinted in *Roman Papers* I, Oxford, 1979, 378–392).

Syme, R. 1974. "History or Biography: The Case of Tiberius Caesar," *Historia* 23: 481–496 (reprinted in *Roman Papers* III, Oxford, 1984, 937–952).

Syme, R. 1977. "How Tacitus Wrote *Annals* I–III," in *Historiographia antiqua. Commentationes Lovanienses in honorem W. Peremans septuagenarii editae*. Louvain. 231–263 (reprinted in *Roman Papers* III, 1984, 1014–1042).

Syme, R. 1979. "Some Imperial Salutations," *Phoenix* 33: 308–329 (reprinted in *Roman Papers*, III, 1984, 1198–1219).

Syme, R. 1986. *The Augustan Aristocracy*. Oxford.

Tibiletti, G. 1953. *Principe e magistrati repubblicani: ricerca di storia augustea e tiberiana*. Rome.

Timpe, D. 1962. *Untersuchungen zur Kontinuität des frühen Prinzipats* (*Historia* Einzelschriften 5), Wiesbaden.

Turpin, W. 1994. "*Res Gestae* 34.1 and the Settlement of 27 B.C.," *CQ* n.s. 44: 427–437.

Weinrib, E. J. 1968. "The Prosecution of Roman Magistrates," *Phoenix* 22: 32–56.

Wickert, L. 1941–1942. "Bericht über Literatur zur früheren Kaiserzeit aus den Jahren 1939 und 1940," *Klio* 34: 127–165.

Wickert, L. 1954. "Princeps (civitatis)," *RE* 22.2: cols 1998–2296.

Woodman, A. J., ed. 1977. *Velleius Paterculus: The Tiberian Narrative*. Cambridge.

Woodman, A. J., ed. 1983. *Velleius Paterculus: The Caesarian and Augustan Narrative*. Cambridge.

Woodman, A. J. 1998. "Tacitus on Tiberius' Accession," in *Tacitus Reviewed*. Oxford. 40–69.

4 *Augustus, War and Peace*†

J. W. RICH

For the theme of the representation and perception of Roman imperial power no individual could be more central than Augustus and no aspect of his reign of greater importance than his role as both great conqueror and bringer of peace. In this paper I shall discuss not only the presentation and perception of this aspect of the first emperor, but also the policies which lay behind the presentation.

IDEOLOGY

Augustus was proclaimed as a great victor in every contemporary medium.[1] The preamble of the *Res Gestae* declares that what follows records the achievements by which "he subjected the world to the empire of the Roman people" (*orbem terrarum imperio populi Romani subiecit*). Early in the document (3.1-4.2) Augustus tells us that "I often waged civil and external wars by land and sea through-

---

† Originally published in L. de Blois, P. Erdkamp, O. Hekster, G. de Kleijn, and S. Mols, eds., *The Representation and Perception of Roman Imperial Power: Proceedings of the Third Workshop of the International Network, Impact of Empire (Roman Empire, c. 200 B.C.-A.D. 476)*, Netherlands Institute in Rome, March 20-23, 2002. Amsterdam: J. C. Gieben, 2003, pp. 329-357.

[1] On war and peace in Augustan ideology see especially E. S. Gruen, 'Augustus and the ideology of war and peace', in R. Winkes (ed.), *The Age of Augustus* (Providence 1985), 51-72; P. Zanker, *The Power of Images in the Age of Augustus* (Ann Arbor 1988), 79 ff.; 172 ff.; 215 ff.; P. A. Brunt, *Roman Imperial Themes* (Oxford 1990), 96-109; 433-480; C. Nicolet, *Space, Geography and Politics in the Early Roman Empire* (Ann Arbor 1991), 15-56; F. V. Hickson, 'Augustus *triumphator*: manipulation of the triumphal themes in the political progam of Augustus', *Latomus* 50 (1991), 125-138; J. B. Campbell, *War and Society in Imperial Rome 31 BC-AD 284* (London 2002), 122-132. In general on the Roman cult of victory and other abstractions see J. R. Fears, *ANRW* II.17.2 (1981), 736-948 (esp. 804 ff., 884 ff. on Augustan developments). E. S. Ramage presents valuable collections of material on Augustan 'propaganda' in Gaul, Spain and Africa at *Klio* 79 (1997), 117-160; 80 (1998), 434-490; 82 (2000), 171-207. See also G. Cresci Marrone, *Ecumene Augustea* (Rome 1993); A. Mehl, 'Imperium sine fine dedi – die augusteische Vorstellung von der Grenzlosigkeit des römischen Reiches', in E. Olshausen und H. Sonnabend (eds.), *Stuttgarter Kolloquium zur historischen Geographie des Altertums* 4, 1990 (Amsterdam 1994), 431-464; K. Balbuza, 'Die Siegesideologie von Octavian Augustus', *Eos* 86 (1999), 267-299.

out the whole world" (*bella terra et mari civilia externaque toto in orbe saepe gessi*), and records among other feats his two ovations, three curule triumphs, 21 imperatorial salutations and 55 *supplicationes*. A later section (26-33) substantiates the preamble's claim of world conquest with a lengthy rehearsal of both military and diplomatic successes.

The theme was on monumental display all over the city of Rome. In the Senate House Augustus erected an altar and statue of Victory.[2] Outside, in the Roman Forum, prows from ships captured at Naulochus and Actium were displayed, following Republican precedents, on specially erected columns and on the new Rostra at the front of the temple of Divus Iulius.[3] Alongside that temple stood Augustus' triple arch, erected, as I have recently argued, to celebrate the Actium victory and later adapted to commemorate the Parthian settlement as well.[4] A short distance away was Augustus' own new Forum, built from his spoils, whose decorations, as Velleius tells us, included *tituli* [inscriptions] of the peoples he had conquered.[5] Elsewhere in the city were other commemorations of Augustus' conquests, for example the obscure Porticus ad Nationes, perhaps the model for the Sebasteion at Aphrodisias.[6] Two Egyptian obelisks were set up in 10/9 BC, with inscriptions recording their dedication to the Sun, "Egypt having been brought into the power of the Roman people" (*Aegupto in potestatem populi Romani redacta*); one was erected on the *spina* of the Circus Maximus, and the other as the *gnomon* of a meridian-instrument, laid out in the northern Campus Martius between Augustus' Mausoleum and the Altar of Pax Augusta.[7] Also in the Campus Martius stood the Porticus Vipsania, completed from Agrippa's designs by his sister. As Pliny tells us (*NH* 3.17), Agrippa planned there "to set the world before the city for inspection" (*orbem terrarum urbi spectandum propositurus*).

---

[2] Dio 51.22.1-2; V. Ehrenberg and A. H. M. Jones, *Documents illustrating the Reigns of Augustus and Tiberius* (Oxford 1967, 2nd ed.) [hereafter, EJ], 51; T. Hölscher, *Victoria Romana* (Mainz 1967), 6-17; *LTUR* 5.150 (E. Tortorici).

[3] Columns: App. *BC* 5.130; Servius, *ad. Georg.* 3.29; *LTUR* 1.308 (D. Palombi). Rostra: Dio 51.19.2; *LTUR* 3.117 (P. Gros).

[4] J. W. Rich, 'Augustus's Parthian honours, the temple of Mars Ultor and the arch in the Forum Romanum', *PBSR* 66 (1998), 71-128.

[5] *RG* 21.1; Vell. Pat. 2.39.2, with Rich 1998, op. cit. (n.4), 123-124.

[6] Servius, *ad Aen.* 8.721; R. R. R. Smith, '*Simulacra gentium*: the *Ethne* from the Sebasteion at Aphrodisias', *JRS* 78 (1988), 50-77.

[7] EJ 14, Pliny, *NH* 36.70-73. Recent studies have shown that the pavement was a meridian-instrument, not a sundial, and have refuted E. Buchner's hypothesis that its equinoctial line intersected with the Ara Pacis: M. Schutz, 'Zur Sonnenuhr auf dem Marsfeld', *Gymnasium* 97 (1990), 432-457; T. Barton, 'Augustus and Capricorn: astrological polyvalency and imperial rhetoric', *JRS* 85 (1995), 33-51, at pp. 44-46.

Brodersen has recently reminded us just how fragile is the basis for the usual view that the Porticus contained a map of the world.[8] However, even if he is right that it merely housed an inscription, the monument must still have been intended as an emblem of Augustan world rule.

Elsewhere in the empire Augustus the victor was celebrated by numerous arches, and by other monuments such as the memorial for the Actium victory erected on the site of his camp and just outside Nicopolis, the new 'Victory City', or the trophies erected at St-Bertrand-de-Comminges and La Turbie in honour of the successes in Spain, Gaul and the Alps.[9] The goddess Victory, often shown surmounting a globe (as probably in the Senate House statue), was one of the commonest types on the Augustan coinage [see Fig. 14.1.8; cf. Fig. 10.14], and this and related themes often appear in private art, for example the Boscoreale cups, where Venus is shown placing Victory on a globe held by Augustus.[10]

When civil wars ended, Octavian/Augustus was (like Caesar earlier) honoured as bringer of peace.[11] Thus the column erected after his victory over Sextus Pompeius in 36 BC bore the inscription: "Peace, long disturbed, he re-established on land and sea".[12] More in the same vein followed the victories over Antony and Cleopatra. In 29 BC, the *augurium Salutis* [augury regarding the well-being (of the state)] was held and the shrine of Janus was closed, both deemed to require universal peace.[13] The closure of Janus was an antiquarian revival of a rite whose attribution to Numa had probably been invented at the time of the only previous historical celebration in 235 BC, and of which Augustus' contemporaries will have been

---

[8] K. Brodersen, *Terra Cognita: Studien zur römischen Raumerfassung* (Hildensheim, Zurich and New York 1995), 268-285. For the usual view of the monument as a map, see especially Nicolet 1991, op. cit. (n.1), 95-122; J. Engels, *Augusteische Oikumenegeographie und Universalhistorie im Werk Strabons von Amaseia* (Stuttgart 1999), 359-377.

[9] For overviews see W. Mierse, 'Augustan building programs in the western provinces', in K. A. Raaflaub and M. Toher (eds.), *Between Republic and Empire: Interpretations of Augustus and his Principate* (Berkeley, Los Angeles and Oxford 1990), 308-333; Ramage, opp. citt. (n.1); D. Kienast, *Augustus: Prinzeps und Monarch* (Darmstadt 1999, 3rd ed.), 417-449. The Actium memorial: W. M. Murray and P. M. Petsas, *Octavian's Campsite Memorial for the Actium War* (Philadelphia 1989). Trophies: G. Charles-Picard, *Les trophées romains* (Paris 1957), 253-311; Ramage 1997, op. cit. (n.1), 125-126.

[10] Hölscher, op. cit. (n.2), 6-47; A. L. Kuttner, *Dynasty and Empire in the Age of Augustus: the Case of the Boscoreale Cups* (Berkeley, Los Angeles and Oxford 1995), 13-34.

[11] On the Roman conception of peace and on honours for Caesar and Augustus as bringers of peace see especially S. Weinstock, 'Pax and the "Ara Pacis"', *JRS* 50 (1960), 44-58, at pp. 44-50. Weinstock's suggestion that Caesar planned to institute a cult of Pax is fanciful, and his rejection of the identification of the surviving monument with the Ara Pacis Augustae is perverse, but the article remains an invaluable collection of evidence.

[12] App. *BC* 5.130.

[13] *RG* 13; EJ p. 45; Livy 1.19.3; Suet. *Aug.* 22, 31.4; Dio 51.20.4.

reminded by Varro's researches.[14] The occurrence of the same phrase in several sources' reference to this closing of Janus suggests that the senate's decree expressly linked it with the establishment of peace 'on land and sea', adapting a formula first used of Hellenistic rulers.[15] About the same time the goddess Pax figured on the coinage of both Italian and Eastern mints.[16]

Later in the reign Augustus continued to be celebrated as bringer of peace. The closure of Janus was decreed twice more during his reign, in 25 BC after his successes in Spain and at an uncertain later date.[17] An altar of Augustan Peace (Pax Augusta) was decreed on Augustus' return to Rome in 13 BC and dedicated in 9 BC, surviving to become for us the most famous of all Augustan monuments.[18] The cult is attested elsewhere too: an altar to Pax Augusta from Narbo appears from its decoration to be of Augustan date, while Strabo records Paxaugusta as the name of a colony.[19] Other provincial celebrations of Augustus the peacemaker include a well-known decree of the Koinon in Asia in 9 BC, in which he is praised as "the saviour who has brought war to an end", and the dedication of a gold statue to Augustus in the Forum Augustum at Rome by the province of Baetica "because by his beneficence and perpetual care the province has been pacified".[20]

Significant though this evidence is, it is clear that Peace was accorded much less prominence in the Augustan media than Victory.[21] There was in any case no contradiction between the

---

[14] Weinstock 1960, op. cit. (n.11), 48. See also R. Turcan, 'Janus à l'époque impériale', ANRW II.17.1 (1981), 374-402; G. Forsythe, *The Historian L. Calpurnius Piso and the Roman Annalistic Tradition* (Lanham 1994), 185-193; *LTUR* 3.92-93 (E. Tortorici).

[15] A. Momigliano, 'Terra marique', *JRS* 32 (1942), 53-64. Cicero had already spoken of Pompey as having established universal peace by land and sea: *Cat.* 2.11 *omnia sunt externa unius virtute terra marique pacata*; cf. *De imp. Cn. Pomp.* 56; *Flac.* 29; *Balb.* 16; *ILS* 8776. The inscription on the Actium memorial at Nicopolis proclaims its dedication *pace parta terra [marique]*: EJ 12; Murray and Petsas 1989, op. cit. (n.9), 76.

[16] *RIC* Augustus 252-253; 476. The goddess Peace also appears on two civic coinages of the Augustan period: *RPC* I.1529 (Pella); 2062 (Nicomedia).

[17] *RG* 13; Suet. *Aug.* 22; Dio 53.26.5; 54.36.2; Orosius 6.21.11; 22.1; R. Syme, *Roman Papers* III (Oxford 1984), 1179-1197; VI (Oxford 1991), 441-450; and see below.

[18] *RG* 12.2; EJ pp. 46; 49; Dio 54.25.3. K. Galinsky, *Augustan Culture* (Princeton 1996), 141-155, is a good recent overview; for further bibliography see Kienast, op. cit. (n.9), 239-240; *LTUR* 4.70-74 (M. Torelli). Note also the statue of Pax dedicated by Augustus, along with statues of Salus Publica and Concordia, in 10 BC (Dio 54.35.2).

[19] See Weinstock 1960, op. cit. (n.11), 48; 54. The altar: *ILS* 3789. The colony: Strabo 3.2.15 (151C). Strabo mentions the colony in his account of Spain. Not otherwise attested, it is perhaps to be identified with Pax Iulia (the modern Beja) in Lusitania. The foundation (or refoundation) will doubtless have taken place in 15-14 BC, when Augustus founded a number of colonies in Gaul and Spain (*RG* 16.1; Dio 54.23.7).

[20] EJ 42 (Baetican statue); 98 line 36 (Asian decree) [trans. Sherk, *RGE*, no. 101]

[21] Rightly remarked by Gruen, op. cit. (n.1); Ramage 1997, op. cit. (n.1), 136 ff.; Ramage 1998, op. cit. (n.1), 462 ff.

commemoration of Augustus as victor and as peacemaker, since in the Roman conception pacification was achieved through victories. Thus Cicero could speak of Macedonia as having been "pacified by many victories and triumphs" (*multis victoriis ... triumphisque pacata*), and claims for triumphs were commonly linked with the pacification of the commander's province.[22] Caesar in *On the Gallic War* repeatedly marks his progress by speaking of part or all of Gaul as "pacified" (*pacata*) by his victories.[23] Augustus himself in the *Res Gestae* asserts that tradition required the closure of Janus when over the whole empire "peace had been won by victories" (*esset parta victoriis pax*), and in his later review of his successes in war he boasts of having pacified the sea, the Gallic and Spanish provinces, Germany and the Alps.[24] Similarly, Velleius, in a brief survey of Augustus' achievements, speaks of his having "pacified the world by victories", and goes on to sketch the pacification of the West, and in particular of Dalmatia, the Alps and Spain.[25]

Nevertheless, there *was* great ambivalence both in Augustus' external achievements and in the ways in which they were perceived and presented. Augustus and those commanding under his auspices conquered more territory than anyone before or after in Roman history. The civil wars had closed with the annexation of Egypt. The achievements of Augustus' sole rule included the conquest of northwest Spain and the Alps and of a vast tract in the Balkans extending as far as the Danube. He also claimed the conquest of Germany as far as the Elbe, only to see it fall out of Roman control in his last years as a result of Varus' disaster. However, his reign also marked the end of steady Roman expansion. The empire at his death could be spoken of as "enclosed by the Ocean and by long rivers",[26] and Claudius and Trajan were the only subsequent emperors to make major additions to the empire. In avoiding expansion, his successors were following the advice which Augustus had left them. Among the documents which Augustus left and which were read out in the senate after

[22] Macedonia: Cic. *Prov. cons.* 4. Triumphs: e.g. Livy 39.29.5; 41.12.10; 41.17.3; Suet. *Iul.* 18.1.

[23] Caes. *BG* 2.35.1; 3.7.1; 28.1; 4.37.1; 6.5.1; 7.65.4.

[24] *RG* 13; 25.1 (*mare pacavi a praedonibus* ["I pacified the sea (by clearing it) of pirates"]); 26.2-3 (*Gallias et Hispanias provincias, item Germaniam qua includit Oceanus a Gadibus ad ostium Albis fluminis pacavi. Alpes a regione ea, quae proxima est Hadriano mari, ad Tuscum pacificavi* ["I pacified the Gauls and the Spains as well as Germany, all the territory bordering on Ocean that stretches from Gades (Cadiz) to the mouth of the Elbe. I pacified the Alps from the region which is nearest to the Adriatic Sea to the Tyrrhenean Sea"]).

[25] Vell. Pat. 2.89.6 (*pacatusque victoriis terrarum orbis*); 90.1; 91.1. Note also 2.126.3, where Velleius includes among the blessings of Tiberius' reign the universal diffusion of *pax augusta* [Augustan peace] (the only occurrence of the phrase in a literary source).

[26] Tac. *Ann.* 1.9.5: *mari Oceano aut amnibus longinquis saeptum imperium.*

his death was a summary of the resources of the empire, and to this summary, written in his own hand, he had appended the advice that the empire should be kept within its bounds.[27] Thus, by the end of his life, Augustus had concluded that the expansion to which he had made so notable a contribution should go no farther.

Later writers sometimes downplay Augustus' conquests, apparently influenced by their knowledge of the sequel and in some cases by their own prejudices against expansion. Thus Suetonius, writing under Hadrian, who had abjured expansion, passes over the conquests very briefly, stressing instead Augustus' restraint in his dealings with foreign peoples, and he later remarks on Augustus' insistence that battles or wars should not be begun unless the prospective gain exceeded the loss risked.[28] Florus, who criticizes the *inertia* of Augustus' successors, makes much more of Augustus' wars, but still ends his work with an effusion on Augustus' establishment of universal peace.[29] Cassius Dio, who makes no secret of his opposition to expansion in his own day, regularly depreciates Augustus' wars and perversely claims that he both preached and practised the policy of not extending the empire throughout his reign. This distorted view led him to interpret as a general statement against imperial expansion a letter sent by Augustus to the senate in 20 BC, which must in fact have had a more limited application and probably referred primarily to the decision to leave Armenia and other territories as client kingdoms rather than annexing them as provinces.[30] The emperor Julian, in his satire *The Caesars*, makes Augustus boast that "I did not give way to boundless ambition and aim at enlarging the empire at all costs, but assigned for it two

---

[27] Tac. *Aug.* 1.11.4. The failure of Suet. *Aug.* 101.4 to mention this advice is not an argument against its authenticity. According to Dio 56.33.3-6 the warning against expansion formed part of a separate document devoted to advice; this elaboration is certainly fictional and may be Dio's own work. It is uncertain whether the summary of resources with its appended advice against expansion was read along with the other documents at the first senate meeting, before Augustus' funeral (so Dio), or separately at the second session on 17 September at which Augustus' deification was decreed (so Tacitus; EJ p. 52 for the date). Tacitus' language is naturally interpreted as meaning that Augustus had added the advice in writing, not orally, *contra* J. Ober, 'Tiberius and the political testament of Augustus', *Historia* 31 (1982), 306-328. It is in any case unlikely that Tiberius would have presumed to invent the advice, as Ober maintains.

[28] Suet. *Aug.* 21; 25.4. At 21.2 Suetonius cites the oaths which Augustus administered to some barbarian chieftains and his practice on hostages as evidence of how much "he lacked the desire to increase empire or military glory by whatever means" (*tantum afuit a cupiditate quoquo modo imperium vel bellicam gloriam augendi*). The passage does not allege that he lacked such desire altogether, as supposed by, e.g., Gruen 1985, op. cit. (n.1), 67 n. 92, and Brunt 1990, op. cit. (n.1), 465, disregarding *quoquo modo*.

[29] Florus 2.34. Successors' *inertia*: Florus 1. *praef(atio)* [preface] 8.

[30] Dio 54.9.1. Other references to the supposed policy of non-expansion: 53.10.4; 56.33.5-6; 41.7. See Brunt 1990, op. cit. (n.1), 106; 462; 466-468; J. W. Rich, *Cassius Dio. The Augustan Settlement (Roman History 53-55.9)* (Warminster 1990), 17; 183.

boundaries defined as it were by nature herself, the Danube and the Euphrates".[31]

It was not only later writers who misinterpreted Augustus' intentions. Contemporary perplexities can be traced in the evidence of the poets. Parthia was the principal business which Augustus' predecessors had left unfinished. Crassus' invasion of Parthia had ended in his defeat and death at Carrhae in 53 BC, and since then the Parthians had been the Romans' great enemy. Caesar's planned invasion had been pre-empted by his death, and further humiliations had followed: the Parthians had invaded Syria in 40 BC, defeating and killing the legate L. Decidius Saxa; Antony had invaded Parthia in 36 BC, but his rearguard under Oppius Statianus had been annihilated, and winter had forced him to withdraw under Parthian harassment. The Parthians still held captives and standards from Crassus', Decidius' and Antony's armies. Other peoples too remained in defiance, including the Britons: revolt in Gaul had prevented Caesar from carrying out the conquest of Britain which he had essayed through his invasions in 55-54 BC, and no subsequent commander had taken up the challenge.

In the first years of Augustus' sole rule, Virgil, Horace and Propertius make frequent prophecies of grand conquests for Augustus which would extend Roman rule to the ends of the earth and over Parthia in particular. Several of Horace's poems also look forward to the subjugation of Britain. Horace's Regulus Ode provides a concise formulation:

> caelo tonantem credidimus Iovem
> regnare: praesens divus habebitur
> Augustus adiectis Britannis
> imperio gravibusque Persis.
>
> In heaven his thunder taught us Jupiter
> Is king. Augustus will be held a god
> Amongst us, when to the empire
> He adds the Britons and grim Persians [*sc*. Parthians].[32]

The poets may be taken as reflecting public expectations and as writing what they thought might please the emperor himself. The Roman public, then, expected Augustus to embark on great wars of

---

[31] Julian *Caesares* 326C.
[32] Hor. *Carm*. 3.5.1-4. For expected Parthian and British conquest see also Hor. *Carm*. 1.35.29-32; cf. *Epod*. 7.7-10, *Carm*. 1.21.15. For other prophecies of Parthian and wider conquest see Verg. *Georg*. 3.32-33; 4.61; *Aen*.7.603-606; Hor. *Sat*. 2.1.14-15; *Carm*. 1.2.51-52; 1.12.53-57; 1.29.1-5; 2.9.18-24; 3.3.43-48; Prop. 2.10.13-18; 3.4.1-6.

foreign conquest like those of Pompey and Caesar, and above all to subjugate the Parthians by force of arms.[33]

The expected attacks on Parthia and Britain never took place. Whether Augustus ever contemplated an invasion of Britain remains uncertain. Dio's reports that he was planning an invasion in 34, 27 and 25 BC may perhaps derive from contemporary rumours, but it is unlikely that he was seriously considering such an enterprise in those years.[34] With Parthia Augustus consistently pursued a diplomatic solution. This bore fruit in 20 BC, when he induced the Parthian king Phraates to surrender the Roman captives and standards in return for Roman friendship, and he continued to rely on diplomatic methods in his dealings with Parthia throughout the rest of his reign.

Even after the settlement of 20 BC expectations of Parthian conquest were not wholly abandoned. Thus Propertius speaks of Parthian trophies as postponed for Augustus' adopted sons Gaius and Lucius to win, and, on the eve of Gaius' departure for the East in 1 BC, Ovid prophesied the triumph he would celebrate over Parthia. In the event, Gaius restored good relations, as Augustus had no doubt always intended, meeting the new king Phraataces in person in AD 2.[35]

Horace, however, takes a different line in poems written after the settlement of 20 BC and one which is closely in accord with the picture Augustus himself was to present in the *Res Gestae*. World rule and universal peace are no longer presented as in the future, to be accomplished by Augustus' expected wars of conquest, but as having been already achieved by his military and diplomatic successes. The Parthian settlement was at the heart of this claim: Augustus maintained, with little or no justification, that he had 'compelled' the Parthians to return the Romans' standards and spoils and to seek their friendship as 'suppliants', and they are represented on the coinage and elsewhere as surrendering the standards on bended

---

[33] For full discussion of the poets' treatment of external policies and expectations see H. D. Meyer, *Die Aussenpolitik des Augustus und die augusteische Dichtung* (Cologne 1961), with the criticisms of Brunt 1990, op. cit. (n.1), 96-109, and W. Schmitthenner, *Gnomon* 37 (1965), 152-162. There is no need to suppose that Horace was offering a personal critique of Augustus' inactivity, as suggested by R. Seager, '*Neu sinas Medos equitare inultos*: Horace, the Parthians and Augustan foreign policy', *Athenaum* 58 (1980), 103-118. On the poets' relationship with the Augustan regime see above all P. White, *Promised Verse: Poets in the Society of Augustan Rome* (Cambridge, Mass. 1993).

[34] Dio 49.38.2; 53.22.5; 53.25.2; Rich 1990, op. cit. (n.30), 156-157.

[35] Prop. 4.6.80-82; Ov. *Ars am.* 1.177-228; *Rem. am.* 155-158. Gaius' meeting: Vell. Pat. 2.101; Dio 55.10a.4.

knee.³⁶ Further support was supplied by the fortuitous arrival, about the same time, of embassies from the Scythians and Indians.³⁷ Hence Horace's proud boast in the *Carmen Saeculare* [Secular Hymn]:

> iam mari terraque manus potentis
> Medus Albanasque timet securis,
> iam Scythae responsa petunt superbi
> nuper et Indi.

> Now the Mede [*sc.* the Parthian] fears the forces strong by land
> And sea and the Alban axes; now
> The Scythians, formerly proud, and the Indians
> Seek responses.

In the following lines Horace celebrates the return of Peace and Plenty along with the old Roman virtues.³⁸ These diplomatic successes along with the recent victories in Spain and the Alps are adduced as attesting universal acceptance of Roman authority in several other of Horace's poems of the period, and sometimes the Parthians' submission is explicitly linked with the closure of Janus.³⁹ The celebration of Augustan peace and world rule is later taken up by Ovid, notably in the closing lines of the *Metamorphoses* and in his treatments of Janus and the Ara Pacis in the *Fasti*.⁴⁰

The claim that Augustus had achieved world rule appears not only in the poets, in the *Res Gestae* and in art, but also in a writer as sober as Strabo. The conception of the Roman empire as effectively coterminous with the inhabited world runs through Strabo's universal geography.⁴¹ He recognises, of course, that some of the regions of which he treats, such as Britain, Parthia and India, still lay outside the empire, but he contrives to suggest that what was outside the

---

[36] *RG* 29.2: *Parthos trium exercitum Romanorum spolia et signa reddere mihi supplicesque amicitiam populi Romani petere coegi.* Kneeling Parthians: Hor. *Epist.* 1.12.28; *RIC* Augustus 287-289, 304-305, 314-315; R. M. Schneider, *Bunte Barbaren* (Worms 1986), 18-97. For other sources on the settlement of 20 BC see Rich 1990, op. cit. (n.30), 180-181. For its commemoration in art see especially Zanker 1988, op. cit. (n.1), 186-192.

[37] Listed along with other embassies from far-flung peoples at *RG* 31. Other sources include Strabo 15.1.4 (686C); 15.1.73 (719-720C); Suet. *Aug.* 21.3; Florus 2.34.62; Orosius 6.21.19. Augustus received an Indian embassy while he was in Spain and a second in Syria in 20 BC.

[38] Hor. *Carm. Saec.* 53-60.

[39] Hor. *Epist.* 1.12.25-29; 1.18.54-57; 2.1.253-256; *Carm.* 4.5.25-28; 4.14.41-52; 4.15.4-9; 4.15.21-24. The same associations reappear later at Florus 2.34. Similarly, the cuirass of the contemporary Prima Porta statue of Augustus [see Chapter 11, below, Figs. 11.7-11.8] depicts the Parthian surrender of the standards with flanking figures representing other submissive peoples.

[40] Ov. *Met.* 15.822-839; 860; *Fasti* 1.277-288; 1.711-718.

[41] See K. Clarke, *Between Geography and History: Hellenistic Constructions of the Roman World* (Oxford 1999), 307-328; Engels 1999, op. cit. (n.8), 303-313; 337-358; D. Dueck, *Strabo of Amasia: A Greek Man of Letters in Augustan Rome* (London and New York 2000), 96-129.

empire was either not worth conquering or had already effectively submitted or both. Thus he argues that the annexation of Britain would not be cost-effective and that the Britons' embassies to Augustus show the island to be already virtually subject to Rome. The Dacians too he represents as having come near to submission to the Romans, claiming that it was only their hopes of the Romans' German enemies that prevented their complete subjection. As for the Parthians, while he elsewhere speaks of them as rivals of the Romans, he optimistically concludes his sketch of the stages by which the Romans had acquired universal hegemony by adducing the Parthians' return of their spoils, entrusting of royal princes to Augustus as hostages and reception of one of these princes as king as evidence that they had gone far towards accepting Roman supremacy and were on the point of submitting themselves entirely to the Romans.[42]

Such claims were, of course, grossly exaggerated. The despatch of embassies was in itself not a mark of submission, whether from remote peoples such as the Indians and Scythians or from the much closer Britons. Augustus boasted in the *Res Gestae* that his army had "obliged the Dacians to submit to the commands of the Roman people", but in reality all that had been achieved against them had been the repulse of Dacian raiders and on one occasion a punitive expedition across the Danube.[43] Augustus had indeed erased the disgrace of past Roman defeats at Parthian hands, but at the cost of accepting peaceful co-existence with this powerful neighbour. It is no accident that we are given no details of the manner in which the Roman standards and captives were returned: we may be sure that in reality no Parthian bended the knee. Phraates' despatch of his sons to Rome served his own domestic convenience, and Vonones, sent back by Augustus to take the throne at Parthian request in AD 6, was ousted six years later.[44]

There were, however, long-established features of the Roman outlook which made it easier for Augustus and his loyal supporters

---

[42] Britain: Strabo 4.5.3 (200-210C), well discussed by D. C. Braund, *Ruling Roman Britain* (London 1996), 80-89. Dacia: 7.3.13 (305C). Parthians as rivals: 11.9.2 (515C). Effective universal rule and Parthians near submission: 6.4.2 (288C); cf. 17.3.24 (839C). There is no need to explain the apparent inconsistencies in Strabo's statements about the Parthians in terms of different stages of composition: so rightly Dueck 2000, op. cit. (n.41), 113-115; *contra* R. Syme, *Anatolica* (Oxford 1995), 365-366; Brunt 1990, op. cit. (n.1), 436-437. Similar interpretations of the Parthian royal hostages: *RG* 32.2; 33; Suet. *Aug.* 21.3.

[43] *RG* 30.2: *exercitus meus Dacorum gentes imperia populi Romani perferre coegit*. For the expedition across the Danube see EJ 43a; the commander was probably M. Vinicius, as argued by R. Syme, *Danubian Studies* (Bucharest 1971), 26-39.

[44] Strabo 16.1.28 (748-749C); Jos. *AJ* 18.41-49; Tac. *Ann.* 2.1-2.

to claim that he had brought the world under Roman rule. The Romans, like the Greeks, had a firmly Mediterranean-centred view of the world. This had made it possible for them to be spoken of as world rulers by Polybius and other Greeks since the second century BC, and Romans themselves had made such claims from at least the early first century. The vast conquests of Pompey and Caesar had further strengthened the case, and both had been acclaimed as extending Roman rule to the ends of the world.[45] Such views were facilitated not only by the limitations of contemporary geographical knowledge, but also by the ambiguities of the Roman conception of empire, which embraced not only those directly ruled in provinces but also the Romans' other friends and allies – kings, peoples and cities. Not since the early second century had they been obliged to treat with another nation on truly equal terms, and the line between friends and subjects had long been conveniently blurred. It was thus easy enough to hope that the friendship concluded with the king of Parthia might evolve into a client relationship like that with an Amyntas or a Herod and to speak as though it had already done so.[46]

Nevertheless, while the claim that Augustus had subjected the world to the empire of the Roman people stood in a well-established Roman tradition, Augustus was making a dramatic breach with the tradition in basing this claim as much on diplomatic successes as on military victories. The Parthian settlement was the first time that the Romans had resolved a major dispute with a foreign power by diplomacy rather than by force of arms, and, as we have seen, this outcome ran counter to the public's expectations. For reasons of policy Augustus decided to make a peaceful settlement, despite the pressures of tradition and popular anticipation. To compensate, he was obliged to represent the settlement as a bloodless victory, and the fervour with which it was celebrated by the poets, in the coinage and in art reflects the regime's eagerness to portray it as a great Roman success.

As I have argued elsewhere, the honours which Augustus accepted for his Parthian success were, even more than on other occasions, the outcome of a delicate negotiation between those conferring the honours (in this case, the senate) and their recipient. By a becoming parade of modesty Augustus avoided accepting honours which

---

[45] On pre-Augustan claims to Roman world rule see especially Nicolet 1991, op. cit. (n.1), 29-56, citing the evidence.
[46] Cf. Brunt 1990, op. cit. (n.1), 433-438. On the Roman conception and organization of their empire see A. W. Lintott, *Imperium Romanum: Politics and Administration* (London and New York 1993), 16-42.

would have contrasted too sharply with the bloodless character of his Parthian success, but he ensured all the same that it received exceptional commemoration. The *princeps* insisted on maintaining his by now established practice of entering the city quietly rather than in ovation or a curule triumph. He declined a new arch, but agreed that additions commemorating the settlement should be made to the Actium arch, in the form of figures of Parthians offering up standards. He declined a temple of Mars Ultor on the Capitol to house the standards, but went on to build a much larger temple to that god and partly for that purpose in his own new Forum.[47]

By contrast, the commemoration of the great Augustan wars of conquest is comparatively low-key. To some extent, this may reflect the accidents of survival. Thus Kuttner has argued plausibly that the Boscoreale cups celebrate Tiberius' triumph of 7 BC and derive from a lost monument.[48] However, it is striking how few contemporary coin types relate to the wars in central Europe: the conquest of the Alps in 15 BC is commemorated only in a small group of Lugdunum issues showing one or two soldiers (perhaps to be identified as Tiberius and Drusus) offering a branch to Augustus seated on a tribunal, while no coin issues directly relate to the great wars in Germany and the Balkans in the following years.[49] Much larger issues produced at Lugdunum over the same period show Apollo and Diana in an explicit and strangely belated celebration of the victories at Actium and Naulochus.[50]

The relatively low prominence accorded to the great victories in central Europe is no doubt to a large extent due to the fact that they were won not by Augustus himself nor by the (still infant) Gaius and Lucius whom he intended to succeed him, but by his stepsons Tiberius and Drusus. They were allowed to accumulate military

---

[47] Rich 1998, op. cit. (n.4), with earlier bibliography. On the origins of the temple of Mars Ultor and the Forum Augustum, I am in substantial agreement with M. Spannagel. *Exemplaria Principis: Untersuchungen zu Entstehung und Ausstattung des Augustusforums* (Heidelberg 1999), 15-255, on which see my review at *BMCR* 2002.03.21.

[48] Kuttner 1995, op. cit. (n.10).

[49] Soldier(s) offering branch: *RIC* Augustus 162-165. The twelve year old C. Caesar's service with the German legions in 8 BC (Dio 55.6.4) is commemorated on *RIC* Augustus 198-199. The scene shown on *RIC* Augustus 200-201 is plausibly interpreted by Kuttner 1995, op. cit. (n.10), 94-123, as representing the offer of child hostages by Gallic chieftains. The barbarian offering a *vexillum* [military standard] on *RIC* Augustus 416 is probably a Gaul rather than a German: Augustus is not known to have recovered standards from Germans, but claims to have done so from Gauls at *RG* 29.1.

[50] *RIC* Augustus 170-173; 179-183; 190-197; 204. For a different view of the commemoration of the successes in Germany see R. Wolters, 'Germanien im Jahre 8 v. Chr.', in W. Schlüter and R. Wiegels (eds), *Rom, Germanien und die Ausgrabungen von Kalkriese* (Osnabrück 1999), 591-636, at pp. 606-615.

honours, but only by a carefully staged process, culminating in Tiberius' triumph in 7 BC.[51] By then, commanders outside the imperial family had ceased to hold triumphs. Augustus himself continued to accept military honours, taking *supplicationes* [thanksgivings involving offerings of wine and incense] and imperatorial salutations and dedicating the laurels from his *fasces* on his return to Rome after a salutation. However, after the Spanish war of 26-25 BC, he no longer campaigned in person, and he had in any case resolved to hold no more triumphs, enhancing the glory of his triple triumph of 29 BC by preserving its uniqueness.[52]

POLICIES

What then were the policies which lay behind this varied record of conquest and diplomacy with its grandiose presentation and shifting public perceptions? Widely divergent answers to this question are offered by modern scholarship.

It was until comparatively recently generally assumed that Augustus' external policies were defensive and aimed at the preservation of peace throughout the empire and the establishment of secure frontiers. On this view, Augustus undertook the great advance in central Europe simply because he conceived it as necessary to secure the empire from external threats.[53]

The grand scale of Augustus' expansion to the Danube and the Elbe is an obvious difficulty for this thesis, and some have accordingly sought instead to explain this advance primarily in terms of a search for a shorter frontier. The most fully developed exposition of this view is that of Syme. For Syme Augustus was concerned not so much with frontiers as with communications, and it was to Illyricum that he attached most importance. The civil wars had revealed the possibility of a split between the eastern and western halves of the empire, and to avert this Augustus advanced to the Danube to secure the land route from Italy to the Balkans by the Save valley. With the advance to the Danube decided on, it seemed prudent to advance also to the Elbe, to provide a shorter line of communications for the more

---

[51] See further J. W. Rich, 'Drusus and the *spolia opima*', CQ 49 (1999), 544-555.
[52] See further Hickson 1991, op. cit. (n.1).
[53] W. A. Oldfather and H. V. Cantor, *The Defeat of Varus and the German Frontier Policy of Augustus* (Urbana 1916), 54-70, conveniently surveys older views. For a clear statement of the traditional view see Meyer 1961, op. cit. (n.33), 1-13. See also H. E. Stier, 'Augustusfriede und römische Klassik', ANRW II.2 (1975), 3 ff.

efficient protection of the empire against possible threats from beyond the frontier.⁵⁴

Syme's imaginative conception has been widely followed, but is surely fanciful. It was only in the later empire that Illyricum and its land route attained the strategic importance which so engaged Syme. It is unlikely that Augustus would have thought that there was much risk of the empire splitting on territorial lines, let alone that he would have conceived of an advance in Illyricum as a security against such a danger. In view of the Romans' ignorance about the geography of central Europe before his invasions, Augustus could hardly have discerned the supposed advantages of the Elbe as a frontier. Recent work has in any case effectively challenged the notion that the Roman imperial frontiers were ever conceived as linear and 'scientific', and it is altogether improbable that Augustus would have undertaken the huge advance into central Europe in the pursuit of such a chimera.⁵⁵

Other scholars have challenged the defensive interpretation of Augustus' aims and have argued instead that he sought unlimited expansion and aspired to the conquest of the whole known world. This thesis has been most cogently stated by Brunt.⁵⁶ Brunt's arguments have persuaded so many scholars that his view has now become orthodoxy.⁵⁷ This doctrine accords better than the traditional defensive interpretation both with the huge scale of Augustan expansion and with the emphasis on Augustus' victories

---

⁵⁴ R. Syme, in *CAH* X (Cambridge 1934), 340-381, esp. 351-354. For Syme's later restatements of his view see *Danubian Papers* (above, n.43), 13-25; *History in Ovid* (Oxford 1978), 51-52; *Roman Papers* VI (Oxford 1991), 129-141, 372-397.

⁵⁵ Roman frontiers not linear or 'scientific': see especially B. Isaac, *The Limits of Empire: The Roman Army in the East* (Oxford 1992, rev. ed.), esp. 372-418; C. R. Whittaker, *Frontiers of Roman Empire: A Social and Economic Study* (Baltimore and London, 1994), 1-97; S. Mattern, *Rome and the Enemy: Imperial Strategy in the Principate* (Berkeley, Los Angeles and London 1999), esp. 109-122. For critiques of Syme's theory see Brunt 1990, op. cit. (n.1), 102; 455-456; N. J. E. Austin and B. Rankov, *Exploratio: Military and Political Intelligence in the Roman World from the Second Punic War to the Battle of Adrianople* (London and New York 1995), 125-127.

⁵⁶ P. A. Brunt, review of Meyer 1961, op. cit. (n.33), *JRS* 53 (1963), 170-176, reprinted in his *Roman Imperial Themes* (above, n.1), 96-109. Brunt amplifies and in some respects modifies his view at *Roman Imperial Themes* 433-480.

⁵⁷ Brunt is followed by e.g. C. M. Wells, *The German Policy of Augustus* (Oxford 1972), 1-13; A. R. Birley, 'Roman frontiers and Roman frontier policy: some reflections on Roman imperialism', *Transactions of the Architectural and Archaeological Society of Durham and Northumberland* 3 (1974), 13-25; Ober 1982, op. cit. (n.27); P. Garnsey and R. Saller, *The Roman Empire: Economy, Society and Culture* (London 1987), 7; Nicolet, op. cit. (n.1), 29-30; T. J. Cornell, in J. W. Rich and D. G. J. Shipley, *War and Society in the Roman World* (London and New York 1993), 139-142; Mattern 1999, op. cit. (n.55), 89-91, 107; Kienast 1999, op. cit. (n.9), 332 ff. Austin and Rankov 1995, op. cit. (n.55), 127-128, doubt whether Augustus aimed at world conquest, but suppose that he sought expansion of the empire without a clear idea of how far he would advance.

and on his extension of empire in the *Res Gestae* and other media. Augustus' advice to his successors against expansion is not a difficulty, since on any view it represents a departure from the policy which he had himself earlier pursued. However, the supposition that Augustus aimed to conquer the whole world by force of arms is uncorroborated speculation and is supported neither by the contemporary testimony nor by Augustus' actions. It is true that the poets in the 20s BC envisaged military conquests extending to the ends of the earth, but, as we have seen, their expectations of British and Parthian wars came to nothing, and their later claim that Augustus has already achieved world rule through his diplomatic and military successes gives no support to Brunt's thesis. Although the Romans greatly underestimated the extent of the regions beyond the boundaries of their empire, they recognized that the unconquered territory was very large.[58] Augustus' forces launched no more than a punitive expedition across the lower Danube against the Dacians, and he decided not to extend hostilities beyond the Elbe, instructing his generals (probably from 8 BC) not to pursue emigrating tribes beyond it.[59] L. Domitius Ahenobarbus' crossing of the Elbe in AD 1 was not a breach of that instruction, since he contented himself with establishing friendship with the tribes on the farther bank and establishing an altar to Augustus.[60] Augustus could, of course, have envisaged that further advances beyond the Elbe and lower Danube might be made at some later date, but we have no warrant for supposing that he entertained such notions.

The greatest weakness of Brunt's thesis is its failure to account for the avoidance of war with Parthia. Brunt claimed that the conquest of Parthia had merely been postponed until after that of central Europe.[61] That is most implausible. If Augustus had intended to conquer Parthia as public opinion had expected, he would surely have accorded it the highest priority. That war with Parthia should be avoided if at all possible was evidently an axiom of his policy from which he never wavered.

Both Syme's and Brunt's hypotheses share the assumption that Augustus set his sights firmly on a single, overriding goal and pursued it consistently at any rate down to Varus' disaster, but it is surely more likely that his external policies evolved over the course of his

---

[58] On the Romans' conception of the extent of the regions outside the empire see Brunt 1990, op. cit. (n.1), 107-108; 449-450; 455-456; Nicolet 1991, op. cit. (n.1), 57-122; Mattern 1999, op. cit. (n.55), 24-80.
[59] Strabo 7.1.4 (291C).
[60] Dio 55.10a.2; Tac. *Ann.* 4.44.2.
[61] Brunt 1990, op. cit. (n.1), 105-107; 456; 460-464.

long reign. There is thus some attraction in the view of Gruen that, behind the grandiose rhetoric, Augustus was a simple pragmatist in these matters, responding to events as they arose.[62] However, this presents, in my view, too passive a picture to give an adequate explanation of the many external initiatives of at least the first half of Augustus' reign and in particular of the great advance into central Europe.

An adequate account of Augustus' external policies should allow for their evolution over time. It should set them against the background of the traditional expectations and assumptions of Roman dealings with external peoples. And, I would like to suggest, it should relate them more closely to internal political imperatives than has generally been customary.[63]

One such imperative we have already noticed, namely the popular expectation that he would embark on great wars of conquest. If he was not to disappoint, Augustus had either to satisfy these expectations or offer an acceptable substitute. Another imperative was Augustus' own dynastic aspirations. If he was to succeed in founding a dynasty, he needed to provide both his intended successors and other members of his family with the opportunity to acquire glory and charisma. It was clearly with this in mind that Augustus withdrew himself from frontline command at a relatively early age and from 15 BC entrusted the important campaigns in central Europe to Tiberius and Drusus. Augustus must have planned that Gaius and Lucius should have at least commensurate opportunities, but fate prevented him from achieving whatever designs he had for them.

What has not, to my mind, attracted sufficient notice is how closely Augustus' external policies were integrated with his solutions to the problems of the army and of his own position in the state.

His victory over Antony left Octavian/Augustus in control of an army of some sixty legions, in which many veterans were clamouring for their rewards. The huge ensuing demobilization reduced the army to a force of 27 or 28 legions, with their accompanying auxiliary troops, stationed in some seven provinces. In a radical departure from earlier practice, Augustus thereafter avoided raising

---

[62] E. S. Gruen, 'The imperial policy of Augustus', in K. A. Raaflaub and M. Toher (eds.), *Between Republic and Empire: Interpretations of Augustus and his Principate* (Berkeley, Los Angeles and London 1990), 395-416; id., 'The expansion of the empire under Augustus', in *CAH*² X (1996), 147-197; cf. id., 'Augustus and the ideology of war and peace' (above, n.1).

[63] The importance of political and dynastic motives from Augustus' wars is rightly stressed by Campbell 2002, op. cit. (n.1), 4-9; B. M. Levick, 'Augustan imperialism and the year 19 BC', in A. F. Basson and W. J. Dominik (eds.), *Literature, Art and History: Studies on Classical Antiquity in Honour of W. J. Henderson* (Frankfurt 2003), 305-322.

new legions for specific occasions, opting instead to meet Rome's military needs from the permanent establishment, with units being redeployed as required, and as a result he was able to develop a planned solution to the great problem of the rewards for discharged veterans.[64]

Octavian laid the basis for his own position in the state in the great settlement of 28 and 27 BC, by which he established his monarchy in a republican guise, and for which he was rewarded, among other honours, with the name Augustus. New light has been thrown on the settlement by a recently discovered aureus, dated by its obverse legend to Octavian's sixth consulship (28 BC). The reverse, which shows Octavian seated on a curule chair and holding out a scroll and bears the legend LEGES ET IVRA P R RESTITVIT ("he had restored their laws and rights to the Roman people") [= Fig. 3.1, above; cf. pp. 10 and 92 for a new interpretation of the legend], accords with his statement in the *Res Gestae* that the settlement took place over his sixth and seventh consulships, and shows that Dio was guilty of radical distortion in compressing the whole settlement into an offer to surrender power made in a single senate meeting in 27 BC. The first stages of the settlement, carried out in 28 BC, probably included not just the annulment of Octavian's illegal and unjust acts, but also other measures such as the reform of the treasury and the restoration of free elections. For the final stage, at the senate meeting of 13 January 27 BC, were left the most crucial matters: the armies and the provinces.[65]

The appointment of provincial governors presented Octavian/Augustus with a particularly delicate problem. If his claim to have transferred the republic to the control of the senate and people was to have any substance, he could not continue to appoint the governors as before, but he could not surrender the choice of military commanders without jeopardizing the control of the armies on which his power ultimately depended. The solution which he devised was one of characteristic brilliance. He announced the transfer of the provinces in the senate, but made sure that there would be protests, and then, after a show of reluctance, consented to resume the bulk

---

[64] For convenient overviews of Augustus' military reforms see K. Raaflaub, 'The political significance of Augustus' military reforms', in W. S. Hanson and L. J. F. Keppie (eds.), *Roman Frontier Studies 1979* (Oxford 1980), 1005-1026 [= Chapter 6, below]; L. Keppie, *The Making of the Roman Army* (London 1998, rev. ed.), 134-171; Kienast 1999, op. cit. (n.9), 320-332.

[65] J. W. Rich and J. H. C. Williams, '*Leges et iura p. R. restituit*: a new aureus of Octavian and the settlement of 28-27 BC', NC 159 (1999), 169-213. In general on Augustus' constitutional powers see now J.-L. Ferrary, 'À propos des pouvoirs d'Auguste', *Cahiers Glotz* 12 (2001), 101-154 [Engl. trans. = Chapter 3, above].

of the military provinces, leaving the remainder to the Roman people. This compromise permitted the resumption of sortition for the proconsuls of the public provinces, while Augustus continued to appoint the governors of his own provinces, who as his *legati* were no longer eligible for imperatorial salutations or triumphs.[66]

A justification was, however, needed for the retention of most of the military provinces, and Augustus supplied this by declaring that he was keeping them for a limited period only in order to carry out a programme of empire-wide pacification. As Dio puts it, "he retained the stronger provinces on the grounds that they were insecure and dangerous and either had enemies on their borders or were capable of launching a serious rebellion on their own", and he accepted the provinces only for ten years, promising to restore them to order within that time and to return them sooner if he completed the task more quickly.[67] The justification conformed to and built on traditional assumptions. As we have seen, commanders had commonly claimed to have pacified their provinces.[68] Pompey had been credited with worldwide pacification through his campaigns against the pirates and in Asia, not only in Cicero's speeches but also in the text of a law.[69] Augustus had been acclaimed as the bringer of peace throughout the empire by land and sea through his ending of the civil wars. He now undertook to make this claim good by accepting the command of the insecure provinces with the declared objective of pacifying both them and their neighbours.

Augustus doubtless always intended that at the expiry of the ten years it should be found that further time was needed to complete the pacification, and so indeed it proved. Dio tells us that, with fresh shows of reluctance, he accepted a five-year renewal in 18 BC, soon afterwards extended to ten, and further renewals, each time for ten years, in 8 BC, AD 3 and AD 13.[70] From Tiberius' accession in

---

[66] In general on the provincial settlement see Rich 1990, op. cit. (n.30), 141 ff. F. Millar, '"Senatorial provinces": an institutionalized ghost', *Ancient World* 20 (1989), 93-97 (reprinted in his *Rome, The Greek World and the East* I (Chapel Hill and London 2002), 314-320), rightly reminds us that those provinces not retained by Augustus were transferred to the Roman people, not the senate, and so should be spoken of as public, not senatorial provinces.

[67] Dio 53.12.2. Ten years: Dio 53.13.1.

[68] Above, nn. 22-23.

[69] Cicero: *Prov. cons.* 31, "there is no people that has not either been so utterly destroyed that it scarcely exists or so tamed that it remains submissive or so pacified that it takes delight in our victory and imperial rule"; other passages cited at n.15 above. Law: Lex Gabinia Calpurnia de Insula Delo, lines 19-20, *imperio am[pli]ficato [p]ace per orbe[m terrarum confecta]* ["its empire has been increased and peace established throughout the world"] (M. H. Crawford, *Roman Statutes* I (London 1996), 346).

[70] Dio 53.16.2; 54.12.4-5; 55.6.1; 12.3; 56.28.1; 39.6. Dio describes these extensions as renewals of the 'leadership' (*prostasia*) or 'supremacy' (*hegemonia*). This may merely reflect his

AD 14 the division of the provinces became permanent. From now on it was accepted that the emperor should hold the provinces which required a military garrison, and this conception is reflected in the way in which the contemporary Strabo and later Suetonius report Augustus' division of the provinces.[71]

The familiarity of the division of the provinces as a permanent feature of the imperial system has perhaps led us to overlook the fact that at the outset the promise of pacification cannot have been just an idle pretext. If Augustus had done nothing to implement his promise, he would have exposed the settlement as an empty charade. Thus Augustus was committed, particularly in the first part of his reign, to carrying out the programme of pacification. This will in any case have chimed well with his other interests: it required him to be absent from Rome for extended periods, a prudent device to allow the new system to bed down, and it enabled him to meet the challenge of satisfying public expectations of conquest.

So, I would argue, Augustus' external policies should be interpreted in terms of the fulfilment of the undertaking of pacification given in January 27 BC, and, particularly in the first part of the reign, the rhythm of those policies can be seen to be related to the renewals of the provincial division. In conclusion, I shall briefly sketch the outlines of such an interpretation.[72]

IMPLEMENTATION

The principal provinces which fell to Augustus in the division of 27 BC were Spain, Gaul, Syria and Egypt. This made good sense in terms of the programme of pacification: there had been recent disturbances in Gaul and Spain, Syria bordered Parthia, and Egypt was a major new acquisition, not yet fully brought under control. These provinces held the majority of the legions, but between five and eight legions overall remained in three public provinces, namely Africa,

---

interpretation of the significance of the division of the provinces, but it may alternatively indicate that Augustus accepted an informal oversight of the *res publica* at the same time: see Rich 1990, op. cit. (n.30), 139-140; Rich and Williams 1999, op. cit. (n.65), 211-212; *contra*, Ferrary 2001, op. cit. (n.65), 113-115 [= Chapter 3, above, pp. 97-99].

[71] Strabo 17.3.25 (840C) (Augustus took "those that needed a military garrison"); Suet. *Aug.* 47 ("he himself took control of the more vigorous provinces, which could not be governed by annual magistrates either easily or securely").

[72] For recent overviews of Augustus' conduct of external affairs, citing sources and further bibliography, see Gruen, opp. citt. (n.62); Kienast 1999, op. cit. (n.9), 332-377 (acutely noting the link with the division of the provinces at pp. 333, 352, 525). See also J. Bleicken, *Augustus: eine Biographie* (Berlin 2000), 565-618; W. Eck, *The Age of Augustus* (Oxford 2003), 93-104 [= 2nd ed. (Oxford 2007), 123-136].

Illyricum and Macedonia. Africa was of relatively little military importance, and Augustus could not plausibly have claimed in 27 BC that the Balkan provinces needed pacification. He himself claimed to have pacified Illyricum by his campaigns of 35-33 BC, celebrated on the first day of the triple triumph of 29 BC. As for Macedonia, the proconsul M. Licinius Crassus had recently achieved remarkable successes beyond the frontiers of the province, killing an enemy commander with his own hands and advancing to the Danube.[73]

Augustus began his programme of pacification in Spain, heading there in his first extended absence from Rome, from 27 to 24 BC. In Spain, he embarked on the conquest of the north-west, the only part of the Iberian peninsula to have remained outside Roman control. That this campaign was the first stage of the promised pacification was symbolically marked by the reopening of the temple of Janus and its second closure when he finished campaigning in 25 BC. Augustus' own campaigns did not end all resistance, but his legates, followed by Agrippa, completed its elimination before the ten-year period was up.[74]

Meanwhile in Egypt, the first three of Augustus' prefects were all militarily active. C. Cornelius Gallus subdued Upper Egypt and both he and the third prefect P. Petronius engaged with the Ethiopians. These activities could be represented as part of the programme of pacifying the troubled provinces and the regions beyond their frontiers. The expedition of the second prefect, Aelius Gallus, into Arabia was an unprovoked quest for glory and profit, although the proximity of southern Arabia to the Horn of Africa and so to Egypt's southern neighbours may have provided some shred of justification.[75] Although Aelius Gallus enjoyed little success, Petronius established a lasting settlement with the Ethiopians. It could thus be claimed that the pacification of Egypt and the neighbouring regions had been completed within the first ten-year period, and thereafter the legions stationed in Egypt seldom saw action.

Proconsuls pursued the same quest during these years. Two proconsuls of Africa, L. Sempronius Atratinus and L. Cornelius Balbus, campaigned beyond the provincial frontiers, earning what proved

---

[73] For Crassus' exploits and their significance see Dio 51.23-27; J. W. Rich, 'Augustus and the spolia opima', *Chiron* 26 (1996), 85-127.

[74] For the Spanish campaigns see Rich 1990, op. cit. (n.30), 160, with further bibliography. Janus: Dio 53.26.5; above, n.17.

[75] Cf. Strabo 16.4.22 (780C), our only evidence for the motives of Aelius Gallus' expedition, implausibly interpreted as a flanking move against Parthia by C. Marek, 'Die Expedition des Aelius Gallus nach Arabien im Jahre 25 v. Chr.', *Chiron* 23 (1993), 121-156.

to be the last triumphs celebrated by commanders who were not members of the imperial family. Nothing is known of Sempronius' campaign other than the bare fact of his triumph, but about Balbus' we are better informed: he subjugated the Garamantes, a remote desert people, and Pliny preserves the names of the communities and natural features of which images were displayed in his triumph.[76] Marcus Primus, proconsul of Macedonia, was less fortunate, being prosecuted for *maiestas* on his return. His offence, however, was not, as is usually supposed, making unauthorized war beyond the frontiers but attacking a friendly nation, the Odrysian kingdom in Thrace.[77] His reason for launching the assault remains obscure.

The Parthian question, as we have seen, was the most urgent external issue facing Augustus, and, to meet public expectations, it was essential that the matter should be satisfactorily resolved within his first ten-year period. He may at first have hoped that the pretender Tiridates would succeed in ousting king Phraates, but, when Tiridates failed, Augustus prepared for a diplomatic settlement. The policy was announced in 23 BC, when Phraates' son, who had been brought to Augustus by Tiridates, was handed over to his father's envoys with the stipulation that in return he should hand back the Roman standards and prisoners.[78] The main purpose of Augustus' Eastern journey of 22-19 BC was to secure Phraates' compliance, and this was achieved when Augustus reached Syria in 20 BC. Augustus had evidently decided from the outset on the policy of avoiding war with Parthia to which he adhered throughout his reign. The reason is not hard to seek. Crassus and Antony had failed disastrously in their attempts to conquer Parthia, and Augustus had no grounds for confidence that he would be more successful. If he had attempted the conquest of Parthia and failed, he would have suffered a grave loss of prestige at home, and his supremacy might even have been put at risk. It would have been folly for Augustus to hazard all he had achieved on such an enterprise if an acceptable diplomatic solution could be found.[79]

---

[76] *NH* 5.36-37.
[77] Dio 54.3.2; Rich 1990, op. cit. (n.30), 175-176.
[78] Dio 53.33.1-2. For Augustus' earlier dealings with Tiridates see Dio 51.18.2-3; Justin 42.5.6-9.
[79] For judicious assessments of Augustus' Parthian policy see D. Timpe, 'Zur augusteischen Partherpolitik zwischen 30 und 20 v. Chr.', *Würzburger Jahrbücher für die Altertumswissenschaft* 1 (1975), 155-169; A. N. Sherwin-White, *Roman Foreign Policy in the East* (London 1984), 323-341; J. B. Campbell, 'War and diplomacy: Rome and Parthia, 31 BC-AD 235', in J. W. Rich and D. G. J. Shipley (eds.), *War and Society in the Roman World* (London 1993), 213-240.

Also in 20 BC, an appeal from Armenia provided Augustus with a pretext for ousting the hostile king Artaxes in favour of his brother Tigranes. Augustus thus succeeded in re-establishing the Roman claim, first asserted by Pompey, to determine who should rule the Armenian kingdom. This claim was to prove the principal irritant in subsequent Roman relations with Parthia. The strategic position of Armenia between Roman Anatolia and the Parthian empire may partly account for the significance which Augustus and his successors attached to the claim, but the most important factor was probably just that Roman prestige was committed.

Thus by the time the first ten-year period expired in 18, Augustus was able to show very substantial progress in delivering the promised pacification. Roman prestige had been restored in the East; northwest Spain, which had eluded Roman control for nearly two centuries, had been brought to heel; and Roman arms had penetrated far into Africa and Arabia. Already in 22 BC he had made a first step towards the promised restoration of his provinces to the Roman people, detaching Cyprus from Syria and handing it and Gallia Narbonensis back.[80] However, when the question of renewing Augustus' term was considered in 18 and again at each of the subsequent renewals, the senators will have argued that the remaining provinces were not yet secure enough to be returned to the people, and on this occasion the argument was strengthened by the fact that Gaul had so far received relatively little attention. Augustus maintained his stance that the provincial division was only temporary by accepting the renewal of his provinces for just five years, claiming that that would suffice.

The principal tasks which Augustus set himself for this five-year period, and may indeed have announced when accepting it, were carried out during his absence in Gaul and Spain in 16-13 BC, his last extended absence from Italy: he himself re-organized the Gallic provinces, while the Alps were conquered by his legates, principally his stepsons Tiberius and Drusus. It has often been claimed that Augustus decided on the conquest of the Alps in preparation for the later advance into Germany.[81] However, control of the Alps was not essential for the advance beyond the Rhine, and the conquest is better explained in its own right, as the next stage in the Augustan pro-

---

[80] Dio 53.12.7; 54.4.1.
[81] E.g. K. Kraft, *Gesammelte Aufsätze zur antiken Geschichte und Militärgeschichte* I (Darmstadt 1973), 190 ff.; Wells 1972, op. cit. (n.57), 44-46; Kienast 1999, op. cit. (n.9), 359-360. *Contra*, K. Christ, 'Zur augusteischen Germanienpolitik', *Chiron* 7 (1977), 149-205, at pp. 167-189.

gramme of pacification. The imposition of peace and order on this region which was so close to the heart of the empire and yet had remained for so long outside the Roman people's control was fully in accord with the objectives of that programme. The conquest of the Alps may have been part of the plans which Augustus had formed when he announced the pacification programme in 27 BC, and, if not, must certainly have been included in his plans since Terentius Varro's campaign against the Salassi in 25 BC.

So by 13 BC it could be claimed that Augustus had brought peace to all the provinces assigned to him, and this is surely what is implied by the decreeing of the Altar of Augustan Peace on his return to Rome in that year. The gradual restoration of provinces to the Roman people was probably continued by the division of Hispania Ulterior and transfer of the southern portion as the new public province of Baetica.[82] However, it would not at all have suited Augustus for his task to be thought at an end. New frontiers of pacification were needed and were supplied by the great expansion into central Europe, which began in 12 BC.

Recent disturbances provided the pretexts for the advance into central Europe. There had been recurrent fighting in the Balkans since about 18 BC.[83] The Sugambri and other German tribes crossed the Rhine in 16 BC, inflicting a defeat on M. Lollius; Augustus hastened his departure from Rome, but, before he reached Gaul, Lollius had imposed a settlement.[84] A further incursion in 12 BC provided the immediate pretext for Drusus' invasion of Germany, but it must have been planned well in advance: Drusus had at his disposal a fleet and a canal from the Rhine to the IJsselmeer (the *fossa Drusiana*), both of which would have taken a considerable time to construct, and it is likely that the redeployment to new bases on the Rhine had been in progress for some years.[85] Thus the decision that a major offensive would in due course be launched in central Europe is likely to have been taken no later than 16 BC, in the aftermath of the German invasion and Lollius' defeat.

It is disputed when Augustus first formed the design of expanding in central Europe, but it seems to me most likely that his decision was prompted by the German invasion of Gaul in 16 BC and the contem-

---

[82] Best dated c. 13 BC: Rich 1990, op. cit. (n.30), with further bibliography.
[83] Dio 54.20.2-3; 24.3; 28.1.
[84] Dio 54.20.4-6; Vell. Pat. 2.97.1; Tac. *Ann.* 1.10.3; Suet. *Aug.* 23.1; Obsequens 71. The invasion is to be dated to 16 BC in view of the agreement of Dio and Velleius, rather than 17 BC with Obsequens.
[85] The 12 BC incursion: Dio 54.32.1. Preparations: Dio 54.32.2-3; Strabo 7.1.3 (290C); Tac. *Ann.* 2.8.1; Suet. *Claud.* 1.2; Wells 1972, op. cit. (n.57), 93 ff.

porary disturbances in the Balkans.[86] The exclusion of the Balkan provinces from Augustus' original share shows that expansion in this region had not figured in his initial plans, and it was probably the renewed uprisings there that led to the change in policy. German threats to the peace of Gaul are reported on several occasions in the years before 16 BC.[87] However, the major incursion of that year gave the issue a new urgency. Dio tells us that, having taken only a five-year renewal of the division of the provinces in 18 BC, Augustus soon after accepted an additional five years.[88] If he had already decided on the advance into central Europe by 18 BC, it is hard to see why he did not take a ten-year renewal at that point. It is a tempting conjecture that Augustus took the further five-year extension in 16 BC before his departure for Gaul and in the immediate aftermath of the German invasion, and that the new threats from Germany and in the Balkans were given as the justification.

Internal political imperatives – the need to justify the continued division of the provinces and to provide the princes of the imperial house with further opportunities to win military glory – necessitated further warfare and expansion, but central Europe was not the only possible direction. An alternative option was Britain, and it may well be that, if the Germans and the Balkan peoples had not drawn attention to themselves, it would have been there that Augustus would have turned next. He could readily have claimed, as Caesar had done before and Claudius was to do later, that the security of Gaul required the subjection of Britain to Roman rule. He had disappointed the public over Parthia, but could easily have satisfied their expectations of British conquests.[89]

---

[86] For a survey of views see Christ 1977, op. cit. (n.81), 149 ff.

[87] Dio 51.20.5; 51.21.6; 53.26.4; 54.11.12. It is uncertain whether Agrippa's resettlement of the Ubii on the left bank of the Rhine (Strabo 4.3.4 (194C)) took place in 39/8 BC or 20/19 BC: see J.-M. Roddaz, *Marcus Agrippa* (Rome, 1984), 384-388; Kienast 1999, op. cit. (n.9), 356-357.

[88] Dio 54.12.5.

[89] On Augustan policy towards Britain see Braund 1996, op. cit. (n.42), 76 ff. Brunt 1990, op. cit. (n.1), 103-104, infers from Hor. *Carm*. 4.14.41-52, that the British embassies to Augustus, adduced by Strabo in justification of the failure to invade (above, n.42), had already arrived by the time of the poem's composition in or soon after 15 BC. However, Horace here lists peoples against whom military or diplomatic successes had been achieved as showing awe or veneration for Augustus: "you the previously untamable Cantabrian, the Mede and the Indian, you the nomadic Scythian now revere ... you the Sygambrians who glory in slaughter now venerate after laying down their arms" (in the case of the Sugambri the reference must be to Lollius' settlement: Dio 54.20.6). By contrast the Britons are introduced only obliquely, in association with Ocean ("Ocean, full of whales, which thunders up against the (shoreline of the) remote Britons"). This suggests that by 15 BC no diplomatic success had yet been achieved against the Britons and that public opinion may still have envisaged the possibility of an invasion.

In Illyricum the original intention may have been merely to re-establish the settlement which Augustus had achieved in his campaigns of 35-33 BC. This may explain why that region was originally allotted to Agrippa; the despatch to Germany of Tiberius and Drusus, who had the greater need to acquire military glory, suggests that Augustus regarded this as the more glamorous assignment. However, Agrippa's death led to Tiberius' transfer to Illyricum, and the Roman aims in the Balkans probably became more extensive as the fighting dragged on. In Illyricum itself Tiberius encountered repeated resistance, while L. Calpurnius Piso was summoned with reinforcements from Galatia-Pamphylia to deal with an uprising in neighbouring Thrace. By 8 BC Roman control had been extended up to the Danube along the whole of its lower and middle course. One consequence was the demilitarization of the public provinces in this region. Illyricum was transferred to Augustus, and the legions were stationed there and in what was to become the new imperial province of Moesia, relieving the proconsuls of Macedonia of military command and leaving Africa as the only public province whose proconsul commanded a legion.[90]

In Germany too the Romans' plans may have evolved in the course of the campaigns. Drusus began by advancing against the Sugambri and their allies both by sea and by land, up the Lippe valley. The defection of the Chatti obliged him to extend operations to the Main valley in 10 BC and in 9 BC he advanced as far as the Elbe, but died on the way back. Tiberius in 8 BC brought the warfare to what was proclaimed as a successful conclusion, celebrated in his triumph of 1 January 7 BC. How much had been accomplished by these campaigns has been much disputed. Archaeology has shown that Roman military occupation in Germany was confined for the most part to the right bank of the Rhine and its immediate hinterland, and some hold that the campaigns aimed not at conquest but merely at demonstrating Roman power. Dio's minimizing of Tiberius' achievements in 8 BC lends some support to this view.[91] Other literary evidence, however, reveals that it is a misconception. As these sources show, all the tribes remaining in Germany up to the Elbe performed acts of surrender (*deditiones*); the Sugambri, the principal belligerents, were deported west of the Rhine; the Marcomanni and Suebi avoided submission by migrating eastwards, and it was surely now

---

[90] Dio 53.12.4; 54.34.4; Rich 1990, op. cit. (n.30), 141; 214.
[91] Dio 55.6.1-4.

that Augustus ruled against pursuing the fugitives beyond the Elbe.⁹² This settlement satisfied traditional Roman expectations of conquest. It was indeed far from establishing full provincial government in the newly conquered region, but the same had been true of the initial phases of many earlier conquests, for example central Spain in the early second century or Caesar's Gaul.⁹³

At the start of the year 8 BC Augustus accepted a ten-year renewal of the division of the provinces after the usual protestations of reluctance.⁹⁴ There was now no need to seek out new regions requiring pacification in order to justify the renewal. It would take a long time for the great new conquests to be absorbed and Roman control in these lands to be consolidated. This in itself provided sufficient foundation for the argument that the territories which Augustus had pacified were not yet secure enough to be handed over to the Roman people and its proconsuls. Although ten-year renewals and ritual protestations continued to the end of Augustus' reign, the division of the provinces had now effectively become permanent.

One mark of this change may be the ending of the use of the Janus ritual to mark phases of pacification. The shrine was closed for the second time, as we have seen, in 25 BC. We do not know when it was reopened: it may well have remained shut until Augustus went out to Gaul in 16 BC immediately following the German invasion of that year.⁹⁵ The third closure is equally mysterious. Dio records a senatorial decree ordaining that the shrine be closed in 11 BC, not implemented because of renewed hostilities in the Balkans. It may well be that there was no third closure and that the shrine remained open from 16 BC until the reign of Nero.⁹⁶

---

⁹² Cassiodorus, *Chronica Minora* 2.135 ("all the Germans between the Elbe and the Rhine surrendered to Tiberius Nero", perhaps from Aufidius Bassus); Strabo 7.1.3-4 (290-1C); Vell. Pat. 2.97.4; 2.108.2; Tac. *Ann.* 2.26.3; 12.39.2; Suet. *Aug.* 21; *Tib.* 9.2; Eutropius 7.9; Orosius 6.21.24.

⁹³ The view taken here (as already at Rich 1990, op. cit. (n.30), 223-224) is similar to that of Wolters 1999, op. cit. (n.50). Other views are surveyed by J. Deininger, 'Germaniam pacare. Zur neueren Diskussion über die Strategie des Augustus gegenüber Germanien', *Chiron* 30 (2000), 749-771.

⁹⁴ Dio 55.6.1.

⁹⁵ The shrine can hardly have been opened when Augustus left for the East in 22 BC, as suggested by Syme 1984, op. cit. (n.17), 1181. Although Augustus may have used threats to ensure Parthian compliance, an announcement of war would have been inappropriate at a time when he was seeking to confirm the friendly relations initiated in 23 BC (above, n.78). If the shrine had been opened in 22 BC, it would surely have been closed again after the Parthian settlement, and this closure is unlikely to have gone unrecorded.

⁹⁶ Dio 54.36.2; Rich 1990, op. cit. (n.30), 163; 216. Suet. *Aug.* 22, states that Augustus closed the shrine thrice, but Augustus himself merely states that the senate thrice decreed its closure (*RG 13*). Orosius' statement (6.22) that the shrine was closed in 2 BC (on his reckoning the year of Christ's nativity) is a patent Christianizing fiction. Syme 1984 and 1991, opp. citt. (n.17), argues for closure in 7 BC, reopening in 1 BC.

Augustus doubtless envisaged further military initiatives after 8 BC. Major new campaigns would be needed to enable the princes of his family to win laurels, above all his intended successors Gaius and Lucius. Possibly he was now reserving Britain for them. Fate, however, decreed otherwise. The death of Drusus and Tiberius' withdrawal to Rhodes in 6 BC left Augustus for a time with no available commander from the imperial house. When the nineteen year old Gaius was sent east in 1 BC, the objectives were not primarily military, despite Ovid's expectations, but rather to show him off to the eastern provinces and to re-establish good relations with Parthia. In the event he did engage in some campaigning, in Arabia and, fatally, in Armenia.[97] However, the great wars that Augustus must have planned for the young princes were forestalled by the deaths of Lucius in AD 2 and Gaius in AD 4.

When Tiberius was restored to favour after Gaius' death, the initiative was resumed: rebellion in Germany was crushed with the sweeping campaigns of AD 4-5, and for AD 6 an advance was planned against the Marcomanni and their ruler Maroboduus. This action, like Augustus' previous advances, was represented as necessary for the security of territories under Roman rule, in this case at least a very specious justification.[98] However, the Marcomanni were spared: the Pannonian Revolt supervened, followed in AD 9 by Varus' disaster and the loss of all that had been gained in Germany.

It was doubtless these disappointments of his final years which led to the new policy of not extending the empire beyond its bounds which Augustus enunciated in his posthumous advice. Its significance, however, remains ambivalent. In Germany, in particular, it is not clear where Augustus wished the bounds of empire to be set. The Rhine was the effective limit of Roman control at the time of his death, but the presence of a substantial army on the Rhine under the command of Germanicus suggests that he had not abandoned the hope of re-establishing Roman control up to the Elbe. That certainly was Germanicus' plan, and it was left to Tiberius in AD 16 to order the final withdrawal to the Rhine.[99]

It is likely enough that until his last years Augustus envisaged that Roman expansion would continue and that over time Roman claims

---

[97] On Gaius Caesar in the East see F. E. Romer, 'Gaius Caesar's military diplomacy in the East', *TAPA* 109 (1979), 199-214; Syme 1978, op. cit. (n.54), 8-11; Syme 1995, op. cit. (n.42), 317-334.

[98] Vell. Pat. 2.109.

[99] For the view that Augustus still regarded the Elbe as the boundary see e.g. Kienast (1999), op. cit. (n.9), 373-375.

to world rule would come increasingly to correspond to the realities. However, he did not envisage universal conquest by force of arms, for towards Parthia it was his settled principle that the Romans should proceed by diplomacy rather than by military might. Augustus' external policies were in any case not shaped by a global strategic conception. They evolved over time, and were determined above all by internal political imperatives and by his personal ambitions for himself and his successors, with a central part being played, particularly in the first half of his sole reign, by the programme of pacification which he presented as the justification for the division of the provinces by which he perpetuated his power.[100]

---

[100] Earlier versions of this paper were given at the Rome conference which gave rise to this volume [= de Blois et al. (2003)] and also at Aberystwyth, Exeter, Leeds, Manchester, Newcastle, Paris and Perugia. I am very grateful to the audiences on these occasions for their comments.

5 Livia and the Womanhood of Rome†¹

NICHOLAS PURCELL

I

See how Fortune has raised you high, and commanded you to occupy a place of great honour; so, Livia, bear up that load. You draw our eyes and ears to you, we notice all your actions, and the word of a *princeps*, once spoken, cannot be concealed. Stay upright, rise above your woes, keep your spirit unbroken – in so far as you can. Our search for models of virtue, certainly, will be better when you take on the rôle of first lady of Rome (*Romana princeps*).²

These words were written by a Roman *eques* just after he had taken part in the funeral of Livia's son Drusus in 9 B.C.; they derive from a poem known conventionally as the *Epicedion Drusi* [*Funeral Lament for Drusus*] or *Consolatio ad Liviam* [*Consolation to Livia*].³ Drusus, consul in that year, had died of an illness on cam-

---

† Originally published in the *Proceedings of the Cambridge Philological Society*, n.s. 32 (1986), 78-105.
¹ Versions of this paper have been given at a seminar at St. Andrews and at the Cambridge Philological Society: I am grateful to the audience on both occasions for suggestions and comments. Livia has not been well served by historical scholarship in recent years; one exception is the interesting article of Marleen Boudreau Flory, 'Sic exempla parantur: Livia's shrine to Concordia and the Porticus Liviae', *Historia* 33 (1984) 309-30. Useful material is collected by Gertrude Grether, 'Livia and the Roman imperial cult', *AJPh* 67 (1946) 222-52. For basic reference the survey of Lotte Ollendorff in *RE* 13 (1926) 900-24 is to be recommended. I have not seen H. Willrich, *Livia* (1911). One aim of the present collection of material and attempt to interrogate it is to show how much more can be attempted with the quite copious evidence than has been to date.
² *Consolatio ad Liviam*, 349-56:
 en posuit te alte Fortuna locumque tueri
  iussit honoratum: Liuia, perfer onus.
 ad te oculos auresque trahis, tua facta notamus,
  nec uox missa potest principis ore tegi.
 alta mane, supraque tuos exsurge dolores
  infragilemque animum, quod potes, usque tene.
 ac melius certe uirtutum exempla petemus
  cum tu Romanae principis edis opus.
³ For the authenticity of the *Consolatio*, once doubted, see the edition of E. Baehrens, *Poetae Latini Minores* vol I (1879) 97-101; for the equestrian rank of its author, *Consolatio* 202. For

paign east of the Rhine; for his successes against the Germans he had been about to receive various honours at Rome, including a triumph. Among these one of the more outstanding was the banquet for the principal women of the city which his mother and step-sister (Julia, Augustus' daughter by Scribonia) were to give in his honour; a celebration which they had previously organized for Drusus' brother Tiberius, to commemorate the pacification of Pannonia.[4] But 'a cortège not a triumph is your lot, and the tomb, rather than the citadel of Jove, awaits Drusus'.[5] To form part of the official consolation of the bereaved mother, alongside private efforts like the *Consolatio* itself, she was awarded the privileges of mothers of three children and a series of statues in prominent places in the city. This disastrous episode in the long saga of the 'woes of Caesar Augustus'[6] presents the historian with a striking introduction to Livia Drusilla, the wife of the *princeps*; she herself is produced as nothing less than *Romana princeps* [first lady of Rome], or *princeps femina* [leading woman] in the Roman polity.[7] We see her fully involved in the public life of the Augustan state. It is this public rôle that I want to examine in this paper.

Is the expression *princeps femina* an absurd hyperbole? Is our equestrian author quite wild in using a phrase which is almost an oxymoron, combining as it does a firmly political word full of the connotations of the highest *auctoritas* in the *res publica*, with the essentially and basically unpolitical, apolitical idea – as it was to the ancient world – of womanhood? And if he is not, if a real context for this phrase can be found in the thought-world of Augustan Rome, are we dealing with a paradox designed to heighten the glamour of Augustus and his immediate circle, or with some wider association of the female with the *res publica*?

The personality of Livia the human being is, naturally enough, the preserve of speculation or historical fiction. The images of her which were projected to the Roman world in her lifetime and afterwards,

---

the date and composition of the *Consolatio*, with recent bibliography, John Richmond, *ANRW* II 31.4 (1981) 2768-83. He argues for a date between A.D. 12 and A.D. 37, mainly on literary grounds which I am not qualified to assess; but the *terminus post quem* of the dedication of the temple of Castor by Tiberius in A.D. 6 will not stand, since the rebuilding in honour of his relationship with Drusus, like that of the Temple of Concord, was planned already in at least 7 B.C. If the piece is not Augustan, a Claudian date is clearly most appropriate historically; the issue does not greatly affect the argument of this article.

[4] Dio 55.2.4 For the preparation for triumphs by women see also Ovid *Pont*. 3.4.95 f.; Dio 55.8.2.

[5] *Consolatio* 27-8.

[6] Cf. *Consolatio* 66-74, esp. 71-2. The theme is elaborated by Seneca *Marc*. 2-4.

[7] For the phrase *princeps femina*, cf. Ovid *Pont*. 3.1.125.

composed of value-judgements and reported actions, are the proper raw material of history. It is a copious array of material, too, and it is odd that there have been no proper syntheses, let alone interpretations. There has even been a general lack of sidelong considerations of Livia's part in the Augustan principate in discussions where it has an important contribution to make. The most likely cause of this neglect is the overwhelming attention paid to the person of Augustus himself at the expense of all his associates. While clearly the product of the events and atmosphere of the principate, this exclusiveness is not, I believe, the intentional self-presentation of the first *princeps*, which is why I will in this account be playing down the first of the two possibilities mentioned above, that peculiarities in the role of Livia can be satisfactorily explained simply in terms of the honour that they did Augustus.

While monarchic views of the principate prevailed, and while Augustus tended to be perceived as the founder of that monarchic principate *tout court*, Livia was just one of the many historical figures completely over-shadowed by the great protagonist. She was seen as a mere appendage, demoted into being simply the vehicle for the transmission of the divine and royal blood. She became simply one of the stock inhabitants of the *aula* [court], a scheming woman at the court with only the wiles of womankind to assist her meddling ambitions. Petticoat-power, one might say, and the emperor Caligula has been translated as calling her 'Odysseus in petticoats'.[8]

The translation says it all. Caligula's phrase was *Ulixes stolatus*. He understood Julio-Claudian Rome and the role of women in it well enough not to use of Livia a phrase with the nuance of cumbersome undergarments. The *stola* of the phrase was the dress of the *matrona* [matron, i.e., married woman], so respectable a garment that to be called just *stolata* in the formal language of documents of the imperial period was a sufficient indication of high rank.[9] It was the equivalent of the *toga*, a garment whose use was sharply defined and controlled. That women had an equivalent of the *toga* is a striking feature of Roman life, and all the more important when the *toga* itself was becoming increasingly the symbol of the better sort of Roman citizen, the kind who took the responsibility of forming a part of the *res publica* seriously. Women too formed a part of the *res publica*, and had their part to play in its formal existence. Now that we have

---

[8] Suet. *Calig.* 23.2.
[9] On the *stola RE* 4A (1932) 58-62, and cf. Festus p.112 L 'they called matrons just those who had the right to wear the stola'. Examples of the phrase *stolata femina* ['stolate woman']: *CIL* III 5225, 5283, 5293, 6155.

come to see more clearly how Augustus was the architect – over fifty years – not just of a set of constitutional innovations but of a complete remodelling of the social structure of the *res publica*, it is high time that all the constituent parts received adequate attention. Alongside the parts to be played by the senator, the *eques*, the freedman, the soldier and so on there was a new expression of what was to be expected of the women of Rome; and in developing that the example of Augustus' own household, and above all of Livia, was paramount.

This article is about a frontier – the frontier between the domestic and the public, between affairs of state and of the family, between politics and household management, between forum and atrium. Our approach, as historians, to the Augustan age must explore this boundary, as it is central to understanding the changes in the Roman polity which we label *res publica restituta* [the Republic restored], 'Augustus' constitutional position', 'the founding of the Empire' or 'the social reforms of the *nouus status* [the new state of affairs]'. All these developments were, whether planned or not, a matter of redefining the demarcation between the political world and the household world. That demarcation has been considered too simply; it is not an obvious, single, easily perceived on-off line, but a remarkably nuanced zone of transition, whose geography has to be painstakingly reconnoitred before explanation can begin. Livia, as the quotation above suggests, did cross the frontier, and the complex processes by which she did so may help us to understand its nature; for crossing it the reward was, finally, deification; the penalty, a scurrilous vilification in the popular tradition which goes beyond most ancient invective in its hostility.

II

'For she had become puffed up to an enormous extent, surpassing all women before her, and would even make a regular habit of receiving in her house any of the senate and people who wanted. This is a fact that was entered in the public records.' Dio goes on to note with wonder how Livia shared Tiberius' principate to the extent of their receiving addresses and issuing pronouncements jointly.[10] Petticoat-power? Or the natural result of Augustus' policy? The phenomenon

---

[10] Dio 57.12.2 'Her status had swollen far beyond that of any woman of the past, so that she had long received in her house at her *salutatio* [daily ritual greeting ceremony] the senate and any of the plebs who wanted to – and these occasions were entered in the public records'; and he goes on to allege that 'she set about managing everything else as if she were ruling alone'.

would not have surprised the author of the *Consolatio*: What good, he asks, is it to the wretched Livia, to be so virtuous? The passage is worth quoting, as it is so ineptly revealing:

> What good are your good habits, and a lifetime purely spent in pleasing so great a man so much? What use is it to have wrapped chastity up in such a bundle of virtues that it takes least position among your praises? Why should you have kept your heart righteous in times that were not and held your head up among all their vice?

So far the praise certainly seems conventional enough. But the author proceeds –

> What good is it not to have harmed anyone though you were in a position to harm; that no-one has lived in terror of your slaves; what good that your political strength has not romped through voting-assembly or forum and that [most sinisterly bland] you have called a halt short of where you were allowed to ... ?[11]

This is our *Romana princeps* again, a woman who has not usurped influence by feminine wiles, but a public figure to whom a vast amount is allowed – the word is *licet* – and whose virtue is the moderation of the statesman as much as the submission of the wife. Her power is quite simply *auctoritas*: what was its basis?

In the Roman past, especially as interpreted and transmitted by Livy, the women of the city had played a public role on many occasions. In moments of crisis they acted in concert to intercede with the Gods. Their role in officially expressing public grief, which we met at the funeral of Drusus, goes right back to the last rites of the first consuls of the Republic in Livy or to the exequies of Sulla and Julius Caesar.[12] They might help in more mundane ways by the

---

[11] *Consolatio* 41-50:
> quid tibi nunc mores prosunt et puriter actum
> omne aeuum et tanto tam placuisse uiro?
> quidque, pudicitia tantum inuoluisse bonorum,
> ultima sit laudes inter ut illa tuas?
> quid tenuise animum contra sua saecula rectum,
> altius et uitiis exercuisse caput
> nec nocuisse ulli et fortunam habuisse nocendi,
> nec quemquam seruos extimuisse tuos
> nec uires errasse tuas campoue foroue
> quamque licet citra constituisse modum?

[12] For the early involvement of women in Roman religion, J. Gagé, *Matronalia* (1963). An important rôle-model was of course the *Virgines Vestales* [Vestal Virgins], on whom see Mary Beard, *JRS* 70 (1980) 12-27. Their sacral, public, rôle ensured that they could move outside the normal female world. For Livia's position in relation to them Dio 60.5; 59.3.4; Suet. *Calig.* 15.2; see also Boudreau Flory, *Porticus Liviae*, 320-1 and below, pp. 174-176 with nn. 32 and 40. Official grief: the first consuls, Livy 2.7.4 cf 2.16.7; Sulla, Gran. Lic. 33.4; Caesar, Suet. *Iul.* 84. 4.

gift of their adornments. Thus the *coetus* [meeting] of the *matronae* at the time of the Gallic sack decided to contribute to the needs of the state, and they were duly honoured afterwards with a formal vote of thanks and the right to *sollemnis laudatio* [solemn eulogy].[13] This was the tradition which lay behind and linked the famous examples of matronly probity in the Republic, Quinta Claudia and virtue vindicated by the Gods, or Cornelia the mother of the Gracchi.[14] The episode of Hortensia and the Triumvirs is also of great interest for the public role of the *ordo matronarum* [order of matrons].[15] The Triumvirs in 42 B.C. attempted to tax the wealthy women of Rome. They chose to identify a group of 1400 of the richest women, order them to produce a valuation of their property, and pay a certain fixed percentage to the State. In protest the women assembled and made formal petition to Antony's mother, Octavian's sister Octavia and Antony's wife Fulvia. The first two received them courteously, for all the world like male politicians: Fulvia insulted them by driving them away. This they made the excuse for holding a formal public meeting in the Forum in front of the Triumvirs; Hortensia delivered a speech which in Appian's version has reminiscences of the debate on the *lex Oppia* in Livy (below, pp. 173-174) and is striking for its sense of the history of Rome's women. The whole action was clearly seen as quite unproper and desperate but the women were protected from the *coercitio* [coercion] of the magistrates by popular support and outcry. The result was a reduction of the group bearing the burden from 1400 to 400. What impresses here, apart from the courage and initiative of the women and the eloquence of Hortensia, is the way in which the women were used to behaving in ways analogous to the male political world. It was not their actual doings here that were irregular, simply that they were doing them in the male public world. The presence of *principes* [leading citizens] among them is noteworthy too; the pre-eminence of Livia is partly foreshadowed by the activities of some of these women, perhaps most notably Fulvia.[16] This is a rather different rôle from the more restrained and passive

---

[13] Livy 5.25.8, 50.7.

[14] For Claudia see Cic. *Har. resp.* 27; Diod. Sic. 34.33.2, both accounts involving *matronae* alongside the men of the city. Livy 29.14.12. has a rather different version. The early accounts were contradicted by Diodorus' source, Valerius Antias, who substituted a Valeria for Claudia as *castissima matronarum* ['the most chaste of matrons']; see T. P. Wiseman, *Clio's cosmetics* (1979) 94-9, 115-16. Cornelia, *RE* 4 (1901) 1592-5.

[15] App. *BC* 4.5.32-4; Val. Max. 8.3.3.

[16] Fulvia, *RE* 7 (1912), 281-4. Her remarkable career certainly involved acting politically and adopting male roles, but whereas Livia was advanced through the barriers gradually by more or less legal paths, Fulvia, in more troubled times, simply ignored them. The comparison is instructive.

public virtue of Claudia or Cornelia, still revealed in the last days of Republic by, for example, the fortitude of the wife of Lepidus, sitting at her wool-working as the rioters burst in to the patrician *domus* [house].[17]

The moral rectitude of the *matrona* was something much more than being loyal, subservient, faithful, obliging, the virtues of the harem: the Greek scholar who said that the Romans call *matronae* what the Greeks know as οἰκοδεσποίναι [mistresses of the house][18] was being misleading, for womanly virtue at Rome had a truly public face, and should not be dismissed as if it were simply domestic goodness of so striking a kind that the state occasionally condescended to notice it. We are prepared to accept that male virtues such as *grauitas* [seriousness of purpose], *fides* [trustworthiness], *abstinentia* [self-restraint] and so on form an important part of a directly political public image; we should not be slow to recognize that something analogous is true of the *matrona* too. Both the public rôle and the expression of the virtues which underlay it continue well beyond the Republic.

Very scattered evidence tells us of a formal organization of the *matronae* on the model of the senate. The most explicit comes from the worst of sources; the Scriptores Historiae Augustae, and within it from the least reliable of the *Lives*, that of Varius Elagabalus.[19]

The perverted antiquarianism of the author, in his search for curious inversions for the emperor, turns to the field of women's public rôle. His account may express partly the distaste which was felt at the time for the public role of Julia Soaemias Bassiana. Elagabalus is said to have had her bidden to the senate as a member on the first meeting after his accession and to have ensured that she took her place among those who authenticated *senatus consulta* – a process which the author feels the need to gloss. He also describes the *conuentus matronalis* [gathering of matrons] which met for religious purposes on the Quirinal, and how this was converted into a female senate. The description of the status quo is made more plausible by an allusion to the *consularis coniugii ornamenta* [insignia of marriage to a man of consular rank], about which we happen to know from a passage of Ulpian. A woman who marries a consular gains a consular status herself, which she retains even if, when widowed, she marries a man of lower status. This right needed to be

---

[17] Asconius *Mil.* 38.
[18] Lydus *De mens.* 4.29.
[19] *Heliog.* 4.1-4. On the subject see now R. J. A. Talbert, *The senate of imperial Rome* (1985) 160-1, cf. 493-4.

asked for, and was conferred by Caracalla on Julia Mamaea.[20] The text of Ulpian tells us nothing about whether this privilege was conferred on the Quirinal hill as the biographer alleges (cf. n.33). But the other texts in this chapter of the *Digest*[21] confirm that women gained the status of *clarissima* [most distinguished] or *consularis* [of consular rank] from their husbands and sons, and so the biographer is right in his nuance when he says that Elagabalus' innovation was to let a *clarissima* behave like a senator. Later in the *Historia Augusta*[22] we hear how Aurelian likewise planned to recreate this *senaculum* [lit. 'minor senate'], creating in it a hierarchy in which seniority went to those whom the senate had granted priesthoods. Here the idea is not scorned; but Elagabalus' mother was said to have passed a series of *senatusconsulta ridicula de legibus matronalibus* [absurd senatorial decrees on the laws about married women], minutely regulating clothing, deportment and transport.[23] In 1911 Stuart Hay, the author of a general work on Elagabalus, took the *Historia Augusta* literally. His words have a somewhat period feel: 'Today, despite the fact that we have progressed by eighteen centuries, it is generally believed in governmental circles that such matters are possibly best settled by women, and such useful, not to say necessary functions concerning the polite amenities of civilised existence would be most readily conceded by authority to their sex, if only such would content and assuage that feline animosity which has of late disturbed social gatherings, even the intercourse between authorities in the state and ladies seeking a useful outlet for their superfluous energies'.[24] The studies of Teufer, on the history of *Frauenemanzipation* [women's emancipation] in 1913, and Santo Mazzarino, who much more recently wrote of the *femminismo parlamentaristico* [parliamentary feminism] of the age of Elagabalus, may be compared.[25] These quaint bits of the history of scholarship may serve to shed further light on why this subject has been ignored or misunderstood for so long. Today, perhaps, what we may extract from these passages of the *Historia Augusta* is the consciousness that they show of the possibilities and limits of the involvement of women in the public life of the state. Johannes Straub has shown clearly that

---

[20] *Dig.* 1.9.12 pr.
[21] *Dig.* 1.9.1 and 8.
[22] *Aurel.* 49.6.
[23] *Heliog.* 4.4.
[24] Stuart Hay, *The amazing Emperor Heliogabalus* (1911) 122-3.
[25] J. Teufer, *Zur Geschichte der Frauenemanzipation in alten Rom, eine Studie zur Livius* 34, 1-8 (1913).

they are extremely unlikely to be historical, but this is because the author has presented a coherent pastiche of anecdote and opinion culled from the antiquarian and historical tradition.[26] While we may be able to say nothing about the third century, we may well have preserved here some traits of the tradition about the periods which we are more closely involved with.

Straub has shown that the *locus classicus* for the biographer's material is the spectacular set-piece debate on the repeal of the Lex Oppia which opens Livy 34, and in which fears of *muliebris seditio* [womanly dissension] are given a full rhetorical display in the speech of Cato. The womenfolk of Rome and its region poured in to Rome to win the abolition of this sumptuary law, which had been introduced twenty years before in the crisis after Cannae, and Cato alleges that the point of the agitation is 'that we may glitter with gold and purple; that we may ride in *carpenta* [two-wheeled carriages] through the city on feast days and not-so-festive days as if in triumphal procession to celebrate the abolition of law and order and the taking prisoner of your votes.' Cato's speech, and the counter-attack of L. Valerius the tribune, are Livy's own; and it is important that Cato is defeated. The whole elaborate scene is given this prominence by Livy in order to point up not the austerity of Cato, but the successful moderation which wins the day and secures the abrogation of the law. Valerius says a good deal that is of vital significance for Augustan Rome, producing a résumé of the contributions of women to previous Roman history: he goes on to say 'all the other *ordines* [note 'other'] have felt the recent change for the better – should it be only to our wives that the benefits of peace and public quiet should not reach? We use purple, dressed in the *toga praetexta* [purple-bordered toga] as magistrates or priests; so do our children, and we allow magistrates in municipalities and colonies to do so, and even at Rome that lowest of breeds, the *magistri* ['masters'] in charge of city-districts [a clear anachronism] – and all this not just in life, but also to be cremated in. Will it be only women then that we forbid to use purple?'[27] The style of thought here is deeply Augustan. The division of society is that observed by the theory and practice of so many Augustan laws and *senatus consulta* and reflected in the epigraphy of the members of the different groups, whether freedmen, *magistri* or colonial magistrates; moreover, the preoccupation with

---

[26] Johannes S. Straub, 'Senaculum, id est mulierum senatus', *Bonner Historia-Augusta-Colloquium* 3 (1964-5) 1966, 221-40.
[27] Livy 34.1-7.

badges of office and signs of status bears the mark of that age, keen as it was to define where everyone belonged in society and to keep them in it. We may compare, for example, the detailed regulations about seating at spectacles of the *Lex Iulia theatralis*.[28] That catered precisely for women too, as any such social legislation obviously must; and Valerius' case against Cato is essentially the argument of the need for an all-inclusive and consistent social legislation against the unfair and divisive mood of the Lex Oppia.

The atmosphere of Augustan Rome lies at the heart, then, of the literary web which joins the debate on the Lex Oppia with the fantastic excesses of Elagabalus. From that period comes independent attestation of most of the aspects of the life of the *matronae* that we have noticed. In the *Aeneid* the *matres* [mothers] of Latium pray collectively around their queen and princess for the defeat of the invader, all participating in the incensing of the temple; on Aeneas' shield beside the Salii, the Luperci and the *ancilia* [small oval shields] 'the pure *matres* were escorting the sacred objects through the city in their upholstered carriages'.[29] In the rituals of the *ludi saeculares* 110 *matronae* represented the years of the *saeculum* [century; more precisely, a period of 110 years].[30] And at the centre of these observances it is natural to find Livia: 'and let Livia make offerings to the Gods, along with her good daughters-in-law, for the safe return of her son – long may such offerings be appropriate! And with her, equally, the *matres* and the women who, above all accusation, serve the pure hearthfires with unending virginity'.[31] This is the context of the *Consolatio Liviae* and of Livia's involvement in the preparation of both triumph and funeral.

From this period on the reality of the Augustan pattern is clearly demonstrable. The association of the *matronae* with the Vestals, alluded to in the last passage, receives confirmation from the younger

---

[28] Elizabeth Rawson, 'Discrimina ordinum: the Lex Iulia Theatralis', *PBSR* 55 (1987) 83-114, reprinted in her *Roman Culture and Society: Collected Papers* (1991) 508-45. See also, for special privileges in the theatre for Livia, n.45 below. For the law in action in a context which shows the parallelism between the *ordo matronarum* and the *ordo equester* in Julio-Claudian society, Suet. *Calig.* 26.4 on a disaster in the Circus when Caligula attempted to use club bearers to clear crowds who were taking up their seats in the middle of the night: 'he treated the other orders with insolence and violence ... in the course of the uproar more than twenty Roman knights were crushed and a similar number of matrons, as well as a countless crowd of others'.

[29] Virg. *Aen.* 11. 477-85; the Homeric model gives all the ritual action apart from the lament and the stretching out of hands to the priestess of Athene, Theano (*Iliad* 6. 297-311). Aeneas' shield: *Aen.* 8. 663-6. Cf. the propitiation of Juno Regina by the *matronae* in Tac. *Ann.* 15.44.

[30] *CIL* VI 32323, l.123 f, cf. the gathering on the Capitol, l.707-80.

[31] Ovid *Trist.* 4.2.11-14, in a passage running through all levels of Roman society.

Pliny.³² The *conuentus matronarum* [gathering of matrons] appears occasionally in the historical tradition.³³ It also furnishes philosophical reflections which echo down the texts from Seneca the Elder to St. Jerome.³⁴ The inscriptions of the Latin communities of Italy and the provinces, reflecting as they always do the imitation of the social institutions of the capital, provide further confirmation.

The *mulieres* are a prominent subdivision of the municipal polity. At Lanuvium there was a *curia* of women [i.e., an official body comprising the women of the community] whose members came to receive benefactions alongside the decurions and Augustales of the town – on one occasion a 'double banquet'.³⁵ They have certain public roles, for instance, as at Rome, at public funerals; at Pisa in A.D. 2 one of the recognitions of the demise of C. Caesar is *matronas quae in col(onia) n(ostra) sunt sublugere* ['that the married women who are in our colony should mourn him'].³⁶ At Naples by A.D. 71 there was an οἶκος γυναικῶν [meeting-house for women], headed by a priestess who was, to judge by the honours she received from the town-council, one of the most prominent individuals in the city; her name, Tettia Casta ['Casta' means 'chaste'], is also relevant.³⁷ But they would also take the intitiative: at Surrentum the local *matronae* collected enough money to dedicate a statue of a priest, or more likely a priestess, of Venus in the temple of that deity.³⁸ The complex links of imitation and veneration which bound the life of the municipalities to that of the capital came out in this area most vividly in the female priesthoods of particular imperial women, or the *divae Augustae* [deified female members of the imperial family] as a collec-

---

³² Pliny *Ep.* 7.19.1-2, a duty for the *matronae* to perform organised 'on the authority of the pontiffs'. Cf. Ovid *Pont.* 4.13.29.

³³ Suetonius (*Galba* 5.1, which may have influenced the Historia Augusta) reports a quarrel at the *conuentus matronarum* between Agrippina and Domitia Lepida; Claudius' reception of an embassy of Alexandrian Jews 'while he was with Agrippina and the *matronae*' is mentioned in a papyrus, *P. Berol.* 511.2. Sen. *Suas.* 2.21 portrays a woman arguing in front of the *matronae* over the custody of children. A real setting for such a *conuentus* on the Quirinal is suggested not only by the passage in the *Life of Heliogabalus* but by the findspot beneath the end of the hill of the dedication of Sabina to the *matronae*, CIL VI 997, and by the long associations of the *matronae* of Rome with their Sabine predecessors (note the empress' name). See, for one example, Columella 12, *pr.* 'that old custom of Sabine and Roman mistresses of households has died out'. The *matronae* were under the particular protection of Iuno Curitis: Festus s.v. *caelibari hasta*, p. 55 L. Further epigraphic evidence for them: CIL VI 31075, a *feriale* [calendar of holidays] which refers to *matronae cum carpentis* [married women with two-wheeled carriages] and 32327, regulations as to which incenses they are to use.

³⁴ Jer. *adv. Jov.* I 47 (PL 23, 289 B); cf. *Ep.* 43.3.3.

³⁵ CIL XIV 2120 *epulum duplum*; cf. 2110, perhaps not unconnected with the important local cult of Iuno Sospita.

³⁶ CIL XI 1421, line 24 [= ILS 140; trans. Sherk, *RE*, no. 19].

³⁷ IG XIV 760.

³⁸ CIL X 688.

tivity. The *sacerdos* or *flaminica* [priestess] of Livia or her dozen or so divified heirs over the next two and a half centuries served to promote the standing of the great woman so honoured in the *res publica* as a whole, and invested the local priestess with something of that rôle in her own community.[39]

All these *matronae* of course, despite their services to Rome, suffered from the burdens of their legal status. As Gaius the jurist pointed out, in his day all women were bound by *tutela* [legal guardianship], and the only exceptions apart from the Vestal Virgins owed it to the right of having three children as established by Augustan law.[40] It is relevant to our theme that those *matronae* who fulfilled their public role of procreation were rewarded by the state with rights guaranteed by the public law. There was an ancient precedent – from before the Twelve Tables the Vestal Virgins had enjoyed this freedom from *tutela* in honour of their priesthood, and it was on this that the Augustan exemption was modelled. Independence as an honour was a concept in ancient Rome, even for women, it seems. Where did Livia stand?

In 35 B.C. Octavian made a remarkably original and innovative grant to two of his female relations.[41] Perhaps it marks the beginning of his pointing-up of the alienness of Antony's relationship with Cleopatra; perhaps it represents a moment in his pursuit of factitious dynastic respectability. What must be stressed is that it is typical of the deviser in that, while traditional in flavour and nuance, in substance it was revolutionary and novel. By law or *senatus consultum* or triumviral edict (we are not told which) Livia and the dynast's sister Octavia received the sacrosanctity of tribunes of people and freedom of financial action. The importance and public nature of the occasion was pointed up by the public dedication of statues to the honorands. Each of the halves of the honour released these women from an important part of the traditional burdens which promoted the social control of women in Roman society.

The financial liberation, first, amounted to the removal of *tutela*. That Livia won the *ius trium liberorum* in 9 B.C., as we have heard,

---

[39] I know of no general study of these priestesses and their branch of the imperial cult; it was particularly well developed in Spain: see Nicola Mackie, *Local administration in Roman Spain A.D. 14-212* (1983) 62-4, 85-6, and *ead.* 42 for a comparison of these posts with the sevirate as a means of incorporating marginal social groups in municipal life – and costs. For a brief account of the evidence, Grether, *Livia and the imperial cult*, 249-50.

[40] Gaius I. 145.

[41] Dio 49.38.1 'To Octavia and to Livia he gave statues, and the right to administer their own business without a supervisor, and sacrosanct immunity on the model of that of the tribunes of the plebs.' The context dates the grant to the last months of 35.

is no obstacle to that view, as this right brought more advantages than the simple removal of *tutela*.⁴² That is clear from the parallel award to the Vestals, who had never been subject to *tutela*, of the *ius trium liberorum* in A.D. 9.⁴³ Financial emancipation was something which could be awarded by stages, and Augustus, in A.D. 9, further refined his action of 35 B.C. by a grant to a privileged band of *matronae*, including Livia, of immunity from the *lex Voconia* so that they might inherit more than 100,000 sesterces at a time.⁴⁴ We are firmly in the tradition of the *lex Oppia* here; the history of sumptuary legislation at Rome shows clearly how it was through conspicuous display of accumulated wealth in ornament that aristocratic women had been accustomed to play something of a public part, and how that had been the target of repressive legislation which had the effect of markedly diminishing the freedom of action of such women. This is the first load of disadvantage that Octavian lightened.

The tribunician *sacrosanctitas* [sacrosanctity] is more interesting. It is definitely a public perquisite; it presupposes some degree of political exposure. By this act Octavian explicitly recognises that Livia and Octavia, in pursuit of their proper rôle at Rome, will be independent enough of him to need other protection. It is a privilege which resembles the granting to various categories of women, by the *lex Iulia theatralis*, of special seats in the theatre – it is to be accepted that certain women are to have a public function; but it remains true that, because of that, they need specially protected treatment. In this context another outward and visible sign of Livia's public status is of some interest. At some date (unfortunately unknown) she received the right to use the elaborate ceremonial vehicle known as the *carpentum*.⁴⁵ Entitlement to various methods of transportation had always been a complex question among the female élite of Rome: we noticed the subject among the 'absurd senatorial decrees' of Elagabalus' *senaculum* and in the debate on the *lex Oppia*. Part of the point is that the *décor* of the vehicles was an occasion for spectacular display, and so comes under our previous heading.⁴⁶

---

⁴² Livia granted the *ius trium liberorum*: Dio 55.2.5; cf. above, p. 166.

⁴³ Dio 56.10.2.

⁴⁴ Ibid. 'Contrary to the *lex Voconia* whereby no woman was allowed to inherit properties worth more than 25,000 denarii, he permitted some women to do this.'

⁴⁵ Dio 60.22.2. The *carpentum* was one of the commemorative honours appointed by Caligula for his mother: Suet. *Calig.* 15.1 and by Claudius for his, Suet. *Claud.* 11.2. The grant to Livia may date to Livia's illness of A.D. 22, when the *carpentum* first appears on coins: Grether p. 237.

⁴⁶ For attacks on the luxury of vehicles, and transportation as a status symbol, Pliny *HN* 34.17, cf. 33.49. For Cato's attack on these in his censorship in a speech *De uestitu et uehiculis* [*Concerning dress and vehicles*], Malcovati, *ORF*, 93 with refs.; also Suet. *Claud.* 16; Martial

The two-wheeled *carpentum*, and its companion vehicle with four wheels, the *pilentum* [carriage], were highly evocative of the great women of the past.[47] But it is also important to see it as a form of mobility, and notice how it was a vital ingredient in Roman social control to circumscribe the ease of personal movement.[48] Women on the move are highly significant in the tradition, usually in more or less ritual, processional contexts; we regularly meet the idea of an *agmen mulierum* [column of women].[49] The author of the *Consolatio*, to give one example, makes great play with Livia's plan to process to meet the returning Drusus.[50] Again, the controls have only been slackened by a point or two: the *sacrosanctitas*, the *carpentum*, the theatre-seats all say 'this woman is allowed to take a few steps out into the public, male world; so observe the limits which she is defining by her extraordinary privilege.' Livia's masculine honours, remarkable though they were in their emancipatory extent, were not remotely normative except in this inverted way: they were really the reverse of a movement towards a serious change in the social role of women, and so are no exception to the repressive stabilizing intended by Augustus' social programme as a whole.

So Livia was allowed, encouraged, impelled to step out into the public world, alongside Octavia, in 35 B.C. The unprecedented event was properly publicized and advertised. There can be no doubt about the reality and the seriousness of the change, but much more can be said about the kind of transition: what type of inception in the Roman public world was expected of Livia – and what actually came to happen?

Most remarkable, for a Roman woman, was the atmosphere of

3.72; and SHA *Heliog.* 29.1 – his *uehicula* were jewelled or gilded, since he despised the ordinary categories of silver, ivory or bronze. The SHA believes in this regimented calibration of décor; cf. *Heliog.* 4.4 for *sellae* [sedan chairs] and *Alex. Sev.* 43.1, *Aurel.* 46.3 for *uehicula* in general.

[47] Ovid *Fast.* 1. 619. The *carpentum* in Livy is the vehicle of the formidable womenfolk of the kings, Tanaquil and Tullia: 1.34.8; 48.5, 7. Their associations were cultic, as is best shown by their prominence alongside the Luperci and the Salii on the Shield of Aeneas (*Aen.* 8.666) 'chaste mothers were parading holy objects through the city on cushioned carriages'. The *sacra* long remained the principal occasion for their use: Livy 5.25.9, cf. above, p. 170, for the *matronae* and the Gallic sack.

[48] Careful control of the *lectica* [a litter]: Suet. *Iul.* 43 (use restricted by status age and calendar); *Claud.* 28 (use granted as great honour to the freedman Harpocras); *Dom.* 8 (notorious women denied use). It may be guessed that the regulations about traffic in Rome and other cities are concerned with this as well as with utilitarian issues. The *lectica* and its equipment was a very intimate part of the belongings of the *materfamilias*: *Dig.* 32.1.49, *pr.* The wider context is, of course, the various restrictions on movement between one locality and another and the tendency in Roman regulations to specify boundaries very carefully.

[49] For the *agmen mulierum* see Gagé, *Matronalia* 111 f.

[50] E.g. *Consolatio* 33 'I shall go out to meet him, and throughout the towns I shall be called fortunate.'

magistracy which was conferred by the *sacrosanctitas*, as it was, much later in her life, by her being granted a single lictor as priestess of Augustus (below, n.74). But this could only form a part of the significance; it was more appropriate that Livia should emphasize more those functions which, while characteristic of great public figures, were somewhat more domestic in mood. Livia's position can only be understood through the perception that there was a graded range of activities lying between the totally domestic and the completely public, not a sharply defined boundary. Her rôle was developed through subtly exploiting a variety of positions in that range, at its most public verging on the male political world, but more often making use of the less sensitive intermediate zones of the range of possibilities. So it is that we must investigate Livia the patron and Livia the mediator, two intimately linked rôles. Livia was to speak for and protect a particular constituency in Roman society, as a *patrona* [female patron] (we may compare here the word *matrona*), as a figurehead, indeed as a *princeps*. The most obvious member of this constituency is the *ordo matronarum*, recipient of many public honours under the tutelary presence of Livia – we have encountered the banquets which formed part of this, and in Section III below some religious examples are discussed. But the *ordo equester*, male though it was and second in the Augustan order, is also found in quite close association with the *princeps femina*; we have seen their presence at the funerals of her family, and may remember their devotion in the season of her own ill-health in A.D. 22.[51] Livia thus played a vital part in the network which bound the *ordines* of Roman society to the narrow élite around Augustus at the top; in the final analysis, her representation of these groups was approved lest some adversary of the system should attempt to win political kudos by addressing himself to this constituency. But Livia was more than an ordinary Augustan super-patron; she also fulfilled the function of imperial mother, beside Augustus' *pater patriae*, and deriving influence from the *auctoritas* of his position. She thus foreshadowed her imperial successors who actually took the appellation *mater* in various forms.

Within the family she acted as refuge for the erring Julia; it was she who advised the young Claudius that he should drop his early plans for writing history, it was with her that Augustus discussed Claudius'

---

[51] For the funeral of Drusus, *Consolatio* 199 f.; cf. Dio 55.2.1. For that of Augustus, Suet. *Aug.* 100.2; Dio 56.31.1. See also Dio 59.11.2, the funeral of Drusilla. For the illness of A.D. 22, Tac. *Ann.* 3.71; the *equites* sought for their *uotum* [vow] a temple of Fortuna Equestris and settled eventually on one with that designation at Antium.

peculiarities.⁵² Beyond the ties of kin we find her interceding for conspirators, notably, in the great dialogue in Dio, for Cinna Magnus; to her, through his own wife, the exiled Ovid addresses one of his pleas.⁵³ In the citizen body as a whole she is the compassionate fount of philanthropic charity.⁵⁴ Outside even that she is to be found interceding for foreign cities, mediating their causes to the male potentates of the family; they worshipped her in return as θεὰ εὐέργετις [divine benefactress].⁵⁵ Hers was the responsibility for the hostage children of princes; it was to her that Cleopatra had hoped to turn to find mercy.⁵⁶ In these ways the sympathetic mother and the kind-hearted wife became an imperial institution, and it is not surprising that embassies and petitions were addressed regularly to her (cf. n.10); and scarcely more so, except in human terms, that it can be alleged that Augustus spoke in private with her on all matters of a certain seriousness from a text which would then form a record of their discourse!⁵⁷ She became a guarantrix and instrument of the Augustan peace (compare her links with the cult of *pax* [peace], below p. 187); the discussion must turn to religion next, as such phenomena at Rome were never without their religious dimension.

III

Among the historical moments which gave the *matronae* of Rome their justification for public pride was the changing of the heart of Coriolanus. The event was commemorated four miles from the city on the Via Latina by a temple of Fortuna Muliebris [Womanly

---

⁵² Julia: Tac. *Ann.* 4.71.5; Suet. *Claud.* 41.2 (Antonia and Livia dissuade Claudius from writing political history); *Claud.* 4 (Augustus to Livia on the subject of Claudius). We note Tiberius, about to depart for Rhodes, reading his will to Augustus and Livia (Dio 55.9.8).

⁵³ Cinna Magnus: Dio 55.14-22. Compare the Hortensia episode (p. 170), and the way in which the *plebs* takes the side of the women, a pattern repeated in Julio-Claudian times, and probably reciprocated (cf.n.83). Ovid: the most important passage is *Pont.* 3.1 in which the exile asks his wife to intercede with Livia on his behalf (114). The *comitas* [companionship] of Livia is not much in evidence: *sentiat illa te maiestatem pertimuisse suam* ['make sure that she sees that you are thoroughly in awe of her greatness'] (155-6). See R. Syme, *History in Ovid* (1978) 44-5, with other, more casual, allusions.

⁵⁴ Livia's philanthropic activities: Dio 57.16.2 (fire victims in A.D. 16); 58.2.3 (payment of dowries). Compare Boudreau Flory, *Porticus Liviae*, 319.

⁵⁵ Patronage of allied cities: the key text is the subscript of Augustus to Samos preserved at Aphrodisias (Joyce Reynolds, *Aphrodisias and Rome* (1982) Doc. 13 and pp. 104-6) 'I am favourably disposed towards you, and I should like to oblige my wife, who is enthusiastic about your cause, but not to the point of subverting my own customary practice.' Compare Dio 54.7.2, Augustus' favour to Sparta because of its services to Livia. Livia as 'divine benefactress': Grether, *Livia and the imperial cult*, at 231.

⁵⁶ Client princes connected with Livia: Jos. *AJ* 17.10. Cleopatra: Dio 51.13.3.

⁵⁷ Suet. *Aug.* 89.

Fortune]. The blinkering of scholars by the narrow limits chosen for topographical reference-books to the city of Rome has helped obscure the fact that this was one of the Roman temples restored as part of the Augustan religious revival [cf. ch. 9, below]. This we know from the massive marble fragments of its frieze, which fortunately enable us to reconstruct part of the dedicatory inscription. The temple, it transpires, was restored by Livia. Moreover she describes herself with a nomenclature which reveals her independence and self-importance; she uses a filiation before the name of her husband, and is recorded as *Drusi f., uxor [Caesaris Augusti]* [daughter of Drusus, wife of [Caesar Augustus]].[58] A Severan reconstruction in which Julia Domna took part is also attested on the same fragments. When the *matronae* of Rome had dedicated the original temple in 493 B.C. its statue took the trouble to reassure them that they had done well – so unusual was their initiative – *rite me matronae dedistis* ['it was right and fitting for you to dedicate me, matrons'], it exclaimed – twice.[59] The temple, it seems, became a centre of the religious activities of the *ordo matronarum*, its worship 'un culte d'encadrement des catégories feminines' ['a cult in which female categories were encapsulated'].[60] How that worked in the middle Republic is for ever obscure; it is as an image of the past in the consciousness of Augustan Rome that it is accessible to us. Livia acted to display the ancient image in a modern form in rebuilding the venerable suburban shrine in the latest architectural taste. Her action in rebuilding the temple of Bona Dea Subsaxana [lit. 'The Good Goddess below the Rock'], another women's goddess *par excellence*, is a direct parallel, and it has been argued that she also rebuilt the ancient temples of Pudicitia Plebeia ['Plebeian Chastity'] and Pudicitia Patricia ['Patrician Chastity'].[61] The shrine of Concordia ['Concord'] for which Livia was responsible was dedicated on 11th June, the festival of the Matralia, rich in associations with the women's cult of Mater Matuta and connexions with the worship of Vesta.[62] In this case the message involved matrimonial loyalty and the sacredness of the relations between spouses. That Livia should dedicate with Tiberius the temple to the dead Augustus which marked his deification is entirely

---

[58] *CIL* VI 883; see now Stefania Quilici Gigli, 'Il tempio della *Fortuna Muliebris*', *MEFRA* 93 (1981) 2, 547-63. With the nomenclature we may compare the extraordinary proposal that Tiberius should take Livia's *nomen* after A.D. 14: Dio 57.12.4.
[59] Dion. Hal. 8.56; Plut. *Coriolan*. 57, with Val. Max. 1.8.4 cf. 5.2.1. Livy 2.40.11-12.
[60] Gagé, *Matronalia*, 48-63.
[61] Bona Dea: Ovid *Fast*. 5.157-8, remarking that Livia was consciously imitating her husband's building activities. Pudicitia: R. E. A. Palmer, *RSA* 4 (1974) 140.
[62] The case is made by Boudreau Flory, *Porticus Liviae*, at 313-17.

congruent with the development of such a theme.⁶³ To some of these aspects of Livia's religious behaviour we shall return.

First, however, we should pause to observe that, if the background to these actions is deeply traditional and their antecedents of properly hoary antiquity, Livia's actions are unprecedented. The *monumenta* [monuments] of an increasingly monumental Rome had been the political display-pieces of the great *men* of the state, and Livia as builder was adding her contribution to that process. On top of the religious buildings first mentioned we find Livia involved with the Augustan rehabilitation of the Esquiline, with the construction of the provision-market north of the Porta Esquilina, the Macellum Liviae, and, more spectacularly, the Porticus Liviae which provided a setting for Livia's shrine of Concordia. It is worth pointing out that the latter celebrated Tiberius' triumph of 7 B.C., and that in this way Livia could almost consider herself a *triumphator* by proxy in the putting up of *monumenta*. A recent account has analysed the moral and political messages in this project very well, showing how the new building counters the luxury of the house of the dissolute Vedius Pollio, which had previously stood on the site.⁶⁴ In all this we should recognize the direct personal involvement and agency of Livia, whose participation was vital to the picture which was being presented. The effect would have been spoiled if she had been only passively associated with these plans, and we remember that she had been given the financial independence which made it possible for her to take as active and formal a responsibility for them as any male politician (above, pp. 176-177).⁶⁵

The temple is the most spectacular type of religious benefaction. There were others. Livia dedicated a statue of a young child of Germanicus (who died before maturity) in a temple on the Capitol

---

⁶³ Dio 56.46.3, stressing the partnership of Livia and Tiberius in action. Pliny *HN* 12.94 attributes construction of the temple solely to Livia.

⁶⁴ Boudreau Flory, *Porticus Liviae* esp. 324-30. This article should be consulted for the Porticus Liviae and its associations, and clears up many of the problems associated with it. For the *macellum* see (for the sources) Platner and Ashby, *Topogr. Dictionary*, s.v.; the best discussions is that of Claire De Ruyt, *Macellum – marché alimentaire des romains* (1984) 166. It is perhaps significant that a building devoted to the provision of the wherewithal for household management and daily life should have been dedicated by the *materfamilias* of the *domus Caesarum*.

⁶⁵ Although Dio (54.23.6; cf. 55.8.2 and n.64) says 'he placed the name of Livia in the dedicatory inscription' it does not remotely do justice to Livia's involvement to say with Sarah Pomeroy, *Goddesses, whores, wives and slaves* (1975) 184, just that 'Augustus named the Porticus Liviae and the Macellum Liviae in honour of his wife'. Even other women in the imperial circle took to building: note Agrippa's sister Polla decorating the 'racetracks' of the Campus Martius and building (Dio 55.8.3) a great porticus in the same part of the city; and cf. the position of Octavia and the mysterious Basilica Antoniarum Duarum (Platner–Ashby s.v.).

which Suetonius calls Venus Capitolina; he further records that Galba chose the same setting for a dedication of an extremely valuable necklace.[66] There was a temple of Venus on the Capitol which was rich in good omen for the régime, the temple of Venus Victrix; dedicated on the same day as the temple of Apollo Palatinus, it housed a cult intimately linked with the worship of Fausta Felicitas and Genius Populi Romani. The triple observation is prominent in the Augustan calendars.[67] This is likely to be the setting chosen by Livia for her offering on behalf of Germanicus' son, perhaps his firstborn son, and for the – as it turned out, less auspicious – dedication of Livia's protégé and admirer Galba. We see here a nice instance of the impact on a traditional cult of the favour of the imperial system; the old triple cult-place which involved Venus Victrix becomes known as *the* sanctuary of Venus on the Capitol.[68] This is the public aspect of the relationship between Livia and the family of Germanicus, now hard to perceive against the glare of the tradition of *odia nouercalia* [step-motherly hatreds] which emerges so strongly in Tacitus.[69]

Livia the builder, Livia the dedicator: these are part of the public role of Augustus' spouse. As *Romana princeps* she deals with the divinities in whose hands the *res publica* reposes, on behalf of the sections of the *res publica* with which she is most concerned – the *ordo matronarum* and the family of which she is mother. The latter case arises naturally from the traditional responsibility for the general welfare of that family, and more particularly of the husband, which fell to her. The supereminent status of that family made Livia's case an unusually public matter, and most of all when it left the realm of the merely human. It had already been an estate of Livia which was dignified by the Gods with the signs of the fortune of the dynasty which was to arise from Livia's motherhood, the wonderful miracle of the chickens and bay-trees which gave to her Prima Porta establishment the name *Ad Gallinas Albas* ['At the White Hens']. One of the interpretations of the omen was that Livia should have the might of Augustus in her complete control.[70] From this tutelary function it was an easy transition to being the celebrant of the divine honours of the dead spouse. So, after Augustus' death, it was Livia who became

[66] Suet. *Calig.* 7.7; *Galba* 18.
[67] Platner–Ashby, s.v. Venus Victrix, citing the evidence from the calendars.
[68] Platner–Ashby, s.v. Venus Erycina for a different identification; but this temple's existence in even the late Republic is not documented.
[69] See, for example, *Ann.* 1.32; Ollendorff 919-20 suggesting that tension succeeded family amity, an unnecessary resolution of the paradox.
[70] Dio. 48.52.4; cf. also Pliny *HN* 15.30 and Suet. *Galba* 1.

his principal priestess, and it was she who paid out a million sesterces to the senator who witnessed the evidence of Augustus' apotheosis.[71] As we saw (above, n. 63) she and Tiberius acted jointly in building the new temple to Augustus. She was joined at the pyre in her personal five days' vigil by the *equites*, in rather the same way as they had been involved in the funeral of Drusus (above, n. 51). Two passages in Dio may be fitted together interestingly here. Livia set up in A.D. 14 a three-day festival in her own household which was observed by later emperors, but this may have been intended as rather more than a domestic observation of the *familia Caesaris* [imperial household], if it is the same occasion as the dedication of a statue to Augustus in her house over which she violently disagreed with Tiberius.[72] She was intending to feast the senate and *equites* and their wives to celebrate this occasion. She had on other occasions too, like all great Roman magnates, emphasized her standing in the state by deliberately crossing the boundary between public and private in this way. Tiberius demanded that the senate ratify the proposal, and that then he host the men, Livia the women. Here we see clearly a withdrawing towards the conservative tradition from the innovative and independent practice of Augustus which produced so much of what we have been discussing. It is not that Dio, our source for the funeral honours of Augustus, apologises for giving so much prominence to Livia in these transactions;[73] it is a role which he finds strange in the monarchic circumstances of the later principate, and objectionable after the similar behaviour of the Severan empresses, and he interprets it as if it were a sign of the political ambitions of Livia. But it is better taken as a clear sign of the way in which the new cult was best presented to the Roman world – as a family observance which had an impact on the state; not a purely political phenomenon, but not just the domestic honours of a *paterfamilias*, which were catered for separately. It is noteworthy that Livia, as priestess, received the right to be preceded by a single lictor.[74] The public role of the female head of the family which had been allowed to develop for fifty years could not simply be abandoned.

One of Livia's actions in honour of the dead and divine Augustus happens to have had a little more attention from the tradition. On the 23rd April A.D. 22, the feast of the Vinalia, Livia and Tiberius jointly dedicated a statue to 'Divus Augustus Pater' ['Deified

---

[71] Dio 56.46.2.
[72] Dio 56.46.5 and 57.12.5.
[73] Dio 56.47.1.
[74] Dio 56.46.2.

Augustus the Father'] at the Theatre of Marcellus. It might be thought that this was a relatively commonplace action, but the occasion is mentioned in Tacitus and is noticed, more importantly for our purposes, in the Fasti Praenestini ['Calendar from Praeneste'].[75] The dedication of honorary statues to the living and dead at Rome, which we have now met twice in this discussion, represents a minutely graded set of potential honours which is not readily familiar to us, but which should have more attention. On this occasion the neighbourhood of one of the great Augustan dynastic monuments makes the act specially significant. The associations and subtle messages of acts like this also pertained in the towns of the Roman world. At Forum Clodii in A.D. 18 the *duouiri* established a whole series of dynastic festivals and set up statues of Augustus, Tiberius and Livia.[76] Quite apart from the other festivals there was to be a distribution of sweet wine and cakes on the day when the statues were dedicated. Since that was at a time of year when the town was less frequented, they chose to move it to the day in early March when Tiberius had taken on the post of *pontifex maximus*. Presumably the statue at the theatre of Marcellus was the occasion for some similar handout to the urban *plebs*.

The practice of marking occasions in the life-history of politicians, and observing their anniversaries, is something of which the long history of monarchy has made the modern world aware. No need, therefore, to take it for granted: especially not when it is elaborated to the extent found in Augustan Rome. The calendars are one of the most remarkable creations of the period; a major expression, and, on this scale, a novel one, of the impact on the public world of the essentially personal concerns of the ruling circle. The attitude is a historical one. The lives of Augustus and his associates are punctuated with notable occasions, and every year of everyone else's life is punctuated by the anniversaries of those occasions; the religious observances and public entertainments linked with the anniversaries move similarly in a measured cycle through the buildings and monuments whose grandeur and permanence guarantee the perpetuation of the cycles through the *saeculum*. The statues, offered as a consolation to Livia in 9 B.C. (above, p. 166), prominent in the heart of Rome, were there to indicate forever the moment of bereavement and the proper reaction of the community to it; and to assist the recapitulation of that significant set of occurrences at all times in the

---

[75] Tac. *Ann.* 3.64; Fasti Praenestini in Degrassi, *Inscr. It.* XIII, 2 (1963), p. 131.
[76] *CIL* XI 3303 = *ILS* 154 = EJ 101.

future. But some of these commemorations were less grim. The one which the decurions of Forum Clodii were observing was the birthday of Livia on 30th January. The celebration was highly suitable. Cake and sweet wine was then, as the inscription says, made available to the women of the villages dependent on Forum Clodii, and it was to be handed out at the temple of the Bona Dea.[77] The connection between the image of Livia and the women's world could hardly be more explicitly or regularly and impressively made.

It is important that Livia's birthday was held to be significant. The Arval brethren are found sacrificing to her on that day after her death, in A.D. 38, and Tacitus records a disloyal jibe at the priests' banquet on the occasion in A.D. 32, but it is not clear on what occasion it became an official celebration: it does not occur in other calendars, but the celebration at Forum Clodii does indicate that it was observed before her death. More importantly, this was the day when Augustus chose to dedicate the Ara Pacis.[78] Her parents naturally share the glory: we have a scatter of dedications to her father M. Livius Drusus Claudianus and to her mother Alfidia. After Livia's deification by Claudius, both parents received dedications at Samos in the precinct of Hera, in which they are described as 'responsible for the greatest benefits to the universe'.[79] It is perhaps not surprising, given this grandiloquence, that the relatively obscure origin of Alfidia became a feature of the hostile tradition; there was even some doubt as to which Italian town she originated from.[80] The main point of these attentions is obvious; it is dynastic, and the still more important celebration of the wedding-day of Augustus and Livia (below), belongs in this context too. But there may also be a more than simply dynastic significance.

One of the hyperbolic titles common on dedications to Livia and reminiscent of the praises of Claudianus and Alfidia is nothing less than *genetrix orbis* [she who gave birth to the world].[81] The status of her descendants is perhaps not enough to explain this. It is perhaps also useful to look at Augustus' wish to emphasize how important

---

[77] Ibid. The choice of site receives extra appropriateness from Livia's involvement with the restoration of the principal temple of this goddess in Rome, above p. 181 and n.61. The text of the inscription should not be interpreted (*pace* Boudreau Flory, art. cit. (n.1) 320) as referring to a *uicus ad Bonam Deam*, but to the site of the banquet.

[78] *CIL* VI 2028c, l. 2; Tac. *Ann.* 6.5. Dedication of the Ara Pacis: Augustan calendars, references in Platner–Ashby s.v. The presence of Livia in the decoration is of course noteworthy. For her official iconography, W. H. Gross, *Untersuchungen zur Livia-Ikonographie*, Abh. Ak. Wiss. Göttingen, Phil.-hist. Kl. (1962).

[79] *IGRR* IV 982-3.

[80] Suet. *Tib.* 5; *Calig.* 23.2, and T. P. Wiseman, *Historia* 14 (1965) 333-4.

[81] *CIL* II 2038 (Anticaria, Baetica) = EJ 123, cf. 124.

the bearing of children in general was to the prosperity of the *orbis terrarum* [lit. 'the orb of the lands'; i.e., the whole world]. Livia's own three children were something of an example, even if they were by two different husbands; she was awarded the right of the *ius trium liberorum* at the moment of loss of one of them as we saw earlier – a move which perhaps seems paradoxical to us (above, p. 166). In rather the same vein, the day of her marriage to Augustus was an even more important date in the calendars than her birthday, and was the day chosen by Claudius as the appropriate moment for her deification.[82] The theme of prosperity and sufficiency was also linked by her associations with the cult of Ceres. This does feature in the epigraphic record, but, since Livia is syncretized with a very wide variety of deities in inscriptions, it is perhaps more significant that she is linked with Ceres, indeed represented as Ceres holding a handful of ears of corn, also on coin-types of Augustus and Claudius.[83]

The other divine associations of her coins are with Iustitia [Justice] and Pax [Peace].[84] Here we enter another complicated set of associations. Rome's women, like those of many cultures, had a tradition of acting to save their brothers, husbands and children in times of danger – a tradition which was vividly expressed in Augustan Rome in Livy's account of the seizure of the Sabine women and their role in the hostilities between Roman and Sabine which followed.[85] The asso-ciation of Livia with domestic *pax* on the coinage and in dedications as to 'Diana Pacilucifera Augusta' ['August Diana Bringer of Peace and Light'] is a natural one, and the dedication of the Ara Pacis on Livia's birthday clinches it.[86] Justice is more complicated, and reminds us yet again that the position of Livia was not officially limited to the setting of domestic examples. We have noticed (above, pp. 179-180) Livia's moderating of Augustus' decisions by the constant supplying of good advice, and her role as mediatrix for suppliants, above all in the matter of the pardoning of Cornelius

---

[82] Fasti Verulani, Jan. 17th 'holiday in accordance with the senatorial decree because on that day Augusta married the deified Augustus': Degrassi, *Inscr. It.* XIII, 2, p. 161. Deification: *CIL* VI 2032. This was also the day chosen for the dedication of the Ara Numinis Augusti in A.D. 5 or 9: L. R. Taylor, 'Tiberius' *Ovatio* and the Ara Numinis Augusti', *AJPh* 58 (1937) 185-93.

[83] Ceres and abundance: Grether, *Livia and the imperial cult,* 226-7 (the altars, dedicated in A.D. 7, to Ceres Mater and Ops Augusta), cf. 232. The coins: *BMC* 1, Augustus no. 544, Claudius no. 224. See also *ILS* 121 (Gaulus). Compare Livia's generosity in the matter of dowries for the needy (Dio 58.2.3), and that in return some people were hailing her as Mother of the Country: cf. above, p. 179, and Dio 57.12.4. A discussion of 'the Empress Mother' at Grether, 233 f., relating the idea very closely to Livia's being *Tiberius'* mother.

[84] Grether, 236-7 for *iustitia*; compare her general rôle outlined above on p. 179. For *pax* and *concordia*, Boudreau Flory, art. cit. (n. 1) is now the best guide.

[85] Livy, 1.13.

[86] EJ 130 (Corinth). For the Ara Pacis, cf. n. 78.

Cinna. Cassius Dio makes Livia's speech to the sleepless Augustus about the merits of clemency in the case of this conspiracy one of his major set-pieces in the Augustan narrative, and the theme derived something of its popularity from Seneca's *De clementia* [*On Clemency*].[87] But the theme was prominent in the favourable tradition much earlier, and Velleius actually sets Livia's good influence in its divine context when he calls Livia 'a woman of the highest possible standing, and in all respects more like a god than a human being, someone whose influence (*potentia*) was never perceptible except in the removal of a threat or the granting of a promotion'.[88] Livia's divine *iustitia* entails a position of power in the state, Velleius' *potentia* and the *fortuna nocendi* [the opportunity to harm] of the *Consolatio* [line 47, quoted above, p. 169, and n. 11]. *Potentia* is not an unambiguous virtue, indeed it is often simply pejorative, and it is most important that even Velleius does not attempt to deny the *potentia*, simply to say that it was a thoroughly good thing in practice. The same can be said of the notion of *concordia*, which Barbara Levick has recently explored fruitfully: Livia's involvement in the cult of this virtue, which sets the precedent for various assertions of the harmony between the *princeps* and his spouse, is as sinister a sign as all attempts to display such public agreement.[89] But this too is a clear sign of the public standing of the relationship. We may consider how unnecessary and indeed distasteful it would seem in a post-classical monarchy for there to be public celebration of the mutual co-operation and lack of disagreement between head of state and spouse!

In due course it was natural enough that Livia herself should become, officially, a goddess, though the official recognition of the fact at Rome did not take place until A.D. 42: in the provinces, especially in the east, she had received divine honours already in her lifetime.[90] The process was closely analogous to that by which the divinity of Augustus became widely accepted: one particularly striking Italian inscription is dedicated by a freedman *Genio Augusti*

---

[87] Sen. *Clem.* 7. 1-12.
[88] Vell. Pat. 2.130.5.
[89] B. M. Levick, 'Concordia at Rome', *Scripta Nummaria Romana: essays presented to Humphrey Sutherland* (1978), 217 ff. at 227-8; for its more domestic connotations, Boudreau Flory, art. cit. (n. 1) 314-22.
[90] The amplest collection of evidence for the worship of Livia is Grether, *Livia and the Roman imperial cult*. Ovid already can say (*Fast.* 1.536) 'in this way Augusta Iulia will be a new divine power'. The delay in deification, like the delay in executing the provisions of her will in A.D. 29 (Tac. *Ann.* 5.1; Dio 58.2.1-3ª, cf. 59.1.4 and 2.4) and the ignoring of the excessive honours paid to her, reflects how sensitive and difficult her position in the state had become. Note that Dio (*cit.*) explicitly says that the arch voted to her was an honour never before offered to a woman.

et Ti. Caesaris, Iunoni Liuiae [To the Genius of Augustus and Ti(berius) Caesar, to the Juno of Livia], where the parallelism is given a revealingly traditional form.[91] It was natural that the new cult should continue the expression of the connection between the imperial system and the womanhood of the city that the public rôle of the living Livia had fostered. Claudius made it compulsory for women taking oaths to do so in the name of Livia, and we find the *matronae* involved in later cases of the deification of imperial women.[92] Livia also, as goddess, continued to play a very prominent part in the life of the imperial *familia*. The cult of Augustus which she had established on the Palatine became hers too, and its functionaries were drawn from the household of the emperors. But, once again, that throws into relief the public nature of the other worship. The moment of apotheosis is relatively unimportant – it simply represents another threshold crossed, another gradation in the long readjustment of Livia's position. Imperial cult was not a matter of 'on' or 'off' – in the case of Livia we have seen over this section how her rôle was gradually inserted into the system of religious behaviour, with one form of involvement shading into another. To be divine was the culmination of the 'coming out' of Livia Drusilla; in the Roman *res publica* to be the object of the state's religious observances was to be as public as was well possible. By 42, then, more than a decade after her death, Livia had completed the passage of the frontier.

IV

'In the religious good order of her household she was up to ancient standards: she was affable to a greater extent than was considered proper among the women of the past; as a mother she was overbearing and over-influential, as a wife easy-going and obliging – so she was well adjusted to the tricks of her husband and to the insincerity of her son.'[93] In his obituary account of Livia, Tacitus is relatively kind – rather surprisingly. She is not, here at least, an example of 'the imperial woman interfering in politics'. So the

---

[91] *CIL* XI 3076 (Falerii) = *ILS* 116. For the *matronae* and the cult of Iunones of various kinds, Gagé, *Matronalia*, 63 f.; for the parallelism of *genius* and *iuno*, Grether, 225. But Livia was also linked in various ways with the goddess Iuno, and it would be unwise to make too schematic a separation between the forms.

[92] Dio 60.5, cf. 59.11.3 (a similar honour for Drusilla); compare the use of Livia's name in the Egyptian marriage-oath, Grether, 242; Boudreau Flory, art. cit. (n. 1) 319 (*Matronae* and the deification of Iulia, daughter of Titus, Martial 9.1.7).

[93] Tac. *Ann.* 5.1: *sanctitate domus priscum ad morem, comis ultra quam antiquis feminis probatum, mater impotens, uxor facilis et cum artibus mariti simulatione filii bene composita.*

passage makes a good starting-point for a general discussion of aspects of the tradition which concern the *domus*. It is probably not necessary to go through the more conventional and predictable praises in which works like the *Consolatio* abound.[94] Much more interesting are two slightly unexpected and unnecessary forms of praise – for her beauty and for her pleasantness. The tradition is at some pains to stress that Augustus loved Livia – if only to excuse the rather abrupt circumstances of their betrothal and marriage.[95] It is not clear if the emphasis on these aspects is designed to explain the picture of harmony which was presented to the public and emphasized by Augustus' last words 'Livia, remember our marriage and farewell', with its flavour of the sanctity of Augustan marriage;[96] Livia's *comitas* does not need to be part of that tradition, however, and indeed could be seen as contrasting with it. However that may be, these aspects of the public image were quickly appropriated by the satirical tradition; it is from such claims that the rumours which abound in the rich gossipy layers of Suetonius and Dio draw their appropriateness – who can judge their veracity? We may only pause for a moment at the glimpse Dio gives us of the marriage-feast of Octavian and Livia and the pert and mischievous remarks of one of the 'psithyroi' – 'young boys, naked by and large, whom the women usually have around them for entertainment', – but Livia the procuress for Augustus' lusts is taking *facilitas* [affability] a long way: the contest of beauty between Livia and Maecenas' wife Terentia is right for one outstanding in beauty; the virtues of chastity and being obliging and tolerant to her husband are put forward as her own explanation of her political power.[97]

These slurs on Livia's character are not, of course, by any means the most serious. If we begin to look at the core of the hostile

---

[94] These include *lanificium* [wool-working] (Suet. *Aug.* 73). Compare Dio 54.16, on Augustus' making Livia a model of wifely virtue, and Pliny *HN* 14.60; 19.92 on her taste for humble wine and therapeutic elecampane salad. It is worth observing that Livia's modesty was protected with Draconian strictness; a chance encounter with some naked men all but resulted in their execution and provided an opportunity for her *clementia*: Dio 58.2.4. Standard praises: Vell. Pat. 2.75; 2.130.5.

[95] Dio 48.34.3: the dawning of his love is linked with the first shaving of his beard; cf. Tac. *Ann.* 5.1 'Caesar, smitten by her beauty, immediately detached her from her husband ...'. See also Ovid *Pont.* 3.1.117 'the beauty of Venus, the habits of Juno'.

[96] Suet. *Aug.* 99.1 *Livia, nostri coniugii memor uiue, ac uale.* Ovid's estimate (*Trist.* 1.161-4) is that Augustus and Livia are the only people worthy of each other: cf. *Fast.* 1.650 and *Consolatio* 380.

[97] The *psithyroi*, Dio 48.44.3; Livia the procuress, Suet. *Aug.* 71.1; the contest with Terentia, Dio 54.19.3; the political rewards of chastity. Dio 58.2.5 'when someone enquired of her how she had subjected Augustus to her authority, and what she had had to do, she replied that it was through the strictest moral self-control' ... and by ignoring his sexual indiscretions.

tradition we find things which take us further out into the public world. Most spectacular is the charge of poisoning. The hostile accounts involve her in the deaths of Marcellus, Lucius and Augustus himself.[98] Why does this extreme charge take its place in the anti-Livia tradition?

In the first place it is simply the inverse of the image of dynastic solidarity which Augustus was keen to project; Livia who was the linch-pin of the family network is presented as the agent of the destruction within. It is also the natural result of speculation about household politics and the rise to prominence of Tiberius. Evidence like the correspondence about the young Claudius quoted by Suetonius was naturally a help in promoting this picture of the differences of opinion which were, no doubt, a natural enough fact of aristocratic life. But there is a more interesting angle. Roman *matronae* had often been thought guilty of *ueneficium* [poisoning], because the charge was actually a natural inversion of a little-appreciated aspect of the tutelary position that the *matrona* held in the *domus*. Some key texts are to be found in a little-used source, Marcellus *De medicamentis* [*On Remedies*], in which various recipes are attributed to noble women of the Augustan age including Octavia and Antonia Minor as well as Livia. One example will suffice:

> an ointment for chill, listlessness, and pain of nervous tension, which if used in winter allows no part of the limbs whatsoever to grow cold: it contains 1 scruple sweet marjoram, 1 scruple rosemary leaves, 1 lb fenugreek, a *congium* [a Roman liquid measure equivalent to ⅛ of an amphora] of Falernian, 5 lb Venafran oil. Let it all soak in the wine (except for the oil) for 3 days, then mix in the oil and cook the preparation on charcoal that is not too hot until the wine evaporates, then strain through a double layer of linen and, while the oil is still hot, add ½ lb of Pontic beeswax. Keep the drug in a pottery or tin vessel. It is helpful when rubbed in gently to all the limbs. Augusta Livia used to use this recipe.[99]

However it is to be interpreted, the tendency to attack Livia in this way is an important fact. She was held to have done exactly the reverse of what she was claimed to do. The symbol of family unity was accused of destroying the family. Why this extreme charge?

The answer, in my view, is provided by the crossing of the boundary between private and public which we have been examining. Had it not been so definitely expressed by Augustus, the attacks on Livia

---

[98] Marcellus, Dio 53.33.4; Gaius and Lucius, Tac. *Ann.* 1.3; Dio 55.10^a.10; Augustus, Tac., *Ann.* 1.5; Dio 56.30.1-2 with some circumstantial details; Aurelius Victor *Epit* 1.27: Agrippa Postumus, Dio 57.3.6. Cf. Dio 57.18.5^a, Livia's pleasure at the death of Germanicus.

[99] Marcellus *De medicamentis*, ed. G. Helmreich (1889), 35.6, compare Pliny *HN* 19.22. For the hostilities within the family Dio 55.32.2; 57.3.3.

would have been limited to our first type – allegations about the sexual mores of the imperial couple. But Livia the *princeps femina*, the historical figure, had to be attacked appropriately, and the historiography of imperial poisoning developed from the tradition of *matronae ueneficae* [married women who were poisoners] in response to that need.

V

What should we conclude? First, that Livia's position in Augustus' *res publica* was an extremely complex one, which needs detailed analysis, and for which there is considerable underused evidence. But second, and more importantly, that our categories of boudoir-influence and bedroom politics, of the hidden domestic strength of women in an enclosed household, are not adequate for understanding this position. There are important ways in which Livia's activity and status are public and political in the full male sense to which we are used in the Roman world. She fulfilled these male roles to a much greater extent than was ever under the principate tolerated from male freedmen, for example. I have argued that the unprecedented magnitude of her success in this area is responsible for the violently hostile tradition which at once belittles her position by representing it as that of the scheming woman (we are very lucky to have just enough evidence to correct that view) and attempts to subvert it by making her guilty of crimes which deliberately invert her professed virtues. This hostility is even latent in the encomiastic versions of the author of the *Consolatio* and Velleius, as it was presumably in the very full sources used by Cassius Dio. But I also argued that Livia's success is not just a personal achievement reflecting either her acumen or the singular standing of Augustus. If it were simply that, it would still be a fascinating breach of the Roman proprieties. But it is intimately linked with the place of the women of the upper-class (and, I suspect, though it is another story, of other social groups too) in the *nouus status*; it is justified by historical tradition and takes its forms from it; and it is accompanied by changes in the social role of the *matrona* which echo down through succeeding generations.

In concluding it is appropriate to make three disclaimers. First, it must be remembered that the discussion of Livia's image is scarcely talking about a human being. My theme has been a status and its expressions. If we may fancy that we catch glimpses of the people under the gems and gold and purple, of the occupant of the *carpentum*, that adds to our pleasure but, with the evidence as it is, may not enter the argument. It follows, secondly, that I need make no apology within the terms of reference of my paper for interpreting these seeming *muliebria* [women's matters] with my inevitably male analytical framework. For what we have been discussing remains firmly a male world created largely by male political impetus for male observers. Indeed a central point has been that the activities, precedents and forms are *not* part of the female world, which is why it is so interesting to find Livia so involved in them. Thirdly, I should not wish to be misunderstood as being optimistic about the position of women in imperial society. If I have been arguing that advances through barriers could be made, that was not to suggest that concepts such as *Frauenemanzipation* or *femminismo parlamentaristico* are remotely appropriate. The example of Livia was only occasionally followed by the imperial women who succeeded her, and none of them achieved quite the *fastigium* [pinnacle] which she enjoyed; and that that example was based on a new role for the *ordo matronarum* did not save that *cadre* from being the defenceless object of scathing legislation, like the *senatus consultum* from Larinum, and insultingly hostile attitudes, like that of Valerius Maximus, during the reign of Livia's son.[100]

Those disclaimers are necessary and proper. But in the last paragraph I should like to make one observation of a very general kind which investigating this set of problems has suggested to me. It seems to me that exclusive study of a downtrodden group in ancient society can in effect share in the oppression which that group experienced in Antiquity. With the best intentions in the world, single-minded researchers have locked slaves in an academic *ergastulum* [workhouse] and penned women into a γυναικεῖον [women's section] of the library shelves. Instead of this scholarly *apartheid* I think that research into these sharply defined social categories could very pro-

---

[100] The example of Livia: we have observed how Octavia stands closely beside Livia in the early Augustan period (see above, pp. 170 and 176: the Hortensia episode and events in 35 B.C. respectively), but from her death in 11 B.C. no woman of the *domus Caesarum* received any honours remotely analogous to those of Livia during the latter's lifetime, though it is possible that the elder Julia would in better circumstances have done so. This will have been one of the problems faced by Agrippina the Elder. She and Antonia received honours like those given to Livia, under Gaius (Suet. *Calig.* 15.1-2; Dio 59.3.4 and 11.2) along with Gaius' sisters. Claudius continued the observance of Antonia (Suet. *Claud.* 11.2) and extended those of Livia to deification, as we have seen. Livia's accumulation of rights formed an explicit model in the case of the grants to Drusilla (Dio 59.11.2) and subsequently to Messalina (60.22.2) and Agrippina the Younger (61.33.12). By that stage these rights had become an institution, like the *cuncta principibus solita* ['all the usual imperial titles'] of the imperial successions themselves, and the tralatician tendency diminished the individual honour of the elements. Repressive and hostile attitudes to women in the Tiberian age, B. M. Levick, *JRS* 73 (1983) 97-115 (the SC from Larinum).

ductively focus on what institutions, structures, attitudes and mores helped weaken the definitions. Then we could cease simply to reproduce the ancient official version – which would be antiquarianism – and, instead, reinterpret using our own perceptions and questions – which is history. So I would like to think that by seeing Livia and the *matronae* in male terms in a male world we can add something to the study of ancient women; and that by regarding her as 'just another example of a woman but one who happened by good luck to find herself in a position of great influence' we would be still playing the game of Stuart Hay, Cassius Dio and Valerius Maximus. What could be less congenial to the historian than that!

POSTSCRIPT

The two decades since this article was published have thoroughly remedied the previous neglect of the subject. Pride of place should go to A. A. Barrett, *Livia: First Lady of Imperial Rome* (2002). His bibliography includes many recent items relevant to these themes, mostly not repeated here. For images of Livia and their context, see S. E. Wood, *Imperial Women: A Study in Public Images, 40 B.C.–A.C. 68* (1999); E. Bartmann, *Portraits of Livia; Imaging the Imperial Woman in Augustan Rome* (1999). The social and political background is interestingly illuminated by K. Milnor, *Gender, Domesticity and the Age of Augustus: Inventing Private Life* (2005), and on a smaller scale by S. Treggiari, "Women in the Time of Augustus," in K. Galinsky, ed., *The Cambridge Companion to the Age of Augustus* (2005) 130-147; J. P. Hallett, "Queens, *princeps* and Women of the Augustan Élite: Propertius' Cornelia-Elegy and the *Res Gestae Divi Augusti*," in R. Winkes, ed., *The Age of Augustus* (1987) 73-88; and M. Dettenhofer, "Zur politischen Rolle Der Aristokratinnen zwischer Republik und Prinzipat," *Latomus* 51 (1992) 775-795.

On the particular question of the dating of the *Consolatio ad Liviam*, see A. Fraschetti, "Sulla datazione della consolatio ad Liviam," *RivFil* 123 (1995) 409-427, and "Indice analitico della *consolatio ad Liviam Augustam de morte Drusi Neronis filii eius qui in Germania de morbo periit*," *MEFRA* 108 (1996) 191-239 (arguing for an Augustan date).

PART II
Res publica restituta

Introduction to Part II:
Res publica restituta

After the disruption and dislocation of the civil wars, one of the characterising features of Augustus' principate was the much-vaunted "restoration of the Republic" (*restitutio rei publicae*). The historian Velleius Paterculus, writing later in the reign of Augustus and under Tiberius, describes with great enthusiasm the "summoning back" of the "traditional form of the state" once the civil wars had been extinguished (2.89.3):

> The civil wars were brought to an end in their twentieth year; foreign wars were laid to rest, peace summoned back, the frenzy of arms lulled to sleep everywhere; vigour was restored to the laws (*restituta vis legibus*), authority to the courts, majesty to the senate; the power of magistrates was reduced to its old-fashioned limit, the only exception being that two praetors were added to the existing eight. That ancient traditional form of the state was summoned back (*prisca illa et antiqua rei publicae forma revocata*).

Similarly in the eulogy that he delivered at his wife's funeral, known to us from an inscribed version of the text of which various sections have been found in and around Rome, a husband (whose name is lost) commented with wistful relief on the joys of peace and political stability brought about by Augustus after years of political and personal turmoil during the civil wars: "After the world had been pacified and the Republic res[tor]ed, tranquil [and blessed] times once again befell us."[1] A major part of this restoration was achieved by the political settlement that was reached whereby all the key groups in Roman society (the senate, the army, the people, and, not

---

[1] The so-called Laudatio Turiae: *ILS* 8393 = EJ² 357, column ii, lines 35–36; trans. Cooley no. T37: *pacato orbe terrarum res[titut]a re publica quieta deinde n[obis et felicia] tempora contigerunt*. The entry for 13 January from the damaged calendar from Praeneste (the Fasti Praenestini) has been restored to read: *corona quern[a uti super ianuam domus imp. Caesaris] Augusti poner[etur senatus decrevit quod rem publicam] p. R. rest[i]tui[t]*: "[The senate decreed that] a crown of oak-leaves be placed [above the door of the house of Imp(erator) Caesar] Augustus [because] he restored [the *res publica*] of the Roman people" (EJ² p. 45; trans. Sherk, *RE* no. 1; Cooley no. C5, both to be modified in the light of Mantovani 2008: 32–33); cf. *RG* 34.

least, the victorious Octavian) agreed, formally or tacitly, to the new arrangements (the *novus status*) of 28–27 BC.[2] The articles in Part I of this volume have explored various aspects of the political process and the political solution. However, the "restoration of the Republic" also involved an unprecedented degree of reform and transformation in many other areas of Roman life.

The physical fabric of the city of Rome and its urban amenities were significantly enhanced during Augustus' principate, as we shall explore in greater detail in Part III; in this section Werner Eck examines the nature and effects of the changes in Rome's urban administration in Chapter 7, while in Chapter 9 John Scheid discusses the refurbishment of existing temples and the construction of many new ones in Rome and its immediate territory, as well as developments in the religious life of the city, especially at the level of the local neighbourhoods (*vici*). The Roman army was thoroughly revamped, as the conception of it as a citizen militia in which all Roman citizens were expected to serve on a rotating basis was abandoned and replaced by the institution of a standing army with much longer fixed terms of service for citizen legionaries and non-citizen auxiliaries. A series of administrative changes was put in place that affected life in the city of Rome, the regions of Italy, and the Roman provinces both in the East and in the West for many years to come. A renewed emphasis was also placed upon religion and religious ritual, while a far-reaching programme of moral and social reform attempted, *inter alia*, to regulate marriage (especially among the upper strata of Roman society), to control adultery and illicit sexual activity, and, in general, to reinforce traditional status distinctions and social boundaries. The essays presented in Part II deploy a variety of methodological approaches to explain some crucial elements of this process of transformation.

A central question for historians to address is the degree to which Augustus had a conscious, carefully prepared plan for introducing these wide-ranging changes. Or did circumstances play a determining role, affecting at least in part the nature and timing of the reforms that were implemented? Various contrasting responses to such questions are presented in the papers that follow.

In his article on the reforms of the Roman army (Chapter 6), Kurt Raaflaub certainly gives Augustus much credit for the changes that occurred in this sphere. Professor Emeritus of Classics and History

---

[2] As Augustus himself put it (*RG* 34.1), it was "with unanimous consent" that he was "in possession of complete power" (*per consensum universorum potens rerum omnium*).

at Brown University in Providence, Rhode Island, the Swiss-born and Swiss-trained historian has published important work in both Greek and Roman political and intellectual history.[3] Here Raaflaub takes a broad approach, arguing that the implications of the military reforms can only be fully appreciated if they are studied in terms of their immediate political context, their historical background, and their consequences. Raaflaub's interest in Greek and Roman political theory comes through clearly here, as he identifies some of the main structural problems that the army had caused for the stability of the Republican political system. And despite the obvious perspicacity that Augustus showed in devising these reforms, Raaflaub underlines, by means of a structural analysis, the continued theoretical potential of a now professional army to disrupt the political process at Rome. To prevent this from happening, the *princeps* had to nurture a close personal bond with the soldiers and, in particular, to choose his legionary commanders with care. While Raaflaub's emphasis on the importance of patron–client bonds for military recruitment and for the relationship between army leaders and the soldiery in the late Republic is arguably overplayed,[4] his analysis clearly illustrates how important these army reforms were to the political position of Augustus and his successors.[5]

The second chapter in this section, "The Administrative Reforms of Augustus: Pragmatism or Systematic Planning?", presents a radically different view of the first *princeps*. Its author is Werner Eck, who was Professor of Ancient History at the University of Cologne from 1979 until his retirement in 2007 and remains one of the world's leading Roman historians. He has devoted much of his scholarly energy to the senatorial and equestrian aristocracy in the imperial period and to issues of administration in the city of Rome, Italy, and the provinces.[6] In his customarily lucid and lapidary style, Eck here argues that Augustus did not devise any master plan of administrative reform at the start of his principate; he simply reacted to the various situations that presented themselves, with the result that, eventually, after a series of experiments and shifts in direction,

---

[3] Raaflaub 1974; 1985 (English edn, 2004); Raaflaub and Samons 1990.
[4] For cogent arguments that patron–client relations were not important in military recruitment in the late Republic, see Brunt 1988: 259–262 (new material in a substantially revised version of Brunt 1962) and 435–438.
[5] On the army reforms, see further Momigliano 1938; Keppie 1984: 145–171; Campbell 1984 provides a full analysis of the political relationship between the emperor and the army from Augustus to the early third century; on the key question of Augustus' settlement of army veterans, see Keppie 1983 (updated at Keppie 2000: 249–262); Mann 1983.
[6] For a selection of his many major contributions, note Eck 1970, 1979, 1995, 1996, 1997a.

some elements of an administrative framework were put in place that were to have a lasting effect on how the city of Rome, the regions of Italy, and the provinces of the Roman Empire were managed.[7]

As far as the moral reforms are concerned, the personal influence of Augustus is more patent. "By new laws passed on my own initiative I restored many ancestral practices that were already becoming obsolete in our times and I bequeathed to posterity many exemplary practices for people to imitate" is how he chose to describe these reforms in the *Res Gestae*.[8] It was in 18 BC that Augustus used his tribunician power to propose laws that bore his name (*leges Iuliae*) on a whole range of subjects. Most notable were the *lex Iulia de adulteriis*, criminalising adultery and outlawing illicit sexual activity, and the *lex Iulia de maritandis ordinibus*, which required Roman citizens to marry and produce legitimate offspring, as well as defining from among which status-groups members of the upper orders of Roman society might select their marital partners. The marriage law, which was later to be modified in the face of protests by the *lex Papia Poppaea* introduced by the consuls in AD 9, contained strong incentives to encourage marriage and procreation and stern penalties to punish those who refused to comply. One of the most striking features of these laws is that Augustus made matters that had hitherto been left to the male head of the household (*paterfamilias*) to regulate within the family now the public concern of the Roman state, with transgressions treated as criminal, rather than civil, offences.[9]

Moral decline was used by Roman authors as one of the main explanations for the political crisis of the late Republic (cf. Sall. *Cat.* 10–13; Livy *Preface* 10–11), and so these laws were in part designed to address the perceived cause of these earlier problems. But they also gave Augustus the opportunity to attempt to reconstruct social and moral practices according to the traditional set of principles that he personally espoused as *princeps*. In "Family and Inheritance in the Augustan Marriage Laws" (Chapter 8), an article written early in his career, Andrew Wallace-Hadrill argues that the aim of the marriage laws was more far-reaching still.[10] In addition to their professed

---

[7] A similar interpretative tendency is present in Eck's general history of the age of Augustus: Eck 2003 = 2007; more briefly, Eck 2008.

[8] RG 8.5: *legibus novi[s] m[e auctore l]atis m[ulta e]xempla maiorum exolescentia iam ex nostro [saecul]o red[uxi et ipse] multarum rer[um exe]mpla imitanda pos[teris tradidi]*.

[9] For a good summary of the moral legislation, see Treggiari 1996; for further more detailed studies, see the works cited in the Introduction, p. 3, n. 5.

[10] For further discussion on the rest of Wallace-Hadrill's work on Augustus, see the Introduction, pp. 25–26.

function of stimulating the birth-rate, they also sought to stabilise the property regime of the Roman elite, in that the availability of legitimate children as heirs would ensure the steady transmission of property from one generation to the next and hence help to perpetuate traditional status distinctions within Roman society. In making his case, Wallace-Hadrill combines social, political, and legal history to provide fresh insights into Augustus' thinking in this crucial, and much discussed, area of social reform.

Religious regeneration lay at the very heart of the "restitution of the Republic." Again, Augustus was proud to boast in the *Res Gestae* that in 28 BC he had "restored 82 temples of the gods in the city on the authority of the senate, passing over none that at that time required refurbishment."[11] John Scheid, who since 2001 has held a prestigious chair at the Collège de France after serving since 1983 as directeur d'études ("director of studies") at the École Pratique des Hautes Études in Paris, is one of the world's leading specialists on Roman religion. He firmly holds that Augustus developed a clear religious programme even as early as the triumviral period.[12] In "To Honour the *Princeps* and Venerate the Gods" (Chapter 9), he shows that, given traditional Roman concepts of the relationship between humans and gods, any restoration of the state *ipso facto* required the restoration of religious institutions and cult places. Augustus' project subtly connected repair of dilapidated cult places with the revival of cults that had been allowed to lapse, and these revivals and the new cults that were introduced were all harnessed to boosting the prestige of the *princeps* and of his family. Eventually Augustus permitted ritual acts to be carried out to honour his *genius* (his divine protective spirit), then to honour the *Lares Augusti* ("the Augustan Household Gods"), most strikingly at the crossroads of all 265 urban *vici* of the city of Rome, which were equipped with altars for the purpose. Such rituals were made all the more memorable by the joyous festivals and games that accompanied them.[13] These important religious innovations were thus very much inscribed into the urban landscape and constituted an essential stage, Scheid argues, in the development of emperor worship at Rome. In this article, Scheid brings together a plethora of crucial issues to demonstrate the central

---

[11] *RG* 20.4: *duo et octoginta templa deum in urbe consul sex[tu]m ex [auctori]tate senatus refeci, nullo praetermisso, quod e[o] tempore [refici debeba]t.*

[12] See also Scheid 1999 and 2005. For his definitive work on the Arval Brethren (a priestly college revived under Augustus), Scheid 1990 and 1998a. For a succinct account of his views on Roman religion in general, Scheid 1998b = 2003. He is also responsible for a major new scholarly edition of the *Res Gestae*: see Scheid 2007.

[13] For the urban neighbourhoods of Rome under Augustus, see now Lott 2004, esp. ch. 4.

place that religion played in the *restitutio rei publicae* and in the legitimation of the *princeps* and his family. In line with much current thinking on Roman religion (which he himself has done much to shape), he places great emphasis on ritual acts as lying at the very heart of Roman religious practices.[14] In short, his article makes a major contribution to our understanding of how religious life at Rome was affected by political change.

---

[14] Also emphasised, for instance, in Price 1984; Beard et al. 1998; Rives 1995 and 2007.

6 The Political Significance of Augustus' Military Reforms †

KURT A. RAAFLAUB

I

Suetonius writes in ch. 49 of his life of the Deified Augustus:

> Of his military forces he assigned the legions and auxiliary units to the various provinces ... The remainder he employed partly for the protection of Rome, partly as palace-guards ... He also standardized the pay and allowances of all the soldiers, wherever they were stationed, designating the duration of service and the rewards due on its completion according to each man's rank, in order to keep them from being tempted to revolt after their discharge on the excuse that they were either too old or too poor to earn an honest living. In order to have sufficient funds always available for maintaining the soldiers and paying the rewards due to the veterans, he established a Military Treasury, supported by new taxes.

This is a brief summary of Augustus' military reforms which partly emerged as the result of experiments and a series of changes during his entire reign, partly were introduced by specific legislation in 13 B.C. and A.D. 6. From other sources we know enough about the details: the amount of pay; the duration of service (12 years for praetorians, 16 for legionaries after 13 B.C., extended to 16 and 20 years respectively plus five years of service in special reserve units in A.D. 6; some more for the auxiliaries); the conditions of discharge, especially the kind and amount of retirement rewards (down to 13 B.C. usually consisting of a piece of land, afterwards of a lump sum equalling about the pay of 13 years); the origin of the enormous capital necessary for both these purposes (before the establishment of the *aerarium militare* from Augustus' private fortune, afterwards from a 5% inheritance and a 1% sales tax); the marked difference in status, rewards and treatment between auxiliaries, legionaries and the praetorians who enjoyed many special privileges.

† Originally published in W. S. Hanson and L. J. F. Keppie, eds, *Roman Frontier Studies 1979* (BAR International Series 71), Oxford: British Archaeological Reports, 1980, III, pp. 1005-1025. [A more fully annotated German version of the same article ("Die Militärreformen des Augustus und die politische Problematik des frühen Prinzipats") was later published in G. Binder, ed., *Saeculum Augustum. I. Herrschaft und Gesellschaft* (Wege der Forschung 266), Darmstadt: Wissenschaftliche Buchgesellschaft, 1987, pp. 246-307.]

Even more important than the details is the basic significance of those reforms. They formally institutionalized the Roman army as a standing army of professionals. They replaced the insufficient temporary improvisations of the Republic by a permanent organization that was far better able to serve the needs of the empire and therefore basically remained unchanged during the next two centuries. And they represented in many respects a valid and final answer to some of the most difficult social and political problems of the Late Republic – problems which the Senate had never managed to solve and which had decisively contributed to the succession of civil wars, to military dictatorship and the breakdown of the Republic. To obtain a clear understanding of the political significance of Augustus' military reforms is, therefore, a matter of prime importance for every attempt to understand the emergence, character and significance of Augustus' Principate.

A proper understanding can only result from appropriate questions. That one has to start with a careful examination of the problems Augustus had to face and of the solutions he offered – individually and in their mutual relation – is obvious enough. On that basis the following questions seem to be especially important: (1) Were the reforms of Augustus, if compared with the problems and needs, adequate, that means: were they radical, comprehensive and efficient enough? In other words: did he really solve the problems or did he only cure some of the most obvious symptoms? (2) Since the military reforms are only one part of a comprehensive rearrangement of the social and political order (which Sir Ronald Syme has called the "New State"), what is their place in this complex system? How do they relate to regulations and measures in other political areas? (3) The effectiveness of reforms has to be measured by the disappearance or recurrence of the problems which they were designed to solve. How, then, did the relationship between armies and state or society develop in the decades after Augustus? Are there any events or phenomena that reveal problems comparable to the ones at the end of the Republic?

My premise, accordingly, is simple, obvious and demanding at the same time. The military reforms, as central as they may be, can only be judged adequately, if they are analyzed in the framework of their political context, their historical background *and* their consequences and effects. It is necessary, therefore, to go back at least to Marius and the important changes connected with his name, to follow later developments at least down to the period of the next great civil war of A.D. 68-69, and to comprise the whole complex of political problems which Augustus had to face.

Modern scholars usually include only one or two of these *three* historical dimensions in their study of periods that appear as the "threshold" or "border area" (rather than "line") between two distinctly different epochs. The reign of Augustus, which obviously marks such a fundamental transition, is no exception. It is generally approached either from the side of the Republic and then seen as the very end of a specific epoch, or from the Empire and therefore taken as the very beginning of a new era, or else studied rather narrowly by itself. But hardly ever is it comprehended as the central piece of a long period (extending over at least about two hundred years) of gradual transition and only occasional abrupt changes in almost every area of Roman constitutional, political and social life. Here, as elsewhere, only a "three-dimensional" approach which deliberately bridges the threshold between the epochs can give us the full historical perspective and understanding.

In this paper I intend to present a first (and preliminary) summary of the results that can be reached by such a broad approach. I shall therefore concentrate on the main lines of development and on showing the complexity of the problems involved. After a brief study of the preconditions and the details of the regulations of Augustus I shall especially try to find a more differentiated answer to the question of their effectiveness and appropriateness. By applying this method of analysis to one important part of the settlement of Augustus, I hope to contribute to a better overall understanding of the possibilities of and limitations on solving political and social problems under the specific conditions that characterized the Principate of Augustus.

II

What, then, was the nature of the problems to be solved? They were, roughly, the result of a basic contradiction between theory and practice of the Late Republican military system. In theory (which determined the legal situation, the institutions and the official policy of the Senate) the traditional principles of the citizen-militia of a city-state were still valid. All citizens who met the census-requirements were obliged to serve in a fixed number of yearly campaigns; armies were formed by senatorial decree, temporarily and in emergencies only. In practice, however, since Marius the recruitment of volunteers, mainly from the mass of rural proletarians, had become the rule. For this new type of soldier service was a means to secure a living rather than a civic duty; the hope for material rewards like good pay, rich booty and especially an adequate veteran "pension" was his main incentive. The Senate, which had never regulated or even legalized, only tolerated the improvisation of Marius, was, for several reasons, unable and unwilling to fulfill these demands. Instead, the commanding generals became leaders and representatives of the soldiers and their interests, in military life and beyond. The traditionally close and personal relationship between soldiers and generals thereby was considerably intensified and developed into a specific kind of patronage and clientele that was based on effort and personal loyalty on one side, military and social responsibility and success on the other.

To understand the political implications of this "army-*clientela*" one has to consider two characteristic features of Roman society. First, despite the recent changes in the social composition of the armies, the traditional identity of soldiers and citizens was still generally valid. Consequently, soldiers on leave or veterans could vote and, if necessary, even form effective pressure groups in the assembly. Second, the original unity of military and civil competence in the Roman magistracy was still expressed by the simultaneousness or at least succession of civil and military functions in the pattern of political careers. A general could, therefore, not only use his soldiers or veterans for direct political blackmailing by military force, he could also, after the end of his command, exploit the voting power of his veterans in order to achieve certain political goals. Thus the army-*clientela* could be transferred directly into political *clientela*. Since the veterans could not permanently be present in Rome, this specific kind of support could probably be activated only for votes on a few special topics (like agrarian bills, regulations or extensions of provincial or extraordinary commands), in elections and in emergencies for the protection of their patron (*patronus*). But these were the most important occasions for the formation of personal power.

These are the main preconditions of a process in which the Roman proletarian soldiers, led by unscrupulous and power-hungry members of the senatorial aristocracy that had long since lost its unity and homogeneity, became a decisive factor in political life. In the course of this process the use of armies for political purposes was not only steadily increasing and refined, but the soldiers became increasingly aware themselves of their important role. The result and climax was the development of something like an independent policy of the legions in the years after Caesar's assassination. Led by their centurions and tribunes, the soldiers forced their generals to avoid unnecessary battles and conclude treaties and alliances. Their political goal was to maintain the unity among the heirs of Caesar and thereby to improve the chances for the realization of the promised distribution of money and, much more important, of land.

To sum all this up in two ugly but appropriate catchwords: the lethal crisis of the Republic was characterized by the militarization of politics and the politicization of the military. This was not the only but certainly the most important and immediate factor that caused the breakdown of the Republic. Whoever undertook to end the age of the civil wars and establish a sound and lasting political order faced in the first place the necessity of eliminating this factor. When Octavian emerged as victor and sole ruler after Actium, it was, indeed, his most urgent and important task to make sure that the soldiers and officers unlearned their political role and that the military and political spheres were henceforth clearly separated from each other again.

III

It is pretty safe to assume that Augustus had to attack the problems on two levels. He had ideally to exclude, or realistically at least to reduce as far as possible, (a) the need and readiness of the soldiers to interfere (or to be used as an instrument) in politics; and (b) the probability or even the possibility of any political use of military power by anyone (except, of course, by the Princeps himself).

Before we enter the discussion of these two aspects we have to consider Augustus' freedom of action and range of possibilities. On first sight, one is tempted to think that they were almost unlimited. Not only did Augustus after Actium in fact control the entire military and political power and was he apparently able to use it at will; but there are indications that a majority of his contemporaries after three generations of civil wars desperately expected him to restore peace once and for ever and that they were ready to accept rather profound changes and the establishment of some kind of a unified and superior political and military leadership, because they understood that only a strong *princeps civitatis* [leading man of the state] could prevent the outbreak of new civil strife.

But there were decisive limitations. First, Augustus had to work with the existing components of Roman society and politics. He especially had to base his planning on the existing capacities. For example, there was, for several (practical and other) reasons, simply no way to completely and quickly replace the senatorial class in political, administrative and military leadership. Second, he had bound himself by the promises he had given when he faced the necessity of winning the support of the leading classes for the struggle against Sextus Pompeius and Antonius. The "restoration of the Republic" was from then on promise and program, inevitable and compulsory for the establishment of peace and order as well as for his own credibility. Whatever we think about the realization of this program, in several important matters Augustus had no choice. He could not replace the citizen army at once by mercenaries or any alternative military system. He could not completely change the traditional unity of civil and military functions in Roman magistracies. And he could not exclude the Senate or individual senators from the administration of the provinces.

Third, there was the unfortunate experience of Caesar, the Dictator. And Octavian was a rather cautious man. The mistakes of his adoptive father certainly influenced his considerations quite distinctly. The lesson was clear: a dictatorship based only on military power and the enthusiasm of the lower classes without strong support in the upper classes was bound to fail. It was, under these circumstances, at present not advisable, if not impossible, to try to rule Rome without or against the Senate and especially the old nobility.

Keeping all this in mind, let us now turn to Augustus' actual measures.

IV

In order to depoliticize the armies he had first of all to reduce their need and readiness to assume a political role. He therefore had to eliminate the reasons that had in the past induced or even forced them to politicize. This could be done (a) by fulfilling old promises and complying with the justified demands of the soldiers, and (b) by eliminating their dependence on their commanding generals for pay and rewards during and after their service.

To take care of the veterans, accordingly, was Augustus' most urgent concern. Between 41 and 13 B.C., several hundred thousand men were settled in a vast number of colonies in Italy and the provinces. The land assignments, at least down to the years after Actium, however, were dictated by immediate necessities; they satisfied the soldiers (who had expressed their demands once more very clearly in the mutiny of Brundisium of 30 B.C.), they eliminated the legacy of the civil wars and at the same time helped to reduce the armies to a reasonable size. Despite a few additional measures the pressure of these emergency-actions for a long time prevented

Augustus from developing a general solution for the problem in the future.

Such long-term solutions were the aim of his military reforms of 13 B.C. and A.D. 6, which I have described above. In essence, he thereby officially recognized and legally regulated the professional status of the soldiers and their corresponding social and material needs. While retaining in principle the character of the army as an army of Roman citizens, he nevertheless was able to draw the necessary consequences from the century-long development since the creation of the proletarian army by Marius.

The introduction of clear and binding regulations at the same time was designed to eliminate the traditional dependence of the soldiers upon their generals. They now received their pay and retirement rewards from the emperor or the financial administration in Rome, no longer from their temporary commander. The previous form of army-*clientela* was thus considerably weakened. It could be expected that the inclination of the soldiers toward following a general into a political revolt would henceforth be reduced. Our sources mention this quite rightly as the main purpose of the reforms.

V

It was, however, obvious that by merely satisfying the basic material needs of a professional army – as big an improvement as that might have been – further political interventions could not sufficiently be prevented. Strong supplementary measures which made an inappropriate use of the armies, if not impossible, at least very difficult, were indispensable. The legal and practical preconditions for such measures had been created early. Already in 38 B.C., Augustus had underlined the importance of his military leadership by assuming an unprecedented *praenomen*, "Imperator". In 29 B.C., it was accepted and given permanence by the Senate; from then on it was part of the titulature of the Princeps. The long-term proconsulship which was voted to him in 27 B.C. made him governor of the three most important military provinces of Spain, Gaul-Germany and Syria. He thereby not only became the supreme commander of at least four-fifths of the armed forces with the right of nominating the generals of armies and legions, but was also able to exert a dominant influence on decisions concerning "foreign policy" in the most important frontier regions. His control in these two areas became almost absolute when Illyricum was added to his share in 12 B.C. and the Macedonian legions were moved out of the province into the recently conquered territories of Moesia later in his reign, so that Africa with one, at times two, legions remained the only senatorial military province.

This long-term concentration of the supreme command of almost the entire armed forces in the hands of one person was, despite certain precedents in the Late Republic, unique and new. Its basic significance is obvious. Using those powers, Augustus in subsequent years introduced a vast complex of measures which were indispensable for the stabilization of his own position and the political order.

1 The drastic reduction of the number of legions, resulting in a dangerously unfavorable relation between the size of the empire (especially the length of the frontiers) and the size of the army, must have been motivated not only by financial considerations and calculations of the available manpower, but also very much by reasons of internal security; the fewer the legions the smaller the probability of revolt.

2 Similar considerations could have been responsible for the decision to distribute the legions and auxiliary troops in scattered camps all along the border of the empire and thereby to avoid any large concentrations in the same area. We know little about the location of the legions in the time of Augustus, but the existing indications make it probable that garrisons with two legions were exceptions, actually confined to Germany. Relatively little power was thus concentrated in one place; potential troublespots could be isolated and played off against each other. That some of the most serious troubles later originated in areas of such (permanent or temporary) concentrations proves the accuracy of Augustus' assessment.

3 That the legions were stationed in the frontier regions, as far away from Italy and Rome as possible, certainly was a (psychologically and politically advantageous) demonstration of the break with the past (the civil wars), of the geographic separation of civil and military spheres and of the (at least officially) sole and only future purpose of the army: the defense of the frontiers, warfare against external enemies. One should, however, be aware that Augustus thereby sacrificed the goal of a complete reintegration of the soldiers into Roman society. The split between unarmed and armed citizens, which had emerged during the civil wars with disastrous consequences, was perpetuated and deepened. Military professionalism soon led to the development of a military class with the well-known effects visible already in 68-69, but much more clearly in the late 2nd and 3rd centuries.

4 Besides these more technical precautions, Augustus concen-

trated his efforts in the development and consolidation of a uniquely close relationship between the soldiers and himself and his family. Here as in many other areas he drew the logical conclusions from the experiences of three generations of civil wars. He, as all the great men of the Late Republic, had won his powerful position through the loyalty of his victorious armies. Their loyalty had been carefully built upon successful leadership and generous patronage. Like his adoptive father he had, after his final victory, inherited with the command also the patronage of all existing Roman troops. He was not going to give it away anymore; command and patronage of the whole army were henceforth monopolized by the Princeps and his family – at least as far as possible. As long as all the soldiers and all the veterans felt (and were frequently and strongly enough reminded) that they were the clients of the Princeps and only the Princeps, as long as no conflicting loyalties were given a chance to develop, there was little danger of political interference. Every action connected with the army, from recruitment to warfare and triumph, to reward and discharge, had henceforth to happen in the name of and through agents of the Princeps. A few examples may illustrate that.

The *sacramentum* [oath of allegiance] was sworn to the Princeps by all units, even those stationed in senatorial provinces. Donatives were distributed to the soldiers from the private treasury of the Princeps, not only after victories and at triumphs, but also on important political occasions. Especially revealing is what Cassius Dio reports about the presentation of C. Caesar, the presumptive successor, to the army in 8 B.C.: "Augustus granted money to the soldiers not as to victors ... but because then for the first time they had Gaius taking part with them in their exercises" (55.6.4). The discharge benefits in land or money were distributed by the Princeps and, at least until A.D. 6, out of his money. Augustus himself tells us how many hundreds of millions he spent for land purchases or cash rewards for no less than 300,000 veterans (RG 3.3, 16.1-17.2). His personal representatives distributed the money to the soldiers in the provinces at the occasion of their discharge. All the dozens of veteran colonies he founded of course bore the name of either *colonia Julia*, *Julia Augusta* or *Augusta*: a powerful and permanent reminder. And when the financial demands of his discharge program finally forced him to transfer these expenses to a new public treasury, he made sure that the initial funding came again out of his pocket and that only cities and (foreign) vassal kings, but not Roman individuals, were allowed to contribute to it: there must not be any conflicting merits and claims.

5 The treatment of the centurions was a matter of special concern because, in the last civil wars, they had been the leaders and speakers of the legionaries and therefore exerted strong political influence. Augustus offered them high material advantages, generally improved their status and increased their competences, and created for them a new and differentiated career-scheme that included the possibility of social promotion into the *ordo equester*. The centurions thus became a privileged corps of officers; they owed everything to the Princeps, they thanked him with unconditional loyalty, and henceforth represented an important element of stability.

6 However, the allegiance of soldiers, officers and veterans was not based only on material rewards or on social care. It was formed and developed through personal contact, leadership and success. Here, too, the Princeps, his family and his trusted friends claimed a rather rigorous monopoly. The armies and legions were (with few exceptions) commanded by *legati Augusti*, officers who were nominated by and acted in the name and under the *auspicia* of the supreme commander. All their actions and successes, therefore, were in fact attributed to the Princeps, which is best illustrated by the 21 salutations as *imperator* he claims in the *Res Gestae* (4.1), and the 55 thanksgivings [*supplicationes*] "offered to the immortal gods on account of the successes on land and sea gained by me or my legates acting under my auspices" (4.2). To be hailed as *imperator* and to celebrate a triumph soon became the exclusive privilege of the Princeps and his family-members. The last triumph celebrated by a person not belonging to this circle dates to 19 B.C., the last *imperator* acclamation to A.D. 24. The importance attributed by Augustus to military success and triumph as the basis for an especially close relationship between general and army is further underlined by the fact that only very few of the early *triumphatores* are known to have obtained another important military command afterwards.

It was the natural consequence of this principle that all major military actions should actually be led by the Princeps himself or at least by his closest relatives. It is therefore significant that even after 27 B.C. Augustus personally commanded the last stages of the pacification of Spain and Gaul and was at least present himself in the East for some time; that he delegated his stepson Tiberius to regulate the Armenian succession and negotiate the restitution of the standards from the Parthians in 19 B.C.; that he sent his young grandson C. Caesar to a similar mission twenty years later; that he was present in Gaul when the drive toward shorter and safer frontiers in the Rhine and Danube areas was launched with the conquest of Raetia and Noricum; that these conquests were conducted by Drusus and Tiberius, etc. Further, it should at least be mentioned here that consequently also Augustus' external policy (at least as far as it included the possibility of military engagements) must largely have depended on considerations of internal security, and that the Princeps obviously only abandoned his cautious policy of consolidating already conquered territories and started a new program of systematical expansion when his own family finally could provide able commanders for the big armies necessary for such conquests.

VI

It is hardly necessary to continue along these lines. There can be little doubt that Augustus' comprehensive program of recognizing and fulfilling the basic needs of a professional army and monopolizing its leadership and patronage indeed succeeded in reducing to a great extent the danger of its detrimental politicization. This certainly is an impressive political achievement that deserves our appreciation or admiration, even though its long-term effectiveness has often been overestimated in modern scholarship. There is no space here to deal with individual opinions. The vast majority of scholars, however, seems to agree that the system of Augustus, based on the two pillars that have been described above, was sufficient to pacify the armies for two centuries. In this view, the civil wars of 68-69 and 193-197 appear as "interruptions" or "accidents", as grave but still surprising eruptions of disobedience which should actually have been excluded by this system.

This conclusion seems to me to be questionable. It is the purpose of the following discussion to find out how far it can be maintained. The primary question is: were Augustus' measures in the military sphere really comprehensive and fundamental enough to permanently eliminate the danger of a new politicization of the armies? My doubts are based on the following considerations.

1 Some of Augustus' measures, e.g. the change of address from "Comrades" to "Soldiers" (Suet. *Div. Aug.* 25.1) or the establishment of the *aerarium militare* as a state treasury, show a deliberate effort to rationalize his relationship to the armies, to put some distance between Princeps and soldiers. Nevertheless, the army remained a personal army. For several reasons this could not be avoided. It was even indispensable because, in view of the basically unchanged social and political structures, the army could not really be confined to the function of defending the frontiers. For the sake

of peace and stability (and contrary to the appearance and official representation that have been mentioned above), its duty also was to secure the power and rule of the Princeps. To be sure, in the place of a plurality of possibly competing personal armies there remained only one now; and the Princeps had indeed concentrated the whole army-*clientela* on his person and was determined to prevent the formation of rival *clientelae*. Nevertheless, the old mechanisms were still working. Since it had only been possible to achieve stability by intensifying and expanding the very methods which previously had prevented stability, the possibility remained that in changed times and circumstances these same methods might again threaten stability. Even if *clientela* was generally taken as a strong obligation, even if it was hereditary, it still could be replaced or superseded by other obligations; temporary allegiances or advantages might prevail.

2 The loyalty of the client had always largely depended on the success and care of the *patronus*. Certainly, Augustus had fulfilled the demands of the soldiers and improved their situation tremendously. Accordingly, it can be argued, the social needs of soldiers and veterans no longer were a political issue. Nevertheless, there were upsetting factors. It took quite a long time until the new regulations worked satisfactorily; in A.D. 14, the complaints about their failure were the main reason for severe difficulties. Moreover, the pay of the soldiers was, as far as we can see, hardly generous; nor was it ever adapted to inflation between Caesar and Domitian. One further gets the impression that even the retirement rewards, if compared with the costs of land, did not allow the veterans to establish themselves very comfortably. All this helps to explain why the profession of soldier soon lost so much of its attraction, especially in the traditional Roman recruiting areas – a process which can clearly be derived from the statistics listing the origin of the legionaries in different periods.

It is hardly surprising, therefore, that donatives more and more were considered to be a regular part of the pay; they were taken as a right, no longer as an exceptional and voluntary gift. In general, such material considerations again became very influential, even more than one should expect anyway; and that means that they could play a decisive role in determining loyalties. Furthermore, the privileges and power bestowed on the centurions created tensions between soldiers and officers that occasionally erupted in ugly acts of revenge and could, under certain conditions, be exploited by the generals. To loosen discipline thus became a possible method of gaining popularity and forming bonds of loyalty against the Princeps.

3 Augustus had, as far as possible, concealed the fact that the army also had to serve as the main guardian of internal stability. His successors departed from this policy; for several reasons they emphasized this function which was mainly exercised by the praetorian guard. From Tiberius on, it was concentrated in Rome and was increasingly used to exert pressure on the Senate and to influence political decisions. In this context, the donatives became a means of securing the loyalty of the troops in critical situations, especially at the discovery of (real or alleged) conspiracies or at imperial successions. In such cases, unlike after victories or at triumphs, the troops did not receive a reward for an extraordinary military achievement, but rather because they had simply declared their loyalty or even because they had failed to show any disloyalty. The consequences were grave: loyalty again became venal, the donatives became the precondition of loyalty, the troops "made" the emperor. Certainly, they preferred to transfer their allegiance within the family of the Princeps because they were bound by *clientela* and were interested in the continuity of their material privileges. The ascendance of Claudius is a characteristic example for this attitude. But if there was a choice of possibilities, money could influence the decision for one candidate and against the other. Such was the case of Nero. From this point to the proclamation of an outsider who excelled by birth and social prestige, it might have been a smaller step than one is inclined to think. And this was probably even more true for legionaries, who did not enjoy the special privileges of the praetorians.

4 Certainly, until A.D. 68, and then again until 193, no major civil war broke out. We should not forget, however, that between the ascendance of Tiberius and the death of Nero there were several military revolts. Even though, before 68, they failed without exception, an examination of them provides us with some useful clues.

In A.D. 42, for example, the governor of Dalmatia, L. Arruntius Camillus Scribonianus, tried to instigate his troops to revolt against the emperor. He had been one of the Senate's candidates to succeed Caligula and feared now, like others, the suspicion and revenge of Claudius. His attempt failed completely; after only five days the soldiers decided to stick to their oath of allegiance. However, initially they had accepted the proposal of revolt, and what caused them to change their minds was not their bad conscience because they had planned to break their oath, but the political program of their leader. When he promised the restoration of freedom and the Republic, they could only think about trouble, disorder and civil war, nothing desirable.

Usually, however, such revolts did not fail because the soldiers refused to participate. Quite the contrary. Two early cases may illustrate that (there are more).

In A.D. 18, Tiberius sent Germanicus to the East. He had watched the successes and the popularity of his nephew among the troops in Germany with increasing suspicion in the years before and decided to prevent similar developments in the East. Cn. Calpurnius Piso was installed as governor of Syria and obviously had clear orders to secure the loyalty of the Syrian legions and keep them from any close attachment to Germanicus. According to Tacitus,

> On reaching the army in Syria, Piso was lavish with gifts, bribes, and favours even to the humblest soldiers. He replaced centurions of long service and the stricter among the tribunes by his own dependants and bad characters. He allowed the camp to become slack, the towns disorderly, and the men to wander in undisciplined fashion round the countryside. The demoralization was so bad that he was popularly called "father of the army". (Tac. *Ann.* 2.55.5)

However exaggerated this picture may be, it vividly recalls the methods Sulla had used to spoil his army and prepare it for the imminent civil war. Piso had acted on orders of Tiberius, and the outcome of events later prevented him from using the weapon he had sharpened. But the weapon had been there.

Soon after the death of Augustus, in A.D. 14, a mutiny broke out first among the Pannonian, then among the German troops. It was caused by the discontent about the setbacks in the realization of Augustus' military reforms, by the exhaustion of the soldiers, the lack of homogeneity among the troops and their hatred against the centurions; in short, mostly by the effects of the military catastrophes of A.D. 6 and 9. The legions therefore mainly asked for social and financial redresses; in Germany they also wanted Tiberius to be replaced by the more popular Germanicus. The loyalty of Germanicus and the other generals, as well as the clever use of favorable circumstances, finally brought the revolt down. But it is most revealing to read the comment of Velleius Paterculus who, after all, was a contemporary and an experienced officer:

> The army ... wanted a new leader, a new order of things, and a new Republic. Nay, they even dared to threaten to dictate terms to the Senate and to the emperor. They tried to fix for themselves the amount of their pay and their period of service. They even resorted to arms; the sword was drawn; their conviction that they would not be punished came near to breaking out into the worst excesses of arms. All they needed was someone to lead them against the State; there was no lack of followers. (2.125.1-2)

The situation of A.D. 14 certainly was extraordinary. The first and therefore especially difficult and uncertain succession in the Principate coincided with exhaustion and widespread, probably rather justified, discontent among the troops. But a system devised to exclude political interference by the military could only be efficient if it also worked under extraordinary circumstances. Exhaustion and discontent of the soldiers hardly were anything surprising in a Roman army; one simply had to expect that from time to time and build a sufficient safety margin into the system.

The analysis of all military revolts down to A.D. 68 provides us with a clear result. Only once did the initiative originate, as in 14, at least partly with the troops. Characteristically, these were, in 68, the German legions whose long-term commanders Nero had forced to commit suicide, whose pay was delayed, and who, by crushing the revolt of Vindex, had been elated by military success. Even here, however, it remains a strong possibility that their general, L. Verginius Rufus, had been actively involved in the plot. In all other cases the generals took the initiative when they succeeded in gaining popularity and (at least temporarily) the following of the legions against their distant *patronus* in Rome. Two conclusions seem obvious: (a) the loyalty of the troops was indeed no firm and unbreakable factor; and (b) the most serious problem was not the troops but the army commanders.

5 To sum up these considerations. There are enough reasons not to attribute the lack of successful military revolts down to A.D. 68 and again to 193 only or even mainly to the effectiveness of Augustus' military reforms proper or of his attempt to monopolize the army-*clientela*. Rather, we have to consider another decisive factor: civil wars had only become possible because soldiers *and* generals had been united in their determination to fight for their individual interests against their common opponent, the Senate. Civil wars could, therefore, only be prevented, in the future, if the possibility and interest of soldiers *and* generals to use their military power for political ends could be reduced to a minimum. That means: the depoliticization of the armies presupposed the depoliticization of the generals. Accordingly, we have to discuss again, and in more detail, the problems of military leadership.

VII

Facing this situation, Augustus had to devise a system of safeguards that made it impossible and unnecessary or uninteresting for generals to interfere in politics. His task was made especially difficult because, as I have pointed out above, he had to respect the framework of Republican traditions and structures as well as the existing capacities. Radical solutions were therefore excluded. He could, for example, not generally recruit his legionary and army commanders from the equestrian class (which, moreover, at present hardly was able to provide enough skilled and experienced personalities); more than a few exceptions were impossible. Accordingly, a basic precondition of his success was his ability to win the cooperation of at least large parts of the senatorial class and especially its leading families. The details of this life-long process have been carefully investigated by several scholars and are very illuminating.

What he gained thereby was on the one hand credibility for his program of *res publica restituta* [the Republic restored] and support for his goal of peace, order and stability, on the other hand a supply of personnel in reserve for the leading positions in the army and the provinces. This, however, was at the same time useful and problematical. Many senators could still rely on a centuries-old system of family relationships and *clientelae* in Rome, Italy and the provinces; they therefore possessed enormous social prestige, they were proud, ambitious, independent – potentially powerful and therefore dangerous. It was essential that they be kept away, if not from office and honour, at least from the sources of real power. The competences deriving from his extensive proconsulship and his unchallenged *auctoritas* enabled Augustus to exercise a tight and almost complete control on all promotions into the top military positions. All the measures he introduced to secure his monopoly of leadership and patronage of the army were at the same time components of a personnel policy that was based on an elaborate and comprehensive system of safety controls. This personnel policy deserves a closer look. Its main content, which careful prosopographical research by many scholars during the last decades has taught us to understand, can be summarized in two principles: (a) only a strictly limited group of most reliable persons was admitted to the highest military positions at all; and (b) a system of administrative provisions was designed to make it most difficult even for those chosen men to develop more than a minimal amount of personal power. This can be illustrated by the following details.

1 Members of the clan of the Princeps (including the husbands of numerous female family members), his close friends, his fellow combatants of the early days and again their relatives were given high priority. Such close relationships were traditionally seen as warranty

of loyalty and reliability. The descendants of the leading *populares* of the Late Republic had generally much better chances than those of the families most closely connected with the narrow optimate oligarchy and with the enemies of Caesar. Members of this second group were allowed to reach the consulate and to govern senatorial provinces, but only very few who had either joined Octavian early or married into his clan got positions in the provinces of the Princeps. After 23 and especially after 12 B.C., members of the old Republican nobility appear frequently in the consular *fasti* [official list of consuls]. This was the demonstration of their reconciliation with the "New State" – but not more. Between 12 B.C. and A.D. 2, only three noble consulars entered the ranks of *legati Augusti*. Of 26 remaining nobles who did not serve in the provinces of the Princeps, thirteen governed at least senatorial provinces, thirteen none at all.

The *nobiles* were, however, still well represented in the governorships. Their share was especially high in the very honorable senatorial proconsulates of Africa and Asia (75%). In the big military provinces of the Princeps they were less successful: they obtained still almost 50% in Spain and Illyricum, only one third in Syria and Germany. Even more interesting is the comparison with the figures for the patrician nobility. Augustus himself promoted many noble families to patrician rank as a sign of especially high distinction: 29% of the senators were patricians, but they obtained 53% of the consulships, 52% of the important priesthoods. On the other hand, they got only between 25 and 33% of the governorships. Again, Augustus was obviously very generous in allowing the senatorial nobility to occupy the most honorable positions, but he was clearly less enthusiastic in admitting those men to the positions controlling the real power. The beginning of the later sharp division between senators with purely civil and those with military careers is clearly visible.

Besides the members of his own and his friends' families, and besides a few *equites* to whom Augustus entrusted the top positions in Egypt and in some recently conquered territories, he mainly employed "new men" [*novi homines*] in his provinces. Between 40 and 50% of the governors of Spain, Gaul-Germany and Syria are sons of senators of non-consular rank. One has to compare those figures with the Late Republican ones to understand the real proportions of this enormous change. Those men who owed their promotion into the social elite to the Princeps alone could be expected to be absolutely reliable. Like the centurions, but on a higher level, they represented an element of stability, especially since, lacking the usually indispensable amount of inherited social prestige, they could hardly become a challenge for the Princeps himself – at least not yet. Their families together with the old noble clans formed the new nobility of the early Principate. And not unexpectedly, their sons were treated with much more reluctance. Only a few of them are known to have reached the same high positions in military provinces as their fathers had before. Obviously with good reason: high office, governorships and military commands of ancestors bestowed high social prestige on their descendants. The Vitellii, for example, belonged to the *homines novi* ["new men"] of Tiberius. The youngest of four brothers was three times consul and became the most trusted lieutenant of Claudius. His son was made governor of Lower Germany by Galba – without previous military distinction. He was welcomed by the army "with open arms, as a gift from the gods. After all, here was the son of a man who had held three consulships ..." (Suet. *Vit.* 7). Tacitus simply remarks: "That seemed to give him enough legitimacy" (*Hist.* 1.9). Only a few weeks after his arrival he was proclaimed emperor by the troops.

2 The careers and performances of the generals were carefully planned and supervised. As soon as they became not only successful, but too proud of themselves, too ambitious or too independent, their careers came to a quick end. Their commands were usually short. The three years that Maecenas recommends in Dio's famous speech (52.23), and that appear as a rule in the second century, are attested under Augustus only in very few cases; they may have been more frequent, but longer commands certainly were extremely rare. Two or three years were long enough to get familiar with the specific problems of a province, too short for the development of dangerously close ties with the army, especially if the command of larger operations was reserved for members of the immediate entourage of the Princeps.

Even our scanty material allows us to see that a sequence of several such short governorships in different provinces formed the normal pattern of the surprisingy short careers. In addition, those commands were usually separated by years of leave, civil functions in Rome or senatorial governorships. The same person could exercise two commanding functions in the same region, but hardly ever in the same province. In the few exceptional cases, the persons involved were among the closest friends of the Princeps. Also very rare are subsequent governorships of members of the same family in the same province. And the same is true for contemporary commands of close relatives in several military provinces, again with obvious good reasons that are aptly illustrated by the difficulties caused to Tiberius and especially Caligula by Cn. Cornelius Lentulus Gaetulicus, who for many years governed Germania Superior with four legions, while his father-in-law commanded another four legions in Lower Germany and a brother-in-law very probably was in charge of Pannonia with three legions.

All these measures seem to me to indicate a certain tendency. During the Late Republic active generals had used their armies to exert political pressure in order to secure an exceptionally powerful position in political life faster and more effectively than was possible through the normal career-patterns. As a result, the ultimate goal of political ambition no longer was to become *princeps senatus* [first man of the senate], i.e. the most distinguished of the former consuls, but to belong to a very small group of potentates whose power was based on the long-term command of several provinces and legions rather than on their influence in the Senate. Now, under Augustus, this plurality of *principes*, who still (at least formally) had competed for primacy among equals, had finally been replaced by one Princeps whose position, moreover, no longer was open to competition. Since, therefore, the previous main target of senatorial ambition had become unattainable – and had to be unattainable for the sake of lasting peace and stability – this ambition itself had to be redefined and given a new orientation. The new pattern of senatorial careers accordingly provided, in addition to the traditional magistracies and governorships in senatorial provinces, a series of new civil offices and the prestigious and rewarding positions in the provincial administration and command of the armies of the Princeps. This, however, implied an almost complete change in the character of office. The dependent *legatus*, closely controlled and limited in his freedom of action, replaced the independent, king-like *proconsul*. At the same time the offices of the traditional senatorial career, including the consulate, increasingly lost their political significance. Previously political competition in Rome had always aimed at obtaining influence, power and rule in a very basic and concrete sense. It might, therefore, not be exaggerated to conclude that the internal pacification of Rome could, in the last resort, only be realized by depoliticizing the entire senatorial aristocracy. In spite of the program of *"res publica restituta"*, the time of Augustus saw the (very cautious, but obvious) beginning of this process. It should be added that, by assigning for the first time in Roman history some legionary and provincial commands permanently to *equites*, and by introducing the basic components of what was later fixed as the equestrian *tres militiae* ["three military posts"], Augustus also laid the foundations of the slow but inevitable process of demilitarization of the senatorial class and its replacement by the *ordo equester* – which was itself created and organized as such by Augustus.

VIII

It is time to summarize the results of our discussion. The internal pacification of the empire was not only, perhaps not even mainly, due to Augustus' military reforms proper. Their effect certainly should not be underestimated. They satisfied the most urgent needs of the soldiers, they secured a basis for their professional existence and their pension and thereby considerably reduced their readiness to interfere in politics. This readiness was further decreased by the monopolization and careful cultivation of the army-*clientela* by the Princeps and his family. But the very nature of such a professional army (which, moreover, for political reasons could not be fully integrated into Roman society but was forced to live a secluded life on the edges of the civilized world) *a priori* limited the effect of these measures. The chances of a revival of its political activity could therefore be minimized but not eliminated; the latent inclination of the soldiers to politicize continued to exist. This danger could only be checked effectively on the political level, by controlling the leadership of the armies. The Senate and personnel policy of Augustus, therefore, was most important for his program of internal pacification. Only a restricted group of tested and trustworthy men, bound to the Princeps by close personal ties, was henceforth allowed to handle the delicate instrument of real power – and their possibilities to handle it were restricted and tightly supervised.

The solution which Augustus developed for the separation of the political and military spheres, therefore, was broad and comprehensive. It was successful because it combined all the *three* possible and necessary factors: the social care for and material satisfaction of soldiers, officers and veterans; the intensive, steady cultivation of the personal ties of *clientela*; and the diligent provision for and supervision of trustworthy leadership. The skilful combination of these *three* elements was so effective that the system was able to survive, even if one or the other component occasionally failed or was neglected by the successors. The reign of Tiberius, for instance, was marked by some extremely long governorships. The reasons may have been complex, but the names of the persons involved show that he selected his men very carefully. In addition, his long career as commanding general provided him with such a bonus of loyalty within the armies that, after the mutinies of A.D. 14, there were only minor difficulties. Caligula was overthrown without the participation of the provincial armies. He did not live long enough to destroy the reputation he enjoyed with the soldiers as a son of Germanicus; and, whatever his shortcomings in other areas, he obviously was well aware of the fundamental significance of a close relationship to the armies. Claudius lacked any such personal relationship when he became emperor. But he made up for that by personally visiting and leading his troops at the end of the first stage of the conquest of Britain.

The system only broke down when Nero neglected all three of its components at once. He did not care about the material needs of the army and let pay and retirement rewards fall into arrears; he not only did not establish any personal relationship to the soldiers but, by his extravagant behaviour, antagonized especially parts of the important corps of centurions; he not only made grave mistakes in the selection of governors, but by arbitrarily putting to death some successful commanders, he decisively alienated the corps of his generals. It is, therefore, surprising not that the breakdown finally occurred but that it occurred so late (and this again can at least partly be explained by some provisions introduced by Augustus). The attempt of the German legions to proclaim Verginius as emperor, the revolt of the Spanish troops under Galba and the subsequent civil wars, accordingly, were no accidents; they were logical and inevitable. Under the specific circumstances of Nero's later reign the permanent but latent tendency of the armies to reassume their political role was bound to break into the open.

Contrary to appearances, then, the complex of problems that so largely had been responsible for the end of the Republic had not really been solved. Under the conditions of the Augustan Principate, with its deliberate and necessary continuation of most of the fundamental Republican structures, these problems could not be solved; they could only be brought under control and suppressed. To insist on this negative statement does not mean that Augustus failed or is to be blamed for the failure of later generations. On the contrary, he did all that could be done, and he did it thoroughly and with deep insight. It rather means that over-optimistic and sometimes superficial judgments of modern observers ought to be corrected. Illegitimate interference of armies in politics could and can never be stopped or prevented by measures on the military level only. Adequate changes and provisions on the political level are indispensable, probably even more important; there is no lack of later, even contemporary evidence. And so the secret of Augustus' successful suppression of the politicization of the armies is to be found rather more on the political than on the military side. The events after the assassination of Domitian and Commodus were going to prove that again.

NOTE

Earlier drafts of this paper have been read at Brown University in Providence and the Free University in Berlin. I am grateful to my colleagues at both universities and to others who have read the text (esp. to G. Bowersock, Ch. Fornara, M. Krebs, R. MacMullen, Chr. Meier and J. van Sickle) for valuable comments and suggestions. The responsibility for the published text rests of course entirely with me. Due to the complexity of the problems involved and the limited space available the format of a lecture has basically remained unchanged. I hope soon to be able to present a thorough documentation and more detailed discussion in a forthcoming publication. For most readers my main sources of information (ancient and modern) will be obvious. However, a few remarks on the state of research and some selected references to important or most recent publications seem to be necessary.

I Modern scholarship on the period and problems covered by this paper generally shows two remarkable gaps. One of them concerns the temporal dimension: the lack of a wide-spaced diachronic approach which "bridges" the "threshold" between the Late Republic and the Principate has been described above (part I). H. H. Scullard's *From the Gracchi to Nero* (3rd ed. London 1970) or R. MacMullen's *Roman Social Relations, 50 B.C. to A.D. 284* (New Haven and London 1974) are a few exceptions. The other *desideratum* is an equally comprehensive synchronic inclusion of the whole range of Roman society. For a long time research on the crisis of the Late Republic and the emergence of the Principate has been preoccupied with one part of society only. Both the students of prosopography, trying to clarify the composition and changes of the "parties" struggling with each other (best represented by R. Syme's already classic *The Roman Revolution*), and the students of the working principles of Roman political life and of the structural characteristics of Roman "constitution" and institutions (from M. Gelzer's *Die Nobilität der römischen Republik* [1912 = *Kleine Schriften* I (1961) 18ff. = *The Roman Nobility* (trans. R. Seager, Oxford 1969)] to Chr. Meier's *Res publica amissa* [Wiesbaden 1966]) have tended to concentrate almost exclusively on the upper classes and to neglect the remarkable influence of the will and needs of the lower classes, the proletarian masses, the soldiers. In reaction to this one-sidedness, some scholars (most prominently P. A. Brunt in numerous publications, e.g. in "The Army and the Land in the Roman Revolution", *JRS* 52 [1962] 69ff. [updated version in his *The Fall of the Roman Republic and Related Essays* (Oxford 1988), pp. 240-275 = ch. 5], and in *Italian Manpower* [Oxford

1971]; or, e.g. H. Aigner, *Die Soldaten als Machtfaktor in der ausgehenden römischen Republik* [Innsbruck 1974], esp. pp. 148ff.; H. Schneider, *Wirtschaft und Politik. Untersuchungen zur Geschichte der späten römischen Republik* [Erlangen 1974], esp. pp. 250ff.; Id., *Die Entstehung der römischen Militärdiktatur. Krise und Niedergang einer antiken Republik* [Köln 1977]) more recently have focused their attention on the social and economic situation and the important historical function of the Roman and Italian lower classes in the period of the "Roman Revolution". As necessary and important, however, as it is to stress those neglected aspects, the result often enough is again unbalanced and unsatisfactory. This is clearly visible even in some of Brunt's conclusions (cf. e.g. *JRS* 52 [1962] p. 84, or *Social Conflicts in the Roman Republic* [London 1972], p. 149), and it is amazingly obvious in the works of Schneider (passim) and Aigner (e.g. l. c. p. 176: "It is necessary to stress that Augustus ... stopped the 'Roman revolution' at the level with which he was in the main preoccupied: at the level of the reintegration into society of the arms-bearing proletarians."). By concentrating on either the upper or the lower classes one is bound to miss factors which are indispensable for a proper understanding. A comprehensive explanation of the fundamental changes that were witnessed and brought about by Augustus and his contemporaries therefore has to take into account the role of all social classes. In the context of this paper, it needs especially to be emphasized that the power struggles within the nobility, the permanent collision of individual pretensions to a form of power which was increasingly taken as absolute and separated from its original aristocratic basis, were as necessary a precondition for the civil wars and the breakdown of the Republic as the social misery and discontent of the proletarian soldiers (cf. above, end of part VI). I am, of course, not the first to insist on the importance of Augustus' tight control of military leadership. And most of my "facts" are well known. Rather, it is my aim to reach, on the basis of systematical considerations, a more balanced and comprehensive understanding and to attribute the proper weight to each of the several social and political factors that made it possible to overcome the threat of civil war and found the *pax Augusta* [Augustan peace].

II The following bibliographical notes are, of course, by no means supposed to be complete. Recent systematic bibliographies have been published by K. Christ, *Römische Geschichte. Eine Bibliographie* (Darmstadt 1976), and M. Clauss, "Ausgewählte Bibliographie zur lateinischen Epigraphik der römischen Kaiserzeit (1.-3.Jh.)", in *ANRW* II.1 (1974), pp. 796ff.; cf. esp. pp. 819ff.

1 For the political role of the soldiers in the Late Republic cf. mainly E. Gabba, *Republican Rome, the Army and the Allies* (Berkeley and Los Angeles 1976), pp. 1ff. and 20ff. P. A. Brunt, "The Army and the Land ...", l.c. R. E. Smith, *Service in the Post-Marian Army* (Manchester 1958). F. B. Marsh, *The Founding of the Roman Empire* (2nd ed. London 1927), is still very valuable. Cl. Nicolet, *Le métier de citoyen dans la Rome républicaine*

(Paris 1976), pp. 122ff., 150ff., 173ff. [= *The World of the Citizen in Republican Rome* (trans. P. S. Falla, Berkeley 1980)], and *Rome et la conquête du monde méditerranéen*, vol. I: *Les structures de l'Italie romaine* (Paris 1977), pp. 300ff., covers both the technical and political aspects. The shortcomings of J. Harmand, *L'armée et le soldat à Rome de 107 à 50 av. notre ère* (Paris 1967), have sharply been pointed out e.g. by M. Rambaud, "Légion et armée romaine", *REL* 45 (1967) pp. 112ff. The dissertations of H. Aigner (l.c.) and E. Erdmann, *Die Rolle des Heeres in der Zeit von Marius bis Caesar. Militärische und politische Probleme einer Berufsarmee* (Neustadt/Aisch 1972), are useful but leave many questions open (see my review in *Gnomon* 49 (1977) 486ff.). For the years after 44 cf. W. Schmitthenner, "Politik und Armee in der späten Römischen Republik", *Histor. Zeitschr.* 190 (1960) 1ff. H. Botermann, *Die Soldaten und die römische Politik in der Zeit von Caesars Tod bis zur Begründung des Zweiten Triumvirats* (München 1968).

2 Augustus' military reforms: V. Gardthausen, *Augustus und seine Zeit* (2 vols. Leipzig 1891-1904), pp. I 626ff. with II 340ff., still gives the most complete references. A. Momigliano, "I problemi delle istituzioni militari di Augusto", in *Augusto: Studi in occasione del bimillenario augusteo* (Rome 1938), pp. 195ff., provides a useful survey of the scholarship. Short chapters e.g. in: A. H. M. Jones, *Augustus* (London 1970), pp. 110ff. M. Hammond, *The Augustan Principate in Theory and Practice during the Julio-Claudian Period* (2nd ed. Cambridge, Mass. 1968), pp. 148ff. F. Vittinghoff, *Kaiser Augustus* (Göttingen 1959), pp. 75ff. All of these, of course, have to be consulted for other aspects too. For Augustus' supreme command cf. esp. H. Nesselhauf, "Von der feldherrlichen Gewalt des römischen Kaisers", *Klio* 30 (1937) 306ff. For the *praenomen imperatoris* cf. R. Syme, "Imperator Caesar. A Study in Nomenclature", *Historia* 7 (1958) 172ff. [= Chapter 1 above]. J. Deininger, "Von der Republik zur Monarchie. Die Ursprünge der Herrschertitulatur des Prinzipats", *ANRW* I 1 (1972) 982ff. For the monopolization of the army-*clientela* cf. A. von Premerstein, *Vom Werden und Wesen des Prinzipats* (München 1937), pp. 13ff., esp. 99ff. (the sections on the "*Kaisereid*" [oath of allegiance to the emperor] now have to be modified: cf. P. Herrmann, *Der römische Kaisereid* (Göttingen 1968). V. Fadinger, *Die Begründung des Prinzipats* (Berlin 1969) 272ff.). R. Syme, *The Roman Revolution* (Oxford 1939), pp. 276ff. and passim. J. Gagé, *Les classes sociales dans l'empire romain* (2nd ed. Paris 1971), pp. 59ff. For Augustus' dealing with the centurions cf. B. Dobson, "The Significance of the Centurion and 'Primipilaris' in the Roman Army and Administration", *ANRW* II 1 (1974), 392ff., with rich references. For the colonization program cf. F. Vittinghoff, *Römische Kolonisation und Bürgerrechtspolitik unter Caesar und Augustus* (Mainz 1951). F. T. Hinrichs, "Das legale Landversprechen im Bellum civile", *Historia* 18 (1969) 521ff. P. A. Brunt, *Italian Manpower* (Oxford 1971), pp. 332ff. A more recent but hardly satisfactory discussion in H. Chr. Schneider, *Das*

Problem der Veteranenversorgung in der späten römischen Republik (Bonn 1977), pp. 206ff.

3 For the armies of the early Principate cf. G. Webster, *The Roman Imperial Army of the First and Second Centuries A.D.* (London 1969). G. R. Watson, *The Roman Soldier* (London 1969), both mainly concerned with the technical aspects. M. Grant, *The Army of the Caesars* (New York 1974), whatever its other shortcomings, at least underlines the political problems. Cf. further H. G. Pflaum, "Forces et faiblesses de l'armée romaine du haut-empire", in: *Problèmes de la guerre à Rome*, ed. P. Brisson (Paris 1968), pp. 85ff. J. Harmand, "Les origines de l'armée impériale. Un témoignage sur la réalité du pseudo-principat et sur l'évolution militaire de l'occident", *ANRW* II 1 (1974) 263ff. For the social and economic problems of the professional army and the veterans cf. Watson, l.c. 89ff. Brunt, *Italian Manpower* 342ff. Id., "Pay and Supernumeration in the Roman Army", *PSBR* 18 (1950) 50ff. Esp. important: G. Forni, *Il reclutamento delle legioni da Augusto a Diocleziano* (Milano and Roma 1953), esp. 28ff., 119ff.; and, more recently: "Estrazione etnica e sociale dei soldati delle legioni nei primi tre secoli dell'impero", *ANRW* II 1 (1974) 339ff., esp. 390ff. Forni also provides the basic statistics for the change of recruiting areas in the 1st and 2nd century A.D. The development from military professionalism to military class is discussed by J. Gagé, l.c. 133ff., 249ff. However, the political function of the army during the Principate has not been system-atically discussed in recent years. For a discussion of some important aspects cf. J. Bleicken, *Verfassungs- und Sozialgeschichte des römischen Kaiser-reiches*, vol. I (Paderborn 1978), pp. 213ff. For a discussion of the military revolts down to 68 one has to refer to the biographies of the individual emperors. For 68/69 cf. G. E. F. Chilver, "The Army and Politics A.D. 68-70", *JRS* 47 (1957) 29ff. P. A. Brunt, "The Revolt of Vindex and the Fall of Nero", *Latomus* 18 (1959) 531ff. [= *Roman Imperial Themes* (Oxford 1990), pp. 9-32 = ch. 2]. H. Grassl, *Untersuchungen zum Vierkaiserjahr 68/69 n. Chr. Ein Beitrag zur Ideologie und Sozialstruktur des frühen Prinzipats* (Diss. Graz 1972).

4 For Augustus' relationship to the upper classes (and many related problems) cf. mainly R. Syme's *Roman Revolution* (a work to which this paper owes much more than it shows). The thorough analysis of P. Sattler, *Augustus und der Senat. Untersuchungen zur römischen Innenpolitik zwischen 30 und 17 v. Chr.* (Göttingen 1960), and "Julia und Tiberius. Beiträge zur römischen Innenpolitik zwischen den Jahren 12 vor und 2 nach Chr.", in: id., *Studien aus dem Gebiet der Alten Geschichte* (Wiesbaden 1962), 1ff., now in: *Augustus*, ed. W. Schmitthenner (Darmstadt 1969), pp. 486ff., covers at least a large part of Augustus' reign. For the control of military leadership and the careers of *legati Augusti* cf. E. Birley, "Senators in the Emperor's Service", *Proc. Brit. Acad.* 39 (1953) 197ff. "Beförderungen und Versetzungen im römischen Heere", *Carnuntum Jahrbuch* (1957/58) 3ff. Birley's conclusions have been slightly modified but

basically confirmed in several publications of G. Alföldy (e.g. in "Die Generalität des römischen Heeres", *Bonner Jahrbücher* 169 (1969) 233ff.), W. Eck (e.g. in "Beförderungskriterien innerhalb der senatorischen Laufbahn, dargestellt an der Zeit von 69 bis 138 n. Chr.", *ANRW* II 1 (1974) 158ff.) and others. Criticism and doubts are expressed e.g. by F. Millar, "The Emperor, the Senate and the Provinces", *JRS* 56 (1966) 156ff. [= *The Roman Republic and Augustan Revolution* (Chapel Hill and London 2002), pp. 271-291 = ch. 11]. B. Campbell, "Who were the 'viri militares'?", *JRS* 65 (1975) 11ff. The conclusions of all these scholars, however, are mostly based on evidence of the second half of the first and the second centuries. For the first half of the first century and the time of Augustus the sources are much poorer. How much of the later system was already fully developed by Augustus himself remains therefore uncertain to some extent. The available source material has carefully been collected and arranged by R. Szramkiewicz, *Les gouverneurs de province à l'époque augustéenne*, 2 vols. (Paris 1976). Despite its lack of historical perspective and penetration, this work is extremely useful for its statistics. Here, at last, is a synchronic study on the governors of all provinces of the empire in a given period. For many questions this is much more helpful than the diachronic studies concentrating on the administration of one single province that are so popular among prosopographists (cf. also W. Eck, l.c. 158-161). A similar systematical study for the subsequent period from Tiberius to Nero is (despite R. Syme's *Tacitus*) most desired. H. H. Pistor, *Prinzeps und Patriziat in der Zeit von Augustus bis Commodus* (Diss. Freiburg 1965), and A. Bergener, *Die führende Senatorenschicht im frühen Prinzipat (14-68)* (Diss. Bonn 1965), at least fill some parts of the gap. Again, some discussions of the problems involved can be found in more recent biographies of individual emperors. Cf., e.g., for Tiberius: R. Seager, *Tiberius* (Berkeley and Los Angeles 1972). G. Alföldy, "La politique provinciale de Tibère", *Latomus* 24 (1965) 824ff. W. Orth, *Die Provinzialpolitik des Tiberius* (Diss. München 1970).

7 The Administrative Reforms of Augustus: Pragmatism or Systematic Planning?†*

WERNER ECK

translated by Claus Nader

In his biography of Augustus, Suetonius describes – in chapters 34 and following – the measures that the first *princeps* took to reconstruct Roman public life after the turmoil of the civil wars and to configure it according to his own principles. In this section a striking sentence is to be found in chapter 37:

> *quoque plures partem administrandae rei publicae caperent, nova officia excogitavit: curam operum publicorum, viarum, aquarum, alvei Tiberis, frumenti populo dividundi, praefecturam urbis, triumviratum legendi senatus et alterum recognoscendi turmas equitum.*

> [To allow more men to take part in the administration of the state, he devised some new official posts: the supervision of public works, roads, aqueducts, the channel of the Tiber, the distribution of grain to the people, the urban prefecture, the board of three for the selection of the senate and another for the review of the companies of knights (*equites*).]

---

† Originally published in German as "Augustus' administrative Reformen: Pragmatismus oder systematisches Planen?" in W. Eck, *Die Verwaltung des römischen Reiches in der Hohen Kaiserzeit*, Basel: F. Reinhardt, 1995, 83–102, a revised and expanded version of an article of the same title first published in *Acta Classica* 29 (1986), pp. 105–120. [Editor's note: I would like to thank the author for his generous cooperation in the translation of his article and for updating some of the references.]

* The following ideas were developed during several seminars at the Universities of Saarbrücken and Köln; they took their present form as lectures given in Capetown, Durban, Johannesburg, Pretoria, and Oxford. I would like to thank many participants at these lectures for their stimulating criticisms. I have maintained the lecture format and only the most important references will be cited in the notes (with some additions for this translation). The following works are cited in abbreviated form: Brunt, *JRS* 73 (1983) = P. A. Brunt, "Princeps and Equites," *JRS* 73 (1983), 42ff.; Eck, *Italien* = W. Eck, *Die staatliche Organisation Italiens in der Hohen Kaiserzeit*, Munich 1979; Eck, *Verwaltung* = W. Eck, *Die Verwaltung des römischen Reiches in der Hohen Kaiserzeit*, Basel 1995; Kienast, *Augustus* = D. Kienast, *Augustus: Prinzeps und Monarch*, 3rd edn, Darmstadt 1999; Pflaum, *Procurateurs* = H.-G. Pflaum, *Les procurateurs équestres sous le Haut-Empire romain*, Paris 1950. For the whole subject of the article see also W. Eck, *The Age of Augustus*, Oxford 2003, pp. 77ff. = 2007, pp. 89ff.

This statement is striking in two different ways. First, the reasons given for the introduction of these new posts are not connected to any practical needs. According to Suetonius, Augustus' motives stemmed from his desire to strengthen the bonds between senators and the *res publica*, evidently as a reaction against their widespread preference for withdrawing from public life while maintaining their socio-political status. Second, Suetonius does not say anything about the new equestrian officials whom Augustus entrusted with various public duties: for example, the prefects of Egypt, the financial procurators in the provinces, or the equestrians who were charged with various administrative tasks in the city of Rome closely linked to Augustus. In fact, there is no mention of these officials at all in the whole of Suetonius' biography of Augustus.

Suetonius' statement stands in stark contrast to the view that has developed in the modern scholarly literature about administrative change under Augustus. On the one hand, scholars have emphasised the practical need to improve Rome's administration: given the general deficiency in terms of administration that existed previously, considerable action was required, but this was incompatible with the traditional, aristocratic character of the Roman state. Only after power had become concentrated in Augustus' hands alone and aristocratic competitiveness, which had hitherto prevented any reform of the administration of the *res publica*, had been curtailed was Augustus able to respond to the critical needs that had built up. The important result of this was that henceforth equestrians were brought in to take on administrative duties alongside senators. Here Augustus' political aim was to create a counterbalance to the still powerful influence of the senate. Thus the promotion of equestrians can be seen to have played a role in the power struggle between the (monarchical) victor of the civil war and the (aristocratically minded) senate.[1]

---

[1] These aspects have been emphasised in a variety of ways in the modern scholarly literature and it is unnecessary to elaborate on them fully here; a few references will suffice. Christian Meier, for example, speaks of the "limited means of administration of the res publica," in *Res publica amissa*, Wiesbaden 1980, p. 37; cf. C. Meier, *Die Ohnmacht des allmächtigen Diktators Caesar*, Frankfurt 1983, p. 278: "the entire administration was reorganised" ("Die gesamte Verwaltung wurde neu organisiert"). "Deficiency in administration": H. Galsterer, *Herrschaft und Verwaltung im republikanischen Italien*, Munich 1976, p. 3; H. H. Scullard, *From the Gracchi to Nero*, London 1970, p. 234: "thus an efficient system was established"; "vast administrative service"; W. Dahlheim, *Geschichte der römischen Kaiserzeit*, Munich, 1984, p. 40: [the assignments given to the equestrians] "originated in the necessity to monitor the power of senators in all important areas of administration and military affairs" ("der Notwendigkeit, die Macht der senatorischen Herren in jedem wichtigen Bereich der Verwaltung und des Heeres überwachen zu müssen"). Pflaum, *Procurateurs*, p. 4: "a social class which ... could constitute a counterweight in this balance of powers" ("classe sociale qui ... pouvait

Suetonius' position stands in clear opposition to that held by modern scholars, in that the goals and intentions ascribed to Augustus by Suetonius and modern scholars are very difficult to reconcile with one another. On the other hand, they are somewhat similar in so far as they both presuppose a consistent political vision on the part of Augustus. Moreover, modern scholars reckon that Augustus' reforms were a response to the crisis of the late Republic. As a result, neither in Suetonius nor in modern scholarship does one specific factor, which is of fundamental significance for understanding Augustus' policy, receive sufficient attention: namely, the factor of change over time. Augustus held legitimate sole power for more than forty years, a period in which circumstances and conditions hardly remained the same. Long-term developments and immediate political requirements had an important influence on the measures that Augustus took. These included, for example, the process of becoming familiar with a new political system, situations of military crisis, famine, or issues within Augustus' own family or circle of supporters. What at the end of the Augustan period or from the perspective of the developments of the centuries that followed may be viewed as apparently consistent policies responding to particular goals did not necessarily start out as such.

As a result, we need to pose two questions. (1) In what specific circumstances during his long reign did Augustus carry out his measures of administrative change? (2) What were the reasons that led Augustus to bring equestrians into administrative positions, and what influence did they have in the context of these positions and of the circumstances that the community itself needed to deal with?

January of the year 27 ushered in, after a good deal of preparation, a fundamentally new political order, which in terms of its essential components would not be modified. The regulations of 13 January were not a legal division of power, but rather a political measure of pacification that reconciled the legal needs of the *res publica* with the demands of the power-holder Augustus. As far as administrative change is concerned, the specific results of this political act were, all in all, minimal.[2] Admittedly, the provinces now saw governors who

---

constituer un contrepoids dans cette balance de puissances"). Compare also W. Eck, "Die Ausformung der ritterlichen Administration als Antisenatspolitik?" in *Opposition et résistance à l'Empire d'Auguste à Trajan* (Entretiens Fondation Hardt 33), Geneva 1987, pp. 249–283 = Eck, *Verwaltung*, pp. 29–54.

[2] For example, the overtly general statement at H. Bengtson, *Grundriss der römischen Geschichte mit Quellenkunde I*, Munich 1970, p. 260: "the development of the principate made a significant impact on the administration of the Empire as well" ("auch in der Verwaltung des Reiches bezeichnet die Entstehung des Prinzipats einen tiefen Einschnitt"), is therefore not strictly applicable.

were differentiated by their titles: proconsuls in the provinces of the Roman people (*provinciae populi Romani*), whose number only fluctuated to a small degree and by the end of the Augustan period had reached the canonical figure of ten, as opposed to legates of Augustus with propraetorian power (*legati Augusti pro praetore*) in the provinces controlled by Augustus himself (*provinciae Caesaris*). The change and distinction in nomenclature, however, should not lead us to suppose that there were significant modifications in the nature and intensity of Roman provincial administration.[3] The circle from which both types of governors were selected remained one and the same; it comprised senators, who held office within both Augustus' and the Roman people's spheres of responsibility. Personal qualifications and personal levels of experience were essentially identical in each category.

Evidently the principle of annual terms in office was not maintained for *legati Augusti*, since Augustus himself did not receive yearly assignments for his group of provinces. A similar method had been employed by Pompeius in 55 when he sent L. Afranius and P. Petreius as legates to Spain, where they remained in office until his defeat in 49. The extension of legates' terms of office to several years cannot be used to prove that there was an intensification in administrative activity. This could only have been achieved by an increase in the number of subordinate administrative personnel or by their decentralisation, and neither of these things occurred. Indeed most of all in the Augustan period the activity of legates in most provinces was focused to a considerable extent on actively leading the army, particularly during the wars of expansion. In this respect their potential military effectiveness may well have been a significant factor in their appointment by Augustus, as well as his estimation of their political loyalty. It seems that considerations regarding legates' overall administrative effectiveness did not in any decisive way influence the adoption of the Pompeian model.

Similarly Cassius Dio (53.15.3-5) places in the year 27 the first appointment of procurators in all provinces of the Roman Empire.[4] On the basis of this passage, a key focal point for Dio appears to have been – from the anachronistic perspective of later developments – that the system drew its significance most of all from the fact that it

---

[3] Emphasised by F. Millar, "The Emperor, the Senate, and the Provinces," *JRS* 56 (1966), 156ff. (reprinted in F. Millar, *Rome, the Greek World and the East. 1: The Roman Republic and the Augustan Revolution*, eds H. M. Cotton and G. M. Rogers, Chapel Hill and London 2002, pp. 271ff.).

[4] Strabo 17.3.25 speaks only of procurators in the provinces controlled by Augustus.

was centred fundamentally on tax collection. However, procurators could not in any way have played such a systematic and official role in this period; apart from their title, which advertised the fact that they originated within the private legal sphere, procurators in all provinces governed by proconsuls did not have any responsibility for the finances of the *res publica*.[5] When Augustus entrusted the administration of his private wealth outside Italy to procurators, this was *a priori* a private legal action that did not require the senate's approval, nor did Augustus bring it before that body for confirmation. It is impossible to prove that patrimonial procurators in the proconsular provinces were already at this time responsible for the collection of public revenues (with the exception of *tributum*); besides, it is quite improbable for political reasons, especially in the early years of Augustus' reign.

It would be far more important to know how the procuratorial system developed in the provinces controlled by Augustus. In other words, we need to find out at what point quaestors stopped being sent to these provinces. To be sure, during Pompeius' time in Spain this still happened, even though the direct administration of the province was now in the hands of a legate.[6] Our admittedly scanty source material does not attest any quaestor who was assigned to a legate of Augustus. As a result, we may conclude, though not with complete confidence, that the appointment of an Augustan legate brought to an end the use of quaestors. This is quite likely. Most of all, the number of quaestors appointed annually supports the argument. To be sure, Caesar had designated forty quaestors each year. But since Velleius Paterculus (2.89) stresses that Augustus in 27 at the latest returned to the former system of magistracies except in the case of the praetorship, there could only have been twenty quaestors once again in office. Since six or seven of them, if not more, were traditionally needed each year in Rome and Italy,[7] the remaining number would have already been insufficient by the year 27, since quaestors had to be appointed in at least sixteen provinces. The only

---

[5] When Dio 53.15.3 merely excludes *phoroi* (tribute) in the senatorial provinces, this does not mean anything for the Augustan period; rather, it reflects later developments. That can clearly be seen from Strabo 17.3.25 (cf. n. 4).

[6] An attested example is Q. Cassius Longinus in 52: see Broughton, *MRR*, II: 236; cf. W. Eck, "Sulpicii Galbae und Livii Ocellae – zwei senatorische Familien in Tarracina," *LF* 114 (1991), 93ff.

[7] Two quaestors attached to the consuls, two urban quaestors, perhaps three for the *calles*, i.e., for southern Italy, Ostia, and Ravenna: see Mommsen, *Staatsrecht* (3rd edn), II: 571ff. The date from which there were two (or more?) "quaestors of Augustus" (i.e., later, emperor's quaestors) is not attested. But since he, in his function as proconsul, was presumably entitled to these quaestors for his provinces, they must have been appointed on a regular basis.

possible solution to such a shortfall would have been to increase the number of quaestors, but this evidently did not happen. It would have conflicted with Augustus' efforts to reduce the size of the senate to its former limit of 600 members. So the decision to stop sending these officials to the provinces controlled by Augustus was a consequence of the return to Republican practices regarding state magistracies; the abandonment of the policy was a result of the limited availability of personnel. Accordingly, the appointment of freedmen or equestrian procurators to administer the finances in the provinces controlled by Augustus was not an aggressive move directed against the senate, but simply a means of replacing officials, who were insufficient in number, within the recently re-established structure of the *res publica*. Apart from that, Augustus' quaestors (*quaestores Augusti*) should be seen as a type of support-staff allocated to the *princeps* on the basis of his consular imperium (*imperium consulare*) for the provinces that had been transferred to his control, once again in conformity with Republican precedent. Naturally, neither these quaestors nor Augustus himself travelled to these provinces; they remained at his side and so usually in Rome.

In whatever particular way this development occurred, the sending of procurators of freedman or equestrian rank to the provinces certainly did not take place with the intention of categorically changing or improving the existing method of collecting taxes. From what we know of the Augustan period, the previous mode of tax collection was not modified in any way. In point of fact, the system of leasing contracts for the collection of taxes, wherever it existed, was evidently retained. Moreover, whenever new taxes were instituted, such as the 5 per cent inheritance tax, which Augustus introduced initially in AD 6 and which pertained exclusively to Roman citizens and hence territorially first and foremost to Rome and Italy, the task of collecting them was still assigned to *publicani*.[8] In this regard, without any hesitation, the old system remained in place. The *publicani* were basically not discredited as servants of the *res publica*, but, on the contrary, continued to undertake important responsibilities on the state's behalf as a matter of course. The only thing they no longer held was political power. Therefore, the recently added provincial procurators were not in any way officials who directly undertook the collecting of taxes from individuals liable to pay them. In fact, just like the quaestors elsewhere, they stood between the private tax collectors or communities and, respectively, the treasury

---

[8] See Eck, *Italien*, pp. 129ff.

of Saturn (*aerarium Saturni*) or Augustus in his capacity as the power-holder responsible for the province.

With the exception of Egypt, these were the only organisational and administrative changes that occurred in regards to personnel in the provinces. The overall impression is one of far-reaching continuity with the previous Republican period, particularly when we consider the number of officials who were entrusted with certain tasks. A substantial rise in their number did not take place, nor was there an immediately noticeable increase in the supply of subordinate officials.[9] Greater "efficiency" in provincial administration and, as a result, a clear reduction in the number of complaints from Rome's provincial subjects, in any case, cannot be attributed to this aspect of state activity. To be sure, the shifting of political power and the possibility of devising in the city of Rome measures concerning the provinces were far more important than any direct administrative changes.

A similar observation can also be made for Italy, the core region of the Empire.[10] As regards state administration, Italy was almost a power vacuum, since its annual magistrates were directly linked to the city of Rome. First of all, it was the local magistrates in the towns of Italy who were responsible for putting into effect generally binding regulations issued from Rome, not officials whose usual and regular realm of operation was Italy outside Rome and who were directly dependent on the senate or on Augustus. To be sure, Augustus organised Italy into eleven regions, but so far it is impossible to connect this creation of territorial districts with any specific activities of the Roman state and, to a much lesser degree, with administrative ones; in other words, with activities that recurred on a more or less regular basis. The only event that took place at regular intervals and was perhaps organised according to these regions was the recording of the local census results.[11] This cannot, however, be confirmed by any firm evidence. But even if this were correct, a new administrative system for Italy could not have been created, since there is no evidence for the appointment of officials

---

[9] It seems likely that the use of military staff (*officium*) for "civilian" purposes was not introduced by Augustus. See further M. A. Speidel, "Geld und Macht. Die Neuordnung des staatlichen Finanzwesens unter Augustus," in A. Giovannini (ed.), *La révolution romaine après Ronald Syme: bilans et perspectives* (Entretiens Hardt 46), Vandœuvres/Geneva 2000, pp. 113ff.

[10] See further Eck, *Italien*, but not limited to the Augustan period.

[11] See, though not entirely satisfying, W. Simshäuser, ANRW II 13 (1980), 410ff.; for a convincing overview of the problem, see U. Laffi, "L'organizzazione dell' Italia sotto Augusto e la creazione delle *regiones*," in L. Labruna, M. P. Baccari, and C. Cascione (eds), *Tradizione romanistica e costituzione*, Naples 2006, pp. 933ff.

permanently assigned to such an activity. This, in particular, would have been a basic requirement for a fundamental change in the administration of Italy.

In just two areas did Augustus create permanent administrative institutions and associated state officials for Italy: the so-called *cursus publicus* and the *cura viarum*, responsible for administering the major public roads outside Rome.[12] In both cases Augustus' motives are relatively clear. During the Republic local officials in the communities outside Rome had not been given responsibility for the public or military roads (*viae publicae* or *viae militares*); rather, Roman state magistrates had taken care of them ever since the construction of the Via Appia. In particular, it was military considerations that made this necessary. Furthermore, construction of these roads was never restricted to the territory of any one particular community; it therefore required coordination from a higher level. Both conditions – politico-military requirements and the need for an operation that extended over the territories of all local cities – still applied in the Augustan period. Besides, Augustus' need for political security depended no less on receiving fast and reliable information. This resulted in the creation of the *cursus publicus*.[13] Precisely when this occurred we do not know. We may assume, however, that it did not happen very late in Augustus' reign; it could hardly have taken place later than the period from 20 to 10 BC. Local magistrates became crucial in ensuring the day-to-day functioning of the *cursus publicus*, but its coordination Augustus seems to have transferred to a specific official known as the "prefect of the vehicles" (*praefectus vehiculorum*).[14] This prefect was selected by Augustus from men of equestrian rank; he was, therefore, one of the first officials chosen from this socio-political group.

Earlier still, Augustus had himself taken on supervision of the public roads (the *cura viarum*), but certainly not with the prime intention of keeping in his own hands an important instrument for the effective exercise of power; rather, his assumption of this responsibility was necessary for military and administrative reasons, because the network of roads and bridges had suffered greatly in the previous decades. Once the civil wars had come to an end, Augustus sought to induce his victorious colleagues of senatorial rank to use their respective spoils for the reconstruction of the neglected and

---

[12] See Eck, *Italien*, pp. 25ff., 88ff.
[13] Suet. *Aug.* 49f.; see also recently W. Eck, "Tacitus, Ann. 4,27,1 und der *cursus publicus* auf der Adria," *SCI* 13 (1994), 60ff.
[14] W. Eck, *Chiron* 5 (1975), 380f.; Eck, *Italien*, pp. 89ff.; cf. Brunt, *JRS* 73 (1983), 70.

partially destroyed roads of Italy.[15] He mentions in the *Res Gestae* (20.5) that he himself took on the repair of the Via Flaminia from Rome to Ariminum (Rimini), including its bridges. The remaining roads were supposed to be repaved by other triumphant generals. In other words, the notion that aristocrats should bear responsibilities on behalf of the *res publica*, a traditional Republican principle, was hereby being put into practice.[16] But most of these aristocrats refused to respond to Augustus' request. Only Calvisius Sabinus and Messalla Corvinus initiated construction work on the Via Latina and the road leading to Tusculum and Alba.[17] Augustus' plan to address public concerns with the traditional assistance of Roman aristocrats had, therefore, failed. This did not become clear until 20, when he, by means of a resolution from the senate, took on the "supervision of the roads" and appointed "supervisors of the roads" (*curatores viarum*) from the group of expraetors to assist him in the day-to-day execution of his duties; their position as public officials was symbolised by the two lictors carrying *fasces* who were assigned to them.[18] Augustus, therefore, had not by any means aimed to take over the management of the Italian road system all by himself; rather, he made this decision primarily because he realised that a more traditional approach to resolving the problems in this area would turn out to be either ineffective or even impossible to carry out. Therefore, it seems certain that he did not introduce the later custom of appointing eight *curatores viarum*. It was only under Nero or Vespasian that it evidently became customary to appoint eight of these officials. If these offices had already been in existence in the 20s BC, this would have been mentioned in our sources, as a comparison with offices of similar rank suggests. However, since there are very few attestations of *curatores viarum* before the age of Nero, we must conclude that, under Augustus, the organisational format for this office was different and that it involved a considerably smaller number of officials who worked together as colleagues.[19] What the format for this office was, we cannot tell for certain. Yet it is quite plausible that, in general, practical needs were satisfied, despite the very limited format in terms of personnel.

As in the provinces, so also, it appears, in Italy the action needed was generally quite small, at any rate as far as organisational changes

---

[15] Suet. *Aug.* 30.1.
[16] Cf. I. Shatzman, *Senatorial Wealth and Roman Politics*, Brussels 1975, pp. 90f.
[17] For example, ILS 889; AE 1969/1970, 89; Tib. 1.7.57ff.
[18] Dio 54.8.
[19] Eck, *Italien*, pp. 43f.; idem, "*Cura viarum* und *cura operum publicorum* als kollegiale Ämter im frühen Prinzipat," *Klio* 74 (1992), pp. 237ff. = Eck, *Verwaltung*, pp. 281ff.

that led to the appointment of new administrators were concerned. The city of Rome, however, presents a rather different impression. The passage of Suetonius cited at the start of this chapter explicitly mentions appointments, apart from the *cura viarum*, related to the centre of power. If an administrative deficiency was noticed in a precise sense in any area, then it was very possibly here.

As early as 28 BC, there was a change in the management of the treasury of Saturn: instead of quaestors, two prefects (*praefecti*) of praetorian rank were appointed. But already by the year 23 a return to the previous system had taken place: now two praetors, i.e., two regular annual magistrates, were appointed by lot to look after the administration of the treasury.[20] It was impossible to return to officials of quaestorian rank because quaestors now took up office at the age of 25 (rather than at 30, as had previously been the practice), an age at which they, as individuals, had only just reached full legal capacity. To entrust the management of the entire public treasury to such officials would presumably have demanded too much of their capacities. Nevertheless, here as well, the Republican method of selection by lot was still used, which demonstrates that considerations of specific, practical competence did not play any role in their appointment.

When M. Vipsanius Agrippa died in 12 BC, in his will he made Augustus heir to part of his wealth and a group of 240 of his slaves. These slaves had been employed in maintaining the aqueducts that Agrippa had constructed, the *Aqua Iulia* and the *Aqua Virgo*, as well as the inner-city waterworks he had built.[21] As Frontinus states in his work *On the Water Supply of the City of Rome* (*Aq.* 98), for more than twenty years Agrippa had acted as a quasi-supervisor of the aqueducts (*curator aquarum*) without ever actually having received any such official appointment. By providing his own slaves, he acted in a similar manner, for example, to Egnatius Rufus, who, as a powerful aristocrat, used his own funds to put an end to a deplorable state of affairs regarding fires for the citizens of Rome.[22] Presumably, the continued use for more than two decades of a private format for organising such projects, and not just limited to the year in which Agrippa was aedile, was only possible under the changed political circumstances. It is remarkable, however, that Augustus only came to devise a public legal solution after he had become Agrippa's heir. The solution he chose in 11 BC did not create a direct instrument

---

[20] M. Corbier, *L'aerarium Saturni et l'aerarium militare*, Rome 1974, pp. 17f.
[21] Frontin. *Aq.* 98ff.
[22] Vell. Pat. 2.91.3; Dio 53.24.4.

for himself because the slaves he had recently inherited from Agrippa were made public slaves (*servi publici*) and hence became the property of the Roman people. They were entrusted to a college (*collegium*) of three senatorial *curatores aquarum*, the leader of which was a man of consular rank.[23] As a result, a form of organisation was now established within an area of public supply involving a resource that was essential for the bulk of the population of Rome on a daily basis; the model adopted was to be maintained, in its essential features, for centuries to come. Once again, two observations are in order. It was only after Augustus had come to realise that a traditional solution – namely, Agrippa's private initiative – was no longer practicable that he implemented a new system. This, however, was triggered by a specific need rather than primarily by any motivation to provide more senators with public responsibilities, as Suetonius claims. For, what is more, this possibility had already arisen earlier. It should definitely be emphasised that the board of three was by no means fully occupied in supervising the water supply. Moreover, as is quite clear from a *senatus consultum* of the year 11 BC, the *curatores aquarum*, just like the *curatores viarum*, had other senatorial duties to perform, in particular as members of the judicial panels.[24] Presumably, it was even possible for any of the *curatores aquarum* to hold another public office at the same time.

Besides the supervision of the roads and the water supply, Suetonius attributes the supervision of the channel of the river Tiber (*cura alvei Tiberis*) as well as the supervision of public buildings of the city of Rome, both sacred and profane, to the reforms introduced by Augustus. This could well be true in the case of the supervision of the sacred temples, works, and public places (*cura aedium sacrarum et operum locorumque publicorum*), though it is hard to substantiate.[25] With regard to the *cura alvei Tiberis*, however, Suetonius' claim is demonstrably false. To be sure, there were reasons for administrative measures to be taken in this area because of the numerous and partially disastrous floods of the Tiber. In his narrative of quite a number of years, Cassius Dio repeatedly describes such

---

[23] Frontin. *Aq.* 99ff.; see, in general, C. Bruun, *The Water Supply of Ancient Rome: A Study of Roman Imperial Administration*, Helsinki 1991; W. Eck, "Organisation und Administration der Wasserversorgung Roms," in *Wasserversorgung im antiken Rom 1*, Frontinus Gesellschaft (1982), 63–77 = Eck, *Verwaltung*, pp. 161ff.

[24] Frontin. *Aq.* 101.1.

[25] This assumption is based only on Suetonius; there is no specific evidence for such an official in the Augustan period. Cf. A. E. Gordon, *Quintus Veranius consul A.D. 49* (University of California Publications in Classical Archaeology 2.5), Berkeley 1952, pp. 279ff.; W. Eck, *Klio* 74 (1992), 237ff.; A. Kolb, *Die kaiserliche Bauverwaltung in der Stadt Rom*, Stuttgart 1992.

catastrophes.[26] Nevertheless, no direct actions were taken to deal with even some of the repercussions of such frequently recurring natural disasters apart from the appointment of a special official, sometimes a consul, by the senate or the emperor himself. Only in the year AD 15, following a particularly disastrous and catastrophic flood, did Tiberius arrange for the appointment by lot of *curatores alvei Tiberis*.[27] In an emergency they were immediately available and, whenever the situation was particularly urgent, they could perhaps dedicate themselves to their responsibilities with greater intensity than regular, annual magistrates. These officials should not be considered one of Augustus' innovations, since, just like the urban prefecture (*praefectura urbis*), they only became a regular feature of Roman life under Tiberius.[28] Only at that time did the urban prefect take command of the urban cohorts (*cohortes urbanae*), which were themselves certainly created by Augustus. Admittedly, it is still debatable when the four cohorts were first established. For they were the true police-force of Rome, an enormous step forward compared to the anarchic conditions of the late Republic. Only by means of ad hoc measures had it been possible in the past to deal with emergencies.[29] Although the praetorians were regularly at Augustus' disposal for political and military protection from the year 27 BC onwards,[30] they should not be seen as a police-force in any civic or administrative sense. The first attestation of the existence of the urban cohorts occurs in the context of the year AD 5, when they are mentioned in a description of military dispositions under Augustus,[31] but this does not provide any information about the date when these four units were created. If they had been established at the same time as the praetorians, in the year 27, then this could be seen to be the result of an analysis of the causes of the late Republican crises in the city of Rome.[32]

---

[26] See, for example, Dio 53.20.1 (27 BC); 53.33.5 (23 BC); 54.1.1 (22 BC); 54.25.2 (13 BC); 55.22.3 (AD 5); 56.27.4 (AD 12).

[27] Dio 57.14.7; see also Tac. *Ann.* 1.76.1; J. Le Gall, *Le Tibre, fleuve de Rome dans l'antiquité*, Paris 1953, pp. 135f.

[28] See Tac. *Ann.* 6.11.3; P. Lambrechts, "Studien over romeinsche instellingen," *Philologische Studiën* 8 (1936/1937), 3–18.

[29] H. Freis, *Die cohortes urbanae*, Epigraphische Studien 2 (1967), 3ff. With regard to the problematic concept of policing in Rome, W. Nippel, "Aufruhr und Polizei in der späten römischen Republik und in der frühen Kaiserzeit," in *Der Mensch in seiner Umwelt*, Humanistische Bildung 6 (1983), 85ff.; also "Policing Rome," *JRS* 74 (1984), 20ff.

[30] Dio 53.11.5.

[31] Tac. *Ann.* 4.5.3.

[32] Of course one could assume from Suet. *Aug.* 49.1 that Suetonius believed that the *cohortes urbanae* were already established in 27 BC. However, compare the discussion with regard to this problem in Freis (cit. n. 29), pp. 4ff.

But this need not be the case, as the development of the night-watch (*vigiles*) indicates. During the late Republic smaller or larger fires frequently broke out in the city of Rome, but no administrative solution was devised to deal with them.[33] The urgency of this problem and the experiences of the inhabitants of Rome may be gauged from the political success that Egnatius Rufus achieved by establishing a unit of fire-fighters during his year as aedile. He presumably made use of his own slaves, who, specifically purchased for this purpose, were deployed in combating fires in the city of Rome.[34] This, in any case, was a traditional way for a Roman aristocrat to win popularity during his term as aedile. Nevertheless, political success did not lead to a permanent solution. After witnessing Egnatius Rufus' political success, Augustus himself created a permanent group of 600 slaves, but they remained at the disposal of the aediles currently in office, who changed on a yearly basis. Whether we are dealing with public slaves or with slaves owned by Augustus himself is unclear.[35] An improvement in the general situation presumably took place even though the manpower resources deployed did not relate in any meaningful way to the expansion in the built-up area of Rome. But Augustus operated basically within a Republican framework since the aediles were normally the appropriate officials responsible for such tasks. It seems, however, that this system did not function with any great effectiveness since the necessary speed of action could not be attained. The latter had to await a regulation devised in 7 BC.

Once the fourteen regions of the capital had been established, the respective magistrates of the urban neighbourhoods (*vici*) were evidently given fire-fighting responsibilities and, therefore, power over this group of slaves.[36] Since these *vicomagistri* also resided in the specific areas of the city for which they were each responsible, a prompt response to emergencies was in all likelihood guaranteed. Furthermore, the *vicomagistri* themselves in turn reported to senators (tribunes of the plebs, aediles, or praetors), who were assigned by lot to these fourteen districts. In this way the office was kept under senatorial control.[37]

---

[33] Cf. P. K. Baillie Reynolds, *The Vigiles of Imperial Rome*, London 1926, pp. 18f.; O. Robinson, "Fire Prevention at Rome," *RIDA* 24 (1977), 377ff. See now R. Sablayrolles, Libertinus miles. *Les cohortes de vigiles*, Rome 1996, pp. 6ff.
[34] Vell. Pat. 2.91.3, 92.4; Dio 53.24.4f.
[35] Dio 54.2.4; cf. 53.24.6 mentioning that aediles were instructed to include fire-fighting among their duties; see also Baillie Reynolds (cit. n. 33), pp. 20f.
[36] Dio 55.8.6f.
[37] Dio 55.8.7f.; cf. Baillie Reynolds (cit. n. 33), pp. 22f.

However, the definitive form of organisation had still not been found. After a clearly devastating fire had spread across various districts and destroyed a vast area of the city in the year AD 6, seven cohorts of night-watchmen (*cohortes vigilum*) were created, either 3,500 or 7,000 in total strength; that is, depending on whether there were 500 or 1,000 men per cohort. The assignment of each of these units to two of the fourteen districts and the decentralised stationing of these forces ensured a more efficient response to fires.[38] In this manner, the previous Republican system, which had involved the deployment of slaves for such assignments, was abandoned; instead of slaves, the new regulations now entailed the use of freedmen, who received regular pay, as a means of assuring the necessary motivation level.[39] Most importantly, however, one single individual was appointed to command all the units: the prefect of the night-watch (*praefectus vigilum*), who was, from the start, a man of equestrian rank. According to Cassius Dio, Augustus originally intended to disband the night-watch (*vigiles*) quite quickly, but their usefulness and the obvious need for them convinced him to keep them on.[40] Unless Dio's comment conceals some hidden agenda stemming from a political debate over the deployment of the *vigiles* that we can no longer grasp,[41] it provides further evidence for the fact that Augustus, even in such a vital area that obviously needed to be re-organised, did not in any way seek from the start to assert a firm control that would enable him to gain power over the senate in an important area of public life. Only as a result of experimentation forced upon him for a variety of reasons and quite late in his reign – in AD 6 – was a solution found that finally resolved these problems and which then remained in force for several centuries.

This careful process of experimentation over a period of almost thirty years can also be observed within a second, vital sector of inner-city life in Rome: namely, in the safeguarding of the grain supply for the population of the capital. In this, two separate aspects need to be distinguished: on the one hand, the distribution of free grain to a large part of the urban plebs and, on the other, the supply of grain for the city markets, where it could be bought by any Roman. During the late Republic, only the grain handouts (*frumen-*

---

[38] Dio 55.26.4f.; Baillie Reynolds (cit. n. 33), pp. 22ff.; Sablayrolles (cit. n. 33), pp. 249ff.; W. Eck, "Auf der Suche nach Personen und Persönlichkeiten: *Cursus honorum* und Biographie," in *Biographie und Prosopographie. Festschrift zum 65. Geburtstag von A. R. Birley*, ed. K. Vössing, Stuttgart 2005, pp. 53ff.
[39] Suet. *Aug.* 25.2; Strabo 5.3.7; Dio 55.26.4.
[40] Dio 55.26.4.
[41] Perhaps to allay political fears on the part of some of his opponents.

tationes) normally required the attention of government officials, who were, from Caesar's time onwards, the two "aediles of Ceres" (*aediles Cereales*).⁴² It was only probably for a five-year period that Pompeius assumed "supervision of the grain supply" (*cura annonae*) and also looked after the provisioning of cereals; this was an effective measure, but at the same time an exceptional one.⁴³ In connection with the difficulties caused by the powerful fleet of Sextus Pompeius in the 30s, Octavian came to realise how delicate an issue Rome's grain supply really was.⁴⁴ It was particularly in this context that the urban plebs became a political factor. Nevertheless, his first measures after the establishment of sole rule involved just grain handouts. This occurred for the first time in 22 BC in the wake of a menacing famine, when he himself, following Pompeius' example, took over the *cura annonae*.⁴⁵ It seems that Augustus did not create a system for the acquisition of grain similar to the one devised by Pompeius, which was implemented by means of *legati*. Rather, each year Augustus designated two former praetors, who had held office at least five years previously, as special officers for the distribution of grain.⁴⁶ The entrusting of a duty to higher-ranking officials in Rome usually points to the increased importance of that duty, at least from a political point of view. But in this case that was not necessarily the case. Moreover, we need to take account of the fact that, considering the general reduction in the age at which Republican magistrates up to and including praetors held office, the aediles, who were traditionally responsible for the grain handouts, now entered office at approximately the age of 27 instead of between 37 and 40, as had previously been the case. So when Augustus from 22 BC onwards selected the "grain supervisors" (*curatores frumenti*) from a pool of men who were at least 35 years old, he may have considered it necessary to avoid the negative impressions that might have resulted from the general inexperience of considerably younger officials compared to those appointed under the previous system. It should be pointed out, however, that these officials were selected by lot in the Republican fashion and were, without exception, senators. In this

---

⁴² G. Rickman, *The Corn Supply of Ancient Rome*, Oxford 1980, p. 59. Of course this does not mean that the aediles, occasionally, as well as other magistrates, were not also occupied with the influx of grain into Rome (see Rickman, pp. 34ff.); this is particularly clear from the new document from Larisa: P. Garnsey, T. Gallant, and D. Rathbone, "Thessaly and the Grain Supply of Rome during the Second Century B.C.," *JRS* 74 (1984), pp. 30ff.
⁴³ Rickman (cit. n. 42), pp. 55ff.
⁴⁴ App. *B.Civ.* 5.66ff., 71f.; Vell. Pat. 2.77.1; Suet. *Aug.* 16.1.
⁴⁵ *RG* 5; Dio 54.1.4.
⁴⁶ Dio 54.1.4.

way the senate's responsibilities in this area were certainly given recognition, as is also clear from the *senatus consultum* that was connected with the appointment of these *curatores*. Four years later modifications had already taken place with regards to their method of appointment and their number had been increased to four. According to Dio, these officials were to take on the distribution of grain one after the other.[47] What is striking about this new regulation is the reference to the successive rotation of these officials, now doubled in number, in carrying out their duties. If this new system were only implemented to deal with an increasing number of tasks, then its operational details would not make any sense. Since the office was only concerned with the immediate execution of the task at hand, it may be assumed that the senators involved were annoyed at the time-consuming and unrewarding nature of an office that did not have much prestige. Neither Augustus nor any other individual had much influence on who was appointed to this office, since every magistrate had to nominate someone of praetorian rank; from this group four prefects or grain supervisors were selected by lot. None of this had anything to do with practical experience or efficiency.

Furthermore, no permanent solution was yet devised to tackle the fundamental problem of Rome's grain supply, because no efforts were made to ensure the regular import of grain from outside Rome, especially from the provinces. Even in the years AD 5 to 7, when Rome was hit by a famine that was so devastating that foreigners had to be expelled from the city en masse, the remedy chosen first was to appoint (in addition?) two men of consular rank who were supposed to ensure greater efficiency in the supply mechanisms.[48] Since two lictors were assigned to them in AD 7,[49] it seems plausible that their activity extended outside the city of Rome as well.

It is certain, however, that, shortly afterwards, an equestrian prefect of the grain supply (*praefectus annonae*) had been appointed on a permanent basis, because such an official was clearly in office by AD 14.[50] Augustus' immediate motives for this step forward are not attested anywhere in our sources. But it seems quite obvious that if we take into account the prior example of the *praefectus vigilum*, we need to seek these motives in the area of practical needs. All previous measures demonstrated that annually changing magistrates, no

---

[47] Dio 54.17.1.
[48] Dio 55.22.3, 26.1ff., 31.4; Suet. *Aug.* 42.3.
[49] Dio 55.31.4.
[50] Tac. *Ann.* 1.7.2; see H. Pavis d'Escurac, *La préfecture de l'annone. Service administrative impériale d'Auguste à Constantin*, Rome 1976, pp. 29ff.

matter how they were appointed, were unable to achieve a reliable and long-lasting system of supply. With regard to direct distribution within the city of Rome, these one-year "officials" may have been sufficient, but not for the regulation of the flow of grain from overseas. The fundamental factor in Augustus' decision to appoint an equestrian rather than a senator in the city of Rome as his immediate representative for the grain supply (*annona*) stemmed, without doubt, from the need to devote attention to this matter on a permanent basis. This first took place more than thirty years after Augustus had personally taken on the supervision of the grain supply.

These were the essential administrative changes in so far as they manifested themselves in institutional terms in the appointment of certain permanent officials. We have not yet mentioned the two praetorian prefects (*praefecti praetorio*), who, from 2 BC onwards, commanded the praetorian cohorts.[51] This omission is intentional because the praetorian prefects of the Augustan period are irrelevant to the question of administration. With no other office does its later significance get so frequently transferred back to its origins in an anachronistic manner. Yet it is clear that the administrative and judicial duties that were increasingly assigned to the prefects in the second and third centuries AD simply did not exist – even in the most basic form – during the Augustan period. This also holds true partially for the *praefectus annonae* and the *praefectus vigilum*.[52]

This last observation leads one to ask what overall significance equestrians had in Augustus' administrative system and, more specifically, if there were political reasons for appointing members of the *ordo equester* to certain tasks. For even in recent scholarship on Augustus these measures are ascribed, in one way or other, to his tendency to have to take a stand for political reasons against the senate and its demands. For Augustus, the transfer of responsibilities to the equestrians created a counterbalance to the senate.[53]

One might assume that such a motive was very probably a factor in the appointment of Cornelius Gallus to the prefectship of Egypt (*praefectura Aegypti*).[54] For to entrust such a financially lucrative region, in which three legions were stationed, to an equestrian must

---

[51] Dio 55.10.10.
[52] See Kienast, *Augustus*, p. 113; Brunt, *JRS* 73 (1983), 59ff.
[53] See the literature cited in n. 1 above; also in W. Eck, "Die Ausformung der ritterlichen Administration als Antisenatspolitik?" in *Opposition et résistance à l'Empire d'Auguste à Trajan* (Entretiens Hardt 33), Geneva 1987, pp. 249–283 = Eck, *Verwaltung*, pp. 29ff.
[54] Compare, for example, the sources cited at Brunt, *JRS* 73 (1983), 61, n. 132; also Kienast, *Augustus*, pp. 64f.

have been, in this particular situation, an exceptional measure since it required a law (*lex*) to be specially introduced authorising the bestowal of proconsular *imperium* on an equestrian.[55] One might surmise that the role Egypt had played in the power struggle between Octavian and Antonius required a more careful approach. It was certainly much harder for an equestrian than it was for a senatorial official to stake a general political claim with the hope of gaining the necessary support from influential senators at Rome and in the provinces. In a highly significant analysis of the relationship between *princeps* and *equites*, P. A. Brunt argued that Augustus had pragmatic reasons for appointing Cornelius Gallus, since the latter was quite familiar with conditions in Egypt and had already commanded legions there during its conquest in 30 BC.[56] And this may well have been seen as an indispensable qualification in the case of the prefects who succeeded Gallus as well. Thus, the fact that Gallus was an equestrian was a mere accident. But since senators had certainly been part of Octavian's military staff in 30 BC, and among them were individuals with similar qualifications, this explanation for the appointment of an equestrian raises considerable doubts.

There were no other permanent equestrian governors under Augustus. The prefects who, for instance, held office in Judaea, Raetia, and also perhaps Noricum were not responsible for provinces, but rather just for sections of provinces. In point of fact they were always subordinate to a senatorial legate, as in the case of Judaea, where the prefect was subject to the legate of Syria. The prefect of Raetia was also subordinate to a military commander on the Rhine. Only in the case of Sardinia is the situation unclear.[57] In any case, these sub-governors did not play any role in issues of political power or security. Militarily they were unimportant, the prefect of Sardinia included, in particular because all of them were subordinate to senators. The reason for their appointment by Augustus presumably varied from one province to the next; it should certainly not be seen as having been caused by problems over security. On the other hand, as we have already seen, the appointment of procurators from the ranks of equestrians and, to a degree, freedmen in place of quaestors was possibly simply motivated by the

---

[55] *Dig.* 1.17.1 (Ulpian).
[56] Brunt, *JRS* 73 (1983), 62f.
[57] Arguing against, for example, Pflaum, *Procurateurs*, 46 for Sardinia (still under Vespasian), as well as G. Meloni, *L'amministrazione della Sardegna da Augusto all'invasione vandalica*, Rome 1958; G. Walser, "Via per Alpes Graias," in *Beiträge zur Geschichte des Kleinen St. Bernhard-Passes in römischer Zeit*, Stuttgart 1986, pp. 17, 19.

practical constraint of the number of senators available for such tasks.[58] In no way does this amount to any tendencies against the senate.

It still remains to discuss the equestrian officials who were introduced at Rome by the *princeps* himself. Here we do not need to consider C. Maecenas, since his influence rested on his unofficial position. The first point to note is the rather advanced date at which equestrian prefects were appointed in the city of Rome: 2 BC for the praetorian prefects, perhaps AD 6/7 for the prefect of the nightwatch, a position that, according to Dio, Augustus wanted to eliminate sooner rather than later, and, finally, between AD 8 and 14 for the prefect of the grain supply. The prefects, so it seems, made their initial appearance at a time when Augustus' position was very firmly entrenched rather than at the beginning of his reign, when some kind of threat to his position might still be assumed to exist. In terms of political power, only the praetorian prefects had any kind of potential, which possibly found its expression through the collegiality that was a feature of their office, but their power only involved control over the military and had nothing to do with administrative power. One of the praetorian prefects could always intervene to avert a critical situation with regards to issues of power.

This, however, was not the case with the *praefectus vigilum* and the *praefectus annonae*. Both positions seem to have been designed in such a way that senators were probably never considered for them at all, for a number of reasons. To deal with the grain supply, as well as to try to prevent serious fires, Augustus experimented with various possible solutions; here, with the exception of the *vicomagistri*, only senators had been given responsibility for the tasks at hand. In the end, all these models turned out to be ineffective. One of the reasons may have been the inexperience of the officials and, even more, the limitations caused by the fact that each office lasted just one year. In any case, the first *praefectus annonae* held office for several decades.[59] On the other hand, the *praefectus vigilum* was required to be continually on call day and night, which was hardly compatible with a senatorial position.[60] A senator as *praefectus annonae* would never have been able to take part in meetings of the

---

[58] Cf. above, p. 238.

[59] C. Turranius Gracilis was *praefectus annonae* from at least AD 14 to 48: see Pavis d'Escurac (cit. n. 50), pp. 317ff.

[60] *Dig.* 1.15.3.3 (Paulus). We need to consider, however, what was discussed above (p. 239) in regard to the *curatores aquarum* or *viarum* and their availability for judicial responsibilities.

senate. Shouldn't we at the very least see practical requirements such as these as a fundamental reason for the advancement of equestrians in place of senators? Since, in particular, there were no direct Republican precedents for a permanently maintained fire brigade, senators did not lose control of any area in which they had previously been involved. All we know points in this direction rather than towards measures that were allegedly characterised by a mistrust of senatorial officials. The essential reasons are more likely to be found in practical requirements that arose from specific situations.

It is possible to draw the following conclusions from the foregoing discussion:

1. The measures that Augustus took with regard to Roman administrative institutions were not in total very numerous.[61] Moreover, his actions were concerned to a relatively small degree with Italy and the provinces and focused to a much greater extent on the city of Rome.
2. These measures did not stem predominantly from any overarching scheme that Augustus had devised to secure his own power and weaken those who had previously held power. In fact, most of his administrative reforms were closely related to the needs and difficulties that arose in all their clarity and urgency over the course of four decades. The reason for Augustus' interventions cannot, therefore, be attributed to any analysis on his part of a deficiency in terms of administration that had caused the fall of the Republic, especially when we consider that most of the definitive changes took place quite late: namely, in the last decade of Augustus' life.
3. In his early years in power, Augustus exclusively appointed senators to hold the new posts that he introduced, and he relied quite overwhelmingly on them later in his reign as well. This occurred, so it would appear, once again mainly for reasons of administrative necessity rather than, as Suetonius claims, out of a prime concern to reinforce the links between senators and the *res publica*. At the same time we should not abandon Suetonius' idea in its entirety. Equestrian officials, who were much less numerous than their senatorial counterparts, were not appointed to strengthen Augustus' political position, but primarily to meet

---

[61] This does not express how deeply Augustus affected the daily life of the citizen by means of his wide-ranging programme of legislation; on this, see Kienast, *Augustus, passim*. But this did not have any direct impact on Rome's administrative structure.

practical demands. In the area of such practical demands also belongs, among others, Augustus' initiative to restore the number of senators to 600, its former Republican level.

On his death, Julius Caesar left behind a variety of major proposals still in the planning stage.[62] It appears that this would not have been the case if Augustus had died earlier than he did. His policies developed slowly and in stages and, if one disregards his desire to secure power, depended on situations; they were motivated by particular circumstances much more than by any desire to shape the Empire according to a set of consistent ideas. That Augustus' reign was so stable was a not insignificant consequence of this kind of pragmatic political approach.

---

[62] On this, see M. Jehne, *Der Staat des Diktators Caesar*, Köln 1987.

8 Family and Inheritance in the Augustan Marriage Laws†*

ANDREW WALLACE-HADRILL

> Finally in his sixth consulship Caesar Augustus, securely in control, cancelled the orders he had issued as triumvir and laid the legal foundations for use in peace under principate. The bonds were more bitter from then on; watchers were set over us, with the inducement of rewards from the *lex Papia Poppaea*; the aim was that if men shirked the privileges of parenthood, the state as common parent should lay claim to their vacant possessions. (Tac. *Ann.* 3.28)

In a remarkable excursus, Tacitus casts the Augustan marital laws as the culmination of the whole history of Roman legislation. Two points emerge forcefully from his account: the laws were regarded as in some sense fundamental to the principate; and yet they were no easy laws, but ones that chafed bitterly. Both points are borne out by other ancient witnesses. That they were fundamental is still maintained by a panegyrist of Constantine, scarcely more than a decade before in 320 the essential provisions were repealed as conflicting

---

† Originally published in the *Proceedings of the Cambridge Philological Society*, n.s. 27 (1981), 58-80.

The following works are referred to by author and date of publication only.
R. Astolfi, *La lex Iulia et Papia* (1970).
P. A. Brunt, 'The Augustan Marriage Laws', in *Italian manpower* (1971), Appendix 9, 558-66.
P. Csillag, *The Augustan laws on family relations* (1976).
J. Goody, J. Thirsk, E. P. Thompson, *Family and inheritance: rural society in Western Europe 1200-1800* (1976).
M. Humbert, *Le remariage à Rome* (1972).
D. Nörr, 'Planung in der Antike. Uber die Ehegesetze des Augustus', in *Freiheit und Sachzwang. Beiträge zu Ehren Helmut Schelskys* (1977).
L. F. Raditsa, 'Augustus' legislation concerning marriage, procreation, love affairs and adultery', *ANRW* II 13 (1980) 278-339.
S. Riccobono, *Acta Divi Augusti* (1945) 166-98.
A. Watson, *The law of succession in the later Roman Republic* (1971).
 For full bibliographical references see Raditsa (1980).

* I am grateful to the members of the Society, before whom this paper was delivered on 7 May 1981, for their comments. I have profited enormously from discussion of the subject with Peter Brunt, John Crook and Peter Garnsey; naturally they are not to be taken as sanctioning my views. After delivering the paper, I discovered that some of my ideas were shared with Keith Hopkins. I include references to the chapter of his forthcoming book [i.e., *Death and Renewal* (1983)] which he generously showed me in typescript; our arguments are however independent.

Family and Inheritance   251

with Christian ideals of celibacy. To feel how bitterly they chafed it is enough to read the Latin love elegists.[1]

What then were these laws for? It has proved surprisingly difficult to discover why they were considered worth putting up with, how indeed they could have been supposed to have the slightest effect, let alone proving fundamental. Indeed, there is an 'official' explanation. Yet it rings hollow, and suspiciously so.

Officially, the laws were designed to stimulate the birthrate and secure the state's military manpower. The theme is clear in the Augustan poets.[2] Propertius protests against the first attempts at legislation: 'nullus de nostro sanguine miles erit' ['no one from our bloodline will become a soldier']. The same picture emerges from Horace's idealisation of the Sabine farmer-soldier; and one may guess it was the main drift of the old censorial oration of Metellus Macedonicus which Augustus read to the people and the senate.[3] Yet Brunt has shown conclusively that the laws can have had no effect on most of the peasantry from whom the legions were recruited.[4] The demonstration is simple. The laws operated through a series of rewards and penalties. In their nature these could only affect either the substantial property owners, those who sought office locally and at Rome, or freedmen, particularly the better off. The only provision likely to affect the 'ordinary' man was that bachelors were banned from certain shows, or were assigned separate seats. Even this is obviously only of significance to the urbanite, not to that 'rusticorum mascula militum proles' ['the manly offspring of country-born soldiers'] so adept with his Sabellian mattock. The younger Pliny is quite frank about the limitations of the law: 'vast rewards and corresponding penalties encourage the propertied (*locupletes*) to rear children, but for the poor, a generous princeps is the sole reason for bringing them up' (*Pan.* 26.5).[5]

---

[1] *Pan. Lat.* 7 (6) 2.4 'quare si leges eae ... vere dicuntur esse fundamenta rei publicae ...' ['wherefore if those laws ... are truly said to be the foundations of the state']. The 'si' implies however a note of doubt. On the elegists and public morality see in general R. Syme, *History in Ovid* (1978) 199-214.
[2] See G. Williams, 'Poetry in the Moral Climate of Augustan Rome', *JRS* 52 (1962) 28-46; J. H. W. G. Liebeschuetz, *Continuity and change in Roman religion* (1979) 90-100.
[3] Prop. 2.7.14; Hor. *Odes* 3.6.37-41; for the speech of Metellus, Aul. Gell. *NA* 1.6; Suet. *Aug.* 89.2. See also *Pan. Lat.* 7 (6) 2.4 'quasi fontem humani roboris semper Romanis exercitibus ministrarunt' ['as if they always provided the source of strength for Roman armies'].
[4] Brunt (1971) esp. 562-6.
[5] Plin. *Pan.* 26.5. The *Gnomon* of the Idios Logos 32 rules that only men worth over 100,000 HS [sesterces] (i.e. members of the first census class) were affected; the lower limit for women was 50,000 HS, id. 30. Humbert (1972) 143 n. 7 thinks these levels may not be the original Augustan ones. For further details of rewards for parenthood see conveniently Brunt (1971) 563, and in detail Astolfi (1970) 333-41; Csillag (1976) 164-74. Riccobono (1945) remains a useful compendium of the texts.

Of course it was not easy to design rewards and penalties that *would* affect the peasant. It was generally supposed that the humble imitated their social superiors (a topos going back to Plato), and certainly emperors tried to play this card. Augustus sat in the theatre with his great-grandsons on his lap to quieten protest; and Claudius granted early retirement to a gladiator with four sons, advertising publicly that this was a lesson of the rewards of paternity.[6] But I think we do Augustus and his successors an injustice if we suppose they seriously expected this legislation to affect the general birthrate. The only practicable measure would have been a system of child allowances, such as adopted by modern states.[7] Now of course Trajan's alimentary schemes were a step in that direction and Pliny loudly welcomes parallel measures at Rome as encouraging the poor to raise infants to serve under the colours.[8] Yet the professed intentions of raising Italian troops are belied by actual imperial recruitment patterns. From Augustus on, the area of recruitment gradually shifts from Italy to the provinces; and it is quite clear that even non-citizens were enrolled and granted citizenship on the spot. It is incredible that this was due to the paucity of citizen manpower in Italy. Italians were spared because they were unwilling to serve. The length of service and the distance of the frontiers from home were surely the crucial factors; it is only in the Praetorian Guard, based in Italy, that Italians are still regularly found after the first century A.D.[9] One can hardly maintain that emperors simultaneously imposed marital legislation primarily in order to raise troops and yet failed to recruit them. So the military theme is *ideological*. As Veyne says à propos the *alimenta* [alimentary schemes], it seems as if states that wish to encourage childbearing for other reasons like to play on the emotive citizen-soldier ideal. Even English pamphleteers like Defoe and Petty stressed this theme when their real motives were quite other.[10]

Talk of soldiers is designed to set the patriotic blood thumping. But it brings us no nearer to understanding why it was felt necessary to subject the propertied classes to the burden of oppressive legislation. The aim of this paper is to explore an aspect of reproduction that has

---

[6] For the topos, see the collection of references in A. J. Woodman, *Velleius Paterculus: the Tiberian narrative* (1977) 245. For the incidents cited, Suet. *Aug.* 34.2; *Claud.* 21.5.

[7] The point was made by Bouché-Leclerq when the French were debating how to promote their birthrate in the late 19th century: 'Les lois démographiques d'Auguste', *Rev. Hist.* 57 (1895) 241-92.

[8] Plin. *Pan.* 26. 3 'alimentisque tuis ad stipendia tua pervenirent' ['so that they might pass from your alimentary schemes to the military pay you provide'].

[9] See P. A. Brunt, 'Conscription and volunteering in the Roman imperial army', *Script. Class. Isr.* 1 (1974) 90-115.

[10] P. Veyne, *Le pain et le cirque* (1976) 652.

been neglected in this context. One of the functions of the institution of marriage, at least among the well-to-do, is to act as a vehicle for the transmission of property from generation to generation.[11] The thesis of this paper, crudely put, is that Augustus aimed to encourage the family in order to stabilise the transmission of property, and consequently of status, from generation to generation.

MARRIAGE LAWS AND INHERITANCE

It is by no means unparalleled for states to discourage celibacy and reward the production of children. In Sparta failure to marry (ἀγαμία) was an offence, as were late marriage (ὀψιγαμία) and mésalliance (κακογαμία). The penalty appears to have been a fine. Incorrigible bachelors were also subject to strong social stigma. Production of children was rewarded: fathers of three or four sons were exempted from military service and other burdens.[12] Modern dictatorial regimes have also proved anxious to multiply the birth-rate.[13] Notable are the incentives established by Stalin in Russia; higher taxes for celibates and small families, generous maternity benefits, and graded decorations ('Motherhood Medals') for good breeders. The Romans too believed in a traditional abhorrence from celibacy: laws against it were attributed to Romulus.[14] But what sets the Augustan laws apart, it seems, from all others, is that they operated primarily through intervening in the pattern of inheritance.

Certainly the scope of *praemia* [rewards] and *poenae* [penalties] was wider than matters of inheritance. Parenthood brought some advantages in selection for political office; immunity in some cases from local financial burdens and the duties of guardianship; it could free a woman from the disadvantages of legal minority (*tutela*), and a freedman from his obligations of service to his patron.[15] Nevertheless, it was the provisions affecting inheritance which were regarded as central. They formed the centre of discussion in ancient legal writers (as in modern); they are the most frequently alluded to by ancient sources; and it was these that brought in their wake the regime of *delatores* [accusers] which Tacitus so resented.

---

[11] For recent discussion of the role of property-transmission in Athenian marriage, and specifically in the institution of *engye* [marriage/surety] see E. J. Bickerman, 'La conception du mariage à Athènes', *BIDR* ser. 3.17 (1975) 1-28, and J. P. Gould, *JHS* 100 (1980) 43-6.
[12] For references, P. A. Cartledge, 'Spartan Wives: liberation or licence?', *CQ* n.s. 31 (1981) 84-105 at 95.
[13] Raditsa (1980) 286-8 draws attention to fascist interest in encouraging procreation.
[14] Brunt (1971) 559.
[15] Riccobono (1945) 174-80. Further see n. 5 above.

These considerations seem to me to justify the adoption of an unusual tactic. By considering the marriage laws in their role as inheritance laws, it may be possible to cast light on their background and aims. We can ask just what was the pattern of transmission of property (and consequently status) the legislation sought to promote, what were its desired and actual consequences in Roman society. The tactic has a secondary advantage. The social implications of inheritance patterns is a topic on which there is a growing body of literature by students of other societies.[16] While I can offer no parallel for the Roman situation, it is at least helpful to be aware of the practices of other societies in order to put into perspective the peculiarities of Roman society.

As an approach shot, I shall raise a possibility not previously considered in detail. Augustus carries the responsibility for the extinction of the republican nobility. May it not have been his intention to smash old and established families by ensuring the fragmentation of their estates?[17]

One of the most striking features of the testamentary practice of the Roman aristocracy is that there was no tradition of impartibility, that is to say, no expectation that 'the family estate' would pass to a single heir. By contrast, primogeniture and entail were crucial for the survival of the post-feudal aristocracy of Europe.[18] In the mid-eighteenth century it was conjectured that the dissolution of entails and the consequent fragmentation of noble estates had been a prime factor leading to the English civil war. When the Protestants wanted to destroy the power of the Irish Catholic nobility in 1704, they simply enacted that their estates must 'descend to all and every the sons of such papists ... share and share alike ...'.[19] The ancients too were well aware of the consequences of partibility. Aristotle is sharply critical of the Spartan rewards for fathers of three and four: 'it is obvious that, if there were many children, the land being distributed as it is, many of them must necessarily fall into poverty'.

---

[16] I have found particularly useful the collection of essays edited by Goody *et al.* (1976). See also Goody's papers reprinted in *Production and reproduction* (1976); Lawrence Stone's *Family, sex and marriage in England 1500-1800* (1977); and various articles in the *Journal of Family History* (1976-).

[17] This is apparently the view of Csillag (1976) 45. For Augustus and the 'doom' of the nobility, Syme, *Roman revolution* (1939) 490-508 is classic.

[18] For the contrast between Rome and early modern Europe see E. Rawson, 'The Ciceronian Aristocracy and its Properties', in M. Finley (ed.) *Studies in Roman property* (1976) 85-102. Her views need to be modified in view of E. R. Treggiari, 'Sentiment and Property', in A. Parel and T. Flanagan (eds.) *Theories of property* (1979) 53-85; nevertheless the basic contrast still seems to me valid.

[19] Both examples from J. P. Cooper, 'Patterns of inheritance and settlement by great landowners', in Goody *et al.* (1976) 192-327 at 193-5.

Family and Inheritance

Hence, he supposes, the inequitable pattern of land tenure and the shortage of Spartiates.[20] How far the republican nobility achieved effective impartibility by disadvantaging some sons is a question we cannot answer; but at least it should be a fair conjecture that one of the reasons for low birthrate in the late republic was the fear of overburdening the estate with heirs. What were the implications of Augustus' laws for great estates?

In this light, the crucial question is how many children the law required. The figure of three springs instantly to mind. It was the *ius trium liberorum* that privileged *orbi* [men without children] like Martial, Pliny or Suetonius were granted by the emperor.[21] Three surviving children were necessary to secure exemption from *tutelae* [legal guardianships] or *munera* [obligatory public services]. To be senior consul, indeed, it was necessary to have as many children as possible; what is more, they must be surviving and *in potestate* [under the legal control (of their father)], though death on the battle front was allowed as survival. But though the full range of legal advantages was reserved for parents of three, escape from the crucial disabilities did not require so many children. To burden the estate with three surviving children might indeed be catastrophic. But for purposes of *capacitas*, ability to take under wills, one surviving child was enough.[22] But what if it died? That was a real enough possibility: it is calculated that the chances of a child surviving its parent in a pre-industrial society with low life-expectancy are only 1 in 3.[23] The legislator saw this, and laid down a complicated scale. One child surviving into puberty secured full *capacitas*; or two children surviving to 3 years; or three surviving to the *nominum diem*, the day of name-giving. How many were born was of course irrelevant; for infanticide was a substitute for birth-control, and evidently one of the practices the law needed to check.[24]

---

[20] Arist. *Pol.* 1270 b 1-7.
[21] On the *ius trium liberorum* see Steinwenter, RE 10 (1919) 1281-4; Astolfi (1970) 99-102 and 174-9.
[22] Juvenal 9.87-90 makes it quite clear that a single child was sufficient for full *capacitas*: further children brought other advantages, 'commoda praeterea iungentur multa caducis / si numerum si tres implevero' ['besides many advantages will be yoked to the caduciary property, if I fill up the number to bring it to three']. Csillag (1976) 83 is wholly misleading on this point.
[23] See the tables in J. Goody, *Production and reproduction* (1976) 133-4. By these calculations, given a 2 in 3 probability of the child dying before the father, even with an average of 3 children per family, only 40.9% of families would produce a male heir; 24.2% would have daughters only; 35% would remain childless. The chances of one child surviving to puberty, as envisaged in the Augustan laws, are naturally considerably higher.
[24] These details derive from *Tit. Ulp.* 16.1a on transmission between man and wife. Astolfi (1970) 175 takes them to be of general application. For *nominum diem* [the name-giving day] some prefer *nonum diem* [the ninth day]; there is no material difference, as name-giving

The aim of destroying estates, then, can hardly be attributed to Augustus. His scale is in fact nicely calculated to make the production of a single heir as easy as possible. But the case of rich freedmen (worth over 100,000 HS [sesterces]) was very different. The patron had a claim to a share of the estate, unless there were a full three surviving children left as *heredes* [heirs].[25] The implications are very interesting: it would be almost impossible for a freedman worth 100,000 HS but no more to leave any heir who would in turn be in the first census class. So it looks as if the only status Augustus wanted to diminish was that of the freedman *parvenu*.

Perhaps in this connection we should take note of another phenomenon. It is a well-attested practice under the early empire for rich freedmen to secure a place in the local senate for their sons by a munificent benefaction to the town. So a freedman from Carsulae frankly records that he built an aqueduct and distributed *denarii* to the populace in recognition of his son's election to the duumvirate.[26] In cases where the freedman was likely to lose half his estate to his patron or his patron's family, it is possible that such benefactions may have operated as a dodge, designed to buy in advance prestige for the son and heir, before the patron could lay hands on the estate.

However this may be, the essential point that has been gained is that the law might have different implications for freeborn and ex-slave. So long as we regard the sole purpose of the laws as to multiply children, the differentiation is concealed. But when they are interpreted as inheritance laws, the provisions emerge as carefully nuanced.

FAMILY AND 'OUTSIDERS'

Once the path has been cleared of the misconception of Augustus as the enemy of old family estates, it is possible to understand his attitude to the family properly. The first point which I wish to underline is simple enough. It is common in the literature on Augustus' laws to speak of them as *compelling* citizens to marry and beget children.[27] This is of course technically wrong; but worse, it conceals the degree of freedom of choice that remained open. Every citizen could decide

---

took place on the ninth (possibly eighth) day. Its significance is that name-giving involved the decision to rear the child.

[25] See below, n. 40.

[26] For the practice, M. L. Gordon, *JRS* 21 (1931) 65-77; P. D. A. Garnsey in B. Levick (ed.), *Essays in honour of C. E. Stevens* (1975) 167-80.

[27] So e.g. Csillag (1976) 81. So too Humbert (1972) 146-7 speaks of 'the obligation to remarry', 'being constrained to remarry'. In this sense Humbert overplays his valuable discussion of the conflict between the laws and the Roman ideal of the *univira* [woman with a single husband throughout her life].

whether to opt for the advantages of 'obeying' the law or the advantages of 'disobeying' it. The advantages of *orbitas* [childlessness] is a topic on which the sources incessantly complain. What were the disadvantages? Reduced to its simplest form, the law stated that a man or woman of child-producing age was not entitled to take under wills (*capax*) unless married and with children; the childless married (*orbus*) might only take half of any bequest.[28]

But to this rule there was (or so one reads in most of the modern handbooks and discussions of the laws) a very considerable exception: relatives to the sixth degree of relationship could inherit irrespective of marital status.[29] One only need reflect on the inheritance practices of our own and other societies to see how important an exception this is. In almost all the literature on inheritance, it is taken for read that property will be transmitted within the family. The crucial differences consist in different ways of transmitting property within the family: notably in the contrast between practices of partibility and impartibility, that is whether the estate goes to a single heir (and if so, whether by primogeniture, by ultimogeniture – 'borough English' –, or by parental choice) or whether it is divided among the children (and if so on what system, and what part daughters play, and so on).[30] Of course, the literature is tilted towards the study of relatively primitive societies. Perhaps the Romans should be compared to more sophisticated, urbanised societies. Yet I doubt whether we could find one on which the Augustan laws with such exemptions could have made much of an impact. Legacies to friends have been a common enough phenomenon in early modern and contemporary Western society; yet it is dubious whether any legal inducements to marry could at any period have been built out of restrictions of freedom in this respect.

In view of this, we must ask whether so large a circle can really have been exempted from the laws. There is indeed room for doubt about the extent of the exceptions: the evidence only allows us to be confident that close family (to three degrees of relationship) was exempted, though the indications that extended family was also let off are strong.[31] But what makes the privileged position of family in

[28] Stated at Gaius *Inst.* 2.286. On the 'rewards for childlessness' see below nn. 54 and 61.
[29] Thus Buckland, *A text-book of Roman law* ed. 3 (1963) 293; M. Kaser, *Römische Privatrecht* I (1971) 724; Brunt (1971) 564. For detailed argument see Appendix (below, pp. 271-274)
[30] So Goody in Goody *et al.* (1976) 14: 'Inheritance is the transmission of ... material property at death ... It is everywhere dominated by kinship and conjugality; property is usually redistributed among the "relatives" ...'. P. 13 for the different types.
[31] See Appendix.

rules affecting inheritance intrinsically plausible is the powerful sentiment attested after the legislation as well as before. Family was regarded as having a claim as of right to inheritance of property. The sentiment is articulated most explicitly in a passage of Pliny's *Panegyric*.[32] Trajan had made some adjustments to the operation of the *vicesima hereditatum*, the 5 per cent tax on inheritance established by Augustus to raise revenue for military pensions. Close family (we do not know how close) was exempted from the operation of this law; and Pliny explains the logic. He describes the tax as tolerable for heirs as long as they were outsiders (*extranei*) but burdensome for members of the family (*domestici*). Hence the exemptions, 'for it was obvious how painful, in fact how downright intolerable men would find it for a portion to be scraped and nibbled away from the possessions which they had earned by their blood, gentility and common share in rites, possessions which they never took as a windfall from outside, but as their own, always held by the same hands and to be passed in turn to their closest kin'.[33] This is highly charged language and Pliny roots it in ancient Roman sentiment by invoking archaic terminology. *Gentilitas* [kinship] and the share in *sacra* [religious rites] had meaning for the traditional republican aristocracy; indeed, by the *ius gentilicium* [law concerning a *gens*, i.e., wider kinship group] property without an heir ultimately devolved on the *gens*. But this had already become obsolete in the first century B.C. and common *gens* and *sacra* can have meant little in practical terms to the families of the early empire.[34]

Pliny's distinction between family and outsiders (*extranei*) is fundamental. He clearly regards the state as having no claim on property transmitted within the family, and what is said of the *vicesima hereditatum* must apply equally to the marital laws. Pliny's attitudes are supported by the moralistic collection of anecdotes by Valerius Maximus on 'wills which were rightly cancelled' (7.7) and on 'wills which could rightly have been cancelled but were allowed to remain' (7.8.1–4). Both classes show clearly what a Roman writing after the passage of the marital laws regarded as right and proper. One of the preoccupations that emerges most strongly is the absolute right of close family to inherit. The rights of the son though supposed dead (7.7.1), emancipated (2) or disinherited (3) are taken for granted.

[32] Plin. *Pan.* 37-40 on the *vicesima*. On this tax see Wesener, *RE* VIII A (1958) 2471-7.
[33] *Pan.* 37.2 'manifestum erat quanto cum dolore laturi seu potius non laturi homines essent destringi aliquid et abradi bonis, quae sanguine gentilitate sacrorum denique societate meruissent, quaeque numquam ut aliena et speranda sed ut sua semperque possessa ac deinceps proximo cuique transmittenda cepissent'.
[34] On the *ius gentilicium* and its disappearance see Watson (1971) 180-2.

Notable is the case where Augustus prevents a mother entering a second marriage with an old man and disinheriting her two children (4). Daughters too have a strong claim, and it is regarded as very odd when a mother makes only one of her two daughters heir (7.8.2). In absence of children, agnates have the strongest claim: all sympathies are with Pompeius Reginus, who was passed over by his brother for *alieni* [those in someone else's legal power]; he could have taken up the case in court, but preferred not to (7.8.4). But even remoter family are conceived of as having a prior claim over outsiders. Metellus Nepos, consul in 57 B.C., in making an outsider his heir passed over not only his brother, but all the numerous Metelli, let alone the Claudii to whose *gens* he also belonged (7.8.3). At least in an aristocrat, it was regarded as odd to ignore what Pliny calls 'gentilitas sacrorumque societas' ['kinship and common share in sacred rites'].

None of this is very surprising to us. But what most societies take for granted, the Romans regarded as a duty. The implication is that there was strong temptation to do otherwise. Granted the exception of family (however defined) Augustus' marriage laws could only have effect insofar as there was a widespread social convention, at least among the upper classes, of leaving property outside the family. Exactly the same is implied by the limitation of the *vicesima hereditatum*: the state depended for a revenue of very considerable proportions on the assumption that property would be willed outside the family.[35] And of course this pattern is widely attested. One thinks of that stock figure of Roman satire, the *captator* [legacy hunter], hunting bequests for a living: how else was Ulysses to patch together again his estate on return to an Augustan Ithaca, than by courting rich and filthy bachelors and offering the services of his wife? Here was the world in which the childless flourished, and paternity brought crippling disadvantages. Plutarch devotes a little essay to the contrast between the natural love of offspring in the animal world, and the horror of children among humans. Who does not love the rich bachelor; and what man does not lose his friends when he produces a son and heir?[36]

---

[35] This is stressed by Keith Hopkins in his forthcoming book [since published as *Death and Renewal* (1983), esp. ch. 4]. He calculates (but doubts) an implied annual volume of inheritance outside the immediate family of over 1300 million HS [*Death and Renewal*, 243 and n. 56].

[36] Hor. *Sat.* 2. 5; Plut. *de amore prolis* esp. 497 A–C. For the endless texts on legacy hunting see L. Friedländer, *Sittengeschichte*, ed. 10, I 248-53; Mayor's commentary on Juvenal, index s.v. *captatio*, *orbus*. Keith Hopkins (forthcoming [*Death and Renewal*, 238-47]) has an illuminating discussion of the phenomenon.

Satire offers an exaggerated stereotype. But the truth underlying it constitutes the central and distinctive feature of Roman practice. The laws belong to the context of a pattern of conventions linked by a causal nexus. People (the rich) generally left at least some of their estate outside the family: the childless were courted for their estate: childlessness flourished: families declined: so more people left property outside the family. Here is the spiral into which Augustus sought to break.

PROTECTION OF THE FAMILY

We are now able to define a little more sharply the pattern of transmission of property which Augustus wanted to encourage. Social pressure urged men to leave property outside the family, to *extranei*; Augustus countered these pressures by making it harder to leave to outsiders, unless they were family men (or women) themselves, and so less likely to leave property in turn to outsiders. A brief look at some of the details may support the contention that Augustus wanted property to stay 'in the family'. Three main types of transmission are involved; between outsiders, between man and wife, and between master and slave.

(a) Extranei

As we have seen, we must considerably modify the common summary of the law, 'bachelors could not take under wills, and bequests to them were confiscated by the state'. It is only in inheritances and legacies outside the family that the restriction applies. Nor did *caduca* [property left vacant where there were no legitimate heirs] go straight to the state. Family had first claim, and with them any heirs or legatees who had children; only failing them did the state profit.[37] Both points may be illustrated by the sodomite of Juvenal's ninth Satire. He does a favour to the infertile old man, by fathering a child on his wife. The old man has a lot to be grateful for:

> iura parentum habes, propter me scriberis heres,
> legatum omne capis nec non et dulce caducum. (9.87-8)

> [You have the rights of parents; because of me you'll be written down as heir; you take every legacy including that quite sweet vacant property.]

But one must assume that once provided with a child, the old man is unlikely to leave much of his winnings outside the family. Education

---

[37] Riccobono (1945) 192-5; see also Appendix.

is an expensive business, and he will want to see his son well set up. And indeed, he proves all too stingy in rewarding the stud for his priceless services.

We may note that the new rules applied to women as well as men. The *lex Voconia* of 169 B.C. had banned women from being instituted as heirs; but Augustus exempted mothers of three. These, it might be assumed, would pass on property to their needy children.[38]

(b) Man and wife

Transmission of property between spouses is a difficult area. They belong to different families; yet together they procreate a common one. Pre-Augustan law was very suspicious of exchanges between man and wife: gifts *inter vivos* [between living people] were banned absolutely. Augustus' new rules were complex, yet derived their logic from the desire to keep property 'in the family'. Donation *inter vivos* was still forbidden; and the husband's power over the dowry severely restricted. But after the husband's death, the widow might inherit property if they had a common child; and she might take a certain proportion if she had children by another union. The logic is plain: the wealth of two families should not intermingle unless there were a new family to which it would eventually flow. This is corroborated by an exception to the rules: if man and wife were within the six degrees of relationship to each other, they might inherit from each other though childless.[39]

(c) Master and slave

For inheritance purposes, a slave or an ex-slave belonged to his master's (or her mistress') *familia*. The master was still quite at liberty to free a slave and make him his heir in his will (necessarily the slave was childless in the eyes of the law). This was a real enough possibility, because if you suspected your estate was negative, you could leave your debts to a slave as *heres necessarius* [required heir].

But conversely, a freedman's property did not escape the master's *familia*. By the praetor's edict, half the freedman's estate reverted to the patron or his descendants; though, if the freedman had a child, his estate escaped the patron. Augustus made escape harder; only a

---

[38] The rules affecting women are numerous and complicated: see best Humbert (1972) 146-70. Humbert well brings out the anxiety to protect the inheritance rights of children that underlies these and other rules, 207-63.

[39] *Tit. Ulp.* 15-16 for the rules; Humbert (above) for the implications. Contrast the disabilities of women in Athenian law, Bickerman (n. 11).

freedman father of three escaped completely. If he had only one or two children, the patron shared (a half or a third). This point has already been discussed; but note here that the family is closing in.[40]

According to my reading of the laws, then, Augustus was trying to stabilize property and status. If wealth was to escape the hands of an old family, it would have to flow to a new one, where, it might be calculated, it would stay for at least one generation. But there are still plenty of questions to answer before we can make sense of what Augustus was doing. Why did Romans have so strong (and unusual) an urge to leave wealth to outsiders? Why did Augustus think it to his advantage to obstruct this urge? And did the legislation, so long retained, actually have any significant effect?

OFFICIUM IN THE WILL

To make further progress towards understanding Augustus' laws, we need to relate them more closely to the testamentary practice of the late republic. The laws presuppose an extraordinarily strong urge to leave property to *extranei*. Whether we see Augustus as harnessing this urge in an attempt to raise the birthrate, or, as I would prefer, as trying to bring this urge under control, a first step towards interpreting Augustus' intention must be to explain why the urge existed in the first place.

It is at this point that the going becomes difficult, and the ancient historian comes up against familiar problems of lack of evidence. One lesson that the comparative material teaches quite clearly is that we cannot understand patterns of inheritance by looking at the laws and rules alone. Local conditions produce varieties in practice out of the same basic rules and customs. What we need is a large corpus of republican wills for analysis, and that we can never have.

The limitations of the evidence may be illustrated simply. It makes a great difference to our understanding of Roman inheritance to know what proportion of Romans in fact died intestate. This matters for the Augustan laws too, because they did not affect intestate succession. What sort of people made wills, and why? The standard view that all Romans had a 'horror of intestacy' came under attack from Daube; but his suggestion that will-making was an upperclass practice was undermined by Crook.[41] However the evidence is largely anecdotal; and without an extensive corpus of wills for

---

[40] On freedmen's property see Riccobono (1945) 189-91; Astolfi (1970) 229ff.
[41] D. Daube, 'The Preponderance of Intestacy at Rome', *Tulane Law Review* 39 (1965) 253ff.; J. A. Crook, 'Intestacy in Roman Society', *PCPS* n.s. 19 (1973) 38-44.

analysis we cannot establish the sort of pattern which would reveal why some people made wills and others did not.[42]

As it happens, modern historians have since the Daube–Crook debate started to ask exactly this question. The debate is still in its infancy. But the documentary basis for an answer exists, and it appears that the answer will not be an easy one. On the one hand, a study of early modern Banbury shows, what we might be inclined to suspect, that the well-off were relatively more likely to leave wills than the poor. On the other hand, a study of the fen village of Willingham throws up precisely the opposite pattern: the poor made wills more frequently than those with relatively large holdings.[43] The lesson that emerges is that it is not just a matter of wealth. People leave wills because there are all sorts of reasons why they do not want their belongings to devolve according to local intestate custom.

Now in the case of the Romans, we should surely take notice of the anecdotal evidence that suggests they were unusually disinclined to die intestate. It was felt to be somehow a dishonour. But why? There are doubtless many factors; but the one that is particularly interesting in the context of Augustus' laws is the habit of naming friends in the will.[44] The standard method must have been to leave legacies to friends. Of course friends were also remembered by being named together as heirs 'in the third grade', who would only succeed in the rare event of the decease or abnegation of the primary and secondary heirs. Augustus so honoured his closest friends; Julius even named some of his murderers in the second grade.[45] For lack of close family, friends might also be instituted as heirs in the first grade. So the outsider as legatee is only one of several possibilities. But it is one on which it is worth focussing.

There is abundant evidence, at an anecdotal level, that under the late republic you were conventionally expected to leave bequests to your friends. Indeed, it could be a matter of shame not to be so remembered. Cicero boasts that nobody cut him out of their will when he was in exile; and in a famous passage of the *Philippics* he engages in a slanging-match with Antony on this topic. Antony has alleged that nobody named Cicero; Cicero counters, is 20 million sesterces in bequests from friends really a sign of contempt? As for

---

[42] For some documents that do survive see Amelotti, *Il testamento romano attraverso la prassi documentale* 1 (1966).
[43] Richard T. Vann, 'Wills and the Family in an English Town: Banbury, 1550-1800', *J. Fam. Hist.* 4 (1979) 346-67; on Willingham, Margaret Spufford in Goody *et al.* (1976) 169-72.
[44] See W. Kroll, *Die Kultur der ciceronischen Zeit* 1 (1933) 110-12.
[45] Suet. *Aug.* 101. 2; *Jul.* 83. 2.

Antony, he is remembered, but by the most disreputable people, and ones on whom he has never even set eyes.[46]

The will in fact expressed one's pattern of obligations. The first duty was of course to the family; but the testator should also remember anyone to whom he was bound by ties of *officium* [obligation]. Above all, *clientes* [clients] should remember their *patroni* [patrons]. Atticus inherited the basis of his wealth from an uncle; but the crowd dragged the uncle's body through the streets, because he owed his wealth to the aid of Lucullus as governor of Asia, and he had always proclaimed he would make Lucullus his heir. The story is told by Valerius Maximus, who sympathises with the indignation of the crowd and who is equally shocked by a similar case of a man who failed to remember his benefactor Augustus.[47] Much of Cicero's wealth derived from those to whom he had given his support in court; but he also received from others who owed him obligations, an architect, a Greek philosopher, and businessmen.[48]

The Republican horror of intestacy, then, can be seen in context of the system of *clientela* [clientage]. It could be shocking to die intestate because you would not have expressed your obligations to your *amici* [friends]. This tradition surely goes long back into the republic. Nor can we imagine that Augustus disapproved of it. Suetonius tells us he was quite 'morose' about inspecting the wills of his friends.[49] He felt wounded to be left out; yet the motive was not financial, for if the testator had children, he would hand over his takings to them. Note too the expression for wills used in this passage, *suprema iudicia* [final judgements]. The will for Augustus, as for Romans long before, was the final and decisive judgement of how valuable your friends had been to you.

And yet Augustus' own legislation must have dealt a severe blow to this tradition. Romans continued to remember their friends under the empire (one thinks of the will of Dasumius),[50] but if you were celibate you could make no financial profit out of the ties of *amicitia* [friendship]. So a new possible motive for the legislation presents itself: was Augustus trying to undercut the power of other patrons

---

[46] Cic. *Dom.* 85; *Phil.* 2. 40. Kroll (n. 44) for other passages.

[47] Val. Max. 7. 8. 5 for Caecilius; id. 6 for Augustus; examples 7-9 also involve shocking cases of failure to remember patrons and *amici* [friends]. Thus duty to patrons is the main theme of 8.5-9, just as duty to family is the theme of the rest of chapters 7-8.

[48] See conveniently I. Shatzmann, *Senatorial wealth and Roman politics* (1975) 409-14 on Cicero's inheritances; 50-3 on the importance of inheritances as a source of wealth in general.

[49] Suet. *Aug.* 66. 4. On the varied practices of emperors in this respect see below n. 51.

[50] *CIL* 6. 10229 = *FIRA* III no. 48. Note also the assumption of Pliny (*Ep.* 7.20.6) that he and Tacitus would be left legacies by those who were not even close friends, of which the will of Dasumius is an example.

(particularly the old nobility) and, by hampering one of the bonds on which old patronal power depended, increase the imperial power? Certain emperors were notorious for seeking to raise finances by inducing their subjects to make them their heirs.[51] Should we not also see this as an attempt to engross power? The subject is expected to make the emperor heir alongside his children, because he is now the one to whom he owes his all.[52]

Even if there is something in this suggestion, I do not think it can stand without modification. After all, those with children could still benefit in the traditional way, and if these benefits of patronage were crucial the answer was to become a father. If Augustus had wanted to achieve the effect suggested, he would have done better to make all transmission of property outside the family illegal.

We must therefore focus attention on the position of the bachelor within the system of *clientela* and *amicitia*. It is surely evident that until Augustus' legislation the childless had considerable advantages, both economic and political. Let us return to that figure of satire, the *captator*, and his prey, the rich childless man. To see them in context, it must be appreciated that they belong to the system of *clientela* and *amicitia*, the nexus of exchange of services and bequests. The social paradox is that the *orbus* [the childless man], though so much courted, is in traditional terms the *cliens* [client] of his *captatores*. They are offering him services in the hope of bequests. Take the Horatian Ulysses: among the services he is urged to offer his rich prey (apart from the attentions of Penelope) is his patronage in court. ('Don't bother which of the contending parties is in the right, give your support to the one without children'.) Or take Lucullus and Atticus' uncle Caecilius. Caecilius had always proclaimed that he would make Lucullus his heir; Lucullus may be seen as a *captator* in pursuit of what was to be the basis of one of the great late republican fortunes.[53] The childless had the advantage in securing services that could lift him to wealth and power; and what Augustus does is to cut him out of the chain of inheritance, so that he does not also enjoy the patron's advantages of bequests.[54]

---

[51] See R. S. Rogers, 'The Roman Emperors as Heirs and Legatees', *TAPA* 78 (1947) 140-58; F. Millar, *The Emperor in the Roman world* (1977) 153-8.

[52] For the ideology J. Gaudemet, 'Testamenta ingrata et pietas Augusti', *Studi Arangio-Ruiz* III (1953) 115-37.

[53] Hor. *Sat.* 2.5.27-31 for services in court. Caecilius' fortune is estimated at 10 million HS by Nepos *Atticus* 5. For another example of the patron as *captator*, cf. Juvenal *Sat.* 5. 132-40, where the client is advised to have no children if he desires the attentions of a Virro.

[54] But complaints continue about the advantages of *orbitas*: e.g. Tac. *Ann.* 15.19 'the childless were adequately rewarded in that with much freedom from care and no burdens at all they acquired influence, honours, indeed everything promptly and right there for them'. In the

The point may be illustrated diagrammatically. In the case of a man with a child, a delicate equilibrium is preserved. Wealth flows to him from his parent, and flows in turn to his child (a process described by Pliny [*Pan.* 37.2] in the words 'bona ... sua semperque possessa ac deinceps proximo cuique transmittenda' ['property (that was considered) his own permanent possession to be transmitted in turn to his nearest relative']. He also inherits from friends and clients in recognition of services (Pliny's 'aliena et speranda' ['property of others also to be hoped for']) but correspondingly leaves bequests to friends and patrons who have served him.

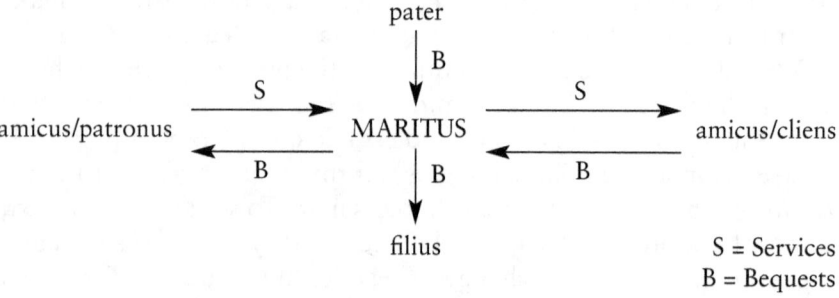

The equilibrium is disrupted by the bachelor or childless. Since he has no *suus heres* [heir of his own] of his own blood, his family property flows into the horizontal line of exchange of services, greatly increasing his purchasing power.

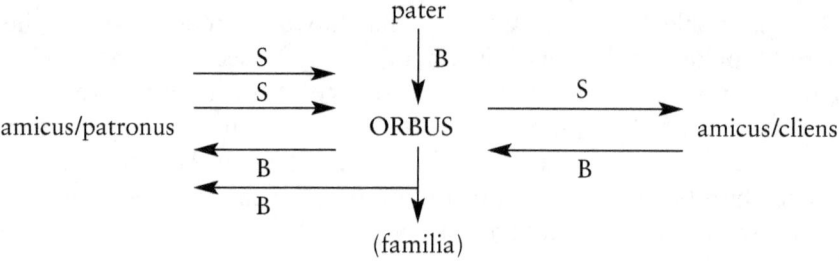

Augustus' limitations of the power of the childless to inherit tends to restore the equilibrium.

---

same vein, the elder Pliny *NH* 14.5 'after childlessness started to gain very great influence and potential and legacy-hunting became a most fertile source of profit ...'.

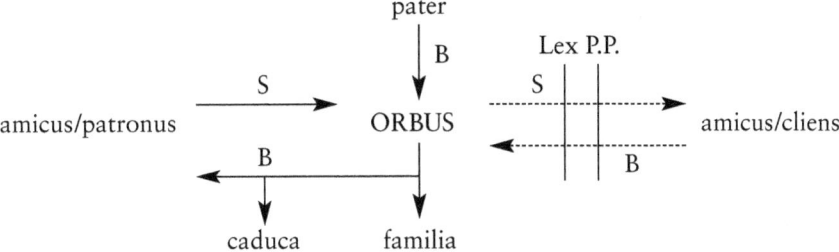

Childlessness and will-hunting in the eyes of Roman moralists were part of the great moral decline.[55] In fact, I have suggested, the use of the testament to acknowledge *officia* [obligations] is likely to be a traditional custom, dating back long before the arrival of Greek wealth and corruption. But perhaps it is fair to guess that Greek wealth did cause a real change. If its effect was to transform the traditional exchange of services more and more into a monetary transaction (as with electoral bribery), testamentary recognition may have been gradually transformed from a token gesture of respect to a real financial benefit worth pursuing.

There is one strong pointer that this is so. At an unknown date, probably early in the 2nd century, a *lex Furia Testamentaria* was passed, setting a maximum ceiling to legacies of 1000 asses (250 HS).[56] Later writers thought that its purpose was to protect the heir, just as the *lex Falcidia* of 40 B.C. that restricted legacies to three quarters of the total estate. But as Gaius points out, the *lex Furia* was ill-designed to achieve this end, for there was no limit on the number of 1000 asses legacies. Modern scholars therefore prefer to see it in line with sumptuary legislation.[57] It probably closely followed the *lex Cincia* of 204 B.C. which limited gifts *inter vivos*, supposedly to stop the payment of advocacy. The *lex Furia* might similarly have aimed at stopping the payment of services by testament. However this may be, the extraordinarily low ceiling on legacies indicates that, in the early second century, testamentary recognition of services was still no more than a gesture. Legacies to members of the family were quite a different matter: the *lex Furia* excepted the six degrees of relationship, just as Augustus' laws seem to have done. But already by the passing of the *lex Voconia* in 169, the *lex Furia* seems to have become a dead letter.

---

[55] So the elder Pliny in the passage cited above.
[56] Watson (1971) 163-7.
[57] So Kaser (n. 29) I 756.

For Augustus to have revived the *lex Furia* would have been impracticable (sumptuary legislation never worked very well). Nor did it cover the case of the man who made his patron an heir, rather than a legatee. To have limited the leaving of property outside the family absolutely would have been to undercut the conventions of *clientela* and *amicitia* in a way which Augustus did not in my view desire. But his marital and inheritance rules, according to my hypothesis, did aim to put a brake on late republican practice. By hampering the testator with children to whom the best part of the estate would normally devolve, and by cutting back the benefits of childlessness, he sought to eradicate what moralists saw as an abuse. He also thereby, as for instance in his legislation on electoral bribery, limited the free play of an aspect of the pursuit of wealth and power in a way an autocrat could not but welcome.

SUCCESS OR FAILURE?

The argument of this paper is that Augustus' marital laws sought to do more than increase the number of Roman citizens. Nor is it enough to account for them as 'eugenic', an attempt to induce the favoured upper classes to reproduce more freely.[58] Certainly their aim was to encourage reproduction; but the specific rules affecting inheritance indicate what the specific advantage of reproduction could be. Among the propertied classes reproduction was necessarily linked with the question of transmission of property; and Augustus' laws sought to stabilize that transmission, and consequently the transmission of status, by advantaging the family man in the pattern of inheritance. The laws struck a blow against the adventurer who, without the ties of family responsibility, could exploit the Roman conventions of will-making to his financial and even political advantage. In the eyes of the legislator who desired order and stability, the flourishing of such adventurers made society volatile and dangerous.

This account of the laws does not seek to exclude other accounts. One should not perhaps underestimate the irrational element of moralistic revivalism, even jingoism.[59] After all, the marital laws were linked with laws against adultery of unprecedented severity in Rome. Adultery is indeed relevant to questions of transmission of

---

[58] Argued by J. A. Field, 'The purpose of the lex Julia et Papia Poppaea', *CJ* 40 (1945) 398-416.

[59] Stressed recently by Raditsa (1980) and R. I. Frank, 'Augustus' Legislation on Marriage and Children', *CSCA* 8 (1975) 41-52.

property: the legitimacy of offspring matters crucially in a society where property and social standing depend on birth. Nevertheless, we need not suppose that those who legislate against adultery do so with a conscious eye on its implications for property and status; their action may well spring from, and be formulated as, moral indignation against improper modes of behaviour. Similarly the marital legislation may well have sprung from irrational feelings of anger and indignation, not from a cool calculation of the social implications of childlessness. But irrational though indignation may be, it does not operate in a vacuum; and my suggestion is that inheritance practices and their practical consequences provide the background against which Augustan indignation makes sense.

As a measure of the extent to which the Romans were conscious of the implications of their marriage laws, we may examine the speeches Dio attributes to Augustus (56.2ff.). The setting is the great protest of A.D. 9 that led up to the reformulation of the laws in the *lex Papia Poppaea*. Augustus assembles the *equites* in the forum, and separating the bachelors from the married, harangues each group as appropriate. The arguments attributed to Augustus are hardly authentic; but at least they offer an insight into how a senator in the third century saw the role of laws that still applied. The theme of population increase is there, as ideology demands: Rome grew great through the numerousness of its offspring (2.2-3); and the good of an imperial state demands a large population 'to work the land, sail the sea, practise crafts and labour, and in time of war to protect our possessions' (3.7). Yet how many of the equestrian audience Dio depicts were liable to father farmers, traders, craftsmen, labourers and legionaries? More to the point is Dio's picture of the private advantages of fatherhood. 'You are right (Augustus addresses the fathers) to imitate your ancestors ... that as they passed down to you the reputation derived from fine achievements, you may pass it on to others, and the possessions which they left to you, you in turn may leave to your own descendants' (3.1-2). 'Is it not a delight to recognise, rear and educate a child as an image of yourself, so that you are renewed in it as it grows? Is it not a blessing on departing from life to leave behind as successor and heir to your substance one sprung from yourself, so that when your mortal nature fades away, you live in your child as successor, and do not fall into the hands of outsiders and perish like a victim of war?' (3.4-5). It is crudely put, but the preoccupation with transmission of property and social standing is clear enough.

No matter what the legislator's intention, in practice a law often has a very different and unforeseen effect. Did Augustus' marriage laws in fact have the intended effect? The question has been the subject of a long and irresolvable debate.[60] We lack the demographical statistics from which to deduce any changing trends. But worse, the Romans also lacked them. They counted the population at large, and proved that it was increasing; but these statistics were incapable of distinguishing the proportion due to citizen reproduction and that due to manumission and enfranchisement. As for social trends among the propertied classes, there was no way of knowing how many people were induced to marry and reproduce by the legislation who would not otherwise have done so. Certainly the laws were not totally effective: contemporaries continued to complain that *orbitas* had all the advantages and flourished.[61]

There is only one effect of which we can be confident. For the first time, the state inserted itself in the scheme of succession (as it did too by the *vicesima hereditatum*). A rich revenue of *bona caduca* [property for which there were no legitimate heirs] and *vacantia* [property without an heir] flowed into the treasury.[62] The state, 'velut parens omnium' ['as though parent of everyone'] profited from disobedience to the law; and it could use those profits (*inter alia*) to convey wealth and status on those of whom it approved. Emperors might use this wealth in grants to the indigent aristocracy, like the too numerous offspring of the grandson of Hortensius.[63] That they did so reflects their assumption that it was good for the state that old families should provide continuity. But they also could endow new men. This sort of social promotion did not hurt emperors, for it was under their control.

This far, Tacitus is justified in his cynical assertion [*Ann.* 3.25] that the motives of the legislation were partly fiscal: 'et augendo aerario sanxerat' ['he had sanctioned it to boost the treasury's revenues']. But it is not enough to talk of the motivation of emperors alone. Augustus introduced his laws with a loud ideological fanfare (notably from Horace). They were intended to meet with the approval of right-thinking men. On the whole, it seems that they did.[64] *Orbitas* was

---

[60] Last, *CAH* X 425-64, believed the laws to have been effective. Recent opinion has swung against him: Brunt (1971) 566; Humbert (1972) 174-8; Nörr (1977) 313-18.

[61] Above n. 54; also Pliny *Ep.* 4. 15. 3 in praise of a man with several children 'in that age in which the rewards of childlessness make it burdensome for many people even to raise just one child'.

[62] See Millar (n. 51) 158-63.

[63] Tac. *Ann.* 2.37-8. For other examples H. Kloft, *Liberalitas Principis* (1970) 101-4; Millar (n. 51) 297-9.

[64] Nörr (1977) 318-21.

considered a perfectly proper target for legislation, and moralists continued to protest about it. Tacitus' complaints are about the operation of the laws, not their goal of combating childlessness. The spirit of the law chimed with what those 'municipals from the towns of Italy and the provinces that still stuck to the old ways' thought right and proper. Even if the republican aristocracy died out its place was taken by *domi nobiles* [local nobility]. Whether old established local families, or (under Augustus) the beneficiaries of massive land-distributions or even, later, the sons of freedmen promoted to the local senate, they liked to project themselves as good solid family men, not as adventurers risen to sudden prominence. The laws remained not because they were effective, but because it was felt they *ought* to be so.[65] Only after Caracalla turned the law into a naked instrument of fiscality and the consensus was undermined by an alternative, Christian, morality did repeal become desirable.

APPENDIX: *EXCEPTAE PERSONAE*

The proposition that the 'caduciary' clauses of the marital laws did not affect transmission of property within the family is central to my argument; and since the evidence on the point is not wholly clear, it needs to be set out in detail.

Conventionally, the assumption that the circle of those exempted extended to six degrees of relationship, and to the seventh in the case of the *sobrino natus* (i.e. a second cousin once removed) has been based on Frag. Vat. 216 which states that these were 'excepted under the lex Julia'. The passage, citing Ulpian *de officio praetoris tutelaris* [on the office of the praetor who appoints guardians], does not state from what these persons were excepted. Both Voci (*Diritto Ereditario Romano* i, 1960, 426) and Astolfi (1970, 170-4 repeating his arguments from *BIDR* 69 (1964) 220-6) doubt that the exceptions were from the caduciary rules. The problem is that the same fragment goes on to enumerate other exceptions: spouses of relatives to the same degrees (217); relatives by marriage including those who ever were in-laws (218); and connections by a further marriage (step-parents and children) (219). This circle is hopelessly much too wide for exemption from the rules governing *caelibes* [the unmarried] and *orbi*. We know that the laws specifically limited transmission between husband and wife unless they had common children. To extend exceptions to spouses of relatives, let alone in-laws and step-connections, makes nonsense of the whole law. (Astolfi also objects that the exceptions were partly redundant in that spouses of relatives were necessarily not *caelibes* and not therefore

---

[65] Last's chapter (n. 60) remains valuable for its emphasis on the role of Italian municipal morality.

banned from receiving bequests; however, they might be *orbi*, with only rights to the half-portion.) Astolfi suggests that Ulpian's list of exceptions applies to those who could not be forced to bear witness against each other in caduciary proceedings. However this may be, Frag. Vat. 216 is best laid aside for present purposes.

Were there then no exemptions at all for the unmarried and childless? The strongest argument is the silence of Gaius. His *Institutes* discuss the rules for will-making in considerable detail. Three times he mentions the limitations on the *capacitas* of the unmarried and childless, which he states as a general principle without indicating exceptions (2.111; 144; 286). Certainly if there were not indications to the contrary, this would be a strong argument against the exemption of relatives. But it is not enough to undermine contrary evidence. Nowhere in the *Institutes* as preserved does he set out in detail the rules of testamentary succession as defined by the marital laws. We may contrast the Titles from Ulpian which, though also lacunose, sets out in detail the rules for transmission between man and wife. (This is the only passage which explains so vital a question as what exactly 'having children' meant.) The exceptions from the general principle of limitation of the *capacitas* of the unmarried and childless were highly complex: they included absence *rei publicae causa* [on the state's business], the *testamentum militis* [soldier's will], service of the state by provision of corn-supply (after Claudius), and the individual grant of the *ius liberorum*. These were hardly to be set out *en passant*. Thus when Gaius is discussing *fideicommissa* [trusts] he states that they apparently once offered a way round the marital laws, but that this escape had been blocked by the *sc Pegasianum*. In this context the statement 'bachelors, who [sc. *in principle*] could not receive bequests, were apparently allowed *fideicommissa*' is not misleading even if there were other exceptions to the principle.

That certain members of the family were exempted is explicitly stated by the church historian Sozomen in his account of Constantine's reform (*Hist. Eccl.* 1.9). It also seems to me to be implied by the presumptions of Pliny and Valerius Maximus as to what was right and proper (above, pp. 258-259). Can we specify which degrees?

Voci (loc. cit.) believes that children to the third degree were exempted. This is an inference from *Tit. Ulp.* 18.1 which states that those persons were eligible for *caduca*, that is of bequests of portions of bequests which fell through because left to those who were for one reason or another ineligible. *A fortiori* they were able to take bequests in their own names. This surely represents the minimum of family exemptions we must allow; it might also be what Sozomen means by 'very close relatives', and is perhaps all that Pliny and Valerius imply. But it only represents a minimum. What Ulpian is reporting is a change in the caduciary rules by Caracalla. Until that point (as Gaius 2.206-8 shows, cf. *Tit. Ulp.* 1.21) *caduca* were also divided among any with *ius liberorum* who were named as heirs, or failing them named as legatees. Caracalla, to raise additional revenue, cut out the rights of those with *ius liberorum*, only preserving *ius antiquum* [the ancient right] for parents and children of the testator to three grades. Clearly Caracalla was cutting down the beneficiaries of *caduca* to the minimum he could get away with. It is just conceivable that at the same time he cut down the number of relatives who, by *ius antiquum*, were exempted from restrictions on the unmarried and childless, thus increasing the incidence of *caduca*.

What evidence is there for the exemption of a wider range of family than the three closest degrees? Astolfi (1970, 167-9) lays emphasis on the fact that the Augustan laws did not affect intestate succession. Since under the praetor's rules relatives within six degrees (or the cousin's child in the seventh) could lay claim to *bonorum possessio* [possession of goods] when a will was lacking or became void, the same circle ought to have been admitted to testamentary succession, irrespective of their marital status. The argument is reasonable, but not compelling without further evidence.

The most powerful support comes from *Tit. Ulp.* 16.1, the valuable passage in which the rules for transmission between husband and wife are set out. The principle is that husband and wife cannot receive more than one tenth from each other; the exceptions are (1) if they are above or below the legally required ages for producing children; (2) if they are related to each other within six degrees; (3) if the husband is absent *rei publicae causa*; (4) if the recipient of the bequest has the *ius liberorum* in consequence of (a) the grant of this right by the emperor or (b) the production of the requisite number of children in common with the testator. Now since exceptions 1, 3 and 4 all applied to limitations on transmission to the unmarried and childless, the natural inference is that exception 2 also applied.

The argument from *Tit. Ulp.* 16.1 provides strong support to the inference from intestate succession. In view of Augustus' traditionalism it gains further support from the fact that the *lex Furia testamentaria* which limited legacies had the same circle of excepted relatives.

The *Tit. Ulp.* passage is also valuable in suggesting the way in which the rules were put. It starts from the widest possible limitation ('Husband and wife may only inherit one tenth from each other') and then details exceptions, rather than starting from a modified limitation ('Only husband and wife who have children in common may inherit ...'). By analogy we can see that Gaius was right to state as a principle that bachelors could not inherit, rather than formulate a modified principle ('only bachelors who are relatives to such and such a degree may inherit ...'). This phrasing of the law is dictated by legal clarity, not by the order of priorities in the legislator's mind. That the ability of family to inherit is only phrased as an exception to a general principle is no argument against the proposition that the legislator only wanted to limit transmission outside the circle of the family.

This observation has relevance in considering one further possibility. Granted that by Ulpian's time some degrees of family were exempt, was this only a subsequent mitigation of the law and not Augustus' original intention? This is not a very plausible suggestion. There were indeed several subsequent modifications of the *leges Iulia et Papia Poppaea*, but their tendency was generally not to mitigate but to block loopholes. (On this see Humbert (1972) 173; Nörr (1977) 319-20.) Under Tiberius, as Tacitus reports, there were demands in the senate for the modification of the laws; but the complaints were directed against the legal complexities and the unfortunate operation of the laws, not against the principles involved (*Ann.* 3.25). In fact Tiberius made the law tougher. Under Augustus' rules, those above the legally defined age of child-production escaped from the limitations of *capacitas*. This had the unfortunate result that bachelors recovered capacity in their old age; the *sc Persicianum* therefore ruled that those who had lost capacity by refusal to comply with the law could not recover it after passing the age-limit. This in turn raised a snag, that those who produced children over age could still not recover capacity: a *senatusconsultum* under Claudius rectified this anomaly. Under Nero the *sc Calvisianum* stopped older women using this mitigation as an excuse for marrying younger men (*Tit. Ulp.* 16.3-4). Another anomaly under Augustus' rules was that while a childless widow could not inherit from her husband more than one tenth, a mistress with children of her own could (Quint. 8.5.19). This was blocked under Domitian (Suet. *Dom.* 8.3). Adopted children caused another snag: in all Roman law the adoptive child had the status of a natural child, and therefore fulfilled the requirements of the Augustan laws. But a scandalous abuse of adoption caused a furore under Nero (Tac. *Ann.* 15.19) and this loophole was blocked; though what was surely forbidden was temporary and fraudulent adoption for the purposes of securing legal advantages, not the validity of adoption for the purpose of the marital law in general as is sometimes assumed. *Fideicommissa* offered another way round the laws; this was certainly not the intention of Augustus, who offered legal backing to *fideicommissa*, and the anomaly was blocked by the *sc Pegasianum* under Vespasian (Gaius 2.286). Later emperors had to contend with the problem of unwritten understandings (*fideicommissa tacita*), but these were peculiarly difficult to control.

In view of the wealth of detail we possess about later modifications it would seem astonishing that we should hear nothing of so substantial a modification as the introduction of exemptions for relatives. In view of the way known modifications tend to reinforce, not to water down, Augustus' intentions, such a modification would seem at any rate highly unlikely. The only remaining possibility is that the exceptions are one of the ways the *lex Papia Poppaea* modified the *lex Iulia*. However, this is a legal tangle best left alone. The state of our evidence only allows us to discuss the marital laws as finally agreed, and not the separate stages of their enactment.

It seems to me therefore probable but not certain that six (and in one case seven) degrees of relationship were exempted by Augustus; and certain that at least three degrees were so.

9 To Honour the Princeps and Venerate the Gods: Public Cult, Neighbourhood Cults, and Imperial Cult in Augustan Rome†[1]

JOHN SCHEID

translated by Jonathan Edmondson

In his account of his own accomplishments, the *Res Gestae*, Augustus lists an impressive number of repairs, restorations, and constructions of cult places:

> 11. To mark my return, the Senate consecrated an altar of Fortuna Redux [Fortune Returning] in front of the sanctuary of Honour and Virtue near the Porta Capena. It ordered the *pontifices* and Vestal Virgins to conduct a sacrifice at the altar every year on the day on which I returned to the city from Syria, in the consulship of Quintus Lucretius and Marcus Vinicius [12 October, 19 BC]. The senate named this day the *Augustalia* after my surname (*cognomen*).
>
> 12. ... (2) When I returned to Rome from Spain and Gaul, in the consulship of Tiberius Nero and Publius Quintilius [13 BC], after successfully settling matters in those provinces, the senate decided that it should consecrate an altar of the Augustan Peace (*Pax Augusta*) next to the Campus Martius to mark my return. It ordered the magistrates, priests, and Vestal Virgins to celebrate an anniversary sacrifice there each year.
>
> 19. ... I built the senate-house (*curia*) and the adjoining Chalcidicum, the Temple of Apollo on the Palatine and its porticoes, the Temple of the Deified Julius, the Lupercal, the portico next to the Circus Flaminius, which I per-

---

† Originally published in French as "Honorer le prince et vénérer les dieux: culte public, cultes des quartiers et culte impérial dans la Rome augustéenne," in N. Belayche, ed., *Rome, les Césars et la Ville aux deux premiers siècles de notre ère*, Rennes: Presses universitaires de Rennes, 2001, 85–105.

[1] I use the term "imperial cult" because all modern historians use it, even if it is a modern construct. It is a misleading term, since it assimilates various cultic acts that are sometimes very different one from another. If I use it, it is to make myself understandable to my readers, to identify crudely a Roman religious practice. Roman conceptual and cultic realities were different.

mitted to be named the Porticus Octavia after the man who had constructed the previous portico on the same site, the *pulvinar* [i.e., imperial box] in the Circus Maximus, the Temples of Jupiter Feretrius and Jupiter Tonans ["the Thunderer"] on the Capitol, the Temple of Quirinus, the Temple of Minerva, the Temple of Juno Regina ["the Queen"] and Jupiter Libertas ["Freedom"] on the Aventine, the sanctuary of the Lares on the upper section of the Sacred Way, the Temple of the Penates on the Velia, the Temple of Iuventas ["Youth"], and the Temple of the Magna Mater ["Great Mother"] on the Palatine.

20. (1) I restored the Capitol and the Theatre of Pompey, both at great expense, but without inscribing my name on them. ... (4) In my sixth consulship [28 BC], I restored eighty-two temples of the gods in the city of Rome at the senate's suggestion, without neglecting any that had to be restored at this date. ... 21. (1) I constructed on private land the Temple of Mars Ultor ["the Avenger"] and the Forum Augustum with funds derived from the spoils of war.[2]

There are omissions, however, in this list. It passes over in silence some rather spectacular measures such as the installation of the cult of the Lares Augusti in the 265 urban districts (*vici*) of the city of Rome, and it does not mention any building works undertaken in the city's territory. Nevertheless, even this incomplete list of new cult sites gives a clear impression that these constructions must have changed – and indeed they did change – the whole look of the monumental centre and neighbourhoods of Rome. How should we interpret these major building projects, some of which were only completed thirty years after the victory at Actium?

They constitute an important chapter in the history of Rome's urban development, but it was not out of a passion for architecture that these projects were undertaken. Nor was it a question any longer

---

[2] *RG* 11–21 (with omissions): 11. *aram [Fortunae R]ed[ucis a]nte aedes Honoris et Virtutis ad portam | Cap[enam pro] red[itu me]o senatus consacrauit, in qua ponti\[fices et] uir[gines Ve]stal[es anni]uersarium sacrificium facere | [decreuit eo] di[e, quo co]nsul[ibus Q. Luc]retio et [M. Vi]nic[i]o in urbem ex | [Syria redieram, et diem Augustali]a ex [c]o[gnomine] nos[t]ro appellauit. | 12. ... 2. [Cu]m ex H[isp]ania Gal[liaque, rebu]s in iis prouincis prosp[e]\re [gest]i[s,] R[omam redi] Ti(berio) Nerone (et) P(ublio) Qui[ntilio c]o(n)s(ulibus),* (vacat) *aram | [Pacis A]u[g]ust[ae senatus pro] redi[t]u meo consa[c]randam [censuit] ad cam\pum [Martium, in qua m]agistratus et sac[er]dotes [ui]rgines[que] V[est]a[les | ann]iuer[sarium sacrific]ium facer[e decreuit.] ... 19. Curiam et continens eam Chalcidicum templumque Apollinis in | Palatio cum porticibus, aedem diui Iuli, Lupercal, porticum ad cir\cum Flaminium, quam sum appellari passus ex nomine eius, qui pri\lorem eodem in solo fecerat, Octauiam, puluinar ad circum maximum, | aedes in Capitolio Iouis Feretri et Iouis Tonantis,* (vacat) *aedem Quirini, | aedem Mineruae et Iunonis reginae et Iouis Libertatis in Auentino, | aedem Larum in summa sacra uia, aedem deum Penatium in Velia, | aedem Iuuentatis, aedem Matris Magnae in Palatio feci. | 20. Capitolium et Pompeium theatrum utrumque opus impensa grandi refeci | sine ulla inscriptione nominis mei. [...] 4. Duo et octoginta templa deum in urbe consul sex[tu]m ex [auctori]tate | senatus refeci, nullo praetermisso, quod e[o] tempore [refici debeba]t. ... 21. In priuato solo Martis Vltoris templum [f]orumque Augustum [ex ma]n[i]\biis feci.* [This text is taken from the new Budé edition of the *RG* by J. Scheid, *Res Gestae Divi Augusti. Hauts faits du divin Auguste*, Paris 2007.]

of transforming Rome into a new city on the Hellenistic model, as had been the case with the utopian plans of Julius Caesar. On the contrary, even if they had recourse to all the refinement of Hellenistic art and architecture, Augustus' undertakings were firmly rooted in the ideological sphere of traditionalism. He was repairing and reconstructing what had been neglected by his predecessors; he was supplying what the tradition of making vows required him to construct; he was giving the people the kind of luxury spaces that the aristocrats of the late Republic had reserved for their own use.[3] To consider these projects among other things as striking evidence for the piety of the victorious Augustus, faced with the impiety of those who officially bore responsibility for the civil wars, and as a manifestation of self-celebration and flattery does not exhaust their interest and significance. Even if the projects were in part votive offerings linked to Augustus' triumphs and the enormous quantities of booty that resulted from the conquest of Egypt, their aim went far beyond mere sumptuary outlay and celebration of the *princeps*' victories. These buildings, which transformed Rome and gave it the appearance that it would keep throughout the imperial period, expressed and fulfilled something else besides. By recourse to traditional religious categories, they helped to construct, in their own way, the emperor's image. What was this image and how was it diffused?

Augustus' religious efforts, especially the "invention" of the imperial cult, have been assessed in various ways, even by historians who have perceived the religious significance of Augustus' enterprises. In this period Roman religion was in decline and even dead in the eyes of scholars as diverse as Franz Cumont, Kurt Latte, and Jean Bayet.[4] On this view one would expect nothing but propaganda and hypocrisy. Against this negative judgement, which drew its inspiration essentially from a misunderstanding of the importance of ritual in Roman religion, Arthur Darby Nock and Ronald Syme, for example,[5] argued that Augustus did what in fact the Romans were expecting of him; his reforms were crowned with success, since they ensured the survival of ritualist polytheism for at least another three

---

[3] See P. Zanker, *Augustus und die Macht der Bilder*, Munich [1987], (3rd edn), 1997, pp. 35–40, 73–79 (= *The Power of Images in the Age of Augustus*, trans. H. A. Shapiro, Ann Arbor, 1988, pp. 25–31, 65–71).

[4] F. Cumont, *Les religions orientales dans le paganisme romain*, Paris [1929], (4th edn), 1965, pp. 31–34; K. Latte, *Römische Religionsgeschichte*, Munich 1960, pp. 287–289; J. Bayet, *Histoire politique et psychologique de la religion romain*, Paris [1969], 1976, p. 169.

[5] A. D. Nock, "The Augustan Restoration (1925)," in A. D. Nock, ed., *Essays on Religion and the Ancient World*, Oxford 1972, I, pp. 16–25; R. Syme, *The Roman Revolution*, Oxford 1939, p. 447.

centuries. But how should we interpret these reforms? What were they reacting against? It was not a question of a change in religion or a deepening of faith.[6] In line with Roman ritualism, Augustus was reacting solely against the negligence of religious obligations and public cult places caused by the disorder of the civil wars. The restoration of cult places and the rites that were supposed to take place there was one of his main political objectives. The restoration of the state (the *res publica*) at Rome automatically entailed the restoration of religious institutions and public cult places, if they had been neglected or forgotten. In 31 BC that was indeed the situation. Besides, after a civil war – at the end of a century of troubles and civil strife – religious traditions must have appeared neglected and forgotten. The pious restoration of what his rivals had neglected, or even violated, during the conflict was the best way of legitimising his own power. Augustus was perhaps a reactionary, who wanted to restore ancestral practices both within his own family and in public life, but still his religious restorations were a necessary part of his political agenda. His enemies had neglected, confiscated, and almost ruined the Republic, he claimed. He was now returning it to the people, with all its ancestral traditions restored. Historians thus need to deconstruct this political programme and probe Augustus' sincerity, but they must also take account of the fact that Augustus carried it out with tenacity, the people on the whole accepted it, and the main lines of the system established by Augustus survived intact for almost three centuries.

That said, what were the nature and aims of Augustus' restoration of religion? Was it not in fact "more a new construction than a restoration," as Georg Wissowa viewed it?[7] The new construction would in fact have served as a foundation for the imperial cult. This way of thinking, combined with the persistent misunderstanding of the importance of ritualism, still exercises a strong influence on approaches to religion in the age of Augustus and under the Empire. The imperial cult is in fact separated off from religion or viewed as a particular part of state religion, the only part of civic religion that is comprehensible. We can easily grasp the political aims of the imperial cult. Such reasoning allows the imperial cult to be classified under the heading of politics rather than religion; it leads to the con-

---

[6] On this question, see J. Scheid, *Romulus et ses frères. Le collège des frères arvales, modèle du culte public dans la Rome des empereurs* (BEFAR 275), Rome 1990, pp. 679–686.

[7] G. Wissowa, *Religion und Kultus der Römer* (2nd edn), Munich 1912, p. 72 ("mehr ein Neubau als eine Wiederherstellung").

clusion that it was the only element of the old civic ritualism that still had vitality.

Following the example of the cult of the individual common in Fascist regimes of the twentieth century or ambiguous notions invented in this same context, such as the "mysticism" of the *princeps*,[8] scholars have then treated the imperial cult in a summary and incorrect manner to the point where it even loses its substance. And such an oversight cannot be justified by a peremptory declaration that the emperor was a god and that he was honoured as such from the battle of Actium onwards in the cults and on the monuments of Rome.[9] Things were clearly more complicated; they cannot be elucidated either by simplifying approaches or by comparing them superficially to the Fascist regimes of the modern era. To understand a certain number of aspects of the rites that we group under the term "imperial cult," it is advisable to examine them in detail in their full context. The cults and cult places of the city of Rome, restored or created by Augustus, permit such an examination, since they highlight Augustus' methods; for his initiatives were enacted in a particular time and space; they penetrated the everyday.

The spectacular transformation of the public space of Rome and its institutional regime did not occur in a fortuitous and arbitrary manner, dependent on the personal preferences of the *princeps*. It was broadly in keeping with the norms of ancestral religion, and its first objective was to reassert those practices. One needs, therefore, to analyse the innovations brought about by the Augustan restorations according to the rules and principles governing Rome's ancestral cults.

At Rome, the spatial and temporal organisation of human communities formed a united whole; it was composed of divine portions and human portions distributed in a variety of ways. According to Roman modes of thought there were two means of conceiving the time and space that humans and gods shared: a natural calendar desired by the gods, which was acknowledged to be recognised and accepted by humans in the form of an astronomical calendar, and a civil calendar created by magistrates. Similarly certain sacred spaces (temples, for instance) had been created by magistrates or by those who had the institutional power to do so alongside places which were thought to have been conceived and consecrated by the gods them-

---

[8] See, for example, J. Gagé, "De César à Auguste. Où en est le problème des origines du Principat? À propos du *César* de M. J. Carcopino," *Rev. Hist.*, 177 (1936), pp. 279–342.
[9] As, for example, in the most recent book to appear on the subject: M. Clauss, *Kaiser und Gott. Herrscherkult im römischen Reich*, Stuttgart and Leipzig 1999.

selves (sacred woods, bottomless lakes, enormous caverns).[10] In other words, the civic religious calendar and civic religious space were in fact artificial creations, constructed by the authorities, and it was perfectly possible to construct or reconstruct them in a new way, so long as their underlying principles were respected. It was this reality that the calendar and sacred places reflected and it was within this framework that Augustus' initiatives and the "invention" of the imperial cult are to be located.

I shall be concerned here only with the initiatives of Augustus, but it goes without saying that these were often the continuation of previous arrangements and were often pursued further after his death. It is also useful to remember that the common denominator in all decisions creating the imperial cult, accepted by Augustus for the territory of Rome and for the institutions of the Roman state, could be defined as follows: no member of the *res publica* ought to have on earth more honours than Augustus (I am thinking here of the problems of the *imperium maius* [*imperium* greater than that held by others]). As a result, just as he had (at least) the same powers as other magistrates or promagistrates in every area, so he also benefited from specific honours each time the gods were officially invoked. Even if the political benefit of these honours is clear, as well as the fact that this privilege expressed the superhuman quality of Augustus' actions in ritual fashion, the imperial cult was neither a usurpation of divine honours nor deification pure and simple, but rather a particular kind of sharing of the honours paid *on earth* to those who appeared (or wanted) to surpass the human condition and human forms of power.

RESTORATIONS

There would be little point in providing a long commentary on the list of temples restored by Augustus and his friends. One might note that these initiatives went back to the civil war period, to the earliest years of Augustus' career: the headquarters of the college of *pontifices* – the *Regia* in the Roman Forum – was restored from 36 BC onwards by Cn. Domitius Calvinus. More important for our purposes is the fact that Augustus' restoration of temples and cult places allowed him to affect a large proportion of the population of Rome. The scaffolding, the workers, the noise, and other incon-

---

[10] On sacred groves and other natural "divine" places, see the contributions to the colloquium *Les bois sacrés* (Actes du colloque international de Naples, 1989) (Centre Jean-Bérard, 10), Naples 1993.

veniences signalled the event for weeks and months on end. Visits of the man who ordered the work, such as his inspection of the old cult building of Jupiter Feretrius,[11] left people in no doubt about who was responsible for the initiative. Finally, the day of the rededication, a splendid festival, reintroduced a god and temple solemnly back into the religious calendar and religious obligations of the city after decades of neglect or lack of respect, real or imagined. The large number of buildings involved meant that the neighbourhoods of Rome resounded for several years with building-works and the festive brouhaha of inaugurations. But the initiatives went further.

Besides the inscriptions that eventually recalled (or, sometimes, in spectacular fashion did not recall)[12] the name of the pious restorer or dedicator, the day of the dedication was often altered. This could happen since this type of anniversary did not depend on any essential tradition; it amounted to a commemoration by the citizens of a decision taken and not of a day specially reserved for all time for a particular divinity. Augustus and his friends usually made it coincide with a private anniversary within the *princeps'* family.[13] In this way, public festivals coincided with celebrations within Augustus' family. For the Augustan period we are badly informed on other such combinations more directly linked to the imperial cult. A new temple might include, for instance, a statue of Augustus, but before the reign of Caligula we do not hear of public sacrifices being carried out to the Genius (i.e., protecting spirit) of a *princeps* in public cult places in the city of Rome;[14] that is, however, doubtless due to the quality of our evidence for the principates of Augustus and Tiberius. It was always the case that even when the Arval Brethren sacrificed on the Capitol on Tiberius' or Livia's birthday, they did not honour the Genius or the Juno (i.e., protective spirit of a woman) of these two, but only Jupiter.[15] We shall see later that initially the public cult to Augustus' Genius was conducted at a different level. In any case, at

---

[11] Livy 4.20.7.

[12] As in the cases mentioned by Augustus himself: *RG* 20.1.

[13] For a list, see P. Gros, *Aurea Templa: recherches sur l'architecture religieuse de Rome à l'époque d'Auguste* (BEFAR 231), Rome 1976, pp. 32ff.

[14] J. Scheid, *Commentarii fratrum arvalium qui supersunt. Les copies épigraphiques des protocoles annuels de la confrérie arvale (21 av.–304 apr. J.-C.)*, Rome 1998, p. 42, no. 16, line 4 (Caligula).

[15] For example, Scheid, ibid., p. 14, no. 5 (AD 27), f, lines 2–4 (Livia's birthday, sacrifice to Jupiter); p. 18, no. 7 (AD 33), a, I, lines 1–3 (Tiberius' birthday, sacrifice to Jupiter). Independently of this reticence, Tiberius, Livia, and their family were included in the formula of good wishes which opened the announcement of the date of the sacrifice to Dea Dia (Scheid, ibid., p. 10, no. 4, a [AD 21], lines 16–18) or in public vows (first attested on 4 January AD 27: cf. Scheid, ibid., p. 13, no. 5, a-e, lines 4–5).

least after Caligula, offerings were increasingly made to the Genius of the *princeps* at sacrifices that were focused on the *princeps*, and it may be supposed that the emperor's Genius regularly benefited from a (secondary) altar and perhaps from a statue in the imperial shrines in large cult places. After Augustus' death and deification, many cult places were embellished with additional statues or shrines of the Deified Augustus (and later those of other *Divi* too). At the start of the Empire, however, it was more by means of the building-site, the dedication, and the date of its dedication that the *princeps* was linked to the restored temples.

NEW CONSTRUCTIONS

If some of the restored temples were directly connected to Augustus and his triumphs (as with the temple of Jupiter Feretrius, for instance), it was even more the case with the new cult places constructed by or for Augustus during the fifty-year period his Principate lasted. [For their locations, see Fig. 9.1.] In the case of the Temple of the Deified Caesar (18 July 29 BC), the huge Temple of Apollo on the Palatine (9 October 28 BC), that of Jupiter Tonans on the Capitol (21 BC), or that of Mars Ultor ['the Avenger'], these temples celebrated the ascendancy and great deeds of Augustus, while at the same time profoundly restructuring the monumental centre of Rome. As Zanker has emphasised, by the luxury of their facilities and their decoration, these new temples gained the upper hand over the old temples which had been piously restored, but which very much struggled to compete with the Hellenistic splendour of the new temples of the regime.[16] Indeed these decorative elements provided a direct link to Augustus and his family and celebrated the glory of his achievements as well as his piety. In what follows, I would prefer to concentrate on the transformations in social life that these temples brought about.

The Temple of the Deified Caesar restructured the Roman Forum and provided all who worked, were based, or took a stroll in the Forum with a clear image of the links between the Roman people and the family of the Julii. Once the temple was dedicated, this image became quite evident, since the temple was flanked by an arch celebrating Octavian's victory over Egypt and Antony. Prows from Egyptian ships decorated the new rostra that were constructed in

---

[16] Zanker, *Augustus und die Macht der Bilder* (op. cit., n. 3), p. 114 (= *Power of Images*, p. 108).

Map of cult places in and near Rome.
1. Periphery; 2. Urban Centre

1. Mausoleum of Augustus
2. Ara Pacis
3. Ara Providentiae
4. *Horologium* (sundial)
5. Pantheon of Agrippa
6. Capitol: Temple of Jupiter Tonans
   Temple of Jupiter Feretrius
7. Roman Forum: Temple of the Deified Caesar
   Temple of Castor and Pollux
8. Palatine: Temple of Apollo
9. Crossroad (*compitum*) of the Armilustrium
   (with a Dolichenum)
10. Crossroad (*compitum*) of the Via Marmorata
    (with a Mithraeum)
11. Temples of Mars and of Honour and Virtue
    and *Ara Fortunae Reducis*
12. Robigo
13. Fors Fortunae and Dea Dia
14. Fortuna Muliebris

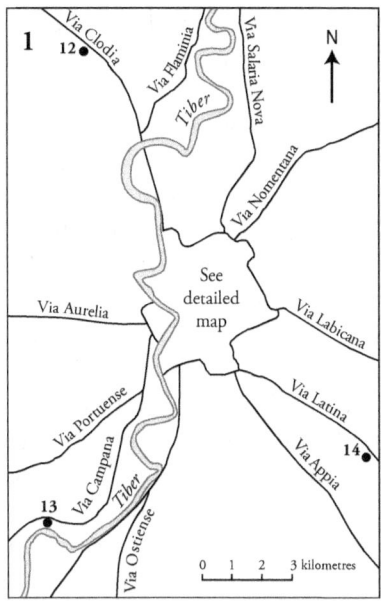

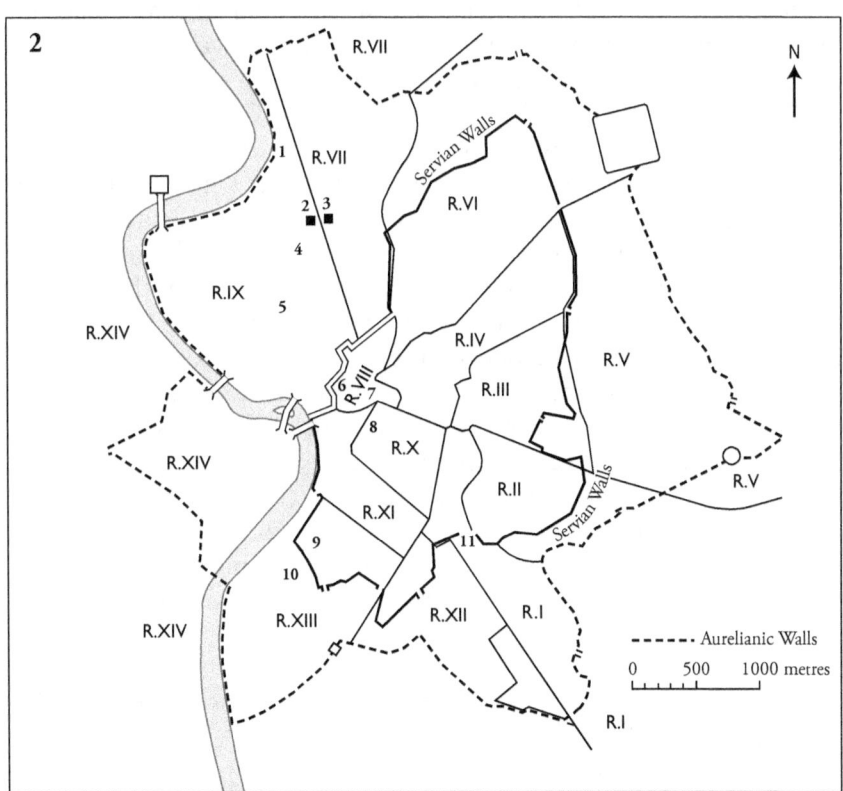

Fig. 9.1. Map of cult places in and near Rome. 1. Periphery; 2. Urban centre

front of the Temple of the Deified Caesar, and four other columns decorated with prows were set up a short distance away in the open square of the Forum, not to mention the other references to his naval victories that could be found in the decoration of numerous public buildings, such as in the new senate-house (*curia*).[17] The old political heart of Rome thus became, to use Zanker's term, a "representational space" for the Julian family. This space, one might imagine, had been appropriated by the *princeps*, even if the meaning of the new memory sites that he established, especially the arches flanking the Temple of the Deified Caesar, was gradually softened and related to the Parthians and the dead young princes Gaius and Lucius Caesar. An anecdote reveals the extent to which the Temple of Jupiter Tonans had similarly appropriated some of the prestige of Jupiter Optimus Maximus ("the Best and the Greatest"). To commemorate an omen about himself, Augustus had had this temple constructed in the *area Capitolina*, on the west side, at the top of the stairs leading up from the Forum Holitorium. Suetonius reports an anecdote about how jealous the "Greatest" (Jupiter Optimus Maximus) became because "the Thunderer" (Jupiter Tonans) started taking worshippers away from him.[18] This implies criticisms of, or at least a justification for, this new temple being built in front of the old Capitoline temple. It was to add an insistently Augustan note in the *area Capitolina*.

The Temples of Palatine Apollo and Mars Ultor, which both celebrated Augustus' victories at Naulochus, Actium, and Philippi, directly transformed the life of the urban neighbourhoods in which they were built. Alongside the Temple of Apollo, the Palatine received a large open square with libraries and porticoes, which immediately made them one of the main centres of cultural and political life in Augustan Rome. The senate held meetings there, so much the more easily since Augustus' house was in the vicinity. In 12 BC.[19] Augustus had the Sibylline Books transferred from the Capitoline Temple of Jupiter to the Temple of Apollo, thus depriving Jupiter of part of his divinatory powers. The Forum Augustum with its Temple of Mars Ultor took over another of Jupiter's prerogatives: senatorial debates on foreign affairs and war, triumphs, and, more

---

[17] *Augustus und die Macht der Bilder*, pp. 85–87 (= *Power of Images*, pp. 79–82), as well as the pages immediately following for a list of symbols of Augustan victory. [See also Hölscher, Chapter 10, below.]

[18] Suet. *Aug.* 91.2; see also *RG* 19; Dio 54.4.

[19] Contrary to what is sometimes imagined, the transfer took place in 12: see J. Scheid, "Auguste et le grand pontificat: politique et droit sacré au début du Principat," *Rev. hist. droit* 77 (1999), 1–19, esp. pp. 17f.

generally, certain tasks of Roman magistrates.[20] A series of Roman state activities was thus diverted towards the new public squares, their porticoes, and basilicas.[21] People were now required to frequent the new spaces, the decoration of which made serious reference to the *princeps* and his exploits. All this is well known. It is appropriate to add that for these new temples and squares, just as for those that had been restored, new religious celebrations were added to the public calendar. Besides the sacrifices and splendid games celebrated during the dedications of these buildings, each subsequent year festivals commemorated the anniversary of their dedication, sometimes with games (for example, the Games of Mars that took place on 12 May and 1 August). It is difficult to know the relative importance accorded the anniversaries of the various temples by Augustus and his successors, but one might suppose that on these anniversaries large banquets or distributions of foodstuffs were organised, which attracted the Roman people on a regular basis to these new cult places. It was, in any case, one means of emphasising the presence of the new cults in Roman state religion.

It was not just the centre of Rome that was endowed with new or restored cults. To judge from two pieces of surviving evidence, Rome's territory equally served to diffuse the glory of the *princeps* and his regime. At the place where the old Via Campana reached the long-established boundary of the territory of Rome, five miles from the city centre, at the modern village of La Magliana in approximately 29–28 BC Augustus saw to the restoration of the sacred grove of Dea Dia, a goddess who provided good heavenly light at the moment of the ripening of the crops.[22] This agrarian cult was established, according to an aetiological myth, by Romulus accompanied by his adoptive brothers, the sons of Acca Larentia. Augustus, who presented himself in this period as a new Romulus, celebrated there with eleven of his peers, some of whom were his former enemies, the return of peace and agricultural productivity, both synonymous in

---

[20] Zanker, *Augustus und die Macht der Bilder* (op. cit., n. 3), pp. 196–217 (= *Power of Images*, pp. 192–215).

[21] It would appear from the current excavations in the Forum of Augustus that a basilica closed off the western part of the square. For discussion, see E. La Rocca, "La nuova immagine dei fori Imperiali: appunti in margine agli scavi," *RM* 108 (2001), 171–213, esp. pp. 192–193 and fig. 14. [Author's note: After further years of excavations, however, it is now clear that there was no basilica: see R. Meneghini and E. Carnabuci, "La nuova *forma* del Foro di Augusto: tratto e imagine; considerazioni sulle destinazioni d' uso degli emicicli," in R. Meneghini and R. Santangeli-Valenziani, eds, *Formae Urbis Romae: Nuovi frammenti di piante marmoree dallo scavo dei Fori imperiali* (*BCom* Suppl. 15), Rome 2006, pp. 157–196.]

[22] For all this, see Scheid, *Romulus et ses frères* (op. cit., n. 6). [For its location, see Fig. 9.1, no. 13.]

the Roman mindset with virtue. We do not know whether the cult of Robigo ("Mildew"), which was similarly linked to the wheat-growing cycle and celebrated each year a month later at the fifth milestone on the Via Claudia,[23] was restored at the same time. These old cults likewise commemorated the archaic boundary of Rome's territory, which henceforth played a symbolic role. They could also evoke in the minds of Romans the idea that Roman territory was protected by the person who had restored the place.

The cult of Dea Dia, which is very well attested, allows us to reconstruct the range of implications of this type of restoration. The cult profited from the traditional popularity of the place. On the same spot was located a temple of Fors Fortuna [Chance Fortune], which attracted a joyous crowd each year on 24 June.[24] This same crowd, one might expect, would return a month later to take part in the sacrifice to Dea Dia, during which the Arval Brethren sacrificed two young sows, a cow, and a lamb, which amounted to at least 400 kg of meat. Even if the priests set aside some of this meat for use at the sacrificial banquets, enough meat was left to organise a distribution before the chariot-races that took place after the priests' banquet.[25] Adding to the traditional and new attractions of the place was the fact that the sacred grove lay on a slope running down to the river Tiber, along which passed day after day the cargoes of wheat that were so essential for Rome's food supply. Indeed, this highly symbolic place, which evoked the *princeps*' concern for the food supply of Rome, could be considered one of the most important forms of what we call the imperial cult. More precisely, this cult, like others, presented Augustus as a second Romulus in the sense that he was restoring cults established by Romulus, benefiting in this way from the superhuman mythical status of their founder. At the same time, Augustus restored the Lupercal on the Palatine, which was associated with the *Luperci* (established by Romulus), the *sodales Titii* (thought to commemorate Romulus' colleague Titius Tatius), and the *Caeninenses* (priests of equestrian rank associated with the cults founded by Romulus at Caenina north of Rome), not to mention the

---

[23] Ovid *Fast.* 4.905–932. [For its location, see Fig. 9.1, no. 12.]
[24] Ovid *Fast.* 6.775ff.
[25] For these calculations, see J. Scheid, "Manger avec les dieux. Partage sacrificiel et commensalité dans la Rome antique," in S. Georgoudi, R. Koch-Piettre, and F. Schmidt, eds, *La cuisine et l'autel: Les sacrifices en questions dans les sociétés de la Méditerranée ancienne* (Bibliothèque de l'École Pratique des Hautes Études, Sciences religieuses 124), Turnout 2005. Note that 400 kg of meat would provide 4,000 portions of 100 g, and so on.

Temple of Jupiter Feretrius, where Romulus deposited the *spolia opima* of Acron, king of Caenina.[26]

The cult of Dea Dia also offered the advantage of spectacular presentations in Rome itself. For the goddess had two cult places: the main one in the sacred grove on the Via Campana, the second in the city of Rome in the house of the current year's president of the Arval Brethren. The sacrifice to Dea Dia, the date of which was eventually fixed on the 17, 19, and 20 or 27, 29, and 30 May, began on the first day at the president's residence. The people of Rome could then see a chosen group of Rome's elite gather, eventually with the emperor, at one of their homes to celebrate an archaic cult there. In some years the gathering took place on the Palatine in the emperor's home. On the second day the fraternity gathered at the fifth milestone on the Via Campana. We do not know if they left Rome in procession, as the *flamen* of Quirinus did when he visited the sacred grove of Robigo. The evening of the following day, they returned to the president's home to conclude the sacred rites. In addition, the Arvals announced each year on 11 January in the *pronaos* [porch] of a temple, usually the Temple of Concord, the dates of the sacrifice to Dea Dia, since they were variable. It is quite legitimate to suppose that the other restored cults benefited similarly from just as much visibility.

On the other bank of the Tiber, at the fourth milestone along the Via Latina [Fig. 9.1, no. 14], Livia restored the ancient sanctuary of Rome's matrons dedicated to Fortuna Muliebris ["Womanly Fortune"] in her role as the leading matron of Rome.[27] Along with the sacred groves of Dia and Robigo, this temple shows how those who travelled to Rome along the consular roads found themselves immediately in the presence of sanctuaries restored or richly enlarged by Augustus and his wife, as if to point out to travellers that they were entering the city of the *princeps*. These old cult places were by no means isolated in their role as the watch-towers of the territory of the city of Rome.

---

[26] I believe that the restoration of the Temple of Jupiter Feretrius, the *fetiales* (who took up in this temple the flint and sceptre that were the symbolic markers of their office), and probably the *Caeninenses* all go back to the same decision taken previously in 32 BC and in view of the declaration of war against Egypt, which was made according to the fetial rite.

[27] *CIL* VI 883; see R. Frei-Stolba, "Recherches sur la position juridique et sociale de Livie, l'épouse d'Auguste," in R. Frei-Stolba and A. Bielman, eds, *Femmes et vie publique dans l'Antiquité gréco-romaine*, Lausanne 1998, I, pp. 65–89, esp. p. 84.

TO HONOUR THE POWER OF THE *PRINCEPS*

The temples mentioned so far made reference, without doubt, to Augustus and his exploits, but the cult celebrated *in honour of* Augustus was addressed to ancestral or new gods and not to Augustus himself, despite certain parallels with Romulus. Gradually, however, other cults and divinities were added to the ones already in existence, and these evoked more directly the divine power of the *princeps*. Before penetrating the old cult places themselves, these cults spread outside Rome and in the neighbourhoods of the city.

The consular roads continued to serve as a stage on which to celebrate the *princeps'* virtues. In 30 BC the people had passed a law that each time Octavian returned to Rome, he would be welcomed by the Vestals, the senate, and the whole Roman people.[28] Octavian refused this honour, but we know that each time he returned from an important journey or in particular circumstances, the question of these returns was posed once again. The debates led, in the end, to the creation of altars and cults, commemorating one particular return or an imperial virtue. The first of these altars is also the most significant.[29]

Augustus had travelled in Greece and Asia Minor from the end of 22 to the autumn of 19 BC. It was during this sojourn abroad that in spring of the year 20 he was able to recover the standards lost during the war against the Parthians. In 19 public order was unstable in Rome to such a degree that there was an ardent demand for the *princeps* to return. Even though Augustus surprised everyone by the speed of his return and re-entered the city discreetly during the night of 12 October, the senate decided to characterise his return as triumphal.[30] Augustus refused various honours, notably a triumphal chariot and triumphal crown, but accepted the construction of a triumphal arch in the Forum, as well as the establishment of an altar celebrating his return (*Ara Fortunae Reducis*) in front of the Temple of Honour and Virtue alongside the Temple of Mars, near the Porta Capena, at the starting-point of the Via Appia and Via Latina [see Fig. 9.1, no. 11]. In the *Res Gestae*, he specified that it was the senate that had consecrated this altar and designated 12 October as a holiday (*feriae*), requiring the pontiffs and Vestals to sacrifice there on subsequent anniversaries of the date of his return and naming this

---

[28] Dio 51.19.2, 20.4.
[29] The Temple of Jupiter Tonans might be considered another cult place linked to Augustus' return.
[30] Dio 54.10.3.

day the Augustalia.³¹ The inscribed calendars specify that the altar was *constituted* [i.e., inaugurated] on 12 October and *dedicated* on 15 December.³²

Looking at things more closely, one can uncover Augustus' whole strategy. The honour accepted in 19 was extraordinary. As Augustus himself emphasised in the *Res Gestae*, the day of the sacrifice had to be given a name derived from his own *cognomen* rather than from that of the divinity honoured: so it was called the Augustalia and not the Fortunalia. From 19 onwards, Augustus received "his own" great festival day similar to Ceres' Cerialia, Vesta's Vestalia, or Saturn's Saturnalia. This honour granted him a privilege fitting for the gods. The privilege did not consist only in what was sacrificed to the gods in commemoration of his quasi-triumph, but also in the day being attributed to Augustus himself,³³ which implied that cult was being offered to his person. In fact, a detailed analysis of the sources reveals rather more complex tactics. The text of the *Res Gestae* appears to imply that the festival was officially known as the Augustalia from the start. No independent source, however, confirms this interpretation. Of the inscribed calendars that have survived, some are fragmentary in the sections covering the month of October, while others that attest this event are dated later than the death of Augustus and so cannot either provide formal proof that the festival was immediately called the Augustalia or provide any *terminus ante quem*.³⁴ According to the evidence that now survives, the name "Augustalia" only seems to have been officially employed from AD 14 onwards. Before this date, the sacrifices were offered to Fortuna Redux to commemorate the "triumphal" entry of 19. Once Augustus was elected *pontifex maximus*, thus removing the (largely imaginary) risk of being criticised by Lepidus, some magistrates celebrated *ludi Augustales* [Augustan games] on their own personal initiative in an irregular fashion, but without any protest on the part of the *princeps*, as, for example, in 11 BC.³⁵

As often occurred, Augustus was not, therefore, opposed to the

---

³¹ *RG* 11 (quoted above, p. 275).
³² Degrassi, *Inscr. It.* XIII.2, p. 519 (*fasti* of Amiternum for 12 October; *feriale* of Cumae for 15 December).
³³ For the creation of these festivals, see A. Fraschetti, *Rome et le prince* (trans. V. Jolivet), Paris 1994, pp. 17–37, esp. pp. 26–27 [= *Roma e il principe*, Rome 1990, pp. 14–41, esp. pp. 19–20].
³⁴ For the details, see Scheid, "Auguste et le grand pontificat" (op. cit., n. 19), pp. 9–12.
³⁵ Dio 54.34.2, with the comments of M. A. Cavallaro, *Spese e spettacoli. Aspetti economici-strutturali degli spettacoli nella Roma giulio-claudia*, Bonn 1984, pp. 251–259, esp. p. 255; J. W. Rich, ed. and trans. *Cassius Dio: The Augustan Settlement (Roman History 53–55.9)*, Warminster 1990, p. 213, *ad loc.*

exceptional tribute of the Augustalia and their games, which *de facto* placed him on a par with the gods. The initiative originated, without doubt, from within his inner circle, but clearly he did not have it included among the major festivals of the Roman state calendar. It was only in AD 14 that the festival found the god it was lacking in the form of Divus Augustus ("the Deified Augustus"), when it became a regular state festival with *ludi Augustales* under the name Augustalia.[36] In 19 BC it sufficed for him to prepare and plan its evolution. Whatever it was, this altar added a very specific nuance to the old Temples of Mars and of Honour and Virtue at the Porta Capena. The location was not gratuitous. It was not only the gate through which Augustus had returned to Rome, but above all an important place of martial cult: the annual procession of knights (*transvectio equitum*) set off from here every 15 July. The procession, dear to the equestrian order, was in this way completely framed by references to Augustus and his family. For the equestrian centuries gathered in the Roman Forum to offer sacrifice in front of the Temple of Castor and Pollux. That meant that the procession passed underneath the arch of Augustus and the ceremony took place between it, the Temple of the Deified Caesar, on one side, and the four Augustan columns with ship-prows on the other. One might also mention the images of the deceased young Caesars, Gaius and Lucius, which were carried in the procession from AD 2 and 4 onwards, and the eventual participation of one of the living young princes as *sevir equitum* [one of the "six men," i.e., leaders, of the equestrians].

The Altar of Fortune and the games (held from 3 to 12 October) that were designed to mark the day indirectly altered the hierarchy among the various sanctuaries. Without possessing a temple, and without even being personally the object of cult, Augustus could appear to compete with the three other divinities, especially from 11 BC onwards. For of all the cult places around the Porta Capena, only the altar of Fortuna Redux had games. Felicitously, but also significantly, these games took up a part of the month of October and were inserted into the calendar between the Roman Games in September and the Plebeian Games in November. It is interesting to note that in line with the military overtones of the place, the fortunate return of Augustus after his "exploits" in the East was defined as a military achievement. The good fortune of his return was in some sense a divinised quality of Mars – or of the *princeps* himself.

---

[36] See Tac. *Ann.* 1.15, with the comments of Nipperdey, Furneaux, or Koestermann.

In the same way, but more clearly, another return was exploited to mark emphatically the point where the consular road coming from the north, the Via Flaminia, entered the city of Rome. When Augustus returned to Rome after his stay in Gaul from 16 to 13 BC, the senate decided to have the Altar of Augustan Peace (*Ara Pacis Augustae*) constructed to celebrate the event [see Fig. 9.1, no. 2].[37] *Constituted* on 4 June 13, the altar was *dedicated* on 30 January (Livia's birthday) in 9 BC. Every year the magistrates and the state priests would sacrifice to commemorate its dedication.[38] Once again, therefore, a cult place directly linked to the *princeps* was set up along the edge of one of the major access routes into the city of Rome. This time, it was one of his virtues that was celebrated, the peace made secure by his actions. And once again the choice of location was not gratuitous. The altar was located near to the entrance to the vast park that surrounded the enormous mausoleum which Augustus had had built from 28 BC onwards and which the traveller would see on his right-hand side as he entered Rome. A place for strolling and for popular pleasures,[39] this space in a way offered itself for the celebration of Augustus' actions. It would also in time welcome other monuments.

In AD 4 another altar similar to that of the Augustan Peace was constructed on the other side of the Via Flaminia, in the Campus of Agrippa, doubtless facing the Altar of Peace: the Altar of Augustan Providence (*Ara Providentiae Augustae*) [Fig. 9.1, no. 3]. As the date of the anniversary of its dedication (26 June) and the reference to it in the *senatus consultum de Cn. Pisone patre* prove, the altar celebrated Augustus' adoption of Tiberius.[40] The landscape that presented itself to those who were passing by or sacrificing at one of these altars was explicit. The benefits of the peace brought back by Augustus were maintained thanks to his providence, which notably involved the selection of a (good) successor in a family whose mausoleum dominated the neighbouring park.

---

[37] Zanker, *Augustus und die Macht der Bilder* (op. cit., n. 3), pp. 177–187 (= *Power of Images*, pp. 172–183); K. Galinsky, *Augustan Culture: An Interpretive Introduction*, Princeton 1996, pp. 141–155.

[38] RG 11.2 (quoted above, p. 275).

[39] Strabo 5.3.8.

[40] Scheid, *Commentarii fratrum arvalum qui supersunt* (op. cit., n. 14), p. 30, no. 12 (AD 38), c, lines 54–57. The mention of the *Ara Providentiae Augustae* in the s.c. concerning *Piso senior* (cf. W. Eck, A. Caballos Rufino, and F. Fernández Gómez, *Das Senatus Consultum de Cn. Pisone patre* (Vestigia 48), Munich 1996, p. 44, lines 83–84; pp. 199ff.) proves that its foundation took place before the fall of Sejanus and that it must have been linked to Tiberius' adoption by Augustus on 26 June AD 4; cf. Scheid, *Romulus et ses frères* (op. cit., n. 6), pp. 425ff.)

According to E. Buchner, the obelisk of the monumental sundial [*horologium*] [Fig. 9.1, no. 4], commemorating the victory in Egypt, which was erected in 10 BC to the west of the Altar of Peace, would have cast its shadow towards the centre of the Altar of Peace on Augustus' birthday.[41] This setting would have enhanced the dramatic effect of the monuments, but doubts have been raised regarding this hypothesis.[42] Nevertheless, the mere presence of this large *horologium*, later restored by Domitian, suffices to illustrate the splendour and originality of the facilities of these parks spreading the imperial ideology. Alongside Augustan Peace and Augustan Providence, the obelisk recalled the historical moment when peace had returned.

Another altar was consecrated by Tiberius on 17 January AD 6 (Augustus' and Livia's wedding anniversary) at an unknown place in Rome to the *Numen Augusti* (the "Divine Power of Augustus").[43] This provided a more general and more direct version of the divine power of action of the *princeps*.

All these Augustan places continued to exercise their influence throughout the imperial period, since they became points of reference for Augustus' successors. Together with other rites and privileges, they had been the first public version in Rome of what we call imperial cult. There can be no doubt that Augustus, his supporters, and a good proportion of the Roman population considered his actions divine, and they were ready to honour him as a god. The example of Caesar's assassination and his own desire to associate the largest number of Romans possible, especially the elite, with his reforms of the state forced Augustus, however, to carry out his work prudently. He drew a clear line between the civic religion of the city of Rome and the initiatives that the cities of Italy and the provinces wished to carry out. In the public cult of the Roman state, only certain elements parallel to what took place elsewhere were possible: first, the insistence on his divine origin – "Son of the Deified One" – and the creation of the cult of the Deified Julius; then the various Romulean enactments; and finally the altars celebrating the divine virtues of the actions of the *princeps*. Initially, the latter cult was assimilated to Fortuna and located in the military setting of the Porta Capena, but from 13–9 BC onwards Peace and in AD 4 Providence became Augustus' personal virtues. As with the immortal gods,

---

[41] E. Buchner, *Die Sonnenuhr des Augustus*, Mainz 1982.

[42] M. Schütz, "Zur Sonnenuhr des Augustus auf dem Marsfeld: eine Auseinandersetzung mit E. Buchners Rekonstruktion," *Gymnasium* 97 (1990), pp. 432–457.

[43] Degrassi, *Inscr. It.* XIII.2, p. 115.

Augustus benefited from the privilege of being associated with abstract divinities, expressing the characteristics and outcomes of his actions.[44] In AD 9 it was his acts as a whole that were celebrated by the cult and altar of his Divine Power.

One might think that these initiatives did not deceive anyone, especially if one compares them with the divine honours that certain individuals and certain cities had paid Augustus, clearly with his approval, or at least with his tacit approval. The example of the Augustalia also reveals the implications of these official initiatives. It is, nonetheless, certain that no direct public cult was authorised. No official sacrifice to the Genius of Augustus is attested during Augustus' lifetime, and the altar of the *Numen Augusti*, as well as the official Ludi Augustales, was the most emphatic outward sign that he would tolerate this. People had to wait quite some time before they saw the custom of publicly sacrificing to the imperial Genius develop.[45] Clearly, as far as Rome's state cult was concerned, Augustus was content to benefit at Rome from all the honours reserved for the immortals, while waiting for himself to be raised to the level of a god. Public festivals celebrated his exploits or events involving him, such as his birthday. In the course of these the magistrates sacrificed to the gods in remembrance of his superhuman acts. More subtly, numerous anniversaries of dedications of temples or altars were aligned with Augustan anniversaries and in this way commemorated *sotto voce* the various stages of his life and career. In everyday life, this meant that a day on which an "Augustan" event was celebrated also saw the celebration of several anniversaries involving temples. Thus 23 September, the first day of the festival marking Augustus' birthday, overlapped with the (new) anniversaries of the Temples of Apollo (Sosianus), Mars *in Campo*, and Neptune *in Campo*.[46] In other words, in addition to the festivities and rejoicing that marked Augustus' birthday, the whole area of the Circus Flaminius in the vicinity of the Theatre of Marcellus was on holiday, doubtless with banquets and distributions of meat resulting from the sacrifices offered. At the same time, these secondary festivals, which were directly related to various supporters of Augustus from the

---

[44] For this category of "secondary" divinities, see J. Scheid, "Hiérarchie et structure dans le polythéisme romain: façons romaines de penser l'action," *Archiv für Religionsgeschichte*, 1.2 (1999), 184–203 [English trans. in C. Ando, ed., *Roman Religion*, Edinburgh 2003, pp. 164–189].

[45] For the hierarchy among immortals gods, *Divi*, and the emperor's Genius, see Scheid, "Hiérarchie et structure dans le polythéisme romain" (op. cit., n. 44), pp. 191–193.

[46] For these temples and the conditions of their restoration, see Gros, Aurea Templa (op. cit., n. 13).

period of the civil wars, offered a sort of commentary on Augustus' exploits.

Another festival, which gradually grew in importance, demonstrates yet again Augustus' reticence. In 30 BC it had been decided that henceforth at the start of each year the magistrates and priests would offer public vows for the well-being of the *princeps* alongside the regular vows for the well-being of the Republic.[47] These vows, the carrying out of which produced enormous quantities of meat,[48] which were perhaps distributed or offered at a banquet,[49] became from the reign of Tiberius onwards one of the great festivals in Rome and throughout the Roman world. It was also the occasion on which to make clear the fact that the *princeps* enjoyed the very same privileges and the same protection as the state itself. In sum, it was a perfect occasion on which to celebrate the new regime and its founder. However, the historical sources on Augustus remain very discreet about these vows, and it is only around AD 23 that they seem to have taken on their definitive form.[50] Augustus was clearly at pains to keep these rites at a modest level. The emphasis was placed instead on the four-yearly votive games for his well-being, celebrated from 28 BC onwards, which at the same time celebrated the victory in the war against Egypt.[51] It was as if he preferred once more to place the accent more on his exploits than on his position.

---

[47] Dio 51.19.7. The historian mentions the priests and priestesses (the Vestals), but in another passage (59.3.4) writes that it involved magistrates and priests, which is confirmed by other documents.

[48] On 3 January each year, the Arvals alone, in carrying out their vows for the well-being of the *princeps*, sacrificed four bovines, which produced 1.2 tonnes of meat: see, for example, Scheid, *Commentarii fratrum arvalium qui supersunt* (op. cit., n. 14), pp. 143 ff., no. 54 (AD 86), lines 1–23. But the Arvals were not the only ones to sacrifice on that day. If we limit ourselves to just the major state officials, we need to add the consuls and at least seven to nine other priestly colleges. Under Tiberius, for example, these magistrates and priests sacrificed 28 extra bovines; in total, at least 32 bovines, or 9.6 tonnes of meat. If all the state bodies doubled the number of victims under Nero, as the Arvals did, one reaches a total of almost twenty tonnes of meat. I owe these estimates to Patrice Méniel.

[49] There is, however, no evidence for this. Even so, the public authorities were in possession of enormous quantities of meat, which they could not store and which they, therefore, had to distribute or sell. The most plausible solution would be to imagine distributions to the people. To get an idea of the possibilities on offer, it is sufficient to consider that twenty tonnes of meat could be made up of 200,000 portions of 100 g (that is, about the total of the *plebs frumentaria* [the plebs who received the grain dole]), or 100,000 portions of 200 g.

[50] For this development, see Scheid, *Romulus et ses frères* (op. cit., n. 6), pp. 290–380.

[51] See *RG* 9.1; J. Scheid, "Les vœux pour le salut d'Octavien de 32 av. J.-Chr. (RGDA 9, 1)," in *Laurea internationalis: Festschrift für Jochen Bleicken zum 75. Geburtstag*, Stuttgart 2003, pp. 359–365.

TO HONOUR THE *PRINCEPS*

It is advisable to nuance what has just been said. The project of Augustus and his supporters was to legitimise the new regime by means of the cult of the *princeps*. As we have just seen, they did not do this directly in cult rituals celebrated by magistrates and state priests. No official temple or official altar was dedicated to Augustus or even to his Genius anywhere within the territory of the city of Rome. Agrippa's plan to have a sanctuary constructed in his own gardens that would carry Augustus' name was modified at the request of the intended honorand. He forbade the placing of his statue alongside those of the twelve gods in the cella of this temple, which was certainly private, but situated in gardens that were open to the public; he was content to see it placed in the temple's *pronaos* [porch].[52] With the marked patience that was characteristic of him, Augustus made those supporters who proposed more radical measures wait and put this all off until after his death; he was content to have himself honoured in state cult solely for his exploits. At another level, however, he went further.

In 30 BC the senate decided that a libation should be offered to his Genius at all public and private banquets.[53] Likewise, probably after Lepidus' death, in the year 13 BC in anticipation of his election as *pontifex maximus*, it was decided that Augustus' Genius should be added to the list of divinities who could be invoked as witnesses in oaths.[54] It was not so much the nature of these practices that was new, because both already existed in domestic cult, where people swore by the Genius of the head of the household (*paterfamilias*), who was also honoured with sacrifices. The novelty lay in the fact that henceforth these practices would be employed in official activities, in which only immortal divinities were usually acknowledged. It is a fine example of the way in which privileges normally reserved for the gods were applied to Augustus; the fact that these same privileges had been granted in 44 BC to Caesar, who had

---

[52] Dio 53.27.3; F. Coarelli, "Il Pantheon, l'apoteosi di Augusto e l'apoteosi di Romolo," in *Città e architettura nella Roma imperiale* (*Analecta Romana*, Suppl. 10), Odense 1983, pp. 41–46; D. Fishwick, "The statue of Julius Caesar in the Pantheon," *Latomus* 51 (1992), pp. 329–336.

[53] Dio 51.19.7. The historian writes that a sacrifice would be offered "to him" (αὐτῷ), but the specific pieces of evidence show that it comprised a libation to his Genius. Cassius Dio elsewhere uses a more specific formula to refer to the same privilege granted Julius Caesar in 44 BC (44.6.1: "to take an oath by his Genius": τὴν τύχην αὐτοῦ). The formula concerning Augustus is elliptical.

[54] The date is deduced from two passages of Horace (*Ep.* 2.1.15ff. and *Odes* 4.5.34), both dating to before 14 July 13 BC.

clearly been deified during his own lifetime, shows that a clear dividing line was being maintained between direct cult and the granting of divine privileges. But so long as Augustus was not formally deified and did not enjoy a public altar or a public temple, things remained this side of a boundary line that was deemed dangerous. Augustus changed tactics. Instead of imposing a cult of the *princeps* from above by the formal creation of a cult, he was happy to enjoy honours equal to the gods in public life, but he authorised – and doubtless encouraged – more direct cult practices at a lower level: i.e., the traditional libations offered between the first and second courses of a banquet and the invocation of his Genius in oaths. These were not state activities, but were in some sense connected practices. Public banquets took place as the closing acts of public sacrifices, once the sacrificial distributions and offerings had already been carried out; libations were offered during that part of the sacrifice involving humans. As for oaths, they accompanied the entry into office of magistrates and did not form a central part of their activity. At the private level, on the other hand, the political risks were fewer. Nevertheless, by means of these new requirements Augustus saw to it that the cult of the emperor's Genius came to form part of all domestic cults, discreetly, without the need for shrines or sacrifices, but by associating it with two already existing domestic and private activities, the banquet and the oath. In the same period a second phase began, which ensured that the cult of the Genius became part of state cult, but at a subordinate level.

From 12 BC onwards, following his election as *pontifex maximus*, Augustus authorised the celebration of *ludi Compitales* ["Games at the Crossroads"], banned since 64 BC.[55] This spectacular measure must have made the Roman plebs rejoice, since they had been forced for more than half a century to celebrate the annual festival of the Compitalia (around 1 January) without games. It was also the occasion for an initiative concerning the cults and cult places of the "crossroads" (*compita*). Starting in 12 BC, at least one urban neighbourhood in Rome, the *vicus* of Jupiter Fagutal,[56] started to honour the Lares Augusti and the Genius of Augustus in the shrine situated at the crossroads that marked the religious centre of the *vicus*. In 9 BC the *vicus* of Honour and Virtue followed suit.[57] And in 7, at the

---

[55] For the chronology and interpretation of all these measures, see the illuminating pages of Fraschetti (op. cit., n. 33), pp. 213–280, esp. p. 264 [= *Roma e il principe*, pp. 204–273, esp. pp. 253–254].

[56] *CIL* VI 452 = *ILS* 3260.

[57] *CIL* VI 449 = *ILS* 3617.

very moment when the new administrative division of the city of Rome into fourteen regions came into force, the majority of the other 265 *vici* inaugurated the same type of cult, each presided over by four freeborn or freedmen "masters" (*magistri*), who were elected in the area involved and assisted by four "ministers" (*ministri*) of servile rank.[58] It is clear from inscriptions and iconographic evidence that it was usually Augustus himself who donated the Lares to the *vici*, to which he occasionally also offered other statues. This all demonstrates the *princeps'* degree of involvement in this initiative. By the reform of the *vici* and the authorisation that he gave to revive the compitalicial games, Augustus completely won over the sympathies of the Roman plebs and laid the foundations for the collective religious organisation of the neighbourhoods of Rome. The evidence for the restoration of the shrines of the Lares under Domitian or Trajan clearly demonstrates that the institution was an unequivocal success.

A certain number of examples – the *vicus* of the Armilustrium on the Aventine or the *vicus* of the Via Marmorata [Fig. 9.1, nos 9 and 10] that stretched between the Aventine and the neighbourhood of Monte Testaccio, for instance – reveal that the "crossroads" of the *vici* served to unify the neighbourhoods and that other similarly new collective cults, such as the cult of Jupiter Dolichenus or of Mithras, were eventually installed there too. Clearly the centres of *vici* as reformed by Augustus had become the public place where the collective religious life of the neighbourhood was conducted. Indeed, this immediate success, as illustrated by the numerous altars that have survived from a variety of *vici*, also established the cult of the emperor's Genius and the Lares Augusti in a lasting manner in the small collective cult places of the regions of the city of Rome. These altars and shrines formed the first sanctuaries of the Genius of Augustus in Rome, and since the *Compitalia* was a public festival,[59] they became public cult places. Put another way, rather than imposing this type of cult at the lofty level of the state in the Forum or on the Capitol, Augustus preferred to integrate it into public cults at a more basic level, so to speak, by taking advantage of a festival and cult places that were evenly distributed across the city of Rome. It is true that he thereby affected a very significant number of citizens, whose principal public religious activity was henceforth conducted in the milieu of what we call the imperial cult. These were not the

[58] For the evolution of the districts of Rome and details of the Augustan reform, see Fraschetti (op. cit., n. 33), pp. 133–285 [= *Roma e il principe*, pp. 123–273].
[59] Fraschetti (op. cit., n. 33), p. 213 [= *Roma e il principe*, p. 204].

only cults celebrated in these places, since we know that other statues and altars were erected there too;[60] but the Lares Augusti and the Genius of Augustus were the titulary divinities of those places. In this way, with the numerous other rites and privileges underlining the superhuman nature of the *princeps*, the reform of the cults at the crossroads allowed the emperor's power to establish itself in the neighbourhoods in a lasting manner, and much more effectively than by the foundation of a temple in the Forum. Beyond the neighbourhoods and the ordinary people, these cults also integrated the cult of the emperor's Genius into state cult as a whole, without injuring too much the political sensibilities of the elite. The reform integrated the religious life of the neighbourhoods into state cult and introduced the cult of the Genius of Augustus into Roman state religion. Gradually all cult places, as well as a good number of public rites, received secondary altars and statues of the emperor's Genius, including shrines of the imperial family (the *domus Augusta*) and, from AD 14 onwards, of the Deified Augustus, not to mention the temple dedicated to the latter.

It would be incorrect, as I said earlier, to attribute all these initiatives, whose evolution and precise nature I have tried here to trace, to an authoritarian cynicism, to religious decadence, and to the hypocritical servility of Augustus' subjects. The historiography of the imperial period is sufficient to show that excessive action is not found in this area, even if some of the senatorial elite at the start of the Empire were forced to think that Augustus "did not leave any honour to the gods."[61] In Roman state cult excess consisted in claiming direct cult during one's own lifetime. Only tyrants did this. A "good" emperor was content, at this level, with a cult to his Genius, his Numen, and his other virtues. He benefited in a different manner from other collective practices, public or domestic, that involved more substantial honours.

It is no less true that the public religious honours addressed to Augustus had a clear religious foundation. By introducing in one way or the other the Princeps as a living partner of the gods (oaths, libations at banquets, *ludi Augustales*, the month of August, *Augustalia*) or as the point of reference for new cults (Fortuna Redux, Pax Augusta, Providentia Augusta, the Genius of Augustus, the Lares Augusti), not to mention giving statues of divinities his

---

[60] For example, in the *vicus* of the Via Marmorata, Apollo Augustus, Diana, Mercurius Augustus, Silvanus, Spes Augusta, and Bona dea Galbilla.
[61] Tac. *Ann.* 1.10.6.

features (Palatine Apollo), Augustus and his advisers were redefining the order of things. The symbolic sharing of time and space between mortals and immortals framed the contours of a terrestrial world in which everyone had his or her own particular place. In Roman ritualism, this model defined the system of the world and allowed it to function. Respect for this model permitted the two types of partner in the city to accomplish their earthly aims. By celebrating the pious submission of mortal Romans to the immortals in a kind of mutually beneficial pact of honours and assistance, everyone was in his or her proper place on earth. The Augustan reforms introduced a third partner into this agreement: the living emperor. Without granting him immortality during his lifetime, the numerous religious measures discussed above invested him, in successive stages and at various levels, with a variety of divine attributes, while people awaited his eventual deification after his death. Such privileges raised him above other mortals and assured him, on earth, of the same honours as the immortal gods were offered. After his death, he even had to receive his immortality by means of a decision taken by humans. As the hierarchy between the "Deified" (*Divi*) and the immortal gods demonstrates,[62] this immortality only related, in the main, to this world and not the other world, which was reserved evermore for the immortal gods. Nevertheless, there was a connection between the moderated honours of state cult and the more or less direct honours granted in the neighbourhoods of Rome and within families, not to mention Italy and the provinces, as well as the comments that writers could make about all this. It is evident that the religious honours paid the *princeps* legitimised and defined his mode of operation and, most of all, conferred upon him responsibilities in all the spaces of the city of Rome that only gods had previously possessed.

Augustus showed the way and it was followed for at least three centuries. Little by little, as we have seen, the cult of the Genius Augusti occasionally became attached to the cult of the other gods. As *principes* were deified, the number of temples and festivals increased, inserted into the calendar and within the civic space of Rome alongside the ancestral festivals and temples. Never, however, were the sensible principles defined by Augustus abandoned, except by "bad" emperors. Clearly those principles corresponded to a Roman conception of the proper order of things.

---

[62] See Scheid, "Hiérarchie et structure dans le polythéisme romain" (op. cit., n. 44).

PART III

Images of Power and the Power of Images

Introduction to Part III: Images of Power and the Power of Images

Few periods of Roman history have provided so many emblematically Roman images as the age of Augustus: the detailed reliefs from the *Ara Pacis*, the Gemma Augustea (Chapter 12, below, Fig. 12.2), the Boscoreale cups, the Portland vase, the Prima Porta Augustus (Chapter 11, below, Figs 11.7 and 11.8).[1] The last of these, a marble statue of the first *princeps* found at the villa owned by his wife Livia on the outskirts of Rome at Prima Porta, encapsulates the rich potential and the memorable, even mnemonic, quality of such imagery. Based on one of the canonical statue types of classical Greece, Polykleitos' Doryphoros ("Spear-Bearer"), probably a copy of a bronze original displayed in a prominent public location, it portrays Augustus as a military leader of youthful vigour, his outstretched right arm with its pointing index finger seeming to urge the Romans on to further military conquests and imperial expansion. His feet are bare, not clad in military boots, making him more reminiscent of a god or hero than a mere mortal. Cupid, riding on a dolphin, tugs at the hem of his tunic, reminding us that Augustus traced his descent from Venus, as did all the *gens Iulia*. The elaborately decorated breastplate (Chapter 11, below, Fig. 11.7) presents at its centre the scene of a Parthian handing over a legionary standard to a Roman commander (or the Roman god Mars). This image celebrates Augustus' recovery from the Parthian king in 20 BC of the standards that had been shamefully lost back in 53 BC when Crassus' army was defeated at the battle of Carrhae. But this diplomatic coup, which was in fact represented to the Roman people

---

[1] For the *Ara Pacis*, see the works cited in the general Introduction, n. 26; Gemma Augustea: Kähler 1991; Pollini 1993; Boscoreale cups: Kuttner 1995; Portland vase: Haynes 1975; Prima Porta: see the following note.

as a great military triumph, is given a cosmic significance by the images that surround the central scene. Above it, a bearded divinity (Caelus [Heaven], Jupiter, or Saturn) holds up and spreads out the canopy of the heavens, as the sun god Sol drives his chariot across the skies and Luna, the moon goddess, is carried off by the winged figure of Dawn. At the base of the cuirass, Mother Earth (Tellus) is shown easily reclining, her cornucopia overflowing with abundance. To the left, just above Augustus' right hip, Apollo rides on a griffin, mirrored on the right side by Diana mounted on a deer. (Diana and Apollo were two of Augustus' most favoured divinities and feature prominently in Horace's *Carmen Saeculare* ("Secular Hymn"), composed for the Secular Games of 17 BC.) Two slumping female figures are shown above Apollo and Diana: on the left, a woman with an eagle-sword, perhaps personifying the East; on the right, a woman holding a dragon-headed trumpet (a *carnyx*), an instrument typically associated with the Gauls (for this detail, see Chapter 11, below, Fig. 11.8). These two women thus represent the defeated peoples of the East and the West, and hence provide further evidence of Rome's imperial dominion under Augustus' charismatic leadership.[2]

Images of power such as this did much to enhance Augustus' authority and prestige and to encourage support for his rule. Not least, they underlined the strong centralised leadership that the Roman state now enjoyed after years of disunity and civil strife. Part III presents four studies that reflect upon the nature and power of the new imagery that pervaded the Empire in the visual forms of portrait sculpture, public monuments, building complexes, and coinage, but also through the rich literature that was created and circulated during the Augustan age.

As the general Introduction has already made clear (above, pp. 22–25), visual evidence has since the 1980s increasingly been integrated into historical accounts of the Augustan age, not least thanks to the work of the distinguished German classical archaeologist Paul Zanker.[3] The article by Maria Wyke (Chapter 11) owes much to Zanker's influence, while Tonio Hölscher's contribution on the diffusion and significance of visual imagery alluding to Augustus' victory at the battle of Actium (Chapter 10), first published in 1985, shows that Zanker was by no means alone in arguing for the importance of

---

[2] On the statue, see Simon 1957 and 1991; Zanker 1988: 188–192. For its findspot at the villa at Prima Porta, Pollini 1987–1988; Reeder 1997a and 1997b.

[3] No extract is presented here from his 1987 book *Augustus und die Macht der Bilder* ("Augustus and the Power of Images"), which needs to be absorbed in its entirety.

visual language for the consolidation of Augustus' power. In fact, Hölscher's brief article anticipates a number of the central themes of Zanker's *Augustus und die Macht der Bilder*.

However, the imagery and subliminal messages conveyed by such visual means raise particular problems of historical interpretation in addition to the basic issue of precisely how they should best be read. To what extent did Augustus have a hand in orchestrating the nature of the images and themes that circulated? Was there a grand scheme in place from the start? Or did this "visual language" take shape through some sort of ongoing dialogue between the *princeps* and the artists and architects of the period? Or was Augustus initially involved in discussions about the basic framework and themes, but then the details were developed without much further direction from the *princeps* or his immediate advisers? What were the mechanisms whereby images that first appeared in Rome were subsequently disseminated in Italy and the provinces?

How to interpret the literature of the period has proved just as controversial. Like most Roman aristocrats, Augustus liked to associate with leading writers, not least since, like many of his social peers, he had literary pretensions of his own (Suet. *Aug.* 84–89). Literature was a central part of the cultural life of the Roman elite during its moments of leisure (*otium*). Furthermore, one of Augustus' closest friends and advisers was the equestrian C. Maecenas, who was even more solicitous in befriending and patronising the best writers of the age; he enjoyed long-lasting relationships with Virgil, Horace, Propertius, and a host of other authors whose works are now lost: Domitius Marsus, Fundanius, Melissus, Plotius Tucca, Viscus, and the evidently very substantial poet Varius Rufus, who was also responsible for the circulation of Virgil's *Aeneid* after its author's death. Contact with Maecenas brought these writers into contact with Augustus too. Hence Horace was selected to compose the *Carmen Saeculare*, while Virgil was encouraged to write the great epic of Augustan Rome, though he baulked at creating an *Augusteid* with Augustus as central figure, preferring to focus instead on Augustus' ancestor, the Trojan prince Aeneas, in his *Aeneid*. To what extent did these social relationships affect the nature of the literature that these writers produced? Is it correct to argue, as Syme did, that this all amounted to an "organisation of opinion"? Or should we envisage a looser relationship between the *princeps* and contemporary writers? On this model, one might argue that the return of peace stimulated a period of intense literary productivity, which naturally led to a whole series of reflections on, and responses to, the political, social, cultural, moral, and religious changes that were taking place.[4]

In addressing these questions, we need to remember that literature did have political ramifications. As T. J. Luce demonstrates in "Livy, Augustus, and the Forum Augustum" (Chapter 13), Livy's accounts of the great figures of Republican history do not agree on all points with the abbreviated versions of their careers devised personally by Augustus for the inscriptions (*elogia*) that stood beneath their statues in the porticoes of the new Forum Augustum, which quickly became a major hub for political and judicial business in Rome after its dedication in 2 BC.[5] Furthermore, the historian from Patavium (modern Padua) also felt the need to distance himself from Augustus' own version of the historical circumstances in which A. Cornelius Cossus in 437 BC had been permitted to dedicate the *spolia opima* ("the rich spoils") after he had killed the king of Veii in single combat. The issue had become politically relevant in 28 BC when Octavian (as he still was) argued that M. Licinius Crassus, who had killed the chief of the Bastarnae when proconsul in Macedonia the previous year, was not eligible to dedicate the *spolia opima* since he was fighting under Octavian's auspices (Livy 4.20.5–11).[6] Furthermore, Augustus became increasingly concerned about the damaging political effects of literature towards the close of his principate. To this period belong the relegation of the poet Ovid to Tomis on the shores of the Black Sea in AD 8 allegedly (so Ovid *Trist.* 2, esp. 207–218) for an "indiscretion" (*error*) and for writing his spoof didactic poem, *The Art of Love*, in playful (obviously too playful) response to Augustus' moral reforms, and the prosecutions of various authors for their scurrilous writings on the charge of *maiestas*, which is usually glossed in English as "treason," but which was strictly speaking related to conduct that "diminished the majesty of the Roman people" (Tac. *Ann.* 1.72; Suet. *Aug.* 55).

The articles that form Part III of this volume make important contributions to such debates about the relationship between artistic or literary imagery and power in Augustan Rome. Tonio Hölscher, Professor of Classical Archaeology at the University of Heidelberg

---

[4] On such questions, Kennedy 1992 and P. White 1993 and 2005 are required reading. Note also Galinsky 1996: 225–287 for a rather different approach, arguing that the writers of the Augustan age "converged" in treating themes important to Augustus.

[5] One should note that many of the texts of these *elogia* are so fragmentary that they can be restored in a variety of ways. Luce relies on the generally sound restorations of Degrassi in *Inscr. It.*, vol. XIII, 3 (1937), but for alternative readings of several by G. Alföldy, one needs to consult *CIL* volume VI.8.2 (published in 1996); for further variations, see Spannagel 1999.

[6] On this much discussed episode, see Syme 1959; Luce 1965; cf. Badian 1993 and Sailor 2006, challenging some arguments of Luce 1990. The poets Virgil and Propertius preferred to take the Augustan line on this matter: see Harrison 1989.

since 1975, has produced a series of studies on the relation between monumental art and political power. His article "Monuments of the Battle of Actium: Propaganda and Response" (Chapter 10) was first published in 1985 in the proceedings of a major conference on the culture of the Augustan age held at the University of Jena in 1982 in what was then East Germany. In it, he develops some of the themes of his earlier work on the iconography of the goddess Victory and builds on concepts explored in his brief monograph, published in 1984, on public monuments and their audience in the late Republic and early Empire.[7] Shortly afterwards, he was to publish an important theoretical discussion on Roman "visual language" (*Bildsprache*) as a semantic system, the main ideas of which were central to Zanker's work on the imagery of the Augustan age. Since the battle of Actium determined the political outcome of the civil wars, it is no surprise that this event was commemorated in a whole series of ideologically charged public monuments and that artistic imagery alluding to Octavian's great victory infused many kinds of Roman public art. Actium elicited literary responses too, most famously in poems by Horace (*Odes* 1.37) and Propertius (*Elegies* 4.6), and in Virgil's description (*ekphrasis*) of the artistic representation of the battle that appeared in the very centre of the shield of Aeneas (*Aen.* 8.675–710).[8] But what Hölscher's study most tellingly examines is the way in which the Actium imagery percolated down to appear on many mass-produced artefacts such as drinking cups and cooking vessels, as well as on higher-value goods such as finger-rings and other types of jewellery. The fact that these items circulated so widely throughout the Roman Empire demonstrates how powerful this imagery was for consolidating Augustus' position.[9]

Just as Actium was central to the repertoire of Augustan visual imagery, so the figure of Cleopatra VII played a vital role in legitimising Augustus' rule. Maria Wyke, since 2005 Professor of Latin at University College London, probes the representations of this Egyptian *meretrix regina* ("whore queen") in Augustan literary texts, especially poetry, but also in visual media, including coin images. Wyke's scholarly interests have to date centred on Augustan love poetry, gender, and reception studies, not least the representation of ancient Rome in twentieth-century film in Italy and Hollywood.[10]

[7] Hölscher 1967, 1984, 1987.
[8] For these and other literary treatments of the battle, see Gurval 1995.
[9] Zanker 1988: ch. 7 develops the theme further.
[10] For a selection of her important work on elegy and gender, see Wyke 1987, 1989, 2002; on reception studies, Wyke 1997 (on cinema; note esp. ch. 4: "Cleopatra: Spectacles of Seduction and Conquest") and 2007 (on the reception of Julius Caesar in Western culture).

In Chapter 11 she demonstrates how social constructions of gender, ethnicity, imperial power, and political legitimation were all at play in forging the Roman image of the Egyptian queen, whose overt sexuality, Oriental exoticism, and regal femininity combined to provide such a valuable foil in Augustan public discourse to the more restrained, traditional Roman style of leadership that was embodied in the first *princeps* himself.

The interplay between literary texts and the monumental topography of the city of Rome forms the central thrust of T. P. Wiseman's article (Chapter 12) on "Cybele, Virgil and Augustus," first published in 1984 in a landmark collection of essays on poetry and politics in the Augustan age.[11] Peter Wiseman, Professor of Classics at the University of Exeter from 1977 until his retirement in 2001, is a rare type of scholar who possesses equal expertise in Latin literature and in Roman social and political history. Since the mid-1980s he has also played a key role in establishing Roman myth as a serious field of study.[12] In the article reprinted here he fuses his interests in the topography of Rome, first nurtured when he was a Rome Scholar at the British School at Rome,[13] in Roman literature, and in Roman myth and religion to grapple with the complex question of the relationship between poetic texts and political authority. How was it, he asks, that Cybele, the Magna Mater (the "Great Mother"), a goddess whose cult was widely believed to involve ritual ecstatic madness on the part of her worshippers and whose priests traditionally had to castrate themselves to enter the goddess' service, not only became a palatable divinity in the religious revival that took place under Augustus, but also proves so valuable to Aeneas at key moments in the narrative of the *Aeneid*? Wiseman's answer requires us to read the Virgilian episodes against the monumental topography of Augustan Rome. This analysis not only clarifies the importance of Cybele in Virgil's *Aeneid*, but also helps to explain the conceptual significance of the location that Octavian chose for his own residence in Rome, which was located on the Palatine in close proximity to the Temple of the Magna Mater, the Temples of Actian Apollo and Victory, and various sites with clear Romulean overtones.[14]

---

[11] Woodman and West 1984.

[12] Literary studies: Wiseman 1979a, 1985, 1992. History: Wiseman 1971. Myth: Wiseman 1995 and 2004.

[13] See also Wiseman 1974, 1978, 1979b, 1981; note also his contributions to the *Lexicon Topographicum Urbis Romae*: e.g. on the Campus Martius, the Clivus Victoriae, or the Saxum Tarpeium (*LTUR* I, IV, ss.vv.). For the impact of his time in Italy on his scholarship, see Crawford 2003.

[14] For more recent work in this area, Mattern 2000; Pensabene 2002. On Augustus' house:

T. J. Luce, now Emeritus Professor of Classics at Princeton University, also explores the interplay between literary texts and monuments in his article "Livy, Augustus, and the Forum Augustum" (Chapter 13). The new Forum Augustum, dedicated in 2 BC, and Livy's large-scale history of Rome, *Ab urbe condita* ("From the Foundation of the City"), were, Luce justifiably claims, the "two majors monuments to republican history in the Augustan age." His discussion of the conception of the Republican past that the two projects espoused reveals a certain disjuncture between the two both in their general treatment of the past and on specific details. Luce focused throughout his scholarly career on Graeco-Roman historiography and, most of all, on the historiographical techniques of the historian Livy.[15] His analysis here compares the vision of the Republican past developed at length by Livy with Augustus' personal selection of the "great men" (*summi viri*) of the Republic and the brief accounts of their exploits that he prepared for display beneath their statues in the new Forum Augustum, which was in so many ways the ideological centrepiece of Augustan Rome.[16] In so doing, Luce detects a certain ambivalence in the relationship between the *princeps* and the historian, whom Augustus liked, in moments of jest, to call "Pompeianus" as a result of his strong partiality towards Pompey in that part of his history (unfortunately now lost) that dealt with the turbulent events of the civil wars between Pompey and Augustus' adoptive father Julius Caesar, now "Divus Iulius" (the "Deified Julius").[17]

Carettoni 1983; Donderer 1995; Iacopi 2007. On the Temple of Apollo on the Palatine and its relation to Actium, Zanker 1983. "Romulus" had indeed been proposed as a possible new name for Octavian before the senate settled on "Augustus" on 16 January 27 BC (Suet. *Aug.* 7.2).

[15] See Luce 1965, 1977, 1995, 1997. He also translated the first five books of Livy for the Oxford World Classics series (1998).

[16] As emphasised by Zanker (1988: 194–215), arguing that it was "the monument which most fully expresses the new mythology [sc. of Augustan Rome]." For subsequent work on this forum, note Spannagel 1999, with Rich 2002; La Rocca 2001: 184–195; Rinaldi Tufi 2002.

[17] Tac. *Ann.* 4.34, insisting that it did not harm their friendship. Seneca (*Q. Nat.* 5.18) also relates that Livy was highly critical of Julius Caesar, at one point in his narrative musing that it might have been better had he never been born.

10 Monuments of the Battle of Actium: Propaganda and Response†*

TONIO HÖLSCHER

translated by Claus Nader

The battle of Actium not only was the victory that laid the foundation for the Principate, but also served as the point of departure for the new artistic forms of representation (*Repräsentationskunst*) that marked the Augustan age.[1] If we want to identify not just the subject matter of many pieces of visual evidence, but also the real creative dynamics of the period, then we have to ask ourselves, first of all, who were the people responsible for initiating these monuments, how they articulated their message, and how these messages were received by their intended audience. In particular, we need to investigate the ways in which the *princeps* and the senate took the initiative and the kind of audience they were addressing; we need to ask who absorbed the themes of the monuments, in what form the various messages were proclaimed, and whether we can identify any differences between various groups; finally, we need to explore the manner in which these monuments reveal an interplay between Augustus' claim to power and the support he required from the different sectors of the population.

It is crucial to begin by stating that the distinction between the ambitions of a single individual and the consent of society does

---

† Originally published in German as "Denkmäler der Schlacht von Actium – Propaganda und Resonanz," *Klio* 67 (1985), 81–102. [Editor's note: I would like to thank the author for his generous cooperation in the translation of his article and for providing many of the original illustrations.]

* This article was written within the framework of a collaborative research project on "Roman iconology." I should like to express my thanks to the Deutsche Forschungsgemeinschaft, which supported the project.

[1] For previous studies on Actium that incorporate visual evidence, see J. Gagé, *MEFRA* 53 (1936), 37–100; G. C. Picard, *Les trophées romains*, Paris 1957, pp. 253–274; cf. also K. Fittschen, *JdI* 91 (1976), 189–194.

not mean that we are dealing with two fundamentally unconnected elements. As far as the monuments are concerned, it is practically impossible to make a clear distinction between those commissioned by leading politicians and those granted as honours by the senate, the people, and private individuals.[2] When such a distinction is made in this paper, it will be made in order to gain more insight into the reciprocal relationship between the statesman's position and the expectations of society.

To put these questions into sharper historical focus, we need to examine the political monuments of the late Republic, bearing in mind the basic points outlined above. In general terms the situation may be summed up as follows. Monuments that conveyed representational images of Roman politicians were largely restricted to the city of Rome. It was here that the greatest proportion of the spoils of conquest was put on display; it was here that almost all new buildings and works of art were set up.[3] Admittedly during the second century BC, and especially from the time of L. Mummius onwards, pieces of booty were also displayed as public monuments in various cities of Italy and beyond.[4] But new memorials of Roman statesmen were rare outside Rome, being restricted to key locations in the areas in which these leading figures had operated, such as the monument in the form of a pillar honouring Aemilius Paullus at Delphi,[5] to the battlefields of victorious campaigns, such as the trophies of Sulla set up at Chaeronea,[6] or to the boundaries of conquered provinces, such as Pompeius' monument in the Pyrenees.[7] In short, monuments were restricted to those places with which such individuals had a direct

---

[2] This becomes especially evident with monuments initiated by statesmen themselves, those donated by friends and relatives, or at least those that needed the approval of those to be honoured. For honorific monuments in Rome, see G. Lahusen, *Untersuchungen zur Ehrenstatue in Rom*, Rome 1983; id., *Schriftquellen zum römischen Bildnis* I, Bremen 1984.

[3] For booty, see M. Pape, *Griechische Kunstwerke aus Kriegsbeute und ihre öffentliche Aufstellung in Rom*, Hamburg 1975; G. Waurick, *Jahrbuch des Römisch-Germanischen Zentralmuseums Mainz* 22 (1975), 1–46; for buildings and sculpture, F. Coarelli, *Dialoghi di Archeologia* 4–5 (1970–1971), 241–279; also in P. Zanker, ed., *Hellenismus in Mittelitalien* (Abh. Ak. Wiss. Göttingen, Phil.-hist. Kl. 3.Folge, 97/1–2, 1976), pp. 21–51; also in M. Martelli and M. Cristofani, eds, *Caratteri dell'ellenismo nelle urne etrusche* (*Prospettiva* Suppl. 1, 1977), pp. 35–40.

[4] Waurick (cit. n. 3), pp. 12ff., nos 5–6, 8–14, 16–19, 21–32; cf. Plut. *Marc.* 30; Cic. *Verr.* 2.2.3; also 2.4.74ff., 84, 93 (Scipio Africanus); Strabo 6.381; Liv. *Per.* 53; Suet. *Galba* 3, 4; Eutr. 4.14; Frontin. *Str.* 4.3.15 (Mummius). In general, see Cic. *Verr.* 2.1.55.

[5] H. Kähler, *Der Fries vom Reiterdenkmal des Aemilius Paullus in Delphi*, Berlin 1965. In general on dedications in Greece, see M. Guarducci, *Rendiconti della Pontificia Accademia Romana di archeologia* 13 (1937), 41–58.

[6] Plut. *Sulla* 19; Paus. 9.40; *RRC* 373–374, no. 359; Picard (cit. n. 1), pp. 174–181.

[7] Plin. *NH* 3.4.3; Picard (cit. n. 1), pp. 183–186.

personal relationship.[8] It was a form of representation that had a greater influence on the political stage of the city of Rome than in the wider Roman Empire. As a result, such imagery is indicative of Rome's development from city-state to Empire.

The initiative to set up political monuments was often taken by the protagonists themselves. Aiming to publicise their claim to their status as members of the elite, they initiated a veritable "monument war," which occasionally led to considerable jockeying for power and even triggered violent conflicts.[9] Herein lay the explosive significance of representational art (*Repräsentationskunst*). On the other hand, Roman society usually expressed its gratitude and recognition of its leaders in the traditional form of an honorific statue. We should not underestimate the importance of this response to a leading politician's achievements. As a symptom of public response, however, the meaning of an honorific statue still remained limited when compared to later monuments, because both in Rome and in the cities of the Empire statues were as a rule erected by official order, were set up in a single central location, and as a result had the somewhat distancing effect of a political proclamation. As for Italy and the provinces, it should be remembered that the statues set up to honour Romans were usually erected in gratitude for some local benefactions; they were not concerned with the politics of the Empire as a whole.[10] In general, therefore, one gets the impression that the politics of public monuments was strongly focused on the city of Rome and directed in particular towards satisfying the ambitions of politicians rather than winning the consent of the people.

In comparison with this situation, some significant changes took place in the final decades of the Republic, which led on the whole to a fundamental expansion in the range of individuals honoured. Whereas honorific statues of leading politicians had hitherto been concentrated in just a few central locations of the city of Rome, statues were erected for the mint-official Marius Gratidianus, who had reformed the coinage system in 85 BC, in all the urban neighbourhoods (*in omnibus vicis*) by the voting tribes of the Roman

---

[8] See, for example, the depiction that Marius dedicated to the Sanctuary of Marica at Minturnae (Plut. *Mar.* 40), or the tomb of Scipio the Elder with a statue at Liternum (Liv. 42.56); for dedications at Ostia, the harbour for Rome, see F. Zevi in Zanker, *Hellenismus* (cit. n. 3), pp. 52–83.

[9] T. Hölscher in *Tainia: Festschrift R. Hampe* (1980), pp. 355–358.

[10] For Asia Minor, see K. Tuchelt, *Frühe Denkmäler Roms in Kleinasien I: Roma und Promagistrate* (*Istanbuler Mitteilungen* Beiheft 23, 1970), pp. 46–104.

citizen body.[11] In 44 BC it was decided to pay special honours to Julius Caesar by setting up images of him in all the temples of Rome and in all towns, presumably in Italy.[12] It is doubtful whether this decision was actually implemented, but it clearly reveals an intention to present the claims of a leading politician in public, that is, before the eyes of all citizens equally.

To a certain extent there was also a broader response to claims such as this. From the time of Marius onwards, mint-officials issued coins with depictions not only of their own *gens*, but also of leading politicians whom they themselves supported.[13] Themes alluding to the major political figures and their families enjoyed a wider circulation, especially among clients and political supporters, through the media of gemstones and glass-pastes.[14] Especially remarkable is a type of ceramic bowl for the ritual washing of hands that shows a trophy (*tropaeum*) surrounded by various Samnite and other weapons as well as two wreaths, including, on the left, a grass crown (*corona graminea*). The latter establishes a connection with Sulla, who had received this award after his victory over the Marsi.[15] The workshop that produced these bowls must have been situated somewhere in Italy and was presumably quite successful, since the three surviving examples come from Chieti, Aquileia, and Egypt. In this way a leading Roman politician's iconography found its way into the minor arts, i.e., on items of personal use, which were distributed over wide stretches of the Empire.

With this process, the conditions for Augustus' success were established. On the one hand, it strengthened his claims as leader throughout the entire Empire; on the other, it allowed broad support for him to grow, and such imagery found its way even into the private sphere. It is clear that the ambitions of the protagonists in the politics of the

---

[11] Plin. *NH* 34.27; Cic. *Off.* 3.80; Sen. *Dial.* 5.18.1 (= *De Ira* 3.18.1).

[12] Dio 44.4. For further sources referring to depictions of Caesar in Rome, see F. S. Johansen, *Analecta Romana Instituti Danici* 4 (1967), 13–19. Earlier, Verres had tried to accomplish the same in Rome as in Sicily through his extortion from the Sicilians: sources in O. Vessberg, *Studien zur Kunstgeschichte der römischen Republik*, Lund and Leipzig 1941, pp. 75, nos 291–295. For statues of Pompeius in Rome, Vessberg, p. 76, no. 297. Statues of the Marcelli in Tyndaris and other cities of Sicily: Cic. *Verr.* 2.4.86. Statues of Pompeius and Caesar in Asia Minor: Tuchelt (cit. n. 10), p. 60. Also T. Pekary in *Monumentum Chilionense: Festschrift E. Burck*, Amsterdam 1975, pp. 96–98.

[13] *RRC* 2.730–731.

[14] M. L. Vollenweider, *Mus. Helv.* 12 (1955), 96–111; also in *Die Steinschneidekunst und ihre Künstler in spätrepublikanischer und augusteischer Zeit*, Baden-Baden 1966, pp. 17–22.

[15] R. Zahn, *Archäologischer Anzeiger* (1909), 559–569; H. Fuhrmann, *Archäologischer Anzeiger* (1941), 363–364; U. Gehrig, A. Greifenhagen and N. Kunisch, *Führer durch die Antikenabteilung Berlin*, Berlin 1968, p. 201; K. Vierneisel, ed., *Römisches im Antikenmuseum Berlin*, Berlin 1978, pp. 72–73.

period were not in any straightforward sense simply the cause of the acclaim that was manifested, but rather at the same time people's widespread readiness to express their approval of these leaders constituted a precondition for their predominance.

After Actium this notion developed to a quite unprecedented degree. To allow a clear picture of this to emerge, the discussion that follows will be restricted, in geographical terms, to the city of Rome and its immediate vicinity.[16] Rome must have been flooded at that moment with monuments that displayed parts of conquered ships or replicas thereof; these must all have reminded people of Octavian's victory over M. Antonius.[17] Already after the battle of Naulochos the senate had erected in the Roman forum a statue of Octavian on top of a column; prows (*rostra*) from the fleet of Sextus Pompeius were displayed on the column's shaft.[18] Then following the battle of Actium four additional "rostrate columns" (i.e., columns displaying prows, *columnae rostratae*) were erected in his honour; these columns are probably also shown on a denarius minted at this same date.[19] Furthermore, to honour Octavian, the prows of some ships from Antonius' fleet were attached to the speaker's platform at the new Temple of the Deified Caesar in the Forum.[20] *Rostra* also appear on coins of 17–16 BC fixed to an arch erected in Augustus' honour "to commemorate the building of roads" (*quod viae munitae sunt*),[21] as well as on the base of an equestrian statue of Agrippa, as shown on coins minted in 12 BC.[22] In addition, there is the monument that Octavian himself erected: the new senate-house, the Curia Julia, dedicated ten days after his Actian triumph in 29 BC, which, according to the images of it on coins, displayed on top of its pediment an entire sculptural programme that evoked his recently established domination over the entire world.[23] In the centre stood

---

[16] In terms of evidence from the city of Rome, architecture and coinage will not receive any attention here.

[17] See H. Jucker, *Mus. Helv.* 39 (1982), 89–90.

[18] App. *B. Civ* 5.130.

[19] Cf. Verg. *G.* 3.29, with Servius *ad loc.* BMC I, 101, nos 633–636; P. Zanker, *Studien zu den Augustus Porträts I: Der Actium-Typus* (Abh. Ak. Wiss. Göttingen, Phil.-hist. Kl. 3.Folge, 85, 1973), 40–41. This series of coins is repeatedly given an early dating, which is in turn used as an argument for a connection between the *columna rostrata* depicted and an honorific monument after Naulochos (see n. 18): see F. Prayon, *Praestant interna: Festschrift U. Hausmann*, Tübingen 1982, pp. 322–323; but the dating does not seem entirely plausible.

[20] Dio 51.19.2.

[21] BMC I, 75, nos 433–434.

[22] BMC I, 25, nos 122–123. Note also the *rostra* on a base, on which Augustus and Agrippa are sitting: ibid., 23–24, nos 115–117.

[23] BMC I, 103, nos 631–632; G. Fuchs, "Architekturdarstellungen auf römischen Münzen der Republik und der frühen Kaiserzeit", in *Antike Münzen und geschnittene Steine* I (1969),

Figs 10.1 and *10.2*. Frieze with naval trophies and priestly emblems, Rome

a Victory standing on a globe, which was presumably a copy of the famous statue inside the building, and to either side figures that are difficult to interpret, but which clearly allude to the battle of Actium, since they hold an anchor and rudder respectively. How strongly this conception of the *princeps* differed from that shown on other monuments erected in his honour is difficult to determine in the absence of a precise explanation of each element. Nevertheless, the image of Victory standing on the globe may, to a certain degree, represent the self-confidence of the victorious sole ruler, even though Octavian was wise enough to link this image with the senate-house and thereby at the same time to entrust world domination (for those who wanted to see it this way) to the Roman community as a whole.

In this context the frieze in the Capitoline Museum depicting parts of ships and priestly attributes is particularly impressive (Figs 10.1 and 10.2).[24] Soon after Actium, the frieze formulates – in a concept that later found its place on the *Ara Pacis* and in the Forum of Augustus in the juxtaposition of Romulus and Aeneas – an

---

pp. 42–43; P. Zanker, *Forum Romanum*, Tübingen 1972, p. 9. On the statue inside the Curia, see T. Hölscher, *Victoria Romana*, Mainz 1967, pp. 6–17.

[24] H. Stuart Jones, *The Sculpture of the Museo Capitolino*, Oxford 1912, pp. 258–264, nos 99, 100, 102, 104, 105, 107; A. M. Colini, *Bullettino della commissione archeologica comunale di Roma* 68 (1940), 262; J. M. Crous, *RM* 55 (1940), 65–77; E. Simon in W. Helbig, *Führer durch die öffentliche Sammlungen klassischer Altertümer in Rom* II, Tübingen 1966, nos 1382, 1664; F. Coarelli, *Dialoghi di Archeologia* 2 (1968), 191–208; T. Hölscher, *JdI* 99 (1984), 202–209.

Fig. 10.3. Frieze from the Temple of the Deified Iulius, Rome

exemplary link between *virtus* and *pietas*. It has not yet been possible to connect the frieze with any confidence to any specific building, such as the Portico of Octavia or the Temple of Diana. However, we can undoubtedly assume that the frieze belonged to one of those buildings with which Augustus fundamentally transformed the "triumphal" area *in circo* (i.e., in the area of the Circus Flaminius) from the 20s BC onwards. In any case, people must have encountered the symbolism of Actium on public buildings throughout the city. The new ruler showed himself to be omnipresent. Accordingly, as early as 28 BC there were 2,000 silver portrait-statues of Octavian that he could melt down in order to provide votive gifts to mark the inauguration of the Temple of Apollo on the Palatine.[25] Many other portraits of him, made out of other materials, surely remained in place.

A particularly important feature of the emperor's self-presentation may be discerned on the frieze of the Temple of the Deified Iulius (Fig. 10.3).[26] The frieze is composed of archaistic winged goddesses springing forth from plant-tendrils. This iconography derives from a long-established concept of a vegetation deity, which had already found its formal expression as a tendril goddess in Hellenistic art. On the Roman building this motif obviously took on a new and contemporary significance. The figure's wings suggest that it represents a victory goddess, whereas its tendrils point towards Venus' sphere.

---

[25] *RG* 24; Suet. *Aug.* 24; Dio 52.22; see Pekáry (cit. n. 12), pp. 96–108.

[26] M. Floriani Squarciapino, *Rendiconti della Accademia Nazionale dei Lincei* 12 (1957), 270–284; E. Simon in Helbig (cit. n. 24), II, no. 2057; Hölscher, *Victoria Romana* (cit. n. 23), p. 155; M. Montagna Pasquinucci, *Monumenti Antichi* 48 (1971), 255–286.

This combination can be linked to the well-known religious and political vision of Julius Caesar, who honoured his mythological ancestor Venus Genetrix ("Venus the Ancestress") with the epithet Victrix (i.e., "Bringer of Victory") and moreover associated her with Caesar's Victory (*Victoria Caesaris*). The triumvirs had already planned and set in motion the depiction of these Caesarian themes on the temple before the battle of Actium; but when the temple was consecrated in 29 BC, the imagery could now be related to Caesar's heir, who had indeed fixed the *rostra* of his defeated opponent to the front of the temple. In this context it is important to consider the intellectual level of this propaganda. The linking of a mythological ancestor (Venus Genetrix) and a victory goddess (Venus Victrix) is a complex religious and political construct. The use of the long-established archetype of the tendril goddess for this kind of message seems to be a subtle reinterpretation, whereas the archaising style of the image presumes a familiarity with ancient art and a sense of its prestige. In no way were these messages designed for the masses; rather, they targeted an educated, intellectual audience. To be sure, this exclusive approach lay within the tradition of monuments set up to honour leading politicians during the Republic.[27] The same applies to all lavish monuments of the early imperial period: the statue of Augustus from Prima Porta [see Figs 11.7 and 11.8, below], the level of which may be defined by comparison with the closely related Secular Hymn (*Carmen Saeculare*) of Horace, as well as the *Ara Pacis*.[28] Evidently, such monuments were primarily addressed to Rome's upper class. Even after the battle of Actium this class was still the most important group in the Roman state, in front of whom leading politicians had to develop a political profile and legitimise themselves. Only later, during the mid-imperial period, under new social conditions did public art come increasingly to shed this exclusivity.

Moreover, the *princeps*, by adopting a shrewd, calculated policy, tried to persuade individual members of the Roman elite to contribute to the architectural renewal of the city of Rome. In particular, for such undertakings he targeted former supporters of Antonius

---

[27] For this phenomenon in the late Republic and early imperial period see T. Hölscher, *Staatsdenkmal und Publikum vom Untergang der Republik zur Festigung des Kaisertums in Rom* (Xenia 9), Konstanz 1984.

[28] This particularly holds true when one considers the monumental framework that the *Ara Pacis* received in connection with Augustus' sundial (*solarium Augusti*): E. Buchner, *RM* 83 (1976), 319–365; 87 (1980), 355–373. It becomes quite clear that such a structure could be understood and admired on various intellectual levels: there was its complex astrological significance; the slogan-like message that the emperor is "born to bring peace" (*natus ad pacem*); and lastly, the simple meaning of a great monument that contains practical data about time.

who after Actium had switched to the victor's side, so that they could thereby express their general support for the new Principate.[29] Two examples will suffice to demonstrate how successful this policy was.

L. Munatius Plancus' rebuilding of the Temple of Saturn took place either after he had switched to Octavian's side in 32 BC or perhaps even after Actium.[30] According to Macrobius, the gable or the outer edge of the pediment was decorated with Tritons with sea-conch horns,[31] a traditional motif that derived from Hellenistic monuments commemorating naval victories and one that was frequently used to celebrate Actium.[32] Consequently, this building, though erected out of private funds, paid homage to the emperor in its decorative imagery.

The same holds true for the Temple of Apollo *in circo*, although the date of its restoration at some point between the end of the Republic and the start of the Principate admittedly needs further clarification.[33] Its renovation is attributed to C. Sosius, who had initially been a supporter of Antonius. He had won a victory over the Jews, for which in 34 BC he duly celebrated a triumph. He became consul in 32, but had to leave Rome after just a few days in office. After Actium, he switched sides to join Octavian and in 17 BC was jointly responsible as *XVvir sacris faciundis* (i.e., one of the board of fifteen responsible "for carrying out sacred acts") for staging the Secular Games. Given the date of its dedication, 23 September, which was Augustus' birthday, the building was inaugurated after Actium; its style of architectural decoration would date its dedication to *c.* 20 BC, just in time for the secular celebrations.[34] It is controversial whether the temple was designed before or after Actium, i.e., whether before or after C. Sosius switched political sides; recently it has been argued that Sosius only dedicated a new cedar-wood statue of Apollo

---

[29] With regard to Augustus' attitude towards former followers of Antonius, see R. Syme, *The Roman Revolution*, Oxford 1939, pp. 349–351; P. Sattler, *Augustus und der Senat*, Göttingen 1960, pp. 21–22.

[30] CIL XI 6087; K. Fittschen, *JdI* 91 (1976), 208–210.

[31] Macr. *Sat.* 1.8.4; Fittschen (cit. n. 30); E. Simon, *Würzburger Jahrbücher für die Altertumswissenschaft* NF 5 (1979), 264–265.

[32] Hellenistic traditions: T. Hölscher, *Archäologischer Anzeiger* (1979), 338–349; Actium: Fittschen (cit. n. 30), pp. 189–194.

[33] J. Scott Ryberg, *Rites of the State Religion in Roman Art* (Memoirs of the American Academy in Rome 22, 1955), pp. 144–146; G. C. Picard, *MEFRA* 71 (1959), 274–279; E. Simon in Helbig (cit. n. 24), II, no. 1670; B. M. Felletti Maj, *La tradizione italica nell'arte romana*, Rome 1977, pp. 267–272; P. Gros, *Aurea Templa*, Rome 1976, pp. 161–166, 180–189, 211–229.

[34] As we know, the Secular Games were held in the Theatre of Marcellus (before its final inauguration), which stands, not only topographically, in close connection with the Temple of Apollo.

in the temple and that he had nothing to do with the rebuilding.[35] This assertion, however, does not sit well with Pliny's comment (*NH* 36.28) that a Niobid statue-group was located "in the Temple of Apollo Sosianus" (*in templo Apollinis Sosiani*). It is clear that the temple was not named after the donor of a particular statue, but rather after its builder, Sosius. The dating of the temple can then be established from its history. The building's Republican predecessor was situated further to the south than its successor. Its foundations were cut into by those of the Theatre of Marcellus; and so the temple was clearly torn down by Caesar or by the young Octavian in order to provide space for the new theatre. The person who initiated such a measure must have been obliged to provide a new building. It is certain that in 34 BC Octavian could not have left the settlement of the debt owed the divinity to C. Sosius, since the latter was at this point still a supporter of the opposing side. This becomes even more apparent when we realise that we are dealing with Octavian's personal protective divinity, Apollo, who thereby would have been alienated from him. Sosius must, therefore, have been persuaded to build the new temple after the battle of Actium.

Sosius showed his gratitude through the decorative imagery he commissioned for the temple. It is widely maintained that the frieze (Figs 10.4 and 10.5) depicts his own triumph over the Jews in 34 BC.[36] However, this cannot be the case, since the captives who form part of the trophy have Celtic hairstyles. Nor can the frieze depict the inauguration ceremony of the temple itself, since the prisoners-of-war and the accompanying battle-scenes would make no sense in such a scene.[37] Victories against peoples from the north, including Celts, can in this context only be those that Octavian won in the Balkans from 35 to 33 BC, where many Celtic tribes were located. The procession that is shown thus represents the triple triumph of 29 BC, which celebrated the victories in Illyricum, at Actium, and at Alexandria. It is well known that this was Augustus' only triumph and this, therefore, is the only possible interpretation of the frieze. Sosius was very much aware of what he owed to the new ruler, who had shown him clemency.

In what we have considered so far, it was the *princeps* himself who elicited approval from the political elite. At the same time, however,

---

[35] Gros (cit. n. 33), pp. 161–166.

[36] Scott Ryberg (cit n. 33). For well-justified arguments to the contrary, Picard (cit. n. 33).

[37] Picard (cit. n. 33). The interpretation in E. Simon, *JdI* 93 (1978), 210 n. 50, concerning the battle of Pydna poses the problem that other events of the late Republic do not seem to have played a role in representational art in the imperial period.

Figs 10.4 and 10.5. Sections from the frieze of the Temple of Apollo *in circo* (Apollo Sosianus), Rome

Fig. 10.6. Neo-Attic relief with Victory and a trophy

tributes were offered spontaneously as well by the upper classes. A hitherto unnoticed relief from the Museo Nazionale alle Terme shows Victory holding a ship's stern (*aplustre*) in her arm and adorning a trophy with a ribbon (Fig. 10.6).[38] The stern alludes to a naval victory, whereas the lunular shield (*pelta*) on the trophy hints at Eastern enemies; the type of breastplate, the silhouetted outline of the figure, as well as the clearly ordered and, at the same time, nuanced shape of body would all date this piece to the Augustan period. The relief, therefore, celebrates the battle of Actium. A variant version

[38] B. M. Felletti Maj, *Notizie degli scavi* 8th ser., 11 (1957), 328–329; in detail T. Hölscher, *JdI* 99 (1984), 187–214.

Fig. 10.7. Neo-Attic relief with Victory, a trophy, and a warrior

from Liverpool, which shows the lower part of a victory goddess standing in front of a column with a snake coiling up around it,[39] demonstrates that we are dealing not with a single, official state monument, but rather with a popular type of sculptural relief that served the purpose of decorating distinguished residences.[40] The fact that the relief from Rome was found on the Quirinal, one of the smartest residential zones of the city, lends support to this interpretation.

At around the same time another relief-type was created, the best preserved example of which is to be found in the Louvre (Fig. 10.7).[41]

---

[39] B. Ashmole, *A Catalogue of the Ancient Marbles at Ince Blundell Hall*, Oxford 1929, p. 93, no. 250. Hölscher (cit. n. 38). The relief now forms part of the collection of the Merseyside County Museum in Liverpool.

[40] On this type of decorative relief, see now H. Froning, *Marmor-Schmuckreliefs mit griechischen Mythen im 1 Jh. v. Chr.*, Mainz 1981.

[41] V. Poulsen, *Berytus* 2 (1935), 51–56; Hölscher (cit. n. 38).

The relief shows, in the centre, a column supporting a statue of Athena, with a snake coiling up around the column. To the left, Victory holds a ship's stern (*aplustre*) and offers an egg to the snake. To the right, we can see a bearded warrior in a Corinthian helmet, who has lain his shield up against the base of the column. Again, the *aplustre* alludes to a naval victory. The style of the warrior's beard indicates that we are not dealing with a contemporary event. At the same time, however, the relief cannot depict a mythological event, since there are no sea-battles in myth. The only remaining possible interpretation is that the relief depicts a naval battle from ancient history: consequently, not from the Roman past, but from classical Greece. The only sea-battles from this era that were of any general interest during the Roman period were those fought during the Persian Wars, especially the battle of Salamis. Only in this context does the honouring of Athena, as depicted on the relief, make any sense. The classic victories over the Persians served throughout the Hellenistic period as a historical example of the importance of defending the Greek way of life against external, and particularly Eastern, enemies, as is clear, for example, from the so-called small Attalid votive monument.[42] In 2 BC at the height of his reign Augustus presented a re-enactment of the battle of Salamis to celebrate the dedication of his new Forum and to allude programmatically to his victory over Antonius and the East.[43] The rescue of the Athenian *palladion* [statue of Pallas Athene] provided a model of inspiration for Augustus, who felt that he was the preserver of the Roman *palladium* and the guarantor of public well-being (*salus publica*).

Thus, in the Augustan period two types of neo-Attic relief were created that glorified the battle of Actium and the Athenian sea victories against the Persians, which served as a historical model for the Romans. The reliefs decorated distinguished residences, the private realm of the aristocracy. As further testimony, we may add the so-called kitharode reliefs that show the Apollonian triad together with the goddess Victory, which have been correctly related to Octavian's protective divinities at the sea-battles of Naulochos and Actium.[44] These reliefs must also have adorned private residences of the upper class. The type of relief depicting a warrior and the goddess

[42] A. Schober, *Die Kunst von Pergamon*, Vienna 1951, pp. 121–134; cf. B. Palma, *Xenia* 1 (1981), 45–84; T. Hölscher, *Antike Kunst* 28 (1985), 120–136.
[43] Dio 55.10.7; P. Zanker, *Forum Augustum*, Tübingen c. 1968, p. 25.
[44] J. Overbeck, *Griechische Kunstmythologie* IV, Leipzig 1889, pp. 259–268; T. Schreiber, *Die hellenistischen Reliefbilder*, Leipzig 1894, Tables 34–36; A. Oxé, *Bonner Jahrbücher* 138 (1933), 92–94; A. H. Borbein, *Campanareliefs* (RM Ergänzungsheft 14, 1968), pp. 186–187.

of victory, however, must have been particularly important since its subject matter suggests that it operated at a high intellectual level. The relief presupposes Athens was venerated as the classical centre of the ancient world; as a result, it is testimony to a historical consciousness of the exemplary significance of the past from the perspective of the present. Furthermore, it testifies to an exquisite formal taste that oriented itself towards the art of classical Greece and even towards that of the late archaic period. It is a type of "cultivated" art that required a certain level of education to appreciate; its commissioners were evidently members of the Roman upper class who were targeted as the audience for official state monuments such as the frieze on the Temple of the Deified Iulius. These reliefs were the aristocrats' response to official propaganda.

Connected with this perhaps is a relief from the Villa Belletti in Rome,[45] which, in contrast with such indirect pictorial themes, displays a much more explicit pictorial language. The relief shows a military commander in a cuirass stylistically reminiscent of Augustus. He holds a ship's stern and in front of him sits a personification of Africa or Egypt in mourning. The piece is currently untraceable and its function, therefore, difficult to determine. However, given its modest dimensions, it can hardly have belonged to a large public monument. In any case, it may be added to the broad range of political images that recalled the battle of Actium.

Furthermore, under Augustus there was, for the first time, an unprecedented expansion of political imagery such as this into the wider cultural world. A group of terracotta roof-tiles depicts a ship's prow adorned with a trophy (Fig. 10.8).[46] Obviously we are dealing with a representation of the naval victories at Naulochos and Actium, which was also found on coins. Since the preserved examples were fabricated from different moulds, we may assume that they do not originate from one single building. At best, they may have been copies of better-quality roof-tiles that were used for a public building in Rome.[47] It is anyway clear that a motif of imperial art was

---

[45] M. Jatta, *Le rappresentanze figurate delle provincie romane*, Rome 1908, pp. 31–32; J. M. C. Toynbee, *The Hadrianic School*, Cambridge 1934, p. 36, plate 23.1; Hölscher (cit. n. 38), pp. 194ff.

[46] K. Woelcke, *Bonner Jahrbücher* 120 (1911), 152–161; Picard, *Trophées* (cit. n. 1), p. 257; F. Coarelli, *Dialoghi di Archeologia* 2 (1968), 196–197; H. Mielsch, *Römische Architekturterrakotten und Wandmalereien im Akademischen Kunstmuseum Bonn*, Berlin 1971, pp. 24–25, nos 35, 48–49; A. Anselmino, *Terracotte architettoniche dell'Antiquarium comunale di Roma I: Anteflsse*, Rome 1977, pp. 109–110, nos 132–134.

[47] It is mistaken to assign the preserved antefixes to the Curia Iulia (Woelcke, Picard) or to the Temple of Diana (Coarelli) because of the tiles' quality (see Mielsch) and the fact that they do not originate from one single mould (see above). We know of some locations where antefixes

Fig. 10.8. Terracotta roof-tile with naval trophy

distributed on a wide scale. To be sure, this image should not be considered a product for ordinary Romans, since their houses were simply not decorated in such a manner. Nevertheless, a quite ordinary motif such as this was selected from the wealth of imperial symbolic imagery to become a universally applicable decoration.

showing Victory were found; they partially hint at private buildings within a wide area of Rome. The same holds true for the antefixes in the form of a trophy.

Fig. 10.9. Terracotta roof-tile with Victory and Capricorns

This becomes even more obvious when we consider another type of roof-tile that shows Victory flanked by two Capricorns, the birth-sign of Augustus.[48] An early version with palmettes in the background testifies to the origins of this type shortly after Actium (Fig. 10.9). In the late-Augustan period the image was modified: a globe was added and the motif thus became more reminiscent of the famous statue of Victory from the senate-house. Both types are widespread both in Rome and in its vicinity.[49] The emperor, whose birth brought Rome good fortune and was closely linked with Rome's domination of the world, is omnipresent.

A similar diffusion can be seen with various types of gems and glass-pastes. A sardonyx cameo in Boston displays the Actium

[48] See T. Hölscher, *Jahrbuch des Römisch-Germanischen Zentralmuseums Mainz* 12 (1965), 59–71; Mielsch (cit. n. 46), p. 24, nos 34, 46–47; Anselmino (cit. n. 46), pp. 73–74, no. 8, pp. 110–112, nos 135–138.

[49] For findspots, see Anselmino (cit. n. 46).

Fig. 10.10. Sardonyx cameo with Neptune/Octavian on a chariot drawn by sea-horses

imagery in its most distinguished version (Fig. 10.10):[50] Octavian, holding Neptune's trident, rides across the sea in a triumphal chariot (*quadriga*) drawn by hippocamps, while Antonius is shown underneath it, helplessly enveloped by the waves. The symbolism of the marine world has here been utilised to create a lively composition. The findspot of the piece, Hadrumetum (modern Sousse in Tunisia), indicates how much even such small artefacts contributed to the geographical spread of these political images. Even richer in its symbolism is a late-Augustan cameo now in Vienna that depicts a frontal view of the emperor (with his head replaced) on a triumphal chariot drawn by Tritons (Fig. 10.11).[51] The outer Tritons are shown carrying the attributes that symbolised Rome's new dominion shortly after Actium: the Triton on the right holds up a statue of Victory standing on a globe, reminiscent of the statue that stood in the senate-house; the Triton on the left holds an emblem composed of a globe

---

[50] H. P. Laubscher, *JdI* 89 (1974), 248–250.
[51] F. Eichler and E. Kris, *Die Kameen im Kunsthistorischen Museum Wien*, Vienna 1927, no. 5; Hölscher, *Victoria Romana* (cit. n. 23), p. 181 VG 13.

Fig. 10.11. Cameo with Augustus in a *quadriga* drawn by Tritons

flanked by Capricorns and, above, the shield of virtue (*clipeus virtutis*), which was also set up in the senate-house from 27 BC onwards, encircled by a civic crown (*corona civica*). The civic crown had, by this date, become a permanent attribute of the emperor, affixed to the door of his house on the Palatine. Here the attributes of power have evolved into emblem-like elements, which could be used symbolically in a variety of ways in different pictorial contexts. The manner in which such images were in the end reproduced in large numbers in cheap materials is illustrated, for example, by glass-pastes that depict Neptune with the features of a youthful Octavian, resting his foot on a ship's prow (*prora*) and holding a ship's stern in

Fig. 10.12. Gemstone with Neptune/Octavian

his hand (Fig. 10.12).[52] Augustan coins[53] and the Belletti relief reveal how a variety of monuments were available as models for these mass products. It is difficult to establish the precise social circles in which we should locate the owners of such gemstones and glass-pastes, but their varied material and quality suggest a rather broad financial spectrum.

Even simpler are commodities made out of terracotta. Here a type of Arretine cup with reliefs illustrates that compositions depicting the Apollonian triad and Victory pouring a libation found a place in private daily life (Fig. 10.13).[54] This applies to an even greater degree to the production of oil-lamps. One specimen from London has a ship's prow and a centaur throwing a rock depicted on it, apparently another reference to Actium, and seems at present to be the only example of such a motif.[55] More common, however, are types either depicting Victory on a globe (Fig. 10.14) or Victory holding the shield of virtue (Fig. 10.15).[56] Similar versions of these motifs can also be found on various coins.[57] By means of such consumer products these pictorial motifs made their way into the private sphere.

[52] *Antike Gemmen in deutschen Sammlungen IV: Hannover, Kestner-Museum*, Wiesbaden 1975, no. 242. While I strove for completeness with other types, I am restricted to a rather arbitrary selection of gems and glass-pastes. Besides, considering this type only within an urban Roman context would not be sensible. See M. L. Vollenweider, *Die Schneidekunst und ihre Künstler in spätrepublikanischer und augusteischer Zeit*, Baden-Baden 1966, pp. 20–21, 51 n. 23; cf. C. Maderna-Lauter in *Kaiser Augustus und die verlorene Republik*, Berlin 1988, pp. 441–473.

[53] *BMC* I, 100, no. 615.

[54] Oxé (cit. n. 44).

[55] E. H. Williams in *Acta of the XIth International Congress of Classical Archaeology London 1978*, London 1979, p. 239. One faience replica comes from Egypt.

[56] Victory on a globe: H. Menzel, *Antike Lampen im Römisch-Germanischen Zentralmuseum Mainz*, Mainz 1954, p. 58, no. 331. Hölscher (cit. n. 23), p. 182 VG 17. Victory with *clipeus virtutis*: Menzel, p. 41, no. 207; Hölscher, pp. 108–110.

[57] Hölscher (cit. n. 23), pp. 6, 17, 121–122.

Fig. 10.13. Arretine vase with Apollo and Victory

They can hardly be seen as evidence of Augustus' public self-representation; they rather attest to the fact that Augustus' rule found broad and ready acceptance. Once again it is difficult to determine who owned such lamps, but it is certain that they were much easier to obtain than marble reliefs and precious gems and cameos.

The spectrum could easily be widened. Most of all, one could demonstrate that the geographical spread of Augustan images reached the remotest parts of the Empire, especially when one considers the monuments celebrating Actium.[58] Moreover, further themes of Augustan policy, in particular those referring to his religious policies, provide an eloquent image of the Empire and its various population groups being pervaded by pictorial ideas representing the *princeps*. One particularly discernible mechanism for the diffusion of such images was the cult of the Lares [Household Gods] and the Protective Spirit of Augustus (the *Genius Augusti*), with its shrines at each crossroads in the city of Rome. Here the officials, drawn from the ranks of freedmen and slaves, identified themselves in the reliefs on their altars with pictorial ideas drawn from the imperial court. Accordingly, the circulation of such themes underwent a broad expansion both inside and outside Rome.[59] The most important general conclusion to be drawn from an interpretation of the many pieces of evidence which cannot be discussed here would be that the entire reception of this imagery through a cult imposed from above admittedly had, on the one hand, an official starting-point. On the other hand, however, beyond this official framework

---

[58] Examples in K. Fittschen, *JdI* 91 (1976), 192–193.

[59] For further details on the altars at the crossroads shrines, see G. Niebling, *Historia* 5 (1956), 303–331; P. Zanker, *Bullettino della commissione archeologica comunale di Roma* 82 (1970–1971), 147–155. Expansion further afield: see Hölscher, *Staatsdenkmal und Publikum* (cit. n. 27), pp. 29–30.

Fig. 10.14. Oil-lamp with Victory on a globe

there were only a few controlling mechanisms and, overall, no ruthlessly strict ideological centre that could coordinate the political imagery that spread across the Empire in all its manifestations. On the contrary, Augustan ideology was so effective, it would appear, because a political climate was created or fostered in which the reception of the imagery took place of its own accord, as it were, as a form of "spontaneous approval."[60]

In general, it is after the battle of Actium that we can for the first time in Rome identify from the monuments a differentiated image of political behaviour among various groups in Roman society. The *princeps*, by means of his costly monuments, targeted most of all the capital's old aristocracy, which, according to Republican tradition and as a result of the emergence of an Empire from a city-state, was

---

[60] This idea corresponds with the insights of the Heidelberg dissertation of H. Schäfer-Hänlein, *Veneratio Augusti*, Rome 1985. The practice of erecting images of the *princeps* complies with these findings as well.

Fig. 10.15. Oil-lamp with Victory and *clipeus virtutis* (shield of virtue)

still considered an immensely important factor in power relations. This class responded to the *princeps'* messages with images of an exclusive, intellectual calibre. Alongside this, however, images of a rather clichéd simplicity, in particular Victory on the globe, the *clipeus virtutis*, and the *corona civica*, were readily available, and these were well suited for mass production and distribution across a broad spectrum of the Empire's population.

We cannot deduce from the monuments, however, how much conviction and how much opportunism came into play. The evidence can only provide us with a rather general index of the breadth of support, whatever the situation may have been, that Augustus' rule received. The numbers do not add up to an order of magnitude that would be statistically significant.[61] In addition, we need to realise that Augustus' opponents were never represented on monuments. More important than these questions, for which other types of sources can provide reliable evidence, are some more general observations. The extent of the reception of imperial images within the private sphere demonstrates at the very least that resistance to a sole ruler had significantly waned and that it had now become quite common for people to invest their hopes in a single saviour, in the expectation that advantages would be gained from such a situation. From an otherwise not very well-documented perspective, the imagery on these monuments provides us with an idea of how far the Republican state had been eroded since the murder of Julius Caesar. In terms of their sheer quantity, these images provide us with clear testimony to the fact that this style of acclamation, at the same time, represented a loss of political vitality.

---

[61] We can neither guess how widely this consumer production circulated among Augustus' supporters, nor how much of it has survived (nor how much is actually published). In these circumstances, any statistical projections would be invalid.

11 *Meretrix regina:* Augustan Cleopatras†

MARIA WYKE

Propertius asks the reader of his love elegies *quid mirare, meam si versat femina vitam | et trahit addictum sub sua iura virum?* (why are you astonished if a woman drives my life | and drags, bound beneath her own laws, a man? 3.11.1–2).[1] A catalogue of dominating women of myth and history follows, culminating in a lengthy assault on Cleopatra's ambition to rule Rome and praise for Augustus who alone has released the citizenry from such a fearful prospect. But at the poem's close its narrator still remains in bondage to his elegiac mistress and, therefore, locked into the position not of a resistant Augustus but of a Mark Antony enslaved by the *meretrix regina* ('whore queen', 3.11.39). The narrator's life should be no cause of astonishment because it replays the life that Antony had recently led. Throughout the Propertian poetry-books, Jasper Griffin has argued, a parallel is sustained between the life of the lover and the life of Antony: reckless, romantic, and tragically obsessed with a woman who degrades him.[2] Propertius 3.11 lays before its readers a seemingly vitriolic account of Cleopatra's fearsome desires and ambitions in order that they may better comprehend elegy's amatory enslavement. In so doing, the poem deploys motifs for the depiction of the last Ptolemaic ruler that have been traced back to the propaganda spearheaded by Octavian as he agitated for support in the lead up to the battle of Actium, and whose repetition has also been observed in the iambic Cleopatra of Horace *Epode* 9, the lyric Cleopatra of Horace *Ode* 1.37, the epic Cleopatra of Virgil *Aeneid* 8, and the elegiac Cleopatra of Propertius 4.6.

---

† Originally published in Anton Powell, ed., *Roman Poetry and Propaganda in the Age of Augustus*, Bristol: Bristol Classical Press, 1992, pp. 98–140. What follows is the revised and extended version of this article first published in M. Wyke, *The Roman Mistress: Ancient and Modern Representations*, Oxford: Oxford University Press, 2002, pp. 195–243.

[1] See Wyke (2002), ch. 1.
[2] Griffin (1985). On the double-edged comparison between Propertius and Antony in 2.16.35–40, see Miller (2001), sec. 1.

By the time of the battle of Actium in 31 BC, Cleopatra VII had shaped her own image as a protective queen of Egypt and been shaped by her opponents as the eastern enemy of Rome. Her own propaganda, of which there are now few remains, depicted the queen in ways that competed for authority with the propaganda of the ultimate victor, Octavian.[3] Cleopatra's power was variously represented in the verbal and visual discourses of Egypt and Rome, yet the texts that survive from the period close to her death are predominantly male, Roman, and poetic. At this distance, we seem to be witness only to the extreme partiality of the winning side for, within the discursive patterns of Augustan iambics, lyric, epic, and elegy, Cleopatra VII is the defeated enemy of the *res publica* and potent only in her sympotic and erotic perversity. She is the Egyptian whore, a drunkard, mistress of eunuchs, and (almost) of Rome itself. Both this poetic and the later historiographic tradition have been said to create around an opponent of Octavian 'a miasma of romance, glamour, sentiment, and prurience', and to invoke a form of political propaganda against the queen that constitutes 'one of the most terrible outbursts of hatred in history'.[4]

Although twentieth-century historians have often acknowledged the danger of their own complicity with Graeco-Roman judgements of the queen (in the absence of any surviving Graeco-Egyptian accounts), the last Ptolemy has regularly been represented in their works as only an appendage to her two Roman lovers. In the opening paragraph of her biography *Cleopatra* (1999), the Hellenistic historian E. E. Rice warns that:

> Cleopatra VII of Egypt is one of the most famous, if not *the* most famous woman of classical antiquity. Her fortune, or perhaps, misfortune, was that the chaotic historical circumstances of the first century BC – namely a series of Roman civil wars combined with a fateful clash of an increasingly powerful Rome with the Hellenistic Empires of the Greek East – brought about her meeting with two of the most famous figures of Roman history, Julius Caesar and Marc Antony. While these encounters dramatically affected the history of the Mediterranean world, it is our own irresistible fascination with love affairs between larger-than-life historical figures that has ensured Cleopatra's undying fame, for better or for worse.[5]

The marked tendency of twentieth-century historians to break into Shakespearian tragic dialogue when describing the queen's death

---

[3] Hughes-Hallett (1991), 14–15; Rice (1999), 2–3; Foreman (1999), 27.
[4] Respectively, Grant (1972), p. xvii, and Tarn and Charlesworth (1934), 98. Cf. Weigall (1923), esp. 22; Pelling (1996), 4 and 41–6; Rice (1999), 3–6.
[5] Rice (1999), 1.

demonstrates the pervasiveness of one particular ancient fiction, from Plutarch in a direct line of descent through his translators Amyot and North, to Shakespeare and the first 1930s edition of *The Cambridge Ancient History*.[6] Similarly, when Michael Grant, at the outset of his own biography of the queen, invites his readers into the 'story of a woman who became utterly involved, in her public and private life alike, with two men', he borrows his narrative strategy (which allows Cleopatra only the power of sexual allure and absorbs her entirely into a history of Rome) from the ancient historian Cassius Dio who centres Cleopatra's reign around her captivation of two Roman men, Julius Caesar and Mark Antony, and her destruction by a third, Octavian (Dio 51.15.4).[7]

Even where scholars have lingered over Cleopatra in their narratives of Roman history, their narrative alignments are disclosed by such comments as 'she had a wonderful voice and the seductiveness which attracts men', or 'among the women who intervene in the masculine strife for political power, she will always occupy a special position, and ever and anon excite the imagination of mankind'.[8] The Decadent critic Arthur Symons provided the interpretative key to such descriptions when he claimed that 'before the thought of Cleopatra every man is an Antony'.[9] Twentieth-century historians of ancient Rome have structured the queen as erotic object both for the male author of the narrative and for the male reader which that narrative has presupposed.

Nor is the scholar who writes a separate biography of Cleopatra VII's reign in Egypt immune from such erotic fascination. In *The Life and Times of Cleopatra Queen of Egypt* (1914), Arthur Weigall – having just completed a nine-year term as Inspector General of Antiquities for the Egyptian government – constructed for the queen an ambition to restore the lost kingdoms of the Ptolemaic empire (and even to establish world power) through her exploitation of Rome's capacity to aggrandize its clients and allies. Nonetheless he declared that as an historian shapes his picture of Cleopatra 'he cannot fail to fall himself under the spell of that enchantment by

---

[6] Tarn and Charlesworth (1934), 111. Cf. Macurdy (1932), 216–18; Lindsay (1971), 475–6; Foss (1997), 187. No Shakespearian quotation appears in the second edition of the *CAH*, although Pelling (1996), 64, does note the magnificence with which Plutarch, and following him Shakespeare, tell the story of Antony's death.

[7] Grant (1972), p. xv, and reproduced in the Phoenix Press paperback edition published in 2000.

[8] Tarn and Charlesworth (1934), 35, and Volkmann (1958), 219.

[9] Quoted in Hughes-Hallett (1991), 16.

which the face of the world was changed'.[10] At the other end of the twentieth century, following the strategies (and the admission) of Weigall, Michael Foss in *The Search for Cleopatra* (1997) constructs a woman who deploys her sexuality as an instrument of politically perceptive statescraft; yet he invites his readers to 'Imagine her in all the variety and grace and appeal of mature womanhood taken to its utmost possibility, with the mind and a body to captivate a caesar, a world-conqueror, an emperor.'[11] Similarly a recent biography by Laura Foreman, *Cleopatra's Palace: In Search of a Legend* (1999), openly warns against the Cleopatra of the ancient sources as a seductively dramatic but hollow fiction, and observes that already by the Renaissance 'generations of educated individuals across the continent had, like Caesar and Antony before them, fallen under Cleopatra's spell'.[12] Yet a foreword by Franck Goddio, the archaeologist investigating the now submerged royal quarters of ancient Alexandria, belies the biographer's caution. He attaches considerable romantic value to his underwater investigations:

> Above all it was the home of Cleopatra, history's most fascinating woman. It was in Alexandria that she met and mesmerized Julius Caesar, in its now drowned streets that she, a conquerer of conquerors, caroused with Mark Antony. And it was here that she chose for herself death before dishonor.
> More than anything else, it was the drama of Cleopatra's life and loves that drew me to Alexandria and that finally spurred me on in 1992 to undertake the daunting task of locating, mapping, and exploring the remains of the sunken city. (p. 22)

Cleopatra VII appears to have seduced scholars as well as Romans.

The purpose of this chapter is, therefore, to sketch the discursive process whereby an Egyptian queen, the 'glory of her fathers', entered the poetry of the early Augustan period in the shape of a royal mistress charged with such extraordinary political and erotic potency that it has continued to invite its readers to take up the position of either a resistant Octavian or a seduced Antony. Such an examination of the process whereby Cleopatra VII entered Augustan culture to become the most famous of Roman mistresses (whose seductions even jeopardized Rome's dominance of the Mediterranean) addresses questions of poetry's apparent complicity in the social construction of gender, ethnicity, political legitimacy and

---

[10] Weigall (1923 edn.), p. 26 On Weigall's biographies of Egypt's rulers, see Montserrat (2000), 4 and 103–5.
[11] Foss (1997), 9. He immediately poses the question 'Did such a person exist, or was she only a figment of the imagination?', but answers that 'history suggests there was such a woman'.
[12] Foreman (1999), 161 and 27.

empire, its part in the formation of a founding myth of Western culture that predicated Augustan rule on a contest between freedom and tyranny, west and east, male and female.

EMPOWERING WOMEN

The traditional strategies for representing female power which had existed in Ptolemaic Egypt and the validating fictions created by Cleopatra herself both contrast markedly with the images we have inherited from the winning, western side. These validating strategies empower 'woman' not as a despotic enemy who imperils political systems from without, but as a beneficent ruler who protects them from within.

Viewed in the context of the social structures of post-Actian Rome, the queen Cleopatra VII may seem to be a striking anomaly.[13] In ancient Egypt, however, papyri, inscriptions, poetry and prose, temple sculpture, coins, and cult implements all attest to the public powers of the Ptolemaic queens.[14] For example, linked in her coinage with the Pharaonic past, associated with the Egyptian and Olympian deities Isis and Aphrodite, Arsinoe II Philadelphos (c. 316–270 BC) was the first Ptolemaic queen to be worshipped in her own lifetime as a goddess. Towns were named after her, temples erected, and festivals established in her honour.[15] In Hellenistic poetry, the queens often appear as patterns of wifeliness, virtuous in their capacities to maintain the dynastic line.[16] Theocritus *Idyll* 17, an encomium to the poet's patron Ptolemy II Philadelphus, includes praise of Ptolemy's mother Berenice I as outstanding among wise women, while further defining her as a profit to her parents, devout in her conjugal love, and loyal in her production of legitimate children. Gratitude is expressed by the poem's narrator to Aphrodite, who has deified the queen after her death and endowed her with a share of divine prerogatives: placed in Aphrodite's temple, Berenice I now undertakes the goddess's offices in her kindness towards all mortal lovers. Thus queen Berenice I is represented as possessed of positive and public erotic powers.[17] Similarly, Berenice II, addressed as *numpha*

---

[13] Pomeroy (1984), 24 and 26; Hamer (1993), 11–12.
[14] Pomeroy (1984), 28. See, in general, Pomeroy (1984), 13–40; Macurdy (1932), 102–235; Flamarion (1997), 14; Rowlandson (1998), 6 and 24.
[15] Theoc. *Id.* 15.106–11. Fraser (1972), 236–40; Thompson (1973), 4; Pomeroy (1984), 28–39; Quaegebeur (1988), 41–5; Rowlandson (1998), 24–33.
[16] Richlin (1992).
[17] Theoc. *Id.* 17.34–52, for which see Gow (1950), 332–5. Cf. Pomeroy (1984), 31; Rowlandson (1998), 6.

('wife' or 'bride'), provides the narrative frame for the third and fourth books of Callimachus' *Aetia*, a text of fundamental importance to the Augustan poets. The paired books begin with a tribute to a display of Ptolemaic authority on Greek territories (the victory of Berenice's horses at the Nemean games), and close with a description of the queen's conjugal devotion (the tale of the lock of her hair which she vowed for her husband's safety).[18]

The eastern representations of Cleopatra VII clearly belong to this tradition for empowering royal women.[19] The queen is nowhere named in the Augustan narratives, yet her name belongs to a pattern of 'Ptolemies', 'Berenices' and 'Cleopatras' that by its repetitions signified the continuity of the Lagid dynasty.[20] A stele dedicated in 51 BC, the year in which Cleopatra inherited the throne with her brother Ptolemy XIII, represents the queen as a bare-chested and kilted Pharaoh who wears the Double Crown and makes offerings to an enthroned Isis. The accompanying Greek text lists the queen's name and her titles. The combination of Egyptian iconography and Greek inscription signals that the queen who is entitled 'a glory to her father' (*Kleopatra*) and 'father-loving' (*philopator*) is legitimate heir to the authority and political power of both her own father, the Greek-descended Ptolemy XII Auletes, and all her ancestral 'fathers', the native Pharaonic kings.[21] Furthermore, the validating power of such names was clearly recognized by Cleopatra herself for, in 36 BC, she assumed a new title not used by her predecessors. As the queen who was respecting Pharaonic ritual, building temples in upper Egypt, and regaining parts of the lost Ptolemaic empire, she became Queen Cleopatra, the Goddess, the Younger, Father-Loving and Fatherland-loving (*philopatris*).[22] In her Ptolemaic context, Cleopatra was certainly a lover of Egypt, but no seducing *meretrix*.

In her titles and iconography Cleopatra VII, like the other queens before her, played the role of daughter to all the previous kings of Egypt. She also represented herself as mother on monuments and coins, for part of her validating strategies involved the presentation of her son Ptolemy XV Caesar (better known as Caesarion) as

---

[18] Parsons (1977). On the *Coma* [*The Lock of Hair*], in particular, see Fraser (1972), i. 729–30, and, on the translation by Catullus, West (1985).

[19] See, in general, Hamer (1993), 5–18.

[20] Pomeroy (1984), 22; Grant (1972), 31; Bowman (1996), 23.

[21] For an illustration and description of the stele see Bianchi (1998), 188–189, no. 78. Cf. Rowlandson (1998), 37–8.

[22] Maehler (1983), 8; Thompson (1994), 321, Rowlandson (1998), 39. For Cleopatra's participation in Pharaonic ritual see also Tarn (1936) on the stele from Bucheum; Volkmann (1958), 60; Thompson (1994), 321.

Fig. 11.1. Cleopatra's bronze coinage from Cyprus, dated *c.* 47–30 BC

her legitimate heir and co-regent, fit to rule Egypt in the Pharaonic tradition.[23] The birth of Caesarion was celebrated in the words and images of a temple built for the purpose at Hermonthis in Upper Egypt, where Cleopatra's role as mother to her son was assimilated iconographically to the role of Isis as mother to Horus. On the south wall of a surviving temple at Dendera (also in Upper Egypt), a monumental Cleopatra still appears in relief behind Caesarion, both in the dress and posture of the Pharaohs, as they make offerings to the divine mother/son pairs Hathor/Harsomtus and Isis/Horus.[24] Furthermore, as the only Ptolemaic queen to coin in her own right and not as the representative of a king,[25] there appears on Cleopatra's bronze coinage from Cyprus (dated *c.* 47–30 BC) a type of the queen suckling her son and crowned with stephane [diadem], in the manner of Aphrodite/Isis nursing the infant Eros/Horus (Fig. 11.1). The image of fertility as an instrument for the authorization of Cleopatra's power is reinforced by the appearance of a sceptre behind the nursing mother's shoulder on the obverse, and, on the reverse, the type of two cornucopiae – an ancient device of the Ptolemies, employed earlier on the coinage of Arsinoe II – accompanied by the legend KLEOPATRAS BASILISSES ('of Cleopatra the Queen').[26]

Preserving the Pharaonic tradition that closely associated temporal with spiritual authority, Cleopatra represented herself as both a regal

---

[23] Volkmann (1958), 74–7; Flamarion (1997), 50–1; Rice (1999), 46; Southern (1999), 48.

[24] Grant (1972), 99–100; Quaegebeur (1988), 52; Hamer (1993), 14–16; Rowlandson (1998), 38.

[25] Tarn and Charlesworth (1934), 67; Macurdy (1932), 8; Lindsay (1971), 245; Grant (1972), 47–8; Rice (1999), 97; Southern (1999), 21 and 69.

[26] *BMC Ptolemies*, Cleopatra VII, p. 122, no. 2, and pl. 30.6; Burnett et al. (1990), n. 3901; Davis and Kraay (1973), nos. 41, 42, and 46; Volkmann (1958), 76; Grant (1972), 85; Hamer (1993), 8.

and a divine mother. She was regularly identified with the Egyptian mother goddess Isis, in her permanent monumental display on temple walls, in the typology of her coinage, and, most explicitly, in her title *nea Isis* ('new Isis'). The queen dressed her political and social powers in the eroticism of a divine mother nurturing her child. In Egypt, therefore, Cleopatra VII assumed positive, sacred powers as the loving mother of her dynasty and her country, whereas in Rome she would become a model of meretricious perversity who thereby challenged the good ordering of the western world.[27]

Exalted by her divinity, the last Ptolemaic queen may also have been reified as symbol of the conquering east. Among the miscellaneous materials to be found in the third book of the *Oracula Sibyllina* (a collection of which is thought to have been circulating in Rome by the mid-first century BC) are a number of oracles which seem to endorse the conquests of the Ptolemaic dynasty.[28] Two of those oracles personify the powers of the Ptolemaic east in the figure of a woman. At 3.350–80 it is a woman (a *despoina*) who will exact Asia's vengeance for Roman aggression (expressed intriguingly in the invective of sexual promiscuity as if to counterpoint Rome's self-representation in terms of moral probity). Shearing Rome's hair, she will enforce a marriage of enslavement and, with that punishment complete, usher in a Golden Age of peace for both Asia and Europe:

> O Rome, luxurious Rome of gold, you Latin child,
> Virgin drunken with lust in many beds you've run wild,
> but you'll be married without due rites, a slave-slut of despair,
> while still the Queen crops off your delicate head of hair
> and uttering judgements will hurl you to earth from the sky,
> then take up from the earth and set you again on high.[29]

At 3.75–92 it is a widow (a *cherê*) who will take over the rule of the world and then bring on its destruction. A case has been argued for identifying these two female embodiments of the conquering east with Cleopatra herself, and placing their composition respectively in an optimistic period before Actium and in a period of her supporters' disillusionment after the defeat.[30] The prophecy of a glorious world kingdom and a golden age of peace for east and west certainly parallels the discourses of conquest centred around Alexander the

---

[27] See Thompson (1973), 58–9 and 122; Burnett et al. (1990), n. 1245; Hamer (1993), 10–13, and 18; Rowlandson (1998), 39; Gurval (forthcoming [2011]).

[28] Parke (1988), 144. For the eastern provenance of these oracles see Parke (1988), 2 and 6; Collins (1987), 31–2; Lindsay (1971), 355–80.

[29] The translation is taken from Lindsay (1971), 356.

[30] See Collins (1983), 358–61, and (1987), 433–5, who follows Tarn (1932), 137–9. Pelling (1996), 50–1, however, notes sadly that the dating of these oracles is insecure.

Great on which Cleopatra herself had drawn when, for example, she named her son by Antony 'Alexander Helios'.[31] If the identification holds, these oracles assimilate monarch with country or continent in a manner permitted by a pre-existing language for representing the power of the Ptolemaic queens, and, as part of a discourse of resistance to the power of Rome, Cleopatra is transformed into a personification of a righteous and vengeful Asia.[32]

In the years after Actium, however, the Cleopatra who appears at Rome in the poetry of Horace, Virgil, and Propertius exhibits scarcely any of the above features. No name or title is used to identify her. She is once called 'the Egyptian wife' (*Aegyptia coniunx*), but more frequently is entitled only 'queen' (*regina*) or 'woman' (*femina, mulier, illa*). She is described neither as the daughter of kings nor as a mother of kings and, in the Roman narratives, her kingdom seems to consist only of the vanquished.

In Augustan poetry, Cleopatra does not live up to the name the poems deny her: she sheds no glory on her 'fathers'. The queen of Egypt is nameless in the Roman narratives precisely because she is notorious. She has become instead the one exceptional disgrace of a dynasty that claimed descent from the illustrious kings of Macedon when, in Propertius 3.11.40, she is described as *una Philippeo sanguine adusta nota* (the single reproach scorched on the blood of Philip).[33] In Horatian lyric, it is only when confronted by her prostrated kingdom that the queen desires to act more nobly (*generosius*, 1.37.21) and to die without being stripped of her royal status (*privata*, 1.37.31).[34] Moreover, it is not Cleopatra but Octavian who, in *Aeneid* 8.681, is borne into battle resplendent with the glory of the fatherland, the *patrium sidus*.[35] Deprived of name and titles, banished from the dynastic history of Macedonian and Ptolemaic rule, Cleopatra is effectively denied both her paternal ancestral powers and her claims to patriotism.

Just as the Cleopatra of Augustan poetry is denied a role as the fatherland's loving daughter, so she does not appear as good wife, nor as fertile mother. If she is called wife (*coniunx, Aen.* 8.688) or described as demanding a wife's reward (*coniugis pretium*, Prop.

---

[31] See Tarn (1932), 144–8; Volkmann (1958), 122; Grant (1972), 142–4; Collins (1983), 358; Pelling (1988), 256; Hamer (1993), 17–18; Bowman (1996), 34–5; Foss (1997), 185–6.
[32] On the assimilation of female ruler to nation, in a country that has a history of queens, see Warner (1987), 38–60, on Elizabeth I, Queen Victoria, and Margaret Thatcher.
[33] Fedeli (1985), 377–9; Gurval (1995), 196.
[34] Nisbet and Hubbard (1970), 417; West (1995), 189–91.
[35] I am indebted to Duncan Kennedy for this observation.

3.11.31), the adjectives employed to qualify these terms (*Aegyptia* [Egyptian] and *obsceni* [indecent] respectively) signal clearly that for Antony this was no legitimate marriage. Since it was not possible for him to be married to both Octavia and Cleopatra simultaneously or for his foreign 'marriage' to have any legal standing at Rome, from the Roman perspective an *Aegyptia coniunx* is no real *coniunx* at all.[36] Nor can the Augustan Cleopatra be the wedded mother of legitimate offspring, for her claim to the political authority of Julius Caesar, through the alleged parentage of her son Caesarion, conflicts directly with Octavian's claim to be Caesar's rightful heir.[37]

Julius Caesar displayed Cleopatra in Rome neither as his unlawful wife nor as his *meretrix* [whore], but as a divine mother-figure. During the same period as Cleopatra minted her divinely maternal Cyprian coin type, Julius Caesar had placed her gilded statue in the temple of Venus Genetrix at Rome – thus juxtapositioning the Egyptian queen with the mother and founder of the Julian clan. While the deified Berenice I may have supplied a specific Ptolemaic precedent for such shrine sharing, in republican Rome the ascription of such divine authority to a living woman was unprecedented. In Graeco-Egyptian ritual, sacred architecture, coinage, and literature, the Ptolemaic queens exercised the fertile erotic powers of an Aphrodite/Isis mother figure, but no Augustan poem reproduces Caesar's provocative gesture.[38] Instead the texts substitute such general devices for the delineation of Octavian's eastern enemy as drunkenness (Hor. *Ode* 1.37.14, Prop. 3.11.56) and excess (particularized as the unmanly luxury of mosquito nets at Hor. *Ep.* 9.15–16 and Prop. 3.11.45). Where Cleopatra's sexual behaviour is mentioned at all it is in the guise of 'the whore queen of incestuous Canopus' (*incesti meretrix regina Canopi*, Prop. 3.11.39); the kind of woman who wears herself out in intercourse with her own slaves (*famulos inter femina trita suos*, Prop. 3.11.30), and emasculates the men who are present at her court (*Ep.* 9.13–14, *Ode* 1.37.9–10).

Neither daughter, wife, nor mother, Cleopatra has scarcely any physical presence at all in the Horatian and Virgilian narratives. At best the queen is drunk with sweet success (*Ode* 1.37.11–12) or pale with fear of her coming death (*Aen.* 8.709). Only barking Anubis and the rattling sistrum which, in the *Aeneid*, accompany the

---

[36] See Reinhold (1988), 221 on Plutarch's comments; Lindsay (1971), 240; Rice (1999), 55; Southern (1999), 50 and 122.
[37] Dio 49.41.1; 50.1.3; 51.3.5. Zanker (1988), 34; Grant (1972), 87–8; Aly (1992), 50.
[38] App. *BC* 2.15.102, and Dio 51.22.1–3. On which, see Lindsay (1971), 67–8; Reinhold (1988), 158; Aly (1992), 52.

queen into battle might suggest the dissonance of barbarian speech. In Propertian elegy, Cleopatra takes on a little more substance. At 4.6.22, the weapons of the losing side at Actium are clutched shamefully in the hand of a woman. In 3.11, more significantly, the dying Cleopatra possesses a tongue that once had spoken, hands that are now enchained, and a body steeped in poison (3.11.52–5). When, however, the elegiac narrator claims to have witnessed the physical effects of venom on the queen's body (*spectaui* ['I watched'], 3.11.53), it becomes apparent that the author has put on display in poetry not Cleopatra's death at Alexandria in 30 BC, but its Roman simulacrum – the visual representation of the vanquished which will have been carried in the triple triumph at Rome in 29 BC.[39] Similarly, the Cleopatra of the *Aeneid* is not presented as a woman of flesh and blood, but as a woman of metals such as silver and gold, already a visual image on a shield now further delineated in the words of a poetic ekphrasis [description of an artefact].[40] In both poetic contexts, Cleopatra's failing body is distanced as a work of art designed for the voyeuristic pleasure of her Roman spectators.

The Egyptian Cleopatra assumed positive powers through her identification with the goddess Isis. For the poetic Cleopatra of the Augustan narratives, however, assimilation to Isis brings with it connotations of disorder, dissonance, and barbarous animality. The Roman poems do not name Isis explicitly in association with Cleopatra but bring the goddess in indirectly through her cultic attributes.[41] Virgil's epic narrative of Actium and Propertius' elegy 3.11 both depict Cleopatra in possession of a sistrum (a musical instrument used regularly in the fertility rites of Isis and appearing frequently in visual depictions of the goddess to signal her powers), and supported by Anubis (the god who in the myth of Isis assisted her in restoring Osiris to life).[42] In the *Aeneid*, the sistrum is not an instrument of worship but a native Egyptian means for summoning up armies (*Aen.* 8.696), and Anubis, in the company of all the monstrous shapes of the Egyptian gods, barks his opposition to the pantheon of Rome (8.698). The hierarchical oppositions of which the sistrum and Anubis form a part are set out in Propertius 3.11: Cleopatra loses because she dared to oppose 'our' Jupiter with her

---

[39] See Plut. *Ant.* 86, and Dio 51.21.7–8. Cf. Fedeli (1985), 384, on Prop. 3.11.53–4.
[40] See e.g. West (1975) for the ekphrastic techniques of the Virgilian narrative, and Putnam (1998), 119–88.
[41] As Malaise (1972), 246–7; Witt (1971), 55.
[42] Toynbee (1934), 41; Witt (1971), 39 and 198.

barking Anubis (3.11.41) and the Roman trumpet with the *crepitanti sistro* [jangling rattle (distinctive of the cult of Isis)] (3.11.43).[43]

Thus the Cleopatra of the Augustan poets exhibits a certain anonymity. She holds the relationships neither of daughter, nor mother, nor legitimate wife, and possesses no individuating physical features. Remaining somewhat distanced and reified, she becomes an artful and artifical symbol of an entire nation. Within eastern discourses for the authorization of imperial power, 'woman' is reified as righteous and vengeful Asia. She becomes, however, the personification of effeminate and conquered Asia in the competing discourses of the west.

The sympotic, epic, and elegiac Cleopatras of Augustan poetry all constrain the queen within the limits of a sexualized role as vanquished opponent of the Roman state, which may suggest that these texts are operating as the authoritative voice of Augustus in matters Actian. Yet the persistence with which the Horatian, Virgilian, and Propertian Cleopatras are associated with abuse of political power, with drunkenness, immorality, bestiality, effeminacy, and a perverse sexual dominance, takes on a recognizably more longstanding and entrenched discursive shape. For the rhetorical patterns of Octavian's agitational propaganda that emerged in the 30s BC (and to which these poetic motifs have been traced) could not constitute mere inventions of the moment but, in order to prove persuasive with their intended addressees (the veteran colonies, the propertied classes of Italy's towns, the Roman senate), they had to draw on pre-existing structures of thinking they then mirrored and exploited.[44]

The poetic fictions of a queen who is surrounded by the paraphernalia of an eastern despot are clearly grounded in a discursive tradition whose history transcends the immediate control of individual Augustan poets, their individual poetic utterances, and the specific political agendas of their patrons. The features of these fictive Cleopatras are clearly articulated with the overlapping structures of ancient gender and orientalism – 'the complex system of signifiers denoting the ethically, psychologically and politically "other" by which the West has sought to dominate and have authority over the East'.[45] So, before literary critics attempt to discriminate between individual poetic fictions according to such categories as period of

---

[43] Hardie (1986), 98; Putnam (1998), 145.
[44] Pelling (1996), 41–6, and Feeney (1992), 3.
[45] Hall (1989), 2 and 99, following Said (1985), 3. For Cleopatra's deployment in the modern orientalist discourses of colonialism, see Hughes-Hallett (1991), Flamarion (1997), 140–8, and Wyke (2002), ch. 7.

production, patronal relations, genre, context, or narrative voice, it is essential to elucidate the broad conceptual patterns which underlie the writing of Cleopatra into Augustan Rome as a *meretrix regina*.[46]

Edith Hall placed the invention of the oriental 'barbarian' in the specific historical circumstances of the fifth century BC and demonstrated the ways in which tragic drama provided cultural authorization for the perpetuation of the stereotype.[47] In Aeschylus' *Suppliants*, the sons of Aegyptus (the prototypes of the Egyptian people) are unfavourably contrasted with their philhellenic relatives the Danaids as violent, arrogant, gluttonous, and treacherous barbarians, and Egyptians are in general ridiculed as crocodiles, beer-drinkers, and papyrus-eaters.[48] The Athenian polarization between Greece and its other then became the model for subsequent constructions of Roman identity through definition of the other, or reverse self.[49] Despite its traditional depiction as the cradle of wisdom, its association with a miraculous fertility, and its gradual entry from the second century BC into Rome's sphere of political influences, Egypt nevertheless held an important place in Rome's discourses of orientalism.[50] The visit of Scipio Aemilianus to Egypt about 140 BC was later pictured by the Graeco-Sicilian historian Diodorus Siculus as a confrontation between the Roman general's practicality and strength and the Ptolemaic king's effeminacy and luxurious incompetence;[51] while the first documented rhetorical assault on Egypt by a Roman occurs in a defence speech Cicero delivered in 54 BC, where he attempted to undermine the testimony of Egyptian witnesses by describing Alexandria as the home of all tricks (*praestigiae*) and deceits (*fallaciae*).[52]

Egypt's place in Rome's discourses of orientalism was reinforced by the subsequent civil conflicts in Alexandria and the murder of Pompey. Recording the background to his involvement in the Alexandrian wars of 48–47 BC over Cleopatra's claims to the Ptolemaic throne, Julius Caesar presaged the tactics of Octavian's propaganda campaign against Antony when he noted disparagingly

[46] For the priority of conceptual systems over individual literary expressions see Goldhill (1986), 111–13, on anthropologically based readings of Greek tragedy, and Wyke (1989) on Paul Veyne's readings of Latin love elegy. Cf. Said (1985), 13 on modern orientalist literatures.
[47] Hall (1989), 1 and 103.
[48] Smelik and Hemelrijk (1984), 1870–2.
[49] Hannestad (1988), 54; Marshall (1998), 49.
[50] See, in general, Balsdon (1979), 68–9; Malaise (1972), 244–51; Smelik and Hemelrijk (1984); Reinhold (1988), 227–8; Takács (1995), 33–4; David (2000), 51–8.
[51] Diod. Sic. 33.28b.1–3. On which, see Gruen (1984), 714–15; Lampela (1998), 21–2.
[52] Cic. *Pro Rab. Post.* 35, on which see Smelik and Hemelrijk (1984), 1921–2.

that the Egyptian general's armies included Roman soldiers 'who had by now become habituated to the licentiousness of Alexandrian life (*Alexandrinae vitae ac licentiae*) and had forgotten the good name and orderly conduct of the Roman people (*nomen disciplinamque populi Romani*) and had taken wives by whom most of them had children', *Civil Wars* 3.110.2.[53] After the battle of Actium and the conquest of Egypt in 30 BC, the unique policy of isolating Egypt which Augustus pursued further fostered the pre-existing pattern. Government of Egypt was allocated to a prefect of equestrian (rather than senatorial) rank who was directly appointed by and answerable to the *princeps* (rather than the state). While members of the Roman elite were not allowed to visit Egypt without the permission of Augustus, Egyptians were not allowed to serve in the Roman army or enter the senate. Such official prohibitions marked the country as both a unique and a distant realm, and one which was now under the authority of the *princeps* (although, officially, he had added it to the empire of the people of Rome).[54] It is that particular historical context which lends a strong political resonance to the poetic construction of Cleopatra as Egyptian: she is the Egyptian wife (*Aen.* 8.688), the whore queen of Canopus (Prop. 3.11.39), nourished by the waters of the Nile (*Aen.* 8.711–13), drunk on the wine of Mareotis (*Ode* 1.37.14).

The ideological resonance of the poetic Cleopatra's identification with Isis also must be understood in a larger historical context – that of Roman religious practice and prohibition. Although the worship of Isis constituted the most popular cult that spread to Rome from Egypt, in the early principate its Italian adherents practised beliefs that were neither centred on the Augustan state nor controlled by it.[55] Three times already between 58 and 48 BC, the altar of Isis on the Capitol had been destroyed on the orders of the senate in order to affirm that only it had the right to confer official religious status. Cleopatra's presence in Rome before the assassination of Caesar may have given the cult higher visibility and encouraged the triumvirs to vote it a temple in 43 BC. But the official gesture towards the deified Caesar and his Egyptian consort was an empty one, the temple never erected. Three years after Actium, to further an atmosphere of religious renewal, Octavian himself debarred the practice of the Isis

---

[53] Monaco (1992), 262.
[54] Smelik and Hemelrijk (1984), 1922–4; Reinhold (1988), 227–8; Hamer (1993), 23; Bowman (1996), 37–8; Flamarion (1997), 110–11: Rowlandson (1998), 10–11; Southern (1999), 36 and 145.
[55] Toynbee (1934), 40; Malaise (1972), 159–70.

cult from within the boundaries of the *pomerium*, and, in 21 BC, from within the first milestone of the city. Isis never gained a place in the official calendar of the Augustan state religion.[56] It is in this historical context that the sistrum and Anubis become transformed by Augustan representations of Cleopatra into markers of incongruity, of exotic 'otherness', of animality and, especially, of eastern discordance. Within the logic of Roman orientalism, the alien and the bestial Anubis of Propertius 3.11 must be defeated by the familiar anthropomorphic divinity Jupiter, the bark and the rattle must be drowned out by the clear sounds of Rome's trumpet.[57]

In the narrative patterns of fifth-century tragic drama the barbarian is shaped as an inversion of Athenian civic ideals and is associated, therefore, with tyranny and female power.[58] Societies that marginalize women in the political arena locate female rulers outside their own political structures in an alien social order, as a means of highlighting that order's perceived peculiarity and their own 'normality'.[59] In Athenian drama, women are ascribed political authority in proportion to the perceived barbarity of the community to which they belong and Athens is being opposed.[60] In the ethnographic tradition as well as in drama, gender roles are reversed in the world of the other: Egyptian customs and laws, according to the account of Herodotus, were 'for the most part the converse of those of all other men' and required, for example, that women go out to trade, while the men remain at home weaving.[61] Similarly, Diodorus Siculus (who lived in Egypt between 60 and 56 BC and wrote his universal history at Rome in the period of the second triumvirate) imputed to the worship of Isis Egypt's now notorious gender reversals: 'This, they say, is the reason that it was handed down that the queen should receive greater power and respect than the king and that, among private individuals, the woman should be master of the man, and in the dowry-contracts husbands should agree to obey the wife in all matters.'[62]

---

[56] Malaise (1972), 365–89; Zanker (1998), 109; Ciceroni (1992); Takács (1995), 75–80; Beard, North, and Price (1998), esp. 230–1 and 250.

[57] Roman abhorrence for the Egyptian theriomorphic gods is detailed in Smelik and Hemelrijk (1984), 1854–5. Cf. Malaise (1972), 211 and 246–8.

[58] Hall (1989), 1 and 50. See also Hartog (1988), 212–14, for the schema of inversion in the historiographic tradition.

[59] Macdonald (1987a), 8; Hall (1989), 201.

[60] Hall (1989), 95.

[61] Hdt. 2.35. On which, see Hartog (1988), 213; Hall (1989), 202 and 208; Smelik and Hemelrijk (1984), 1873–80; Rowlandson (1998), 3.

[62] Diod. Sic. 1.27.1–2; the translation is taken from Rowlandson (1998), 11. On the passage, see Smelik and Hemelrijk (1984), 1895–8.

Tyranny and aberrant female power are likewise the two principal features which give shape to the Egyptian queen of Augustan poetry. In the political writings of the late republic, the championship of *libertas* [liberty] against the threat of *seruitus* [servitude] or *regnum* [monarchy] became the validating slogan for insurrection. After Actium, *libertas* was appropriated (and redefined as a form of *securitas* [security]) to validate the incipient autocracy, so that Augustus commenced his *Res Gestae* with a claim to have liberated the republic.[63] Confronting long-standing constructions of oriental tyranny with the republican slogan of liberty, the poetic narratives of Actium construct an anomalous and eroticized female despotism by which the *libertas* of the Roman male is dangerously imperilled. If, in *Epode* 9, the Antonian soldier is in bondage to a woman (*emancipatus feminae*, 9.12) and in service to wrinkled eunuchs, Octavian is thereby rendered the champion of male liberty in the Actian sea-battle, seeking to free the Antonian slave from a woman's chains.[64] In Virgilian epic, Augustus sails into that battle made radiant by the star of his fathers – both the deified Julius Caesar and the fatherland (*patrium sidus*, *Aen.* 8.681). He is also escorted by the fathers (*patribus*, *Aen.* 8.679) and the people of all Italy and partnered by his trusted general Agrippa. Whereas, instead of the Roman fathers and a named general, Antony brings the assorted hordes of the orient and a nameless Egyptian 'wife' (*Aen.* 8.685–688).[65] In Propertian elegy, after the battle is won, sea nymphs clap the freed standards (*libera signa*, 4.6.62) of the fatherland (*patriae*, 4.6.24) which had been forced shamefully to confront a woman's javelins (*pilaque femineae turpiter apta manu*, 4.6.22), and Rome, thanks to its saviour Augustus, becomes a city no longer terrified by woman's warfare (*femineo Marte*, 3.11.58).[66] By demanding a sympotic celebration of the death of Cleopatra and a dance beaten out with a freed foot (*pede libero*, *Ode* 1.37.1), the Horatian ode points a parallel with the Alcaic celebration of the death in battle of the hated tyrant Myrsilus.[67] This time, however, death has come to a female tyrant, a *regina*, whose court once consisted of diseased men.

This persistent equation of the relation of west to east with that

---

[63] Wirszubski (1960), esp. 87–91 and 100–6; Earl (1967), 59–60 and 64; Reinhold (1988), 108; Kennedy (1992), 31; Galinsky (1996), 54–7.
[64] Otis (1968), 59; Pelling (1996), 42; Gurval (1995), 147–50.
[65] Smelik and Hemelrijk (1984), 1853–5; Quint (1989), 6–7 and 9; Hardie (1986), 98; Putnam (1998), 142; Keith (2000), 76.
[66] Mader (1989), 190–7.
[67] Otis (1968), 54–5; Nisbet and Hubbard (1970), 411; West (1995), 182–3; Lowrie (1997), 145–6; Oliensis (1998), 143: Gurval (forthcoming [2011]).

of male to female provides, within the logic of ancient orientalism and gender, the necessary authority for domination and conquest.[68] The womanish easterners enthralled by their Egyptian queen need imposed upon them the masculine order of the west, embodied in the figure of Octavian/Augustus.[69] A sense of urgency then attends the whole process for, following the orientalist pattern that calls for the west's control of the east in order to stop the east's designs on the west,[70] the Capitol is depicted as compelled to conquer Cleopatra in order to prevent Cleopatra's plans for subjecting it (*Ode* 1.37.5–12, Prop. 3.11.39–46).

In the Augustan narratives, Cleopatra is a nameless, scarcely individuated *meretrix regina*, a dangerous anomaly who represents the 'otherness' of the east and whose characteristics thereby lend poetic authority to the supremacy of the west. Positive images of the political power of women were not, however, entirely alien to the Roman state. Precisely in this same period, a representational language was being developed for some specific women as good servants of Rome's political interests, despite a republican historiographic tradition that had deployed women in possession of political power as signifiers of moral decline and the breakdown of social order. Whether, for example, the participation of Sallust's Sempronia in the Catilinarian conspiracy of 63 BC is an historiographic fiction or the documentation of an elite woman's genuine political interests, her characterization in *Bellum Catilinae* 25 underscores the dubious character of the conspiracy and demonstrates by counterpart its leader's lack of *virtus*. Sempronia's departure from the matronly norm expected of a consul's wife into the domain of political intrigue is categorized in terms of financial extravagance, an aggressive sexuality (her desires were so ardent that she sought men more often than she was sought by them), and transgressions of gender; Sempronia was, in sum, a woman 'who had often committed many crimes of masculine daring' (*quae multa saepe uirilis audaciae facinora conmiserat*, 25.1)[71] In the early principate, even members of the imperial family such as Augustus' wife Livia and his daughter Julia, who were shaped by the state machinery as paragons of the wifely virtues, could attract the charge of excessive political authority (especially in the matter of

---

[68] Cf. Said (1985), 206 and 309 on the discourses of modern orientalism.
[69] Quint (1989), 8–9 and 21.
[70] See Hall (1989), 195–7.
[71] See Paul (1985); Boyd (1987); Bauman (1992), 67–8; Hemelrijk (1999), 84–6 and 90; Wyke (2002), ch. 1. For the collocation of social and political disorder with transgressions of gender roles in the cultural discourses of Augustan Rome, see also Wallace-Hadrill (1985); Edwards (1993); Bauman (1992), esp. 10–11.

control over the dynastic succession) and with it the invective pattern of promiscuity and poisoning.[72]

Nonetheless, in the 30s BC, a language was being created to endorse the role of specific women in Roman political activity. Already, shortly after the marriage of Antony and Octavian's sister in 39 BC, silver cistophori and gold aurei were minted in the east to commemorate the treaty of Brundisium that the marriage had been designed to seal. Innovatively Antony's coinage celebrates Octavia's role in forging a political alliance by displaying her head on the reverse, his on the obverse.[73] It is also clear that, in the years immediately preceding Actium, still more audacious attempts were made by Antony to incorporate Cleopatra within Roman political structures and, particularly, to exploit her authority in the east within Roman systems for designating and sustaining power.

Two sets of coin types disclose the distinct techniques employed by Cleopatra and Antony to integrate each other into their respective political and iconographic systems. One series of bronze coins from Chalcis, dated around 31 BC, has Cleopatra for its mint authority. A portrait head of the queen appears on the obverse accompanied by her name and title BASILISSES; on the reverse appears a type of Antony, who is evidently the subordinate figure of the pair since it is Cleopatra's regnal year 21 which is inscribed first around Antony's portrait head, instead of year six of a new dating system designed to declare their joint sovereignty over the east and Rome.[74] Another series, this time of silver denarii, dated around 32 BC, has Antony for its mint authority (Fig. 11.2). A head of Antony appears on the obverse with an Armenian tiara behind him and the legend ANTONI ARMENIA DEVICTA (of Antony, Armenia conquered). The coinage is linked iconographically to the republican tradition for signalling Roman victories over eastern despotism. On the reverse, however, there appears a portrait of Cleopatra redesigned to look like her Roman patron's, yet crowned with a diadem and accompanied by the legend CLEOPATRAE REGINAE REGUM FILIORUM REGUM (of Cleopatra, Queen of Kings and of her Sons who are Kings). A ship's prow lies in the foreground. While Cleopatra's coinage attempts to

---

[72] See Purcell (1989) [= Chapter 5, above]; Richlin (1992); Bauman (1992), 99–129; Bartman (1999), 35–40; Hemelrijk (1999), 80–1; Wood (1999), 38–9 and 75–141. Cf. Wyke (2002), ch. 9, on historiographic accounts of the political intrigues and sexual excesses of the empress Messalina.

[73] Carson and Sutherland (1956), 151–2; Kleiner (1992), 361–3; Bartman (1999), 59 and 213–14; Wood (1999), 41–51.

[74] Brett (1937), 460–61. *BMC Phoenicia*, 54 no. 15 and pl. 7.10, identifies the origin of the coinage as Berytus, but see Burnett et al. (1990), n. 4771.

Fig. 11.2. Silver denarius of Antony, dated *c.* 32 BC

endorse Antony's role in the east by assimilating it to the Ptolemaic dynastic system, Antony's coinage attempts, remarkably and paradoxically, to incorporate Cleopatra's royal powers and dynastic ambitions within Roman republican strategies for designating a general's triumph: a client queen's Egyptian ships have brought aid to another Roman victory over oriental tyranny (for which she and her sons have been rewarded with additional territories by the triumvir).[75]

It was apparently to counter such extraordinary moves as these (and motivated most immediately by Antony's rejection of Octavia when she visited him in Greece to supply troops) that from 35 BC there began to accrue to Octavian's sister and to his wife extraordinary and innovative honours which served to elevate them both above other Roman *matronae*, and to distinguish them from Antony's Egyptian *meretrix*. They were provided with freedom from *tutela* [legal guardianship], tribunician sacrosanctity, and public statuary – the latter connected in the past almost exclusively with male service to the state. If, as has been conjectured, the statues of Octavia and Livia were placed on public display in the temple of Venus Genetrix near that of Cleopatra, they would have provided viewers with an opportunity to make tangible and unfavourable comparison between the gilded whore of Antony's Egypt and the loyal wives of Octavian's Rome.[76] During the course of the prin-

---

[75] *BMCRR* 2, no. 180. See Volkmann (1958), 148; Kent (1978), 275; Smith (1998b), 132–4 and pl. 75.21-4; Smith (1991), 209; Lindsay (1971), 56–60; Kleiner (1992), 364–5; Hamer (1993), 8–10; Pelling (1996), 41; Wood (1999), 46; Southern (1999), 113–16; Rice (1999), 56–7 and 98.

[76] Volkmann (1958), 138; Purcell (1986), 85 [= Chapter 5, above p. 176]; Bauman (1992), 91–8; Flory (1993); Bartman (1999), 62–7; Wood (1999), 27–35.

cipate, Livia was to become assimilated to personifications of *iustitia* [justice] and *pax* [peace] on Augustan coinage and the *Ara Pacis* reliefs of 9 BC, and marked out as an emblem of chastity and marital harmony, fertility, and prosperity. By the final years of the regime, Livia would even be appealed to in poetry as the *Romana princeps* [first lady of Rome], a guide to the appropriate public virtues for women. The most important woman in the Augustan state thus became identified gradually as a model of chaste womanhood, the first wife and mother, and a benefactor of family life, in a manner that (somewhat ironically) closely resembles Ptolemaic strategies for validating female rule.[77]

Any attempt to accommodate Cleopatra within Roman systems for political validation and to justify her public powers in these new Roman terms would, however, have been fraught with difficulty, because her state functions extended far beyond the limits that were being laid down carefully even for Livia (as benefactor, mediator, and mother of the people). While Livia was only ever associated with victory and carefully distanced from acts of war or their triumphal aftermath,[78] the Ptolemaic queen exercised authority in the military sphere.

Within Roman discursive systems, a militant woman was traditionally and persistently a transgressive figure, a non-woman or a pseudo-man, who overturned all established codes of social behaviour. The patterns of invective which could be brought to bear on a specific woman operating in the military domain can be seen at play in the abuse heaped on Antony's previous wife, Fulvia, when in 40 BC she summoned reinforcements for his brother besieged in Perusia. Sling-bullets employed during the siege of Perusia, the *glandes Perusinae*, are inscribed with insults against both sides, but include threats of sexual assault against Fulvia such as *Fuluiae landicam peto* (I aim at Fulvia's cunt). An epigram of Martial (11.20), which claims to quote a poem composed by Octavian himself at the time of the battle, follows a similar pattern, denigrating Fulvia's military activities through her supposedly parallel sexual initiatives. Fulvia, portrayed as jealous of her husband's philandering with Cleopatra, demands of Octavian *aut futue, aut pugnemus* (fuck me or let's fight). The battle of Perusia then takes place only to ensure

---

[77] Purcell (1986) [= Chapter 5 above]; Bauman (1992), 124–9; Bartman (1999), esp. 72–101; Wood (1999), 75–141.
[78] Bartman (1999), 84–6.

the continued health of Octavian's *mentula* [prick].⁷⁹ In subsequent historiographic texts, Fulvia's participation in warfare is bound up closely with fictions of the 'non-woman'. According to Velleius Paterculus, the only part of the militant Fulvia that was female was her anatomy: *nihil muliebre praeter corpus* (2.74.2). Plutarch's Fulvia not only lacks due feminine interest in spinning and housekeeping, but plays the man in wishing to rule the ruler and command the commander: *archontos archein, strategountos strategein* (*Ant.* 10.3). The potential for this form of invective to be transferred wholesale to the figure of Cleopatra is fully realized in Plutarch's biography of Antony, where his wife passes on to his whore a man already thoroughly trained in the habits of *gynaikokratia* (feminine rule).⁸⁰

The Horatian, Virgilian, and Propertian Cleopatras can seem to operate within precisely such invective patterns as these. Their Egyptian queen transgresses all the social and political constraints which Roman society imposed (ideally) upon its women. Operating outside cultural structures construed as 'natural', she is a fatal monstrosity (*fatale monstrum, Ode* 1.37.21), both deadly and doomed.⁸¹ Nameless, in possession of no individuating physical features, represented largely in terms of political, religious, ethnic, and gender difference, the Cleopatras of Augustan poetry can be read as part of a narrative of Actium and Alexandria which turns Roman civil war into an heroic Caesar's fight against tyranny, female dominance, and the perils of the orient. The poetic reification of Cleopatra renders her a suitable second term in the binary oppositions between west and east, male and female, which these texts appear to articulate.⁸²

AUGUSTAN VICTORY

There are aspects of the Augustan poems, however, which do not seem to be straightforwardly critical of Cleopatra nor unambiguously supportive of Octavian. Many critics have hesitated over the double poetic similes which lead into the second half of the Horatian

---

[79] Hallett (1977), 154–5 and 160–3; Lindsay (1971), 171–6; Welch (1995), 193–4; Galinsky (1996), 372; Pelling (1996), 16.

[80] Volkmann (1958), 96; Bauman (1992), 83–9; Hemelrijk (1999), 90–1; Bartman (1999), 58–9.

[81] Pomeroy (1984), 26–7.

[82] See Quint (1989), 3–4, on the Roman texts. The Greek conceptual system of hierarchical oppositions based on male/female is discussed by DuBois (1982). Maclean (1980) surveys its impact on the Renaissance structuring of femininity. See also Said (1985), 7, on orientalism; Greene and Kahn (1985), 3–4, on gender; Yeğenoğlu (1998) on the importance of their intersection.

ode on Cleopatra's defeat (1.37.17–20), where the hawk and the soft doves, the hunter and the hare, illustrate Octavian's pursuit of Cleopatra across the sea from Actium back to Egypt. Some have read the next stanza's *fatale monstrum / quae* (1.37.21) as a pivotal phrase that now turns the reader's point of view and sympathies away from the cruel Roman hunter and toward his defenceless quarry, restoring to the 'fateful marvel' humanity, gender, nobility, and courageous agency.[83] As noted at the opening of this chapter, Jasper Griffin has argued that the first-person, authorial voice of the Propertian elegy 3.11 effectively pushes the love poet into the role of an Antony who willingly accepts submission to his dominating beloved. For the poem employs Cleopatra as an example of the kind of woman who can hold men like the narrator voluntarily enchained.[84]

More tentatively, Page duBois has explored the implications of the ekphrastic narration of Roman history in the *Aeneid* – a verbal description of visual images on a shield – and observes that the poetic convention allows the epic hero (who gazes on the shield) to mediate the audience's relationship to narrated history, and places in the foreground the hero's act of incomprehension; while Robert Gurval has argued that, despite its exaltation of Actium as a cosmic struggle for order over chaos, *Aeneid* 8 locates the frightful gods Mars, Dirae, Discordia, and Bellona (War, Furies, Discord, and Battle) neither on one side nor the other, but at the centre of the struggle.[85] Propertius 4.6 has been read as a witty parody of the triumphal celebration of Actium, or at least as a depiction of a winnerless victory since it entails merely the defeat of a woman.[86] Even Horace's *Epode* 9, which has generally been read as an unequivocal and immediate celebration of Antony's flight from Actium, has been closely scrutinized by Gurval for potential political ambivalence: introduced as a *mixtum carmen* (a poem of shifting tones, 9.5), it opens optimistically but ends with the enemy not yet captured, the narrator fearful for the renewal of civil war.[87]

In seeking to put these apparent poetic ambiguities or ambivalences into an historical context, it is important to note that surviving depictions of Cleopatra occur at Rome only in the *poetry* composed

---

[83] As e.g. Commager (1958); Johnson (1967); Otis (1968), 51; Mader (1989), 184–8; DeForest (1989); Monaco (1992), 263; Hendry (1993), 143–7; West (1995), 187–91; Oliensis (1998), 139–45; Gurval (forthcoming [2011]). Cf., more cautiously, Lowrie (1997), 150–64.
[84] Griffin (1985), 32–47. Cf. discussions of the political ambivalence of Prop. 3.11 in Mader (1989), 188–200, and Gurval (1995), 189–207.
[85] DuBois (1982); Gurval (1995), 209–47; Putnam (1998), 119–88.
[86] Johnson (1973); Gurval (1995), 249–78.
[87] Gurval (1995), 137–59.

around and after Actium. Yet, in the aftermath of Actium, the Augustan poetry which began to create its own fictions of Cleopatra was only one of many sites that displayed and explored the new powers and political authority vested in the *princeps*. After Octavian's victories at Actium and Alexandria, his ascendancy was also articulated through civic ceremonies and religious rituals, through the changing topography of the city of Rome, through new monuments, coin types, inscriptions, and testimonials that proclaimed Augustus himself as their author.[88] Yet, where we might expect to find attempts to produce wholly unambiguous images of Octavian's victory, in these state rituals, monuments, coins, or inscriptions, Cleopatra scarcely figures at all.

Augustan poetry and, therefore, its fictive Cleopatras should not be read in isolation from the whole system of discourses within which validation of Augustan autocracy was played out. Firstly, the Augustan state itself continually recognized the word and, specifically, the poem as a tool for sustaining political power. According to the evidence of the later historians and biographers such as Suetonius, from the death of Julius Caesar in 44 BC to the suicide of Antony in 30 BC, graffiti, lampoons, letters, speeches, pamphlets, and edicts were all employed as instruments in the pursuit of political power.[89] After the initial deployment of invective to undermine the credibility of Antony, and after the declaration of war against Cleopatra in October 32 BC for which legitimacy was sought through the re-enactment of an ancient (perhaps even fabricated) fetial ritual,[90] the post-Actian period witnessed numerous instances of the spoken word and the displayed text employed to buttress the new regime. Most pervasively, the personal name 'Augustus', once voted by the senate and people in 27 BC, lent to the *princeps* a sacred aura of venerability on every repetition as one divinely bestowed with the power to foster growth.[91] Official narratives, stamped with the authority of an Augustus who speaks for himself in the first person, were prepared and publicized throughout the relevant period: an autobiography was composed to deny any usurption of power, and this was followed by the monumental *Res Gestae*. Itself both word and image, the *Res Gestae* was engraved on two bronze columns and

---

[88] Brunt and Moore (1967); Yavetz (1984); Millar and Segal (1984); Zanker (1988), 79–339; Reinhold (1988); Gurval (1995); Galinsky (1996); Habinek and Schiesaro (1997).
[89] See esp. Scott (1929) and (1933); Charlesworth (1933); Zanker (1988), 33–77; Pelling (1996).
[90] See Reinhold (1981–2); Reinhold (1988), 94; Volkmann (1958), 170; Pelling (1996), 54.
[91] Millar (1984), 37; Galinsky (1996), 315–18.

displayed in front of Augustus' Mausoleum as a permanent epigraphic key for understanding the other visual displays of Augustan achievement by which it was surrounded.[92]

Testimony to a belief in the persuasive powers of oracular poetry is to be found both in the new location provided for the Sibylline books and in the constraints attached to their consultation. Recopied in 18 BC, and transferred by Augustus six years later to two gilded bookcases deposited in the base of Apollo's cult statue in the new Palatine temple, the *libri Sibyllini* [Sibylline books] were brought physically adjacent to the residence of Augustus and effectively under his jurisdiction. Consulted only by decree of the senate, the political importance of these texts was both manifest and unparalleled.[93] Yet the establishment of a library adjoining the Palatine temple, to house works in both Greek and Latin (and in later years to hold meetings of the senate), demonstrates that a much broader range of literature was also subjected to Augustus' public ratification and formed part of a strategy for his own cultural accreditation.[94] Furthermore, any sharp distinctions in Augustan culture between the propagandist possibilities of monument, religious ritual, and poetic production would have been blurred at least temporarily when, in 17 BC, a Horatian choral ode (the *Carmen Saeculare*) was performed first before Apollo's temple on the Palatine and then before Jupiter's on the Capitoline as the culminating point of the three-day celebration of the Secular Games, of which Augustus, along with Agrippa, was the chief officiant. An oracle calculating the length of a *saeculum*, cataloguing the order of the ceremonies, and specifying the performance of a choral hymn had conveniently been found in the recopied Sibylline books.[95]

Secondly, while the Augustan state can recognize the political strength of poetry alongside that of rituals and monuments, Augustan poetry often ascribes to itself a parity with those same rituals and monuments, or even offers itself as a challenge to their presumed superiority.[96] A passage of Virgil's *Georgics*, most likely written around the time of the triple triumph of 29 BC and the dedication of the Palatine temple to Apollo in 28 BC, deploys metaphors of a triumph and a temple to characterize an envisaged epic narrative

---

[92] Elsner (1996). Cf. Yavetz (1984).
[93] Parke (1988), 141; Collins (1983), 319–20; White (1993), 124; Galinsky (1996), 102 and 216.
[94] Galinsky (1996), 218; Yavetz (1984), 32 n. 131.
[95] See Fraenkel (1957), 364–82; Zanker (1988), 167–72; White (1993), 123–7; Galinsky (1996), 100–6; Feeney (1998), 28–38 [reprinted in Ando (2003), ch. 5].
[96] See Fowler (2000), 193–217.

as a Caesarian temple of poetry and its poet as a triumphator, parading a hundred chariots before it in victory games (3.10–36). In the metaphoric idioms of the Horatian and Propertian texts, lyrics are a loftier monument than pyramids (*Odes* 3.30.1–5), and elegiacs are more lasting (Prop. 3.2.17–26).[97] The Augustan poems categorize themselves as social acts rather than personal artforms when they address directly Maecenas, Augustus, or the Roman populace at large. They also characterize their poets as priests or prophets of public ceremonial, rather than as private artists, when they use the title *uates* [seer].[98]

The poetic narratives of Cleopatra's defeat themselves dissolve distinctions between ritual, monument, and poem. The Horatian Cleopatras of *Epode* 9 and *Ode* 1.37 appear in the context of a call for the ritual, sympotic celebration of victory. The Propertian elegy 3.11 offers its own verbal simulacrum of Cleopatra at the same time as it makes its poet witness to the ritual display of her visual simulacrum in the triumphal procession of 29 BC. As part of an ekphrasis on the shield of Aeneas, the Cleopatra of Virgilian epic takes on material shape and monumental proportions. Similarly, the subsequent and dependent elegiac Cleopatra of Propertius 4.6 appears within a poetic aetiology of an Augustan monument (the ubiquitous temple of Apollo on the Palatine) and within a narrative which describes itself simultaneously as poetic performance and act of ritual worship. Thus, at the precise points where the Ptolemaic queen enters Augustan poetry as the *meretrix regina*, those narratives relate the poetic to both ritual and monumental celebrations of Roman victory.

Augustan poetry thus *demands* comparison with other contemporary discursive mechanisms for the propagation of an image of the principate. Ever since Ronald Syme claimed, in *The Roman Revolution* (1939), that the Augustan poets were merely fulfilling a requirement to design formulas by which the Roman elite could accept the new regime, the relationship between poetry and the *princeps* in the post-Actium period has been much debated.[99] Many critics have observed that, on Syme's model, literature and art concede second place to politics: Augustan culture can only be responsive, for (or, more infrequently, against) Augustus. In

---

[97] Vance (1973), 112; White (1993), 175–7; Galinsky (1996), 240, 275, and 350–1; Kraggerud (1998), 1–20; Habinek (1998), 110–14.

[98] Santirocco (1986), 22.

[99] A representative sample would include Powell (1992), White (1993), Gurval (1995), Galinsky (1996), Barchiesi (1997), Habinek (1998), Fowler (2000), 173–92.

The Roman Cultural Revolution (1997), Thomas Habinek and Alessandro Schiesaro have called for a more holistic approach to Augustan cultural production – as Augustan poetry itself demands – in which culture ceases to be construed as a purely aesthetic activity independent from, and subordinate to, politics. Augustan culture is instead a process, and a set of intersecting practices and discourses: verbal and visual, closer to or more distant from the orbit of the *princeps*. On this definition, Augustan poetry does not merely reproduce the propaganda of Augustus, but refracts, interrogates, or even enables the social, political, and economic changes that were taking place under the new regime. In order better to analyse whether the Cleopatras of Augustan poetry are refractions, interrogations, subversions, or creations of the new cultural order, it is therefore necessary to compare them to other mechanisms for representing the victor and the vanquished in the post-Actium period, mechanisms to which they allude and respond.

Outside the narratives of the Augustan poets, most of our evidence for ancient constructions of Cleopatra as vanquished enemy of the *res publica* comes from historians and biographers such as Velleius Paterculus, Plutarch, or Dio.[100] These historiographic works reproduce, in one form or another, the same chauvinisms of sex and race as appear in the Augustan poetry-books. The speech which Dio assigns Octavian before the commencement of battle at Actium, for example, encourages the Roman soldiers to fight on two counts; because the opposing commander is an Egyptian woman (and it would be unworthy of the Roman ancestors who overthrew the likes of Pyrrhus, Philip, Perseus, and Antiochus for their descendants to be trodden underfoot by a female), and because the opposing armies are Egyptian (and it would be disgraceful to bear the insults of the sort of people who are a woman's slaves). Cleopatra once again is mannish and her orientalized Antony unmanned.[101]

Yet it is difficult to extract from these later accounts Cleopatra's precise function in the consolidation of Augustus' position at Rome during the years immediately after his victory.[102] In the absence of substantial extracts of both Augustus' autobiography and contemporary prose histories, few later statements regarding his direct propagandist strategies can now be corroborated except, perhaps, by

---

[100] For which see, respectively, Woodman (1983); Pelling (1988); Reinhold (1988). The full range of texts are reviewed by Becher (1966).

[101] Dio 50.24.3–7. Cf. Vell. Pat. 2.87.1 and Plut. *Life of Ant.* 53–5. See Reinhold (1988), 109–10; Brenk (1992), 160; Flamarion (1997), 82–3.

[102] As Tarn (1931), 173.

their widespread repetition: in one case, we are told by Dio's history that Augustus claimed Antony's Roman legions were made to guard Cleopatra's palace in Alexandria (50.5.1) and by Servius' commentary on the *Aeneid* that this claim appeared in Augustus' own account of the period (*ad Aen.* 8.696). The later prose narratives, moreover, are often composed for a different audience of Greeks in the east and shaped by the political perspectives, analogical interests, and literary traditions (such as the Greek romance) of different cultures and centuries.[103] Finally, in both ancient and modern studies, lurid depictions of Antony's captivation and Cleopatra's suicide have a tendency to overshadow the few details which the texts also supply for Cleopatra's propagandist functions in the immediate post-Actian phase of celebration and consolidation.

As part of a propagandist scheme closely associated with Augustus himself, most attention seems to have been focused on Cleopatra in a limited period immediately before and after the battle of Actium, when she appears within a larger discursive pattern of political agitation that articulates Octavian's pursuit and achievement of power as a war of liberation by Italy against an external, eastern enemy.[104] In the many public rituals and ceremonies of this period, Cleopatra has an integral function only in the declaration of war and the triumphal celebration. Several of the ancient historians agree that in October 32 BC war was declared formally against Cleopatra alone, using the full panoply of fetial rites, and thus was proclaimed a national crusade in defence of *Romanitas* ['Romanness'], the West, and the Male Principle.[105] Similarly, during the triple triumph of August 29 BC, celebrated for victories over Illyria, at Actium, and (climactically) in Egypt, an effigy of Cleopatra is said to have been present in the parade of the vanquished, in addition to two of her surviving children, Alexander Helios and Cleopatra Selene.[106]

All the other surviving evidence suggests that, in the public celebrations of Actium, victory and the struggle to obtain it were signified by more abstract tokens – it was Egypt or the east, not a specific Ptolemaic queen, that had been defeated. It was the day of Alexandria's capture (and Antony's death), not the day of Cleopatra's suicide, which was declared a holiday by resolution of the senate, and

---

[103] Reinhold (1988), 6–7; Pelling (1988), 8; Brenk (1992); Pelling (1996), 4.
[104] On which, see Galinsky (1996), 39–41.
[105] Plut. *Ant.* 60.1; Suet. *Aug.* 31; Dio 50.4.4, 6.1, 26.3–4. See Reinhold (1981–2), 102; Flamarion (1997), 80–1.
[106] Dio 51.21.7–8; Prop. 3.11.53–4. See Gurval (1995), 4–5 and 19–36; Hamer (1993), 20–1.

the day of Octavian's entry into that city was recorded publicly in the *Fasti* as one on which he had saved the state not from the clutches of a female despot but simply from 'terrible danger' (*rem public. tristiss. periculo liberauit*).[107] The monumental taxonomy of domination which constitutes the *Res Gestae* follows a similar pattern of abstraction. Not one of Augustus' opponents appears in it by name. Sextus Pompeius becomes an anonymous pirate supported by runaway slaves, and Antony a faction. Cleopatra, however, is rendered completely impersonal – a territory rather than a political party – when her defeat becomes the addition of Egypt to the empire of the Roman people (*Aegyptum imperio populi Romani adieci*, RG 27.1).[108]

There is also little evidence to suggest that Cleopatra had a role to play in the monumental iconography which featured so significantly in Augustus' refurbished Rome. The Palatine temple to Apollo which was dedicated on 9 October 28 BC (and which has often been interpreted as the most visible and prominent monument to the Actian victory in Rome) commemorated victory exclusively in the abstract or mythological idioms of Apollo's achievement as saviour and divine avenger of mortal hybris. A votive statue of the god before the temple signalled victory at sea metonymically, in the shape of ships' prows, while the depiction in ivory on the temple doors of Apollo's rout of the Gauls at Delphi in 278 BC and his mythic slaughter of the Niobids constitutes at best a veiled metaphor for or allegory of Octavian's divinely sanctioned defeat of Antony, as does the depiction on terracotta plaques of Apollo confronting Hercules.[109] Similarly, the statues of the Danaids (set between the columns of the temple portico according to Propertius 2.13) could only at best allude indirectly to the conquest of Egypt, and even the detail of their allegorical function has been much disputed. While, for some, the gender of the Danaids, their Graeco-Egyptian ethnicity, and their traditional condemnation in art and literature for the impious slaughter of their husbands might evoke Cleopatra, for others their earlier function as prototypes of the Greeks battling against the barbarous other (enacted in Aeschylus' *Suppliants*) renders the slaughter of their

---

[107] For references to the appropriate Augustan documents see Volkmann (1958), 213; Tarn and Charlesworth (1934), 108 and n. 3; Gurval (1995), 19–85.
[108] Brunt and Moore (1967), 2; Gurval (1995), 15–16 and 146; Elsner (1996), 39–40.
[109] See Zanker (1988), 85–9; Kellum (1997), 159–61; Fantham (1997), 127–8. Gurval (1995), 213–24 argues that such imagery would have been resonant beyond any immediate reference to Actium.

Egyptian relatives an evocation and legitimation of civil war between the western Octavian and the eastern Antony.[110] The statues and reliefs belonging to the temple of Apollo focus on the quality of divine victory over anonymous hubristic hordes or purge, through myth, the conflicts of Roman civil war, but they do not focus, as does Augustan poetry, on the mortal specifics of a particular Ptolemaic queen's defeat. Here Cleopatra is concealed rather than revealed as Rome's enemy.

The precise design and location in Rome of an arch to commemorate the Actian victory are still much disputed. This renders its identification with arches illustrated on some denarii equally contentious. If, as is generally the case, the Actian arch is thought to have been single-vaulted, it may be identifiable with a coin type that displays an arch crowned by a triumphant statuary group of Octavian standing in a quadriga, and exhibiting additionally only disembodied standards on its socles. A high degree of abstraction would then be attached to the monumental iconography for victory. Moreover, it is now disputed whether such an arch was ever erected, and archaeological study of the *forum Romanum* suggests that, if erected, it was soon supplanted by a much grander, triple-vaulted arch celebrating Rome's triumph over Parthia.[111]

Aligned with other public discourses of the principate explicitly through their illustration of monuments or ritual acts or literary topoi (such as the departure of Aeneas from Troy), and minted to pay the army and generally to support the economic life of both Italy and the provinces, coins nevertheless were not the foremost instruments of Augustus' validation at Rome. Coin types and their slogans which proclaimed military success often relied for comprehension on the detail provided previously by the celebration of a triumph. Nevertheless, Augustan coins were invested with substantial discursive power and were designed to draw on images of maximum political potency.[112] Yet no coin throughout this period depicts a vanquished Cleopatra.

Of the coins minted during the triumviral period and the early principate many depict the victor of a sea-battle or the fruits of victory, but nowhere is Cleopatra a part of the victory symbolism.

---

[110] Contrast Kellum (1997), 159–61 with Galinsky (1996), 220–2. Gurval (1995), 124–6, argues instead that the sanctuary simply honoured Apollo and the myths associated with him.

[111] See Nash (1961), 92–101; Coarelli (1985), 258–308; Nedergaard (1988); Hannestad (1988), 58–62; Reinhold (1988), 146; Gurval (1995), 5, 8, and 36–47.

[112] See Wallace-Hadrill (1986), 68–70, for this description of the status of coins. Cf. Consigliere (1978), 7–11 and 120–1.

Fig. 11.3. Coin issued to celebrate the Actian victory

There appear, instead, impersonal tokens such as ships' prows and marine creatures, divine patrons such as Venus and Apollo, or personifications such as Victory standing on a globe. So impersonal is the typology and so detached from the specific features of the sea-battle at Actium that it is difficult to distinguish it (if at all) from that designed to celebrate Octavian's earlier sea-battle at Naulochus in 36 BC.[113] One coin type shows, standing on a ship's prow, a copy of the 'Victory of Samothrace' – a statue which the Macedonian Antigonus had set up to commemorate his victory over Ptolemy II at Cos (Fig. 11.3). If it can be reliably dated to the post-Actium period, the design implies that Actium belongs to a celebrated tradition of victories over the Ptolemaic dynasty, but suppresses any detail of that dynasty's most recent representative and subsumes the queen Cleopatra into a more comfortable history of victory over kings.[114] On coins which celebrate the capture of Egypt (and can, therefore, be more reliably dated), it is a crocodile that takes Cleopatra's place. Some rare gold and silver coins dated to 28–27 BC, but of uncertain mint, display a head of the then Octavian Caesar on their obverse and, on the reverse, carry the legend AEGYPT. CAPTA accompanied by a crocodile (Fig. 11.4).[115] Similarly, abundant coppers from the mint at Nîmes which were distributed widely through the west in the period 10 BC to AD 14 display on the reverse a captive crocodile and a palm tree and, on the obverse, heads of Augustus and Agrippa.[116]

Victories at Actium and in Egypt, and the forces ranged at that

---

[113] Sutherland and Carson (1984), 30–1; Zanker (1988), 82; Gurval (1995), 8–9 and 47–65.
[114] *BMC* 1, nos. 616 and 617. Tarn (1931), 179–83; Tarn and Charlesworth (1934), 113; Hannestad (1988), 57; Simon (1986), 84; Kent (1978), 18–19 and pl. 35.123.
[115] *BMC* 1, no. 655, and cf. nos. 650–4. See also Kent (1978) no. 124; Wallace-Hadrill (1986), 68; Sutherland and Carson (1984), 38; Gurval (1995), 64.
[116] Sutherland and Carson (1984), 26–7 and pl. 3.154–5.

Fig. 11.4. Coin issued in celebration of the capture of Egypt, dated *c.* 28–27 BC

time against Octavian, are all depicted, in this iconographic pattern, in terms of material or animal tokens, divine personifications, or – more distantly still – in terms of illustrations of monumental depictions of tokens and personifications. They are never depicted in terms of vanquished opponents or suppliant peoples. Yet opponents and peoples do appear in Augustan coin types signifying conquests and submissions when those conquests and submissions have ceased to be associated with either Cleopatra or Antony. The supplicating barbarian, for example, becomes an especially popular image after the restoration of the Roman standards from Parthia in 20 BC, an event which is far more personalized in the *Res Gestae* than was the conquest of Egypt: 'I forced the Parthians to restore to me the spoils and standards of three Roman armies and to ask as suppliants for the friendship of the Roman people' (29.2). The triple-vaulted Parthian arch (thought to have soon replaced the simpler 'Actian' arch in the Roman forum) was elaborately carved with suppliant bowmen and slingers.[117] Large numbers of denarii issued at Rome show on the obverse the head of a divinity such as *Liber* or *Honos* and on the reverse the legend CAESAR AUGUSTUS SIGN. RECE. (Caesar Augustus, the standards restored) accompanied by the type of a bareheaded Parthian – perhaps king Phraates himself – who kneels in breeches and cloak offering a standard and holding out his left hand in supplication.[118] The installation of a client king in Armenia was also commemorated in a coin series minted at Rome in 18 BC, showing the head of *Liber* on the obverse and, on the reverse, the legend CAESAR DIVI F. ARME. CAPT. (Caesar, son of the Divine, Armenia

---

[117] Galinsky (1996), 155–6; Gurval (1995), 282.
[118] BMC I, nos. 10–17 and 56–8; Zanker (1988), 183–92. Cf. Kent (1978), 277–8 and no. 131.

captured) accompanied by the type of an Armenian king who, wearing the tiara and long robe that signified an eastern monarch, kneels and extends both hands in a gesture of submission.[119]

Although this intersecting network of rituals, monuments, coins, and writings testifies to the importance of military victories and conquests in Augustus' claims to power,[120] there seems to be a certain hesitancy in authorizing the political ascendancy of the *princeps* through the representation of a specific woman as vanquished opponent. The discourses of power most closely supervised by Octavian and the subsequent Augustan state are not static but change through time. The agitational rhetoric of the triumviral period of the 30s BC changes, in the post-Actium period, into a more restrained rhetoric of integration that would allow for both the legitimation of new government and the reconciliation of former foes. In this shifting scheme, Cleopatra herself carries only a brief ideological potency centred around the time of the military campaigns, and by the time of the triumphs in 29 BC is already being subsumed into a less problematic celebration of the conquest of Egypt. Even that conquest gradually ceases to possess its original political resonance, being replaced soon after 20 BC by 'the suppliant Parthian' as a more pervasive representation of surrender to Augustan military might.[121] In the post-Actium period, no lasting image of Cleopatra has survived in the discourses of power closest to the *princeps*. Within the framework of the representation of Actium and Alexandria as moments of victory in a war of liberation from the tyranny of the east, the Roman Antony could not be represented, but neither, it would seem, could Cleopatra. In games, festivals, libations, dedications, public statuary and monuments, there are only Apollos and Victories, and a general triumphant, while ships' prows and crocodiles stand in for the actual opponents. Why, then, does Cleopatra VII appear so briefly in the most 'official' victory symbolism?

THE PROBLEMATIC FEMALE

One explanation for the abstraction of the coin types which celebrate Actium and Egypt lies in the evident gendering of the iconography of victory and the vanquished which traditionally occurred in Roman coin issues. Coins which mark conquest or submission disclose a

---

[119] *BMC* 1, nos. 18 and 19, and Hannestad (1988), 55. Cf. *BMC* 1, nos. 43 and 44.
[120] Smith (1987), 98; Zanker (1988), 185.
[121] Gurval (1995), esp. 135–6. Cf. Yavetz (1984), 1–5; Feeney (1992), 1–2.

Fig. 11.5. Coin issued in celebration of Julius Caesar's Gallic victories, dated *c.* 48 BC

spectrum of types ranging from named enemies through to material tokens and personifications of Victory. In that spectrum, representations of women are more closely aligned with the general than the particular.

One of the earliest examples of a coin type which marks the specific military achievements of a living magistrate is a series of silver denarii minted at Rome in 58 BC jointly by M. Scaurus and P. Hypsaeus. The side devoted to Scaurus records the surrender of the Arabian king Aretas of Nabataea, who appears on his knees holding an olive branch beside a camel and is identified clearly by name.[122] Many similar designs followed, such as the silver denarii of 56 BC which were minted by Sulla's son and display on the reverse an enchained Jugurtha being surrendered by king Bocchus of Mauretania to an enthroned Sulla.[123] None such design displays a woman as the specific conquered opponent.

In the spectrum of coin types depicting conquest and submission, and in order of increasing abstraction, women first appear not in the category of 'specific opponents' but in that of 'typical prisoners' and, even here, their iconographic function is still differentiated from that of their more substantial male counterparts. An issue of denarii minted in Spain around 46–45 BC, for example, celebrates Julius Caesar's conquests in Gaul by displaying a portrait head of Venus on the obverse and, on the reverse, Gallic trophies surrounded by two figures – a kneeling or seated male whose hands are tied behind his

[122] *BMCRR* 2,591, no. 16, or *RRC* no. 422, 1b. See Kent (1978), 15 and pl. 17.60; Hannestad (1988), 26.
[123] *BMCRR* 1,471, no. 3824, or *RRC* no. 426, 1. See Hannestad (1988), 22; Kent (1978), 16 and pl. 18.69.

Fig. 11.6. Coin marking Julius Caesar's victories in Gaul, dated *c.* 48 BC

back, and a seated female who, in a gesture of grief, rests her head in her right hand. Since only the male is enchained, the female figure has been read as signifying both a captive Gaul and a grieving *Gallia*. It is then as both representative prisoner and personification of the province that the woman mourns.[124] Gallic female is similarly differentiated from Gallic male on a pair of silver denarii minted around 48 BC. On one coin, the portrait head of a bearded (and therefore barbarian) male displayed on the obverse is matched, on the reverse, with the type of a charioteer leading a naked warrior who brandishes spear and shield (Fig. 11.5). On the other coin, the portrait head of a long-haired (and therefore barbarian) female on the obverse is matched, on the reverse, with the type of Artemis, the goddess of Massalia, who holds a spear and rests her right hand on the head of a stag (Fig. 11.6).[125] While the male is associated with the ferocious military agents in Caesar's Gallic wars, the female is linked more impersonally to the symbol of an acquiescent Gallic city.

Further along the spectrum, where victory is designated by the category of 'personified countries' rather than 'typical prisoners', the female replaces the male altogether on the standard coin type. Instead of representative inhabitants of surrendered or restored territories, the coinage displays ideal female personifications of whole peoples.[126] A denarius minted at Rome in 71 BC, for example, carries on the obverse the helmeted bust of *Virtus* and, on the reverse, the legend SICIL. accompanied by an armed warrior raising up a fallen female figure. The gesture towards the woman alludes symbolically

---

[124] See Hannestad (1988), 22–3 on *RRC* no. 468, 1.
[125] *BMCRR* I, 513, nos. 3994 and 3996; *RRC* no. 448, 2a and 3. See Kent (1978), 271.
[126] See Toynbee (1934), 7–23; Smith (1988a), 71.

to the benefits conferred on Sicily by Marius, the grandfather of the minter, when he ended Sicily's second slave war.[127]

In conventional patterns for the Roman iconography of the vanquished, therefore, the female form functions largely as a personification or at best as a representative prisoner in coin types, never as a specific opponent, and her attributes characterize a nation not an individual.[128] The figure of Cleopatra VII clearly cannot fit into such a system and is absent from the coinage which pays tribute to the powers of Augustus.

This pattern for gendering the iconography of victory and the vanquished extends into every visual sphere. Thus on the breastplate of the famous statue of Augustus from Prima Porta, the centrepiece is devoted to the representation of a Parthian surrendering the standards to a Roman commander (or the god Mars) (Fig. 11.7). Persian dress, bow and quiver, and royal diadem identify the suppliant male figure as the Parthian king Phraates IV. On the edges of the breastplate, on either side of the Parthian king, appear figures of grieving females (Fig. 11.8). Their attributes, instead of marking the women as specific vanquished opponents, assist in the process of reification. The eagle-sword and the dragon-trumpet are additional signifiers of client states restored or territories captured in both east and west.[129] Thus the specific male opponent and the specific military achievement lie, literally, at the heart of a monument which sets out the anatomy of Augustan victory symbolism. The female personification and her generalized gestures remain marginalized on either side.

The relative abstraction of such 'official' discourses celebrating victory at Actium and the conquest of Egypt is, thus, explained by the requirements of victory symbolism at Rome. Depictions of Roman Antony would have resonated with civil war associations, while the Egyptian foe Cleopatra VII was highly problematic as a *female* opponent. In Rome's traditional displays of military conquest, the female functions as an abstraction, and the entire possibility of differentiating between a symbolic order of female personifications such as Victory, Justice, or the Nation Vanquished, and the actual order of soldiers, generals, and defeated foes depends largely on the absence of women from the military sphere.[130] Where war is defined as a masculine activity and highly-esteemed masculine qualities are

---

[127] *RRC* no. 401, 1. See Hannestad (1988), 23.
[128] Toynbee (1934), esp. 9–10.
[129] Zanker (1988), 188–92; Hannestad (1988), 55; Galinsky (1996), 107 and 155–64.
[130] See Warner (1987), for a more general discussion of the role of women in victory symbolism.

Fig. 11.7. Statue of Augustus from Prima Porta, detail of cuirass

attached to military pursuits, a specific female opponent is suggestive of a paired and perverse gender reversal, and she can therefore operate as a derogation of her male military opponent: Dio portrays the militant Boudicca as transgressing the bounds of normal female behaviour, and sets up her opposition to Rome as an illustration of Nero's effeminacy and Rome's social disorder.[131] Thus the delineation of a specific female opponent would fit uneasily into

---

[131] See Macdonald (1987a), 6, and (1987b), 44–5 on Dio 62.

Fig. 11.8. Detail of breastplate of statue of Augustus from Prima Porta

the intricate symbolic network of gender and imperialism which constitutes Rome's validating system for warfare, and would disturb the system's operations. If any dignity accrues to Cleopatra in the poetic description of her death at the end of Horace's *Ode* 1.37 it is, from the Roman perspective, because in her final moments she *transcends* the condition of woman – *nec muliebriter / expavit* ['she was not afraid like a woman'] (1.37.22–3).

It is not only as a result of the Roman grammar of conquest that Cleopatra VII is rendered problematic as a symbol of Augustan claims to power. The queen's suicide also generates substantial difficulties as an image of Augustan victory, for in the ideology of conquest a Roman general would kill a king in battle, or accept his submission and lead him and his children in a triumphal procession of the vanquished. Cleopatra's suicide thus denied to the triumph of 29 BC her physical presence as an assured token of that submission.[132] Some historians have argued that Cleopatra's death may have been ordered or connived at by Octavian, since (according to Dio 43.19.3–4 and Appian, *BC* 2.15.101–2) the appearance of her sister Arsinoe in the triumphal procession of Julius Caesar in 46 BC had stirred Roman spectators to sympathy rather than patriotic pride.[133] Cleopatra, however, had been constructed as the cause of war, and the story of her death by snake-bite left space for a defiant and regal figure to emerge: in prose narratives, epitomes, and commentaries, the tale is repeated that Cleopatra herself cried out against appearing in a Roman triumph; while the circumstances of her death could be read as entirely in keeping with the emblematic apparatus of the Pharoahs, a conclusive reassertion both of royalty and godhead which boldly denied that the final victory belonged to Octavian.[134]

Finally, the potential ambiguity in exposing for Roman consumption representations of the Ptolemaic queen is not lost even on ancient commentators. Dio notes that in 29 BC, by senatorial decree, Octavian removed many public dedications but not the gilded statue of Cleopatra that Julius Caesar had placed in the Temple of Venus Genetrix. Dio relishes the paradox that in continuing to display the sculpted image of the defeated queen, the Romans might yet be

---

[132] Smith (1987), 115–17, and see *RG* 4.3 for Augustus' own boast that he led nine kings or children of kings in triumph.

[133] On which, see Aly (1992), 51; Gurval (1995), 22–5.

[134] See Pelling (1988), 318–19, and (1996), 64–5, where he argues that modern scepticism about the ancient accounts of Cleopatra's death may be misplaced. Cf. Volkmann (1958), 205–7; Lindsay (1971), 431–6; Reinhold (1981–2), 136; Pomeroy (1984), 28; Hamer (1993), 21–2; Whitehorne (1994), 186–96; Marasco (1995), 320–1; Rowlandson (1998), 40–1; Southern (1999), 143–5; Gurval (forthcoming [2011]).

adding to her glorification (51.22.1–3).¹³⁵ It is as if, for Dio, the visual discourses of Augustan victory lacked the register of invective, but could only be viewed as positive assertion.¹³⁶ There inhere within the Augustan Cleopatras elements which can contradict and throw into question her once dominant ideological function at Rome as a validator of civil war. The queen can frustrate attempts at representational conquest.

Earlier in this chapter, a certain anonymity was observed in the poetic representations of Cleopatra during the years that followed Actium. She possesses no name, no individuating physical features, and none of the physical presence customarily accorded the poetic barbarian such as the golden locks and golden dress, the striped cloaks and the milky-white necks, the spear-carrying hands and the protected bodies of the Gauls who, elsewhere on the shield of Aeneas, are caught ascending the Capitol (*Aen.* 8.657–62). The extent of Cleopatra's reification, moreover, grows with time. In the later poetic narratives of the *Aeneid* and Propertius 4.6 there are no mosquito nets and no eunuchs, no drunkenness or sexual depravity, only the conflict of divine forces embodied in the sanctified Augustus and the Isiac Cleopatra. Nonetheless, after the triumphs of 29 BC, the very presence of Cleopatra in these poetic narratives marks a significant departure from other modes of cultural production of the period, whether rituals, monuments, coin issues, or inscriptions. For Augustan poetry plays with its fictions of Cleopatra long after she has ceased to carry any burden of validation in more 'official' spheres. Long after her image had once been carried in the triumphal procession of 29 BC, poetic fictions of Cleopatra continue to be composed and distributed.

In the absence of the historiographic Cleopatras of the contemporary prose tradition, the poetic Cleopatras of the Augustan age are an important and intriguing anomaly. Furthermore, the Augustan poets focus precisely on those issues that elsewhere render Cleopatra problematic as a signifier of victory. They engender and individuate the battle of Actium as the defeat of a specific militant woman: Propertius, in particular, reminds his readers that for Romans a triumph over one woman (*una mulier*) is no real triumph at all (4.6.65–6). They frequently colour the queen's regal suicide in tragedy or pathos: Horace, most famously, concludes his call for sympotic celebration in *Odes* 1.37 not with Augustus Caesar the

---

¹³⁵ See Reinhold (1988), 157–8; Flory (1993), 295–6.
¹³⁶ I am grateful to Andrew Wallace-Hadrill for this point. Cf. Powell (1992), 148 on the relative incapacity of Augustus' iconographic propaganda to register apology.

hunter, but with the Egyptian quarry who, with calm resolution (*voltu sereno*, 1.37.26), manages to elude him in death. And by explicitly linking their poetic Cleopatras to other Augustan mechanisms for the depiction of victory – triumphs, temples, decorative armour, religious ritual – they everywhere draw attention to the question of *how* to represent Cleopatra publicly and to the *difference* of poetry.

The difference of Augustan poetry could be read in two distinct ways. On the one hand, it works towards creating a new more abstracted representation of Cleopatra and Actium better to suit the early principate's political climate of integration rather than agitation. From Horace *Epode* 9 through to Propertius 4.6, ambivalence and ambiguity are gradually weeded out to culminate in a confident myth of cosmic struggle, where the point of view rests with a divinely favoured Augustus ever resisting the forces of femininity and barbarism. On the other hand, Augustan poetry interrogates (and, in places, subverts) the validating strategies of the regime through its continued display of the troublesome *meretrix regina*, persistently putting a tragic Cleopatra before its readers in order, like a remonstrating Antony, better to disclose the uncomfortable truths of a civil war. Yet, either way, the depiction of Cleopatra in the poetic narratives of Augustan Rome, the position from which her features are assembled, is always that of the Roman and the Male and the texts themselves work to construct a reader according to that model. Nowhere do they deploy Cleopatra's own Ptolemaic strategies for validating female rule, as Julius Caesar and Antony in turn had cause to do, nor do they write from her point of view (however imagined). It is only in the much later tradition of the *meretrix regina* that mechanisms are employed (poetic or otherwise) to solicit from her consumers an identification, as woman, with the female seducer of the masters of Rome.

WORKS CITED

Aly, A. A. 1992. "Cleopatra and Caesar at Alexandria and Rome," in Carratelli et al. 1992: 47–61.

[Ando, C., ed. 2003. *Roman Religion*. Edinburgh: Edinburgh University Press.]

Balsdon, J. P. V. D. 1979. *Romans and Aliens*. London: Duckworth.

Barchiesi, A. 1997. *The Poet and the Prince: Ovid and Augustan Discourse*. Berkeley, Los Angeles, and London: University of California Press.

Bartman, E. 1999. *Portraits of Livia: Imaging the Imperial Woman in Augustan Rome*. Cambridge: Cambridge University Press.

Bauman, R. A. 1992. *Women and Politics in Ancient Rome*. London: Routledge.
Beard, M., North, J., and Price, S. 1998. *Religions of Rome*. 1. *A History*. Cambridge: Cambridge University Press.
Becher, I. 1996. *Das Bild der Kleopatra in der griechischen und lateinischen Literatur* (Deutsche Akademie der Wissenschaften zu Berlin, Sektion für Altertumswissenschaft 51). Berlin: Akademie Verlag.
Bianchi, R. S., ed. 1988. *Cleopatra's Egypt. Age of the Ptolemies* (Brooklyn Museum Exhibition Catalogue). New York: Brooklyn Museum.
Bowman, A. K. 1996. *Egypt After the Pharaohs: 332 B.C.–A.D. 642. From Alexander to the Arab Conquest*. London: British Museum Press.
Boyd, B. W. 1987. "*Virtus effeminata* and Sallust's Sempronia," *TAPA* 117: 183–201.
Brenk, F. E. 1992. "Antony-Osiris, Cleopatra-Isis: The End of Plutarch's *Antony*," in P. A. Stadter, ed., *Plutarch and the Historical Tradition*. London: Routledge. 159–182.
Brett, A. B. 1937. "A New Cleopatra Tetradrachm of Ascalon," *AJA* 41: 452–463.
Brunt, P. A. and Moore, J. M., ed. and trans. 1967. *Res Gestae Divi Augusti. The Achievements of the Divine Augustus*. Oxford: Oxford University Press.
Burnett, A. M., Amandry, M., and Ripolles, P. P. 1990. *Roman Provincial Coinage*. 1. *From the Death of Caesar to Vitellius*. London: British Museum.
Carratelli, G. P., Del Re, G., Bonacasa, N., and Etman, A., eds. 1992. *Roma e l'Egitto nell'antichita classica* (Atti del I Congresso Internazionale Italo-Egiziano). Rome: Istituto Poligrafico e Zecca dello Stato.
Carson, R. A. G. and Sutherland, C. H. V., eds. 1956. *Essays in Roman Coinage Presented to Harold Mattingly*. Oxford: Oxford University Press.
Charlesworth, M. P. 1933. "Some Fragments of the Propaganda of Mark Antony," *CQ* 27: 172–177.
Ciceroni, M. 1992. "Introduzione ed evoluzione dei culti egizi a Roma in età repubblicana. La testimonianza delle fonti letterarie," in Carratelli et al. 1992: 103–107.
Coarelli, F. 1985. *Il Foro Romano*. 2. *Periodo repubblicano e augusteo*. Rome: Quasar.
Collins, J. J. 1983. "Sibylline Oracles," in J. H. Charlesworth, ed., *The Old Testament Pseudepigrapha*. 1. *Apocalyptic Literature and Testaments*. London: Darton, Longman, and Todd. 317–472.
Collins, J. J. 1987. "The Development of the Sibylline Tradition," *ANRW* II.20.1: 421–459.
Commager, S. 1958. "Horace, *Carmina* 1.37," *Phoenix* 12: 47–57.
Consigliere, L. 1978. *"Slogans" monetarii e poesia augustea*. Genoa: Istituto di Filologica Classica e Medievale.

David, R. 2000. *The Experience of Ancient Egypt*. London: Routledge.
Davis, N. and Kraay, C. M. 1973. *The Hellenistic Kingdoms: Portrait Coins and History*. London: Thames and Hudson.
DeForest, M. M. 1989. "The Central Similes of Horace's Cleopatra Ode," *CW* 82.3: 167–173.
DuBois, P. 1982. *History, Rhetorical Description and the Epic: From Homer to Spenser*. Cambridge: D. S. Brewer.
Earl, D. C. 1967. *The Moral and Political Tradition of Rome*. London: Thames and Hudson.
Edwards, C. 1993. *The Politics of Immorality in Ancient Rome*. Cambridge: Cambridge University Press.
Elsner, J. 1996. "Inventing *imperium*: Texts and the Propaganda of Monuments in Ancient Rome," in J. Elsner, ed., *Art and Text in Roman Culture*. Cambridge: Cambridge University Press. 32–53.
Fantham, E. 1997. "Images of the City: Propertius' New-Old Rome," in Habinek and Schiesaro 1997: 122–135.
Fedeli, P. 1985. *Properzio: Il libro terzo delle elegie*. Bari: Adriatica Editrice.
Feeney, D. 1992. "*Si licet et fas est*: Ovid's *Fasti* and the Problem of Free Speech under the Principate," in Powell 1992: 1–25.
Feeney, D. 1998. *Literature and Religion at Rome*. Cambridge: Cambridge University Press.
Flamarion, E. 1997. *Cleopatra: From History to Legend*, trans. A. Bonfante-Warren. London: Thames and Hudson.
Flory, M. B. 1993. "Livia and the History of Public Honorific Statues for Women in Rome," *TAPA* 123: 287–308.
Foreman, L. 1999. *Cleopatra's Palace: In Search of a Legend*. London: Discovery Books.
Foss, M. 1997. *The Search for Cleopatra*. London: Michael O'Mara Books (in association with BBC Timewatch).
Fowler, D. 2000. *Roman Constructions: Readings in Postmodern Latin*. Oxford: Oxford University Press.
Fraenkel, E. 1957. *Horace*. Oxford: Clarendon Press.
Fraser, P. M. 1972. *Ptolemaic Alexandria*. 3 vols. Oxford: Clarendon Press.
Galinsky, K. 1996. *Augustan Culture: An Interpretive Introduction*. Princeton: Princeton University Press.
Goldhill, S. 1986. *Reading Greek Tragedy*. Cambridge: Cambridge University Press.
Gow, A. S. F., ed. 1950. *Theocritus*. II. *Commentary*. Cambridge: Cambridge University Press.
Grant, M. 1972. *Cleopatra*. London: Weidenfeld and Nicolson.
Greene, G. and Kahn, C., eds. 1985. *Making a Difference: Feminist Literary Criticism* (New Accents Series). London: Methuen.
Griffin, J. 1985. *Latin Poets and Roman Life*. London: Duckworth.
Gruen, E. S. 1984. *The Hellenistic World and the Coming of Rome*. Berkeley: University of California Press.

Gurval, R. A. 1995. *Actium and Augustus*. Ann Arbor: University of Michigan Press.

Gurval, R. A. forthcoming [2011]. "Dying like a Queen: The Story of Cleopatra and the Asp(s) in Antiquity," in M. Miles, ed., *Cleopatra: A Sphinx Revisited*. Berkeley: University of California Press. 54–77.

Habinek, T. N. 1998. *The Politics of Latin Literature: Writing, Identity, and Empire in Ancient Rome*. Princeton: Princeton University Press.

Habinek, T. N. and Schiesaro, A., eds. 1997. *The Roman Cultural Revolution*. Cambridge: Cambridge University Press.

Hall, E. 1989. *Inventing the Barbarian: Greek Self-Definition through Tragedy*. Oxford: Clarendon Press.

Hallett, J. P. 1977. "*Perusinae glandes* and the Changing Image of Augustus," *American Journal of Ancient History* 2: 151–171.

Hamer, M. 1993. *Signs of Cleopatra: Histories, Politics, Representation*. London: Routledge.

Hannestad, N. 1988. *Roman Art and Imperial Policy*. Aarhus: Aarhus University Press.

Hardie, P. 1986. *Virgil's Aeneid: Cosmos and Imperium*. Oxford: Clarendon Press

Hartog, F. 1988. *The Mirror of Herodotus: The Representation of the Other in the Writing of History*, trans. J. Lloyd. Berkeley: University of California Press.

Hemelrijk, E. A. 1999. Matrona docta: *Educated Women in the Roman Elite from Cornelia to Julia Domna*. London: Routledge.

Hendry, M. 1993. "Three Problems in the Cleopatra Ode," *CJ* 88.2: 137–146.

Hughes-Hallett, L. 1991. *Cleopatra: Histories, Dreams, and Distortions*. London: Vintage.

Johnson, W. R. 1967. "A Queen, a Great Queen? Cleopatra and the Politics of Misrepresentation," *Arion* 6: 387–402.

Johnson, W. R. 1973. "The Emotions of Patriotism: Propertius 4.6," *CSCA* 6: 151–180.

Keith, A. M. 2000. *Engendering Rome: Women in Latin Epic*. Cambridge: Cambridge University Press.

Kellum, B. 1997. "Concealing/Revealing: Gender and the Play of Meaning in the Monuments of Augustan Rome," in Habinek and Schiesaro 1997: 158–181.

Kennedy, D. F. 1992. "'Augustan' and 'Anti-Augustan': Reflections on Terms of Reference," in Powell 1992: 26–58.

Kent, J. P. C. 1978. *Roman Coins*. London: Thames and Hudson.

Kleiner, D. E. E. 1992. "Politics and Gender in the Pictorial Propaganda of Antony and Octavian," *EMC/CV* 36, n.s. 11: 357–367.

Kraggerud, E. 1998. "Vergil Announcing the *Aeneid*: On *Georgics* 3.1–48," in H. P. Stahl, ed., *Vergil's Aeneid: Augustan Epic and Political Context*. London: Duckworth. 1–20.

Lampela, A. 1998. *Rome and the Ptolemies of Egypt: The Development of their Political Relations 273–80 B.C.* (CommHumLitt 111). Helsinki: Societas Scientiarum Fennica.
Lindsay, J. 1971. *Cleopatra*. London: Constable.
Lowrie, M. 1997. *Horace's Narrative Odes*. Oxford: Clarendon Press.
Macdonald, S. 1987a. "Drawing the Lines – Gender, Peace and War: An Introduction," in Macdonald et al. 1987: 1–26.
Macdonald, S. 1987b. "Boadicea: Warrior, Mother and Myth," in Macdonald et al. 1987: 40–61.
Macdonald, S., Holden, P., and Ardener, S., eds. 1987. *Images of Women in Peace and War*. London: Macmillan.
Maclean, I. 1980. *The Renaissance Notion of Woman: A Study in the Fortunes of Scholasticism and Medical Sciences in European Intellectual Life*. Cambridge: Cambridge University Press.
Macurdy, G. 1932. *Hellenistic Queens: A Study of Woman-Power in Macedonia, Seleucid Syria and Ptolemaic Eygpt* (Johns Hopkins University Studies in Archaeology 14). Baltimore: Johns Hopkins University Press.
Mader, G. 1989. "Heroism and Hallucinations: Cleopatra in Horace C. 1.37 and Propertius 3.11," *Grazer Beiträge* 16: 183–201.
Maehler, H. 1983. "Egypt under the Last Ptolemies," *BICS* 30: 1–16.
Malaise, M. 1972. *Les conditions de pénétration et de diffusion des cultes égyptiens en Italie* (EPRO 28). Leiden: E. J. Brill.
Marasco, G. 1995. "Cleopatra e gli esperimenti su cavie umane," *Historia* 44.3: 317–325.
Marshall, E. 1998. "Constructing the Self and the Other in Cyrenaica," in R. Lawrence and J. Berry, eds, *Cultural Identity in the Roman Empire*. London: Routledge. 49–63.
Millar, F. 1984. "State and Subject: The Impact of Monarchy," in Millar and Segal 1984: 37–60 [rev. version in Millar 2002: 292–313].
[Millar, F. 2002. *The Roman Republic and the Augustan Revolution*, eds H. M. Cotton and G. M. Rogers (Rome, the Greek World, and the East 1). Chapel Hill and London: University of North Carolina Press.]
Millar, F. and Segal, E., eds. 1984. *Caesar Augustus: Seven Aspects*. Oxford: Clarendon Press.
Miller, P. A. 2001. "Why Propertius is a Woman: French Feminism and Augustan Elegy," *CP* 96.2: 127–146.
Monaco, G. 1992. "Connotazioni dell'Egitto negli autori latini," in Carratelli et al. 1992: 261–264.
Montserrat, D. 2000. *Akhenaten: History, Fantasy, and Ancient Egypt*. London: Routledge.
Nash, E. 1961. *Pictorial Dictionary of Ancient Rome*. 1. London: A. Zwemmer.
Nedergaard, E. 1988. "Nuove indagini sull'Arco di Augusto nel Foro Romano," *Archeologica Laziale* 9: 37–43.
Nisbet, R. G. M. and Hubbard, M., eds. 1970. *Horace Odes 1*. Oxford:

Oxford University Press.
Oliensis, E. 1998. *Horace and the Rhetoric of Authority.* Cambridge: Cambridge University Press.
Otis, B. 1968. "A Reading of the Cleopatra Ode," *Arethusa* 1: 48–61.
Parke, H. W. 1988. *Sibyls and Sibylline Prophecy in Classical Antiquity.* New York: Routledge.
Parsons, P. J. 1977. "Callimachus: Victoria Berenices," *ZPE* 25: 1–50.
Paul, G. M. 1985. "Sallust's Sempronia: The Portrait of a Lady," *PLLS* 5: 9–22.
Pelling, C. B. R., ed. 1988. *Plutarch. Life of Antony.* Cambridge: Cambridge University Press.
Pelling, C. B. R. 1996. "The Triumviral Period," in *CAH*^{2} X: 1–69.
Pomeroy, S. B. 1984. *Women in Hellenistic Egypt.* New York: Schocken Books.
Powell, A., ed. 1992. *Roman Poetry and Propaganda in the Age of Augustus.* London: Bristol Classical Press.
Purcell, N. 1986. "Livia and the Womanhood of Rome," *PCPS* n.s. 32: 78–105 [= Chapter 5, above].
Putnam, M. C. J. 1998. *Virgil's Epic Designs: Ekphrasis in the Aeneid.* New Haven: Yale University Press.
Quaegebeur, J. 1988. "Cleopatra VII and the Cults of the Ptolemaic Queens," in Bianchi 1988: 41–54.
Quint, D. 1989. "Epic and Empire," *Comparative Literature* 41: 1–32.
Reinhold, M. 1981–2. "The Declaration of War against Cleopatra," *CJ* 77: 97–103.
Reinhold, M. 1988. *From Republic to Principate: An Historical Commentary on Cassius Dio's Roman History Books 49–52.* Atlanta: Scholars Press.
Rice, E. E. 1999. *Cleopatra.* Stroud: Sutton.
Richlin, A. 1992. "Julia's Jokes, Galla Placidia, and the Roman Use of Women as Political Icons," in B. Garlick, S. Dixon, and P. Allen, eds, *Stereotypes of Women in Power: Historical Perspectives and Revisionist Views.* New York: Greenwood Press. 65–91.
Rowlandson, J. 1998. *Women and Society in Greek and Roman Egypt: A Sourcebook.* Cambridge: Cambridge University Press.
Said, E. W. 1985. *Orientalism.* London: Peregrine Books.
Santirocco, M. S. 1986. *Unity and Design in Horace's Odes.* Chapel Hill and London: University of North Carolina Press.
Scott, K. 1929. "Octavian's Propaganda and Antony's *De sua ebrietate*," *CP* 24: 133–141.
Scott, K. 1933. "The Political Propaganda of 44–30 B.C.," *Memoirs of the American Academy in Rome* 11: 7–49.
Simon, E. 1986. *Augustus. Kunst und Leben in Rom um die Zeitenwende.* Munich: Hirmer.
Smelik, K. A. D. and Hemelrijk, E. A. 1984. "'Who Knows Not What

Monsters Demented Egypt Worships?' Opinions on Egyptian Animal Worship in Antiquity as Part of the Ancient Conception of Egypt," *ANRW* II.17.4: 1852–2000.
Smith, R. R. R. 1987. "The Imperial Reliefs from the Sebasteion at Aphrodisias," *JRS* 77: 88–138.
Smith, R. R. R. 1988a. "*Simulacra gentium*: The *ethne* from the Sebasteion at Aphrodisias," *JRS* 78: 50–77.
Smith, R. R. R. 1988b. *Hellenistic Royal Portraits*. Oxford: Clarendon Press.
Smith, R. R. R. 1991. *Hellenistic Sculpture*. London: Thames and Hudson.
Southern, P. 1999. *Cleopatra*. Stroud: Tempus.
Sutherland, C. H. V. and R. A. G. Carson. 1984. *The Roman Imperial Coinage. I. Augustus to Vitellius*. London: Spink.
Takács, S. A. 1995. *Isis and Sarapis in the Roman World*. Leiden: E. J. Brill.
Tarn, W. W. 1931. "The Battle of Actium," *JRS* 21: 173–199.
Tarn, W. W. 1932. "Alexander Helios and the Golden Age," *JRS* 22: 135–160.
Tarn, W. W. 1936. "The Bucheum Stelae: A Note," *JRS* 26: 187–189.
Tarn, W. W. and Charlesworth, M. P. 1934. "The Triumvirs"; "The War of the East against the West"; "The Triumph of Octavian," in *CAH* X: 31–126.
Thompson, D. B. 1973. *Ptolemaic Oinochoai and Portraits in Faience: Aspects of the Ruler-Cult* (Oxford Monographs on Classical Archaeology). Oxford: Clarendon Press.
Thompson, D. B. 1994. "Egypt, 146–31 B.C.," in CAH^2 IX: 310–326.
Toynbee, J. M. C. 1934. *The Hadrianic School: A Chapter in the History of Greek Art*. Cambridge: Cambridge University Press.
Vance, E. 1973. "Warfare and the Structure of Thought in Virgil's *Aeneid*," *Quaderni Urbinati di Cultura Classica* 15: 111–162.
Volkmann, H. 1958. *Cleopatra: A Study in Politics and Propaganda*, trans. T. J. Cadoux. London: Elek Books.
Wallace-Hadrill, A. 1985. "Propaganda and Dissent? Augustan Moral Legislation and the Love Poets," *Klio* 67: 180–184.
Wallace-Hadrill, A. 1986. "Image and Authority in the Coinage of Augustus," *JRS* 76: 66–87.
Warner, M. 1987. *Monuments and Maidens: The Allegory of the Female Form*. London: Picador.
Weigall, A. 1923. *The Life and Times of Cleopatra Queen of Egypt: A Study in the Origin of the Roman Empire*. London: Thornton Butterworth (1st edn, 1914).
Welch, K. E. 1995. "Antony, Fulvia, and the Ghost of Clodius in 47 B.C.," *G&R* 42.2: 182–201.
West, D. A. 1975. "*Cernere erat*: The Shield of Aeneas," *PVS* 15: 1–6.
West, D. A., ed. and trans. 1995. *Carpe Diem: Horace Odes I*. Oxford: Oxford University Press.

West, S. 1985. "Venus Observed? A Note on Callimachus, Fr. 110," *CQ* n.s. 35: 61–66.

White, P. 1993. *Promised Verse: Poets in the Society of Augustan Rome.* Cambridge, MA: Harvard University Press.

Whitehorne, J. 1994. *Cleopatras.* London: Routledge.

Wirszubski, C. 1960. *Libertas as a Political Idea at Rome during the Late Republic and Early Principate.* Cambridge: Cambridge University Press.

Witt, R. E. 1971. *Isis in the Graeco-Roman World.* London: Thames and Hudson.

Wood, S. E. 1999. *Imperial Women: A Study in Public Images, 40 B.C.–A.D. 68.* Leiden: E. J. Brill.

Woodman, A. J., ed. 1983. *Velleius Paterculus: The Caesarian and Augustan Narrative (2.41–93).* Cambridge: Cambridge University Press.

Wyke, M. 1989. "In Pursuit of Love, the Poetic Self and a Process of Reading: Augustan Elegy in the 1980s," *JRS* 79: 165–173.

Wyke, M. 2002. *The Roman Mistress: Ancient and Modern Representations.* Oxford: Oxford University Press.

Yavetz, Z. 1984. "The Res Gestae and Augustus' Public Image," in Millar and Segal 1984: 1–36.

Yeğenoğlu, M. 1998. *Colonial Fantasies: Towards a Feminist Reading of Orientalism.* Cambridge: Cambridge University Press.

Zanker, P. 1988. *The Power of Images in the Age of Augustus*, trans. H. A. Shapiro. Ann Arbor: University of Michigan Press.

12 Cybele, Virgil and Augustus†

T. P. WISEMAN

What I myself have found most astonishing is that despite the influx into Rome of countless peoples who are in duty bound to honour their ancestral gods by their own native customs, the city, unlike many cities in the past, has never adopted any of these foreign practices publicly. Any rites Rome has introduced in response to oracles, such as those of the Idaean Goddess, she celebrates according to her own traditions, rejecting all fabulous claptrap. The annual sacrifices and games that the praetors hold for the Goddess are according to the laws of Rome. Her priest and priestess, however, are Phrygians; it is they who carry her through the city, begging alms in her name as their custom is, wearing pectoral images and beating tambourines as their acolytes play the Mother's hymns for them on the pipes. But it is contrary to the law and the senate's decree that any native Roman should process in a spangled robe begging alms to the music of the pipes, or celebrate the Goddess's orgies in the Phrygian manner. So careful is the city about religious customs other than its own; so much does it abominate all empty show that lacks decorum (Dion. Hal. 2.19.3–5)

This passage, internally datable to after 23 B.C.,[1] is part of Dionysius' account of the excellent institutions of the Romans, attributed by him to Romulus; since good government rests first on the favour of the gods, Romulus established temples and altars, but banned from Roman cult all myths that degraded the gods and were therefore 'wicked, useless and indecent'.[2] No castration of Uranus, no Cronos devouring his children – and, we may add, no Attis, whose self-

---

† Originally published in Tony Woodman and David West, eds, *Poetry and Politics in the Age of Augustus*, Cambridge: Cambridge University Press, 1984, pp. 117–128.
I am very grateful for helpful suggestions from Nicholas Horsfall.

[1] Praetors were put in charge of the annual *ludi* only in 22 B.C. (Dio 54.2.3); before that, the *ludi Megalenses* [games/festival of the Magna Mater (the Great Mother), i.e., Cybele] were the responsibility of the curule aediles (Liv. 34.54.3, Cic. *Har. resp.* 27, Ascon. 70c, etc.).

[2] Dion. Hal. 2.7.2–2.29.2, on the organisation of the state. Religious customs are discussed at 18.2–23.6, among the institutions that encouraged piety, temperance, justice and courage in war (18.1); 18.3 for the myths that were πονηροὺς καὶ ἀνωφελεῖς καὶ ἀσχήμονας. See Balsdon (1971), who rightly dismisses the idea that Dionysius incorporated a Sullan or Caesarian *Tendenzschrift* [bias]: Dionysius' own analysis is fundamental to the passage (e.g. 19.3, 20.2, 22.1 ad fin., 23.3).

mutilation was essential to the Phrygian goddess's *hieros logos* [sacred story].³ Similarly, no ecstatic frenzies, no mystic initiations, no promiscuous all-night festivals, though they too were all part of her native ritual.⁴

The crucial word in Dionysius' account is δημοσίᾳ, 'publicly'. The Idaean Goddess – Cybele, the Great Mother – was brought to Rome in 204 on the instruction of the Sibylline books (confirmed by Delphi); her temple was completed in 191, and annual *ludi* were instituted in her honour.⁵ The Megalesia were *ludi scaenici et circenses* [festivals that included stage-plays and chariot-races], no different in kind from the other main festivals of the Roman year, and the goddess was honoured by dignified *sodalitates* [associations] of Roman senators, dining frugally at each other's houses in a way wholly consistent with traditional decorum.⁶ Cicero, speaking in the senate, could describe the Great Mother's *ludi* without absurdity as *maxime casti, sollemnes, religiosi* ['especially chaste, solemn, holy'], an example of ancestral piety.⁷

And yet, as Dionysius recognises, the exotic Phrygian element in her worship could not be suppressed. The eunuch Galli were allowed (as an exceptional concession) to beg through the streets on certain days of the year, with the full accompaniment of pipes, tambourines, jewelled robes and corybantic howling.⁸ Moreover, we now know that the worshippers at the Great Mother's temple on the Palatine were from the earliest days in the habit of dedicating votive statuettes of Attis, who had no place in the public cult.⁹ The tension between the popular and 'official' attitudes to Cybele is well illustrated by an episode of 102 B.C., when her high priest at Pessinus came to Rome and announced to the senate that the goddess prophesied victory to

---

³ Dion. Hal. 2.19.1. For the μυστικὸς λόγος [mystic story] of Attis, cf. Neanthes of Cyzicus, *FGrH* 84F37, Paus. 7.17.5 (quoting Hermesianax and a 'Phrygian legend' known also from Arnob. *Adu. nat.* 5.5–7), Diod. Sic. 3.58–9, etc.

⁴ Dion. Hal. 2.19.2. For θεοφόρησις [divine possession/ecstasy], see Menand. *Theoph.* 25–7, Arrian, *FGrH* 156F82; for βακχεῖαι καὶ τελεταί [ecstatic Bacchic ceremonies], Eur. *Bacch.* 73–82 (cf. Hermesianax ap. Paus. 7.17.5, Nicander, *Alexipharmaka* 8 for her ὀργία [secret rites]); for παννυχίδες [all-night festivals], Hdt. 4.76.4, Pind. *Pyth.* 3.78–9 (cf. Pind. fr. 57 B, Eur. *Kretes* fr. 475.13 N for her pine-torches).

⁵ Liv. 29.10.4–11.8, 29.14.5–14, 36.36.3–4; Varro, *Ling. lat.* 6.15, Ov. *Fast.* 4.247–90.

⁶ *Ludi*: see Degrassi, *Inscr. It.* XIII.2, 435 for the evidence of the calendar *fasti*. *Sodalitates*: Cic. *De senec.* 45 (M. Cato), Aul. Gell., *Noct. Att.* 2.42.2, 18.2.11, Verrius Flaccus, *Fasti Praenestini* ad 4 April (Degrassi, *Inscr. It.* XIII.2, 127).

⁷ Cic. *Har. resp.* 24.

⁸ Cic. *De Leg.* 2.22; Lucr. 2.618–23.

⁹ Romanelli (1963), 261–90, 315–17 on the excavations at the temple; his dating of the earliest phase (with which the votive offerings are associated) to the rebuilding of the temple after the fire of 111 B.C. is refuted by Coarelli (1977), 10–13. Discussion of the history of the cult – with the erroneous dating – in Romanelli (1964), 619–26 = (1981), 737–46.

the Romans in the war against the Cimbri and Teutoni. He made a great impression when invited to address the people in his golden crown and his spangled robe shot with gold, but a tribune, A. Pompeius, ordered him from the Rostra with a contemptuous reference to beggars and charlatans. A few days later Pompeius died of fever, and the high priest was escorted on his way by a large and respectful crowd.[10]

It is important to realise that the very elements of the Great Mother's cult which Dionysius gives the Romans credit for not accepting (and which were therefore excluded from the public ritual) did in fact form a conspicuous part of her worship in the late Republic. 'Ecstatic frenzies' and 'promiscuous all-night festivals' are attested by Thyillus, a Greek poet of Cicero's acquaintance, and 'mystic initiations' by Catullus in poem 63.[11]

Catullus' terrible castrating Cybele is not at all the Romanised goddess of the *ludi Megalenses* [games/festival of the Magna Mater (the Great Mother), i.e., Cybele]:

dea, magna dea Cybebe, dea domina Dindymi,
procul a mea tuos sit furor omnis, era, domo,
alios age incitatos, alios age rabidos. (63.91–3)

[Goddess, great goddess Cybebe, goddess mistress of Dindymus, far from my house may all your frenzy remain, O Queen! Drive others to a point of ecstasy, drive others raving mad!]

Compare Varro, in his Menippean satire *Eumenides*:

apage in dierectum a domo nostra istam insanitatem!
(*Saturae Menippeae* 133 Bücheler = 142 Cèbe)

[Begone! Be hanged! Get that insanity away from our house!]

Varro's narrator, searching for sanity in a mad world and hoping to find it in one form or another of philosophy or religion, had tried out the Great Mother's cult, perhaps by initiation; but his experience

---

[10] Plut. *Mar.* 17.9 (ἀγύρτης [begger/charlatan], cf. Alcaeus, *Anth. Pal.* 6.218.1 and Dion. Hal. 2.19.2 and 5 on ἀγυρμοί [crowds of beggars]); Diod. Sic. 36.13. See Morgan (1973), 241–5, suggesting that the political context was the forthcoming dedication of the rebuilt Palatine temple by C. Metellus Caprarius as censor in 101; ibid. 233–4 on the portentous self-emasculation of a slave of Servilius Caepio in honour of the Great Mother in 101 (Obsequens 44a).

[11] Thyillus, *Anth. Pal.* 7.223, cf. Wiseman (1974), 132–3, 140–6. Catull. 63.9, *tympanum tuum, Cybebe, tua, mater, initia* ['your tambourine, Cybebe, your initiation rites, mother']; cf. the fragment of liturgy preserved by Firmicus Maternus (*De errore* 18.1) and Clement of Alexandria (*Protrepticus* 2.15), ἐκ τυμπάνου βέβρωκα, ἐκ κυμβάλου πέπωκα, γέγονα μύστης Ἄττεως [I have eaten from the drum; I have drunk from the cymbal; I have become a mystic of Attis.]. See Vermaseren (1977), 116–19.

convinced him that what was on offer was itself madness. His contempt for the Galli and their effeminate goings-on is reflected equally in Philodemus' ironical epitaph on 'Little Dove', the darling of the gossiping hermaphrodites in their cabin by the Great Mother's Palatine temple.[12] With their high voices, their long perfumed hair and their women's dresses in pink and aquamarine, they were the very antithesis of traditional *uirtus*, and unworthy of the privileges of Roman citizenship.[13]

To the superstitious crowd, Cybele was an awesome power, a worker of miracles; to the rationalising philosopher, she was an allegory of mother Earth; to the Roman statesman, she was the first of the deities annually honoured by the aediles' games.[14] But many Romans in Virgil's lifetime thought of her in terms of madness and high camp – a sinister alien goddess served by a priesthood of contemptible half-men.[15]

Three passages in the *Aeneid* clearly reflect this attitude.[16] First, Iarbas' protest at the transfer of Dido's love from himself to Aeneas:

> et nunc ille Paris cum *semiuiro* comitatu,
> Maeonia mentum mitra crinemque madentem
> subnexus, rapto potitur ... (4.215–17)

[And now this Paris, accompanied by his escort of *half-men*, with his Phrygian bonnet tied on to cover his chin and oily hair, keeps possession of what he has seized by force.]

Secondly, Numanus' taunt to Ascanius, on the contrast between the tough-bred Italians and the effeminate Trojans:

> uobis picta croco et fulgenti murice uestis,
> desidiae cordi, iuuat indulgere choreis,

---

[12] For the plot of Varro's *Eumenides*, see Cèbe (1977), 548–65, with previous bibliography cited there; Cèbe's own reconstruction is vitiated by his erroneous belief that the action is set not in Rome but in Athens. Philodemus, *Anth. Pal.* 7.222; for the cabin, see Wiseman (1982).

[13] Val. Max. 7.7.6 (77 B.C.), *prouisum est ne obscaena Genucii praesentia* inquinataque voce *tribunalia magistratuum polluerentur* [it was decreed that the obscene presence of Genucius *with his contaminated voice* should not pollute the tribunals of magistrates]. Hair: Erucius, *Anth. Pal.* 9.233, cf. Ov. *Fast.* 4.238 (Attis), August. *De ciu.* 7.26 (*madidis capillis* [with hair drenched in unguents]), Firm. Mat. *De errore* 4.1. Dress: Varro, *Men.* 120 Buecheler = 136 Cèbe; Lanciani (1901), 188, on the Attis statue illustrated by Vermaseren (1977), Plate 44; cf. Dion. Hal. 2.19.5, Diod. 36.13.1. See in general Gow (1960), 89–90.

[14] Miracles: e.g. the death of Pompeius (n. 10 above); the vindication of Q. Claudia's chastity (Ov. *Fast.* 4.291–328, etc.); the survival of her statue in the burning temple (Val. Max. 1.8.11). Philosophers: Lucr. 2.598–660, Varro ap. August. *De ciu.* 7.24. Aediles: Wiseman (1974), 159–60.

[15] Half-men: Varro, *Men.* 132 Buecheler = 140 Cèbe, Ov. *Fast.* 4.183 etc. Half-women: Philodemus, *Anth. Pal.* 7.22.5.

[16] See Suerbaum (1967), 196ff., and (on 9.614–20) Horsfall (1971), 1113–15.

Cybele, Virgil and Augustus

et tunicae manicas et habent redimicula mitrae.
o uere Phrygiae, neque enim Phryges, ite per alta
Dindyma, ubi adsuetis biforem dat tibia cantum.
tympana uos buxusque uocat Berecyntia Matris
Idaeae; sinite arma *uiris* et cedite ferro. (9.614–20)

[As for you, your clothes are embroidered in saffron and gleaming purple; sitting around idle is your heart's desire; you love to indulge in dances; your tunics have long sleeves, your bonnets strings to fix them under your chin. O women in fact of Phrygia, for you are not Phrygian men, go run across the heights of Dindyma, where, as you know full well, the pipe rings out its two-valved song for you. The Mother of Ida's Berecynthian drum and boxwood flute summon you; leave fighting to *real men* and give up the sword.]

Thirdly, Turnus' prayer to his spear:

... da sternere corpus
loricamque manu ualida lacerare reuulsam
semiuiri Phrygis et foedare in puluere crinis
uibratos calido ferro murraque madentis. (12.97–100)

[Allow me to fling his body to the ground and use my strong arm to rip off and tear to shreds the breastplate of this Phrygian *half-man*. Let me defile in the dirt his hair all wavy thanks to the hot curling-iron and dripping with myrrh.]

These contemptuous words cannot be dismissed as merely the rhetoric of the Trojans' enemies, for their burden is repeated by Juno in her plea to Jupiter in Book 12 – a plea which receives Olympian assent in the final synthesis of the poem's argument:

ne uetus indigenas nomen mutare Latinos
neu Troas fieri iubeas Teucrosque uocari
aut uocem mutare *uiros* aut uertere uestem.
sit Latium, sint Albani per saecula reges,
sit Romana potens Itala uirtute propago:
occidit, occideritque sinas cum nomine Troia. (12.823–8)

[Do not command the Latins, native to this land, to change their ancient name and become Trojans or be called Teucrians; do not command these *men* to change their language or switch their dress. Let Latium continue to exist! Let there be Alban kings for centuries! Let the Roman line be powerful, drawing strength from Italian manliness. Troy has fallen; let it remain fallen along with its name.]

It is *uox* [lit. voice; language] and *uestis* [dress] that are offensive – and *uiros* [men] in line 825 is there not just for the alliteration but to emphasise their significance. No Roman reader could have failed to sympathise with Juno's argument, or to respond – just two generations after the Social War – to the vision of *Romana potens Itala uirtute propago* [the Roman line powerful, drawing strength from

Italian manliness], so reminiscent of the Augustan pageants in Books 6 and 8.[17] Roman *uirtus* was incompatible with the fancy gear and Phrygian gossip that Roman readers (like Numanus) associated with the Galli of Cybele.

Given all that, it is astonishing how prominent and significant a role the Great Mother herself plays in the action of the *Aeneid*. Her priests may be objects of contempt, but she is a saviour and a miracle-worker, without whom Aeneas' mission could not have been fulfilled.

Her first appearance is indirect. At the moment of despair in burning Troy, Jupiter sends Anchises the omen he has prayed for:

> intonuit laeuum, et de caelo lapsa per umbras
> stella facem ducens multa cum luce cucurrit.
> illam summa super labentem culmina tecti
> cernimus *Idaea* claram se condere *silua*
> signantemque uias. (2.693–7)
>
> [It thundered on the left, and down from the sky slid through the shadows a star dragging a firebrand; it rushed down throwing much light all around. We saw it gliding above the top of the roof of our house and, still burning brightly, it revealed its pathways and then hid itself in the *forest of Mt Ida*.]

Cybele's full title at Rome was Mater Deum Magna *Idaea*, regularly shortened to Mater Idaea.[18] It is to Ida that the star leads the way, and when Anchises in thanks says *qua ducitis adsum*, | *di patrii*, | ... | *uestrum hoc augurium* ['Wherever you lead, I shall follow, *ancestral gods*; ... this is your prophecy.'], the reader may perhaps infer that one of the guiding gods is the Great Mother of Ida. It is she who rescues lost Creusa and keeps her from enslavement by the Greeks, and it is over her sacred mountain that the morning star rises at the end of the book, as Aeneas takes up his burden and sets out.[19]

Aeneas was born on Ida, according to Hesiod, and it was agreed from the *Iliupersis* ['Sack of Troy'] onwards that he escaped to Ida when the city fell.[20] But Virgil makes much more of it than that. Aeneas builds his ships of Idaean timber at the beginning of Book 3, in a passage which concludes with the striking and sonorous line *cum sociis natoque penatibus et magnis dis* [with our comrades and my son, with the guardian deities of the household and the great gods

---

[17] Cf. 6.756–7, 792–3; 8.626, 678, 714–15. *propago* [line, stock] is especially appropriate in the context of Juno's argument: cf. Lucr. 2.617 on the sterility of the Galli.

[18] Degrassi, *Inscr. It.* XIII.2, 8, 126; Liv. 29.10.5 and 14.5, Virg. Aen. 9.619–20, Ov. *Fast.* 4.182, etc.; Dion. Hal. 2.19.3 (p. 381 above) calls her 'the Idaean goddess'.

[19] 2.788 (cf. Paus. 10.26.1), 801; cf. Hunt (1973), 68.

[20] Hes. *Theog.* 1010; Photius, OCT Homer Vol. 5 p. 107.26 (*Iliupersis*), on which see Horsfall (1979), 373–4; Dion Hal. 1.46.3 (Hellanicus), 1.48.2 (Sophocles), etc.

too].²¹ Here too the overtones must not be ignored: whoever or whatever the *magni di* [the great gods] were, in the context the reader may well think of the *magna mater* [great mother], the goddess of Ida. Certainly she is still in Anchises' mind, as he interprets Apollo's 'seek your ancient mother' as an instruction to sail to Crete:

> hinc mater cultrix Cybeli Corybantiaque aera
> Idaeumque nemus, hinc fida silentia sacris,
> et iuncti currum dominae subiere leones.
> ergo agite et diuum ducunt qua iussa sequamur. (3.111–14)

[From here came mother Cybele the object of cult and her Corybants clashing their bronze cymbals and the Idaean grove; from here the reverential silence that marks her rites, and the lions learned to submit to the yoke and pull their mistress's chariot. Come then, let us follow wherever the orders of the gods lead.]

That turns out to be a false hope, and for four books we hear no more of Cybele. But when Aeneas and his followers reach the Tiber mouth at the beginning of Book 7, his prayer of thanks for the 'eaten tables' omen is addressed to (among others) Idaean Jupiter and the 'Phrygian mother'. At the start of Virgil's *maius opus* [greater work], therefore, and the tale of war for which he has just asked the Muse's help, we are reminded of the Great Mother.²² And when she returns to the action in Book 9, it is with a vengeance.

Aeneas is away seeking allies; Turnus, in the hope of luring the Trojans out of their stockade, attacks their ships with firebrands. Virgil pauses for a formal exordium:

> quis deus, o Musae, tam saeua incendia Teucris
> auertit? tantos ratibus quis depulit ignis?
> dicite: prisca fides facto, sed fama perennis. (9.77–9)

[Which god, Muses, averted such destructive conflagrations from the Trojans? Which god drove back such enormous fires from their ships? Tell us! Belief in the event is ancient, but memory of it is everlasting.]

Only now does the reader discover the full significance of the building of Aeneas' ships from Ida timber. The trees were from Cybele's sacred grove, and Jupiter promised his mother that once they reached Italy he would make the ships immortal, as sea-nymphs. Now the fated day was come:

> his primum noua lux oculis offulsit et ingens
> uisus ab Aurora caelum transcurrere nimbus

---

²¹ 3.6 and 12; cf. 8.679 for the only other occurrence of the phrase ('Augustus' at Actium). For the connection of Penates and Magna Mater, see Suerbaum (1967), 187, 189.
²² 7.135–40; 7.33–45 for the address to the Muse.

> Idaeique chori; tum uox horrenda per auras
> excidit et Troum Rutulorumque agmina complet. (9.110–13)
>
> [First, a new light shone into their eyes and a huge cloud appeared to rush across the sky from the east together with dancing groups from Mt Ida; then a voice that made hearts tremble cut through the air and echoed through the columns of Trojans and Rutulians.]

The miracle takes place; the ships dive like dolphins, and re-emerge as goddesses.

But Turnus still presses his attack on the Trojan camp. Aeneas has collected his Etruscan allies, but is unaware of the crisis as he sails the midnight sea:

> Aeneia puppis
> prima tenet rostro Phrygios subiuncta leones,
> imminet Ida super, profugis gratissima Teucris.
> hic magnus sedet Aeneas secumque uolutat
> euentus belli uarios ... (10.156–9)
>
> [Aeneas' ship was first in the line and had Phrygian lions carved on its prow, with Mt Ida towering above, a very welcome sight to the fugitive Trojans. Here great Aeneas sat, pondering in his mind the various possible outcomes of the war.]

Cybele's lions and Cybele's mountain are his insignia, and once again the epithet *magnus* [great] – only rarely applied to Aeneas – may perhaps recall the *magna mater*.[23] As he steers through the night the nymphs that were the Trojan fleet come to warn him of the danger, and he sails to the rescue with a brief prayer for victory:

> alma parens Idaea deum, cui Dindyma cordi
> turrigeraeque urbes biiugique ad frena leones,
> tu mihi nunc pugnae princeps, tu rite propinques
> augurium Phrygibusque adsis pede, diua, secundo.
>   (10.252–5)
>
> [Nurturing Idaean mother of gods, who holds most dear to your heart Dindyma, tower-crowned cities and lions yoked in pairs to the bridle, now may you be my leader in battle, may you duly fulfil the prophecy and take up your position, divine one, alongside the Phrygians and grant them your favour.]

As he appears, striking terror in his foes, he holds aloft the shield that bears *res Italas Romanorumque triumphos* [the history of Italy and the triumphs of the Romans], and his brow blazes like that of

---

[23] *Magnus Aeneas* elsewhere only at 9.737 and 10.830 (5.531 for *maximus*); cf. 1.288 (Iulus), 5.99 and 8.156 (Anchises), 8.341 (Aeneadae).

Augustus at Actium.[24] Yet it is Cybele that grants him the victory – Cybele, whose Phrygian chorus, so despised by the robust Italians, reveals her godhead to mortal sight.[25]

The paradox appears in its most remarkable form in Book 6, at a structurally critical point in the pageant of the future Romans shown to Aeneas by Anchises in Elysium. Between Romulus the founder and Augustus the promised fulfilment, a simile illustrates the city of Rome and its walls, those *altae moenia Romae* [walls of lofty Rome] first mentioned in the seventh line of the poem and referred to in every subsequent prophetic passage as the destiny granted to Aeneas by the gods:[26]

> en huius, nate, auspiciis illa incluta Roma
> imperium terris, animos aequabit Olympo,
> septemque una sibi muro circumdabit arces,
> felix prole uirum: qualis Berecyntia mater
> inuehitur curru Phrygias turrita per urbes
> laeta deum partu, centum complexa nepotes,
> omnis caelicolas, omnis supera alta tenentis. (6.781–7)
>
> [Look, my son, it will be under his (i.e., Romulus') auspices that Rome shall become famous and extend its power across the lands and its spirit to the heights of Olympus. With a single wall will Rome enclose her seven citadels and she will be blessed in the production of many offspring, just like the Berecynthian mother, who rides her chariot through the cities of Phrygia wearing her turreted crown, rejoicing in the gods she has given birth to, embracing a hundred grandchildren, all of them dwelling in heaven, all of them occupying the lofty heights.]

As Austin rightly observes, 'his choice of just this simile to illustrate the all-embracing world-dominion of Rome (and in such a context) is bold and even startling'.[27] So too is his use of Cybele in the narrative. In the light of her cult's reputation in the first century B.C., the prominence Virgil gives to the Great Mother in the *Aeneid* is extraordinary. How can we explain it?

---

[24] 10.270–1, cf. 8.626 and 680–1. Also *stans celsa in puppi* [standing on the lofty poop-deck] (10.261, cf. 8.680).

[25] 9.112, cf. 615 (Numanus); Catull. 63.30, Juv. 6.512, Sil. It. 17.20, etc. At 10.219 and 224 the metamorphosed ships are a *chorus* too.

[26] 6.781–7, on which see West (1969), 46; 1.7, 1.277 (Jupiter), 2.294–5 (Hector), 3.159–60 (Penates), 4.234 (Jupiter), 5.737 (Anchises). *Data/debita moenia* [the walls granted/owed]: 3.85, 3.501, 5.798, 7.145. *Romana arx* [the citadel of Rome]: 8.98, 8.313 (Evander), 10.12. *Romana moenia* [the walls of Rome]: 8.714–15 (Augustus' triumph). Cf. Cruttwell (1946), 22–6 (emphasising Cybele as the wife of *Saturn*), 50–1 (on the *magna moenia* [great walls]).

[27] Austin (1977), 241; for the simile and its significance, see also Grant (1963–4), 7, Galinsky (1969), 224–7. On *felix prole uirum* [blessed in the production of manly offspring], cf. n. 17 above.

A first step, I think, is to recognise an aspect of Virgilian allusiveness that we moderns often forget – the significance of the visible monuments and topography of the city of Rome.

The most conspicuous example comes at 8.306–69, where Evander takes Aeneas and Pallas from the Ara Maxima of Hercules, in the grove by the river, up to the 'city' of Pallanteum, Evander's settlement on the Palatine.[28] The altar of Hercules was in the Forum Bovarium adjacent to the Velabrum.[29] From the Velabrum the Nova Via curved round the northwestern side of the Palatine, gradually ascending to the old Palatine gate, the Porta Mugionia (or Mucionis).[30] Later, the construction of the Horrea Agrippiana and the Domitianic complex behind the temple of Castor was to change the topography completely; but Virgil could expect his readers to visualise a very straightforward walk round the side of the hill, past the Lupercal (343–4) and within easy view of the Capitol (342), the Argiletum (345) and the Janiculum (357–8).[31]

Virgil artfully allows us to view the scene with a sort of double vision: superimposed on the woody slopes of Evander's time we see also the landmarks of the great city – the Porta Carmentalis, the golden Capitol, and 'smart Carinae' and the Roman Forum with Evander's cattle grazing in them.[32] The lowing (*mugitus*) of the beasts places us at the Porta Mugionia, close to the Regia.[33] Evander's humble house is called a *regia* [royal palace] and has a *fastigium* [pediment], as befits the dwelling of a king; but the Roman Regia was

---

[28] *Lucus* [grove] and *urbs* [city]: 8.104, 271, 306, 362 (*sedes*).

[29] Forum Bovarium: Dion. Hal. 1.40.6, Ov. *Fast.* 1.581–2, Tac. *Ann.* 12.24.1. Velabrum: Schol. Veron. *Aen.* 8.104; cf. (for the juxtaposition) CIL 6.1035.5–6, with Wiseman (1981), 41 and 49 n. 39.

[30] Nova Via: Varro, *Ling. Lat.* 5.43 ad fin., 6.24 (Velabrum); Solinus 1.24 (Porta Mugionia), Liv. 1.41.4 with 1.12.3–6 and Dion. Hal. 2.50.3 (Iuppiter Stator temple near Nova Via and Porta Mugionia). For the name of the gate, cf. Varro, *Ling. Lat.* 5.164 and ap. Non. 852 L, Festus (Paulus) 131 L; for its probable position, see Coarelli (1980), 78–9; ibid. 71, 82 for surviving traces of the old Nova Via.

[31] There is an internal incoherence in the passage: according to *ducit* [he leads] at 347, Evander took Aeneas and Pallas across the Capitol; on the other hand, the parallelism of the Capitoline *arx Saturnia* [Saturn's citadel] and the Janiculum at 357–8 strongly suggests that both citadels were being pointed out from a distance, as the repeated *monstrat* [he points out] (337, 343, 345) clearly implies. The easiest solution is to suppose that the 'Capitol' passage was written at a different time and not wholly integrated with the rest. For other such incoherences in the book, cf. 190/236–7 (not to the left if looking from the Ara Maxima), 319–23/602 (who was first in Latium?), 466/521/545 (just Achates, or *Troiana iuuentus* [the Trojan youth]?), 504/597 (*hoc campo* [in this plain], but close to Caere), 652–3/657–8 (did the Gauls hold the Capitol?: Skutsch (1953), 77 n. 7); 531–4, 550, 569–71 (Venus' promise, messengers, attacks by Mezentius – not otherwise mentioned).

[32] 8.338–9, 348, 360–1.

[33] 8.361, Varro, *Ling. lat.* 5.164; n. 30 above.

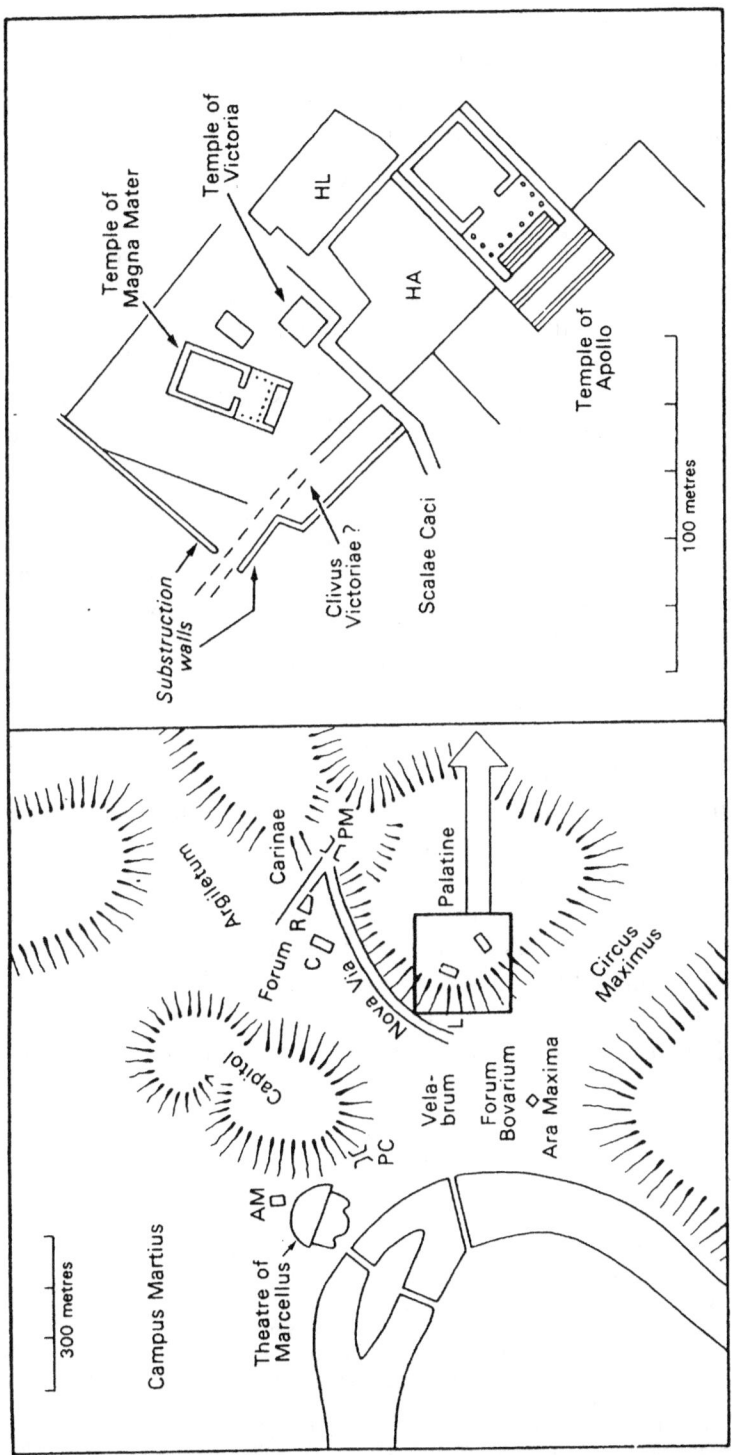

Fig. 12.1. Sketch-map of central Rome and the western corner of the Palatine in the time of Augustus.
Key: AM: Temple of Apollo Medicus; C: Temple of Castor; HA: 'House of Augustus'; HL: 'House of Livia';
L: Lupercal; PC: Porta Carmentalis; PM: Porta Mugionia; R: Regia

the house of the pious and frugal Numa, who is surely meant to be in the reader's mind as Evander welcomes Aeneas:[34]

> aude, hospes, contemnere opes et te quoque dignum
> finge deo, rebusque ueni non asper egenis.
>
> ['Guest, be bold and despise wealth; and mould yourself as well to be fit to be a god; come in, and do not criticise if things look poor and needy.']

For another example of Virgil exploiting his readers' knowledge of the city and its monuments, we may turn to E. L. Harrison's recent analysis of the wounding of Aeneas in Book 12. Why is Iapyx so incompetent a surgeon, if his skill comes from Apollo? Why does Apollo – of all gods – not help Aeneas in his need? Because Virgil wishes to reverse the Homeric situation (*Iliad* 5.311ff.) and give the credit to Venus.[35]

> It is true that on this occasion the patron god of the Augustan regime is the loser as a result of the manoeuvre, but on Virgil's balance sheet he still emerges with enough gains for that to be overlooked. For the adjustments made in his favour were concerned with areas of major significance: the protection of the *gens Iulia*, and the oracular confirmation of the Trojan mission. Here on the other hand it is in his capacity as Apollo Medicus that he is found wanting.

Virgil's readers would see that, and more. The temple of Apollo Medicus had stood since 431 B.C. outside the Porta Carmentalis. It was rebuilt in great style by C. Sosius after his triumph *ex Iudaea* [over Judaea] in 34, and the surviving remains of 'Apollo Sosianus' are considered a masterpiece of Augustan architecture. But that is true only in a chronological sense. Sosius had been proconsul of Syria under Antony in 38–35; as consul in 32 he attacked Octavian, left Rome to join his old leader, and commanded the left wing of Antony's fleet at Actium the following year. The rebuilt temple of Apollo Medicus was the *monumentum* [memorial] of an enemy of the new regime.[36]

Octavian upstaged it in two ways. He put the huge theatre of Marcellus right in front of it;[37] and he built his own temple of Apollo,

---

[34] 8.364–5; cf. 327 for Evander's views on wealth, 455 for his humble house, 100 and 360 for his poverty. *regia*: 8.363 and Servius; Ov. *Tr.* 3.1.30, *Fast.* 6.264, Plut., *Numa* 14, etc. *fastigium*: 8.366; Vitr. 5.6.9, Weinstock (1971), 280–1.

[35] Harrison (1981), 221–3 on *Aen.* 12.391–429: quotations from p. 223.

[36] Liv. 4.25.3 and 29.7 (foundation), 40.31.6 (*Medicus*), Plin. *Nat.* 13.53 and 36.28 (*Sosianus*). Remains: Nash (1968), 28–30. Sosius: evidence collected in Broughton (1952), 393, 397–8, 412–13, 417, 422.

[37] Aug. *RG* 21.1; juxtaposition illustrated in Nash (1968), 29. It was the logical place to put the theatre, on the site of the *scaena* [stage] used for the *ludi Apollinares* [Games of Apollo]

inside the *pomerium*, on the Palatine. Already, in 36 B.C., his agents were buying up the houses of his neighbours at the western corner of the hill, to make room for a great new temple with adjacent porticos. Lighting had struck there, and the *haruspices* declared that the god was announcing his desire for a home in the city proper.³⁸

By the time the new temple was dedicated, on 9 October 28 B.C., Apollo had a new significance: the great naval battle had been fought below his shrine at Actium, and in the victor's version of the conflict he comes with his avenging bow to fight for Rome and Italy against the Egyptian queen and the bestial gods of the East. So Virgil has it in Book 8, with the battle (31 B.C.), the triumph (29) and the Palatine temple (28) presented together as the centre-piece of Aeneas' shield. Propertius, who devoted a whole poem to the temple and the Actium legend, calls the god 'Apollo of the ships'.³⁹

Why did Octavian choose that particular spot, at the western corner of the Palatine overlooking the river, for his house and his Apollo temple? A likely answer can now be given, offering another example of the conceptual significance of Roman topography, and explaining – I believe – why the Great Mother was so important to Augustus, and therefore also to Virgil.

Below the western corner of the Palatine was the Ficus Ruminalis, the fig-tree overshadowing the Lupercal grotto where the she-wolf had suckled Romulus and Remus.⁴⁰ In 296 the aediles Cn. Ogulnius and Q. Ogulnius dedicated there a statue-group of the wolf and twins, paid for by the fines they had exacted from usurers. A little earlier the aedile L. Postumius Megillus had used his money from fines to build a temple to Victoria, which he dedicated as consul in 294.⁴¹ The temple was on the Palatine, and the recent excavations of Prof. Patrizio Pensabene, independently confirmed by a re-examination of the literary and epigraphic evidence, have revealed its exact position. It was almost certainly the small temple whose podium is visible

---

(Liv. 40.51.3), but not where Caesar had planned to put it (Suet. *Caes.* 44.1, *Tarpeio monti accubans* [adjacent to the Tarpeian hill]).

³⁸ Vell. 2.81.3, Suet. *Aug.* 29.3, Dio 49.15.5; the Apollo Medicus temple was *extra urbem* [outside the city] (Liv. 34.43.2, 37.58.3).

³⁹ *Aen.* 8.704ff. (Actian Apollo), 714ff. (triumph), 720ff. (Apollo temple); Prop. 4.1.3 (*naualis Phoebus* [Phoebus of the ships]), 4.6.11–68 (on which see Cairns 1984). For the Actium temple, see Thuc. 1.29.3, Suet. *Aug.* 18.2, Dio 51.1.2; Virg. *Aen.* 3.274–89.

⁴⁰ Dion. Hal. 1.79.8: 'built up against the Palatine on the street leading to he Circus'. Cf. also Val. Max. 2.2.9, Serv. *Aen.* 8.343, Dion. Hal. 1.32.3-4 (below the Palatine hill); Just 43.1.6 (*in radicalis Palatii* [at the foot of the Palatine]); Dion. Hal. 1.79.5 (close to river); Ov. *Fast.* 2.389–92, Serv., *ad Aen.* 8.90 (close to Circus).

⁴¹ Liv. 10.23.11–12; 10.33.9, cf. 29.14.14 (on the Palatine).

immediately to the north of the 'Scalae Caci' ['Stairs of Cacus'], on the crest of the hill above the Lupercal.⁴²

Great substruction walls were constructed at that corner of the hill, which are best interpreted as part of a coherent building programme about 300 B.C.: a partly artificial terrace, with the new Lupercal shrine at the bottom and a Clivus Victoriae [Path of Victory] leading up past the walls to the new temple of Victoria – and also, we may add, to that of Iuppiter Victor, vowed by Q. Fabius Rullianus at the battle of Sentinum in 295.⁴³

The newly-identified site of the temple of Victoria is adjacent to the 'house of Livia' excavated in 1869 and the 'house of Augustus' excavated in the 1960s – two of the houses in the complex of property owned by Augustus, as is now proved by the definitive identification of the Apollo temple immediately to the south-east.⁴⁴ Octavian, that is, chose to live next to the precinct of Victoria, and developed his property in such a way as to give himself two divine neighbours: the goddess of victory on one side and Apollo of Actium on the other. Moreover, the festival of Victoria on the Palatine was the day he chose to celebrate the conquest of Egypt, *quod eo die imp. Caesar Augustus rem publicam tristissimo periculo liberauit* ['because on that day Imp(erator) Caesar Augustus liberated the state from the most serious danger']; it was the first day of the month now renamed *Augustus*.⁴⁵

There were also Romulean associations; the Lupercal was immediately below, and the hut variously attributed to Faustulus, Remus, or Romulus himself was very close by, at the top of the Scalae Caci.⁴⁶ Moreover, it seems clear that the substruction walls in *opus*

---

⁴² Pensabene (1980), 73 and 80 n. 35 (votive inscription ... *L. l. donum soluit Victoriae* [... freedman of Lucius paid (this) as a gift to Victory]); Wiseman (1981), on Dion. Hal. 1.32.3–33.1 (Victoria above Lupercal), *CIL* 6.31059–60, etc. The site of the Victoria temple had already been tentatively suggested by Romanelli (1953), 10 = (1981), 710 and Castagnoli (1964), 185–6.

⁴³ Walls: Coarelli (1980), 127, cf. 12 for the date (fourth century?); illustrated in Nash (1968), 112–13. *Cliuus Victoriae*: Festus 318 L, with Wiseman (1981), 40; see also Panciera (1980), 239–41 for a *uicus Victoriae* [Victory Row], possibly the lower stretch of the *cliuus* in or near the Velabrum. Iuppiter Victor: Liv. 10.29.14 and 18; Dio 45.17.2, 47.40.2, 50.35.1; on the Palatine according to the Regionary Catalogues (*Notitia ad reg. X*), and possibly to be identified with the other small temple podium at the western corner, the so-called *auguratorium*, which is now known to have fourth- or third-century foundations (Pensabene (1980), 71–2). For the terrace, cf. Pensabene (1981), 106 on the identification of tufa blocks pre-dating the Cybele temple; for the precinct and its boundary wall, Pensabene (1980), 73–4 and (1981), 110–11.

⁴⁴ Coarelli (1980), 129–134, with bibliography cited at 378. For the Augustan complex and its pre-Neronian development, see Castagnoli (1964), 188–90, Wiseman (1980), 232.

⁴⁵ Degrassi, *Inscr. It.* XIII.2, 489–90: Fasti Arvales, Praenestini, Amiternini.

⁴⁶ Dio 53.16.4 for the Romulean associations of Augustus' house; ibid. 16.6 and Suet. *Aug.*

quadratum [i.e., masonry of squared stone] were now interpreted as the work of Romulus, the citadel of Roma Quadrata, the symbolic seat of empire:⁴⁷

> [... locus erat ubi Roma con]dita est eaque Roma muro [in speciem quadratam munita est ne]quis at Romam Quadrata<m> [accedere posset. Imperii enim c]aput Romam Quad[rat]am [existimabant].
>
> [... ?This was the place where Rome was foun]ded and that Rome [was fortified] with a wall [in the form of four-square masonry], to ensure that no one [could gain entry] to 'Four-Square Rome'. [For they thought] that 'Four-Square Rome' would be the head [of an empire].

On every side, Augustus surrounded himself with symbols – of victory, and of the foundation of Rome.⁴⁸

The Great Mother had been a part of this topographical complex since 204 B.C., when her image was installed in the temple of Victoria until a permanent home could be built for it, and 191 B.C., when her temple was completed in the precinct of Victoria itself, dwarfing the smaller shrines already there.⁴⁹ As the bringer of victory, against Hannibal and in later wars, she had every right to be there.⁵⁰ Historians and antiquarians did their best to incorporate her into the indigenous traditions of the place.⁵¹ Augustus could not ignore her: somehow, despite the alien mummery of her cult, she had to be assimilated into the complex of associations he had built up around his Palatine house.⁵²

7.2 for his original intention to be called 'Romulus' (cf. Virg. *G.* 3.27). Lupercal: Dion. Hal. 1.32.3–33.1 (Wiseman (1981), 35–7) for the relationship with the Victoria temple. Hut: Solinus 1.18 (Faustulus), Prop. 4.1.9 (Remus), Dion. Hal. 1.79.11 (Romulus).

⁴⁷ *Ox. Pap.* 17 (1927) 2088.14–17, suppl. Piganiol (1937), 374; for the supplements, cf. Festus 310–12 L (q.v., with Solinus 1.18, for the position of Roman Quadrata in this version); Wiseman (1981), 44–5.

⁴⁸ For the 'foundation' ideology, cf. n. 46 above (Romulus); also Festus 310–12 L (Roma Quadrata), Virg. *Aen.* 8.313 (Evander, *Romanae conditor arcis* [founder of the citadel of Rome]). It is explicit at Suet. *Aug.* 7.2.

⁴⁹ Liv. 29.14.2–14, 29.37.2, 36.36.3–4, etc.; cf. n. 9 above. The emerging archaeological evidence suggests that the Magna Mater complex, including a ritual basin for the goddess's *lauatio* [ritual bath], encroached on the area in front of the Victoria temple and may have necessitated the partial removal of its steps: Pensabene (1980), 69–70, (1981), 111–12.

⁵⁰ Liv. 29.10.5 and 8, cf. Cic. *Har. resp.* 27 (Hannibal); Polyb. 21.37.5, Liv. 38.18.9 (Cn. Manlius Vulso in Galatia, 189); Plut. *Mar.* 17.5 (Cimbric campaign: pp. 382-383 above). Vows paid by *imperatores* at Pessinus: Cic. *Har. resp.* 28, whence Val. Max. 1.1.1; e.g. Marius in 99 (Plut. *Mar.* 31.1). For the association of the Magna Mater with Nike/Victoria, see (e.g.) Vermaseren (1977), 30–1 and Pl. 16 (marble relief from Lydia), Daremberg-Saglio, 1193, Fig. 1528 (S. Lorenzo sarcophagus showing *pompa circensis* [procession before a chariot-race]).

⁵¹ E.g.: Romulus' mother became *Rhea* Silvia (Castor of Rhodes, *FGrH* 250F5, Varro, *Ling. lat.* 5.144); cf. Cruttwell (1946), 27–8, drawing a parallel with the woods (*siluae*) of Ida. And it is possible that the cabin that served as the clubhouse for Cybele's priests was identified as the hut of Faustulus or Remus (n. 46 above): Wiseman (1982), on Philodemus 26.3 Gow-Page.

⁵² Cf. Pensabene (1981), 112: the level of the street between the Augustan houses was the same as that of the *area* of Victoria, suggesting that they formed a single architectural complex.

Fig. 12.2. The Gemma Augustea

On the Gemma Augustea, an onyx cameo now in Vienna (see Fig. 12.2), Augustus is shown enthroned next to Dea Roma, receiving Tiberius as he alights from the triumphal chariot in 7 B.C. or A.D. 12. At the top left, behind Tiberius, winged Victoria is the charioteer; at the top right, behind Augustus, a mature divinity in a turreted headdress crowns the *princeps* with a laurel wreath. She is conventionally identified as Oikoumene, the world, but there is no reason at all to resist the natural identification with the *dea turrigera* [turret-crowned goddess], Cybele the Great Mother.[53]

The details of her Augustan rehabilitation are what we see in Virgil. The Phrygian goddess has become the Trojan goddess,[54] protecting Creusa, providing the fleet; the woods of Ida are no longer Catullus' place of horror, but the means of safety for the destined ancestor of Rome. The bringer of victory brings it also for Aeneas;

---

[53] Ov. *Fast.* 4.224, 6.321; cf. *Met.* 10.696, Prop. 4.11.52, Virg. *Aen.* 6.785 (*turrita* [turreted]); Varro ap. August. *De ciu.* 7.24, Lucr. 2.606f., Ov. *Fast.* 4.219.

[54] This aspect was emphasised by Ovid, on whose version see now Littlewood (1981), who perhaps exaggerates the specifically Julian significance of it (at pp. 381–5) but is right to lay stress on the 'canonical Augustan theology' created by Virgil (pp. 381, 386).

like the Roman generals who paid their vows to her, he too prays to the Great Mother before going into action.[55] In the most spectacular of her manifestations, the metamorphosis of the Trojan fleet into sea-nymphs, no reader in Virgil's Rome could fail to recognise Cybele not only as a miracle-worker, but also as the august neighbour of 'Apollo of the ships'.[56]

The Great Mother's most significant appearance, as we have seen, is in the catalogue of Roman heroes in Book 6. The simile of the *Berecyntia mater* [Berecynthian mother], so puzzling at first sight, makes perfect sense if we read it topographically, as one going up from the Forum Bovarium to the Palatine – by the Lupercal shrine, up the Clivus Victoriae past the 'Romulean' walls of the *caput imperii* [head of an empire], to the temple of the Great Mother and the house of Augustus. Virgil gives us, in just that order, Romulus the founder (776–80), *imperium* and the citadel walls (781–3), the Great Mother and her brood (784–7), Rome and the Iulii (788–90), and finally the new founder, Augustus Caesar (791–5).[57] Here, if anywhere, we may be sure that Virgil wrote in full knowledge of, and sympathy with, the image Augustus wished to project to the citizens of Rome.

WORKS CITED

Austin, R. G., ed. 1977. *P. Vergili Maronis Aeneidos liber sextus*. Oxford.
Balsdon, J. P. V. D. 1971. 'Dionysius on Romulus: A Political Pamphlet?', *JRS* 61: 18–27.
Broughton, T. R. S. 1952. *The Magistrates of the Roman Republic*. II. (1st edn). New York.
Cairns, F. 1984. 'Propertius and the Battle of Actium (4.6)', in A. Woodman and D. West, eds, *Poetry and Politics in the Age of Augustus*. Cambridge. 129–64.
Castagnoli, F. 1964. 'Note sulla topografia del Palatino e del foro Romano', *Archeologica Classica* 16: 173–99.
Cèbe, J.-P. 1977. *Varron: Satires Menippees*. IV. Paris.
Coarelli, F. 1977. 'Public Building in Rome between the Second Punic War and Sulla', *PBSR* 45: 1–23.
Coarelli, F. 1980. *Roma* (Guide archeologiche Laterza). Bari.
Cruttwell, R. W. 1946. *Virgil's Mind at Work: An Analysis of the Symbolism of the Aeneid*. Oxford.
Galinsky, G. K. 1969. *Aeneas, Sicily and Rome*. Princeton.

---

[55] *Aen.* 10.252–5; cf. n. 50 above.
[56] See above, nn. 14 (miracles) and 39 (*naualis Phoebus*).
[57] Walls: n. 26 above. *Caput imperii*: p. 395 above. New founder: 6.792–3 (*aurea condet saecula* [golden ages *will he establish*]) and n. 48 above.

Gow, A. S. F. 1960. 'The *Gallus* and the Lion', *JHS* 80: 88–93.
Grant, M. 1963–4. 'Virgil the European', *PVS* 3: 1–11.
Harrison, E. L. 1981. 'Vergil and the Homeric Tradition', in *Papers of the Liverpool Latin Seminar 1981*. Liverpool. 209–25.
Horsfall, N. 1971. 'Numanus Remulus: Ethnography and Propaganda in *Aen.* ix, 598f.', *Latomus* 30: 1108–16.
Horsfall, N. 1979. 'Some Problems in the Aeneas Legend', *CQ* n.s. 29: 372–90.
Hunt, J. W. 1973. *Forms of Glory: Structure and Sense in Virgil's Aeneid*. London and Amsterdam.
Lanciani, R. 1901. *New Tales of Old Rome*. London.
Littlewood, R. J. 1981. 'Poetic Artistry and Dynastic Politics: Ovid at the Ludi Megalenses (*Fasti* 4.179–372)', *CQ* n.s. 31: 381–95.
Morgan, M. G. 1973. 'Villa Publica and Magna Mater', *Klio* 55: 215–45.
Nash, E. 1968. *Pictorial Dictionary of Ancient Rome*. London.
Panciera, S. 1980. 'Olearii', in J. H. D'Arms and E. C. Kopff, eds, *The Seaborne Commerce of Ancient Rome: Studies in Archaeology and History* (*MAAR* 36). Rome. 235–50.
Pensabene, P. 1980. 'La zona sud-occidentale del Palatino', *Quaderni del centro di studio per l'archeologia etrusco-italica* 4: 65–81.
Pensabene, P. 1981. 'Nuove acquisizioni nella zone sud-occidentale del Palatino', *Quaderni del centro del studio per l'archeologia etrusco-italica* 5: 101–18.
Piganiol, A. 1937. 'Le papyrus de Servius Tullius', in R. Paribeni, ed., *Scritti in onore di B. Nogara*. Vatican. 373–80.
Romanelli, P. 1953. 'Problemi archeologici del Foro Romano e del Palatino', *Studi Romani* 1: 3–12.
Romanelli, P. 1963. 'Lo scavo del tempio della Magna Mater sul Palatino e nelle sue adiacense', *Monumenti Antichi* 46: 202–330.
Romanelli, P. 1964. 'Magna Mater e Attis sul Palatino', in *Hommages à J. Bayet* (Collection *Latomus* 70). Brussels. 619–26.
Romanelli, P. 1981. *In Africa e a Roma: scripta minora selecta*. Rome.
Skutsch, O. 1953. 'The Fall of the Capitol', *JRS* 43: 77–8.
Suerbaum, W. 1967. 'Aeneas zwischen Troja und Rom', *Poetica* 1: 176–204.
Vermaseren, M. J. 1977. *Cybele and Attis: The Myth and the Cult*. London.
Weinstock, S. 1971. *Divus Julius*. Oxford.
West, D. 1969. 'Multiple-Correspondence Similes in the *Aeneid*', *JRS* 59: 40–9.
Wiseman, T. P. 1974. *Cinna the Poet and Other Roman Essays*. Leicester.
Wiseman, T. P. 1980. 'Josephus on the Palatine (*AJ* 19.75–6)', *LCM* 5: 231–8.
Wiseman, T. P. 1981. 'The Temple of Victory on the Palatine', *Antiquaries Journal* 61: 35–52.
Wiseman, T. P. 1982. 'Philodemus 26 Gow-Page', *CQ* n.s. 32: 475–6.

13 Livy, Augustus, and the Forum Augustum†

T. J. LUCE

Augustus' forum, dedicated in 2 B.C.,[1] expresses forcibly how the emperor wanted his countrymen to view the sweep of Roman history and his place in it. Although the Temple of Mars Ultor had been vowed on the field of Philippi in 42 B.C. (Suet. *Aug.* 29.2; *RG* 2), forty years passed before it was dedicated. The press of judicial and other business caused the forum to be used before the temple was finished (Suet. *Aug.* 29.1); how long the plans for the forum as a whole had been maturing is not known. It may be that some features had been settled well before 2 B.C., perhaps including the selection of heroes in the Roman "Hall of Fame," whose statues, along with their *elogia* [commemorative inscriptions], were placed in the two porticoes and exedrae on either side of the temple.[2] In any event, it is clear that Livy's history of Rome was well under way when plans for the forum were drawn up, whether we assign an early or late date to them. The first book was completed between 27 and 25 B.C.; very likely the

---

† Originally published in K. Raaflaub and M. Toher, eds., *Between Republic and Empire: Interpretations of Augustus and his Principate.* Berkeley, Los Angeles, and Oxford: University of California Press, 1990, pp. 123–138.

[1] More probably on 12 May of that year (Ov. *Fast.* 5.550–52) than 1 August (Dio 54.5.3): C. J. Simpson, "The Date of the Dedication of the Temple of Mars Ultor," *JRS* 67 (1977) 91–94. I wish to thank E. J. Champlin and B. W. Frier for their comments on an earlier draft of this paper.

[2] The forty-year delay has not been satisfactorily accounted for. That the plans were drawn up in the twenties B.C. does not seem likely to me: T. Frank, "Augustus, Vergil, and the Augustan Elogia," *AJP* 59 (1938) 91–94; and H. T. Rowell, "The Forum and Funeral *Imagines* of Augustus," *MAAR* 17 (1940) 131–43. Nor does Vergil's influence seem probable: H. T. Rowell, "Vergil and the Forum of Augustus," *AJP* 62 (1941) 261–76; contra: A. Degrassi, "Virgilio e il Foro di Augusto," *Epigraphica* 7 (1945) 88–103. See also J. C. Anderson, Jr., *The Historical Topography of the Imperial Fora,* Coll. Latomus 182 (Brussels 1984) 65–100; M. C. J. Putnam, *Artifices of Eternity: Horace's Fourth Book of Odes* (Ithaca, N.Y. 1986) 327–39. Final selections for the Hall of Fame were made no earlier than 9 B.C., when the elder Drusus died; his *elogium* survives: Degrassi, *Inscr. It.* 13.3, D 9. A statue in triumphal garb of Cn. Sentius Saturninus in the forum honored the consul of A.D. 41, not the consul of 19 B.C., as is sometimes claimed (whose praenomen in any case was Gaius): A. R. Birley, *The Fasti of Roman Britain* (Oxford 1981) 360–61.

Fig. 13.1. View of the Forum Augustum, with the Temple of Mars Ultor and part of the exedra of the portico on the south-east side

whole of the first pentad was finished by then.[3] Evidence for dating other portions of the history is lacking, save that the publication of the last twenty-two books was delayed until after Augustus' death in A.D. 14.[4] If we conservatively postulate an even rate of production for Books 6–142 between 25 B.C. and A.D. 14, the average of roughly three and a half books a year would suggest that by, say, 5 B.C. Livy had reached at least Book 75, which answers to the period of the Social War (89 B.C.). In short, Livy's account of much of republican history had probably appeared by 2 B.C.; certainly the books that survive to us had long been known.

It is a commonplace that Livy's achievement "swept the field." His work almost immediately found itself touching on some urgent concerns of the emperor (4.20.5–11), acquaintance with Augustus and the imperial family developed (Tac. *Ann.* 4.34.3; Suet. *Claud.* 41.1), and Livy acquired wide and lasting fame (Pliny *Ep.* 2.3.8; Pliny *HN* 1 *praef.* 16). The Forum Augustum and the *Ab urbe condita* [*From the Foundation of the City*] were thus the two most famous

---

[3] The emperor has the title Augustus, voted on 16 January 27 B.C. (1.19.3), but in the same passage the emperor's second closing of the Temple of Janus in 25 B.C. is not mentioned. Cf. T. J. Luce, "The Dating of Livy's First Decade,' *TAPA* 96 (1965) 209–40.

[4] The superscription to Book 121 reads *qui editus post excessum Augusti dicitur* [which is said to have been released after the death of Augustus]. I am not convinced by L. Canfora's objection to accepting the superscription: "Su Augusto e gli ultimi libri liviani," *Belfagor* 24 (1969) 41–43. It meets, however, with J. Deininger's recent approval: "Livius und der Prinzipat," *Klio* 67 (1985) 269, n.46.

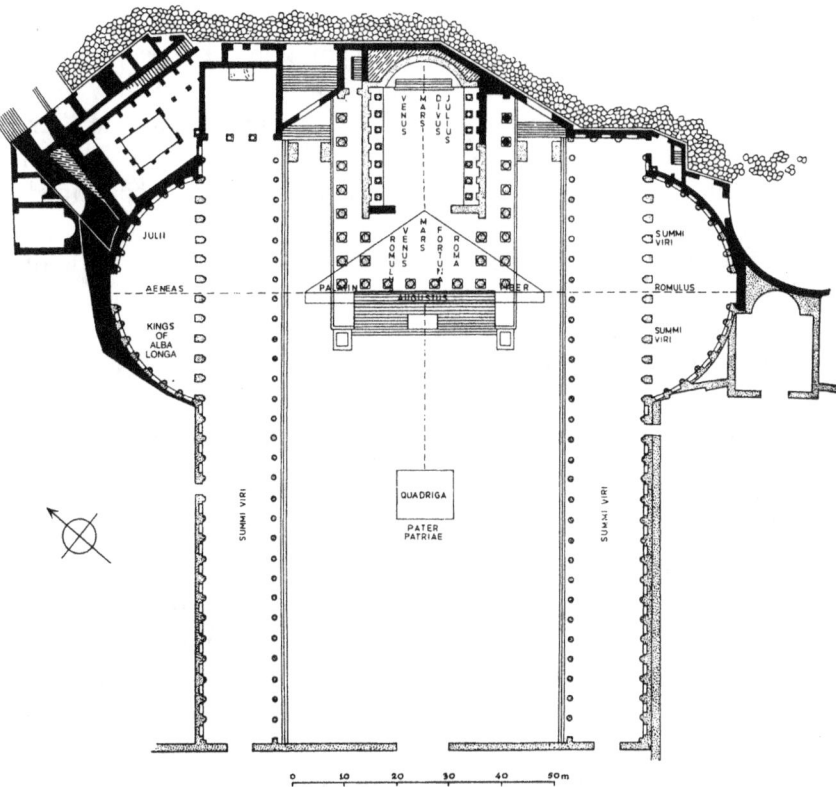

Fig. 13.2. Plan of the Forum Augustum, with a proposed reconstruction of its sculptural programme

monuments to republican history in the Augustan Age, and their creators knew one another. One might therefore expect to see some relationship between their conceptions of the Roman past, whether by influence or reaction. This study will investigate the topic by looking first at their overall conception of Roman history and second at the choice of men made for the Hall of Fame, together with the information contained in their *elogia*, comparing especially those *elogia* of men who also appear in the surviving portions of Livy's history.

I

The forum as a whole was based on a unitary conception of which the Hall of Fame was only a part.[5] On the architrave of the temple,

---

[5] I follow the reconstruction of P. Zanker, *Forum Augustum: das Bildprogramm* (Tübingen 1968). See also id., *The Power of Images in the Age of Augustus* (= *Augustus und die Macht der Bilder* [Munich 1987, transl. A. Shapiro]), esp. 210–15.

which dominated the central space, Augustus' name was emblazoned in large letters (Ov. *Fast.* 5.567–68). The middle of the pediment was occupied by the bearded statue of Mars Ultor, surrounded by Venus, Fortuna, Romulus, the personified Palatine Hill, Roma, and Father Tiber. The cella within held the statues of Mars Ultor, Venus, and the deified Julius, Augustus' adoptive father.[6] The forum contained a large statue of Augustus in triumphal dress driving a quadriga, on the base of which was inscribed PATER PATRIAE (*RG* 35), a title that had been voted earlier in the same year. In the middle of each exedra was a niche of double size. The one on the north contained a statue of Aeneas carrying Anchises on his shoulders, surrounded by statues of Aeneas' Julian descendants. In the central niche on the south Romulus was shown carrying off the *spolia opima*; around him were statues of great men of the Republic, their deeds inscribed on plaques affixed below.[7]

These are the chief features of the Augustan forum, although the whole was considerably more complex than the sketch given here since the site was a repository of mementos and artistic works of all sorts and of diverse decoration.[8] Among the mementos were the standards Crassus and Antony had lost to the Parthians, which Augustus had recovered (by diplomacy) in 20 B.C. (*RG* 29; Dio 54.8.3).

Thus the Forum Augustum was an amalgam of personal and public elements, with pronounced emphasis on the personal. Augustus determined that the fulfillment of his vow at Philippi must be his alone. Accordingly, he purchased privately the land on which the forum was to be placed and would not dispossess those unwilling to sell by having the area declared public land and the project a public undertaking. His purchases produced a more constricted area than he would have liked: clearly one or more landowners were unwilling

---

[6] So E. Strong in *CAH* X, 578, and Zanker (supra n. 5) 20, who does not believe that Julius Caesar also appeared in the Hall of Fame. This supposition receives support from Dio (56.34.2–3), who reports that Caesar's image was not carried in Augustus' funeral procession among the *imagines* [images] of his ancestors on the ground of Caesar's divinity.

[7] Ov. *Fast.* 5.563–66:
> Hinc videt Aenean oneratum pondere caro
>   et tot Iuliae nobilitatis avos,
> hinc videt Iliadem umeris ducis arma ferentem
>   claraque dispositis acta subesse viris.

> "On this side he sees Aeneas weighed down with his beloved burden and so many ancestors of the noble Julian line; on the other side he sees the son of Ilia (i.e., Romulus) carrying on his shoulders the enemy leader's weapons and their famous deeds inscribed beneath the statues of the heroes arranged in sequence."

[8] Cf. Pliny *HN* 35.27, 93–94; see Zanker (supra n. 5) 7–14, 23–24; Putnam (supra n. 2) 332–35.

to sell.⁹ The forum in its final form put great emphasis on his person: the great dedicatory inscription on the temple's architrave, images of his divine ancestors within and without, and his triumphal statue occupying the central space before the temple. Velleius tells us that the names of Spanish and other peoples whom Augustus had conquered were also displayed in the forum (*quarum titulis forum eius praenitet*) [with the inscriptions of which his forum gleams]. Most scholars have supposed that this took the form of an *elogium* on the statue base. This may be doubted: it would compete with the simple PATER PATRIAE on another part of the base and would not have had the prominence that Velleius' word *praenitet* [gleams] suggests. A more suitable place for the names might be the architraves between the upper and lower rows of columns supporting the porticoes, each of which is over 100 m long. The letters would be large, the names running down the long sides of the open area and leading the eye to Augustus' name on the temple's architrave.

The Hall of Fame was subordinate to and supportive of this grand scheme. Surrounding the statue of Augustus' ancestor Aeneas in the central niche in the north exedra were statues of his Julian ancestors, including the fourteen kings of Alba Longa (fragmentary *elogia* of four have survived: D 2–5),¹⁰ Julius Caesar's father (praetor ca. 92, died in 85: D 7) and another member of the clan, Caesar Strabo (curule aedile in 90, died in 87: D 6). These Caesares illustrate the relatively undistinguished record compiled by the Julii in the course of the Republic. Ovid's description (*Fast.* 5.563–66) might be strictly interpreted to mean that the Julii were on one side of the forum, everyone else on the other. But since there was room for up to 108 niches (D 2), it is doubtful that anywhere near 54 Julii could be mustered to fill one side, even allowing for the Alban kings and for those related by marriage or adoption. *Elogia* for Augustus' son-in-law M. Claudius Marcellus (D 8), who died in 23, and for his stepson Nero Claudius Drusus (D 9), who died in 9, were found in the area of the north exedra.¹¹ Zanker is probably right in supposing that

---

⁹ Suet. *Aug.* 56.2: "He made his forum narrower since he did not try to expropriate the neighbouring houses from their owners." The retaining wall to the rear is irregular, and the temple seems to have been pulled forward, partially occupying what should have been an open space between the two exedrae. Yet see the remarks of Anderson (supra n. 2) 66, 74. E. A. Judge, *On Judging the Merits of Augustus*, Center for Hermeneutical Studies in Hellenistic and Modern Culture, Colloquy 49 (Berkeley 1984) 9–10, well emphasizes the private aspects of the forum, noting (in reference to *RG* 21.1) that "in contrast with his public works, this temple was to open the catalogue of his private endowments." Cf. H. T. Rowell (1940: supra n. 2) 141.

¹⁰ Degrassi, *Inscr. It.* 13.3, hereafter cited in the text as D.

¹¹ All Claudii did not stand on the north side, however; the *elogium* for Appius Claudius Caecus (D 12) was found in the area of the south exedra: Degrassi, *Inscr. It.* 13.3, p. 5.

the statues of some *summi viri* [most illustrious men] (as they are called at SHA *Alex. Sev.* 28.6), not related to the Julii, were also on the north side.[12] The division between relatives and nonrelatives was also observed at Augustus' funeral, for which the emperor left detailed instructions (Dio 56.33.1). In the procession three likenesses of Augustus preceded the *imagines* [ancestral images] of the Julii, who in turn were followed by an image of Romulus, which headed up the *imagines* of other Romans (Dio 56.34.2-3).[13] The presence and arrangement of ancestors and of other great Romans are similar in both the forum and the funeral procession.

Why did Augustus appropriate distinguished nonrelations to grace both his forum and his funeral? Suetonius (*Aug.* 31.5) tells us that

> next to the immortal gods he honored the memory of those leaders who had raised the Roman empire from small beginnings to greatness. Accordingly, ... when setting up statues of men in triumphal dress in the two porticoes of his forum, he declared in an edict that he had done so in order that the citizens might measure both himself and succeeding *principes* by the standard set by those men in their lives.

Thus the statues and *elogia* of the forum established a competition by comparison. The *elogia* specify the points of comparison in the choice of achievements that Augustus selected for mention in the case of each honorand. As for Augustus' own *elogium*, he composed it himself; the *Res Gestae* was to be displayed before his mausoleum and to be reproduced for display throughout the Roman world. In a recent article P. Frisch has well argued that the achievements meticulously recorded in the *Res Gestae* were meant to be measured against the achievements of the men whose *elogia* appeared in the forum, and were meant to be found far greater.[14]

In short, the *Res Gestae* is a great comparative document, just as the Forum Augustum is a great comparative monument, with continuous emphasis by statement and suggestion on those matters in which Augustus was the first to do this or that or did more than others or had done so with greater glory and to greater effect. It was not enough for Augustus to claim that he matched or surpassed

---

[12] So also Putnam (supra n. 2) 331.

[13] Agrippa's funeral in 12 B.C. followed the same pattern as that of Augustus (Dio 54.28.5). Drusus' funeral in 9 included images of both Claudii and Julii, although Drusus had not been adopted into the Julian family (Tac. *Ann.* 3.5.1).

[14] "Zu den Elogien des Augustusforums," ZPE 39 (1980) 93-98. Pliny HN 22.6.13, *quod et statuae eius in foro suo divus Augustus subscripsit* ["This the deified Augustus inscribed on his [i.e., Scipio Aemilianus'] statue in the Forum Augustum"], if interpreted literally, would mean that Augustus composed the *elogia* himself. This is improbable. But that he supervised them closely is maintained by most recent scholars, notably Frisch.

the achievements of his linear ancestors, which was the ideal of the nobility throughout the Republic. The chief message of the forum and of the *Res Gestae* is that Augustus matched or surpassed the deeds of all great men of Roman history.

Did Livy subscribe to this claim? Several obstacles stand in the way of a clear view. The first is that we do not know how he regarded the principate as a political institution, as J. Deininger has argued in a recent article.[15] The second concerns the degree of friendship and amount of contact that the two men enjoyed; it might have been fairly close and sustained, but it need not be so interpreted. Moreover, when we come to estimate the significance of Livy's references to Augustus (or the lack thereof: the emperor is not mentioned in the preface), one must allow for the independent stance that Livy was obliged to take in reference to powerful contemporaries if he wished to be judged an honest historian.[16] In postponing publication of Books 121–42 (covering the period 43–9 B.C.) until Augustus was dead, Livy may have been prompted by two seemingly contradictory motives at once: that is, he both feared giving offense for plain speaking and feared being charged with flattery and partisan feeling. There is evidence to suggest that Livy was influenced by both factors. On the one hand, his independence from Augustus is attested by the statement that Tacitus places in the mouth of Cremutius Cordus (*Ann.* 4.34.3). Other examples are his discussion of the descent of the Julii from Julus ("for who could confirm for certain the truth of a matter so ancient?" Livy 1.3.1–3); his evenhanded, somewhat sceptical attitude towards Augustus' version of how Cornelius Cossus won the *spolia opima* (4.20.4–11, cf. 32.4); and his wondering out loud whether it would have been better for the world if Julius Caesar had never been born (Sen. *QN* 5.12.4). On the other hand, he could easily have avoided mentioning the emperor by name altogether; yet his references to Augustus are markedly complimentary.[17]

Thus Livy was probably influenced by both motives. Yet it is doubtful that he believed Augustus to be the last and greatest in a long line of great men of the Republic. Livy viewed Roman history as the joint achievement of leaders and the led; the *mores* of the people as a whole is a constant in his history: how the national

---

[15] Deininger (supra n. 4) 265–72.
[16] See T. J. Luce, "Ancient Views on the Causes of Bias in Historical Writing" *CP* 84 (1989) 16–31.
[17] See 1.19.3, 28.12.12, and *Per.* 59. At 4.20.7 his phrase *Augustum Caesarem, templorum omnium conditorem ac restitutorem* ["Augustus Caesar, the founder and restorer of all our temples"] is a strong, even hyperbolic, expression.

character developed, matured, and decayed.[18] Naturally, the character of individuals is given great prominence, but even his greatest heroes have flaws; more significant is his belief that Rome was the product of a long line of leaders, not of any single individual (see 9.18.9).

On one point in particular Livy and Augustus were in emphatic agreement: history was the great repository of *exempla* [examples] by which one might pattern one's life and against which one might measure the worth of one's own contributions. Livy's remarks in his preface (10) coincide with the emperor's faith in the power of *exempla* in Roman life.

II

Might Livy and his history have suggested to Augustus the choice of certain men as *summi viri*? The large majority needed no Livy to establish their preeminent fame, since most were great *triumphatores*.[19] Furthermore, Augustus' selection was nonpartisan. Marius, a relative by marriage, was there, for example, and his *elogium* survives almost complete. The end of his career is described in this way: *post LXX annum patria per arma civilia expulsus, armis restitutus est. VII cos. factus* ("When he was seventy, he was driven from his country by civil war, and by war he was brought back. He became consul for the seventh time"). Contrast Livy's summation as preserved in *Periocha* 80: *editisque plurimis sceleribus idibus Ianuariis decessit, vir cuius si examinentur cum virtutibus vitia, haud facile sit dictu utrum bello melior an pace perniciosior fuerit. adeo, quam rem publicam armatus servavit, eam primo togatus omni genere fraudis, postremo armis hostiliter evertit* ("Having committed a great many crimes, he died on the Ides of January; if one compares his virtues with his vices, it would be difficult to decide whether he was more serviceable in war or more pernicious in peace – so much so that the country he saved by war he overthrew in peacetime, first by every sort of wrongdoing, and finally in arms like a foreign enemy"). Clearly Livy and Augustus were looking at the same man as an *exemplar* from very different perspectives. On the other hand, Frisch has made out a strong prima facie case for supposing that

---

[18] See T. J. Luce, *Livy: The Composition of His History* (Princeton 1977) 292–94.

[19] Suetonius is wrong to imply that all were in triumphal dress (*Aug.* 31.5); fragments of togate statues have been found, and of those for whom *elogia* survive, neither Appius Claudius Caecus nor L. Albinius celebrated triumphs. On the military functions that were to be performed in the forum, see Dio 55.10.3; Suet. *Aug.* 29.2.

Pompey was included among the *summi viri*,[20] a nonpartisan gesture of which Livy doubtless would have approved.

There are two unexpected choices among the nineteen known *summi viri*. The first is C. Cornelius Cethegus (D 64). It would be a knowledgeable student of Roman history who could without some searching identify this Cethegus, including, one might imagine, Livy himself, although almost all our knowledge of the man comes from his pages. Cethegus' exploits against the Insubres and Cenomani in northern Italy while consul in 197 are recorded at 32.28–31, the debate over his triumph and that of his colleague at 33.22–23.[21] His was a creditable career, to be sure, but it is difficult to believe that Livy's brief account prompted Augustus to make the selection.

The second is L. Albinius (D 11). Once again, it would be a well-informed student of Roman history who could identify him offhand, for he was the plebeian (Livy 5.40.9) who gave the Vestal virgins a ride to Caere in his wagon as they fled the Gauls during the sack of the city in 390. Livy represents our only literary version of the event, since all later accounts derive from his (Plut. *Cam.* 21; Val. Max. 1.1.10; and Florus 1.7). Here, one might think, is a strong prima facie case for supposing that Livy's narrative suggested to Augustus the choice of Albinius, who had no public career of which we know.[22] But, as will be explained below, it is doubtful if even Albinius was suggested by Livy's history.

Elogia survive in some form for ten men whose careers are covered in the extant books of Livy. What does a comparison reveal about Livy as a possible source of information? In two cases no conclusions can be drawn because next to nothing survives.[23] For the other eight many discrepancies appear, both major and minor.

A. Postumius Regillensis (D 10). The few extant words of the *elogium* refer to the presence at the battle of Lake Regillus of the sons of Tarquinius Superbus: [*f*]*iliis et gen*[*tilibus*] [his sons and members

[20] Frisch (supra n.14) 97–98. Pompey's image was carried in Augustus' funeral procession (Dio 56.34.2–3), which reproduced the same conception of Roman history that we find in the Forum Augustum. Note too, that Pompey's *elogium* was among those set up at Vesontio in the Antonine age, which appear to have been patterned after those of the Forum Augustum: Degrassi (supra n. 2) 7; *CIL* I², p. 201, no. xxxviii and vol. XIII, 5381.

[21] Livy otherwise mentions him briefly: 30.41.4–5, cf. 31.49.7 (proconsul); 31.50.7–10 and 32.7.14 (curule aedile); 34.44.4–5, 35.9.1 (censor in 194).

[22] Unless he is to be identified with the military tribune with consular power of 379, whom Livy names as Marcus (6.30.2), Diodorus as Lucius (15.51.1).

[23] For L. Cornelius Scipio Asiaticus (D 15) only a fragmentary part of the inscription on the statue base survives, which gives his names and offices. For L. Papirius Cursor (D 62) the fragmentary *elogium* describes the beginning of the clash with his *magister equitum* [master of the horse], Q. Fabius Ambusti f. Maximus, which agrees with Livy's version at 8.30–36. That the forum contained a statue of M. Valerius Corvinus is known from Aul. Gell. *NA* 9.11.10; no *elogium* survives.

of his *gens*, i.e., kin-group]. For Livy only one son was present (2.19.10: *filius*), who must be Titus, since the other two sons are already dead (Sextus at 1.60.2 and Arruns at 2.6.9). In the version of Dionysius of Halicarnassus both Sextus and Titus are present at the battle (*Ant. Rom.* 6.4.1ff. and 6.5.4).

M' Valerius Maximus (D 60, 78). The *elogium* records his triumph over the Sabini and Medullini; the latter are absent in Livy's version. Dionysius records that at the start of the year the Medullini conspired with the Sabines (4.2.1, 3), but he does not mention them thereafter. The *elogium* named Valerius as the one who ended the secession of the plebs by bringing them back from the Mons Sacer and reconciling them with the senators. Livy credits Menenius Agrippa with these actions (2.32–33). Dionysius' elaborate account gives Valerius a prominent role in the negotiations, but he too names Agrippa as the one who ended the secession (6.57ff. and 6.96). The *elogium* also says that Valerius persuaded the senate to relieve the plebs of their burden of debt; in Livy he signally fails in his effort, prophesying a bad outcome and resigning the dictatorship (2.31.8–10; the secession then follows). The *elogium* also adds some unique or unusual details: Valerius' augurate, his being *princeps senatus* [leading man in the senate], and the precise spot in the Circus where the *sella curulis* was placed for him and his descendants.

M. Furius Camillus (D 61). The *elogium* gives Camillus' victories in his third dictatorship in this order: Etruscans, Aequi, Volsci; Livy reverses the order of conquest (6.2.7–4.3). The elogium speaks of Camillus' settling of the revolt of Velitrae, which according to Livy (6.36.1ff.) began in 370 and was still in progress in 367 when Camillus was declared dictator for the fifth time, specifically to deal with a Gallic war. Livy does not record the actual capitulation of Velitrae: we do not hear of it again after 6.42.4. Plutarch (*Cam.* 41.6–42.1) says that Camillus' fifth and final dictatorship saw the defeat of the Gauls, in the course of which he took Velitrae.

L. Albinius (D 11). The *elogium* reads: [*Cum Galli ob*]*siderent Capitolium,* [*virgines Ve*]*stales Caere deduxit;* [*ibi sacra at*]*que ritus sollemnes ne* [*intermitte*]*rentur, curai sibi habuit;* [*urbe recup*]*erata sacra et virgines* [*Romam re*]*vexit* ("When the Gauls were besieging the Capitol, he conducted the Vestal virgins to Caere; there he saw to it that the sacred rites and ceremonies were not interrupted; and when the city was recaptured he brought the sacred objects and the virgins back"). Both that Albinius brought the Vestals back to Rome and that at Caere he saw to it that the sacred rites were not interrupted are not in Livy. The part about the return is trivial, but

Albinius' actions at Caere are not. For how could a plebeian have anything to do with sacred rites conducted by patricians? This is the chief reason why Borghesi, Hirschfeld, Schwegler, and others have supposed that the *elogium* must refer not to Albinius but to the unnamed *flamen Quirinalis* [priest of Quirinus] in Livy's account (5.40.7).[24] Others, such as Mommsen, find it difficult to believe that an *elogium* in the Forum Augustum would honor a man whose name has not come down to us in any source (yet only the Livian tradition preserves Albinius' name).[25] Moreover, just what might a plebeian do to insure the continuance of the rites? Degrassi suggests, *exempli gratia*, that he might have lent the Vestals the use of his house at Caere. But Albinius was a Roman, not a Caeretan, and it is difficult to believe that an action like the loan of living quarters would be so magnified. The more one ponders the *elogium*, the more problematic it becomes. The information in it cannot possibly come from Livy; it may represent a version radically different from that of Livy.

Appius Claudius Caecus (D 12, 79). The *elogium* preserves the oddities of iterated praetorships and curule aedileships for Caecus, as well as such precise facts as his having been thrice interrex and thrice military tribune. The events of 296 are described in the *elogium* thus: *complura oppida de Samnitibus cepit, Sabinorum et Tuscorum exercitum fudit* ["He captured several towns from the Samnites and routed the army of the Sabines and Etruscans."]. Livy knows of no Sabini, only Sabelli (10.19.20).[26] Moreover, in his version the

---

[24] B. Borghesi, *Oeuvres complètes*, vol. 3 (Paris 1864) 6–7; O. Hirschfeld, *Kleine Schriften* (Berlin 1913) 815; A. Schwegler, *Römische Geschichte*, vol. 3 (Tübingen 1872) 250, n. 3. Most recently, E. A. Judge (supra n. 9) 11, also opts for the *flamen*.

[25] *CIL* I², p. 285, no. 84. B. A. Kellum, in her response to Judge (supra n. 9) 41, opts for Albinius. One of her reasons is that L. Sestius Quirinalis, suffect consul of 23, is supposed to have taken the cognomen from his mother's side of the family (she was an Albinia: Cic. *Sest.* 6 – but see below); in this she follows R. Syme, *CP* 50 (1955) 135, in a review of T. R. S. Broughton's *Magistrates of the Roman Republic*, vols. 1 and 2 (Cleveland 1952); Broughton in vol. 3: *Supplement* (Atlanta 1986) lists the consul as L. Sestius P. f. L. n. Quirinalis Albinianus, the last cognomen derived from ALB on three brick stamps that have Sestius' same (*CIL* 15.1445). Yet it seems odd to select Quirinalis rather than Vestalis as a cognomen to honor the ancestor of Sestius' mother. The *flamen* is not mentioned explicitly as having been given a ride, although in Livy's source(s) the *flamen* clearly accompanied the Vestals and went to Caere (5.40.7–10, 7.20.4). Hence the *flamen* is absent in the accounts derived from Livy. The *elogium* does not mention him. D. R. Shackleton Bailey, *Two Studies in Roman Nomenclature* (State College, Pa. 1976) 6–7, prefers Albanius as the name of Sestius' father-in-law on the basis of the manuscript tradition, although G. V. Sumner in his review, *CP* 73 (1978) 159, opts for Albinius. Even if we follow Sumner and Broughton in preferring Albinius, it does not seem likely to me that the cognomen Quirinalis derives from L. Albinius' exploit during the Gallic sack of Rome. R. M. Ogilvie, *A Commentary on Livy, Books 1–5* (Oxford 1965) 723, identifies the "Lucius" who, according to Aristotle, saved Rome (*apud*. Cam. 22.4) with Albinius.

[26] *Vir. Ill.* 34 is the only other source to agree with the *elogium* on this point. On the oddity, see M. Sage, "The *Elogia* of the Augustan Forum and the *De Viris Illustribus*," *Historia* 28 (1979) 197.

proconsul P. Decius Mus is credited with the victories in Samnium (10.17.1–10); in an aside Livy notes three variants in his sources, none of which answers to the version of the *elogium* (10.17.11–12). Finally, in Livy's narrative of events in Etruria, Caecus cuts a poor figure (10.18).

Q. Fabius Maximus Verrucosus (D 14, 80). The *elogium* refers to events of Fabius' fourth and fifth consulships in 215–214 before mentioning that as dictator (in 217) he saved his *magister equitum* M. Minucius (yet at this point Minucius has been elevated to a position of sharing equal power, according to Livy 22.25.10, 22.26.5–7).[27] Minucius' army hails Fabius *pater* [father] (so also Pliny *HN* 22.10), whereas in Livy, Minucius himself does so (22.30; so also Plut. *Fab.* 13.3). Fabius' two terms each as interrex, quaestor, and military tribune are known only from the *elogium*.

C. Cornelius Cethegus (D 64). Only the letters]ET CENOM[are preserved from the first line of the plaque affixed below the statue base and]VCEM EO[from the second line. As noted above, the reference is to Cethegus' victory and triumph as consul over the Insubres and Cenomani in 197. The reference in the second line is doubtless to the Carthaginian leader Hamilcar, who some historical accounts said was captured in the course of the fighting and led in the triumph. Our knowledge of the variant comes from Livy (32.30.11–12, 33.23.5; cf. Zonaras 9.16), but it is not the version Livy reproduces. For him, Hamilcar's death had come in the year 200 (31.21.18).[28]

L. Aemilius Paullus (D 81). The *elogium* supplies details of his career unmentioned in other sources: interrex, quaestor, and thrice military tribune. It also assigns his victories in Liguria to his first consulship in 182 (so also Vell. Pat. 1.9.3; *Vir. Ill.* 56), whereas Livy puts them in 181 when he was proconsul. The *elogium* also says *copias regis [decem dieb]us quibus Mac[edoniam atti]git delev[it* ["He destroyed the forces of the king within ten days of arriving in Macedonia."]. Yet both Livy (45.41.5) and Diodorus (31.11.1) say it took fifteen days after he entered Macedonia before he defeated

---

[27] Degrassi, *Inscr. It.* 13.3, p. 6, views this as an attempt to sketch at one stroke the events of Fabius' first four consulships. Sage, (supra n. 26) 199, is right to see this as an error, since all other *elogia* give events in chronological order.

[28] At *CIL* I², p. 341, Hülsen notes that although only the tops of the letters EO are preserved, enough is left to show that E, not P, is correct (D]VCEM PO[ENORVM ["leader of the Carthaginians"] would give excellent sense). Yet it is difficult to see how Hülsen's suggestion of EO[RVM ["of them"] could be right: there seems to be no room for POENI, much less CARTHAGINIENSES, to appear earlier, to which EO[RVM could refer (unless in this version Hamilcar is credited as a *dux* of the Insubres or Cenomani!). EO[DEM PROELIO or TEMPORE ["at the same battle" or "at the same time"]?

Perseus' forces. The *elogium* has too little room to supply [*quindecim dieb*]*us* [within fifteen days] and too much for [*XV dieb*]*us*. Bormann's restoration (*CIL* 11.1829), which Degrassi follows, is probably correct: the *elogium* thus gives a reckoning different from our other sources. Moreover, in the sentence before the one just discussed, the *elogium* reads: *iterum cos. ut cum rege*/[*Per*]*se bellum gereret, ap*/[... *f*]*actus est* ["He was appointed consul for a second time .... when he was waging war with king Perseus"]. The obvious restoration is *ap*[*sens f*]*actus est* ["was appointed in absence"] (so Bormann; there is not enough room for Mommsen's *a p*[*opulo*] ["by the people"]). Scholars have been reluctant to accept the restoration, because it disagrees with the version of Plutarch (*Aem*. 10); nor is there any mention in Livy of Paulus' absence (44.17–18). Yet Bormann's restoration is likely to be right.

In the information they provide the *elogia* are independent, quirky, and willful. They like to give the exact number of times a man was interrex, military tribune, and *princeps senatus*, and to preserve such oddities as iterated quaestorships, curule aedileships, and praetorships. Yet they do not seem to differentiate between magistracy and promagistracy or take note of lesser offices (e.g., the fact that Aemilius Paullus was *triumvir coloniae deducendae* ["III vir (i.e., member of a board of three) for founding a colony"] in 194 [Livy 34.45.3–5]). The *elogia* also have a pronounced antiquarian bent, not only in reference to such early personalities as the Alban kings, but, for example, in ferreting out the fact that M' Valerius Maximus (D 60, 78) *princeps in senatu semel lectus est* ["was selected on one occasion as leading man in the senate"] and that the seat at the Circus given him and his descendants was located precisely *ad* [*sacellum*] *Murciae* ["next to the [small shrine] of Murcia"] (so also Festus, p. 464L). Most striking, however, are the many disagreements not only with Livy but with all other extant sources concerning the achievements of the *summi viri*.

When *Quellenforschung* [source criticism] was in its heyday, speculation inevitably arose as to the sources of the *elogia*. The claims of such late annalists as Valerius Antias and Licinius Macer and of Atticus' *Imagines* by way of Verrius Flaccus have been advanced.[29] But such guesses were bound to seem feeble, given the

---

[29] *RE* 5.2 (1905) 2447, s.v. Elogium (A. von Premerstein); Degrassi, *Inscr. It.* 13.3, p. 6; and Frisch (supra n. 14) 91 with n. 5 review these efforts. An anonymous referee believes the most likely candidate to be Varro's *Hebdomades*, or *De imaginibus*, compiled in 39 B.C., which featured portraits of seven hundred famous Greeks and Romans from all spheres of endeavor, each picture accompanied by an epigram in verse and a brief *elogium* in prose.

vast time span covered by the *elogia* (from the fall of Troy to the death of the elder Drusus) and what must have been a remarkably wide-ranging search for the sometimes arcane and unique information found in them. Mommsen believed that the sources themselves were authentic and reliable, but that those responsible for using them were careless and unlearned. Yet, as Degrassi has noted, the number of certain errors that we can detect are few.[30]

We now know of another and more probable candidate as a source, which was contemporary, lengthy, markedly antiquarian, and covered events from the fall of Troy down to, one would guess, at least the 120s B.C. I refer to the eighty volumes of the *annales maximi* [lit., "greatest annals"], which, as B. W. Frier has argued in a recent book, were almost certainly an Augustan compilation.[31] To my mind Frier has convincingly shown that the eighty-volume edition mentioned by Servius (*ad Aen.* 1.373) cannot be the same as the jejune *annales pontificum maximorum* [annals of the chief pontiffs] that Cicero spoke of (*De Leg.* 1.5–6), which reported only dates, persons, places, and deeds in a chronicle devoid of all ornamentation (*De or.* 2.51–53). Frier argues that all references to this eighty-volume edition derive from the Augustan antiquarian Verrius Flaccus. The edition contained the most detailed account of Roman history we know of, beginning with Aeneas' departure from Troy. Book 4, for example, dealt with individual Alban kings; around Book 9 the history of the Republic began, since the story of the statue of Horatius Cocles appeared in Book 11 (which answers to the period covered in Book 2 of Livy). If the *annales maximi* stopped in the 120s B.C., when the *pontifex maximus* P. Mucius Scaevola ceased to put up the *tabulae dealbatae* [whitened notice-boards] (Cic. *De or.* 2.52), then some seventy books were devoted to a period of republican history that Livy covered in around sixty. Frier has characterized the nature of the antiquarian information preserved from citations from the early books: often late republican in formulation, prone to favor

---

[30] Degrassi, *Inscr. It.* 13.3, p. 6; the only significant error, in his view, is Paulus' defeat of the Ligurians as consul rather than as proconsul.

[31] *Libri Annales Pontificum Maximorum: The Origins of the Annalistic Tradition*, PAAR 27 (Rome 1979). I have seen no convincing refutation of Frier's main thesis, despite the reservations and alternate hypotheses of some: e.g., T. J. Cornell, "The Formation of the Historical Tradition of Early Rome," in I. S. Moxon, J. D. Smart, A, J. Woodman, eds., *Past Perspectives: Studies in Greek and Roman Historical Writing* (Cambridge 1986) 71 with n. 21; R. Drews, "Pontiffs, Prodigies, and the Disappearance of the *Annales Maximi*," *CP* 83 (1988) 289–99; cf. Ps. Aurelius Victor, *Les origines du peuple Romain*, ed. J.-C. Richard (Paris 1983) 9–48, esp. 38–48. I would presume that the *tabulae pontificum* [records of the *pontifices*] that Cato and Cicero knew were available for "consultation" by researchers such as Varro, but we do not hear of anyone actually using them or citing information from them.

odd and trivial variants, intricate and sometimes bogus in combining bits of information from sources of widely different provenances and credibility.[32]

In at least one instance we can perhaps see how the compilers of the *elogia* may have worked with their antiquarian material. The *elogium* of Manius Valerius Maximus (D 60, 78) states that he was augur, which R. M. Ogilvie discounts as an antiquarian reconstruction, believing with Mommsen and others that the guess was based on Livy (3.7.6), who for the year 463 notes the death of the augur Marcus Valerius. Manius, already an old man in 494 (Dion. Hal. *Ant. Rom.* 6.39.2), could scarcely have survived another thirty years. Ogilvie concludes that "the identification of the augur with the dictator need be no more than a guess by the author of the Elogium who in an endeavor to fill out a biography gathered and combined material from every source. ... The testimony of the Elogium can be discounted as an antiquarian reconstruction."[33]

The purpose of the eighty-volume edition "remains mysterious," as Frier concedes.[34] But that its provenance was Augustan seems certain, and Frier has made out a plausible case for supposing that it was compiled shortly after 12 B.C., when Augustus succeeded Lepidus as *pontifex maximus*. The *annales maximi* were so named, Verrius Flaccus claimed in a novel interpretation, not because of their size, but because the *pontifex maximus* compiled them.[35] A flurry of religious activity connected with Augustus' new position quickly followed after 12 B.C., especially in the area of sacred records. Moreover, Augustus had about him specialists who were historical and antiquarian experts: those who had helped earlier to compile the *fasti Capitolini* [Capitoline lists of consuls] and *acta triumphalia* [records of triumphs], those who gathered the information for the *elogia* (whatever their sources), and those who late in the reign compiled the lists of the major priestly colleges.[36] I believe that Frier's proposed dating makes sense, and would suggest that in the decade after 12 B.C., as the compilation for the eighty-volume *annales maximi* was under way, it provided much or all of the information for the *elogia* as well. Certainly the research for the *annales maximi* must have been wide-ranging; Frier's detailed analysis of the legend of

---

[32] Frier (supra n. 31) 50–67, esp. 55–56 (on the descent of Julus) and 60–66 (on the statue of Horatius Cocles).
[33] Ogilvie (supra n. 25) 407–8. He emends the M. Valerius of Livy's MSS to M' at 2.30.5.
[34] Frier (supra n. 31) 196.
[35] Paulus (W. M. Lindsay's Teubner edition of 1913, p. 113), summarizing Verrius. See Frier (supra n. 31) 47–48, 195.
[36] Frier (supra n. 31) 196–200.

Horatius Cocles' statue shows how complex the reconstruction by the compilers could be, involving aetiological explanations based on "archival notices," arcane religious lore, literary verses, topographical siting, and the like.

The *elogia* thus pursue an independent course in the information they provide about the *summi viri*, disagreeing not only with Livy, but on some points with all other sources that survive to us. The disagreements with Livy, however, are curiously many, especially when we consider that the *elogia* for the most part select for mention the highlights of the careers of famous men: doubly curious, given that most *elogia* are very fragmentary and given how brief the few are that survive complete, or nearly complete; triply so, given the fame that Livy's history enjoyed.

The suspicion arises that on particular points the *elogia* may have deliberately been making correctives or ripostes to Livy's version of events: for example, L. Albinius is credited with providing much more than a ride to Caere for the Vestals. The *elogium* of Appius Claudius Caecus is pointed in its disagreement about Caecus' victories in Samnium. Livy gives full credit for them to Decius Mus, and adds three variants (10.17.11–12): that Fabius Maximus deserved even greater credit than Decius for the victories; that the new consuls, Caecus and Volumnius, shared the glory; and that Volumnius alone earned it. The *elogium* selects the one variant that Livy fails to report: the credit goes to Caecus alone (or primarily). Disagreement is even more marked in the *elogium* of M' Valerius Maximus. At 2.18.5–6 Livy rejects the possibility that Valerius' nephew was chosen dictator in 501, because of a law requiring that dictators be consulars. Yet at 2.30.5, when he reports that the uncle, a nonconsular, was appointed dictator, he takes no notice of his dictum a few pages earlier that would invalidate such an appointment. The *elogium* (D 60, 78) is firm on the matter: *priusquam ullum magistratum gereret dictator dictus est* ["He was appointed dictator before he held any magistracy."]. And where in Livy, Valerius signally fails in his effort to relieve those oppressed by debt, in the *elogium* he fully succeeds. Finally, in the *elogium* Valerius ends the secession of the plebs, but in Livy, Menenius Agrippa does so.

In conclusion, Livy and Augustus agreed on the exemplary value of history, although for Livy the emphasis was on imitation or avoidance in the conduct of one's personal life and public career, whereas for Augustus it was on the achievements against which he and succeeding *principes* should be measured in the judgment of posterity. But in all else there is little common ground. I do not believe that Livy viewed Augustus as having surpassed the achievements of all *summi viri* of the past or that he thought Roman history reached its acme in Augustus' lifetime (Livy's preface trenchantly rejects any such interpretation, at least up to ca. 25 B.C.).[37] Moreover, it does not appear that Livy's history suggested to Augustus any of the choices of the men whom we know to have been represented in the forum. As for the information set forth in the *elogia*, the numerous and marked differences between Livy and the exiguous fragments show that those men whom Augustus assigned to gather and select the information treated Livy's version of Roman history with calculated indifference. Augustus accepted their suggestions. The friendship between the emperor and the historian may not have been as close or congenial as some have supposed.

At first glance the *elogia* appear harmless enough; it is only on closer inspection that the many disagreements come into view. I have a picture of Livy touring the Hall of Fame on his first go-round with cheerful approval; but when he stopped to inspect the *elogia* at greater leisure, disappointment and annoyance supervened, to be replaced in the end by sharp irritation.

---

[37] Recently A. J. Woodman, *Rhetoric in Classical Historiography* (London, Sydney, and Portland, Oreg. 1988) 128–40, has argued that Livy, like Horace, developed an admiration for Augustus during the course of the principate.

PART IV

The Impact of Augustus in the Roman Provinces

Introduction to Part IV: The Impact of Augustus in the Roman Provinces

In the year 9 BC the general council (*koinon*) of the Greeks of the province of Asia issued a decree declaring that henceforth all cities of the province would recognise the "ninth day before the Kalends of October" (i.e., 23 September) as the start of their New Year. In so doing, they were enthusiastically taking up a suggestion of the Roman proconsul of Asia, Paullus Fabius Maximus, a close friend of Augustus.[1] The language in which the council chose to justify this far-reaching decision is revealing:

> Since Providence, which has [divinely] disposed our lives, having employed zeal and ardour, has arranged the most perfect culmination for life by producing Augustus, whom for the benefit of mankind she has filled with excellence, as if [she had sent him as a saviour] for us and our descendants, (a saviour) who brought war to an end and set [all things] in order; [and since with his appearance] Caesar exceeded the hopes of [all] those who received [glad tidings] before us, not only surpassing those who had been [benefactors] before him, but not even [leaving any] hope of [surpassing him] for those who are to come in the future ... for this reason, with good luck and for (our) salvation, it has been decreed by the Greeks in Asia that the first month of the New Year shall begin for all the cities on the ninth day before the Kalends of October, which is the birthday of Augustus, in order that each time the day might correspond in each city, (the Greeks) shall use the Greek day along with the Roman; they shall make the first month – "Caesar," as previously decreed – begin on the ninth day before the Kalends of October, the birthday of Caesar. (*OGIS* 458 = EJ² 98 = *RDGE* 65, trans. Sherk, *RGE*, no. 101, with slight modifications)

Augustus was "filled with excellence," a "benefactor" surpassing all previous and future benefactors, a "saviour who brought war to an end and set all things in order." The Greeks of Asia and mainland Greece had become accustomed to issuing honorific decrees praising

---

[1] For Paullus Fabius Maximus, see Syme 1986: 403–420. For the new calendar of Asia, Laffi 1967.

the manifold virtues of Hellenistic monarchs and then Roman magistrates, in which they often hailed them as "saviours and benefactors";[2] and some of the language found in this decree owes much to those rhetorical precedents. But the far-reaching implications of the council's decision should not be downplayed. Henceforth all the cities of the province of Asia were to operate on the same solar calendar of twelve months rather than according to a heterogeneous variety of local practices. Their year would now begin on Augustus' birthday, which was to become the first day of the month "Caesar." The rhythms of life from then on would be calibrated according to a new Roman system, a system shared by all cities of the province and one that fixed attention for now and for the future on Augustus (in Greek, *Sebastos*, "the revered one," or simply *Kaisar*, i.e., "Caesar") and, not least, on the day of his birth.

This is just one isolated example of the many profound changes that affected the lives of the fifty million or so inhabitants of the Roman Empire during the age of Augustus. Many provincials had seen their world turned upside down during the "Roman revolution," which, as Fergus Millar has reminded us, was a distinctly pan-Mediterranean event.[3] In the 40s and 30s BC large numbers had been drafted into, or volunteered to fight in, the armies led by rival Roman dynasts. During their time under arms, many saw service in several sectors of the Mediterranean. Of those who survived the wars, how many, one wonders, returned to their place of origin? Most of them were demobilised and settled in colonies of veterans established by Augustus in Italy and across the Empire in Africa, Sicily, Macedonia, the Spanish provinces, Achaea, Asia, Syria, Gallia Narbonensis, and Pisidia, as Augustus himself enumerated with great care in the *Res Gestae* (*RG* 28). The Augustan age was one of unprecedented geographical mobility, some of it enforced rather than voluntary.[4]

The administrative reorganisation of many of Rome's existing provinces and the addition of several new ones after further peoples had been "reduced into the power of the Roman people" entailed a long and complex process of political, social, and cultural transformation across the Empire. The inhabitants of all the provinces were now subject to periodic censuses, which required them to put on record details of all family members and the landed and moveable

---

[2] See, e.g., Gauthier 1985; Gruen 1984: 166–172, 184–198; Ma 2000: 182–214.
[3] Millar 1984b; note also Woolf 2005.
[4] On veteran settlement in Italy Keppie 1983, with an update at Keppie 2000: 249–262; in the provinces, Brunt 1971b: 589–610.

property that they owned. The census records then provided a more formal basis for assessing the tax payments that provincials were liable to contribute to the Roman state, except in those privileged cities that were exempt from Roman taxation. In areas where cities were thinly distributed or non-existent, new urban centres were created and given clearly delimited territories. Changes in the civic status of communities were widespread. Some towns were granted the status of Roman colonies with full Roman citizenship; others became municipalities with the Latin rights of citizenship, whereby local magistrates became full Roman citizens on taking up office; a few were given "freedom and autonomy" and exemption from taxation, while others that had possessed this privileged status during the Republic saw it removed.

Urban centres throughout the Empire were embellished with public buildings, monuments, and statues that emphasised the new political relationship with Rome and, most importantly, with Augustus and other members of the *domus Augusta* ("Augustan household"). And even some communities outside the formal control of Rome saw similar developments: in the East in Judaea, for instance, with the extensive building programmes of Herod the Great; or in the West in Mauretania, where king Juba II monumentalised the city of Caesarea (modern Cherchel in Algeria) to the extent that it would not have looked out of place in the very heart of the Empire. (This process of reorganisation was by no means complete at the time of Augustus' death in AD 14, since there was much work to be done in a number of regions; and throughout the imperial period the perceived loyalty or disloyalty of provincial communities could lead to further promotions or demotions in status.)[5]

Given the sheer magnitude of the territory that formed part of the Roman Empire under Augustus (see map, above, p. xxx), stretching from the Atlantic shores of modern Portugal to the deserts of Syria, from the Rhine valley to the Sahara in Africa, it is no surprise that we have large amounts of information available with which to examine the impact of Rome in a great variety of geographical and cultural settings; and this material continues to increase in quantity each year with further archaeological and epigraphic discoveries. Any balanced account of the history of Rome during the Principate,

---

[5] On these questions, see Nicolet 1988 = 1991: esp. chs 6–7 (census and land cadastres); Sherwin-White 1973 (status of cities); Bowman 1996 and Ando 2006 (on provincial administration); Gleason 2006 (cities in the Greek East); Edmondson 2006 (cities in the western provinces). On Herod, see L. M. White 2005; on Caesarea in Mauretania, Leveau 1984.

including studies of Augustus and his age, needs to address the impact of Roman power across the vast and culturally diverse Empire.

It is impossible in a volume such as this to do justice to the sheer range of topics one might wish to have included. Something on the modifications in the day-to-day administration of the provinces that took place under Augustus would have been valuable, although here one needs to be careful not to retroject back to the Augustan period practices and procedures that only took hold more gradually.[6] An assessment of the extent to which local economies were transformed as provinces became increasingly linked to supplying the city of Rome and exchanging goods with other regions within the Roman Empire would reveal much about the economic ramifications of the reorganisation of the provinces. In any such analysis, it should not be assumed that there was little economic interchange in the pre-Augustan period, and it might be difficult to muster sufficient evidence from individual provincial zones over a relatively restricted time-period.[7] The social changes that occurred under Augustus are another crucial subject, as local Italian and provincial elites were recruited into the Roman equestrian and even senatorial orders and service in Rome's armed forces opened up some possibilities of social mobility for many provincials of the "middling sort."[8] The nature of cultural change across the Empire has been a problem that has continued to generate intense debate, as many scholars have become dissatisfied with earlier interpretations that relied too readily on the problematic concept of "Romanisation" to explain the complex process of transformation of local cultures under Roman rule.[9] In the end, I have chosen to include here two studies that employ very different methodologies to address the impact of Augustus on provinces at opposite ends of the Empire. The first focuses on a single city in the

---

[6] See the remarks on this by Eck, Chapter 7, above. On provincial administration more generally, Eck 1995 and 1997a.

[7] See the recent chapters in Scheidel et al. 2007 on the early Roman Empire by D. Kehoe (production, 543–569), N. Morley (distribution, 570–591), W. Jongman (consumption, 592–618), and E. Lo Cascio (the state and the economy, 619–647), and on regional development by P. Leveau (western provinces, 651–670), S. Alcock (eastern Mediterranean, 671–697), D. Rathbone (Egypt, 698–719), and D. Cherry (frontier zones, 720–741).

[8] Syme elucidated many aspects of this process; the rise of the Italian elite is a major theme of Syme 1939; for the provincial elite, see, e.g., Syme 1958b and 1999 (the posthumous publication of a work drafted in 1934).

[9] The bibliography is enormous, but see, e.g., in general: Mattingly 1997; Fentress 2000; MacMullen 2000 (on the Augustan period specifically); on the western provinces: Blagg and Millett 1990; Keay and Terrenato 2001; Woolf 1998 (on Gaul, emphasising the importance of the Augustan period for cultural change); Mattingly 2004 (on Britain); on the eastern provinces: Woolf 1994; Alcock 1997.

province of Lusitania in the west of Roman Spain, while the second looks more broadly at changes across the cities of the Greek world following Octavian's victory at Actium.

Walter Trillmich in his study of "Colonia Augusta Emerita, Capital of Lusitania" (Chapter 14) provides a very closely argued analysis of the foundation and early development of this veteran colony, founded in 25 BC on the site of modern Mérida in Spain. As a research member of the Deutsches Archäologisches Institut (DAI; German Archaeological Institute) from 1977 onwards, eventually serving as director of the DAI headquarters in Berlin from 1996 until his early retirement in 2004, Trillmich is a classical archaeologist who has concentrated in particular on the study of Roman sculpture and the iconography of Roman coins. During his extended period at the Madrid department of the DAI from 1980 to 1996 he established himself as one of the leading experts on the archaeology of Roman Spain in general and Mérida in particular.[10] In October 1987 he was responsible for organising with Paul Zanker a major international conference in Madrid on "Stadtbild und Ideologie: Die Monumentalisierung hispanischer Städte zwischen Republik und Kaiserzeit" ("Cityscape and Ideology: The Monumentalising of the Cities of Roman Spain between Republic and Empire"), which aimed to examine the impact of Augustus on the urban landscapes across the Iberian peninsula. This took place right at the time that Zanker's book on Augustus and the power of images appeared, and so, as Trillmich comments in a recent postscript to his article (see p. 464, below), the influence of Augustus was arguably overemphasised at this event, given the nature of the archaeological data then available. It was at this conference that Trillmich presented the original version of the essay that appears here for the first time in an English translation.

The Augustan period was certainly one of significant change in the Iberian peninsula. In the law of January 27 BC granting Augustus his provinces, he retained control of the two existing Hispanic provinces, Hispania Citerior and Hispania Ulterior, which he continued to govern through his own appointed *legati Augusti propraetore* ("legates of Augustus with propraetorian power"). But at some point between 27 and 13 BC the decision was taken to divide Hispania Ulterior into two new provinces of Hispania Ulterior Lusitania and Hispania Ulterior Baetica, and the latter was transferred from Augustus' group of provinces to those controlled by the

---

[10] For some of his major works, see Trillmich 1976, 1978, 1988, 1993.

"senate and people of Rome" with a proconsul henceforth selected by lot in the senate to govern it. But these administrative questions are not Trillmich's focus. Rather, he uses his expertise as a classical archaeologist to examine the initial design, early growth, and ideological significance of the colony of Augusta Emerita.

Trillmich sees Emerita as the most "Augustan" of cities in Roman Spain, and uses numismatic evidence to make the argument that it was designed symbolically to proclaim that peace now extended to the far western edge of the Empire. He goes on to analyse the deliberately impressive engineering skills that the Romans displayed in laying out the new city before turning to the ideological significance of some of its major building complexes: the theatre, funded by M. Agrippa; the amphitheatre, funded by Augustus; and the colony's earliest main temple and associated forum. These buildings were initially constructed of local granite, but were later embellished with high-quality marble decoration, probably in the late-Augustan period, or so Trillmich then believed. Most of all, a porticoed square was added alongside the original forum that was decorated in a style very reminiscent of the Forum Augustum in Rome, with caryatids and *clipei* (shield roundels) with heads of Medusa and Jupiter Ammon gracing the portico's attic, and togate statues displayed in niches along the portico's back wall, which would appear to be modelled on the gallery of heroes displayed in the Forum Augustum, as discussed by Luce in Chapter 13, above.

Since the publication of Trillmich's study in 1990, this interpretation has been strikingly confirmed by the secure identification of elements of a statue-group representing Aeneas, his father Anchises, and his son Ascanius, as well as two small sections of an inscribed *elogium* (commemoration) of Aeneas.[11] The central problem, however, of Trillmich's analysis is his dating of the programme of marble decoration. He now admits that this may well have been not a late-Augustan phenomenon, but a late-Claudian or early Neronian variant on Augustan ideological models (see his revised views in the Appendix to his article, pp. 464–467, below). This usefully illustrates the point that arguments based on archaeological data must always be treated as provisional. New discoveries, as in the case of Mérida, have the potential to overturn previous hypotheses. But it is through the proposing of fresh theories based on existing data and by their

---

[11] For the statue-group, see Chapter 14, below, Fig. 14.12 (an illustration added to those in the original article), and the bibliography cited in the Appendix, n. 127. For the *elogium* of Aeneas (*AE* 1996, 864a–b), see de la Barrera and Trillmich 1996. For the Forum Augustum as a model for Italian and provincial architectural complexes, see Gros 2006.

later confirmation or refutation in the light of new evidence that real progress can be made.

The final contribution (Chapter 15) is an extract from Glen Bowersock's important monograph on *Augustus and the Greek World*, first published in 1965. In it, he relies in the main on literary evidence, not least Strabo's *Geography*, and inscriptions for his analysis of the impact of Augustus on the cities of the Greek East. After his initial studies at Harvard, Bowersock went to Oxford to take a second BA before completing his DPhil thesis there under Ronald Syme in 1962. He then returned to the United States to become Professor of Classics and History at Harvard before moving to the Institute for Advanced Study at Princeton in 1980, where he remained Professor of Ancient History until his retirement in 2006. The influence of his doctoral supervisor is clear in many of his publications, not least the chapter here reprinted from his first book. This is most noticeable in the emphasis Bowersock places upon the social and political relationship between members of the local elite in the Greek cities and Augustus and his family. But in his overall approach Bowersock was also inspired by the great French epigrapher Louis Robert (1904–1985), who elucidated the political, social, and cultural history of many remote corners of the Greek East under Roman rule by confronting epigraphic and literary sources with his unparalleled understanding of the physical topography of the areas he discussed.[12]

Bowersock's "Greek world" is broadly defined to include mainland Greece, the Aegean islands, Asia Minor, Syria, Judaea, Egypt, and Cyrenaica (modern Libya), and several of these regions receive attention in his chapter on "The Cities of the Greek World under Augustus."[13] In it, he explores Augustus' relations with these cities through his contact with their elites either as individuals or as members of local city councils or as representatives of regional confederations (*koina*). He argues for an Augustus who actively engaged in the affairs of the Greek world, and not just during his travels in the Greek East from 22 to 19 BC, as he sought to repair the damage that the region had suffered during the civil wars, when it had largely sided with his rival M. Antonius. Augustus' preference for working through local elites meant that the latter had frequently to take part in embassies despatched by their cities to the *princeps* wherever he happened to be residing, and this continued to be the

[12] For a selection of his work, see Robert 1935, 1946–1965, 1969–1990.
[13] For his later work on the Greek East, see, e.g., Bowersock 1969, 1973, 1983, 1984, and 2002 (on Augustan Athens). On Augustus' pontificate, note Bowersock 1990a. He is also a major figure in the study of late antiquity: see, e.g., Bowersock 1978, 1990b, and 2000.

standard mechanism of communication between provincial communities and the emperors that succeeded Augustus.[14] Bowersock's chapter also allows us to grasp something of the detailed and time-consuming process of political reorganisation and cultural renewal that was needed after the civil wars. Most of all, it raises the important question of how historians, when discussing the relationship between the Roman imperial state and its provinces, should weigh the relative importance of directives imposed from above (through the direct intervention of the *princeps* or the Roman provincial governor) and responses to the changed political circumstances that emanated from the provincial communities themselves.

---

[14] A process since elucidated greatly by Fergus Millar: see Millar 1977 (*passim*) and 1988b.

14 Colonia Augusta Emerita, Capital of Lusitania †

WALTER TRILLMICH
translated by Claus Nader

Of all the cities of Roman Hispania, the city of Emerita is without doubt the most Augustan. Its foundation – which, as Cassius Dio reports,[1] took place in the year 25 BC after the (supposed) end of the

---

† Originally published (in German) as "Colonia Augusta Emerita, die Hauptstadt von Lusitanien," in Walter Trillmich and Paul Zanker, eds, *Stadtbild und Ideologie: Die Monumentalisierung hispanischer Städte zwischen Republik und Kaiserzeit* (Abh. Bayer. Ak. Wiss., Phil-hist. Kl., N. F. 103, Munich, 1990, pp. 299–316, with Spanish summary (here omitted), pp. 317–318.

[Editor's note: It has been necessary to reduce considerably the number of illustrations for this translated version, but the selection has been made in full consultation with the author, to whom I am grateful for his generous cooperation and for his help with the illustrations. Illustrations included here are given in the form Fig. 14.1; references to illustrations in the original German version, even those excluded here, are given in square brackets in the form [Taf. 23a]. I have taken the opportunity, in consultation with the author, to include a recent plan of the city of Emerita as Fig. 14.2 and two illustrations (Figs 14.8b and 14.12) of important sculptural finds and reconstructions published since the appearance of the original article in 1990. Figs 14.8–14.9 replace the original Taf. 25–26 to allow some of the more complete *clipei* and caryatids not yet published in 1990 to be included. W. Trillmich has also kindly provided a brief update to his article (see below, Appendix), illustrating how arguments based on archaeological evidence are often provisional and may be confirmed, modified, or overturned by later discoveries. All references to *Stadtbild* are to the volume in which this essay was first published (in German): for full details, see above.]

* For various reasons none of our friends and colleagues from Mérida was able to participate in the colloquium in Madrid in 1987, which we very much regret. As a substitute, the task has fallen to me to provide a sketch of the appearance of the Colonia Augusta Emerita. I have limited myself to relatively few monuments and for illustrations have used images of the sculptural material known up to the year 1980. I am aware of, and have taken into account, the extraordinarily important new discoveries made since 1980; their publication, however, must be reserved for another occasion. [For some of the more recent scholarship, see Appendix, below, pp. 464–467.] My heartfelt thanks to the former and current directors of the Museo Nacional de Arte Romano, José Alvarez Sáenz de Buruaga and Dr José María Alvarez Martínez, and all their colleagues for their longstanding friendship and their frequent invaluable assistance with my studies on Augusta Emerita.

For reasons of space, reference to the scholarly literature is here restricted to the most important items. [For a full bibliography on Roman Mérida, see now A. Velázquez Jiménez, *Repertorio de bibliografía arqueológica emeritense* I–II, Cuadernos emeritenses 6 (1992) and 19 (2002), III (2010).]

[1] Dio 53.26.1.

Cantabrian war (*bellum Cantabrum*)[2] – signalled to the western Roman Empire that war was now at an end and an era of peace beginning under the auspices of Augustus. The city's name, "Emerita," appears by itself, without any additional distinctive titles, on the coins of the provincial issue of P. Carisius (see p. 430 and Fig. 14.1.6 [= Taf. 22, 6]), and this alludes to this specific historical moment. The "image" of the newly founded city on the coins evokes the same message: works of peace now take the place of great accomplishments in war. The entire city of Emerita is a monument to Augustus, the bringer of peace; it is the western counterpart to Actium-Nikopolis.

1 THE MESSAGE OF THE COINS: THE FOUNDATION OF EMERITA AS A SYMBOL OF THE PACIFICATION OF THE WEST

The coinage is the most reliable guide to the specific historical context of the foundation of Emerita, as in many other cases, most of all because it preserves in an officially authorised and comprehensive manner its original programmatic conception. One can only understand the silver provincial coinage issued in Hispania by the general P. Carisius (Fig. 14.1.1–6 [= Taf. 22, 1–6]),[3] who presumably also served at the same time as provincial governor,[4] if one arranges the various types into groups according to their thematic content. In this way, the coins' programme can be revealed, as K. Kraft has

---

[2] A. M. Canto discussed the history of the foundation of Emerita at our colloquium: see *Stadtbild*, 289–298. Her contribution contains full references to the scholarly literature on what has been up till now quite a controversial and difficult topic. I refrain from commenting on her new theory about the three-stage foundation of the city, most of all because I do not agree with her arguments. I shall only note this about Cassius Dio's terminology at 53.26.1 (cf. Canto, *Stadtbild*, 290): *ktizein* naturally had in Dio's time the sense of "founding." Since Dio does not use the word *apoikizein* [to found a colony], we may assume that Emerita was not founded as a colony (by Augustus) but received that status only later, a point that is consistent with the change in nomenclature of the city on coins (see below, p. 448 and nn. 77–78). Cassius Dio's account of the instructions Augustus gave regarding the soldiers discharged from his army may be interpreted to mean that he gave orders "to found in (far away) Lusitania a city which is (today) called Augusta Emerita" (or "which was then called Augusta Emerita"). Canto's theory of a supposed previous settlement dating to the Caesarian period is in archaeological terms a phantom. The inscriptions, discussed and illustrated in summary form by J. Alvarez Sáenz de Buruaga, *Museos* 1 (1982), 5–7, which give the city's name as C.I.A.E., are surely of less official character than the legend on the city's coins, and can easily be read as *C(olonia) I(mmunis) A(ugusta) E(merita)*.

[3] For these coins, which have nothing to do with the later civic coinage of Emerita and which are unlikely to have been produced there, as is repeatedly claimed, see the following convenient collections: Vives IV 61f., plates 140–141, 2; *BMCRE* I 51–55, plate 5; Giard I 161–166, plates 41–43.

[4] For Carisius, see G. Alföldy, *Fasti Hispanienses* (1969) 131f., with references and bibliography.

demonstrated for the so called "triumphal coinage" of Octavian.[5] Such an analysis also shows that the silver coinage minted in Hispania forms the western counterpart to Octavian's triumphal coinage minted in the context of his political struggle with Antony and Cleopatra; it is based upon very similar criteria, in terms of both its ideology and propaganda.

Of the five *denarius* types of Carisius' coinage, two issues (Fig. 14.1.1-2 [= Taf. 22, 1-2]) have heraldically arranged weaponry depicted on their reverse. On one of these types a *falcata* is shown:[6] i.e., the curved, single-bladed Hispanic short sword, well known in Rome; another type has a strange face-like helmet, crowned with antlers;[7] both these images clearly demonstrate that we are dealing with captured weaponry.[8] Two further *denarius* types show military trophies (*tropaea*) (Fig. 14.1.3-4 [= Taf. 22, 3-4]). One type has a shackled, kneeling barbarian in its lower half;[9] another[10] has a frequently overlooked dragon-headed trumpet (*karnyx*) located beneath the base of a victory monument made up of round shields.[11] It is very obvious that both these types allude to a defeated enemy. Ancient ethnology was notoriously imprecise; and, as a result, this Gallic trumpet is here associated with the Cantabrians, who are treated as generic "western" barbarians.

The "world-historical" claim of the triumphal imagery on these four *denarius* types becomes clear when one examines the *quinarius* type that belongs to this same coin series (Fig. 14.1.5 [= Taf. 22, 5]).[12] In numismatic and iconographic terms, it is clearly reminiscent of a coin-type produced c. 100 BC to glorify Marius' victory over the

---

[5] K. Kraft, *Zur Münzpragung des Augustus*, SBer Frankfurt VII, 1968, Nr. 5 (1969) 205–225. For discussion on the dating of the so-called triumphal coinage, see W. Trillmich in *Kaiser Augustus und die verlorene Republik* (Exhibition catalogue, Berlin 1988) 506–507, cat. no. 323. Whether these coins were issued in preparation for the struggle with Antonius and Cleopatra or only after their defeat is still hotly disputed; the resolution of this question is of lesser significance at least for the thesis to be elaborated here, regarding the parallels between them and the later propaganda on the coins minted in Hispania.

[6] Vives IV 61, nos 1–2, plate 140, 1–2; BMCRE I 51, nos 277–279, plate 5, 1–3; Giard I 161f. nos 1028–1034, plate 41.

[7] Vives IV 61, nos 6–8, plate 140, 6–8; BMCRE I 52, nos 280–282, plate 5, 4–5; Giard I 162f. nos 1044–1054, plate 42.

[8] Cf. A. M. de Guadán, *Las armas en la moneda ibérica* (no date, c. 1979) 59f., 66ff., 77.

[9] Vives IV 61, no. 5, plate 140, 5; BMCRE I 53, no. 287, plate 5, 8; Giard I 161, plate 42a–c; 162, no. 1035, plate 42.

[10] Vives IV 61, nos 3–4, plate 140, 3–4; BMCRE I 52f., nos 283–286, plate 5, 6–7; Giard I 163f. no. 1055–1064, plate 42.

[11] This can be seen particularly in an example in Glasgow: A. S. Robertson, *Roman Imperial Coins in the Hunter Coin Cabinet* I (1962) 25, no. 126, plate 4. On the Gallic *karnyx*, see Daremberg–Saglio I 2 (1887) 925f., s.v. carnyx.

[12] Vives IV 62, nos 11–12, plate 140, 11–12; BMCRE I 54, nos 293–297, plate 5, 13–14; Giard I 164, nos 1065–1076, plate 43.

Fig. 14.1: 1–6. Silver provincial coinage issued by P. Carisius in Hispania, 25–23 BC.

Cimbri. On the *quinarius* type issued by the quaestor C. Fundanius,[13] for example, we also find a kneeling, shackled barbarian and a *karnyx* at the base of a trophy being crowned by the goddess Victory. The various pictorial elements on the *denarius* types of Carisius just discussed (Fig. 14.1.3–4 [= Taf. 22, 3–4]) also allude to earlier Roman coin types, and all of these images may even derive from a single model: a triumphal monument that celebrated Marius' victory over the Cimbri.[14] By commemorating his exploits in the Cantabrian war, Augustus was thus comparing himself to, and styling himself as a direct heir of, C. Marius.

To complement his victory in the East, Augustus required a great victory in the West, so that he could present himself as the bringer of peace across the entire world. This theme is addressed on the breastplate of the Prima Porta statue of Augustus [see Chapter 11, above, Fig. 11.7]. On the side showing the rising sun sits a woman who embodies the peoples of the East; on the opposite side a seated woman is depicted representing the peoples of the western provinces [see Chapter 11, above, Fig. 11.8]; the standard with its wild boar and the dragon-headed trumpet help to identify her in this way.[15]

Augustus needed this kind of geographical completion of his military successes as urgently as he needed a victory in a foreign war (*bellum externum*) to counterbalance his victory in the civil war at Actium. (This war was never officially recognised as a civil war, of course, even though that is precisely what it was in everyone's

---

[13] *BMCRR* I 233, nos 1696ff., plate 32, 8; *RRC* 328, no. 326/2, plate 42.

[14] On this cf. T. Hölscher in *Tainia: Roland Hampe zum 70. Geburtstag* ... (1980) 356f., with further bibliography.

[15] For detailed depictions of the personifications, see E. Simon, *Augustus. Kunst und Leben in Rom um die Zeitenwende* (1986) 55, figs 55–56; cf. P. Zanker, *Augustus und die Macht der Bilder* (1987) 184, fig. 148b; T. Hölscher in *Kaiser Augustus und die verlorene Republik* (Exhibition catalogue, Berlin 1988) 386ff., cat. no. 215 with fig. and bibliography.

experience.) So the victory over the mountain-peoples of northern Hispania was seen by Augustus as extraordinarily important, at least for a few years, until the "victory" over the Parthians overshadowed all his previous successes. He closed the doors of the Temple of Janus for the second time "after his victories had given birth to peace throughout the entire Roman Empire by land and sea" (*cum per totum imperium populi Romani terra marique esset parta victoriis pax*, *RG* 13) and Agrippa, who actually brought the Cantabrian war to a conclusion,[16] later declined a triumph[17] – something he presumably did not do entirely of his own accord.

That success in war was only one necessary condition for the creation of world-wide peace was a fundamental theme of Augustan propaganda. Indeed Carisius' programme of coinage did not end with themes of war against, and victory over, western barbarians. A fifth and final *denarius* type of the same series (Fig. 14.1.6 [= Taf. 22, 6])[18] shows a city gate with two passageways and, behind it, a circuit of city walls with pinnacles; the city's name, EMERITA, rich in significance [emphasising that it was a city founded for *emeriti* (demobilised veteran soldiers)], is inscribed between the towers flanking the gate. As far as the programmatic context of the *denarius* series is concerned, image[19] and text can only mean that war was over once and for all; the future belonged to works of peace and to the founding and building of cities.[20]

Thus the *denarius* coinage of Carisius comprised two types with weapons, two with trophies, and one with a heraldic view of the city of "Emerita"; we may thus establish a tripartite division with a thematic sequence of "War – Victory – Peace," just as we can with the images on the reverse of three *denarius* types from the slightly earlier, so-called "Actium coinage" (Fig. 14.1.7–9 [= Taf. 22, 7–9]).[21] In that coin series there is yet another tripartite division with precisely the same themes (Fig. 14.1.10–12 [= Taf. 22, 10–12]):[22]

[16] Rightly Hor. *Epist.* 1.12.26f.
[17] Dio 54.11.6 (discussing the year 19 BC).
[18] Vives IV 62, nos 9–10, plate 140, 9–10; *BMCRE* I 53, nos 288–292, plate 5, 9–12; Giard I 162, nos 1036–1043, plate 42.
[19] On the depiction of the city, see also M. Pfanner, *Stadtbild*, 88, with nn. 76–77.
[20] It is significant that the *aes* coinage of Carisius is restricted to a single type with a reverse image that is not dedicated to the theme of war and victory, but again shows a view of Emerita: Vives IV 62, nos 16–18, plate 140, 16; *BMCRE* I 54, note *; Giard I 165, nos 1077–1079, plate 43.
[21] K. Kraft, *Zur Münzpragung des Augustus* (1969) 206f., plate 1, 4–6; Zanker, *Macht der Bilder* (n. 15) 61f., fig. 41; W. Trillmich in *Kaiser Augustus und die verlorene Republik* (1988) 484, fig. 211, fourth line.
[22] Kraft, op. cit., 211–214, plate 2, 18–20; Trillmich in *Kaiser Augustus ...* (1988) 506ff., cat. nos 323–325.

Fig. 14.1: 7–12. So-called "Actium" series of coinage: silver denarii (nos 7–10, 12) and gold aureus (no. 11), issued by Octavian, *c.* 29–28 BC.

Mars (Ultor, who helped bring victory at the battle of Philippi) with his weapons stands for (just) war (Fig. 14.1.10); Diana (who helped bring victory at the battle of Naulochos) with a trophy represents victory and triumph (Fig. 14.1.11); and Apollo (who helped bring victory at Actium) is connected with the image on the reverse of a priest with a bull and cow tracing the *sulcus primigenius* [i.e., the inaugural furrow ploughed as part of the foundation ritual] of a newly founded city, a symbol of peace, at last achieved and now definitive (Fig. 14.1.12). Konrad Kraft connected this image with the foundation of Nikopolis after the battle of Actium,[23] which is highly plausible given the programmatic context of the three coin types. In any case it cannot be a coincidence that of all cities it was Emerita that took up this imagery, which is rarely found elsewhere in the West, on its local coinage minted after the year 2 BC, putting it on no fewer than four coin types, two of which are illustrated here (Fig. 14.1.13–14 [= Taf. 22, 13–14]).[24] Whether or not it was definitely planned by Augustus himself as he established this first new foundation in Hispania, the city of Emerita in the late-Augustan period at any rate saw itself, according to the message of these coins, as the western Nikopolis. The monumental design and first-class sculptural decoration that the city received at that time justifiably boosted the self-esteem of the citizens of Emerita in a variety of different ways, as we shall later see.

[23] Kraft, op. cit., 213f.
[24] Vives IV 63, no. 20, plate 141, 4; no. 22, plate 141, 6 (cf. here Fig. 14.1.14 [= Taf. 22, 14]); 64, no. 31, plate 142, 1; nos 32–33, plate 142, 2–3 (cf. here Fig. 14.1.13 [= Taf. 22, 13]). I cannot here discuss the chronology of the city coinage of Augusta Emerita; important for our purposes is the large chronological gap between the issuing of the prototype coins (here Fig. 14.1.12 [= Taf. 22, 12]) and the resumption of the theme of the *sulcus primigenius*.

Fig. 14.1: 13–14. Bronze *asses* issued by local mint at Emerita, late Augustan (after 2 BC)

2 BUILDINGS OF THE "FOUNDATION PERIOD"

Emerita's initial buildings look modest, at least in an artistic sense and in terms of the materials employed in their construction. The basic ideological claim of the colony's "foundation period" lies most of all in the immense size of the whole urban layout (see Fig. 14.2a–b)[25] and in its individual monuments, in particular the utilitarian public buildings, which proved that, as far as Roman architecture was concerned, there were no technical difficulties that could not be overcome. On the contrary, the Romans confronted the challenge of the natural surroundings, took the task in hand, and finished the job.

Time and again we read that the city of Emerita was built at a carefully chosen location on the banks of the river Anas at a point where an island situated in the middle of the river facilitated its crossing. But the river is considerably narrower in other places, where it is easier to cross than here, as pointed out by M. Pfanner (*Stadtbild*, 90 and 99, fig. 31). It must be admitted that it is quite unlikely that the bridge over the Guadiana (Fig. 14.3 [cf. Taf. 5h])[26] straddled that island so that it might coincide with the *decumanus maximus* [main east–west street] of the newly built city;[27] rather, the bridge was probably the very first item on the agenda when it came to conceiving Emerita's overall layout.[28] It was far from being a "tool of war," as A. Schulten, only able to imagine the bridge teeming with armies clanging their weapons, once claimed.[29] Rather, this bridge served as an eloquent symbol for the pacification of this part of the world, for

---

[25] Cf. Pfanner, *Stadtbild*, 85, with n. 72; for bibliography on the urban layout of Emerita, ibid., nn. 94, 100.

[26] Alvarez Martínez, *Puente*; see also P. Gazzola, *Ponti Romani* II (1963) 121f., no. 161.

[27] So Pfanner, *Stadtbild*, 90.

[28] Cf. Richmond 104; Alvarez Martínez, *Puente*, 70f. with plate 14: the bridge is certainly older than the reinforcement wall along the riverbank.

[29] A. Schulten, *Mérida. Das spanische Rom* (*Deutsche Zeitung für Spanien*, Barcelona 1922) 12.

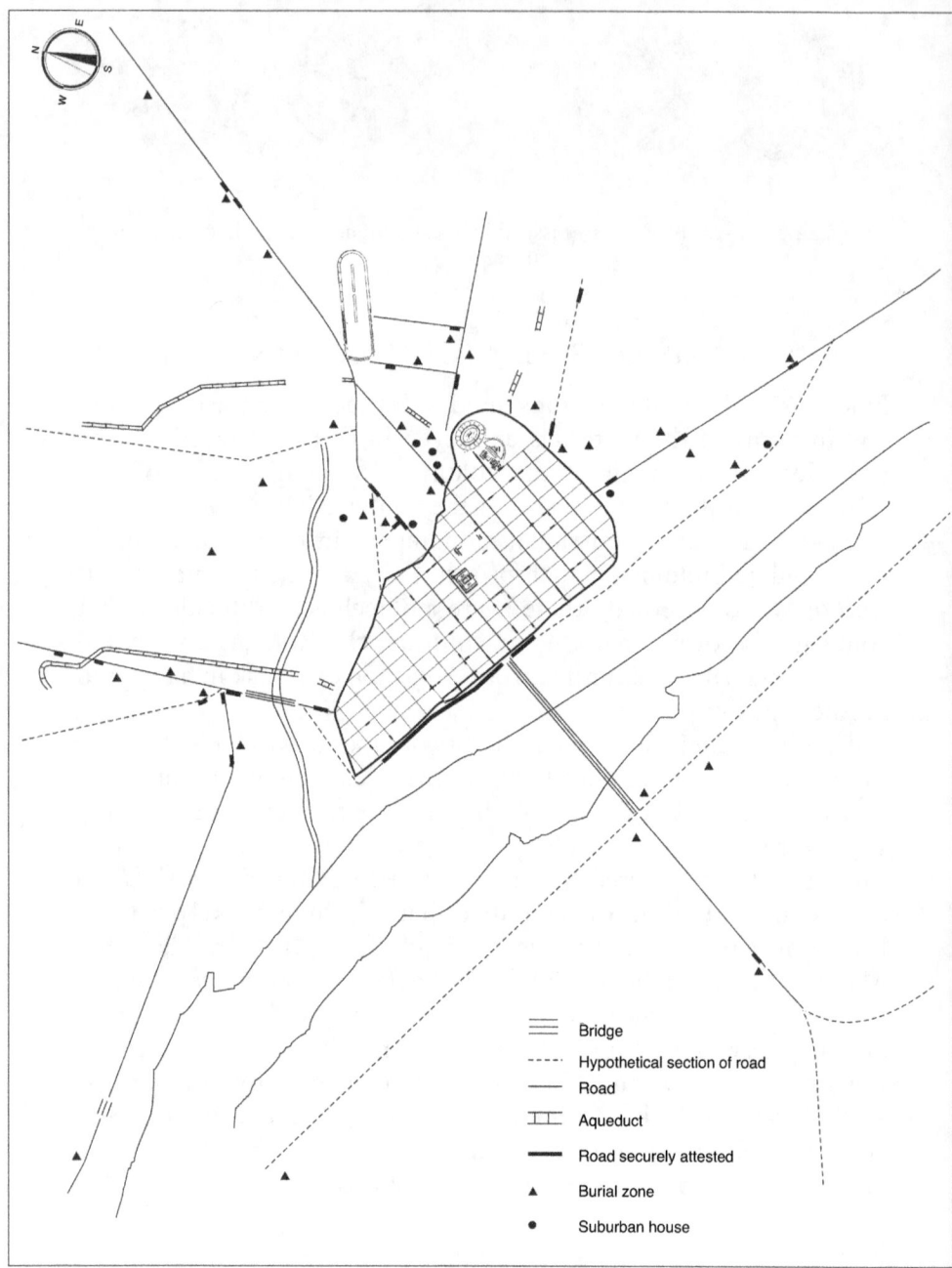

Fig. 14.2a. Plan of Emerita and environs (Consorcio de la Ciudad Monumental de Mérida)

Colonia Augusta Emerita, Capital of Lusitania 435

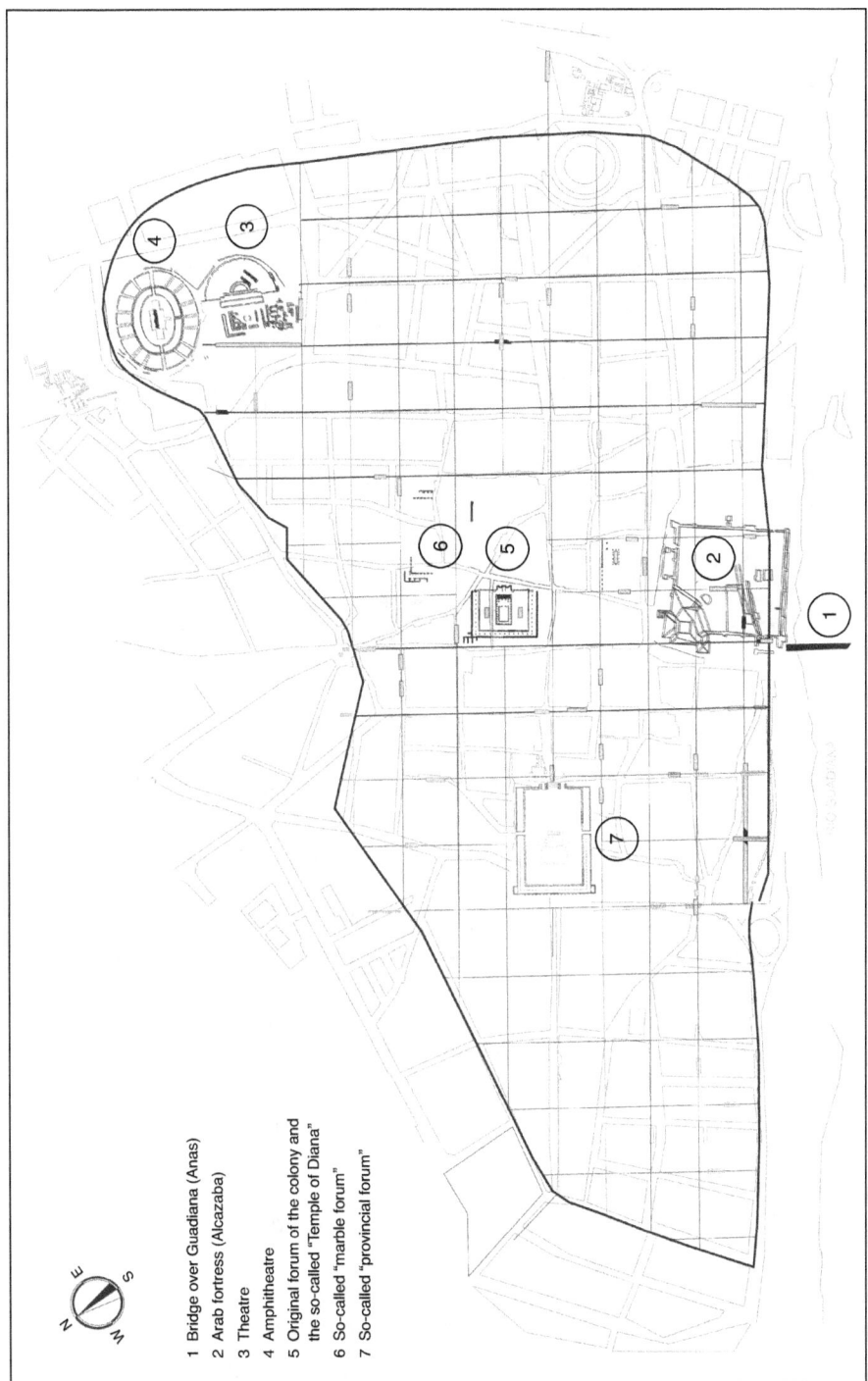

Fig. 14.2b. Plan of urban centre of Emerita (Consorcio de la Ciudad Monumental de Mérida)

1 Bridge over Guadiana (Anas)
2 Arab fortress (Alcazaba)
3 Theatre
4 Amphitheatre
5 Original forum of the colony and the so-called "Temple of Diana"
6 So-called "marble forum"
7 So-called "provincial forum"

Fig. 14.3. Bridge over the river Anas (Guadiana)

the final integration of the far west into Augustus' Empire. One of the roads[30] that led to Emerita started from Olisippo (Lisbon), where the Atlantic marked the end of the inhabited world. More than just to assist crossing the river, which is at this point extraordinarily wide, the island was also a challenge for the engineers[31] and additionally a pretext for the architect to design the bridge in two sections that were technically and formally distinct. Given the bridge's enormous span of almost 800 metres, this had the aesthetic advantage of avoiding monotony in terms of its design. The orientation of the new city's main *decumanus* was aligned with the course of the bridge.

As one approached from the west and crossed this almost endless bridge, one would gaze in wonder for quite some time at the façade of Emerita, the city of peace, rising up along the other bank. One would walk towards its splendid gate, which, we may imagine, resembled the one shown on the heraldic image of the city on its coins (cf. Fig. 14.1.6 [= Taf. 22, 6]). This is even clearer since the actual

---

[30] For the location of Emerita at an important road junction, see Alvarez Martínez, *Puente*, 19ff., with fig. 3 and further literature.

[31] The "tajamar," discussed by Alvarez Martínez, *Puente*, 65–70 and 84 with fig. 12, was in my opinion designed to divide the water of the river into two streams and, more importantly, to serve as a strikingly artistic fortification of this island.

discovery a few years ago of remains of part of a gate with towers and two passageways at the end of the bridge on the city side of the river.[32] The entirely non-military design of this gate on the same axis as the bridge and *decumanus maximus* shows that it functioned as the entrance to the city rather than as a barrier.[33]

On his arrival, the traveller would see on either side the impressive reinforcement of the riverbank[34] (on which the walls of the Arab fortress with its towers now rest [Taf. 23a]), strengthened and subdivided by buttresses, with the actual city wall 20 metres behind [Taf. 23b].[35] The Romans could easily have constructed the city, which did not have a harbour or even a landing-berth because of the difficulties in navigating this particular part of the Anas,[36] some distance away from the river on elevated terrain, but the Romans needed to emphasise that the Anas had also been "reduced into the power of the Roman people" (*in potestatem populi Romani redactum*) by means of this great feat of engineering and the remarkable reinforcement of the riverbank. The buttressed wall, which in fact only needed to keep the river within its limits when the water level was high and which was supposed to protect the city walls at all times from the danger of being undermined by water, functioned as an artificially constructed gigantic terrace, on which the entire city sat enthroned.

Large outlets for sewers, carefully protected with metal grilles, are clearly visible at fairly regular intervals along its broad façade.[37] Generally, these openings are rectangular, but the outlet right alongside the bridge, which ran underneath the *decumanus maximus*, is capped with an arch, composed of two adjoining cut ashlar blocks; this marks it out as belonging to a particularly important street [Taf. 23c].[38] Thus even the sewers were integrated into the imposing and carefully planned city façade: visitors could immediately see that they

---

[32] Cf., provisionally, J. M. Alvarez Martínez in *Ciudades superpuestas*, 40, with the figure on p. 50.

[33] For an evaluation of such Augustan "fortification" architecture, see Pfanner, *Stadtbild*, 88.

[34] Richmond 105f. and plate 3, A; Alvarez Martínez, *Puente*, 70–73 and plate 52; cf. n. 28 (above). To this day, the riverbank reinforcement is more or less well preserved for 250 m upstream from the bridge.

[35] Emerita's city wall is virtually unpublished; see briefly Richmond 101f., 106f.; Alvarez Martínez in *Ciudades superpuestas*, 39f., with plan on p. 47; Pfanner, *Stadtbild*, 88, 105 fig. 36.

[36] Cf. Alvarez Martínez, *Puente*, 10f. It is remarkable that there is no attestation for a landing even though we may assume that there was local river traffic in the vicinity of Mérida.

[37] Richmond 105f.; Alvarez Martínez, *Puente*, 72. These openings for the sewers provide precious information about Emerita's street plan; the frequently published and consulted plan with the layout of the sewers (e.g., M. Almagro, *Guia de Mérida*, 8th edn, 1979, fig. 2 following p. 24) is, however, in many respects hypothetical and imprecise; cf. Alvarez Martínez, loc. cit.

[38] Cf. Alvarez Martínez, *Puente*, plate 14.

had entered a modern city, one which was, from the very beginning, equipped with an impressive infrastructure.

The imposing character of the city's fortifications and its other technical facilities, such as its lavish water-supply system, as well as the masonry of the buildings that date to the "foundation period," were all discussed some time ago by I. A. Richmond,[39] later by A. M. Canto,[40] and more recently by M. Pfanner.[41] The technical (and stylistic) similarities of the rusticated masonry used for both bridges[42] (see Fig. 14.3 [= Taf. 5h] for the bridge over the Guadiana), the aqueducts (especially the Los Milagros aqueduct [Taf. 7a]),[43] the façades of the theatre [Taf. 8i][44] and amphitheatre [Taf. 8h],[45] and even the water tower at the remote Cornalvo reservoir are, in fact, so strong that they constitute sufficient grounds for dating all these buildings to the same period.

The four building inscriptions that survive from the theatre (Figs. 14.4a–b [= Taf. 8a and 23e]),[46] with the name of Agrippa, the building's donor, in the nominative, make it quite clear that the construction of Emerita was closely linked to Agrippa's presence in Hispania. The very particular city plan, its street grid and connected infrastructure, its civil engineering projects, and its imposing public

---

[39] Richmond, *passim*.

[40] A. M. Canto, "Sobre la cronología augustea del Acueducto de Los Milagros de Mérida," in *Homenaje a Sáenz de Buruaga* (1982) 157–176.

[41] *Stadtbild*, 62 and fig. 8; 104, fig. 34; Taf. 8f,h,i.

[42] Guadiana bridge: see above n. 26. Albarregas bridge: Richmond 106 plate 3, b; Alvarez Martínez, *Puente*, 75ff.; also compare P. Gazzola, *Ponti Romani* II (1963) 137f. no. 186 (strangely dating it to the Trajanic-Hadrianic period).

[43] A. Jiménez Martin, "Los acueductos de Emerita," in *Bimilenario* 111–125 (with divergent date); cf. Canto, loc. cit. (above, n. 40); recently, Alvarez Martínez in *Ciudades superpuestas*, 42f; cf. also Pfanner, *Stadtbild*, 103ff.

[44] Most important literature regarding the theatre of Mérida: J. R. Mélida, "El teatro romano de Mérida," *RevArchBiblMus* 19 (1915), 1–38; J. Menéndez-Pidal y Alvarez in *Bimilenario*, 207–211; J. Alvarez Sáenz de Buruaga, "Observaciones sobre el teatro romano de Mérida," in *Actas del Simposio "El Teatro en la Hispania Romana", Mérida 1980* (1982) 303–316, with further literature. Cf. also Pfanner, *Stadtbild*, 97ff., figs 30 and 32; H. von Hesberg, *Stadtbild*, 355ff.

[45] J. R. Mélida, *El anfiteatro romano de Mérida*, MemJuntaSupExcav 1918, no. 2 (published 1919); id., *El anfiteatro y el circo romanos de Mérida*, MemJuntaSupExcav 1920–1921, no. 4; J.-Cl. Golvin, *L'amphithéâtre romain: essai sur la théorisation de sa forme et de ses fonctions* (1988) 109f. no. 77 (with further literature), plate 30; on its façade, see ibid., 318f., with parallels. Cf. also the following remarks.

[46] The two inscriptions on granite blocks (beneath the south-western tribunal, as shown in Fig. 14.4a [= Taf. 8a]): *CIL* II 474 = *ILS* 130. Formerly inscribed in bronze: Richmond 115f. with fig. 4 (reconstruction) and plate 6, b. Fig. 14.4b here [= Taf. 23e] shows the northern of the two main entrances to the orchestra with the building inscription above: M • AGRIPPA • L • F • CO[S • TERT] / TRIB • POTEST • T[ERT]. The inscription shows signs of repair (in the area of the letters L and F) (cf. also below, n. 84), but this took place later – when the entrance to the theatre was changed and modified by the addition of columns, for the erection of which parts of the former gate-posts were chiselled off, as is clearly shown in the photograph.

buildings, of which only the temple in the forum will be examined in this paper in any detail (see below, pp. 441ff.), must have been constructed quite a few years after the presumed foundation of the veteran settlement in 25 BC.

The inscription mentioning Augustus from the amphitheatre (Fig. 14.5a–b [= Taf. 23f–g]) provides the most precise evidence for the duration of Emerita's first phase of expansion.[47] According to the emperor's titulature, this building was more or less completed or at least inaugurated and functioning by the year 8/7 BC. The Agrippa inscriptions from the theatre, mentioned above, are relevant in this context too; they refer to his third consulship and third year of *tribunicia potestas*, which means that the theatre could not have been completed before the year 16/15 BC. The building process may have continued well beyond this date and possibly also after the donor's death in 12 BC. In any case, Agrippa's granite theatre was completed before the process of "marble refurbishment" (*Marmorisierung*) began at Emerita – a process that we can confidently place in the late-Augustan period (see below, p. 448)[48] and which affected all the early

[47] Mélida, op. cit. (n. 44; 1919) 31–34, plate 17; J. Menéndez-Pidal y Alvarez, "Restitución del texto y dimensiones de las inscripciones históricas del anfiteatro de Mérida," *AEspA* 30 (1957), 205–217; L. García Iglesias, Epigrafía romana de Augusta Emerita (unpublished dissertation, Madrid 1972–1973) 111–115, nos 35–37. The fragments shown in Fig. 14.5a–b [= Taf. 23f–g] belong to two different inscriptions (different in terms of the structure of their texts, but obviously related as far as their content is concerned) that were fixed to the two unequally large tribunals built into the middle of the amphitheatre's two long sides. A third inscription with the same text, but arranged in three lines, was published by Menéndez-Pidal (loc. cit., 207ff., fig. 3), who also discusses at length the execution of the mouldings and bracket holes for a later facing of the western and eastern *tribunalia* with these inscriptions (loc. cit., 214ff.; cf. below, n. 48). At this time I cannot comment on the epigraphic problems (the fragment Mélida shows on the left of plate 17b, in my opinion, clearly shows the number XII and cannot be interpreted as [COS] XII[II], as claimed by many authors); for the discussion here, the reference to Augustus' sixteenth year of *tribunicia potestas*, which relates to the year 8/7 BC, is important and decisive.

[48] Apparently, the extensive "marble refurbishment" took place just a few years after the completion of the granite buildings, as we can see from the previously mentioned tribunal inscriptions from the amphitheatre. The clearly verifiable marble facings of the western and eastern *tribunalia* [tribunals] and, therefore, the covering up of the already affixed dedicatory inscriptions of Augustus (Fig. 14.5a–b [= Taf. 23f–g]; cf. n. 47) could make us believe that we are dealing with measures taken at a much later point, perhaps thanks to renovations undertaken by an emperor or official who, so to speak, would have been usurping applause for Augustus' munificence on the building. The third of the Augustan inscriptions (Menéndez-Pidal, loc. cit., 207, fig. 3), however, for certain remained uncovered and legible. Perhaps during the process of refitting parts of the amphitheatre with marble (the podium as well as the first rows of seats certainly received this treatment; cf. Menéndez-Pidal y Alvarez, *AEspA* 28 (1955), 292–300), they were detached from their original placement and moved to a more suitable location, just as occurred with the Agrippa inscriptions in the theatre (see below, p. 449 and Fig. 14.4a [= Taf. 8a]; contrary to J. Menéndez-Pidal, *AEspA* 30 (1957), 207f., I do not believe that there were also *tribunalia* above the entrances on the long axis; Golvin, loc. cit. (n. 45), seems to overlook this theory, not discussing it at all). Everyone then could see who the donor of the amphitheatre was. One would like to assume that the texts on the *tribunalia*, which were obscured by the marble facing, were also once again displayed on these revetment plaques.

Fig. 14.4a–b. Theatre, Emerita: dedicatory inscriptions of M. Agrippa, 16–15 BC, set up (a) over the *aditus maximus* in the orchestra and (b) over the north entrance to the orchestra

Fig. 14.5a–b. Amphitheatre, Emerita: dedicatory inscriptions of Augustus, 8/7 BC

large-scale buildings except the temple in the forum in the city centre. Perhaps this was for religious reasons connected to its original plan of design.

The main temple from the "foundation period" is, without doubt, the one that stands on a high podium with a rather old-fashioned profile. It has been known since the seventeenth century as the "Temple of Diana" (Fig. 14.6a–b [= Taf. 24a–b])[49] and recently it has been restored in an extraordinarily unfortunate manner, whereas, as I have already stated, it was more respected in antiquity. The hexastyle, peripteral temple stands in the centre of a public square paved

---

The chance of being able to identify parts of these new marble inscriptions (and, therefore, to pinpoint precisely the year in which the revetment in marble of one of the large-scale buildings from Emerita's "foundation period" took place), raised by Menéndez-Pidal, *AEspA* 28 (1955), 300, is by no means unrealistic.

[49] J. M. Alvarez Martínez, "El templo de Diana," in *Bimilenario*, 43–53, plates 17–22, with plan at p. 45, fig. 2 (but see below, n. 68); also id., *Ciudades superpuestas* 39, 40, 48 (e); cf. also T. Hauschild in *Homenaje a Sáenz de Buruaga* (1982) 145–156; Pfanner, *Stadtbild*, 93f., fig. 27. With regard to the capitals: Alvarez Martínez in *Bimilenario*, 48, plate 20, b–d; J. L. de la Barrera Antón, *Los capiteles romanos de Mérida*, Monografías Emeritenses 2 (1984) 27 no. 1 (still situated at the building robbed of its layer of stucco), 33f., no. 20 with many figures (stuccoed capital), 72f., 79; cf. also M. A. Gutiérrez Behemerid, *Capiteles romanos de la península ibérica*, Studia Archaeologica (Valladolid) 77 (1986) 18f.; H. von Hesberg, *Stadtbild*, 343f. with nn. 19–29 on this stuccoed capital and its dating.

Fig. 14.6a–b. So-called "Temple of Diana," Emerita, with detail (b) of the corner of the "rostra" in front of the temple

 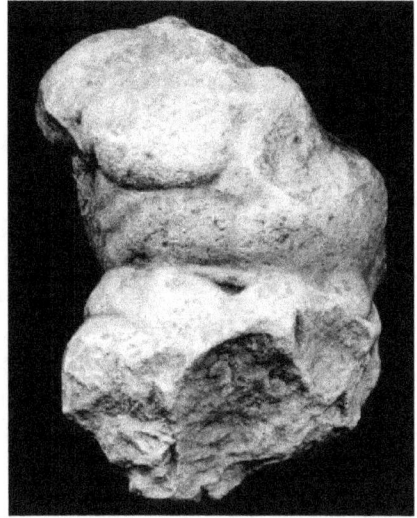

Fig. 14.7a–b. Colossal statues of an emperor found near the "Temple of Diana"

with large granite slabs. The square was bounded on the west and north by the *cardo* (the modern calle A. Zamora Vicente) and the *decumanus maximus* (the calle Santa Eulalia) respectively; it can, therefore, be identified with confidence as the (main) forum dating back to the time of the city's foundation.[50]

The full extent of the square, apparently surrounded by a cryptoporticus (visible at the western edge of the excavated area), which was presumably topped by a portico, has not yet been determined with certainty.[51] At least along its western side a row of shops (*tabernae*) opening outwards could have been located in the gap between the cryptoporticus and the *cardo maximus* [main north–south street]. The water basin[52] located in the open square to the west of the temple resembles the water installations recently discovered in excavations around the podium of the peripteral temple in Évora (Roman Ebora), which is probably somewhat later in date.[53]

Now that speculative attempts to identify it as a Temple of Diana, a Temple of Jupiter, or a Capitolium have been abandoned, there is more or less a scholarly consensus that the temple was linked to the

---

[50] Cf. M. Pfanner, *Stadtbild*, 99, fig. 31 (plan) [see now also Fig. 14.2, above].
[51] J. M. Alvarez Martínez, "El foro de Augusta Emerita," in *Homenaje a Sáenz de Buruaga* (1982) 53–68, 145–152.
[52] *Bimilenario*, plate 21b.
[53] T. Hauschild, "Untersuchungen am römischen Tempel von Évora," *MM* 29 (1988), 208–220.

imperial cult.[54] However, not one of the arguments so far advanced for this hypothesis is convincing; the only piece of evidence[55] that is in any way valuable is the colossal imperial statue (Fig. 14.7a [= Taf. 24c–f]),[56] now in Seville, which was found in Mérida in the calle Romero Leal (no. 22), i.e., in the area of this forum.

Here we are dealing with part of a seated statue in the round (1.11m tall), comprising the upper body, of the widely diffused Jupiter-type,[57] which was particularly popular during the reign of Claudius. In fact, the torso from Mérida has a particularly close affinity with the seated statue of Augustus from the Claudian portrait-group from the so-called "old forum" (Foro Vecchio) at Leptis Magna.[58] The wreath ribbons with their sharp wavy folds, visible on the shoulders, are very similar to those found on the statues of Claudius from the statue-group (just mentioned) from Leptis[59] and from the theatre at Caere.[60] Since there are a number of reasons to date the torso to the Claudian era, its sagging, full shape provides an additional indication that the statue perhaps represented this same emperor. The statue's sheer scale and its unfinished back, however, do not necessarily prove that it was used as a cult image and, similarly, the presence of an over-life-size statue of an emperor inside a temple, or in its vicinity, does not permit us to conclude with certainty that this emperor enjoyed cult here.

There can scarcely be any doubt that this Jupiter-statue functioned as a portrait. Furthermore, it seems that a whole series of portraits of members of the imperial family had been assembled in the "old" forum of Emerita. The head of Agrippina the Younger now in Madrid certainly comes from Mérida,[61] and may be identical with one of the female heads found in the calle Berzocana according to

---

[54] Cf. J. M. Alvarez Martínez in *Bimilenario*, 50f., with earlier literature.

[55] Discussed for the first time by Alvarez Martínez, loc. cit., 51.

[56] *EREP* 183f., no. 206, plate 151; C. Maderna, *Iuppiter, Diomedes und Merkur als Vorbilder für römische Bildnisstatuen*, Archäologie und Geschichte 1 (1988) 176, JT 18, plate 11, 1 with further literature.

[57] With regard to the type, see Maderna, loc. cit., 24ff. and cat. 163ff., JT 1–39; cf. H. G. Niemeyer, *Studien zur statuarischen Darstellung des römischen Kaisers*, Monumenta Artis Romanae 7 (1968) 59ff., 107ff., nos 95ff.

[58] Niemeyer, loc. cit. 106, no. 89, plate 30; Maderna, loc. cit., 166, JT 3, plate 6, 1.

[59] Niemeyer, 106, no. 90, plate 31; Maderna, 191f., JT 43, plate 6, 2.

[60] Niemeyer, 105f., no. 88, plate 29,4; Maderna, 167f., JT 5, plate 7, 2; cf. M. Fuchs, *Untersuchungen zur Ausstattung römischer Theater in Italien und den Westprovinzen des Imperium Romanum* (1987) 80, no. C I 3.

[61] *EREP* 44, no. 35, plate 31; W. Trillmich, *MM* 15 (1974), 193, plate 45; H. Jucker, *JdI* 91 (1976), 233, fig. 8; W. Trillmich in *Homenaje a Sáenz de Buruaga* (1982) 115f., no. E (with further literature); K. Fittschen and P. Zanker, *Katalog der römischen Porträts in den Capitolinischen Museen* III (1983) 7, no. 5, n. 4: Type II, d; S. Sande, *ActaInstRomNorvegiae* 5 (1985), 193, n. 127, no. 4. See also n. 62.

P. M. Plano García,[62] while excavations in 1973 revealed a fragment of a head that may well portray Antonia the Younger. Further discoveries of this excavation, which J. M. Alvarez Martínez is currently preparing for publication, include the body of a woman dressed in a *stola* and the nude upper torso of a male figure (see Fig. 14.7b), which likewise probably bore a portrait in the insert-hole for the head.[63]

A further indication that the main temple of Emerita was linked to the emperor is perhaps provided by its ground plan. As the excavations directed by J. M. Alvarez Martínez clearly established,[64] the back of the temple faced towards the *decumanus maximus*; its main side with the entrance faced towards the south-west, looking out over the square. The few ideas that have been propounded about the design of the steps leading up to the podium are imprecise at best. This part of the temple has not yet been completely excavated. Nevertheless, a series of clues suggests that the temple was not accessible by means of a set of stairs that extended across the entire width of its frontage; rather, it must have been reached by way of a platform attached to its front that was fitted with a set of lateral staircases.[65]

J. M. Alvarez Martínez's observation that, with the exception of the extra-wide central intercolumniation, all the spaces between the columns across the front of the temple were closed off with high metal-grille fences is a point in favour of the solution of a "smaller" access to the temple.[66] A broad set of stairs would have worked against this strongly "channelled" access into the inner temple. On the other hand, two lateral narrow and, moreover, presumably reverse sets of steps would have slowed down the process of entering the temple and would have been quite well suited to a restricted point of entrance.

That apart, there is not the slightest trace of a set of stairs; on the contrary, clearly visible are remains of a kind of "rostra" that formed

---

[62] P. M. Plano y García, *Ampliaciones a la Historia de Mérida* ... (1894) 28. This head of Agrippina formed part of the Monsalud collection in Almendralejo together with the togate statue discussed below (cf. n. 106 and Taf. 27), and it was in fact mounted onto it: see J. R. Mélida, *Catálogo Monumental de España. Provincia de Badajoz* I (1925) 355, no. 1486, plates 125, 180. That it originated in Mérida is not in doubt: it appears, for instance, in Plano y García, loc. cit., plate 1 alongside another togate statue (Fig. 14.13a [= Taf. 28b]) in what was then the Mérida municipal museum.

[63] Compare the same insertion system (which was not very common with nude statue types) on the colossal torso illustrated here as Fig. 14.7a [= Taf. 24c–f]. [For the new colossal torso, Fig. 14.7b, see J. M. Alvarez Martínez and T. Nogales Basarrate, *Forum Coloniae Augustae Emeritae: "Templo de Diana"* (2003) 200–204, no. 2 and plate 56a–d.]

[64] *Bimilenario*, 46, 48.

[65] A possibility also raised by T. Hauschild, MM 29 (1988), 219, with further examples from Hispania.

[66] *Bimilenario*, 48. Compare the similarly restricted entrances to the temples in Rome cited in nn. 70–71.

the front of the actual podium of the temple. Fig. 14.6a [= Taf. 24a] shows the temple's south-western front after the demolition of the modern noble mansion (*palacio*) that was previously attached to it:[67] most of all, one can see by looking at the smooth finish of the nearest plinth profile block that a building structure, which was designed independently from the actual podium, was supposed to be connected to its front. In fact, at a distance of about 9 metres from this worked block one can make out, in an area not yet fully excavated, the south-west corner of the platform that stood in front of the temple's podium. This corner comprises a three-sided pilaster and, to the east of it, three or four blocks (see Fig. 14.6b [= Taf. 24b]).[68] This in turn suggests that access to the temple was not via a frontal stairway, but rather by means of two lateral flights of stairs that were cut into this platform. If this conjecture about the design and function of the temple's actual frontage turns out to be correct, then it must have been about two to three metres wider than the temple's current width.[69] This would correspond to the two earliest temples known to have had similar entrance arrangements: the Temple of Venus Genetrix in the Forum Iulium, inaugurated by Caesar in 46 BC and completed by Augustus,[70] and the Temple of Divus Iulius in the Forum Romanum.[71]

Both these temples were clearly connected with the imperial cult. The "rostra" in front of them with their lateral, narrow sets of stairs

---

[67] For a photograph showing its previous state, see *Bimilenario*, plate 17b.

[68] It is also hinted at on the plan published by J. M. Alvarez Martínez, *Bimilenario*, 45, fig. 2. The scale (1:100) given there is incorrect; it is approximately 1:200. The labels giving the modern street (calle Romero Leal) and the square ("Foro") need to be placed much further to the south-east of the columns along the front of the temple. Nothing remains of the so-called "stairway" ("escalinata"), which was apparently imagined as a wide free-standing set of stairs.

[69] Compare the apparently similar relationship on the temple of Évora: Hauschild, *MM* 29 (1988), 218f. Hauschild, as opposed to the previous literature (ibid., 216 with n. 28), inclines towards similar lateral sets of stairs at Évora as well (cf. n. 65, above).

[70] Nash I, 33, 424ff. For a plan of the original design with the temple's actual entrance way narrowed down to the three central intercolumniations, see F. Coarelli, *Rom. Ein archäologischer Führer* (1975) 105f.; P. Gros, *Aurea Templa* (1976) plate 22, 1; cf. R. B. Ulrich, "The Temple of Venus Genetrix in the Forum of Caesar in Rome: The Topography, History, Architecture and Sculptural Program of the Monument" (Dissertation Microfilm, Ann Arbor 1984); idem, *RM* 93 (1986), 405–423 (plan of the renovation under Trajan: 408, fig. 1).

[71] Nash I, 512ff.; B. Andreae, *AA* (1957), 174 fig. 26; M. Montagna Pasquinucci, *Athenaeum* 52 (1974), 144–155; P. Zanker, *Forum Romanum. Die Neugestaltung durch Augustus* (1972) 12ff., figs 13 and 24; F. Coarelli, op. cit. (n. 70), 84, 86; Gros, op. cit. (n. 70), plate 10, 2; F. Coarelli, *Il Foro Romano II: Periodo repubblicano e augusteo* (1985) 230ff., 269ff., 272 fig. 71; H. Hänlein-Schäfer, *Veneratio Augusti*, Archaeologica 39 (1985) 255ff., plates 66, b to 69. Like the Temple of Venus Genetrix (cf. n. 70), this temple can only be entered through the three middle column bays at the front. For coins depicting the temple, which show clearly that the "rostra" planned at the outset were wider than the temple façade and that the lateral sets of stairs were not visible from the front, see W. Trillmich in *Kaiser Augustus und die verlorene Republik* (Exhibition, Berlin 1988) 501f., no. 308, with refs.

leading from the back upwards were designed with liturgical needs in mind. Not all temples with such reverse lateral stairs were dedicated to the imperial cult; comparable access solutions,[72] however, appear particularly frequently, as with the Temple of Roma and Augustus of Tiberian date at Leptis Magna,[73] the Temple of Vespasian in Pompeii,[74] and the Trajanic Temple of Victoria Parthica Augusta in the forum at Timgad.[75] While nothing is preserved at the "Temple of Diana" in Mérida of the side stairways[76] or of the podium stretching across the front of the temple except for the remains of the front of a moulded base, which could be due to the fact that the podium – as, for example, at Leptis Magna – was not built of solid masonry, but rather was hollow on the inside. On the analogy of the Temple of Roma and Augustus at Leptis Magna, it is possible that the previously mentioned portrait-statues of the imperial family were perhaps set up on or up against the platform that ran across the front of the temple.

Naturally it is not possible to identify the divinity who occupied the temple on the basis of a proposed reconstruction of its system of access. In any case, the proposed solution would refute the recently revived theory that the temple was the colony's Capitolium, which is already ruled out anyway by its peristyle-shaped ground-plan. At this moment, I cannot comment on relevant ideas concerned with the city's legal status at the time of its foundation. Hopefully J. M. Alvarez Martínez's forthcoming publication will soon offer us answers to all these questions, as well as proposals about the design

---

[72] Here it should be mentioned that the cella of the sanctuary of Munigua (cf. Pfanner, *Stadtbild*, 79ff. with figs 21-22 and plate 6) is only accessible via a wider podium running across its front, which is reached by means of two sets of reverse stairs on its side: *MM* 19 (1978), 291, fig. 1 (plan). Depiction of these small sets of stairs on the north side: *Actas del V CongrNacArqueología, Zaragoza 1957* (1959), 280; *Neue deutsche Ausgrabungen im Mittelmeergebiet und im Vorderen Orient* (1959), 340, fig. 8. This system of access could provide clues about the cult at the sanctuary of Munigua. See also F. Coarelli, "Munigua, Praeneste e Tibur. I modelli laziali di un municipio della Baetica," *Lucentum* 6 (1987), 91-100, esp. 95-97, with figs 7-9.

[73] S. Aurigemma, *Africa Italiana* 8 (1941), 1-94; plan 3, fig. 1; a better plan (1:500) at A. di Vita, *Orientalia* 37 (1968), 201ff, plate 37. Cf. H. Hänlein-Schäfer, op. cit., 226ff. A 53, with further refs.; see recently W. Trillmich in *Estudios sobre la Tabula Siarensis*, Anejos AEspA IX (1988), 53ff., with notes 13ff.

[74] E. La Rocca et al., *Guida archeologica di Pompei* (1976) 118ff.; Hänlein-Schäfer, op. cit., 133ff. A 5 (with further refs.); Coarelli, op. cit. (n. 72), fig. 9.

[75] J. Lassus, *Visite à Timgad* (1969) 34-37, figs 14-17; Chr. Courtois, *Timgad, antique Thamugadi* (1951) 28f., 32.

[76] Solutions other than reverse, lateral sets of stairs are possible; cf. the Temple of Roma and Augustus in the Forum at Ostia from the early imperial era, on which the two lateral stairways lead towards the frontal "rostra" and are situated at right angles to the temple's main axis: G. Calza, *Scavi di Ostia* I (1953) 115f., fig. 30 and suppl. 8; cf. Hänlein-Schäfer 130ff., A 4 with plates 2-8 and further refs.

and layout of the main temple of Emerita in its "foundation period."

During the later years of the reign of the first *princeps*, the granite-grey city of Emerita was transformed into "Augusta" Emerita, a "city of marble," which took as its model the city of Rome as restored by Augustus (Suet. *Aug.* 28.5). It is not possible to discuss here whether there is a causal and chronological relationship between the new building programme at Emerita and a change in the city's legal status or its elevation to the status of capital of the newly created province of Lusitania. In any case, Emerita's coins, which took over the theme of a city-view from Carisius' older provincial issues, are now inscribed not only with EMERITA, but also almost always with the name AVGVSTA.[77] In abbreviated versions of the city's name on Augustan and Tiberian coins (C A E or similar)[78] the element C(olonia) emphasises Emerita's privileged legal status.

As for the date of the start of Emerita's urban remodelling, the best indication is provided by the fact that Emerita's "marble forum," which we shall examine in greater detail below (pp. 450ff.), is a genuine copy of the Forum Augustum at Rome, inaugurated in the year 2 BC. This date corresponds excellently with the results of research (which cannot be discussed here) on the programmatic structure of the Augustan city coinage of Emerita, which started to be minted precisely in the year 2 BC. The portraits and honorific inscriptions from various locations in the theatre[79] similarly show that this building was refurbished and decorated with marble in the late-Augustan period. Stylistic criteria can provide only an approximate date for the completion of these large-scale projects; however, everything indicates that Augustus' Emerita was only completed under Claudius.

The *Marmorisierung* of Emerita for the most part took place completely *ex novo*, that is, through the erection of totally new building complexes; on the other hand, it also affected buildings that had already been completed in the foundation period,[80] which we may

---

[77] Vives IV 62, no. 19, plate 141, 3 (Augustan; after 2 BC); 64, no. 36, plate 142, 6; 65, no. 45, plate 143, 5; nos 51–53, plate 144, 1–3; 66, no. 55, plate 144, 5; no. 62, plate 145, 1 (Tiberian).

[78] Vives IV 63, no. 23, plate 141, 7; no. 24, plate 141, 8; no. 26, plate 141, 10; Tiberian: Vives IV 64, no. 37, plate 142, 7; 65, no. 43, plate 143, 3 etc. on various coin types.

[79] Cf. n. 110, as well as D. Boschung, *Stadtbild*, 391ff.

[80] A special case may be the gigantic temple in the forum in the north-western part of the city, across which the *cardo maximus* runs and whose entrance is formed by the three-gated "Arch of Trajan" (cf. Pfanner, *Stadtbild*, 99, fig. 31): Alvarez Martínez in *Ciudades superpuestas*, 42 with images on pp. 52–53; idem in *Historia de la Baja Extremadura*, ed. M. Terrán Albarrán, I (1986) 135 (figure), 155ff. with nn. 480, 484; cf. also H. von Hesberg, *Stadtbild*, 361, plate 41a; Pfanner, *Stadtbild*, 94 with n. 94. From this one gets the impression

also call the city's Agrippan phase. In some areas drastic measures were undertaken, as on the massive three-gated entrance arch to the north-western forum: here the attractive façade of the passageway was chiselled off in order to attach a marble facing.[81] The *scaenae frons* [scene building at the back of the stage] of the theatre received the same treatment, at least at the level of its already complete granite plinth,[82] as did the amphitheatre, where the podium and front rows of privileged seating were subsequently revetted with marble.[83]

On the other hand, building elements of the initial phase were occasionally treated like relics and reused in other appropriate places. The two granite blocks inscribed with dedicatory inscriptions of the donor Agrippa (one of which is shown in Fig. 14.4a [= Taf. 8a]) had perhaps once formed part of original theatre's *scaenae frons*, apparently built into the structure's side arches. They were cut to size and reinstalled in another location, probably underneath the two *tribunalia* so that the inscription could still be easily read[84] (in similar fashion to the way in which Hadrian later reused for his new Pantheon the text of Agrippa's dedicatory inscription that had once adorned the original temple). In general, even long after his death M. Agrippa was remembered at Emerita as the crucial person in the city's initial building phase, as is demonstrated by the large, splendid monument dating to the Claudian period, from which we have recently reconstructed a relief plaque that shows Agrippa in the act of sacrifice.[85]

There is no need here for any further treatment of the marble refurbishment of the large-scale buildings of the foundation period; the phenomenon is discussed in detail by M. Pfanner and H. von Hesberg in their contributions to this volume [i.e., *Stadtbild*]. As regards the entirely new "marble forum," parts of which have only recently been excavated, just a few aspects will be discussed briefly here: the sculptural decoration of marble-clad Mérida, its programmatic signifi-

---

that only the podium was completed at the time it was decided to refurbish it with marble, since the upper part of the building was built entirely of marble.

[81] Cf. also Pfanner, *Stadtbild*, 102 with fig. 33 and plate 8d–e.

[82] Cf. Pfanner, *Stadtbild*, 101f. with fig. 32 and plate 8a–c; with regard to the date of the marble stage façade, see comprehensively H. von Hesberg, *Stadtbild*, 356ff.

[83] On the marble refurbishment of the amphitheatre, see above p. 439, with nn. 47–48 and Fig. 14.5a–b [= Taf. 23f–g]; see also n. 84 (below).

[84] Cf. the remarks of Pfanner, *Stadtbild*, 102, with plate 8; von Hesberg, *Stadtbild*, 360. Similarly one can imagine the refurbishment of the amphitheatre from the relocation of one of the inscriptions commemorating the benefactions of Augustus in the year 8/7 BC (J. Menéndez-Pidal y Alvarez, *AEspA* 30 (1957), 207f. fig. 3; cf. also n. 48).

[85] W. Trillmich, *MM* 27 (1986), 279–304, plates 39–48; for its dating to the Claudian period, ibid., 298f. with plate 49. Cf. also n. 109 (below).

450   The Impact of Augustus in the Roman Provinces

cance and problems regarding its artistic manufacture, especially the question of workshops and building operations. On these topics, numerous pieces of new information are now available thanks to an intensive study, generously permitted by J. M. Alvarez Martínez, of the latest discoveries. These can only be briefly discussed in what follows. At the same time, we will frequently refrain from using this specific evidence, relying instead on already published material to illustrate the arguments being advanced. Even given these limitations, we can at least determine the directions in which further research needs to go and perhaps also reach some initial conclusions that are generally plausible.

3 TOWARDS AN *URBS MARMOREA*: PROCESSES, DECORATIVE PROGRAMMES, AND THE QUESTION OF WORKSHOPS

In 1934 fragments of some large architectural reliefs with shield-roundels (*clipei*) (Fig. 14.8a–c [replacing Taf. 25a–f]) and caryatids (Fig. 14.9a [= Taf. 26c], 14.9b–c [replacing Taf. 26d]) were discovered built into a modern sewer channel in Pancaliente on the north-west edge of the modern town of Mérida, and hence had clearly been removed from their original location. As M. Floriani Squarciapino was the first to realise, they belonged to a building that in its conception copied the decoration of the Forum Augustum and imitated it in its design.[86] *Disiecta membra* of this obviously important building complex have been found dispersed all over the city; nevertheless, the finds are concentrated in one particular area, which allows us to establish the complex's approximate extent. Excavations took place in 1980 in its north-eastern corner,[87] more precisely underneath house no. 13 in the calle Sagasta, which had already in the nineteenth century provided us with significant sculptural finds.[88] Now it is clear that a large square, surrounded by a portico with a water channel running in front of it, all built entirely of marble, was located along the north-east side of the original forum that contained the "Temple of Diana." The attic level of this porticoed hall was decorated with caryatids standing above the columns, while *clipei* were affixed above the spaces in between the columns, just as in the

---

[86] *Bimilenario*, 55–62, plates 23–30; for further literature on the finds from Pancaliente, see W. Trillmich, *MM* 27 (1986), 281, n. 14.

[87] For references, see W. Trillmich, *MM* 27 (1986), 280f., nn. 10–11; see further Alvarez Martínez in *Historia de la Baja Extremadura* I (1986) 155.

[88] As discussed by W. Trillmich, *MM* 27 (1986), 279f.

Fig. 14.8a–c. Clipei with heads of Jupiter Ammon and Medusa from the "marble forum"

Forum of Augustus in Rome,[89] the only difference being that at Emerita the caryatids were sculpted in relief rather than fully in the round. The portico's back wall was designed in such a way that the pilasters set up along it corresponded with the columns that stood along the front of the portico. Between each pair of pilasters a recessed niche was cut into the wall to hold a statue, with the individual portrayed identified on an inscribed plaque set up underneath.[90]

---

[89] Concerning the Forum Augustum and its reconstruction, see, among others, P. Zanker, *Forum Augustum. Das Bildprogramm*, Monumenta Artis Antiquae 2 (no date; *c*. 1968); E. Simon, *Augustus. Kunst und Leben in Rom um die Zeitenwende* (1986) 46ff.; P. Zanker, *Augustus und die Macht der Bilder* (1987) 196ff.; recently (with sources and numerous images) various authors in *Kaiser Augustus und die verlorene Republik* (1988) 184ff., cat. nos 77–92.

[90] Cf. the photo published by J. M. Alvarez Martínez in *Ciudades superpuestas*, 53.

From the material known before the new excavations were undertaken, we were already able to distinguish two types of *clipei*: those with the head of Jupiter Ammon and those with the head of Medusa, each of which are found in at least three different variants, based on the details of the border surrounding the central image (Fig. 14.8a–c [cf. Taf. 25a–c and e–f]).[91] The new and much better preserved *clipei* from the calle Sagasta (Fig. 14.8a, c)[92] reveal that each of the four corners of the basically rectangular slabs was filled with a large open flower.

Among the caryatids[93] we can likewise distinguish two types (Fig. 14.9a [= Taf. 26c], 14.9b–c [cf. Taf. 26d), which are essentially similar in their subject matter, but which derive from two quite different artistic designs.[94] Among the items that have long formed part

[91] Some brief explanations are in order regarding the typology of these *clipei* [Taf. 25a–f]:
(a) without inventory number: *clipeus* with head of Ammon (remains of hair on forehead, horn on the left, part of right eye); inner border: pearl bar; outer border: cord-like design. From Pancaliente; max. height: 78 cm. *EREP* 415f., no. 417, plate 297c; *Homenaje a Sáenz de Buruaga* (1982) 39, fig. 5.
(b) without inv. no.: *clipeus* with head of Ammon (mouth survives with left half of beard); inner border: braided staff; outer border: smooth ring. From Pancaliente; max. height: 65 cm. *EREP*, plate 297d.
(c) inv. no. 4423: *clipeus* with head of Ammon (remains of nose, mouth with moustache and lower part of beard); inner border: cord-like design, outer border: smooth ring. From Pancaliente; max. height: 90 cm. *EREP*, plate 297b; *Bimilenario* 58, plate 26b.
(d) without inv. no.: *clipeus* with Gorgon's head (remains of forehead with part of the eyes; left half of hair, with head wing); inner border: egg-and-dart; outer border: laurel wreath. From Pancaliente. Max. height: 90 cm. *EREP* plate 297a; *Bimilenario* 58, plate 27a.
(e) without inv. no.: *clipeus* with Gorgon head (remains of snakes entwined in front of crease of neck); inner border: egg-and-dart; outer border: oak wreath. From Pancaliente. Max. height: 59 cm. *MemMusAProvinc* 4 (1943), 46 under no. F, plate 6, 3 (left; incorrectly adjoined); *AEspA* 17 (1944), 179 no. a, fig. 34 top (left; incorrectly mounted).
(f) inv. no. 8161: *clipeus* of the Gorgon series; inner border of the lost middle part: egg-and-dart, outer border: tendril. Found by accident in the calle Santa Eulalia (= *decumanus maximus* of Emerita); deposited in the museum in 1953. Max. height: 50 cm.
[92] One of these [Fig. 14.8b] is illustrated by Alvarez Martínez in *Ciudades superpuestas*, 51. [Fig. 14.8a = Museo National de Arte Romano inv. no. 33002; J. L. de la Barrera, *La decoración arquitectónica de los foros de Augusta Emerita*, Bibliotheca Archaeologica 25 (2000) 79–80, cat. no. 245 and plate 95; Fig. 14.8b = inv. no. 33000; de la Barrera 79, cat. no. 243 and plates 92–93; Fig. 14.8c = inv. no. 33001; de la Barrera 80, cat. no. 247 and plate 97.]
[93] For the caryatids found at Pancaliente: *AEspA* 17 (1944), 180, fig. 24; *EREP* 420, nos 420–423, plate 30of; *Bimilenario*, plate 24a–d.
[94] Here Fig. 14.9a [= Taf. 26c] (Type A): inv. no. 4398. From Pancaliente. Max. height: 132 cm. On the figure's left shoulder remains of the ends of two corkscrew-shaped locks falling along the neck as well as the raised fringe of a cloak which covers her head and was worn over the peplos by the girl, who holds it in her left, relaxed hand. The right arm was raised in a gesture of support. Taf. 26d (Type B): inv. no. 4401. From Pancaliente. Max. height: 90.5 cm. As in the previous piece, above the fibula the ends of two locks of hair fall along the neck to the shoulders. Stance and arm gesture are identical with the caryatids of Type A, except in this case the left and right sides of the image are reversed (in both types these two variants exist). The design of the robe is, especially in its style, much different from Type A. For the completely preserved new caryatids of Type B, see Fig. 14.9b–c and below, with n. 99. [Fig. 14.9b = inv. no. 33003; de la Barrera (cit. n. 92) 105, cat. no. 371 and plate 127; Fig. 14.9c = inv. no. 33004; de la Barrera 105, cat. no. 372 and plate 134.]

of the Mérida museum's collection are two fragments of heads, for which there is no information about their findspot. Nevertheless, they can be connected with some confidence with the caryatids from the marble forum. One of them [Taf. 26a], which E. Kukahn published in 1970 in a strangely deficient article as an image of Meter from the second century AD[95] and which was then forgotten, carries a braided basket (*kalathos*) above her veil. The earlier assumption[96] that this piece belonged to a caryatid is now confirmed by the discovery of just such a *kalathos* at the site of calle Sagasta no. 13.[97] The second, even more fragmentary head [Taf. 26b][98] shares a number of characteristics – its form as a relief, the veil, the two neck-length locks of hair – and is of exactly the same dimensions. As a result, it can only be interpreted as the head of another caryatid from the marble forum. The female figure has a slightly different hairstyle and, in place of the *kalathos*, supports an architectural element resembling a capital on top of her veiled head. With the help of newly discovered and as yet unpublished fragments, we still need to clarify whether these two types of head can be associated with the two body types previously identified.

In connection with these two heads, a recently discovered, but unfortunately headless torso of a caryatid of the second type (Fig. 14.9b)[99] helps to reveal how these caryatids functioned as architectural supports: these female figures supported a building element (probably the attic frieze) not only on their heads, but also on top of a raised right or left arm, with its hand bent backwards and carrying a large vase decorated with reliefs. This design is exceptionally unusual for this type of buttressing figures and its stylistic origins still need to be explored. A preliminary sketch by U. Städtler (Fig. 14.10) provides a rough idea of the appearance of these caryatids.

The "inventory" of statues displayed in this forum, of which, as

---

[95] Inv. no. 7479. We do not know anything about its origin; it has been in the museum's collection since 1948. Max. height: 32 cm. E. Kukahn, "Una cabeza de Meter en Mérida," *XI CongrNacArqueología, Mérida 1968* (1969), 735f., fig. 1. Traces of two twisted locks of hair are preserved behind the ears; to the left side of the head, a larger part of the outline of the relief may be seen.

[96] *MM* 27 (1986), 282, n. 16.

[97] Inv. no. 33181 (unpublished). Ironically, as we were taking a photograph for plate 26d in the storeroom in the Alcazaba in the year 1979, we propped up the torso of the caryatid by resting it on a fragment of a *kalathos*, which we did not then recognise as such. The fragment has not resurfaced since then.

[98] Inv. no. 20744; previously in the storeroom located at the Roman theatre, but this does not tell us anything about the actual origin of the piece. Max. height of section remaining: 31 cm.

[99] Inv. no. 33003. Found in 1980 in the excavation of the corner of the forum in the calle Sagasta: J. M. Alvarez Martínez, *Ciudades superpuestas*, fig. on p. 50.

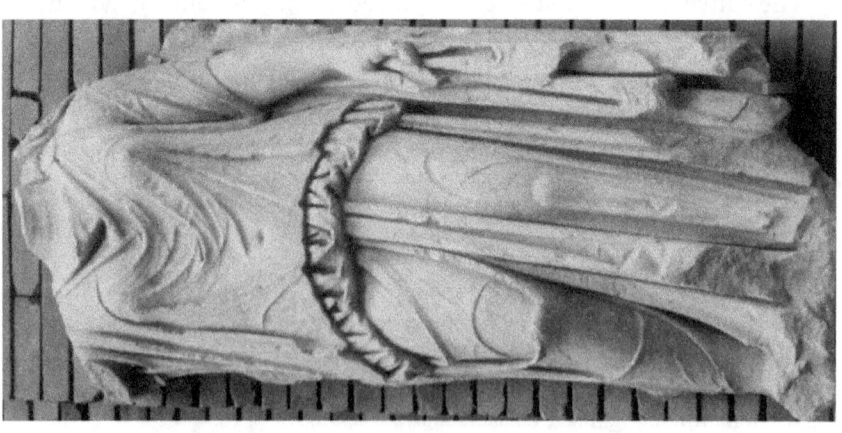

Fig. 14.9a–c. Caryatids from the "marble forum"

Fig. 14.10. Reconstruction of Caryatid from the "marble forum"

pointed out above, only a small corner is so far known, is of the greatest importance for our understanding of the ideological message and artistic realisation of this exceptionally ambitious building programme. The sensational new finds of 1980 and 1986 demonstrate that we are dealing in programmatic terms with a rather faithful copy of the Forum Augustum in Rome in terms not just of its architectural decoration, but of its sculptural layout as well. This all underlines the very ambitious claims of the provincial capital.

The head of a youthful male figure with short beard, now mounted on the central togate statue displayed along the far wall of the main display hall of the Museo Nacional de Arte Romano in Mérida, has a broad band with no trailing ribbons tied around his equally short hair.[100] This provides decisive information about one part of the

---

[100] Inv. no. 33677; found on the site of calle Sagasta no. 11/13 during a clean-up campaign in 1986; unpublished (except for a photo of it on the front page of the Madrid newspaper *ABC* of 20 September 1986, in an article covering the opening of the new Mérida museum).

programme: evidently we are dealing here with a king wearing a diadem. Since its portrait features do not match any other known sculptural conception dating to the early imperial period, it cannot depict, for instance, a client king such as Juba II, but must represent an idealised image of a king, very probably a king of early Rome.

A fortunate circumstance furnishes important information about another part of the sculptural programme: a robed statue of very unusual type (Fig. 14.11 [= Taf. 28c]),[101] which was discovered at the end of the nineteenth century at house no. 13 in the calle Sagasta, bears the inscription AGRIPPA along the left edge of its plinth. This shows that members of the imperial family were also depicted in this forum.

The ever stronger parallels with the sculptural layout of the portico of the Forum of Augustus in Rome ultimately lead us to conjecture that the fragment of an enormous cuirassed statue,[102] with its left leg thrust forward in a wide stride, may perhaps represent the remains of a statue of Romulus or of an Aeneas group, depicted in a style not unlike that of the colossal sculptures recorded from the Forum Augustum.[103] [The recent discovery of parts of a statue of Anchises and the re-identification of a statue long thought to represent Diana as Ascanius have allowed a very plausible reconstruction of this Aeneas group: see Fig. 14.12.]

A more detailed examination of the programme of the forum's layout must be reserved for future discussion. The sensational meaning of these sculptural finds will be obvious to anyone who has seen the items exhibited in the museum at Mérida. This paper will conclude with a brief discussion of some key questions related to the production of this extraordinarily rich sculptural decoration, in terms of its programmatic significance as well as its artistic importance.

Among the fortunate new finds from this corner of the "marble forum" are four togate figures that were discovered fallen to the ground in front of their respective wall niches.[104] Three of them are on display in the museum at Mérida. They increase the overall number of *togati* with the workshop inscription "*ex of(f)icina* ..."

---

[101] Inv. no. 93; P.M. Plano y García, *Ampliaciones á la Historia de Mérida* ...(1894) 27f., plate 1; *EREP* 186f., no. 210, plate 155 (with literature; see further *MM* 27, 1986, 280, n. 8).

[102] Inv. no. 33676, likewise stemming from the cleaning-up campaign of 1986 (cf. n. 100).

[103] Cf. the literature cited above in n. 89; further references in W. Fuchs, *ANRW* I 4 (1973), 615ff.; *LIMC* I (1981), 381, 390, nos 146–154, with a collection of references to the Aeneas group.

[104] One of which (inv. no. 33005) is illustrated by J. M. Alvarez Martínez in *Homenaje a Sáenz de Buruaga* (1982) 57, fig. 4.

Colonia Augusta Emerita, Capital of Lusitania

Fig. 14.11. Statue of a man ("Agrippa" statue) from the "marble forum"

["from the workshop of ..."] to six. Already in the late-nineteenth century, within about a decade, two *togati* were discovered at the same location: one remained in Mérida (Fig. 14.13a [= Taf. 28b]),[105] while the other passed into the collection of the Marqués de Monsalud before eventually ending up in Madrid [Taf. 27a–f].[106] We, therefore, have at our disposal a group of six masterpieces, each with a quite individual artistic character. However, they can all be closely connected to one another since they can all be shown to have been produced in the same single workshop and, in addition, we can verify that they were all displayed as a group in the same physical setting. Any examination and partial reconstruction of the artistic context of, and the processes that lay behind, the production of the entire sculptural decoration of the marble forum and, so it would appear, of other buildings at Emerita must begin from a stylistic analysis of these togate figures.

---

[105] Inv. no. 94; Plano y García (op. cit., n. 101), 28; *EREP* 184f., no. 207, plate 152; *Homenaje a Sáenz de Buruaga* 46, fig. 12; 56, fig. 3.

[106] Madrid, Museo Arqueológico Nacional, inv. no. 13431: Plano y García, loc. cit.; *EREP* 188, no. 215, plate 157; M. Almagro in *Bimilenario*, 134, plate 54, a–b. I am very much obliged to the museum's director, Dr José Maria Luzón Nogué, for readily issuing me permission to examine, photograph, and publish the statue.

Fig. 14.12. Reconstruction of the statue-group of Aeneas (centre), Ascanius (left) and Anchises (right) from the "marble forum"

It is possible to identify specific stylistic mannerisms of a leading workshop, within which we can already distinguish several master craftsmen [cf. Taf. 27]: for instance, the deeply recessed, hook-shaped crease of the folds in the middle of the fabric; the slight indentations on the cloth's surface, which would appear if one pressed one's thumb against the fabric and which give life, movement, and contrast to the garment; the technically virtuosic wavy edges of the cloth; the bridges in the folds' crevices left behind as a clue to the bravura of the chisel-work; in addition one should note the repeated representations of fine ridges in the fabric, which have nothing to do with the form of the garments, or their draping, flow, or pull, but rather result from the folding of the fabric. Careful observation and delineation of these and other artistic peculiarities of the six togate statues allow us without question to attribute the Agrippa statue (Fig. 14.11 [= Taf. 28c]), which was displayed in the same location, and other works from other contexts too (the theatre, for instance: see below, pp. 460f. to the group of sculptors working at this *officina*.

Apart from the artistic quality of their work, the leading sculptors of this workshop most of all wanted to demonstrate the brilliance and virtuosity of their technique, and their masterpieces had a great impact in Emerita. Some of their characteristic "mannerisms" we find, to give just one example, on a togate statue (Fig. 14.13b [= Taf. 28a])[107] that does not bear the *officina* inscription on its knee and

---

[107] Inv. no. 691. Unpublished. Max. height: 181 cm. Cf. the following note.

Fig. 14.13a–b. Togate statues from the "marble forum"

which in terms of its quality indeed ranks behind the togate statues of that *officina*. At the same time, however, it was without doubt created in imitation of them. One may go so far as to suppose that the togate statue found in Mérida in 1894 (Fig. 14.13a [= Taf. 28b]), so similar in terms of its treatment and style, provided the direct model for it. As for the unsigned togate statue, there is no information unfortunately about its findspot in the museum's inventory; for a long time it was set up on the "Arch of Trajan." However, it is very probably identical with the unpublished togate statue which was discovered around 1880 on the premises of calle de Sagasta no. 13.[108]

---

[108] See Plano y García, op. cit. (n. 101), 28, describing the *togatus* in n. 105: "Only the body of the statue now survives; it is lacking the head, arms and legs [and also the *officina* inscription, one can conclude, from the fact that Plano does not mention it], and although it is also a very good sculpture, it does not come near those related to it."

This would provide the first confirmation that, as far as the embellishment of this marble forum is concerned, there was one leading workshop, which even went so far as to sign its statues and which during the forum's construction phase was given the task of training other sculptors.

One's initial astonishment that the completed public square featured sculptures of first- and second-rate quality standing alongside one another subsides when one takes another look at the forum's architectural decoration. First of all, some of the characteristics of the leading workshop we have just been discussing are also discernible on one of the caryatid types (Fig. 14.9a [= Taf. 26c]). The quality of the execution of these figures in relief that form part of the building's decoration is – one might almost say "naturally" – rather hurried, and yet there can be no possible doubt that they show a stylistic affinity with the products of the same workshop. (Perhaps they were sculpted by other specialised master craftsmen who were distinct from those who sculpted the togate statues.) The caryatids of the second type (Fig. 14.9b–c [replacing Taf. 26d]) display a significantly lower quality of execution than all the examples so far discussed. From this it is clear that people did not object to differences in style and particularly in quality in this row of caryatids that were actually rather eye-catching, since they appeared as a series, even though they were perhaps divided between two separate wings of the portico. A similar phenomenon may be observed elsewhere in Emerita, namely in the theatre.[109]

The sculptural display of the theatre in its second phase has recently been discussed by M. Fuchs and, as far as the portraits are concerned, by D. Boschung.[110] For that reason there is no need to discuss this complex in any further detail here. It is important, however, to note that the slightly larger-than-life-size cuirassed statue with the *palladion* [statue of Pallas Athena] on its chest [Taf. 28d],[111]

---

[109] On the differing grades of quality in the execution of the capitals of the *scaenae frons*, see H. von Hesberg, *Stadtbild*, 355f. On the sacrificial relief mentioned in n. 85, one can also observe a quite striking difference in quality in the carving of the garland area in comparison with the scene with the human figures; the latter is in artistic terms less skilfully worked: see W. Trillmich, MM 27 (1986), 299.

[110] M. Fuchs, *Untersuchungen zur Ausstattung römischer Theater in Italien und den Westprovinzen des Imperium Romanum* (1987) 144f., plates 65, 2–4 (decorative sculptures), 167–169, plates 66–69 (portraits); cf. also the index (p. 201) s. v. Mérida; D. Boschung, *Stadtbild*, 393ff.

[111] EREP 194f., no. 231, plate 163 (with previous literature); P. Acuña Fernández, *Esculturas militares romanas de España y Portugal I: Las esculturas thoracatas*, Biblioteca de la Escuela Española de Historia y Arqueología en Roma 16 (1975) 76ff., no. XVI, figs 51–56.

which M. Fuchs,[112] following K. Stemmer,[113] believed to be Flavian but which was ignored by Boschung, in particular allows us to establish a direct connection with the workshop that was actively involved with work on the "marble forum." Not only do we find specific peculiarities in the treatment of the dress, such as the form of the wad of cloth of the *paludamentum* [military cloak] on the shoulder, that can also be observed on the togate statues; but a series of quite characteristic technical similarities, such as the drill technique along the lower edge of the long leather straps where their connecting bars were left in place and the somewhat coarse and rarely fully bored out fringe-ends, as well as some stylistic similarities (for example, in the form and decoration of the *pteryges* [tongue-shaped flaps attached to the bottom edge of a cuirass] and the tendrils on the lower edge of the cuirass) connect this cuirassed statue quite closely with the colossal cuirassed figure from the "marble forum" (cf. above, p. 456 and Fig. 14.12), although admittedly the latter displays a higher level of quality.

Corresponding similarities may be found on the better of the two other cuirassed statues from the theatre that feature centaurs carrying trophies (see Fig. 14.14a [= Taf. 48a]; notice, above all, once again the typical representation of the folds of the wad of cloth of the *paludamentum*):[114] that it was produced in the workshop of the "marble forum" is beyond doubt. The copy based on this model (Fig. 14.14b [= Taf. 48b])[115] repeats the phenomenon that was already observed on the togate statues with and without a workshop inscription (compare Fig. 14.13a [= Taf. 28b] with Fig. 14.13b [= Taf. 28a]): a less skilled sculptor, apparently an apprentice of one of the workshop's more accomplished masters, produced a copy based on an original model. The two sculptures were set up alongside each other – in this case on the *scaenae frons* of the theatre – despite the fact that their common features displayed some eye-catching differences in terms of quality.

One question that remains open and which needs further examination concerns the origin of this leading workshop and its craftsmen. This workshop in Emerita, however, did not operate in a vacuum with respect to other trained marble sculptors active there.

---

[112] Fuchs, op. cit., 169, with n. 469.
[113] K. Stemmer, *Untersuchungen zur Typologie, Chronologie und Ikonographie der Panzerstatuen*, Archäologische Forschungen 4 (1978) 34, no. III 6, plates 18, 2 to 19, 1.
[114] *EREP* 192f., no. 228, plate 162; Acuña, op. cit., 71ff., no. XIV, figs 43–46; Stemmer, op. cit., 99, no. VIII 2, plate 66, 3–4.
[115] *EREP* 193, no. 229, plate 162; Acuña 73ff., no. XV, figs 47–50; Stemmer 100, no. VIII 4, plate 68.

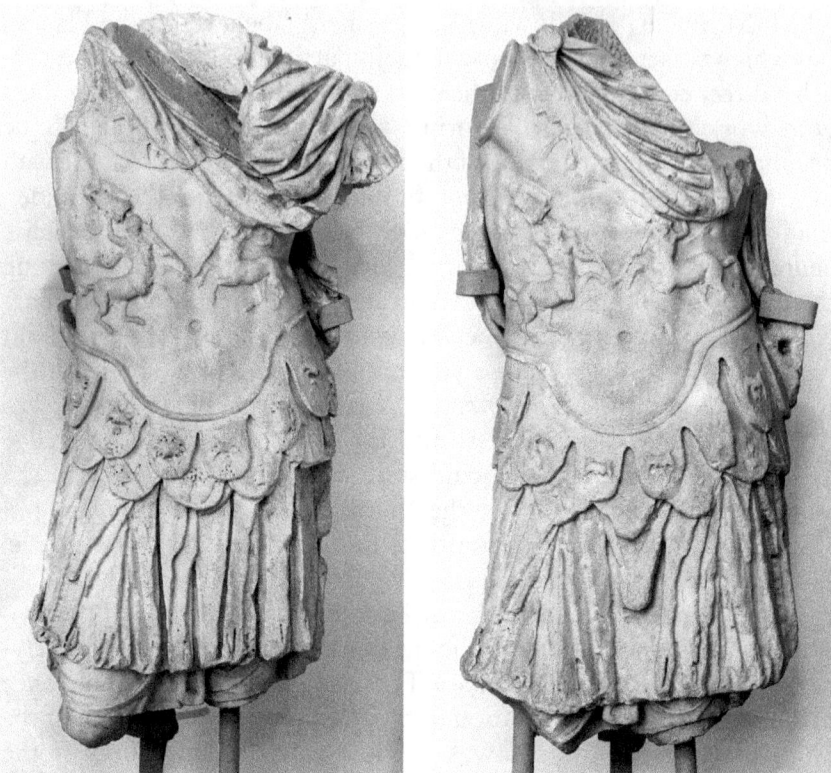

Fig. 14.14a–b. Cuirassed-statues decorated with trophy-carrying centaurs from the theatre

Fortunately, the abundantly surviving private portraits, which need to and can stand as proxy for official monuments, provide us with clues about the situation and sophistication of the local marble sculptors' craftsmanship in the "foundation period."

Very soon after Emerita's foundation, there must have been a considerable demand in the private domain for funerary portraits, which in turn stimulated a flourishing business for sculpture workshops. One example to have survived from the earliest phase of Emerita's history is a male head (Fig. 14.15a [= Taf. 29a])[116] that was originally finished with a layer of stucco; despite the great damage the head has suffered, it can be securely dated to the earliest years of the city on typological grounds and because of the materials used. It is quite apparent that even in those early days portraits were imported or sculptors were summoned who worked at a perfectly

---

[116] Inv. no. 13884, found in the "República Argentina" neighbourhood; i.e., in the area of one of Emerita's necropoleis.

Colonia Augusta Emerita, Capital of Lusitania

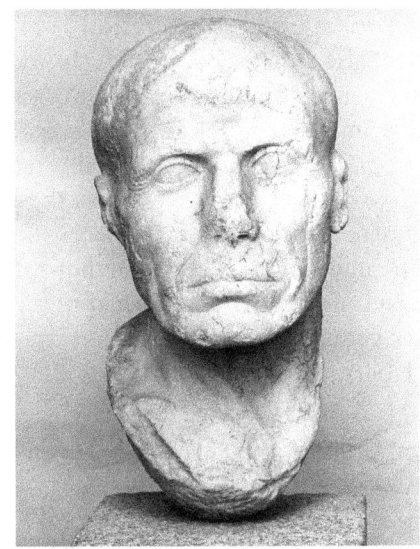

Fig. 14.15a–b. Male portraits from Emerita: (a) in limestone (originally stuccoed?); (b) in marble

good level of quality that indeed matched that of the workshops at Rome, as a well-known portrait of an elderly bald man demonstrates (Fig. 14.15b [= Taf. 29b]).[117] The local workshops that produced portraits took such "masterpieces" as models and examples, and here again it is possible to establish a series of products [Taf. 29b–d][118] that may be classified hierarchically according to their quality in just the same way as may be observed for a later period with the sculptural decoration of Emerita's public buildings (see above, p. 460).

With the better [Taf. 29e][119] and less well executed [Taf. 29f][120]

---

[117] Inv. no. 8895, found by accident in 1963 in the calle General Aranda no. 62; it might not, therefore, be funerary, but perhaps come from an honorific statue: E. García Sandoval, *Ampurias* 24 (1962), 221–224 with plates 1–2; P. Léon, *MM* 21 (1980), 172, plates 36b, 37.

[118] [Taf. 29c]: inv. no. 7131, found during the excavations of 1934–1936 in the peristyle of the theatre: A. Floriano, *AEspA* 17 (1944), 178f., no. 6, figs 17–18; *MemMusAProvinc* 9–10 (1948–1949), 20, plate 3, 2. [Taf. 29d]: inv. no. 684; nothing reliable is known about its origin. R. Lantier, *Inventaire des monuments sculptés pré-chrétiens de la Péninsule Ibérique I: Lusitanie. Conventus Emeritensis* (1918) 15, no. 57, plate 25, 53; F. Poulsen, *Sculptures antiques de musées de province espagnols* (1933) 18, no. 1, plate 9, 14–15; Léon, *MM* 21 (1980), 173, plate 40.

[119] Without inv. no., found during the excavations from 1929 to 1931 in the peristyle of the theatre: J. R. Mélida and M. Macías, *La posescena del teatro romano de Mérida*, MemJuntaSupExcav 118 (1932) 13, plate 11, 3–4; W. Trillmich in *Atti II. Conf. Int. Ritratto Romano: "Ritratto ufficiale e ritratto privato,"* Quaderni de "La ricerca scientifica" 116, 1988, 528f., fig. 2.

[120] Inv. no. 8259; nothing reliable is known about its origin. J. Alvarez Sáenz de Buruaga, *MemMusAProvinc* 16–18 (1955–1957), 177, plate 33,2; Trillmich, op. cit. (n. 119), 529f., fig. 4.

portraits of the "generation" that followed that of the "Republican" realistic portraits of "elderly men," and which clearly came to be influenced by the Augustan portraits of the ruler and the princes of the imperial house, we have reached the era of the city's refurbishment in marble. Sculptors in these local workshops, who knew how to produce portraits such as these, evidently learned their craft from master craftsmen of the workshop responsible for the decoration of the marble forum. It is perhaps no coincidence then that we can find a whole sequence of exceptionally well sculpted works among the private portraits produced in Emerita during the period from Tiberius to Claudius.

APPENDIX (2007)

This article was conceived and written during one of those regularly recurring moments in Roman archaeology when everybody feels overwhelmed by the great influence of the founder of the Principate, Augustus. In 1987 Paul Zanker's celebrated book on Augustus and the power of images (*Augustus und die Macht der Bilder*) appeared in Munich (translated into English in 1988 and into Spanish in 1992), followed in 1988 by the lavish Berlin exhibition on "Caesar Augustus and the Lost Republic" ("Kaiser Augustus und die verlorene Republik"). In those years, the dominant view among German scholars working on Rome's Hispanic provinces was that it had been this emperor, Augustus, who finally, definitely, and, above all, almost at a single stroke brought civilisation to the far West of the Roman Empire. However, already during the conference on "Stadtbild und Ideologie" held in Madrid in October 1987, many of the Spanish participants reacted sharply against this view, pointing out, on the basis mainly of their own excavations, that there seems to have been quite a considerable gap between Augustan ideology and provincial reality, especially in terms of the time it took for those political ideas to become fully realised. In fact, in the case of Emerita, recent excavations, mostly directed by members of Mérida's local archaeological unit, the Consorcio de la Ciudad Monumental Histórico-Artística y Arqueológica, have proved that it took almost a century to get this "Augustan" model town built.

The distinctly Augustan ideological conceptual scheme that lay behind the founding of a city such as Emerita is clearly discernible in the town's name, "Emerita," and in the propagandistic programme of the silver provincial coinage of P. Carisius. This key point can never be invalidated by any new excavations. This town was definitely meant to be a monument of the Augustan peace, now brought to the very far West of the Empire. But the actual realisation of this ideological concept was subject to the natural ups and downs inherent in such a huge project. That is why there are some important corrections that need to be made regarding the chronology of

Emerita's urban development as a whole as well as the dating of several specific monuments that were attributed in my original article to the town's "foundation period."

I still maintain that the almost endless bridge over the river Ana(s), apart from obviously being a vehicle for civilian and military traffic, was meant to be a symbol of the far-reaching power of Rome and the world-wide peace guaranteed by her and especially by the emperor Augustus. At present, however, there is a rather lively discussion going on about the question whether the bridge is earlier than the town as such (as argued in this article, above, p. 433) or vice versa, and whether a ford or wooden bridge existed long before the actual stone bridge was built.[121]

What obviously has to be abandoned is the argument that many of the great engineering works, as well as the theatre and amphitheatre, were constructed at an early date and in the same period, based on their apparently similar technical and aesthetic details (above, pp. 438–441). For example, recent excavations of the Consorcio of Mérida have shown that – in spite of what the building inscriptions seem to tell us – these two huge spectacle buildings were still under construction in the time of the emperor Claudius and, what is more, at that time they still lay outside the ring of the city wall in an area partly occupied by a cemetery.[122]

The main temple of the "foundation period", the so-called "Temple of Diana," and its associated forum have now been fully published, and the old and new sculptural finds belonging to the temple have been fully discussed by T. Nogales Basarrate.[123] It now seems more probable than it did in 1987 that this temple in the very centre of Emerita was dedicated to the imperial cult.[124]

As for the *Marmorisierung* of Emerita, the idea that there was a rather rapid change from a town initially built in granite to a real "Augustan" town of marble must now be abandoned. That process, at least on a large scale, seems to have begun only under Claudius; it continued throughout the reign of Nero and perhaps was brought to completion only under the

[121] See F. G. Rodríguez Martín, "El paisaje urbano de Augusta Emerita: reflexiones en torno al Guadiana y las puertas de acceso a la ciudad," *Revista Portuguesa de Arqueologia* 7 (2004), 365–406, with further bibliography and for the striking theory that the "island" in the Ana(s) is nothing but the result of an artificial draining of the river in order to reduce the force of the waters running next to the reinforcement of the riverbank alongside the city walls.

[122] See P. Mateos Cruz and J. Márquez Pérez, "Nuevas estructuras urbanas relacionadas con el teatro romano de Mérida: El pórtico de acceso," in *Mérida. Excavaciones Arqueológicas 1997. Memoria* 3 (1999) 301–320; J. Márquez Pérez, "Aportaciones al mundo funerario en Emerita Augusta," in *Mérida. Excavaciones Arqueológicas 1998. Memoria* 4 (2000) 525–547; R. M. Durán Cabello, *El teatro y anfiteatro de Augusta Emerita. Contribución al conocimiento histórico de la capital de Lusitania*, BAR International Series 1207 (2004).

[123] J. M. Alvarez Martínez and T. Nogales Basarrate, *Forum Coloniae Augustae Emeritae. "Templo de Diana"* (2003); for the sculpture, see ibid., 66, fig. 8 and plate 94; 191–242, plates 55–73.

[124] See W. Trillmich, "Espacios públicos de culto imperial en *Augusta Emerita*: entre hipótesis y dudas," in T. Nogales Basarrate and J. González, eds, *Culto imperial. Política y poder*, Hispania Antigua Arqueológica 1 (2007) 415–445, esp. 423–434.

Flavians. A large part of the very intense building activity of Emerita's "marble phase" might be due to the presence here of M. Salvius Otho as governor of Lusitania for a whole decade from AD 54 to 64. On the other hand, excavations of the large forum in the northern part of the city have proved that already under Tiberius a whole sector of urban housing was demolished and the *cardo maximus* blocked off, to allow a large marble temple to be erected, which was probably, once again, dedicated to the imperial cult.[125] What is puzzling about that building complex is the fact that part of the architecture of its surrounding square (for instance, the so-called "arch of Trajan") was originally constructed in granite and only later (at some unclear moment) covered with marble architectural decoration.

In the original article I was wrong in assuming that the so-called "marble forum" was built of marble *ex novo* (above, p. 448). As J. M. Alvarez Martínez had already seen[126] and the recent investigations of N. Roering and B. Marr have now confirmed, there was a granite phase prior to the marble embellishment of that portico.

My reconstruction and interpretation of the sculptural decoration of this second phase, which I have been allowed to study and publish by J. M. Alvarez Martínez, have proved to be more successful.[127] Meanwhile it has been shown that we are dealing with some kind of (partial) copy of the sculptural programme of the forum of Augustus in Rome. While in 1987 this fact seemed to prove, once again, the very "Augustan" character of almost every building at Emerita, the rather late date of those sculptures and of the architectural decoration of the portico now seems to point towards a late Claudian or early Neronian dynastic variant of Augustan ideology.[128] One serious error of the original article (above, p. 456) needs to be corrected: the enigmatic statue with the inscription AGRIPPA on its plinth certainly cannot be a representation of M. Vipsanius Agrippa, but rather it belongs to one of a series of statues of the mythical kings of Alba Longa, ancestors of Augustus and of Nero.[129]

As for the section on the artistic and stylistic aspects of Emerita's sculptural decoration (above, pp. 450–464), a number of my more recent articles

---

[125] See J. C. Saquete Chamizo, "L. Fulcinius Trio, Tiberio y el gran templo de culto imperial de Augusta Emerita," *Epigraphica* 67 (2005), 279–308; P. Mateos Cruz, ed., *El "foro provincial" de Augusta Emerita: Un conjunto monumental de culto imperial*, Anejos de AEspA 42 (2006).

[126] *Akten des XIII. Internationalen Kongresses für Klassische Archäologie*, Berlin 1988 (1990) 336–338.

[127] See also W. Trillmich, "Gestalt und Ausstattung des 'Marmorforums' in Mérida. Kenntnisstand und Perspektiven," *MM* 36 (1995), 269–291; idem, "Los tres foros de Augusta Emerita y el caso de Corduba," in P. León, ed., *Colonia Patricia Corduba. Una reflexión arqueológica*, Coloquio Internacional, Córdoba 1993 (1996) 175–195; idem, "Reflejos del programa estatuario del *Forum Augustum* en Mérida," in F. Tarrats, ed., *Actes II. Reunió sobre Escultura Romana a Hispània*, Tarragona 1995 (1996) 95–103; J. L. de la Barrera and W. Trillmich, "Eine Wiederholung der Aeneas-Gruppe vom Forum Augustum samt ihrer Inschrift in Mérida (Spanien)," *RM* 103 (1996), 119–138.

[128] See Trillmich, op. cit. (n. 124), esp. 434–441.

[129] As noted briefly by J. Edmondson, *JRS* 86 (1996), 225.

have refined and explained in greater detail what was simply sketched in the original article. In a series of studies I have discussed in greater depth the specific style of the Roman sculptural workshop active at Emerita for a time around the middle of the first century AD and its effect on local sculptural production.[130] As for portraiture, there is now a complete catalogue of private (i.e., non-imperial) portrait sculpture available, while for the architectural decoration of Emerita's forums there is now an excellent and well-illustrated study.[131] Finally, two up-to-date synopses of Emerita's urban development have recently been published.[132]

---

[130] W. Trillmich, "El modelo de la metrópoli," in J. Arce, S. Ensoli, and E. La Rocca, eds, *Hispania Romana: desde tierra de conquista a provincia del imperio* (exhibition catalogue, Rome 1997) 131–141; idem, "Las ciudades hispanorromanas: reflejos de la metrópoli," in *Hispania. El legado de Roma* (exhibition catalogue, Mérida 1999) 183–195; idem, "Los programas arquitectónicos de época julio-claudia en la Colonia Augusta Emerita," in S. Ramallo Asensio, ed., *La decoración arquitectónica en las ciudades romanas de Occidente*, (2004) 321–335; idem, "La contemporaneidad de lo heterogéneo: Continuidad formal y transformación estilística del modelo urbano en la escultura 'provincial' emeritense", in D. Vaquerizo and J. F. Murillo, eds, *El concepto de lo provincial en el mundo antiguo: Homenaje a la profesora Pilar León Alonso* (2006) 233–247.

[131] T. Nogales Basarrate, *El retrato privado en Augusta Emerita* (1997); J. L. de la Barrera, *La decoración arquitectónica de los foros de Augusta Emerita*, Bibliotheca Archaeologica 25 (2000).

[132] X. Dupré Raventós, ed., *Las capitales provinciales de Hispania 2: Mérida, Colonia Augusta Emerita* (2004); S. Panzram, *Stadtbild und Elite: Tarraco, Corduba und Augusta Emerita zwischen Republik und Spätantike* (2002) 227–312.

15 The Cities of the Greek World under Augustus[†]

G. W. BOWERSOCK

The triumphant Octavian had found the East in unparalleled weakness. The exactions of governors and publicans in the late Republic had been followed by the cruel demands of the tyrannicides and Antony. The kingdom of the Ptolemies was defunct; Asia was bankrupt. Pausanias observed that the fortunes of Greece reached their nadir between the fall of Corinth and the reign of Nero.[1] In the year 45 B.C. Servius Sulpicius sailed from Aegina to Megara and saw desolation on every side.[2] The cities had been drained of money and resources, and food was short. After Actium Octavian attended to his new allies by distributing surplus corn from the war to various destitute cities.[3] But the practical course with which the future Princeps inaugurated his policy for the East was a general remission of debts.[4] The economic strain was relieved, and the Greeks of Asia realized that the victory of Caesar's heir had opened a new era of peace.

The Greek peoples rejoiced to hear that their triumviral patron had been conquered. This was not paradoxical, for their support of Antony had been a matter of necessity; he had been the man of the moment. But Antony's defeat, no less than his victory, would mean an end to privation, and Octavian knew this. While it was fitting for

---

[†] Originally published as Chapter VII of G. W. Bowersock, *Augustus and the Greek World*, Oxford: Clarendon Press, 1965, pp. 85–100.

The following works will be cited in abbreviated form:
Cyrene Edicts   F. de Visscher, *Les édits d'Auguste découverts à Cyrène* (1940)
Magie, RRAM   D. Magie, *Roman Rule in Asia Minor* (1950)
Milet i, 2   *Milet: Ergebnisse der Ausgrabungen und Untersuchungen seit dem Jahre 1899* (ed. T. Wiegand), I.2. *Das Rathaus von Milet* (1908)
Sardis vii   *Sardis VII: Greek and Latin Inscriptions I* (ed. W. H. Buckler and D. M. Robinson) (1932)

[1] Paus. 7. 17. 1.
[2] Cic. *ad Fam.* 4. 5. 4.
[3] Plut. *Ant.* 68. 4–5. On the tesserae used in the distributions at Athens: Rostovtzeff, *Festschrift für Hirschfeld* (1903), 305–11, and Graindor, *Athènes sous Auguste* (1927), p. 37, n. 2; p. 118.
[4] Dio Prus. *Or.* 31. 66.

him to display a certain displeasure toward Antonian partisans, they, like the client dynasts, had no compunction about joining his clientela, now that he was master of the world. Therefore, there was little point in stirring up unnecessary trouble. Octavian was officially angry. A rumour went up that he was abolishing the rights of city assemblies,[5] but there is no evidence that he ever did so. That can only have been a threat, an appropriate demonstration of wrath.

The conqueror allowed himself to confiscate a few masterworks of art. He stole from Greece a statue of Athena by Endoeus and the teeth of the Calydonian Boar, which he exhibited publicly in Rome.[6] Sometimes he offered compensation: one hundred talents of the tribute of Cos were remitted as payment for a painting of Aphrodite Anadyomene, removed from the island and dedicated at Rome to Julius Caesar.[7] Antony had stolen three enormous works of Myron which had stood on a single base on Samos, and one of these was attractive to Augustus, who took it to the Capitol in Rome. As compensation the other two pieces were returned to the Samians.[8] In Egypt Augustus discovered a statue of Ajax which Antony had taken from Rhoeteum; Strabo noted that it was returned.[9] The Emperor was shrewd in that he showed his regard for the East by his restitution of stolen art works, but as a conqueror he was privileged to take what he wanted for himself.

No less than the late Republic, the Augustan Principate reveals great diplomatic activity. The cities presented their cases to the Emperor through their most intelligent and wealthy citizens. The distinguished Potamo of Mytilene, who had twice served as ambassador to Julius Caesar, served again on an embassy to Augustus in 26 B.C.[10] In the years which followed, the interests of that city were to be well cared for at Rome: Potamo's fellow envoy, the poet Crinagoras, remained in the imperial court; and Pompeius Macer, from the family of Pompey's Mytilenean intimate, Theophanes, entered the imperial service, leaving a son to become praetor in A.D. 15.[11] At Miletus C. Julius Apollonius, the son of Caesar's slave, lived long enough to associate himself with the first temple to

---

[5] Dio 51. 2. 1.
[6] Paus. 8. 46. 1 and 4. On art, cf. Bowersock, *Aug.*, pp. 74–75.
[7] Strabo 14. 2. 19 (C 657); Pliny, *NH* 35. 91. The painting deteriorated and was replaced by Nero (Pliny, ibid.).
[8] Strabo 14. 1. 14 (C 637).
[9] Strabo 13. 1. 30 (C 595).
[10] *IGR* 4. 33 [trans. Sherk, *RGE*, no. 97].
[11] On Crinagoras, see Bowersock, *Aug.*, pp. 36–37. For Pompeius Macer, *JRS* 51 (1961), 116–17, n. 42.

Augustus in his city.[12] An offspring of that opulent citizen was highly honoured for his diplomatic successes on behalf of Miletus.[13] The family of Iollas of Sardis, active in diplomacy with Romans of the Republic, was represented in embassies to Augustus.[14] Tralles too sent envoys to the Emperor; the city was noted for the number of wealthy men it contained.[15] The leading ambassador, Chaeremon, was the son of the rich Pompeian, Pythodorus, whose daughter became Queen of Pontus.[16] Embassies made their way to Rome from other places of the East, from Cnidos, Chios, Eresos, Cyrene, Alexandria, Athens, Sparta, and Thessaly.[17]

Augustus knew that the strength of Rome in the East depended upon the support of those very men who represented their cities in embassies to his court. Roman nourishment of the upper classes had begun long before, and Augustus continued it. The cities, in the hands of the right persons, were crucial, and could be made to do much of Rome's work, like the client kings outside the provinces. Augustus was obliged to reconcile astute diplomatic support of a certain class in each city with the maintenance of smoothly functioning local constitutions which would permit that class to predominate. The Emperor could not introduce into Greek cities (*poleis*) Roman constitutions which the Hellenes would not tolerate. But changes had already taken place in the Republic, and Augustus had rather to provide the economic stability necessary for effective local administration.

The Greek city council was originally a body whose membership changed at frequent and regular intervals. It became clear in the days of the Republic that a council of that kind was incompatible with the predominance of the upper class and especially of certain wealthy and educated members of it. Not surprisingly, the *boule* [council] was

---

[12] *Milet* i. 2, no. 7; cf. Bowersock, *Aug.*, p. 8, n. 7.

[13] *Milet*, ibid.; also nos. 6 and 15.

[14] *Sardis* vii. 1, no. 8 [trans. Sherk, *RGE*, no. 104]. The man is mentioned on another inscription from Sardis as giving a donation to the city: *Hellenica* 9 (1950), 8. The republican Iollas: *Sardis* vii. 1, no. 27; cf. Bowersock, *Aug.*, p. 11.

[15] Strabo 14. 1. 42 (C 649) (wealthy men in Tralles). Agathias 2. 17 (embassy of Chaeremon to Augustus in Spain, on which cf. Bowersock, *Aug.*, p. 157, Appendix III).

[16] Cf. preceding note and Bowersock, *Aug.*, p. 8, n. 4 [Strabo 12. 3. 29 (C 555-6) and 14. 1. 42 (C 649). The view of Mommsen that *OGIS* 377 revealed Antony's own daughter as the bride of the younger Pythodorus must be rejected: cf. Dessau, *EE* 9. 691ff. and Magie, *RRAM* ii.1130, n. 60. From the name of the great rhetor of the second century A.D., M. Antonius Polemo, it would appear that the Laodicean family into which Pythodorus married had taken the side of Antony. And one should not overlook Plutarch's contemporary Chaeremonianus of Tralles (Plut. *Quaest. Conviv.* 2.7)].

[17] Eresos: *IGR* 4. 7. The inscription is too fragmentary to reveal much. The other embassies are discussed below: cf. pp. 471 (Cnidos), 471 (Chios), 471-472 (Cyrene), 472-473 (Alexandria), 477 (Athens), 474 (Sparta); for Thessaly, Bowersock, *Aug.*, p. 104.

gradually transformed into a permanent body, with life membership. A parallel with the Roman senate is inescapable. By the beginning of the imperial age most Greek cities of Asia had permanent councils.[18] There was no need for Augustus to make changes.

However, the Emperor interfered on occasion for purposes of enlightened amendment or clarification. He defined the limits of asylum in the sacred territory of Artemis at Ephesus;[19] at Cyme he provided for the return of dedications to the deity to whom they were vowed.[20] A delicate judicial case was referred to him from Cnidos, and he did not hesitate to settle the matter despite the free status of the city.[21] In the cities of Bithynia he revised the law of Pompey by lowering the minimum age for admission to local magistracies.[22] At Chios he confirmed certain privileges granted by Sulla: the island was declared free, and Romans there were to be subject to the laws of the Chians.[23] That was an extraordinary judicial arrangement, without parallel anywhere else.

The edicts from Cyrene show the Emperor again busy with amendment and clarification. As was natural, these documents were the result of diplomatic overtures from the Cyrenaeans. In capital and non-capital trials the Greeks of Cyrene were suffering injustice at the hands of jurors who were Roman citizens; Augustus made fresh and fairer provisions.[24] A new system was announced for facilitating provincial prosecutions of rapacious Roman governors. The effectiveness and the duration of this system are alike dubious, but it appeared, at any rate, to be in the interest of the provincials.[25]

The third edict was an important affirmation of local authority. Pompey, Caesar, Antony, and Octavian had been accustomed to reward their faithful adherents with the Roman citizenship.

---

[18] See Jones, GC, p. 171 and p. 338, n. 29.

[19] Strabo 14. 1. 23 (C 641).

[20] H. W. Pleket, *Greek Inscriptions in the Rijksmuseum at Leyden* (1958), no. 57, reprinted with alterations by Mrs. K. M. T. Atkinson in *Rev. intern. des droits de l'ant.* 7 (1960), 231 ff.

[21] SIG³ 780 [trans. Sherk, *RGE*, no. 103 = Cooley no. H44]. Free status was little more than an honorific title: observe Augustus' interference in Athens, Sparta, Thessaly, Cyzicus, Tyre, and Sidon, all of which were free at the beginning of the Principate. These cases are considered in the present chapter and in Bowersock, *Aug.*, ch. VIII. At Cnidos a slight formality in deference to its free status is noticeable: Augustus remarks that he instructed his 'friend' Asinius Gallus to investigate the situation. In fact, Gallus was proconsul of Asia.

[22] Pliny, *Ep.* 10. 79. 2. Cf. Dio 54. 7. 5.

[23] SIG³ 785 [trans. Sherk, *RGE*, no. 108 = Cooley no. M56], with L. Robert, *REG* 65 (1952), 128.

[24] Cyrene Edicts, i and iv: EJ², no. 311 [trans. Sherk, *RGE*, no. 102 = Shark, *RE*, no. 13 = Cooley no. M60].

[25] Senatus Consultum Calvisianum: *Cyrene Edict*, v [EJ² 311; trans. Sherk, *RGE*, no. 102 = *RE*, no. 13 = Cooley M78]. For the view that the system of extortion trials established in that document neither lasted long nor was very effective, P. A. Brunt, *Hist.* 10 (1961), 199 ff. [= *Roman Imperial Themes* (1990), ch. IV, pp. 64 ff.].

Evidently certain Cyrenaeans, and undoubtedly citizens of other cities of the Greek East, had claimed exemption from local liturgies by virtue of their citizenship. This was bound to lead to trouble in the cities, inasmuch as the very people who had been honoured with the citizenship will have been in most cases the wealthiest. Therefore their claim to exemption meant a serious financial loss to the local administration. Both Julius Caesar and Augustus perceived the difficulties and enunciated that Roman citizenship did not exempt any native Greek from undertaking local liturgies in his own city. Caesar addressed himself to Mytilene, Augustus to Cyrene.[26]

These pronouncements were designed to correct an abuse. They were clarification, not a change in policy or tradition. Bestowals of the Roman citizenship had never entailed local *immunitas* [immunity from taxation]. In surviving instances, a grant of ἀνεισφορία [immunity from taxation] is always specifically added to πολιτεία [citizenship] if it is intended at all.[27] Caesar and Augustus merely pointed out, doubtless to the immense satisfaction of certain city magistrates, that immunity from taxation was not to be arrogated where it had not been bestowed. There is no reason to think that Augustus, unlike Caesar, established by the third edict a class of Roman citizens with minor rights, distinct from those who were citizens at birth.[28] The edict explicitly deals with those who have been honoured with the citizenship, and that was because they were the only Roman citizens in Cyrene who mattered.[29]

In regard to the Greeks in Egypt, Augustus was prepared to alter the existing arrangements, as elsewhere, only to ensure smooth and reliable local administration. Of the four Greek cities in Egypt,[30] Alexandria alone engaged the Emperor's attention. It was a city with a great Hellenistic past and citizens resentful of the Roman yoke; it lacked that quintessential Greek institution, the *boule*, even in a Roman guise. A large admixture of Jews in the population was a potential source of trouble. Although Augustus received

---

[26] *IGR* 4. 33 (col. *b*) [trans. Sherk, *RGE*, no. 83]; 45 (Caesar), *Cyrene Edict*, iii [EJ² 311; trans. Sherk, *RGE*, no. 102 = *RE*, no. 13 = Cooley M60] (Augustus).

[27] Cf. the *SC de Asclepiade* &c. (Bruns, *Fontes*, no. 41 [= *RDGE* 22; trans. Sherk, *RGE*, no. 66]) in which *immunitas* is granted without the citizenship; in Octavian's edict concerning Seleucus of Rhosus granted without the citizenship; in Octavian's edict concerning Seleucus of Rhosus (EJ², no. 301 [trans. Sherk, *RGE*, no. 86]) *immunitas* and citizenship are both explicitly granted.

[28] The class of Roman citizens with minor rights was an invention of Rostovtzeff, *SEHRE*² ii. 559, n. 6.

[29] P. Romanelli, *La Cirenaica romana* (1943), p. 84: 'L'immigrazione diretta di elementi romani dall'Italia è stata certamente finora nulla o quasi nulla' ['Direct immigration of Roman elements from Italy was as yet certainly non-existent or almost non-existent.'].

[30] Naucratis, Alexandria, Ptolemais, Paraetonium: see Jones, *CERP*, pp. 302 ff.

Alexandrian envoys, the *boule* was not restored. Augustus could not be sure of the proud Greeks of that city.[31]

Outside the four Greek cities of Egypt it was difficult in so mixed a population to distinguish Greek from non-Greek, but the distinction had to be made for the simple reason that Greeks were superior to Egyptians and were preferred in positions of authority. The problem was solved in A.D. 4/5 by the creation of a new hellenized aristocracy consisting of two groups: for those in the territory (*chora*) with satisfactory claims to Greek education and origin (who became known as 'those from the gymnasium') and the hellenized residents of the metropoleis. Although these persons were less privileged than ordinary Greeks in paying a poll-tax like Egyptians, they were superior to other Egyptians in paying at a reduced rate.[32] The emperors were to make use of this new class of Greek Egyptians in the lower grades of the civil service.[33]

Augustus liked to leave Greek affairs in the hands of Greeks. His plan emerges in detail in old Greece, which was a country learning how to be a museum; cultivated Romans admired Greece romantically for what she had been.[34] The multiplicity of independent cities, which had once brought glory and disaster, was rapidly disappearing. The descendants of free citizens were becoming the tenants of great estates. To many of the smaller cities nothing remained but their names.[35] Already in the Hellenistic age cities which hoped to survive had sought longevity in alliances and leagues, whereby they might collectively enjoy a greater power and economic stability. Augustus saw at once what his policy should be, here as throughout the East: to provide impetus and direction to what had been happening for some time before.

He encouraged the leagues. In a minor province they were more convenient units than individual cities, and they belonged to the

---

[31] H. A. Musurillo, *Acts of the Pagan Martyrs* (1954), pp. 1–2 (Boule Papyrus) and pp. 84–88. *P. Oxyrh.*, xxv (1959), no. 2435 *verso* records an Alexandrian embassy to Augustus in A.D. 13; lines 56–58 imply that the subject of the embassy was the restoration of the *boule*. Augustus, however, need not be held responsible for having abolished it in the first place. It was restored at last by Septimius Severus: Dio 51. 17. 2–3; SHA, *Sept. Sev.* 17. On anti-Roman Greeks at Alexandria, see Bowersock, *Aug.*, p. 105.

[32] The first *epikrisis* [registration] was inferred by Van Groningen, *Gymnasiarque*, pp. 39–40, to have been in A.D. 4–5; that coincides with the earliest recorded metropolitan exegete in *P. Osl.* 26. (Cf. Jones, *CERP*, p. 475, n. 26.) The arrangements of A.D. 4–5 are described with great lucidity by V. Tcherikover in *Corpus Papyrorum Judaicarum* (1957), i. 59.

[33] Jones, *CERP*, p. 316.

[34] See esp. Cic. *pro Flacc.* 26. 62–63 on the ancient glories of Athens and Sparta in comparison with 'the name of Greece, now disabled and almost broken' (iam fractum prope ac debilitatum Graeciae nomen). Cf. also Bowersock, *Aug.*, ch. VI.

[35] U. Kahrstedt, *Das wirtschaftliche Gesicht Griechenlands in der Kaiserzeit* (1954), *passim*.

evolution of Roman Greece. It should be emphasized that their development has nothing whatever to do with the imperial cult, which appears in none of the leagues in Greece before the reign of Claudius.³⁶ A few great cities flourished under imperial patronage, serving as focal points in the country's economy.

In Laconia the League of the Lacedaemonians had been formed in the time of Nabis under the tyranny of Sparta. Augustus liberated the league from Spartan rule, and the twenty-four cities assumed a new name: the League of Free Laconians.³⁷ It was bound together by a mutual interest in the marble and purple trade.³⁸ In Sparta Augustus installed his over-ambitious partisan, C. Julius Eurycles, and the city was presented with Cythera, Cardamyle, and Thuria as gifts.³⁹ Some time between 7 and 2 B.C. Eurycles will have attempted to reassert Spartan control over the league cities, without success.⁴⁰ But there was no denying that the cities continued to be linked economically to Sparta, which held a complete monopoly over Laconian coinage until the Severan age.⁴¹ An inscription from Gytheum, the arsenal of Sparta, reveals that Eurycles and his son Laco assisted the Free Laconians in some memorable way.⁴² Asopus, another member of the league, received oil from Sparta.⁴³

The Achaean League had also existed in the late Republic; its headquarters were at Olympia.⁴⁴ The participation of Elis demonstrates that the league was not confined merely to the territory of

---

³⁶ The earliest traces of the cult: *Corinth* viii. 2, no. 68; *IG* ii². 3538 (both concerning C. Julius Spartiaticus). On the whole matter of the secular character of the leagues in Greece at the beginning of the Principate, see Larsen, *Representative Government in Greek and Roman History* (1955), pp. 112–13.

³⁷ Strabo 8. 5. 5 (C 366) (formation of the league under Nabis); Paus. 3. 21. 6–7 (Augustus' liberation of the league and its twenty-four cities). On pre-Augustan inscriptions (e.g. *IG* v. 1. 1226, 1227) the league is called κοινὸν τῶν Λακεδαιμονίων ['the confederacy of the Lacedaemonians']; *IG* v. 1. 1161, 1167, 1177, 1243 (imperial) give κοινὸν τῶν Ἐλευθερολακώνων ['the confederacy of the Eleutherolaconians (i.e., Free Laconians)']. Cf. Bowersock, *JRS* 51 (1961), 116. Kornemann, *P–W* Suppl. 4. 929 is confused, perhaps misled by Paus. 7. 16. 9–10 (asserting falsely that all Greek leagues were dissolved in 146 B.C.).

³⁸ Kahrstedt, op. cit., p. 203

³⁹ See Bowersock, *JRS* 51 (1961), 113 and n. 11.

⁴⁰ Ibid., p. 116. It has been suggested to me that the league was still under Spartan domination at this time and was freed as a result of the condemnation of Eurycles. This is unlikely: Augustus would hardly have satisfied the angry family of Brasidas, which brought Eurycles to trial, by depriving Sparta of her league. Note also that Strabo refers without comment (8. 5. 5 [C366]) to Eleutherolaconians. This would be surprising if they had become free just before he was writing: the passage was written between 7 and 2 B.C. and cannot be a Tiberian addition (*JRS* 51 [1961], 115). The liberation of the cities must have happened soon after Actium.

⁴¹ See Head, *HN*² 433–6.

⁴² *AE* 1929. 99, ll. 19–20 [trans. Sherk, *RE*, no. 32]. Gytheum as a league member: Paus. 3. 21. 7. Strabo 8. 3. 12 (C 343) and 8. 5. 2 (C 363) calls the city 'the seaport of Sparta'.

⁴³ *IG* v. 1. 970. Cf. Paus. 3. 21. 7.

⁴⁴ *Inschriften von Olympia*, nos. 328, 333, 367, 401, 415, 420. No. 415 reveals the participation of Elis.

Achaea. The first Princeps maintained the organization he inherited but shifted its centre of gravity. About 14 B.C. Patrae was chosen to be its guardian city: it was admirably located for trade at the western end of the Gulf of Corinth, but it lacked inhabitants and size. Hence the Emperor established a Roman colony on the site and incorporated adjacent Greek villages in a grand synoecism. The earlier colony of Dyme was swallowed up in the new foundation. Augustus went on to extend the territory of Patrae across the Gulf. Calydon and the Aetolian land to the east were absorbed, as well as Naupactus and Oeanthea in Ozolian Locris. The Emperor accorded freedom to his chosen city, the only one in Achaea to which he gave that honour.[45]

Patrae was noted for the abundance and charm of its women, most of whom were textile workers. The traffic in flax, especially the transparent Elean *byssos*, had bound the old Achaean League economically together.[46] As Augustus surely planned, these materials made their way to the new city for processing. The finished products could be conveniently dispatched from Patrae and exported all over the Mediterranean world.

Prospering, the Achaean League incorporated other leagues. There had once been an independent Argolid *koinon* [confederacy], which emerges, late in the reign of Tiberius, as a member of the Achaean League, although it may have joined under Augustus.[47] By the accession of Gaius a huge amalgamation had taken place. The former *koinon* of Boeotians, Euboeans, Locrians, Phocians, and Dorians now belonged to a common organization with members of the Achaean League.[48] The new group styled itself variously: the Achaeans and Panhellenes, more succinctly the Panhellenes, or the Panachaeans. Although Augustus would have approved of the Panhellenes or Panchaeans, it is erroneous to think they were united in his lifetime. The union occurred in his successor's old age.[49]

---

[45] Strabo 8. 7. 5 (C 387) (veteran colony); Paus. 7. 18. 7 (synoecism of Greek cities); Paus. 7. 17. 5 (Dyme); Paus. 10. 38. 9 (Ozolian Locris, except Amphissa); Paus. 7. 18. 7 (freedom). On all this, U. Kahrstedt, 'Die Territorien von Patrai und Nikopolis in der Kaiserzeit', *Historia* 1 (1950), 549 ff., rejecting Pausanias' Augustan date for Dyme and Locris because Strabo is ignorant of these annexations. This argument has no weight, since Strabo was not writing between 2 B.C. and A.D. 14. On relations between Athens and Patrae, see the new inscription in *Hesp.* 28 (1959), 280, with new fragment in *Hesp.* 29 (1960), 83

[46] Paus. 7. 21. 14.

[47] *IG* iv². 665 (Epidaurus). On the Argolid *koinon*: *BCH* 33 (1909), 176–7.

[48] *SIG*³, 767 (Athens; 34/33 B.C.). The large *koinon* was confirmed by Gaius: *IG* vii. 2711, l. 29. *SIG*³, 796A [trans. Sherk, *RE*, no. 73] used to be mentioned in this context, but Momigliano, *JRS* 34 (1944), 115–16, dates it rightly to Nero instead of Tiberius.

[49] Cf. Gaius' action cited in the preceding note. See also U. Kahrstedt, 'Das Koinon der Achaier', *Symbolae Osloenses* 28 (1950), 70–75.

In north-western Greece Augustus caused another synoecism and founded a free city. Nicopolis arose from the camp of the victorious Octavian as an enduring monument of his conquest of Antony. In the late Republic both the Acarnanians and the Aetolians had organized themselves into leagues; Nicopolis replaced them.[50] For practical purposes a synoecism hardly differed from a league, but it was a striking reminder of Actium. Nicopolis gathered into its territory such distant places as Ambracia, Amphilochian Argos, and Alyzia. Anactorium was its commercial centre. Almost every Aetolian was uprooted: those who did not become Nicopolitans fled into Locris to Amphissa.[51]

Nicopolis was a thoroughly Greek city. Romanization was far from Augustus' thoughts. The city's coin legends were all Greek, and so were its inscriptions.[52] The form of its local government was Greek.[53] Even the games with which Octavian celebrated his victory were Greek: the Actia, which were quinquennial, modelled on the Olympics, and supervised by Greeks.[54] And these games were not something new. They had, in fact, been held previously;[55] Octavian only gave them new distinction.

To the east lay two more great cities of Greece, Corinth and Athens. Corinth was Julius Caesar's Patrae. He resurrected a dead city at a commercially vital point by establishing a Roman colony. His obligations to displaced Romans were fulfilled, and the economy of Greece was given some hope of revival. Corinth prospered, growing on the fruits of trade and banking. Undoubtedly it formed a commercial centre for eastern Achaea; a century and a half after Augustus' death it was head of the entire Achaean province, the confluence of trade from Patrae, Athens, and Thessalonica.[56] But Corinth was not a free city, and therein Augustus' plan was made clear. He encouraged another city to head the Achaean province. Caesar's Corinthians had an evil reputation when the Principate was born: the colonists were grave-robbers, and every Roman of fashion

---

[50] Acarnanians and Aetolians: Kornemann, *P–W* Suppl. 4. 921, 923. Nicopolis: Suet. *Aug.* 18; Pliny, *NH* 4. 5; Paus. 10. 38. 4; Strabo 7. 7. 5–6 (C 324–5) and 10. 2. 2 (C 450).
[51] See references in the preceding note, but above all Kahrstedt, *Historia*, 1 (1950), 549–61.
[52] Ibid., 559–60.
[53] Ibid. The Latin inscription from Nicopolis, *AE* 1928. 15 [= EJ² 12, rev. *AE* 1977. 778, trans. Sherk, *RGE*, no. 92 = Cooley H10; it will need further revision after the publication of further new fragments: see K. Zachos, *JRA* 16 (2003), 74–6], does not confirm reports of a colony at Actium (Tac. *Ann.* 5. 10; Pliny, *NH* 4. 5): Kahrstedt, 560, denying that there was a colony.
[54] Strabo 7. 7. 6 (C 325).
[55] Ibid., *P–W* 1. 1213.
[56] Aristides, *Orat.* 46. 23 Keil.

knew about the trade in Necrocorinthia.[57] Augustus' poet lamented the shame.[58] Patrae was the Emperor's answer to Corinth.

Athens, that venerable home of antiquities and pedagogues, was not neglected. Recent excavations now permit remarkable detail and precision about Roman Athens. The so-called Market of Caesar and Augustus, begun through the munificence of the Dictator, was brought to completion after a successful embassy to the Princeps.[59] A temple of Rome and Augustus was constructed on the Acropolis, while in the centre of the agora a vast music-hall was built in commemoration of M. Vipsanius Agrippa, then touring the East with proconsular imperium. Roman architects appear to have been sent to Athens to collaborate with the Greeks.[60] Another extraordinary building appeared: a fifth-century temple of Ares was systematically removed from some unknown site and re-erected in the agora under Augustus[61] – not surprisingly, however, since Ares was the Greek counterpart of the Roman Mars, for whom the Emperor had special regard.[62] And with the emphasis accorded to a fifth-century temple can be compared a revival of fifth-century lettering on inscriptions.[63] The influence of Augustus and the efforts of local partisans may be inferred in these matters, and in others.[64]

Like a few cities in Asia Minor, Athens has bequeathed the names of certain of her eminent philo-Romans by virtue of their tenure of sacred and secular magistracies. When the old Pythais was abolished after Actium, a more modest *theoria* [sacred embassy] to Delphi, the Dodecais, supplanted it. The priest, herald, and exegetes in the five occurrences of the Dodecais under Augustus were the same.[65] These men, in several attested cases, also served as hoplite general or archon.[66] Eucles, for example, was a son of Herod of Marathon

---

[57] Strabo 8. 6. 23 (C 381).
[58] Crinagoras, *Anth. Pal.* ix. 284.
[59] IG iii². 3175, on the gateway to the Roman Forum at Athens.
[60] H. A. Thompson, *Hesp.* 19 (1950), 90 ff.
[61] W. B. Dinsmoor, *Hesp.* 9 (1940), 1 ff.; M. H. McAllister, *Hesp.* 28 (1959), 1 ff., especially 48 ff.
[62] Temple of Mars Ultor at Rome: RG 21, Dio 54. 8. 3 and 55. 10. 1–6. At Nicopolis: Suet. Aug. 18, AE 1928. 15 (ul[tor]).
[63] IG ii². 1040 is the best example of Augustan epigraphical archaism; cf. Raubitschek and Jeffery, *Dedications from the Athenian Acropolis* (1949), p. 149.
[64] e.g. the coinage: cf. Bowersock, *Aug.*, pp. 105–6. Professor S. Dow has kindly informed me of his view, based on IG ii². 1732–3, that there was an Augustan reform of the Athenian courts. The Augustan revival of the Peiraeus, proposed by Day, *An Economic History of Athens under Roman Domination* (1942), pp. 145 ff., rests on the dubious ascription of IG ii². 1035 to the reign of Augustus.
[65] Graindor, *Athènes sous Auguste* (1927), pp. 144 ff. Cf. also J. Day, *An Economic History of Athens under Roman Domination* (1942), pp. 174–5.
[66] e.g. Eucles, five times priest of Pythian Apollo, was both hoplite general and archon

and a member of the distinguished and affluent family which subsequently produced the great Herod Atticus. He assumed from his father the position of overseer of the construction of the Market of Caesar and Augustus, and it was he who went on an embassy to the Emperor to secure the necessary funds for finishing it.[67] He was archon, hoplite general, and five times priest of Pythian Apollo.[68]

Of the important Athenians of this period one is particularly memorable and at the same time mystifying. C. Julius Nicanor came to Athens from Hierapolis in Syria and was a man of enormous wealth.[69] He bought the island of Salamis, which the Athenians had sold after the sack of Sulla, and gave it back to Athens.[70] It was presumably for this act of generosity that he was hailed as the 'New Themistocles'.[71] He was also the 'New Homer', clearly a man of culture.[72] A century later Dio of Prusa recalled the extravagant honours accorded to Nicanor, though he did not mention the strange *damnatio* [condemnation] which the memory of that eminent citizen suffered at an unknown date.[73]

The Augustan system of leagues stretched northward. There had been a league of Thessalians since the fourth century. When Macedonia was humbled, the old league was gradually swollen through incorporation of the regions which encompassed it. Thessalian control spread across Dolopia and penetrated through Phthiotic Achaea as far as the southern confines of Aeniania and Malis. In the east the smaller Magnesian League became a part of the greater Thessalian. In the north Perrhaebia passed from Macedonian to Thessalian domination.[74]

Perhaps because of tumult Augustus saw fit to revoke the freedom which Julius Caesar had granted to Thessalians, but he did not alter

---

(Graindor, pp. 142–3); Polycharmus, five times exegete (Graindor, p. 143), was archon and so was his son (Graindor, *Chronol.*, p. 57); Diotimus, son of Diodorus and five times exegete (Graindor, *Athènes*, p. 143), was archon (Graindor, *Chronol.*, p. 30 and *IG* ii². 1096).

[67] *IG* iii². 3175.

[68] See n. 66 above. On Eucles and other eminent Athenians: Day, op. cit., pp. 172–4.

[69] L. Robert reported in *Hellenica*, 8 (1950), 91 that he had made a study of Nicanor; Attic inscriptions of the Augustan period mentioning Julius Nicanor must be divided between two persons, an Alexandrian and a Syrian. The Alexandrian was doubtless the son of the philosopher, Areius of Alexandria: Suet. *Aug.* 89. 1, cf. Bowersock, *Aug.*, ch. III. The man who bought the island of Salamis came from Hierapolis in Syria (Steph. Byz. s.v.).

[70] Strabo 9. 1. 10 (C 394); Dio Prus. *Or.* 31. 116; Steph. Byz. s.v.

[71] *IG* ii². 3786–9 (statue bases). The view of A. E. Raubitschek in *Hesp.* 23 (1954), 317 ff. is demonstrably untenable: cf. J. and L. Robert, *REG* 68 (1955), 210, n. 79.

[72] See the statue bases in the foregoing note and the inscription considered by Raubitschek in the article cited there.

[73] In *IG* ii². 3786, 3787, and 3789 'New Homer' and 'New Themistocles' have been erased.

[74] Paus. 10. 8. 3. Cf. C. Kip, *Thessalische Studien* (1910), pp. 109, 113, and 129.

the territory of the confederacy.⁷⁵ Its political centre was Larissa.⁷⁶ An inscription reveals how a Roman governor could lighten his work by referring internal disagreements to the league authorities.⁷⁷ It illustrates the recurrent emphasis on local administration in the arrangements of Augustus.

Further north, in Macedonia, the first Princeps accepted the strange political system which had been operating there since 167 B.C. The country had been divided into four parts, a division which lasted at least into the Flavian era.⁷⁸ But it was probably Augustus who brought Macedonia into conformity with the rest of Greece: a Macedonian league emerged under the Principate and united the four divisions in a federal state. The political seat was Beroea, which lay inland, but the economic centre was the port of Thessalonica, a free city.⁷⁹

To consolidate the network of leagues and cities in Greece, Augustus revived the old Delphic Amphictyony. The Augustan Amphictyons were thirty in number, of which the three largest members provided eighteen: the free city of Nicopolis, the Thessalian League, and the Macedonian League each sent six delegates.⁸⁰ The scheme permitted the maximum consolidation of the Greeks with the minimum threat to Rome. The plan was masterful: all thirty Amphictyons were never to assemble together at any one time. Not all of the three largest members sent delegates to every session. Athens with one delegate, Delphi with two, and Augustus' city of victory with six were the only members of the Amphictyony who could be represented at every meeting. The rest sent delegates in turn at regular intervals.⁸¹ The imperial Amphictyony testifies to Augustus' political acumen.

Outside Greece there were at least two leagues already in existence when Augustus became Princeps, and again he encouraged a natural

---

⁷⁵ Grant of freedom from Julius Caesar: App. *BC* 2. 88; Plut., *Caes*. 48. Pliny, however, only lists Pharsalus as free (*NH* 4. 29). On Augustus' action in Thessaly, see Bowersock, *Aug.*, pp. 104 and 160–1 (Appendix III). Above all, Bowersock, *Rheinisches Museum*, 108 (1965): 'Zur Geschichte des römischen Thessaliens.'

⁷⁶ *IG* ix. 2. 261 = EJ², no. 321, line 12: ἐν τῷ ἐνε[στηκότι Θεσσαλῶν τῶν? ἐν Λα]ρίσῃ συνεδρίῳ ['in the council [of the Thessalians established at La]rissa']

⁷⁷ The document cited in the preceding note concerns a boundary dispute which C. Poppaeus Sabinus referred to the Thessalian League.

⁷⁸ Acts xvi. 12; *AE* 1900. 130, altered in *CP* 44 (1949), 89.

⁷⁹ J. M. R. Cormack, 'High Priests and Macedoniarchs from Beroea', *JRS* 33 (1943), 39 ff.; for Macedoniarchs in Thessalonica, p. 43. Cf. Larsen, *Representative Government* (1955), p. 221, n. 24, on Thessalonica. It was free: Pliny, *NH* 4. 36.

⁸⁰ Paus. 10. 8. 4. Cf. Larsen, 'The Policy of Augustus in Greece', *Acta Classica* (Proceedings of the Classical Association of South Africa, 1959), 123 ff.

⁸¹ Paus. 10. 8. 4.

evolution. Traces of a union of cities in Asia early in the first century B.C. become by the time of Antony an organized *koinon*.[82] This body was swift in devoting itself to worship of the Emperor and belongs, therefore, to a history of the imperial cult. It gave the lead to other provinces; *koina* of a similar kind mushroomed in the East without any directive from the Emperor. Meanwhile, Lycia, not yet a province under Augustus, looked after itself by means of a league of twenty-three cities which had been joined together for over a century.[83] In effect, the league did the work of a client king. The usefulness of leagues for local government was demonstrated once more. And the fact that certain of the eastern *koina* occupied themselves particularly with the cult of the Emperor obviously did not preclude their being useful in the same way as the Greek and Lycian *koina*.

It has often been pointed out that the corporate organization of eastern cities in leagues facilitated the bringing of complaints against Roman rule. Inevitably it did, though not to the extent some have imagined.[84] What must always be remembered is that the leagues were things of the East, not created and introduced by Augustus as policy. He inherited many, and allowed others to develop.

Augustus' policy was to create a situation in which the Greek cities would be able to look after themselves as much as possible. He had, of course, to assure himself that the political units were workable and that the right kind of provincials were in control. When he interfered it was to keep the provincial machinery running smoothly. He had begun well with a remission of debts; he then gave the empire the greatest of all possible boons – peace. A succession of earthquakes was the only persistent impediment to recovery, and in response to appeals the Emperor furnished financial aid. Tralles, Laodicea, Thyatira, and Chios all were stricken early in the Principate.[85] In 12 B.C. there were widespread tremors. At that time, the Emperor paid from his own funds the tribute of the province of Asia.[86]

The cities of the East could discern a gentle revival of prosperity. The textile industry at Patrae was flourishing, trade at Corinth was good, and Athens was reaping the benefits of being a centre of Old

---

[82] Traces in early first century B.C.: *OGIS* 439; *IGR* 4. 188 [trans. Sherk, *RGE* no. 58]; Cic. *pro Flacc.* 23. 55–56. The *koinon* under Antony (either 42/41 or 33/32): Preisigke, *Sammelbuch*, 4224 = EJ², no. 300 [trans. Sherk, *RGE*, no. 85]. Cf. Brandis, *Hermes* 32 (1897), 512 ff.
[83] Strabo 14. 3. 2–3 (C 664–5). Cf. G. Fougères, *de Lyciorum Communi* (1898).
[84] P. A. Brunt, *Hist.* 10 (1961), 212 ff. [= *Roman Imperial Themes*, ch. IV, pp. 77 ff.].
[85] Agathias 2. 17 (Tralles); Suet. *Tib.* 8 (Laodicea, Thyatira, Chios). Cf. Bowersock, *Aug.*, pp. 157 and 160 (Appendix III).
[86] Dio 54. 30. 3.

World culture.[87] Strabo observed that Ephesus, by virtue of its favourable location for Asian commerce, was growing more prosperous every day.[88] Second only to Ephesus was Apamea, the former Celaenae, through which passed merchandise from Italy and Greece.[89] Laodicea on the Lycus produced excellent wool, and the exceptionally rich country in the vicinity of Sardis was made to yield despite frequent earthquakes.[90] Cyzicus grew in size and beauty to rival the leading cities of Asia.[91] Tyre in Syria did a thriving business in purple, while the establishment of quinquennial games at Syrian Antioch marked the beginning of its rise to greatness in the empire.[92] Cities, old and new, with names like Caesarea, Sebaste, or Sebastopolis blossomed all over the East.[93] New roads were put through.[94]

By nourishing the life of the cities and entrusting a substantial amount of administrative work to them, Augustus continued the republican tradition of personal dependence on provincials of the upper class. By avoiding a policy of centralization, he eased the strain on Rome; the provincials were profitably occupied with institutions familiar to them. As a patron of the Greek way of life, the Emperor maintained indirectly his own personal pre-eminence, as strong in senatorial provinces as it was in his own. Yet it was precisely because so little was innovatory about Augustus' treatment of the Eastern cities that the hostility and opposition which surged up occasionally in the Republic did so again in his own day. There were still many who hated Rome.

---

[87] Above, pp. 475 (Patrae), 476 (Corinth), 477 (Athens). On the revival of prosperity at Athens, cf. Day, *Economic History of Athens under Roman domination* (1942), pp. 167-71.
[88] Strabo 14. 1. 24 (C 641).
[89] Strabo 12. 8. 15 (C 577).
[90] Strabo 12. 8. 16 (C 578).
[91] Strabo 12. 8. 11 (C 575).
[92] Strabo 16. 2. 23 (C 757) (Tyre). Malalas 9. V95B (0291) on Antioch: cf. G. Downey, *A History of Antioch in Syria* (1961), p. 168. The games were included in the bequest of an Antiochene companion of Augustus.
[93] New foundations under Augustus (page references to Jones, *CERP*): Caesarea, later Caesarea Germanice, in Bithynia (163-4); Sebaste in Asia (72); Caesarea Paneas in Syria (283); perhaps Caesarea Trocetta in Asia (80) and Caesarea of the Proseilemmenitae in Paphlagonia (169). New names for old cities: Caesarea for Tralles (78), Anazarbus (205), and Strato's Tower (273); Sebaste for Pontic Diospolis (170), Paphlagonian Pompeiopolis (169), Elaeussa (207), and Samaria (273); Sebastopolis for Carana (170), Dioscurias (173), Myrrina (398, n. 86), and probably Larba (77). Megalopolis in Polemoniac Pontus may have taken the name Sebasteia under Augustus (171): cf. Anderson, *Anatolian Studies presented to Sir William Ramsay* (1923), 8-10.
[94] E. Gren attributes to Augustus the beginnings of the great road system of Asia Minor: *Kleinasien und der Ostbalkan in der wirtschaftlichen Entwicklung der römischen Kaiserzeit* (1941), p. 44. On the Via Sebaste through Pisidia, which belongs somehow in the context of the Homonadensian War, see R. Syme, *Klio* 27 (1934), 135 ff. On northern roads, D. R. Wilson, 'Historical Geography of Bithynia, Paphlagonia, and Pontus' (unpublished Oxford B.Litt. thesis, 1960), chapter IV.

Chronology

BC

63	23 September	Birth of C. Octavius (later known as Augustus) in Rome.
58	30 January	Birth of Livia Drusilla (later wife of Augustus).
51		Octavius delivers the eulogy (*laudatio funebris*) at the funeral of his maternal grandmother Julia.
49–45		Civil war between the supporters of Cn. Pompeius and Julius Caesar.
48	18 October	Octavius assumes the *toga virilis* ("toga of manhood").
44	15 March	Assassination of Julius Caesar, Octavius' maternal great-uncle; Octavius adopted as Caesar's son in his will.
43	2 January	Octavian receives propraetorian *imperium*; adlected into the senate.
	16 April	Octavian's first acclamation as "Imperator."
	21 April	Victory of Octavian against M. Antonius at the battle of Mutina, in which both consuls, A. Hirtius and C. Vibius Pansa, are killed.
	19 August	Octavian becomes consul for the first time.
	27 November	The *lex Titia* creates the Triumvirate of Octavian, M. Antonius, and M. Aemilius Lepidus, who become *IIIviri r(ei) p(ublicae) c(onstituendae)* ("triumvirs for the ordering of the state"). Proscriptions begin.
42		The *lex Rufrena* deifies Julius Caesar as *Divus Iulius* ("the Deified Julius").
	October	Battle of Philippi; Octavian and M. Antonius defeat the forces of M. Brutus and C. Cassius, who commit suicide.
	16 November	Birth of Ti. Claudius Nero (the later emperor Tiberius), son of Ti. Claudius Nero and Livia Drusilla.
41		War between Octavian and the consul L. Antonius.

		M. Antonius in the East, where he meets Cleopatra at Tarsus in Syria and then travels to Alexandria in Egypt.
40	spring	L. Antonius surrenders to Octavian after the siege of Perusia.
	summer	Octavian marries Scribonia.
	September	Pact of Brundisium between Octavian and M. Antonius. Marriage of M. Antonius and Octavia, Octavian's sister.
	late autumn/winter	Octavian's first *ovatio* (a minor triumph). He assumes the *praenomen* "Imperator."
39	spring	Pact of Misenum between the triumvirs and Sex. Pompeius (son of Pompey the Great).
		Birth of Julia, daughter of Octavian and Scribonia.
38	17 January	Marriage of Octavian and Livia Drusilla after his divorce of Scribonia.
		Sex. Pompeius defeats Octavian off the coast of Italy. Completion of Virgil, *Eclogues*.
37		M. Agrippa's first consulship.
	late summer	Pact of Tarentum extends the Triumvirate for another five years.
36		M. Antonius' unsuccessful Parthian campaign and retreat through Armenia.
		Octavian granted tribunician sacrosanctity (i.e., of a tribune of the plebs).
	3 September	Octavian's forces, led by M. Agrippa, defeat Sex. Pompeius at the battle of Naulochus off Sicily.
	22 September	Lepidus removed from the Triumvirate.
	13 November	Octavian celebrates an *ovatio* for the victory at Naulochus.
35–33		Octavian campaigns victoriously in Illyricum (the Balkans).
34		M. Antonius annexes Armenia. His triumphal celebrations at Alexandria, followed by the "Donations," where Cleopatra and her son Caesarion are declared monarchs of Egypt, Cyprus, and Koile Syria, and her and Antonius' children are given control over other parts of the East: Alexander Helios: Armenia, Media, and (still to be conquered) Parthia; Cleopatra Selene: Libya and Cyrene; and Ptolemy Philadelphus: Phoenicia, Syria, and Cilicia.
33		Octavian's second consulship begins on 1 January. Aedileship of M. Agrippa, who initiates a major programme of public building in the city of Rome.

		The Triumvirate expires at the end of 33 or at the end of 32.[1]
32		M. Antonius divorces Octavia.
		Italy swears an oath of allegiance to Octavian.
		The senate declares war on Cleopatra.
31–23		Octavian consul each year (i.e., his third to eleventh consulships).
31	2 September	Naval battle of Actium, where Octavian's troops, led by M. Agrippa because Octavian was ill, defeat M. Antonius and Cleopatra.
30	1 August	Alexandria falls to Octavian's troops.
	10 August	M. Antonius and Cleopatra commit suicide.
		Egypt annexed as a Roman province.
		Completion of Horace, *Epodes* and *Satires* (or *Sermones*, lit. "Conversations").
29	11 January	Closing of the doors of the Temple of Janus at Rome, symbolising that war was formally at an end.
	13–15 August	Octavian's triple triumph in Rome for his victories in Illyricum, at Actium, and in Egypt.
	18 August	Dedication of the Temple of Divus Iulius and the Julian senate-house (Curia Iulia) in the Forum.
	28 August	Dedication of the Altar of Victory inside the senate-house.
		Completion of Virgil, *Georgics*, and Propertius, *Elegies* I.
28		M. Agrippa holds the consulship (for the second time) with Octavian.
		Restoration of the *iura et leges p(opuli) R(omani)* ("the rights and laws of the Roman people").
		Octavian is named *princeps senatus* ("leading man of the senate"). Census and review of the senate, with Octavian granted censorial powers to carry this out.
		Agrippa marries Claudia Marcella, daughter of Octavian's sister Octavia (Minor).
	9 October	Dedication of the Temple of Apollo on the Palatine Hill.
27		Agrippa consul for the third time with Octavian/Augustus.

---

[1] The problem stems from contradictory sources and from the delay in renewing the Triumvirate after it had first technically ended on 31 December 38. Appian (*Illyr.* 28) suggests that the triumvirs' powers expired on 31 December 32; but Augustus' claim at *RG* 7.1 that he was IIIvir for ten consecutive years (*per continuos annos decem*), if read literally, would require the triumvirate to have ended on 31 December 33.

	13 January	Octavian is granted a large group of provinces, which he is allowed to govern through *legati* ("delegates"), and authorised to display permanently a *corona civica* ("civic crown," i.e., an oak crown awarded to soldiers for saving the lives of fellow-citizens) on the façade of his house on the Palatine.
	16 January	The senate grants Octavian the name "Augustus" and the right to display two laurel crowns and the *clipeus virtutis* ("the shield of virtue") on the façade of his house. He receives a grant of *imperium* for ten years.
27–24		Augustus in Gaul and Spain during the final phase of pacification of northern Spain and during the reorganisation of the Hispanic and Gallic provinces.
26–16		Completion of Properties, *Elegies* II–IV.
25		Second closing of the doors of the Temple of Janus.
		Marriage of Augustus' daughter Julia to his nephew, M. Claudius Marcellus.
		Ovid begins writing the *Amores* (the "Loves").
24–23		Completion of Horace, *Odes* Books I–III.
23		Conspiracies of M. Primus, proconsul of Macedonia, and the consul A. Terentius Varro Murena.
	June	Augustus resigns the consulship and receives tribunician power (renewed annually henceforth on 26 June); his *imperium* to govern his provinces is confirmed and probably becomes *imperium maius quam* ("power greater than") that of other provincial governors. Agrippa is also granted *imperium*.
		Augustus suffers a serious illness.
	after 1 August	Death of Marcellus, who is then buried in the Mausoleum of Augustus.
23–21		Agrippa in the East.
22		Augustus refuses the dictatorship and perpetual consulship, but accepts the *cura annonae* ("responsibility for the grain supply").
22–19		Augustus in Sicily, Greece, and Asia.
21		Agrippa divorces Claudia Marcella and marries Julia, Augustus' daughter.
20–19		Agrippa in Gaul and then Spain, where he completes the pacification of the Iberian peninsula.
		Completion of Horace, *Epistles* Book I.
20		Diplomatic settlement with Armenia and Parthia allows Augustus to recover the Roman standards lost to the Parthians in 53 BC.
		Augustus is given responsibility for the major roads of Italy (*cura viarum*).

Chronology

19	21 September	Death of Virgil, with his major epic poem, the *Aeneid*, not quite completed.
	12 October	Augustus returns from the East to Rome and is granted further privileges. Inauguration of the *Ara Fortunae Reducis* ("Altar of Fortuna Redux," i.e., "Altar of Fortune that Leads Back").
	15 December	Dedication of the Altar of Fortuna Redux.
18		Augustus' *imperium* and *tribunicia potestas* are extended for another five years. Agrippa's *imperium* is renewed and he is granted tribunician power for five years.
18–17		Augustus' moral legislation (*leges Iuliae* regulating *inter alia* marriage among the upper classes, adultery, electoral bribery, manumission of slaves, seating at the theatre).
17	May–June	*Ludi saeculares* ("Secular Games"), for which Horace composes the *Carmen saeculare* (the "Secular Hymn").
		Augustus adopts his grandsons, Gaius and Lucius Caesar, the sons of Julia and Agrippa, born in 20 and 17 respectively.
16	summer	Defeat of M. Lollius, legate of Augustus, in Gaul at the hands of several Germanic tribes.
		Probable date of publication of the second edition of Ovid, *Amores*.
16–13		Augustus in Gaul; Agrippa in the East.
15		Campaigns of Augustus' stepsons, Tiberius and Drusus, in the Alps and Germany.
13		Tiberius holds his first consulship. Death of the former triumvir and *pontifex maximus* M. Lepidus. Augustus' and Agrippa's powers are renewed for another five years.
	4 July	Augustus returns to Rome. Inauguration of the *Ara Pacis Augustae* ("the Altar of Augustan Peace").
		Appearance of Horace, *Odes* Book IV.
12	6 March	Augustus becomes *pontifex maximus*.
	March	Death of Agrippa in Campania. He is buried in the Mausoleum of Augustus.
12–9		Tiberius leads campaigns in Pannonia and Illyricum, Drusus in Germany.
12–8		Completion of Horace, *Epistles* Book II and *Ars Poetica*.
11		Tiberius forced to divorce Vipsania and marry Augustus' daughter Julia.
11–10		Augustus in Gaul.

9		Drusus holds his first consulship.
		Livia granted the *ius trium liberorum* (i.e., privileges granted to freeborn Roman women who had borne three children).
	30 January	Dedication of the *Ara Pacis Augustae*.
	14 September	Death of Augustus' younger stepson Drusus in Germany.
		Completion of the first edition of Ovid, *Ars Amatoria*.
8		Tiberius campaigns in Germany.
		Augustus' powers renewed for a ten-year period. He is also granted censorial power to hold a census.
		Reform of the calendar: the month "Sextilis" is renamed "Augustus." Deaths of C. Maecenas and the poet Horace.
7		Tiberius is granted a triumph to celebrate his German victories.
6		Tiberius' *imperium* is renewed, and he is granted tribunician power for five years, but soon thereafter retires, disgruntled, to the island of Rhodes.
5		Gaius Caesar takes the *toga virilis* and is designated *princeps iuventutis* ("prince of the youth"). Augustus, as consul for the twelfth time, introduces him to Roman public life.
4		Gaius Caesar consul.
2		Lucius Caesar takes the *toga virilis* and is designated *princeps iuventutis*. Augustus, as consul for the thirteenth (and last) time, introduces him to Roman public life.
	5 February	Augustus receives the title *pater patriae* ("father of the fatherland").
	12 May	Dedication of the *Forum Augustum* and the Temple of Mars Ultor.
		Second edition of Ovid, *Ars Amatoria*.
		Augustus' daughter Julia is condemned for adultery, divorced by Tiberius, and relegated to the island of Pandateria.

AD

1–4		Gaius Caesar in the East.
1–8		Composition of Ovid, *Fasti* (incomplete) and *Metamorphoses*.
2		Tiberius returns from Rhodes.
	20 August	Death of Lucius Caesar in Massilia in southern Gaul.
4	February	Death of Gaius Caesar in Limyra in Lycia.
	26 June	Augustus adopts his stepson Tiberius and his grand-

Chronology

		son Agrippa Postumus (son of Julia and Agrippa, born in 12 BC) as his sons; Tiberius adopts his brother Drusus' son Germanicus (born in 15 BC). Tiberius is granted *imperium* and tribunician power for five years.
4–6		Tiberius campaigns in Germany to put down a serious uprising.
6–9		Tiberius campaigns in Pannonia and Dalmatia to put down revolts.
6		Establishment of the *aerarium militare* ("military treasury").
7		Agrippa Postumus relegated to the island of Planasia, and permanently exiled by a senatorial decree in AD 8.
8		Augustus' granddaughter Julia (daughter of Julia and M. Agrippa) and the poet Ovid relegated on separate charges of adultery and conspiracy.
9		Tiberius' *imperium* and *tribunicia potestas* renewed for five years. German forces under Arminius destroy the army of P. Quinctilius Varus in the Teutoburger forest near Kalkriese (north of Osnabrück).
9–12		Composition (in exile) of Ovid, *Tristia* ("Sorrows").
10–12		Tiberius leads campaigns in Germany to avenge Varus' defeat.
12		Germanicus leads campaigns in Gaul and Germany.
	23 October	Tiberius' triumph over Pannonia and Dalmatia.
13		Renewal of Augustus' and Tiberius' powers. Tiberius' *imperium* becomes *imperium maius quam* (i.e., greater than) that of all provincial governors. Augustus and Tiberius are granted censorial power. Ovid's *Letters from Pontus* collected into a book (Book I).
14	11 May	Augustus and Tiberius complete the census.
	19 August	Death of Augustus at Nola in Campania.
	September	Public funeral of Augustus in Rome; burial in his Mausoleum. Livia is adopted into Augustus' family in his will, becoming Julia Augusta.
	17 September	Augustus is consecrated as *Divus Augustus* ("the Deified Augustus"). Tiberius becomes *princeps* as Imp. Tiberius Caesar Augustus.
17		Death of Ovid in Tomis. Posthumous publication of *Letters from Pontus* Book II.
29		Livia dies in Rome and is buried in the Mausoleum of Augustus.
37	16 March	Death of Tiberius at Misenum in Campania.

	4 April	Tiberius is buried in the Mausoleum of Augustus in Rome, but is not consecrated as a god.
42	17 January	Thirteen years after her death Livia is consecrated as Diva Augusta.
1555		Discovery of the bilingual (Greek/Latin) text of the *Res Gestae et Impensae Divi Augusti* on the walls of the Temple of Roma and Augustus in Ancyra (Ankara).
1871		Publication of the first parts of Theodor Mommsen's *Römisches Staatsrecht* ("Roman Constitutional Law").
1887–1888		Publication of the definitive, revised third edition of *Römisches Staatsrecht*.
1891–1904		Publication of *Augustus und seine Zeit* by Viktor Gardthausen.
1903		Publication of Eduard Meyer's important article on "Kaiser Augustus."
1934		First edition of volume X of *The Cambridge Ancient History*, covering "The Augustan Empire, 44 B.C.–A.D. 70" (edited by S. A. Cook, F. E. Adcock, and M. P. Charlesworth).
1936		W. Weber, *Princeps. Studien zur Geschichte des Augustus.*
1937		Posthumous publication of A. von Premerstein, *Vom Werden und Wesen des Prinzipats*.
1937–1938		Major exhibition, the "Mostra Augustea della Romanità" ("Augustan Exhibition of Romanness"), opens in Rome on 23 September 1937 and closes on 23 September 1938.
1938		Publication of *Augustus: Studi in occasione del bimillenario augusteo* in Rome. Inauguration of the reconstructed *Ara Pacis* by Mussolini on 23 September.
1939		Publication of Sir Ronald Syme's *The Roman Revolution* on 7 September.
1947, 1951		Publication of H. Last's articles on Augustus' *imperium maius* and tribunician power.
1953		J. Béranger, *Recherches sur l'aspect idéologique du principat.*
1954		Publication of L. Wickert's detailed article on the principate in *RE*, vol. 22.2.
1960		Publication of A. H. M. Jones' *Studies in Roman Government and Law*, drawing together his important articles on Augustus' *imperium*, his censorial powers, and elections under Augustus.
1965		G. W. Bowersock, *Augustus and the Greek World.*

1970	A. H. M. Jones, *Augustus*.
1981	Opening of the British Museum exhibition on "The Image of Augustus."
1982	D. Kienast, *Augustus. Prinzeps und Monarch* (with second edition in 1992 and third edition in 1999).
1984	Publication of the proceedings of the conference held at Wolfson College Oxford in 1983 to celebrate R. Syme's eightieth birthday: *Caesar Augustus: Seven Aspects* (eds F. Millar and E. Segal).
1987	First publication of P. Zanker, *Augustus und die Macht der Bilder* (with English translation, *The Power of Images in the Age of Augustus*, following in 1988).
1988	Exhibition in Berlin on "Kaiser Augustus und die verlorene Republik" ("Caesar Augustus and the Lost Republic").
	C. Nicolet, *L'inventaire du monde: géographie et politique aux origines de l'Empire romain* (with English translation, *Space, Geography, and Politics in the Early Roman Empire*, following in 1991).
	P. A. Brunt, *The Fall of the Roman Republic and Related Essays*.
1990	Publication of *Between Republic and Empire: Interpretations of Augustus and his Principate* (eds K. A. Raaflaub and M. Toher), papers from a 1989 conference marking the fiftieth anniversary of Syme's *Roman Revolution*.
1996	Second edition of volume X of *The Cambridge Ancient History*, covering "The Augustan Empire, 43 B.C.–A.D. 69" (eds A. K. Bowman, E. Champlin, and A. W. Lintott) and including J. A. Crook's balanced assessment of Augustus.
1998	J. Bleicken, *Augustus. Eine Biographie*.
	First edition of W. Eck, *Augustus und seine Zeit* (with the first edition of an English translation *The Age of Augustus*, following in 2003, with its second, expanded edition in 2007).
2000	Publication of *La révolution romaine après Ronald Syme*, papers from a colloquium in 1999 held at the Fondation Hardt near Geneva celebrating the sixtieth anniversary of the publication of Syme's *Roman Revolution*.
2001	First publication of J.-L. Ferrary's article on the powers of Augustus: "À propos des pouvoirs d'Auguste."

2002   Publication of F. Millar's collected papers on the "Augustan revolution": *The Roman Republic and the Augustan Revolution* (eds H. M. Cotton and G. M. Rogers).

APPENDIX

A. The Consulships of Octavian/Augustus

cos. I	19 August–November 43 BC
cos. II	1 January–31 December 33 BC
cos. III	1 January–31 December 31 BC
cos. IV	1 January–31 December 30 BC
cos. V	1 January–31 December 29 BC
cos. VI	1 January–31 December 28 BC (with Agrippa)
cos. VII	1 January–31 December 27 BC (with Agrippa)
cos. VIII	1 January–31 December 26 BC
cos. IX	1 January–31 December 25 BC
cos. X	1 January–31 December 24 BC
cos. XI	1 January–end June 23 BC
cos. XII	1 January–*c.* 11 April (or 31 July?) 5 BC
cos. XIII	1 January–*c.* 1 August 2 BC

Note: cos. is the standard Latin abbreviation for co(n)s(ul).

B. Salutations as Imperator

Octavian's (later Augustus') successive salutations as *Imperator* appear among his titles on coins and inscriptions in the form *Imp. X*, etc., reflecting the fact that he was granted twenty-one of them between the years 43 BC and AD 13. For full chronological details, see above, Introduction, p. 4 and n. 9.

C. Augustus' tribunicia potestas

Granted first in 23 BC, Augustus' *tribunicia potestas* (tribunician power) ran each year from 26 June to 25 June. The year of his tribunician power was used as a dating mechanism in official documents, as follows:

> *trib(unicia) pot(estate) I* = 26 June 23–25 June 22 BC
> *trib(unicia) pot(estate) II* = 26 June 22–25 June 21 BC
> *trib(unicia) pot(estate) III* = 26 June 21–25 June 20 BC

trib. pot. IV = 20–19 BC
trib. pot. V = 19–18 BC
trib. pot. VI = 18–17 BC
trib. pot. VII = 17–16 BC
trib. pot. VIII = 16–15 BC
trib. pot. IX = 15–14 BC
trib. pot. X = 14–13 BC
trib. pot. XI = 13–12 BC
trib. pot. XII = 12–11 BC
trib. pot. XIII = 11–10 BC
trib. pot. XIV = 10–9 BC
trib. pot. XV = 9–8 BC
trib. pot. XVI = 8–7 BC
trib. pot. XVII = 7–6 BC
trib. pot. XVIII = 6–5 BC
trib. pot. XIX = 5–4 BC
trib. pot. XX = 4–3 BC
trib. pot. XXI = 3–2 BC
trib. pot. XXII = 2–1 BC
trib. pot. XXIII = 1 BC–AD 1
trib. pot. XXIV = AD 1–2
trib. pot. XXV = AD 2–3
trib. pot. XXVI = AD 3–4
trib. pot. XXVII = AD 4–5
trib. pot. XXVIII = AD 5–6
trib. pot. XXIX = AD 6–7
trib. pot. XXX = AD 7–8
trib. pot. XXXI = AD 8–9
trib. pot. XXXII = AD 9–10
trib. pot. XXXIII = AD 10–11
trib. pot. XXXIV = AD 11–12
trib. pot. XXXV = AD 12–13
trib. pot. XXXVI = 26 June AD 13–25 June AD 14
trib. pot. XXXVII = 26 June–19 August AD 14

Glossary

acta senatus	proceedings of the senate
aedilis (pl. *aediles*)	"aedile(s)"; Roman state magistrate(s) traditionally responsible for the upkeep of the city of Rome, the grain supply, and the main state festivals (*ludi*). Each year two plebeian aediles were elected from among the plebeians, two curule aediles initially from among the patricians, but from 367 BC from among the whole citizen body. Also lower-ranking magistrates in municipalities of Italy and the provinces.
aerarium militare	"military treasury," established by Augustus in AD 6 to provide funds to deal with the demobilisation of veteran soldiers
aerarium Saturni	"treasury of Saturn"; i.e., the treasury of the Roman state, located in the Temple of Saturn in the Forum beneath the Capitol
annona	the food supply of the Roman state, especially the grain supply, needed to feed the city of Rome and the Roman army
augur (pl. *augures*)	the "augurs" (sixteen in number from Julius Caesar onwards) formed one of the four main priestly colleges at Rome. They were expert in interpreting omens in the form of the flight of birds, to provide advice to magistrates and the senate whether a particular course of action was favoured by the gods, and in taking the auspices (*auspicia*) (s.v.). They also formally "inaugurated" new buildings, especially temples.
auspicium (pl. *auspicia*)	lit. "watching the birds"; i.e., the interpretation of signs sent by the gods. The "auspices were taken" by magistrates, usually with the expert assistance of the augurs, before major political events such as elections and meetings of the

Glossary

	assembly and the senate and before military campaigns.
censor (pl. *censores*)	Under the Republic two censors were elected every five years to hold a census, conduct a review of the membership of the senate, lease the major public contracts, and scrutinise the morals of the community. Augustus was granted censorial powers to hold censuses in 28 and 8 BC and in AD 14.
cognomen	Roman surname, used to distinguish members of the same *gens*
comitia (pl. in form)	an assembly of the Roman citizen body
comitia centuriata	the assembly of the Roman citizens arranged into 193 voting blocks known as "centuries" responsible for the election of senior state magistrates and declarations of war and peace. The centuries were organised according to levels of wealth and hence military responsibilities, as determined by the census, with the richest Romans comprising a large number of centuries and the poorer citizens restricted within proportionately far fewer voting units.
comitia tributa	the assembly of all Roman citizens arranged in "tribes"; i.e., regionally based voting units. It was important as a legislative body and also elected the more junior magistrates.
concilium plebis	the assembly of the Roman plebs, from which all patricians (s.v.) were excluded. It had the authority to pass *plebiscita* (plebiscites), which had the force of laws and elected the plebeian magistrates (plebeian aediles and tribunes of the plebs).
consilium principis	a modern term used to refer to the emperor's informal advisory council
consul (pl. *consules*)	the two chief annual magistrates of the Roman state, traditionally elected by the Roman citizen body and given *imperium* to enforce orders on Roman citizens and to lead Roman armies. During Julius Caesar's dictatorship and the Triumvirate, the consuls were nominated by the dictator and then the triumvirs often for several years ahead. Formal elections of the consuls returned in 28 BC. It was only with later emperors that certain candidates for this office were "recommended" by the *princeps* and automatically elected.

cos. ord.	*consul ordinarius*; i.e., regular consul who took up office at the start of the year
cos. suff.	*consul suffectus*; i.e., replacement consul who took up office if a *consul ordinarius* had died or stepped down from his position
damnatio memoriae	a modern term used to describe the process whereby all public memory of an individual was expunged after his or her condemnation; it involved the removal of all statues from public places and the erasure of his or her name from inscriptions and even coins
decurio (pl. *decuriones*)	local town-councillor(s) in municipalities in Italy and the provinces
divus (pl. *divi*; fem. *diva*; fem. pl. *divae*)	the title given to deified Roman emperors or to deified members of the imperial family: e.g., Divus Augustus, Diva Augusta
duovir or *II vir* (pl. *duoviri*)	senior local magistrate(s) in a colony or municipality in Italy or the provinces
eques (pl. *equites*)	equestrian(s), knight(s), member(s) of the *equester ordo* (equestrian order), a social order second only to the senatorial order in terms of status and prestige; Augustus fixed the property qualification at 400,000 sesterces and started to use equestrians to fulfil administrative positions in Rome, Italy, and the provinces.
fasces	bundles of rods and axes carried by lictors (attendants), to symbolise a senior magistrate's power
fetialis (pl. *fetiales*)	"fetial(s)"; the college of priests (revived by Augustus) that was responsible for declarations of war and the confirmation of peace treaties. Traditionally declarations of war were marked by the "fetial rite," which involved the *fetiales* ritually throwing a spear into a piece of land just outside Rome that stood symbolically for enemy territory after their earlier demands for reparation of injuries inflicted on Rome had not been heeded by the enemy state.
fiscus	lit. "the basket"; financial account of the emperor
flamen (pl. *flamines*)	priest(s) in charge of the cult of a particular divinity. The three major *flamines* were those of Jupiter, Mars, and Quirinus, and there were another twelve minor *flamines*. The title was eventually used for priests of the imperial cult at the municipal and provincial levels.

Glossary

genius	divine alter-ego or guardian spirit of a Roman male
gens	a kinship unit comprising a group of families who shared the same *nomen* and patrilineal lineage, e.g. the *gens Iulia* was the kinship group of the Iulii, including Julius Caesar and Augustus
haruspex (pl. *haruspices*)	diviner, steeped in Etruscan lore, who interpreted signs sent by the gods
homo novus (pl. *homines novi*)	see *novus homo*
imperator	In the Republic a successful general might be acclaimed as "Imperator" by his troops after a military victory. Taken as his first name (*praenomen*) by Octavian in late autumn/winter 40 BC, from the Flavian period on it became a standard part of the titles of a Roman emperor.
imperial freedman	manumitted slave of the emperor. They were used from Augustus onwards as the emperor's agents in administrative tasks in Rome, Italy, and the provinces. s.v. *procurator*.
imperium	the power to command, invested in senior magistrates (praetors and consuls) and the Roman *princeps*
ius trium liberorum	"right of three children"; a set of legal privileges granted freeborn Roman married men and women who had produced three children
Juno	Roman goddess, consort of Jupiter; also the divine alter-ego or guardian spirit of a female Roman
legatus (pl. *legati*) *Augusti*	legate(s) of the emperor; i.e., a person selected by the emperor to act on his behalf as a governor of a province controlled by the emperor or as an army commander acting under the emperor's auspices
lex annalis	a law that laid down the rules regarding holding public office at Rome, especially the age at which each magistracy could be held
ludi (pl. in form)	a religious festival; games
ludi circenses	games in the circus; i.e., chariot races
ludi saeculares	lit. "Secular Games" celebrating the birth of a new *saeculum* (a defined period of 100 or 110 years). These "Centennial Games" were held in 17 BC for the first time since 146 BC and served as a centrepiece of Augustus' programme of social and cultural regeneration.
ludi scaenici	games on the stage; i.e., theatrical shows

materfamilias	lit. "mother of the household"; mistress of the household, usually the wife of the *paterfamilias* (s.v.)
matrona (pl. *matronae*)	matron; i.e., married woman
nobilis (pl. *nobiles*)	lit. "a known person"; i.e., a person of senatorial rank who could boast a consul among his direct ascendant kin. A looser definition argues that it referred to a senator one of whose direct ancestors had reached the curule aedileship.
nomen	Roman name, especially the name that distinguished one Roman *gens* from another
novus homo (pl. *novi homines*)	lit. "new man"; the first man from a family to enter the senate
optimates	lit. "the supporters of the best men"; politicians who championed the traditional aristocracy and traditional aristocratic values in opposition to the *populares* (s.v.)
ordo equester	s.v. *eques*
ordo senatorius	s.v. *senatus*
ornamenta triumphalia	"triumphal ornaments"; these decorations were awarded to army commanders in lieu of a full triumph, which after the triumph of L. Cornelius Balbus in 19 BC were restricted to emperors and members of the imperial family
paterfamilias	lit. "father of the *familia*"; i.e., the male head of a Roman household, who exercised *patria potestas* ("paternal power") over all members of his family under his power, including its slaves. This would normally not include his wife, unless she had been married *cum manu* (lit. "with hand"), which had become rare by the Augustan period except in a few patrician families.
pater patriae	"father of the fatherland"; a title granted Augustus in 2 BC
patrician/plebeian	patricians were members of certain *gentes* (extended kin-groups) who traced their ancestry back to one of the original senators appointed by Romulus. All non-patrician families were termed "plebeian." A *lex Saenia* of 29 BC granted Octavian the right to adlect a plebeian "among the patricians" as a special honour, which henceforth conferred patrician status on the individual and his family.
pietas	respect or dutiful conduct towards the gods, one's parents, or one's community

pomerium	sacred boundary of a Roman city, especially the city of Rome
pontifex (pl. *pontifices*)	major Roman priest(s) with many public and private duties. The head of the college of *pontifices* was the *pontifex maximus*.
popularis (pl. *populares*)	lit. "supporter of the people"; a politician who sought to gain the support of the ordinary citizens and championed their interests, often in the face of the opposition of more conservative politicians (known as *optimates*, lit. "supporters of the best men")
portorium (pl. *portoria*)	transit toll(s) charged at harbours, provincial frontiers, and the external frontier of the Roman Empire
praenomen	Roman first name
praetor (pl. *praetores*)	praetor(s); the second-highest-ranking annual magistracy of the Roman state after the consuls, they had important judicial duties in Rome during their year in office. Ex-praetors were selected to serve as proconsuls or *legati Augusti* of certain provinces.
princeps (pl. *principes*)	lit. "first citizen"; in the Republic the censors determined who was the *princeps* of the senate; from Augustus onwards, it was used to designate the ruling emperor
proconsul (pl. *proconsules*)	lit. "in place of the consul" (abbreviated as *pro cos*); a magistrate operating "instead of a consul" outside Rome or one who had had his consular power prorogued (i.e., extended) after the end of his year as consul. From Augustus onwards proconsuls served as governors of the so-called "public" or "proconsular" provinces, as opposed to the *legati Augusti* who governed the "imperial" provinces.
procurator (pl. *procuratores*)	lit. "agent" or "representative," used from Augustus onwards to designate the emperor's agents (normally imperial freedmen or *equites*) employed in administrative tasks in Rome, Italy, and the provinces. "Praesidial" procurators governed small provinces such as Judaea, Noricum, or Corsica. Procurators of imperial provinces supervised tax collection and the emperor's properties. Procurators in the public provinces initially administered just the emperor's properties here, but eventually came to

	assist the proconsul in collecting taxes. "Patrimonial" procurators were also appointed to administer the emperor's possessions, including estates.
propraetor (pl. *propraetores*)	lit. "in place of the praetor"; a magistrate operating instead of a praetor outside Rome or one who had had his praetorian power prorogued (i.e., extended) after the end of his year as praetor
provincia	lit., a sphere of command granted to the holder of *imperium*; a province of the Roman Empire
publicanus (pl. *publicani*)	someone who leased a contract issued by the Roman state, in particular a contract to collect Roman taxes in the provinces
quaestor (pl. *quaestores*)	lower-ranking magistrate(s) of the Roman state, twenty of whom were elected annually under Augustus. Their duties were mainly financial. From Augustus onwards two quaestors were assigned to the *princeps*, to assist him in his administrative tasks. Local quaestors were also appointed in certain Italian and provincial municipalities.
quindecimvir(i) or *XV vir(i) sacris faciundis*	member(s) of the board of fifteen responsible for sacred acts, including some state festivals such as the *ludi saeculares* (s.v.)
salutatio	ceremony at which clients came to the homes of their patrons to greet them; in return, they received a handout (*sportula*) of food or, increasingly, money
sella curulis	lit. "curule seat"; a stool on which a curule magistrate (consul, praetor, or curule aedile) sat when conducting public business as a symbol of his magisterial power
senatus	"senate"; council of the Roman state made up of ex-magistrates, which debated issues and passed *senatus consulta* (s.v.) to advise state magistrates. Augustus used censorial powers in 28 and 18 BC to revise the list of its members, reducing it to 600 members, which became its set limit during the Principate, and requiring a property qualification of each senator of one million sesterces. Service in the senate brought with it membership in the *ordo senatorius* for the senator and his direct descendants (to the third generation).

Glossary

senatus consultum (pl. *senatus consulta*)   "resolution(s) of the senate" (abbreviated as S.C., SC or s.c.); technically the formal advice of the senate for a magistrate regarding a particular course of action, written up after the senatorial debate. Texts of these were often published with the magistrate's decree enforcing the policy.

spolia opima   lit. "the rich spoils"; the spoils dedicated by a Roman general after killing the enemy leader in battle

stola   the long, distinctive robe worn on formal occasions by a Roman citizen married woman over a tunic, stretching from the neck to the ankles, a symbol of a Roman matron's chastity

supplicatio (pl. *supplicationes*)   thanksgiving to a god (or gods), involving an offering of wine and incense, often held after military victories

tribunicia potestas   lit. "tribunician power" or powers of a tribune. These powers traditionally included the right to summon the *concilium plebis* (plebeian assembly) and to propose *plebiscita* there, and to intercede on behalf of ordinary citizens against the actions of magistrates. It was granted to Augustus from 23 BC onwards.

tribunus plebis (pl. *tribuni plebis*)   tribune(s) of the plebs; ten annual magistrates elected from among the plebeians to protect the *plebs* from summary actions of other state magistrates, which developed into the right to veto any act of another magistrate; laws that they proposed in the plebeian assembly (*plebiscita*; i.e., "plebiscites") were binding on the entire citizen body from 287 BC

triumph   an elaborate procession through the streets of Rome culminating at the Temple of Jupiter on the Capitol. It was awarded a Roman general who had won a major military victory by a vote of the senate and Roman people. He rode in a triumphal chariot and was escorted by his army, the senate, and the magistrates. The parade also included a display of the spoils captured in the war and enemy captives.

triumphator (pl. *triumphatores*)   a Roman general who had been awarded a triumph (s.v.)

triumviri (III viri) monetales   lit. "the three men responsible for the mint'; moneyers, junior magistrates responsible for the

	production of coinage at the Roman mint
triumviri r.p.c. or *III viri r.p.c.*	*triumviri r(ei) p(ublicae) c(onstituendae)*: "three men for the ordering of the Republic"; official title of the Triumvirate of Octavian, M. Antonius, and M. Aemilius Lepidus established by the *lex Titia* of 27 November 43 BC, renewed in 37 BC
Vestal Virgins	the six priestesses of the state cult of Vesta, Roman goddess of the hearth; they served for thirty years, often beginning in childhood, and were required to maintain their chastity on pain of burial alive. They were granted special privileges, some of which were also granted to Augustus' wife Livia.
virtus	lit. "manliness"; courage, bravery, excellence, virtue

Guide to Further Reading

The main ancient literary sources for the study of Augustan Rome are available in an excellent variety of English editions.[1] Translations of Suetonius' *Life of Augustus*, Tacitus' *Annals*, Plutarch's *Life of Antony* (important for the triumviral period), and the major literary works composed during the age of Augustus by authors such as Virgil, Horace, Propertius, Tibullus, Ovid, and Livy are conveniently available as Penguin Classics, Oxford World Classics, and volumes of the Loeb Classical Library. Books 50–56 of Cassius Dio's *Roman History*, covering the years 31 BC to AD 14, are covered in Ian Scott-Kilvert's 1987 translation in the Penguin Classics series; for Books 44–49, which deal with the death of Caesar and the triumviral period, students will need to consult volumes 4 and 5 of the Loeb Classical Library translation of Dio by E. Cary, first issued in 1916 and 1917 respectively. Appian's *Civil Wars* (translated in both the Penguin Classics and Loeb Classical Library series) is also important for our understanding of the triumviral period.

Useful historical commentaries in English are available on Suetonius' *Life of Augustus* (by J. M. Carter, 1982), on Tacitus' *Annals* 1.1–54 (by F. R. D. Goodyear, 1972), on Plutarch's *Life of Antony* (by C. B. R. Pelling, 1988), and on Cassius Dio as follows: on Books 49–52 by M. Reinhold (1988), Books 53–55.9 by J. Rich (1990), and Books 55–56 by P. M. Swan (2004). A convenient edition and translation of Nicolaus of Damascus' *Life of Augustus*, with historical commentary, by J. Bellemore appeared in 1994. Livy's monumental history is now covered by learned commentaries in English, published by Oxford University Press, on Books 1–5 by R. M. Ogilvie (1965), on Books 6–10 by S. P. Oakley (1997–2005), and on Books 31–45 by J. Briscoe (1973, 1981, 2008, 2012). The history of Velleius Paterculus, composed under Tiberius, provides a rather different slant on Augustus from that found in later works such as Tacitus and Suetonius; a translation is available in the Loeb Classical Library and note also the

---

[1] Given the stated aims of the series, this Guide will deal in the main with works published in English. Readers should also take note of works mentioned in the main Introduction and in the introductions to each Part of the volume. Full details of sources mentioned here and referred to by the editor in the text are given in the Bibliography, below.

edition, with detailed commentary, of A. J. Woodman, *Velleius Paterculus: The Caesarian and Augustan Narratives (2.41–93)* (1983).

Other works written in Greek need to be more fully integrated into interpretations of the Augustan age than has often been the case. It is a pity that Strabo's geography of the known Roman world, composed under Augustus and Tiberius, is only available in the eight-volume Loeb Classical Library translation by H. L. Jones (1917), since this contemporary work throws much light on the Augustan principate: see further K. Clarke, *Between Geography and History: Hellenistic Constructions of the Roman World* (1999), chs 4–6 (pp. 193–336). Dionysius of Halicarnassus' *Roman Antiquities* (in Greek), written in Rome under Augustus, provides a detailed and pointed contrast to Livy's conceptualisation of the history of early Rome: see E. Gabba, *Dionysius and the History of Early Rome* (1991); more briefly, his article, "The Historians and Augustus," in *Caesar Augustus: Seven Aspects* (eds F. Millar and E. Segal, 1984).

To help evaluate the main sources, students will profit by consulting A. Wallace-Hadrill, *Suetonius: A Scholar and his Caesars* (1984); R. Syme, *Tacitus* (2 vols, 1958) or the more straightforward *Tacitus* by Ronald Martin (1981); F. Millar, *A Study of Cassius Dio* (1964). For the literary output of the Augustan age, there are good summaries in E. J. Kenney, *The Cambridge History of Classical Literature. 2. Latin Literature* (1982), pp. 297–494.

Students will also wish to avail themselves of the various collections of translated sources on the age of Augustus now available, since these include not only excerpts from some of the less familiar literary works (including, for instance, the contemporary Greek epigrams of Antipater of Thessalonica and Crinagoras of Mytilene), but also the many coin types and inscriptions (both longer public documents and shorter private texts, especially tombstones and votive dedications) that are vital to our historical understanding and interpretation of the Augustan principate. The best of these is now *The Age of Augustus*, edited by M. G. L. Cooley in the LACTOR series (LACTOR 17, 2003), but note also *Rome, the Augustan Age: A Sourcebook*, edited by K. Chisholm and J. Ferguson (1981), *Augustus to Nero: A Sourcebook on Roman History, 31 B.C.–A.D. 68*, edited by D. C. Braund (1985), with an excellent introductory essay on how best to interpret the varied historical sources, and (more briefly) R. K. Sherk's *The Roman Empire: Augustus to Hadrian*, the sixth volume in the series "Translated Documents of Greece and Rome" (1988). The "classic" sourcebook, with sources excerpted in their original Latin and Greek, remains that of V. Ehrenberg and A. H. M. Jones, *Documents Illustrating the Reigns of Augustus and Tiberius* (often referred to simply as "EJ"), first released in 1949, with a 2nd enlarged edition following in 1955, which was reprinted (with Addenda by D. L. Stockton) in 1976. For the *Res Gestae divi Augusti* (famously described by Mommsen as the "queen of all inscriptions"), readers will find the editions and translations, with helpful historical commentary, by P. A. Brunt and J. M. Moore (1967) and Alison Cooley (2012) the most convenient, but the most up-to-date critical edition of both Latin and Greek versions of the inscription is that of John Scheid (with French translation and historical commentary, 2007).

No one can work on the age of Augustus without reading and digesting the insights of R. Syme's classic, *The Roman Revolution* (1939). In addition, A. H. M. Jones' *Augustus* (1970) and Werner Eck's *The Age of Augustus* (German original, 1998; English translation, 2003; 2nd English edition, 2007), as well as the chapters by Christopher Pelling (on the triumviral period) and John Crook (on Augustus) in the second edition of volume X of the *Cambridge Ancient History* (1996), provide admirably clear and concise historical accounts of the age of Augustus. At the moment in English we lack as comprehensive a survey as that available in German in D. Kienast's *Augustus. Prinzeps und Monarch* (1982; 2nd edn, 1992; 3rd edn, 1999). John Richardson's recent volume on Augustus in the "Edinburgh History of Ancient Rome" series (Richardson 2012) helps to fill the gap. *The Cambridge Companion to the Age of Augustus* (2005), edited by Karl Galinksy, provides a stimulating collection of essays on the political, intellectual, social, religious, artistic, and literary history of the period by major scholars. For a series of essays on the political elite of the Augustan age and their marriage alliances, readers should consult R. Syme's *The Augustan Aristocracy* (1986), the final chapter of which (ch. 30, pp. 439–454) takes the form of a wide-ranging reflection on the Augustan principate: "The Apologia for the Principate."

Modern biographies of key figures such as Livia (by A. A. Barrett, 2002), Tiberius (by R. Seager, 1972, or by B. M. Levick, 1976), or Augustus' daughter Julia (by E. Fantham, 2006) often throw light on important issues in the history of the Augustan age, despite the difficulties inherent in compiling satisfying biographies of individuals from the ancient world; arguably more analytical studies, such as that by Nicholas Purcell on Livia (Chapter 5, above), are more revealing. The best and most detailed account of M. Agrippa is that by J.-M. Roddaz (1984, in French). Not surprisingly, Cleopatra has attracted a host of biographies, but it is very difficult to separate the reality from the myth. More successful than most of these are the catalogue prepared for the British Museum exhibition *Cleopatra of Egypt: From History to Myth*, edited by Susan Walker and Peter Higgs (2001), and Susan Walker's *Cleopatra* (2006), to be read alongside Maria Wyke's essay (Chapter 11, above).

For the late-Republican background to Augustus, readers should consult P. A. Brunt's *Social Conflicts in the Roman Republic* (1971) or, for the more stout-hearted, his more detailed *The Fall of the Roman Republic and Related Essays* (1988). E. S. Gruen's *The Last Generation of the Roman Republic* (1974; rev. paperback edn, 1995) is stimulating and was composed in the tumultuous years of student protest at Berkeley in the late 1960s and 1970s, but pays too little attention to the role that Rome's overseas Empire played in the history of that period (see Michael H. Crawford in *JRS* 67 (1976), 214–217, a review article provocatively entitled "Hamlet without the Prince"). Two recent companion volumes of essays on the Roman Republic are also valuable: Harriet Flower's *Cambridge Companion to the Roman Republic* (2004) and R. Morstein-Marx and N. Rosenstein's (Blackwell) *Companion to the Roman Republic* (2006). M. H. Crawford's *The Roman Republic* (1978; 2nd edn 1992) provides a lively analytical narrative, with much primary evidence quoted (in translation) and woven into the account. It is useful for those studying Augustus to have some understanding in particular of the political career of Julius Caesar. In addition to material in the works just cited, note M. Gelzer, *Caesar: Politician and Statesman* (first published in German in 1921; English trans. of the 6th edn, 1968), Z. Yavetz, *Julius Caesar and his Public Image* (1983), and C. Meier, *Caesar* (first published in German in 1982, with the important review by E. Badian in *Gnomon* 62 [1990], 22–39, the value of which is acknowledged by Meier in later editions of his work, including the English translation of the 3rd edn, 1995).

To understand Augustus' importance for subsequent Roman imperial history, readers will need to consult works such as C. M. Wells, *The Roman Empire* (1984; 2nd edn, 1992), P. Garnsey and R. P. Saller, *The Roman Empire: Economy, Society, and Culture* (1987), M. Goodman, *The Roman World 44 B.C.–A.D. 180* (1997), or A. Garzetti, *From Tiberius to the Antonines* (1974). Fergus Millar's monumental 650-page *The Emperor in the Roman World, 31 BC–AD 337* (1977; rev. edn, 1992) presents an influential (and massively documented) view of how the emperor actually worked and how he related to key groups throughout the Empire.

In addition, readers will want to familiarise themselves with two of the most stimulating recent studies on the age of Augustus: Paul Zanker's abundantly illustrated *The Power of Images in the Age of Augustus* (German original 1987, first trans. into English in 1988) and Claude Nicolet's *Space, Geography, and Politics in the Early Roman Empire* (French original 1988; English trans. 1991). The essays in *Caesar Augustus: Seven Aspects* (eds F. Millar and E. Segal, 1984) and *Between Republic and Empire: Interpretations of Augustus and his Principate* (eds K. A. Raaflaub and M. Toher, 1990) cover many important topics (mainly historical, but some literary) and are required reading. Karl Galinsky's *Augustan Culture: An Interpretive Introduction* (1996) provides a wide-ranging, and very well-illustrated, survey of the literature, art, architecture, and culture of the Augustan age.

Changes occurred in so many areas of Roman life under Augustus that many works that cover Roman social, economic, and religious history over a wider timeframe include important insights on the first *princeps*. So, for instance, Susan Treggiari's *Roman Marriage* (1991), various contributions on Rome in the *Cambridge Economic History of the Greco-Roman World*, edited by Walter Scheidel, Ian Morris, and Richard Saller (2007, especially chs 19–23), or the collaborative work by Mary Beard, John North, and

Simon Price on *Religions of Rome* (1998, especially ch. 4) all contain valuable discussion of key developments that occurred under Augustus. Works on the Roman army, such as Lawrence Keppie's *The Making of the Roman Army* (1984), highlight the Augustan age as a period of crucial change in Rome's military organisation. Archaeological studies of the city of Rome – for example, Diane Favro's *The Urban Image of Augustan Rome* (1996) or the more technical topographical work of Lothar Haselberger and his team, *Mapping Augustan Rome* (2002) and *Urbem adornare ... Rome's Urban Metamorphosis under Augustus* (2007) – illustrate the radical ways in which the urban centre was transformed under Augustus, on which readers may also usefully consult the succinct and well-illustrated *Augustan Rome* by Andrew Wallace-Hadrill (1993) and the helpful review article by John R. Patterson, "The City of Rome: From Republic to Empire," *JRS* 82 (1992), 186–215.

John Rich's article on Augustan imperialism, first published in 2003 (Chapter 4, above), would not have been possible without the foundation laid previously by two triptychs of studies by Peter Brunt and Erich Gruen: Brunt's "Augustan Imperialism," "Laus Imperii," and "Roman Imperial Allusions," which all appear in his volume of collected papers *Roman Imperial Themes* (1990), although the original versions of the first two were published much earlier, in 1963 and 1978 respectively; and Gruen's "Augustus and the Ideology of War and Peace" (1985), "The Imperial Policy of Augustus" (1990), and "The Expansion of the Empire under Augustus" (1996). The far-reaching transformations in Rome's provinces – in terms both of their administration by Rome and of their local economic, social, and cultural frameworks – have been highlighted in a whole host of regional studies, but also in works that take a more synoptic view of how the Roman Empire operated during the principate of Augustus and beyond. Some of the most stimulating regional studies include Glen Bowersock's *Augustus and the Greek World* (1965), Greg Woolf's *Becoming Roman: The Origins of Provincial Civilization in Gaul* (1998), Susan Alcock's *Graecia Capta: The Landscapes of Roman Greece* (1993), and, more recently, Livia Capponi's *Augustan Egypt: The Creation of a Roman Province* (2005) and Antony Spawforth's *Greece and the Augustan Cultural Revolution: Greek Culture in the Roman World* (2012); note also the essays in T. F. C. Blagg and M. Millett, eds, *The Early Roman Empire in the West* (1990), S. Alcock, ed., *The Early Roman Empire in the East* (1997), and E. Fentress, ed., *Romanization and the City* (2000), as well as the series of geographically organised chapters in volume X of CAH^2, including R. J. A. Wilson on Sicily, Sardinia, and Corsica; G. Alföldy on Spain; C. Goudineau on Gaul; J. Wacher on Britain; C. Rüger on Germany; H. Wolff on Raetia; J. J. Wilkes on the Danubian and Balkan provinces; C. R. Whittaker on North Africa; J. Reynolds and J. A. Lloyd on Cyrene; B. M. Levick on Greece and Asia Minor; A. K. Bowman on Egypt; D. Kennedy on Syria; and M. Goodman on Judaea. For broader synoptic works, F. Millar's *The*

Roman Empire and its Neighbours (2nd edn, 1981) is still valuable, although now outdated in terms of its archaeological evidence; see also A. W. Lintott, *Imperium Romanum: Politics and Administration* (1993), especially ch. 7; R. MacMullen, *Romanization in the Age of Augustus* (2000); and C. Ando, *Imperial Ideology and Provincial Loyalty in the Roman Empire* (2000), a closely argued, amply documented, and breathtakingly wide-ranging study. An excellent short account of Augustus' impact on the provinces is to be found in F. Millar's article, "State and Subject: The Impact of Monarchy" (1984), a slightly revised version of which is found in volume 1 of Millar's collected papers, *The Roman Republic and the Augustan Revolution* (2002).

Bibliography

Albrecht, M. von. 1997. *A History of Roman Literature from Livius Andronicus to Boethius*. 2 vols. Leiden, New York, and Cologne.
Alcock, S., ed. 1997. *The Early Roman Empire in the East*. Oxford.
Alföldy, G. 1993. "Two Principes: Augustus and Sir Ronald Syme," *Athenaeum* 81: 101–122.
Alföldy, G. 2000. "Das neue Edikt des Augustus aus El Bierzo in Hispanien," *ZPE* 131: 177–205.
Allen, B. M. 1937. *Augustus Caesar*. London.
Ando, C. 2000. *Imperial Ideology and Provincial Loyalty in the Roman Empire*. Berkeley, Los Angeles, and London.
Ando, C. 2006. "The Administration of the Provinces," in Potter 2006: 177–192.
Ando, C. 2011. "From Republic to Empire," in M. Peachin, ed., *The Oxford Handbook of Social Relations in the Roman World*. Oxford. 37–66.
André, J. M. 1974. *Le siècle d'Auguste*. Paris.
Atkinson, K. M. T. 1960. "Constitutional and Legal Aspects of the Trials of Marcus Primus and Varro Murena," *Historia* 9: 440–473.
Badian, E. 1968. *Roman Imperialism in the Late Republic* (2nd edn). Oxford.
Badian, E. 1982. "'Crisis Theories' and the Beginning of the Principate," in G. Wirth, ed., *Romanitas – Christianitas. Festschrift für J. Straub*. Berlin and New York. 18–41.
Badian, E. 1986. "The Young Betti and the Practice of History," in G. Crifò, ed., *Costituzione romana e crisi della Repubblica. Atti del convegno su E. Betti (25–26 ottobre 1984)*. Naples. 73–96.
Badian, E. 1993. "Livy and Augustus," in W. Schuller, ed., *Livius. Aspekte seines Werkes* (Xenia 31). Konstanz. 9–38.
Baker, G. P. 1937. *Augustus: The Golden Age of Rome*. London.
Barceló, P. A. 2002. "Augustus und die Macht der Worte," *ZRGG* 54.2: 97–121.
Barchiesi, A. 1994. *Il poeta e il principe. Ovidio e il discorso augusteo*. Rome (English tr. = Barchiesi 1997).

Barchiesi, A. 1997. *The Poet and the Prince: Ovid and Augustan Discourse.* Berkeley, Los Angeles, and London.
Barnes, T. D. 1974. "The Victories of Augustus," *JRS* 64: 21–26.
Barrera, J. L. de la and Trillmich, W. 1996. "Eine Wiederholung der Aeneas-Gruppe vom Forum Augustum samt ihrer Inschrift in Mérida (Spanien)," *RM* 103: 119–138.
Barrett, A. A. 2002. *Livia: First Lady of Imperial Rome.* New Haven and London.
Bartman, E. 1999. *Portraits of Livia: Imaging the Imperial Woman in Augustan Rome.* Cambridge.
Barton, T. 1995. "Augustus and Capricorn: Astrological Polyvalency and Imperial Rhetoric," *JRS* 85: 33–51.
Beard, M. 2007. *The Roman Triumph.* Cambridge, MA.
Beard, M., North, J., and Price, S. 1998. *Religions of Rome. 1. A History.* Cambridge.
Bellemore, J., ed. and trans. 1984. *Nicolaus of Damascus: Life of Augustus.* Bristol.
Bénabou, M. 1976. *La résistance africaine à la romanisation.* Paris.
Bengtson, H. 1981. *Kaiser Augustus. Sein Leben und seine Zeit.* Munich.
Béranger, J. 1953. *Recherches sur l'aspect idéologique du principat* (Schweizerische Beiträge zur Altertumswissenschaft 6). Basel.
Béranger, J. 1958. "L'accession d'Auguste et l'idéologie du 'privatus'," *Palaeologia* 7: 1–11 (reprinted in Béranger 1973: 243–258).
Béranger, J. 1973. *Principatus: Études de notions et d'histoire politiques dans l'Antiquité gréco-romaine.* Geneva.
Betti, E. 1982. *La crisi della repubblica e la genesi del principato in Roma* (ed. G. Crifò, intro. E. Gabba). Rome (a collection of essays originally published 1913–1915).
Binder, G., ed. 1987. *Saeculum Augustum. I. Herrschaft und Gesellschaft* (Wege der Forschung 266). Darmstadt.
Binder, G., ed. 1988. *Saeculum Augustum. II. Religion und Literatur* (Wege der Forschung 512). Darmstadt.
Binder, G., ed. 1991. *Saeculum Augustum. III. Kunst und Bildersprache* (Wege der Forschung 632). Darmstadt.
Birkenfeld, G. 1944. *Leben und Taten des Caesar Augustus.* Berlin.
Blagg, T. F. C. and Millett, M., eds. 1990. *The Early Roman Empire in the West.* Oxford.
Bleicken, J. 1990. *Zwischen Republik und Prinzipat. Zum Charakter des Zweiten Triumvirats* (Abh. Ak. Wiss. Göttingen, Phil.-hist. Kl., 3.Folge, no. 185). Göttingen.
Bleicken, J. 1998. *Augustus. Eine Biographie.* Berlin.
Boschung, D. 1993. *Die Bildnisse des Augustus* (Das römische Herrscherbild 2). Berlin.
Boschung, D. 2003. "Die stadtrömischen Monumente des Augustus und ihre Rezeption im Reich," in P. Noelke, ed., *Romanisation und Resistenz*

in *Plastik, Architektur und Inschriften des Imperium Romanum. Neue Funde und Forschungen.* Mainz. 1–12.
Bosworth, A. B. 1972. "Asinius Pollio and Augustus," *Historia* 21: 441–473.
Bowersock, G. W. 1965. *Augustus and the Greek World.* Oxford (ch. 7 reprinted here as Chapter 15).
Bowersock, G. W. 1969. *Greek Sophists in the Roman Empire.* Oxford.
Bowersock, G. W. 1973. "Syria under Vespasian," *JRS* 63: 133–140.
Bowersock, G. W. 1978. *Julian the Apostate.* Cambridge, MA.
Bowersock, G. W. 1983. *Roman Arabia.* Cambridge, MA.
Bowersock, G. W. 1984. "Augustus and the East: Problems of Succession," in Millar and Segal 1984: 169–188.
Bowersock, G. W. 1990a. "The Pontificate of Augustus," in Raaflaub and Toher 1990: 380–394.
Bowersock, G. W. 1990b. *Hellenism in Late Antiquity.* Cambridge.
Bowersock, G. W. 1994. "Ronald Syme (1903–1989)," *Proc. Brit. Acad.* 84: 538–563.
Bowersock, G. W. 2000. *Selected Papers on Late Antiquity.* Bari.
Bowersock, G. W. 2002. "The New Hellenism of Augustan Athens," *Annali della Scuola normale superiore di Pisa*, ser. 4a, 7.1: 1–16.
Bowman, A. K. 1996. "Provincial Administration and Taxation," in CAH^2 X: 344–370.
Bowman, A. K., Champlin, E., and Lintott, A. W., eds. 1996. *The Cambridge Ancient History* (2nd edn). X. *The Augustan Empire, 43 B.C.–A.D. 69.* Cambridge.
Bringmann, K. and Schäfer, T., eds and trans. 2002. *Augustus und die Begründung des römischen Kaisertums.* Berlin.
Brunt, P. A. 1961a. "Lex Valeria Cornelia," *JRS* 51: 71–83.
Brunt, P. A. 1961b. "Charges of Provincial Maladministration under the Early Principate," *Historia* 10: 189–223 (reprinted in Brunt 1990a: 53–95 = ch. 4).
Brunt, P. A. 1962. "The Army and the Land in the Roman Revolution," *JRS* 52: 69–86 (substantially rev., with additions, in Brunt 1988: 240–275 = ch. 5).
Brunt, P. A. 1963. Review-discussion of H. D. Meyer, *Die Aussenpolitik des Augustus und die augusteische Dichtung. JRS* 53: 170–176 (rev. as "Augustan Imperialism" in Brunt 1990a: 96–109 = ch. 5).
Brunt, P. A. 1971a. *Social Conflicts in the Roman Republic.* London.
Brunt, P. A. 1971b. *Italian Manpower, 225 B.C.–A.D. 14.* Oxford.
Brunt, P. A. 1978. "*Laus imperii,*" in P. Garnsey and C. R. Whittaker, eds, *Imperialism in the Ancient World.* Cambridge. 159–191 (revised in Brunt 1990a: 288–323 = ch. 14).
Brunt, P. A. 1982. "Augustus e la *respublica,*" in *La rivoluzione romana: inchiesta tra gli antichisti* (Biblioteca di *Labeo* 6). Naples. 236–244 (in English).

Brunt, P. A. 1984. "The Role of the Senate in the Augustan Regime," *CQ* n.s. 34: 423–444.
Brunt, P. A. 1988. *The Fall of the Roman Republic and Related Essays*. Oxford.
Brunt, P. A. 1990a. *Roman Imperial Themes*. Oxford.
Brunt, P. A. 1990b. "Augustan Imperialism," in Brunt 1990a: 96–109 (ch. 5).
Brunt, P. A. 1990c. "Roman Imperial Illusions," in Brunt 1990a: 433–480 (ch. 18).
Brunt, P. A. and Moore, J. M., eds and trans. 1967. Res Gestae Divi Augusti. *The Achievements of the Divine Augustus*. Oxford.
Bruun, C. 2003. "Roman Emperors in Popular Jargon: Searching for Contemporary Nicknames," in De Blois et al. 2003: 69–98.
Buchan, J. 1937. *Augustus*. London.
Buchner, E. 1976. "*Solarium Augusti* und *Ara Pacis*," *RM* 83: 319–365.
Buchner, E. 1980. "*Horologium Solarium Augusti*. Vorbericht über die Ausgrabungen 1979/1980," *RM* 87: 355–373.
Buchner, E. 1982. *Die Sonnenuhr des Augustus. Nachdruck aus RM 1976 und 1980 und Nachtrag über die Ausgrabung 1980/1981*. Mainz.
Cagnetta, M. 1976. "Il mito di Augusto e la rivoluzione fascista," *Quaderni di Storia* 3: 139–181.
Campbell, J. B. 1984. *The Emperor and the Roman Army 31 B.C.–A.D. 235*. Oxford.
Cardoso, J. 1996. *Um retrato de Augusto: subsídios para o estudo da sua personalidade* (2nd edn). Braga.
Carettoni, G. 1983. *Das Haus des Augustus auf dem Palatin*. Mainz.
Carter, J. M. 1970. *The Battle of Actium: The Rise and Triumph of Augustus Caesar*. London and New York.
Carter, J. M., ed. 1982. *Suetonius*: Divus Augustus. Bristol.
Champion, C. B., ed. 2004. *Roman Imperialism: Readings and Sources*. Oxford.
Chilver, G. E. F. 1950. "Augustus and the Roman Constitution 1939–50," *Historia* 1: 408–435.
Chisholm, K. and Ferguson, J., eds. 1981. *Rome, the Augustan Age: A Sourcebook*. Oxford.
Christ, K. and Gabba, E., eds. 1989. *Römische Geschichte und Zeitgeschichte in der deutschen und italienischen Altertumswissenschaft während des 19. und 20. Jahrhunderts. I. Caesar und Augustus* (Biblioteca di *Athenaeum* 12). Como.
Ciccotti, E. 1938. *Profilo di Augusto, con un'appendice su le leggi matrimoniali di Augusto*. Turin.
Coarelli, F. 1985. *Il Foro Romano. 2. Periodo repubblicano e augusteo*. Rome.
Cohen, D. 1991. "The Augustan Law on Adultery: The Social and Cultural Context," in D. I. Kertzer and R. P. Saller, eds, *The Family in Italy from*

Antiquity to the Present. New Haven and London. 109–126.
Conte, G. B. 1994. *Latin Literature: A History* (trans. J. B. Solodow; rev. D. Fowler and G. W. Most). Baltimore (originally published as *Letteratura Latina: manuale storico dalle origini alla fine dell' impero romano*, Florence, 1987).
Cook, S. A., Adcock, F. E., and Charlesworth, M. P., eds. 1934. *The Cambridge Ancient History.* X. *The Augustan Empire, 44 B.C.–A.D. 70.* Cambridge.
Cooley, A. E. 2009. *Res Gestae Divi Augusti: Text, Translation and Commentary.* Cambridge.
Cooley, M. G. L., ed. 2003. *The Age of Augustus* (LACTOR 17). London.
Corbier, M. 1995. "Male Power and Legitimacy through Women: The *domus Augusta* under the Julio-Claudians," in R. Hawley and B. Levick, eds, *Women in Antiquity: New Assessments.* London and New York. 178–193.
Cotton, H. M. and Yakobson, A. 2002. "*Arcanum imperii*: The Powers of Augustus," in G. Clark and T. Rajak, eds, *Philosophy and Power in the Graeco-Roman World: Essays in Honour of Miriam Griffin.* Oxford. 193–209.
Crawford, M. H. 1978. *The Roman Republic.* London (2nd edn, 1992).
Crawford, M. H. 2003. "Land and People in Republican Italy," in D. C. Braund, E. Gee, and C. Gill, eds. *Myth, History, and Culture in Republican Rome: Studies in Honour of T. P. Wiseman.* Exeter. 56–72.
Crook, J. A. 1996a. "Political History, 30 B.C. to A.D. 14," in CAH^2 X: 70–112.
Crook, J. A. 1996b. "Augustus: Power, Authority, Achievement," in CAH^2 X: 113–146.
De Blois, L., Erdkamp, P., Hekster, O., de Kleijn, G., and Mols, S. eds. 2003. *The Representation and Perception of Roman Imperial Power: Proceedings of the Third Workshop of the International Network, Impact of Empire (Roman Empire, c. 200 B.C.–A.D. 476), Netherlands Institute in Rome, March 20–23, 2002.* Amsterdam.
De Francisci, P. 1938. "La costituzione augustea," in *Augustus: studi in occasione del bimillenario augusteo.* Rome. 61–100.
De Martino, F. 1936. *Lo stato di Augusto. Introduzione.* Naples.
De Visscher, F. 1940. *Les édits d'Auguste découverts à Cyrène.* Louvain and Paris.
Donderer, M. 1995. "Zu den Häusern des Kaisers Augustus," *MEFRA* 107: 621–660.
Drew-Bear, T. and Scheid, J. 2005. "La copie des *Res Gestae* d'Antioche de Pisidie," *ZPE* 154: 217–260.
Duval, N. ed. 1977. *L'onomastique latine.* Paris.
Earl, D. C. 1968. *The Age of Augustus.* London and New York.
Eck, W. 1970. *Senatoren von Vespasian bis Hadrian. Prosopographische Untersuchungen mit Einschluss der Jahres- und Provinzialfasten der*

Statthalter (Vestigia 13). Munich.
Eck, W. 1979. *Die Staatliche Organisation Italiens in der Hohen Kaiserzeit* (Vestigia 28). Munich.
Eck, W. 1984. "Senatorial Self-Representation: Developments in the Augustan Period," in Millar and Segal 1984: 129–167.
Eck, W. 1986. "Augustus' administrative Reformen: Pragmatismus oder systematisches Planen?" *Acta Classica* 29: 105–120 (rev. and expanded in Eck 1995: 83–102; trans. here as Chapter 7).
Eck, W. 1995. *Die Verwaltung des römischen Reiches in der hohen Kaiserzeit* 1. Basel.
Eck, W. 1996. *Tra epigrafia, prosopografia e archeologia. Scritti scelti, rielaborati ed aggiornati* (Vetera 10). Rome.
Eck, W. 1997a. *Die Verwaltung des römischen Reiches in der Hohen Kaiserzeit* 2. Basel.
Eck, W. 1997b. "Provinz – ihre Definition unter politisch-administrativem Aspekt," in Eck 1997a: 167–185.
Eck, W. 1998. *Augustus und seine Zeit*. Munich (English trans. = Eck 2003).
Eck, W. 2003. *The Age of Augustus* (trans. D. L. Schneider). Oxford (2nd expanded edn, 2007).
Eck, W. 2008. "Augustus," in A. A. Barrett, ed., *Lives of the Caesars*. Oxford. 7–37.
Eck, W., Caballos Rufino, A., and Fernández Gómez, F. 1996. *Das Senatus Consultum de Cn. Pisone patre* (Vestigia 48). Munich.
Eder, W. 1990. "Augustus and the Power of Tradition: The Augustan Principate as Binding Link between Republic and Empire," in Raaflaub and Toher 1990: 71–122.
Edmondson, J., ed. and trans. 1992. *Dio: The Julio-Claudians. Selections from Books 58-63 of the* Roman History *of Cassius Dio* (LACTOR 15). London.
Edmondson, J. 2006. "Cities and Urban Life in the Western Provinces of the Roman Empire, 30 BCE–250 CE," in Potter 2006: 250–280.
Edwards, C. 1993. *The Politics of Immorality in Ancient Rome*. Cambridge.
Ehrenberg, V. and Jones, A. H. M., eds. 1949. *Documents Illustrating the Reigns of Augustus and Tiberius*. Oxford (2nd edn, 1955; reprinted, with Addenda by D. L. Stockton, 1976).
Elsner, J. 1991. "Cult and Sculpture: Sacrifice in the Ara Pacis Augustae," *JRS* 81: 50–61.
Elsner, J. 1996. "Inventing *imperium*: Texts and the Propaganda of Monuments in Augustan Rome," in J. Elsner, ed., *Art and Text in Roman Culture*. Cambridge. 32–53.
Étienne, R., ed. 1970. *Le siècle d'Auguste: Choix de textes avec introduction et commentaire*. Paris.
Everitt, A. 2006. *The First Emperor: Caesar Augustus and the Triumph of*

Rome. London (= *Augustus: The Life of Rome's First Emperor*. New York).
Fantham, E. 1996. *Roman Literary Culture: From Cicero to Apuleius*. Baltimore and London.
Fantham, E. 2006. *Julia Augusti: The Emperor's Daughter*. London and New York.
Favro, D. 1996. *The Urban Image of Augustan Rome*. Cambridge.
Feeney, D. 2007. *Caesar's Calendar: Ancient Time and the Beginnings of History*. Berkeley, Los Angeles, and London.
Fentress, E., ed. 2000. *Romanization and the City: Creation, Transformations, and Failures* (*JRA* Suppl. 38). Portsmouth, RI.
Ferrary, J.-L. 1977–1979. "Recherches sur la législation de Saturninus et de Glaucia," *MEFRA* 89: 619–660; 91: 85–134.
Ferrary, J.-L. 1984. "L'archéologie du *De re publica* (2, 2, 4–37, 63): Cicéron entre Polybe et Platon," *JRS* 74: 87–98.
Ferrary, J.-L. 1988. *Philhellénisme et impérialisme: Aspects idéologiques de la conquête romaine du monde hellénistique* (BEFAR 271). Rome.
Ferrary, J.-L. 2001. "À propos des pouvoirs d'Auguste," *Cahiers du Centre Glotz* 12: 101–154 (trans. here as Chapter 3).
Ferrary, J.-L. 2003. "*Res publica restituta* et les pouvoirs d'Auguste," in S. Franchet d'Espèrey, V. Fromentin, S. Gotteland, and J.-M. Roddaz, eds, *Fondements et crises du pouvoir*. Bordeaux. 419–428.
Firth, J. B. 1902. *Augustus Caesar and the Organization of the Empire of Rome*. London and New York.
Fishwick, D. 1987. *The Imperial Cult in the Latin West: Studies in the Ruler Cult of the Western Provinces of the Roman Empire*. I. Leiden.
Fittschen, K. and Zanker, P. 1985. *Katalog der römischen Porträts in den Capitolinischen Museen und den anderen kommunalen Sammlungen der Stadt Rom. 1. Kaiser- und Prinzenbildnisse*. Mainz.
Fraschetti, A. 1990. *Roma e il principe*. Rome.
Fraschetti, A. 1998. *Augusto*. Rome and Bari.
Frei-Stolba, R. 1998. "Recherches sur la position juridique et sociale de Livie, l'épouse d'Auguste," in R. Frei-Stolba and A. Bielman, eds, *Femmes et vie publique dans l'Antiquité gréco-romaine*. Lausanne. 1.65–89.
Gabba, E. 1973. *Esercito e società nella tarda repubblica romana*. Florence (English trans. = Gabba 1976).
Gabba, E. 1976. *Republican Rome: The Army and the Allies* (trans. P. J. Cuff). Oxford.
Gabba, E. 1984. "The Historians and Augustus," in Millar and Segal 1984: 61–88.
Gabba, E. 1991. "L'impero di Augusto," in *Storia di Roma. II. L'impero mediterraneo. II. I principi e il mondo*. Turin. 9–28.
Gagé, J. 1930a. "Romulus–Augustus," *MEFRA* 47: 138–181.
Gagé, J. 1930b. "La Victoria Augusti et les auspices de Tibère," *Rev. Arch.* 5th ser., 32: 1–35.

Gagé, J. 1931. "Les sacerdoces d'Auguste et ses réformes religieuses," *MEFRA* 48: 75–108.
Gagé, J. 1932. "Un thème de l'art impérial romain: la victoire d'Auguste," *MEFRA* 49: 61–92.
Gagé, J., ed. 1935. *Res Gestae divi Augusti ex monumentis Ancyrano et Antiocheno latinis, Ancyrano et Apollonensi graecis.* Strasbourg.
Gagé, J. 1936. "De César à Auguste. Où en est le problème des origines du Principat? À propos du *César* de M. J. Carcopino," *Rev. Hist.* 177: 279–342.
Galinsky, K. 1981. "Augustus' Legislation on Morals and Marriage," *Philologus* 125: 126–144.
Galinsky, K. 1992. "Venus, Polysemy, and the Ara Pacis Augustae," *AJA* 96: 457–475.
Galinsky, K. 1996. *Augustan Culture: An Interpretive Introduction.* Princeton.
Galinksy, K., ed. 2005a. *The Cambridge Companion to the Age of Augustus.* Cambridge.
Galinsky, K. 2005b. "Introduction," in Galinsky 2005a: 1–9.
Galsterer, H. 1990. "A Man, a Book, and a Method: Sir Ronald Syme's *Roman Revolution* after Fifty Years," in Raaflaub and Toher 1990: 1–20.
Gardthausen, V. E. 1891–1904. *Augustus und seine Zeit.* 2 vols. Leipzig.
Garnsey, P. and Saller, R. P. 1987. *The Roman Empire: Economy, Society, and Culture.* London.
Gauthier, P. 1985. *Les cités grecques et leurs bienfaiteurs (IVe–Ier siècle avant J.-C.) (BCH* Suppl. 12). Paris.
Giovannini, A. 1999. "Les pouvoirs d'Auguste de 27 à 23 av. J.-C. Une relecture de l'ordonnance de Kymè de l'an 27 (IK 5, no. 17)," *ZPE* 124: 95–105.
Giovannini, A., ed. 2000. *La révolution romaine après Ronald Syme: bilans et perspectives* (Entretiens Hardt 46). Vandœuvres/Geneva.
Girardet, K. M. 2000. "*Imperium 'maius'*: politische und verfassungsrechtliche Aspekte. Versuch einer Klärung," in Giovannini 2000: 167–227.
Gleason, M. 2006. "Greek Cities under Roman Rule," in Potter 2006: 228–249.
Griffin, J. 1984. "Augustus and the Poets: 'Caesar qui cogere posset'," in Millar and Segal 1984: 189–218.
Griffin, M. T. 1997. "The Senate's Story," *JRS* 87: 249–263.
Grimal, P. 1955. *Le siècle d'Auguste* (Que sais-je? 576). Paris.
Gros, P. 1976. *Aurea Templa: recherches sur l'architecture religieuse de Rome à l'époque d'Auguste* (BEFAR 231). Rome.
Gros, P. 1987. "Un programme augustéen: le centre monumental de la colonie d'Arles," *JdI* 102: 339–363.
Gros, P. 2006. "Le 'modèle' du forum d'Auguste et ses applications italiques

ou provinciales. État de la question après les dernières découvertes," in Navarro Caballero and Roddaz 2006: 115–127.
Gruen, E. S. 1984. *The Hellenistic World and the Coming of Rome*. Berkeley.
Gruen, E. S. 1985. "Augustus and the Ideology of War and Peace," in Winkes 1985: 51–72.
Gruen, E. S. 1990. "The Imperial Policy of Augustus," in Raaflaub and Toher 1990: 395–416.
Gruen, E. S. 1996. "The Expansion of the Empire under Augustus," in *CAH*² X: 147–197.
Gruen, E. S. 2005. "Augustus and the Making of the Principate," in Galinsky 2005a: 33–51.
Gurval, R. A. 1995. *Actium and Augustus: The Politics and Emotions of Civil War*. Ann Arbor.
Habinek, T. and Schiesaro, A., eds. 1997. *The Roman Cultural Revolution*. Cambridge.
Hammond, M. 1968. *The Augustan Principate in Theory and Practice during the Julio-Claudian Period* (rev. edn, with additions). Cambridge, MA (original edn, 1933).
Harris, W. V. 1979. *War and Imperialism in Republican Rome, 327–70 B.C.* Oxford.
Harrison, S. J. 1989. "Augustus, the Poets, and the *spolia opima*," *CQ* n.s. 39: 408–411.
Haselberger, L. 2007. Urbem adornare. *Die Stadt Rom und ihre Gestaltumwandlung unter Augustus. Rome's Urban Metamorphosis under Augustus* (*JRA* Suppl. 64). Portsmouth, RI.
Haselberger, L., Romano, D. G., Dumser, E. A., et al. 2002. *Mapping Augustan Rome* (*JRA* Suppl. 50). Portsmouth, RI (with website http://digitalaugustanrome.org/).
Haynes, D. L. 1975. *The Portland Vase* (2nd edn). London (1st edn, 1964).
Hesberg, H. von and Panciera, S. 1994. *Das Mausoleum des Augustus. Der Bau und seine Inschriften* (Abh. Bayer. Ak. Wiss., Phil.-hist. Kl., N.F. 108). Munich.
Heslin, P. 2007. "Augustus, Domitian, and the So-called Horologium Augusti," *JRS* 97: 1–20.
Hölscher, T. 1967. *Victoria Romana. Archäologische Untersuchungen zur Geschichte und Wesensart der römischen Siegesgöttin von den Anfängen bis zum Ende des 3. Jhs. n. Chr.* Mainz.
Hölscher, T. 1984. *Staatsdenkmal und Publikum. Vom Untergang der Republik bis zur Festigung des Kaisertums in Rom* (Xenia 9). Konstanz.
Hölscher, T. 1985. "Denkmäler der Schlacht von Actium – Propaganda und Resonanz," *Klio* 67.1: 81–102 (trans. here as Chapter 10).
Hölscher, T. 1987. *Römische Bildsprache als semantisches System*. Heidelberg (English trans. = Hölscher 2004).
Hölscher, T. 2000. "Augustus und die Macht der Archäologie," in

Giovannini 2000: 237–281.
Hölscher, T. 2004. *The Language of Images in Roman Art* (trans. A. Snodgrass and A. Künzl-Snodgrass, foreword J. Elsner). Cambridge.
Hönn, K. 1937. *Augustus und seine Zeit*. Vienna.
Hofter, M., Lewandowski, V., Martin, H. G. et al., eds. 1988. *Kaiser Augustus und die verlorene Republik. Eine Ausstellung in Martin-Gropius-Bau, Berlin 7. Juni–14. August 1988: Berlin – Kulturstadt Europas 1988*. Berlin.
Holland, R. 2004. *Augustus: Godfather of Europe*. Stroud.
Holmes, T. Rice. 1923. *The Roman Republic and the Founder of the Empire*. 3 vols. Oxford.
Holmes, T. Rice. 1928–1931. *The Architect of the Roman Empire*. 2 vols. Oxford.
Homo, L. 1935. *Auguste, 63 av. J.-C.–14 ap. J.-C.* Paris.
Hopkins, K. 1978. *Conquerors and Slaves* (Sociological Studies in Roman History 1). Cambridge.
Horden, P. and Purcell, N. 2000. *The Corrupting Sea: A Study of Mediterranean History*. Oxford.
Hurlet, F. 1997. *Les collègues du prince sous Auguste et Tibère: de la légalité républicaine à la légitimité dynastique* (CEFR 227). Rome.
Iacopi, I. 2007. *La casa di Augusto: le pitture*. Milan.
Jones, A. H. M. 1951. "The *imperium* of Augustus," *JRS* 41: 112–119 (reprinted in Jones 1960a: 1–17).
Jones, A. H. M. 1955. "The Elections under Augustus," *JRS* 45: 9–21 (reprinted in Jones 1960a: 29–50).
Jones, A. H. M. 1960a. *Studies in Roman Government and Law*. Oxford.
Jones, A. H. M. 1960b. "The Censorial Powers of Augustus," in Jones 1960a: 19–26.
Jones, A. H. M. 1970. *Augustus*. London.
Judge, E. A. 1974. "Res publica restituta: A Modern Illusion?," in J. A. S. Evans, ed., *Polis and Imperium: Studies in Honour of E. Togo Salmon*. Toronto. 279–311.
Kähler, H. 1991. "Die Gemma Augustea," in Binder 1991: 303–307.
Kajanto, I. 1965. *The Latin Cognomina* (CommHumLit 36.2). Helsinki.
Kajava, M. 1994. *Roman Female Praenomina. Studies in the Nomenclature of Roman Women* (Acta Instituti Romani Finlandiae 14). Rome.
Keay, S. J. and Terrenato, N., eds. 2001. *Italy and the West: Comparative Issues in Romanization*. Oxford.
Kennedy, D. F. 1992. "'Augustan' and 'Anti-Augustan': Reflections on Terms of Reference," in Powell 1992: 26–58.
Kenney, E. J., ed. 1982. *The Cambridge History of Classical Literature. 2. Latin Literature*. Cambridge.
Keppie, L. J. F. 1983. *Colonisation and Veteran Settlement in Italy, 47–14 B.C.* London.
Keppie, L. J. F. 1984. *The Making of the Roman Army: From Republic to*

Empire. London.
Keppie, L. J. F. 1996. "The Army and the Navy," in *CAH*² X: 371–396 (reprinted in Keppie 2000: 20–49, with additional bibliography).
Keppie, L. J. F. 2000. *Legions and Veterans: Roman Army Papers 1971–2000* (Mavors Roman Army Researches 12). Stuttgart.
Kienast, D. 1982. *Augustus. Prinzeps und Monarch*. Darmstadt (3rd edn, 1999).
Kienast, D. 2004. *Römische Kaisertabelle. Grundzüge einer römischen Kaiserchronologie* (3rd edn). Darmstadt (1st edn, 1990).
Kleiner, D. E. E. 1978. "The Great Friezes of the Ara Pacis Augustae: Greek Sources, Roman Derivatives and Roman Social Policy," *MEFRA* 90: 753–785.
Kleiner, D. E. E. 1992. *Roman Sculpture*. New Haven.
Koenen, L. 1970. "Die 'laudatio funebris' des Augustus für Agrippa aus einem neuen Papyrus (P. Colon. inv.nr. 4701)," *ZPE* 5: 217–283.
Koeppel, G. M. 1987. "Die historischen Reliefs der römischen Kaiserzeit. V. Ara Pacis Augustae. 1," *Bonner Jahrbücher* 187: 101–157.
Koeppel, G. M. 1988. "Die historischen Reliefs der römischen Kaiserzeit. V. Ara Pacis Augustae. 2," *Bonner Jahrbücher* 188: 97–106.
Koortbojian, M. 2006. "The Bringer of Victory: Imagery and Institutions at the Advent of Empire," in S. Dillon and K. E. Welch, eds, *Representations of War in Ancient Rome*. Cambridge. 184–217.
Kornemann, E. 1936. *Augustus. Der Mann und sein Werk (im lichte der deutschen Forschung)*. Breslau.
Kraft, K. 1969. *Zur Münzprägung des Augustus*. Wiesbaden.
Kuttner, A. L. 1995. *Dynasty and Empire in the Age of Augustus: The Case of the Boscoreale Cups*. Berkeley.
Lacey, W. K. 1996. *Augustus and the Principate: The Evolution of the System*. Leeds.
Laffi, U. 1967. "Le iscrizioni relative all'introduzione nel 9 a.C. del nuovo calendario della Provincia d'Asia," *Studi Classici e Orientali* 16: 5–98.
La Rocca, E. 1987. "L'adesione senatoriale al 'consensus': i modi della propaganda augustea e tiberiana nei monumenti 'in Circo Flaminio'," in *L'Urbs: espace urbain et histoire Ier siècle av. J.-C.–IIIe siècle apr. J.-C.* (CEFR 98). Rome. 347–372.
La Rocca, E. 2001. "La nuova imagine dei fori Imperiali: appunti in margine agli scavi," *RM* 108: 171–213.
Last, H. M. 1934. "The Social Policy of Augustus," in *CAH* X: 425–464.
Last, H. M. 1947. "*Imperium maius*: A Note," *JRS* 37: 157–164.
Last, H. M. 1951. "On the 'tribunicia potestas' of Augustus," *Rendiconti del Istituto Lombardo di scienze e lettere, Classe di lettere* 84: 93–110.
Laugier, J.-L., Nicolet, C., Petit, P., and Ville, G. 1967. *Rome au temps d'Auguste*. Paris.
Le Roux, P. 2001. "L'*Edictum de Paemeiobrigensibus*: un document fabriqué?" *Minima Epigraphica et Papyrologica* 4, fasc. 6: 331–364.

Leveau, P. 1984. *Caesarea de Maurétanie: une ville romaine et ses campagnes* (CEFR 70). Paris.
Levi, M. A. 1933. *Ottaviano capoparte: storia politica di Roma durante le ultime lotte di supremazia*. 2 vols. Rome.
Levi, M. A. 1951. *Il tempo di Augusto*. Rome.
Levi, M. A. 1986. *Augusto e il suo tempo*. Milan (a reworking of Levi 1933 and 1951).
Levick, B. 1972. "Atrox fortuna," *CR* n.s. 22: 309–311.
Levick, B. 1975. "Julians and Claudians," *G&R* n.s. 22: 29–38.
Levick, B. 1976. *Tiberius the Politician*. London (rev. edn, 1999).
Linderski, J. 1990. "Mommsen and Syme: Law and Power in the Principate of Augustus," in Raaflaub and Toher 1990: 42–53.
Lintott, A. W. 1993. *Imperium Romanum: Politics and Administration*. London and New York.
Lott, J. B. 2004. *The Neighborhoods of Augustan Rome*. Cambridge.
Luce, T. J. 1965. "The Dating of Livy's First Decade," *TAPA* 96: 209–240.
Luce, T. J. 1977. *Livy: The Composition of his History*. Princeton.
Luce, T. J. 1990. "Livy, Augustus, and the Forum Augustum," in Raaflaub and Toher 1990: 123–138 (included in this volume as Chapter 13).
Luce, T. J. 1995. "Livy and Dionysius," *Papers of the Leeds International Latin Seminar* 8: 225–239.
Luce, T. J. 1997. *The Greek Historians*. London and New York.
Ma, J. 2000. *Antiochos III and the Cities of Western Asia Minor*. Oxford.
MacMullen, R. 2000. *Romanization in the Time of Augustus*. New Haven.
Mann, J. C. 1983. *Legionary Recruitment and Veteran Settlement during the Principate* (Institute of Archaeology, Occasional Publication 7). London.
Mantovani, D. 2008. "*Leges et iura p(opuli) R(omani) restituit*: principe e diritto in un aureo di Ottaviano," *Athenaeum* 96: 5–54.
Mashkin, N. A. 1949. *Printsipat Augusta*. Moscow. (Trans. into German as *Zwischen Republik und Kaiserreich. Ursprung und sozialer Charakter der augusteischen Prinzipats*, Leipzig 1954, and into Italian as *Il principato di Augusto*, Rome 1956.)
Massie, A. 1986. *Augustus: The Memoirs of the Emperor*. London.
Mattern, T. 2000. "Der Magna-Mater-Tempel und die augusteische Architektur in Rom," *RM* 107: 141–153.
Mattingly, D. J., ed. 1997. *Dialogues in Roman Imperialism: Power, Discourse, and Discrepant Experience in the Roman Empire* (*JRA* Suppl. 23). Portsmouth, RI.
Mattingly, D. J. 2004. "Being Roman: Expressing Identity in a Provincial Setting," *JRA* 17: 5–25
Mellor, R. 2006. *Augustus and the Creation of the Roman Empire: A Brief Discussion with Documents*. New York.
Meyer, E. 1903. "Kaiser Augustus," *Historische Zeitschrift* 91: 385–431 (reprinted in his *Kleine Schriften*, 2nd edn, Halle, 1924, I.423–474).

Meyer, E. 1918. *Caesars Monarchie und das Principat des Pompejus. Innere Geschichte Roms von 66 bis 44 v. Chr.* Stuttgart and Berlin (3rd edn, 1922).
Meyer, H. D. 1961. *Die Aussenpolitik des Augustus und die augusteische Dichtung.* Cologne.
Millar, F. 1966. "The Emperor, the Senate, and the Provinces," *JRS* 56: 156–166 (rev. version in Millar 2002: 271–291).
Millar, F. 1973. "Triumvirate and Principate," *JRS* 63: 50–67 (rev. version in Millar 2002: 241–270; included in this volume as Chapter 2).
Millar, F. 1977. *The Emperor in the Roman World, 31 BC–AD 337.* London (rev. edn, with afterword, 1992).
Millar, F. 1981. "Style Abides," *JRS* 71: 144–152.
Millar, F. 1984a. "State and Subject: The Impact of Monarchy," in Millar and Segal 1984: 37–60 (rev. version in Millar 2002: 292–313).
Millar, F. 1984b. "The Mediterranean and the Roman Revolution: Politics, War, and the Economy," *Past and Present* 102: 3–24 (rev. version in Millar 2002: 215–237).
Millar, F. 1988a. "Imperial Ideology in the Tabula Siarensis," in J. González and J. Arce, eds, *Estudios sobre la Tabula Siarensis* (*AEspA* Anejo 9). Madrid. 11–19 (revised version in Millar 2002: 350–359).
Millar, F. 1988b. "Government and Diplomacy in the Roman Empire during the First Three Centuries," *International History Review* 10: 347–377 (rev. version in Millar 2004: 195–228).
Millar, F. 1993. "Ovid and the *Domus Augusta*: Rome Seen from Tomoi," *JRS* 83: 1–17 (rev. version in Millar 2002: 321–349).
Millar, F. 2000. "The First Revolution: Imperator Caesar, 36–28 B.C.," in Giovannini 2000: 1–38.
Millar, F. 2002. *The Roman Republic and the Augustan Revolution*, eds H. M. Cotton and G. M. Rogers (Rome, the Greek World, and the East 1). Chapel Hill.
Millar, F. 2004. *Government, Society, and Culture in the Roman Empire*, eds H. M. Cotton and G. M. Rogers (Rome, the Greek World, and the East 2). Chapel Hill and London.
Millar, F. and Segal, E., eds. 1984. *Caesar Augustus: Seven Aspects.* Oxford.
Milnor, K. 2005. *Gender, Domesticity, and the Age of Augustus: Inventing Private Life.* Oxford.
Moatti, C., ed. 1998. *La mémoire perdue: recherches sur l'administration romaine* (CEFR 243). Rome.
Momigliano, A. 1938. "I problemi delle istituzioni militari di Augusto," in *Augustus: Studi in occasione del bimillenario augusteo.* Rome. 195–215.
Momigliano, A. 1940. Review of R. Syme, *The Roman Revolution. JRS* 30: 75–80.
Momigliano, A. 1962. Introduction to Italian trans. of R. Syme, *The Roman Revolution*, Turin (reprinted in A. Momigliano, *Terzo contributo alla storia degli studi classici e del mondo antico.* Rome, 1966. 729–737).

Mommsen, T. 1865. *Res Gestae divi Augusti*. Berlin (2nd edn, 1883).
Moreau, P. 2005. "La *domus Augusta* et les formations de parenté à Rome," *Cahiers du Centre Glotz* 16: 7–23.
Moretti, G. 1948. *Ara Pacis Augustae*. Rome.
Morstein-Marx, R. and Rosenstein, N. 2006. "The Transformation of the Republic," in R. Morstein-Marx and N. Rosenstein, eds, *A Companion to the Roman Republic* (Blackwell Companions to the Ancient World). Oxford. 625–637.
Münzer, F. 1920. *Römische Adelsparteien und Adelsfamilien*. Stuttgart (English trans. = Münzer 1999).
Münzer, F. 1999. *Roman Aristocratic Parties and Families* (trans. T. Ridley). Baltimore.
Murray, W. M. and Petsas, P. M. 1989. *Octavian's Campsite Memorial for the Actian War* (Transactions of the American Philosophical Society 79.4). Philadelphia.
Navarro Caballero, M. and Roddaz, J.-M., eds. 2006. *La transmission de l'idéologie impériale dans l'Occident romain*. Bordeaux and Paris.
Néraudau, J.-P. 1996. *Auguste: la brique et le marbre*. Paris.
Nicolet, C. 1976. "Le cens sénatorial sous la République et sous Auguste," *JRS* 66: 20–38.
Nicolet, C. 1984. "Augustus, Government, and the Propertied Classes," in Millar and Segal 1984: 89–128.
Nicolet, C. 1988. *L'inventaire du monde: géographie et politique aux origines de l'Empire romain*. Paris (English trans. = Nicolet 1991).
Nicolet, C. 1991. *Space, Geography, and Politics in the Early Roman Empire* (trans. H. Leclerc). Ann Arbor.
Nicolet, C., ed. 1994. *La mémoire perdue. À la recherche des archives oubliées publiques et privées de la Rome antique*. Paris.
North, J. A. 1981. "The Development of Roman Imperialism," *JRS* 71: 1–9.
Osgood, J. 2006. *Caesar's Legacy: Civil War and the Emergence of the Roman Empire*. Cambridge.
Paribeni, R. 1950. *L'età di Cesare e di Augusto* (Storia di Roma 5). Bologna.
Pelling, C. B. R. 1996. "The Triumviral Period," in *CAH*^{2} X: 1–69.
Pensabene, P. 2002. "Venticinque anni di ricerche sul Palatino: i santuari e il sistema sostruttivo dell'area sud ovest," *Archeologia classica* 53: 65–136.
Perry, J. S. 2006. *The Roman* Collegia: *The Modern Evolution of an Ancient Concept* (*Mnemosyne* Suppl. 277). Leiden and Boston.
Piganiol, A. 1937. "Les pouvoirs constitutionnels et le principat d'Auguste," *Journal des savants*: 150–166.
Pollini, J. 1987–1988. "The Findspot of the Statue of Augustus from Prima Porta," *BCom* 92: 103–108.
Pollini, J. 1993. "The Gemma Augustea. Ideology, Rhetorical Imagery, and the Creation of a Dynastic Narrative," in P. J. Holliday, ed., *Narrative and*

Event in Ancient Art. Cambridge. 258–298.
Potter, D. S., ed. 2006. *A Companion to the Roman Empire* (Blackwell Companions to the Ancient World). Oxford.
Powell, A., ed. 1992. *Roman Poetry and Propaganda in the Age of Augustus*. London.
Premerstein, A. von. 1937. *Vom Werden und Wesen des Prinzipats* (Abh. Bayer. Ak. Wiss., Phil.-hist. Kl., N.F. 15). Munich.
Price, S. R. F. 1984. *Rituals and Power: The Roman Imperial Cult in Asia Minor*. Cambridge.
Purcell, N. 1985. "Wine and Wealth in Ancient Italy," *JRS* 75: 1–19.
Purcell, N. 1986. "Livia and the Womanhood of Rome," *PCPS* n.s. 32: 78–105 (included in this volume as Chapter 5).
Purcell, N. 1990. "Maps, Lists, Money, Order, and Power," *JRS* 80: 178–182.
Purcell, N. 1995. "Literate Games: Roman Urban Society and the Game of *alea*," *Past and Present* 147: 3–37.
Purcell, N. 1996a. "Augustus," in S. Hornblower and A. J. S. Spawforth, eds. *The Oxford Classical Dictionary* (3rd edn). Oxford. 216–218.
Purcell, N. 1996b. "Rome and its Development under Augustus and his Successors," in CAH^2 X: 782–811.
Purcell, N. 2005. "Romans in the Roman World," in Galinsky 2005a: 85–105.
Raaflaub, K. 1974. *Dignitatis contentio. Studien zur Motivation und politischen Taktik im Bürgerkrieg zwischen Caesar und Pompeius* (Vestigia 20). Munich.
Raaflaub, K. 1980. "The Political Significance of Augustus' Military Reforms," in W. S. Hanson and L. J. F. Keppie, eds, *Roman Frontier Studies 1979* (BAR Int. Series 71), Oxford. III.1005–1025 (included in this volume as Chapter 6).
Raaflaub, K. 1985. *Die Entdeckung der Freiheit. Zur historischen Semantik und Gesellschaftsgeschichte eines politischen Grundbegriffes der Griechen* (Vestigia 37). Munich (rev. English version = Raaflaub 2004).
Raaflaub, K. 1987. "Die Militärreformen des Augustus und die politische Problematik des frühen Prinzipats," in Binder 1987: 246–307.
Raaflaub, K. 2004. *The Discovery of Freedom in Ancient Greece*. Chicago.
Raaflaub, K. and Samons, L. J. 1990. "Opposition to Augustus," in Raaflaub and Toher 1990: 417–454.
Raaflaub, K. and Toher, M., eds. 1990. *Between Republic and Empire: Interpretations of Augustus and his Principate*. Berkeley, Los Angeles, and Oxford.
Raditsa, L. F. 1980. "Augustus' Legislation Concerning Marriage, Procreation, Love-Affairs, and Adultery," *ANRW* II.13: 278–339.
Ramage, E. S. 1987. *The Nature and Purpose of Augustus'* Res Gestae (*Historia* Einzelschriften 54). Stuttgart.

Ramsay, W. M. and Premerstein, A. von. 1927. *Monumentum Antiochenum. Die neugefundene Aufzeichnung der Res Gestae Divi Augusti im Pisidischen Antiochia* (*Klio* Beiheft 19). Leipzig.
Rathbone, D. 1993. "Egypt, Augustus, and Roman Taxation," *Cahiers du Centre Glotz* 4: 81–112.
Rebenich, S. 2002. *Theodor Mommsen. Eine Biographie*. Munich.
Reeder, J. C. 1997a. "The Statue of Augustus from Prima Porta and the Underground Complex," in C. Deroux, ed., *Studies in Latin Literature and Roman History* 8 (Collection *Latomus* 239). Brussels. 287–308.
Reeder, J. C. 1997b. "The Statue of Augustus from Prima Porta, the Underground Complex, and the Omen of the *gallina alba*," *AJP* 118.1: 89–118.
Rehak, P. A. 2001. "Aeneas or Numa? Rethinking the Meaning of the Ara Pacis Augustae," *Art Bulletin* 83.2: 190–208.
Rehak, P. A. 2006. *Imperium and Cosmos: Augustus and the Northern Campus Martius*. Madison, WI.
Rehrmann, F. A. 1937. *Kaiser Augustus, Neuschöpfer Roms, Retter des römischen Reiches und der abendländischen Kultur, Ideal eines genialen und sozialen Friedensfürsten. Jubiläumsschrift zum 2000 jährigen Geburtstage des ersten römischen Kaisers am 23. September 1937*. Hildesheim.
Reinhold, M., ed. 1978. *The Golden Age of Augustus* (Aspects of Antiquity). Toronto.
Reinhold, M. and Swan, P. M. 1990. "Cassius Dio's Assessment of Augustus," in Raaflaub and Toher 1990: 155–173.
Renucci, P. 2003. *Auguste le révolutionnaire*. Paris.
Reynolds, J. M. 1982. *Aphrodisias and Rome* (*JRS* Monographs 1). London.
Riccobono, S. ed. 1945. *Acta divi Augusti. Pars prior. Res Gestae divi Augusti ex monumentis Ancyrano, Antiocheno, Apolloniensi, graece et latine*. Rome.
Rich, J. W. 1989. "Dio on Augustus," in A. Cameron, ed., *History as Text: The Writing of Ancient History*. London. 86–110.
Rich, J. W., ed. and trans. 1990. *Cassius Dio: The Augustan Settlement (Roman History 53–55.9)*. Warminster.
Rich, J. W. 1996. "Augustus and the *spolia opima*," *Chiron* 26: 85–127.
Rich, J. W. 1998. "Augustus's Parthian Honours, the Temple of Mars Ultor, and the Arch in the Forum Romanum," *PBSR* 66: 71–128.
Rich, J. W. 2002. Review of M. Spannagel, *Exemplaria Principis*. BMCR 2002.03.21.
Rich, J. W. 2003. "Augustus, War and Peace," in De Blois et al. 2003: 329–357 (included in this volume as Chapter 4).
Rich, J. W. and Williams, J. H. C. 1999. "*Leges et Iura P. R. Restituit*: A New Aureus of Octavian and the Settlement of 28–27 B.C.," *Numismatic Chronicle* 159: 169–213.

Richardson, J. S. 1976. *Roman Provincial Administration, 227 B.C. to A.D. 117*. London.
Richardson, J. S. 2002. "The New Augustan Edicts from Northwest Spain," *JRA* 15: 411–415.
Richardson, J. S. 2012. *Augustan Rome, 44 B.C. to A.D. 14. The Restoration of the Republic and the Establishment of the Empire*. Edinburgh.
Ridley, R. T. 2003. *The Emperor's Retrospect: Augustus' Res Gestae in Epigraphy, Historiography, and Commentary*. Dudley, MA.
Rinaldi Tufi, S. 2002. "Foro di Augusto: qualche riflessioni," *Ostraka* 11: 177–193.
Rives, J. B. 1995. *Religion and Authority in Roman Carthage from Augustus to Constantine*. Oxford.
Rives, J. B. 2007. *Religion in the Roman Empire*. Oxford.
Rivoluzione romana 1982. *La rivoluzione romana: inchiesta tra gli antichisti* (Biblioteca di *Labeo* 6). Naples.
Robert, L. 1935. *Villes d'Asie Mineure*. Paris (2nd edn, 1962).
Robert, L. 1946–1965. *Hellenica. Recueil d'épigraphie, de numismatique et d'antiquités grecques*. 13 vols. Paris.
Robert, L. 1969–1990. *Opera Minora Selecta. Épigraphie et antiquités grecques*. 7 vols. Amsterdam.
Roddaz, J.-M. 1984. *Marcus Agrippa* (BEFAR 253). Rome.
Rohr Vio, F. 2000. *Le voci del dissenso. Ottaviano Augusto e i suoi oppositori*. Padua.
Rose, C. B. 1997. *Dynastic Commemoration and Imperial Portraiture in the Julio-Claudian Period*. Cambridge.
Rossini, O. 2006. *Ara Pacis*. Rome.
Rowell, H. T. 1962. *Rome in the Augustan Age*. Norman, OK.
Rubincam, C. 1992. "The Nomenclature of Julius Caesar and the Later Augustus in the Triumviral Period," *Historia* 41: 88–103.
Sailor, D. 2006. "Dirty Linen, Fabrication, and the Authorities of Livy and Augustus," *TAPA* 136: 329–388.
Salmon, E. T. 1956. "The Evolution of Augustus' Principate," *Historia* 5: 456–478.
Salomies, O. 1987. *Die römischen Vornamen* (CommHumLit 82). Helsinki.
Salomies, O. 1992. *Adoptive and Polyonymous Nomenclature in the Roman Empire* (CommHumLit 97). Helsinki.
Salway, B. 1994. "What's in a Name? A Survey of Roman Onomastic Practice from *c*. 700 B.C. to A.D. 700," *JRS* 84: 124–145.
Sattler, P. 1960. *Augustus und der Senat. Untersuchungen zur römischen Innenpolitik zwischen 30 und 17 v. Chr*. Göttingen.
Scheid, J. 1990. *Romulus et ses frères. Le collège des frères arvales, modèle du culte public dans la Rome des empereurs* (BEFAR 275). Rome.
Scheid, J. 1998a. *Commentarii fratrum arvalium qui supersunt. Les copies épigraphiques des protocoles annuels de la confrérie arvale (21 av.–304 apr. J.-C.)*. Rome.

Scheid, J. 1998b. *La religion des romains*. Paris (English trans. = Scheid 2003).

Scheid, J. 1999. "Auguste et le grand pontificat: politique et droit sacré au début du Principat," *Rev. hist. droit* 77: 1–19.

Scheid, J. 2001. "Honorer le prince et vénérer les dieux: culte public, cultes des quartiers et culte impérial dans la Rome augustéenne," in N. Belayche, ed., *Rome, les Césars et la Ville aux deux premiers siècles de notre ère*. Rennes. 85–101 (trans. into English here as Chapter 9).

Scheid, J. 2003. *An Introduction to Roman Religion* (trans. J. Lloyd). Edinburgh.

Scheid, J. 2005. "Augustus and Roman Religion: Continuity, Conservatism, and Innovation," in Galinsky 2005a: 175–193.

Scheid, J., ed. and trans. 2007. *Res Gestae Divi Augusti. Haut faits du divin Auguste*. Paris.

Scheidel, W., Morris, I., and Saller, R. P., eds. 2007. *The Cambridge Economic History of the Greco-Roman World*. Cambridge.

Schlüter, W. 1999. "The Battle of the Teutoburg Forest: Archaeological Research at Kalkriese near Osnabrück," in J. D. Creighton and R. J. A. Wilson, eds, *Roman Germany: Studies in Cultural Interaction (JRA* Suppl. 32). Portsmouth, RI. 125–159.

Schmid, A. 2005. *Augustus und die Macht der Sterne. Antike Astrologie und die Etablierung der Monarchie in Rom*. Cologne, Weimar, and Vienna.

Schmitthenner, W., ed. 1969. *Augustus* (Wege der Forschung 128). Darmstadt.

Schnurbein, S. von. 2003. "Augustus in *Germania* and his New 'Town' at Waldgirmes East of the Rhine," *JRA* 16: 93–107.

Schütz, M. 1990. "Zur Sonnenuhr des Augustus auf dem Marsfeld: eine Auseinandersetzung mit E. Buchners Rekonstruktion," *Gymnasium* 97: 432–457.

Severy, B. 2003. *Augustus and the Family at the Birth of the Roman Empire*. New York and London.

Severy, B., ed. 2007. *Reshaping Rome: Space, Time, and Memory in the Augustan Transformation* [= *Arethusa* 40.1]. Baltimore.

Sherwin-White, A. N. 1973. *The Roman Citizenship* (2nd edn). Oxford (1st edn, 1939).

Sherwin-White, A. N. 1984. *Roman Foreign Policy in the East 168 B.C. to A.D. 1*. London.

Shotter, D. C. A. 1991. *Augustus Caesar*. London and New York (2nd edn, 2005).

Shuckburgh, E. S. 1903. *Augustus: The Life and Times of the Founder of the Roman Empire (BC 63–AD 14)*. London.

Siber, H. 1940. *Das Führeramt des Augustus* (Abh. Säch. Ak. Wiss., Phil.-hist. Kl., 44.2). Leipzig.

Simon, E. 1957. "Zur Augustusstatue von Prima Porta," *RM* 64: 46–68.

Simon, E. 1967. *Ara Pacis Augustae*. Tübingen.

Simon, E. 1986. *Augustus. Kunst und Leben in Rom um die Zeitenwende*. Munich.
Simon, E. 1991. "Altes und Neues zur Statue des Augustus von Primaporta," in Binder 1991: 204–233.
Smith, R. R. R. 1996. "Typology and Diversity in the Portraits of Augustus," *JRA* 9: 31–47.
Solin, H. 1982. *Die griechischen Personennamen in Rom. Ein Namenbuch*. Berlin and New York (2nd rev. edn, 2003).
Solin, H. 1996. *Die stadtrömischen Sklavennamen. Ein Namenbuch* (Forschungen zur antiken Sklaverei, Beiheft 2). Stuttgart.
Southern, P. 1998. *Augustus*. London and New York.
Spaeth, B. 1994. "The Goddess Ceres in the Ara Pacis Augustae and the Carthage Relief," *AJA* 77: 65–100.
Spannagel, M. 1999. *Exemplaria Principis. Untersuchungen zu Entstehung und Ausstattung des Augustusforums*. Heidelberg.
Spawforth, A. J. S. 2012. *Greece and the Augustan Cultural Revolution: Greek Culture in the Roman World*. Cambridge.
Stahlmann, I. 1988. *Imperator Caesar Augustus. Studien zur Geschichte des Principatsverständnisses in der deutschen Altertumswissenschaft bis 1945*. Darmstadt.
Stockton, D. L. 1965. "Primus and Murena," *Historia* 14: 18–40.
Strothmann, M. 2000. *Augustus – Vater der res publica. Zur Funktion der drei Begriffe* restitutio – saeculum – pater patriae *im augusteischen Principat*. Stuttgart.
Swan, P. M., ed. 2004. *The Augustan Succession: An Historical Commentary on Cassius Dio's Roman History, Books 55–56 (9 B.C.–A.D. 14)*. Oxford.
Syme, R. 1934. "The Northern Frontiers under Augustus," in *CAH* X: 340–381.
Syme, R. 1939. *The Roman Revolution*. Oxford.
Syme, R. 1958a. "Imperator Caesar: A Study in Nomenclature," *Historia* 7: 172–188 (reprinted in *Roman Papers* I.361–377 and in this volume as Chapter 1).
Syme, R. 1958b. *Tacitus*. 2 vols. Oxford.
Syme, R. 1959. "Livy and Augustus," *HSCP* 64: 27–87 (reprinted in *Roman Papers* I, 400–454).
Syme, R. 1979. "Some Imperial Salutations," *Phoenix* 33: 308–329 (reprinted in *Roman Papers* III.1198–1219).
Syme, R. 1986. *The Augustan Aristocracy*. Oxford.
Syme, R. 1999. *The Provincial at Rome* and *Rome and the Balkans, 80 B.C.–A.D. 14* (ed. A. R. Birley). Exeter.
Talbert, R. J. A. 1984. "Augustus and the Senate," *G&R* n.s. 31: 55–63.
Thomsen, R. 2001. *Augustus: liv og virke*. Aarhus.
Tibiletti, G. 1953. *Principe e magistrati repubblicani: ricerca di storia augustea e tiberiana*. Rome.
Toynbee, J. M. C. 1953. "The Ara Pacis Reconsidered," *Proc. Brit. Acad.*

39: 67–95.

Toynbee, J. M. C. 1961. "The 'Ara Pacis Augustae'," *JRS* 51: 153–156.

Treggiari, S. 1991. *Roman Marriage: iusti coniuges from the Time of Cicero to the Time of Ulpian.* Oxford.

Treggiari, S. 1996. "Social Status and Social Legislation," in *CAH*² X: 873–904.

Trillmich, W. 1976. *Das Torlonia-Mädchen. Zu Herkunft und Entstehung des kaiserzeitlichen Frauenporträts* (Abh. Ak. Wiss. Göttingen, Phil.-hist. Kl., 3.Folge, 99). Göttingen.

Trillmich, W. 1978. *Familienpropaganda der Kaiser Caligula und Claudius. Agrippina Maior und Antonia Augusta auf Münzen* (Antike Münzen und geschnittene Steine 8). Berlin.

Trillmich, W. 1988. "Münzpropaganda," in Hofter et al. 1988: 474–528.

Trillmich, W. and Zanker, P., eds. 1990. *Stadtbild und Ideologie. Die Monumentalisierung hispanischer Städte zwischen Republik und Kaiserzeit* (Abh. Bayer. Ak. Wiss., Phil.-hist. Kl., N.F. 103). Munich.

Trillmich, W., Hauschild, T., Blech, M. et al., eds. 1993. *Hispania Antiqua. Denkmäler der Römerzeit.* Mainz.

Vierneisel, K. and Zanker, P., eds. 1979. *Die Bildnisse des Augustus. Herrscherbild und Politik in kaiserlichen Rom.* Munich.

Vittinghoff, F. 1959. *Kaiser Augustus* (Persönlichkeit und Geschichte 20). Göttingen (3rd edn, 1991).

Volkmann, H., ed. 1942. *Res gestae divi Augusti. Das Monumentum Ancyranum.* Berlin (3rd edn, 1969).

Walker, S. 1997. "Athens under Augustus," in M. C. Hoff and S. I. Rotroff, eds, *The Romanization of Athens: Proceedings of an International Conference held at Lincoln, Nebraska (April 1996)* (Oxbow Monograph 94). Oxford. 67–80.

Walker, S. and Burnett, A. M. 1981a. *The Image of Augustus.* London.

Walker, S. and Burnett, A. M. 1981b. *Augustus: Handlist of the Exhibition and Supplementary Studies.* London.

Wallace-Hadrill, A. 1981. "Family and Inheritance in the Augustan Marriage Laws," *PCPS* n.s. 27: 58–80 (included in this volume as Chapter 8).

Wallace-Hadrill, A. 1982. "The Golden Age and Sin in Augustan Ideology," *Past and Present* 95: 19–36.

Wallace-Hadrill, A. 1986. "Image and Authority in the Coinage of Augustus," *JRS* 76: 66–87.

Wallace-Hadrill, A. 1987. "Time for Augustus: Ovid, Augustus, and the Fasti," in M. Whitby, ed., *Homo viator: Classical Essays for John Bramble.* Bristol. 221–230.

Wallace-Hadrill, A. 1989. "Rome's Cultural Revolution," *JRS* 79: 157–164.

Wallace-Hadrill, A. 1993. *Augustan Rome* (Classical World Series). Bristol.

Wallace-Hadrill, A. 1997. "*Mutatio morum*: The Idea of a Cultural Revolution," in Habinek and Schiesaro 1997: 3–22.
Wallace-Hadrill, A. 2000. "The Roman Revolution and Material Culture," in Giovannini 2000: 283–321.
Wallace-Hadrill, A. 2005. "*Mutatas formas*: The Augustan Transformation of Roman Knowledge," in Galinsky 2005a: 55–84.
Wallace-Hadrill, A. 2008. *Rome's Cultural Revolution*. Cambridge.
Weber, W. 1936. *Princeps. Studien zur Geschichte des Augustus*. Stuttgart and Berlin.
Wells, C. M. 1972. *The German Policy of Augustus: An Examination of the Archaeological Evidence*. Oxford.
White, L. M. 2005. "Epilogue as Prologue: Herod and the Jewish Experience of Augustan Rome," in Galinsky 2005a: 361–387.
White, P. 1993. *Promised Verse: Poets in the Society of Augustan Rome*. Cambridge, MA.
White, P. 2005. "Poets in the New Milieu: Realigning," in Galinsky 2005a: 321–339.
Wickert, L. 1954. "Princeps (civitatis)," *RE* 22.2: cols 1998–2296.
Williams, G. 1962. "Poetry in the Moral Climate of Augustan Rome," *JRS* 52: 28–46.
Winkes, R., ed. 1985. *The Age of Augustus: Interdisciplinary Conference held at Brown University, April 30–May 2, 1982* (Archaeologia Transatlantica 5). Providence, RI, and Louvain.
Winterling, A. 2005. "Dyarchie in der römischen Kaiserzeit. Vorschlag zur Wiederaufnahme der Diskussion," in W. Nippel and B. Seidensticker, eds, *Theodor Mommsens langer Schatten. Das römische Staatsrecht als bleibende Herausforderung für die Forschung* (Spoudasmata 107). Zurich and New York. 177–198.
Wiseman, T. P. 1971. *New Men in the Roman Senate, 139 B.C.–A.D. 14*. Oxford.
Wiseman, T. P. 1974. "The Circus Flaminius," *PBSR* 42: 3–26.
Wiseman, T. P. 1978. "Flavians on the Capitol," *AJAH* 3: 163–178.
Wiseman, T. P. 1979a. *Clio's Cosmetics: Three Studies in Greco-Roman Literature*. Leicester.
Wiseman, T. P. 1979b. "Topography and Rhetoric: The Trial of Manlius," *Historia* 28: 32–50.
Wiseman, T. P. 1981. "The Temple of Victory on the Palatine," *Antiquaries Journal* 61: 35–52.
Wiseman, T. P. 1984. "Cybele, Virgil and Augustus," in Woodman and West 1984: 117–128 (included in this volume as Chapter 12).
Wiseman, T. P. 1985. *Catullus and his World: A Reappraisal*. Cambridge.
Wiseman, T. P. 1992. *Talking to Virgil: A Miscellany*. Exeter.
Wiseman, T. P. 1995. *Remus: A Roman Myth*. Cambridge.
Wiseman, T. P. 2004. *The Myths of Rome*. Exeter.
Woodman, A. J. and West, D., eds. 1984. *Poetry and Politics in the Age of*

Augustus. Cambridge.
Woolf, G. 1994. "Becoming Roman, Staying Greek: Culture, Identity, and the Civilizing Process in the Roman East," *PCPS* n.s. 40: 116–143.
Woolf, G. 1998. *Becoming Roman: The Origins of Provincial Civilization in Gaul*. Cambridge.
Woolf, G. 2005. "Provincial Perspectives," in Galinsky 2005a: 106–129.
Wyke, M. 1987. "Written Women: Propertius' *scripta puella*," *JRS* 77: 47–61.
Wyke, M. 1989. "Mistress and Metaphor in Augustan Elegy," *Helios* 16: 25–47.
Wyke, M. 1992. "Augustan Cleopatras: Female Power and Poetic Authority," in Powell 1992: 98–140 (rev. as "*Meretrix regina*: Augustan Cleopatras" in Wyke 2002: 196–243; included in this volume as Chapter 11).
Wyke, M. 1997. *Projecting the Past: Ancient Rome, Cinema, and History*. London and New York.
Wyke, M. 2002. *The Roman Mistress: Ancient and Modern Representations*. Oxford.
Wyke, M. 2007. *Caesar: A Life in Western Culture*. London.
Yavetz, Z. 1984. "The *Res Gestae* and Augustus' Public Image," in Millar and Segal 1984: 1–36.
Zachos, K. L. 2003. "The *tropaeum* of the Sea-Battle of Actium at Nikopolis: Interim Report," *JRA* 16: 65–92.
Zanker, P. 1968. *Forum Augustum. Das Bildprogramm*. Tübingen.
Zanker, P. 1972. *Forum Romanum. Die Neugestaltung unter Augustus*. Tübingen.
Zanker, P. 1973. *Studien zu den Augustus-Porträts. 1. Der Actium-Typus* (Abh. Ak. Wiss. Göttingen, Phil.-hist. Kl., 3.Folge, 95). Göttingen.
Zanker, P. 1983. "Der Apollontempel auf dem Palatin. Ausstattung und politische Sinnbezüge nach der Schlacht von Actium," in K. de Fine Licht, ed., *Città e architettura nella Roma imperiale: Atti del seminario del 27 ottobre 1981 nel 25° anniversario dell'Accademia di Danimarca* (Analecta Romana Instituti Danici, Suppl. 10). Odense. 21–40.
Zanker, P. 1987. *Augustus und die Macht der Bilder*. Munich (English trans. = Zanker 1988).
Zanker, P. 1988. *The Power of Images in the Age of Augustus*, trans. H. A. Shapiro. Ann Arbor.

Index

Achaea, Roman province, 420
Achaean League, 474–5
Actia, games held at Nikopolis, 476
Actium, battle of, 2, 13, 54, 85, 89, 138–9, 148, 279, 284, 307, 310–33, 344, 349, 354, 355–6, 360, 363, 365, 368, 372, 389, 392, 393, 394, 428, 430–2, 476
administration and administrative practices, 229–49, 422, 468–81; *see also* provincial governors and governance
adopted children and adoptions, 1, 5, 21, 33, 36n, 39, 41, 44, 48, 55, 56, 57, 59, 119, 125, 274, 285, 291, 403
adultery, 3, 198, 200, 268–9, 487, 488, 489
aediles, 63–4, 65, 79, 238, 241, 243, 381n, 384, 393, 403, 407, 409, 411, 484
Aelius Gallus, M., 156
Aemilius Lepidus, M. (*cos.* 46 BC), the *triumvir*, 62–3, 69, 75, 123, 171, 289, 295, 413
Aemilius Paullus, L. (*cos.* 182, 168 BC), 49, 311, 410–11
Aeneas 11, 174, 305, 307, 315, 358, 362, 372, 384, 386–93, 396, 402–3, 412, 424, 456, 458
aerarium militare (military treasury), 203
aerarium Saturni (treasury of Saturn), 234–5, 238
Aeschylus, Athenian tragedian, 346, 361–2
Africa, Roman province, 155–6, 158, 161, 210, 420
Agrippa, M. Vipsanius (*cos.* 37, 28, 27 BC), 5, 10, 45, 48, 51–2, 56–7, 75, 79, 80, 86, 93, 94, 104–5, 107, 110, 113, 114–16, 118–23, 138–9, 156, 160n, 161, 238–9, 295, 314, 357,

363, 438–40, 449, 456, 477
Agrippa Postumus, 56, 57, 488–9
Agrippina the Elder / Maior, 193n
Agrippina the Younger / Minor, 175n, 193n, 444–5
Albinius, L., 407, 408–9
Alexander Helios ('the Sun'), 13, 342, 360, 484
Alexandria, 53, 175n, 319, 337, 344, 346–7, 360, 470, 472–3, 478n
'Donations of Alexandria', 66
allies (*socii*) of the Roman people, 147, 336
Alps, 141, 148, 158–9
ambassadors *see* embassies
amici see friends
amicitia see friendship
amphitheatres, 438–9, 441
annales maximi, 412
anniversaries, celebrations of, 281
annona see grain-supply
Antioch in Syria, 481
Antonia the Younger / Minor, 180n, 191, 193n, 445
Antonius, Iullus, son of the *triumvir*, 42, 43
Antonius, L. (*cos.* 41 BC), 65, 67
Antonius, M. (*cos.* 44 BC), the *triumvir*, 12, 13–14, 33, 42, 55, 61–78, 85–6, 143, 157, 170, 176, 208, 246, 263–4, 314, 317–19, 323, 327, 334–7, 342–3, 346–7, 349, 351–5, 359–62, 364–5, 368, 373, 392, 402, 425, 429, 468–71, 476, 480n, 484–5
Anubis, cult of in Egypt, 343–5, 348
Apamea in Phrygia, 481
Aphrodisias, 9–10, 70–1, 138
Aphrodite, cult of, 338, 343
Apollo, cult of, 148, 183, 282, 284, 293, 299, 304, 308, 316, 318–20, 323, 329–30, 357–8, 361–3, 365, 392–4,

397, 432, 477n, 478
Appian, historian, 62, 66–7, 74, 75–6, 78, 85–6, 113n, 170, 485n
aqueducts, 238–9, 438
Arabia, 3, 156, 158, 163, 366
Ara Pacis Augustae (Altar of Augustan Peace, Rome), 10–11, 12, 19, 138, 139n, 140, 145, 159, 186, 187, 291, 315, 317, 353, 487, 488, 490
archaeological evidence, 10–14, 23–4
Aretas, king of Nabataea, 366
Argolid *koinon* (confederacy), 475
aristocracy, Roman, 39–59, 219–20, 317–19
Armenia, 158, 163, 212, 351–2, 364–5
army, Roman, 2, 3, 6, 19, 50, 125, 127, 152–3, 197–8, 203–28, 232, 347, 362, 420, 495, 497, 498, 501
  commanders, 212–13, 218–22; *see also legati Augusti*
  manpower and recruitment, 252
  revolts, 215–17, 223
Arruntius Furius Camillus Scribonianus, L., 215
Arsinoe II Philadelphus, 338, 340
Arsinoe, sister of Cleopatra, 371
Artaxes, king of Armenia, 158
Artemis, 71, 367, 471
Arval Brethren, priests at Rome, 186, 281, 286–7, 294n
Asia, *koinon* (confederacy) of, 480
Asia, Roman province, 68–9, 112, 113–14, 140, 154, 419–20, 480
Asia, Roman views of, 341
Asinius Pollio, C. (*cos.* 40 BC), 29n, 40, 43
assemblies, Roman voting, 63, 65, 82, 104
Athena, cult of, 174n, 323, 460, 469
Athens under Roman rule, 477–8, 480
Atkinson, K. M., 114
Atticus, T. Pomponius, 75, 79, 86, 264, 265, 411
augurium salutis, 139
augurs, 408, 413
Augusta Emerita *see* Emerita
Augustalia (festival in Rome), 289–90
Augustus/Octavian
  administrative reforms under, 229–49
  army under, 152–3, 203–28
  auctoritas of, 9, 88, 97–8, 108, 109–10, 113–14, 117–18, 122, 179, 218
  birthday of, 11, 12, 18, 292, 293, 318,
419–20
  censorial powers, census under, 100, 105–7, 485, 488, 489, 490
  ceremonial returns to the city of Rome, 288–91
  cities named after, 481
  clients of, 21, 211, 214–17, 222
  coinage under, 10, 23, 54, 83, 92–3, 107, 140, 144–5, 147–8, 187, 314, 324, 329, 353, 356, 363–5, 428–33, 464
  conquests of, 137–64, 277, 303
  consular *imperium*, 90–3, 99–100, 105, 121, 234
  consular privileges, 103, 122
  consulates, 54, 61, 72–3, 79–81, 84–5, 92–3, 99–100, 103, 105, 108, 110, 117, 483, 484, 485, 486, 488, 492
  cura morum (guardianship of morals), 100, 106n
  death of, 126–8, 282, 299, 400, 489
  deification of, 184–5, 188–9, 282, 489
  dictatorship refused, 88, 208, 486
  dynastic aspirations of, 152, 191; *see also* Gaius Caesar, Lucius Caesar, Marcellus, Tiberius
  edicts of, 10, 53, 72, 75, 99n, 110n, 113–14, 117–18, 404, 471–2
  elections under, 7, 63, 65, 82, 92–3, 104, 108–9, 153
  expansion of the Roman Empire under, 137–64
  fasces, right to, 79–80, 100, 104, 149
  freedmen of, 5, 234
  friends of, 218–20, 263, 280–1, 305, 415, 419, 471n
  funeral of, 142n, 184, 402, 404, 407n
  genius (divine spirit) of, 188–9, 201, 281, 293, 295–9, 330
  geographical knowledge under, 25, 145–7
  imperialism under, 21, 37, 137–49
  imperium of, 52, 54–5, 81, 90–129, 234, 483, 486, 487, 488, 489
  imperium maius (quam), 52, 54n, 55, 110–21, 124–5, 280, 486
  juridical powers, jurisdiction of, 74–8, 103n, 109–10
  laws proposed by, 2–3, 104, 108, 174, 177, 200, 250–74
  lictors, right to, 76, 100, 104
  mausoleum of, 5, 11–12, 138, 291, 357, 404, 486, 487, 489, 490
  military campaigns of, 3–4, 51,

137–64, 212–13
military reforms of, 203–28
month of August named in his honour, 298, 394, 488
moral reforms of, 2–3, 88, 198–201, 306
name 'Augustus' granted in 27 BC, 53–5, 79, 97, 126, 356
numen (divine power) of, 53n, 292–3, 298
as *pater patriae*, 54, 87, 123, 126, 179, 402–3, 488
as *pontifex maximus*, 12, 46, 123, 126, 129n, 289, 295–6, 413, 487
powers of, 2, 36–7, 52, 54–5, 60–89, 90–129, 218, 234, 483, 486–7, 488–9, 492–3
praenomen Imperator, 40–59, 69, 70, 126, 209, 484
proconsular *imperium*, 90, 99–100, 102–3, 106n, 209, 218
provincial administration under, 4–5, 25, 153–7, 209–10, 231–5
refusal (*recusatio*) of honours, 124n, 148, 288–9
religious reforms of, 3, 180–3, 275–99
Res Gestae ('Accomplishments') of, 5–6, 9, 55, 84–5, 105, 118, 137–8, 141, 144–5, 211, 212, 237, 275–6, 288–9, 356–7, 361, 404, 420
'restoration of Roman Republic,' 2–5, 10, 34–5, 38, 58, 79–89, 92, 97, 101, 153, 168, 197–8, 201, 208, 215, 278
rise to power, 48–9, 51–53
senate and senators under, 1, 6–7, 9–11, 14, 15, 21, 36–7, 43, 44, 53, 58, 83–7, 95–8, 100–2, 106–7, 109n, 114, 117–18, 122, 126–9, 141–2, 147, 153–4, 156–7, 158, 168, 197, 207–11, 218–22, 229–30, 236, 239, 241–6, 247–9, 284, 288, 291, 295, 298, 309n, 310–11, 314, 347, 356, 483, 485, 486
settlement of 28–27 BC, 79–89, 90–9, 153, 231–4
statues of, 13, 145n, 184–5, 281–2, 295, 298, 303–4, 314, 316, 368–70, 402, 444
tribunician power of, 10, 36, 54, 79, 84, 98, 99–107, 117–19, 122, 123n, 130n, 200, 487, 488, 492–3
triumphs celebrated by, 13–14, 138, 144, 148–9, 156, 212, 277, 282, 288, 314, 319, 327, 344, 355, 357–8, 360, 362, 365, 371, 372, 393, 403, 432
triumphal arch(es) honouring, 138, 148, 282, 284, 288, 290, 314, 362, 364
triumvir r(ei) p(ublicae) c(onstituendae), 40–54, 60–78
slaves of, 59, 241–2

Baetica, Roman province, 140, 159
banks and banking, 476
banquets
 private, 295–6
 public, 166, 175, 285, 293–4, 295–6, 298
barbarians
 cultural construction of at Athens, 346, 348
 cultural construction of at Rome, 142n, 148n, 343–4, 346, 364, 367, 372, 429–31
Bayet, J., 277
Béranger, Jean, 20
Berenice I, queen of Egypt, 338, 343
Berenice II, queen of Egypt, 338–9
Bithynia, Roman province, 112, 471
Bocchus, king of Mauretania, 366
Boeotia, 475
Bononia, pact of, 62
Boscoreale cups, 139, 148
Boudicca, British queen, 369
Bowersock, G. W., 425–6, 468–81, 491
bribery, electoral, 7, 108, 267–8, 487
bridges, Roman, 433–6, 438, 465
Bringmann, K., 120–1
Britain, 143–6, 160, 163, 422n
Brundisium, pact of, 351, 484
Brunt, P. A., 20–1, 36, 38, 104, 150–2, 246, 251, 491
Buchan, John (Lord Tweedsmuir), 16
Buchner, E., 292

Caere, 390n, 407–9, 414, 444
Caesar *see* Julius Caesar
Caesarion, 339–40, 343, 484
calendar, 419–20
Caligula, Roman emperor, 167, 174n, 177n, 215, 220–1, 223, 282
Callimachus, Hellenistic poet, 339
Calpurnius Piso, Cn. (*cos.* 23 BC), 5
Calpurnius Piso, Cn. (*cos.* 7 BC), 216; *see also senatus consultum de Pisone patre*

cameos, 326-9
Camillus, M. Furius, 408
Cantabria, Cantabrians, 429
Capricorns, 326, 328
Caracalla, Roman emperor, 172, 271, 272-3
Carisius, P., 428-31, 448, 464
carmen saeculare (by Horace), 145, 304-5, 317, 357
carpentum, 177-8
caryatids, as architectural decoration, 450-5
Cassius Dio, historian, 2, 6, 62, 80, 85-6, 95, 99, 100-1, 116, 119-20, 128, 142, 154, 161, 168, 188, 211, 232-3, 242, 269, 359-60, 369, 371-2, 427-8
Catullus, Roman poet, 383
censors (magistrates at Rome), 105-6, 177, 251, 383n, 407n
census, local, 5
  at Rome, 100, 105-7, 485, 488, 489, 490
centurions, 206, 212, 214, 219, 223
Ceres, 11, 187, 289
chariot-races, 286, 382
children, 254-7
Chios, 471, 480
Cicero, M. Tullius (*cos.* 63 BC), 40, 41, 43, 45n, 47, 48, 65, 83, 112-13, 116, 140n, 141, 154, 263-4, 346, 382, 412
Cilicia, Roman province, 112
cities, in Roman Empire, 419-81
citizenship, Roman, 56, 66, 69, 73, 252, 384, 421, 471-2; *see also* Latin rights of citizenship
city-walls, 437-8
Claudius, Roman emperor, 141, 179-80, 186, 189, 215, 223, 465
Claudius Caecus, Appius, 58n, 403n, 409-10, 414
Claudius Drusus, Nero *see* Drusus, Nero Claudius, brother of Tiberius
Claudius Drusus, Tiberius *see* Tiberius
Cleopatra VII, queen of Egypt, 12, 13-14, 176, 180, 307, 334-79, 429, 484-5
Cleopatra Selene ('the Moon'), 13, 360, 484
client kings and kingdoms, 142, 147, 180n, 336, 352, 364, 368, 456, 469, 470, 480
clients and clientage in Roman society, 41, 199, 206, 209, 213-15, 218, 264-5, 268, 313
clipei, as architectural decoration, 450-2
Cnidos, 470, 471
coinage
  as historical evidence, 10
  Ptolemaic, 338-41
  Roman, 41-8, 56, 57, 59, 107, 139, 312-13, 329, 351-2, 362-5, 366-8
  Roman provincial, 140n, 351, 432-3, 436, 446n, 448, 474, 476-7
  see also Augustus, coinage under
colonies, Roman, 4, 29n, 47, 140, 173, 175, 208, 211, 345, 411, 420-1, 427-67, 475-6
Compitalia *see ludi Compitales*
Constantine, Roman emperor, 250-1
consular status, 171-2
consuls, 54, 61, 66, 72-3, 79-81, 84-5, 92-3, 99-100, 103, 105, 108, 110, 117, 483, 484, 485, 486, 488, 492
Corinth, Roman colony, 468, 475, 476-7, 480-1
Cornelia, mother of the Gracchi, 170-1
Cornelius Balbus, L., 107, 156-7
Cornelius Cethegus, C., 407, 410
Cornelius Gallus, C., 50, 156, 245-6
Cornelius Lentulus Gaetulicus, Cn. (*cos.* AD 26), 220-1
Cornelius Nepos, Roman biographer, 75, 86
Cornelius Sulla, Faustus, 42, 52, 366
Cornelius Sulla, L. (*cos.* 88, 80 BC), 41, 42, 59, 90-2, 169, 261, 311, 313, 366, 381n, 471, 478
Cos, 469
councils, local, 470-1, 473
court, imperial, 167
Crassus *see* Licinius Crassus, M.
Crinagoras, poet from Mytilene, 469, 477
Crook, J. A., 262-3
cuirass-statues, 460-2
Cumont, F., 277
cura morum (guardianship of morals), 100, 106n
curatores viarum (supervisors of the roads), 236-7
cursus publicus, 236
Cybele, cult of, 381-9, 395-7
Cyme *see* Kyme
Cyprus, 121, 158
Cyrene, 10, 117-18, 471-2, 484

Cyzicus, 481

Dacia and Dacians, 146, 151
Dalmatia, Roman province, 141
Danaids, 346, 361-2
Danube, river, 141, 149-51, 161
Daube, D., 262-3
Dea Dia, cult of, 281n, 285-7
debts, remission of, 468, 480
Deininger, J., 400n, 405
Delphi, 311, 361, 382, 477
Delphic Amphictyony, 479
Diana, cult of, 148, 432
dictator, public office at Rome, 1, 42, 45, 46, 48, 52, 77, 88, 113n, 208, 408, 410, 414, 477, 486
Dio Cassius *see* Cassius Dio
Diodorus Siculus, historian, 346, 348
Dionysius of Halicarnassus, historian, 381-3, 408
Dio of Prusa, 478
diplomacy and diplomats, 68-78, 469-70
Divus Augustus (deified Augustus), 6n, 184-5, 188-9, 282, 290, 298, 489
Divus Iulius (deified Julius Caesar), 1n, 44, 52, 58, 66, 69-70, 71, 77, 138, 282, 292, 295-6, 309, 349, 402, 446
Domitian, Roman emperor, 12, 130n, 274, 292, 297, 390
Domitius Ahenobarbus, L. (*cos.* 32 BC), 66
Domitius Ahenobarbus, L. (*cos.* 16 BC), 151
domus Augusta (imperial family), 26, 56, 182n, 193n, 298, 421
Doris, 475
dowry, 180n, 187n, 261, 348
dress, 384-6
Drusus, Nero Claudius, brother of Tiberius, 13, 148, 158-9, 161, 163, 165-6, 212-13, 403
Drusus Iulius Caesar, son of Tiberius, 128
duBois, Page, 355

earthquakes, 480
Eck, Werner, 198-200, 229-49, 491
effeminacy, Roman views on, 345-6, 369, 384-5
Egnatius Rufus, M., 108, 238, 241
Egypt, 138, 141, 155, 156, 230, 245-6
 Roman views of Egypt and Egyptians, 334-80
Elagabalus, Roman emperor, 171-3
Elbe, river, 141, 149-51, 161-2, 163

elections of Roman magistrates, 7, 63-5, 82, 92-3, 104, 108-9, 153
Elis, 475
elites, local, 425, 470
embassies, 68-78, 469-70
Emerita, 427-67
Ephesus, 49, 51n, 68-70, 71, 73, 471, 481
epigraphic evidence, 8-10
equestrians and equestrian order, 50, 57, 165n, 166, 174n, 179, 184, 212, 218, 219, 221-2, 229-31, 234, 242, 244-5, 245-8, 268, 286, 290, 305, 347, 422
equestrian statues, 13, 314
equites see equestrians and equestrian order
Ethiopia, 156
ethnicity, social construction of at Rome, 334-80
Euboea, 475
eunuchs, 335, 349, 372, 382
Eurycles, C. Iulius *see* Iulius Eurycles, C.
ex-slaves *see* freedmen and freedwomen

Fabius Maximus Verrucosus, Q., 410
famine at Rome, 244
fasces, 47, 79-80, 100, 104, 149, 237
Fascism, 18-19
Ferrary, Jean-Louis, 35-6, 90-136, 491
fetiales (fetials), priests, 79, 287n, 356, 360
fires and fire-fighting at Rome, 238, 241-2, 247-8, 382n
fleet, Roman, 43, 51, 94, 159
Florus, Roman historian, 142
Fors Fortuna, cult of, 286
Forum Clodii, 185-6
forums in Roman cities, 13, 138, 284-5, 315-16, 362, 399-415, 441-57
freedmen and freedwomen, 5, 41-2, 56, 168, 173, 178n, 188-9, 192, 234, 242, 246-7, 251, 253, 256, 261-2, 271, 297, 330
friends (*amici*) and friendship (*amicitia*) of the Roman people, 144, 147, 157, 162n, 364
friends (*amici*) as social relations, 212, 218, 257, 263-6
Frier, B. W., 412-14
frontiers of the Roman Empire, 16, 149-51, 156-9, 209-10, 212-13, 252, 422n
funerals, 10, 114-15, 142n, 165, 168,

169, 174–5, 179, 184, 197, 402, 404, 407n, 483, 489
funerary portraits, 462–4
Fulvia, wife of M. Antonius, 170, 353–4
Furius Camillus, M. *see* Camillus, M. Furius

Gaius ('Caligula'), Roman emperor, 167, 174n, 177n, 215, 220–1, 223, 282
Gaius Caesar, grandson/adopted son of Augustus, 5, 36n, 56, 58, 123, 125, 144, 148–9, 152, 163, 175, 191, 212–13, 284, 290, 487, 488
Galatia-Pamphylia, Roman province, 161
Galba, Roman emperor, 77, 183, 220, 223
Gallia Narbonensis, Roman province, 119, 121, 158, 420
Gallic provinces, 48, 141, 148n, 155, 158, 159–60, 209, 212, 366–7, 486; *see also* Gallia Narbonensis
games, public *see* ludi
Gardthausen, Viktor, 14–15, 490
Gaul *see* Gallic provinces
Gemma Augustea, 396
gemstones, 326–9, 396
gender, social construction of at Rome, 334–80
genius (divine spirit)
  of the *paterfamilias* (head of the household), 295
  of the Roman emperor, 282, 293, 295
  of the Roman people, 183
geographical knowledge at Rome, 25, 145–7
Germania, 4, 12–13, 141, 146, 158–60, 161, 163, 166, 209–10, 216, 221
Germanicus, Nero Claudius (later Germanicus Iulius Caesar), son of Drusus/adopted son of Tiberius, 56, 114–16, 121, 125, 129, 163, 182–3, 216–17
Gibbon, Edward, 2
Girardet, K. M., 96–7, 110, 112, 115
gladiators, 65, 252
grain supply (*annona*), 3, 112, 229, 242–5, 247, 294n, 486
Grant, Michael, 110
Grenade, P., 123
Griffin, Jasper, 334, 355
Groag, Edmund, 17
Gruen, E. S., 152
Gurval, Robert, 355

Hadrian, Roman emperor, 142, 449
Hall, Edith, 346
Hammond, Mason, 15–16
haruspices, 64, 393
Hellenistic motifs in Roman art, 316–18, 322–4
Hercules, 78, 361, 390
Herod the Great, client king of Judaea, 16, 67, 78, 421
Herodotus, Greek historian, 348
Hispania Citerior, Roman province, 43, 50, 81n, 423
Hispania Ulterior, Roman province, 43, 50, 159, 423
historiography at Rome, 350, 399–415
Hitler, Adolf, 18
Hölscher, T., 306–7, 310–33
Horace, Roman poet, 87, 143–5, 270, 304–5, 317, 334, 342–3, 349–50, 354–5, 357–8, 371, 372–3
horologium see sundial
Hortensia, Roman matron, 76, 170
Horus, 340
household gods *see* Lares, Penates
Hurlet, F., 107, 123–4
Hyrcanus II, client king of Judaea, 68, 78

iconographic evidence, 23–4
Illyricum, 37, 120, 149–50, 156, 161, 209, 219, 319, 484, 485, 487
immunity from taxation, 70, 73, 177, 253, 472
Imperator
  as *praenomen*, 40–59, 69, 70, 209, 484
  salutation of generals as, 43, 46–9, 212
imperial cult, 175–6, 186, 188–9, 275–99, 443–7, 474, 480
imperial freedmen, 5, 234
imperialism, Roman, 21, 37, 137–49, 334–80, 428–32
imperium, 52, 54–5, 90–129
imperium maius (quam), 52, 54n, 55, 110–21, 124–5, 280, 486
India, 145–6, 160n
inheritance and transmission of property, 253–68
inheritance taxes, 203, 234, 258–9, 270, 271–4
inscriptions, as evidence, 8–10
intestacy, 262–4
invective, political at Rome, 356
Isis, cult of, 338, 340–1, 343, 347–8
Italy, administration of, 235–7
Iulius Caesar, C. *see* Julius Caesar

Iulius Eurycles, C., 474
Iulius Laco, C., 474
Iulius Nicanor, C., 478
Iustitia, cult of, 187, 188, 353
ius trium liberorum ('right of three children'), 166, 176–7, 187, 255, 272–3, 488

Janus, 53, 67, 84, 139–40, 145, 156, 162, 400n, 431, 485, 486
Jews and Judaeans, 68, 472–3
Jones, A. H. M., 20, 104, 109, 490, 491
Juba II, king of Mauretania, 421, 456
Judaea, 67, 246; *see also* Jews and Judaeans
Julia, daughter of Augustus and Scribonia, 13, 38, 119, 125, 166, 179, 193n, 350, 484, 486, 487, 488, 489
Julia, granddaughter of Augustus, 489
Julia Domna, 181
Julia Mamaea, 172
Julia Soaemias Bassiana, 171
Julian, Roman emperor, 142–3
Julius Caesar, C. (*cos.* 59, 48, 46, 45, 44 BC), 1, 33, 44, 45–8, 51, 69–70, 77, 91–2, 141, 143, 147, 169, 249, 277, 295–6, 313, 317, 319, 343, 346–7, 366–7, 371, 373, 403, 446, 469, 471–2, 476, 477; *see also* Divus Iulius
Juno
    divine spirit of a woman, 188–9, 281
    Roman goddess 174, 276, 385
Jupiter, 143, 281, 284, 304, 344–5, 348, 385–6, 389n, 444
Jupiter Ammon, 451–2
jurisdiction, 75–8
Juvenal, Roman satirist, 260–1

karnyx (dragon-headed trumpet), 304, 429–30
koina (confederacies), 475
Kraft, K., 428–9, 431–2
Kromayer, J., 110
Kyme, 113–14, 471

Lacey, W. K., 94, 101n, 118n
Laconia, 474
Lanuvium, 175
Laodicea, 480
Laodicea on the Lycus, 481
Lares Augusti, 201, 276, 296–8, 330
Last, Hugh, 15–16, 19–21, 490

Latin rights of citizenship (*ius Latii / ius Latinum*), 421
Latte, K., 277
La Turbie monument, 139
laudatio Turiae, 75, 83, 197
leagues of cities in the Greek East, 473–5, 478–80
legacies, 257, 259, 260, 263–8, 273
legati Augusti pro praetore, 4, 80–1, 85, 93, 96n, 103n, 109, 125, 154, 158, 212, 219, 221, 232–3, 246, 423, 486, 487
Lepidus *see* Aemilius Lepidus, M.
Leptis Magna, 444
Levi, M. A., 20
Levick, B., 128
lex Aelia Sentia, 102n
lex annalis, 108
lex Falcidia, 66, 267
lex Fufia Caninia, 102n
lex Furia testamentaria, 267–8, 273
lex Gabinia, 94, 111–12
lex Iulia Caesaris, 92, 94, 96
lex Iulia de adulteriis, 3, 198, 200, 268–9, 487
lex Iulia de ambitu 108, 487
lex Iulia de maritandis ordinibus, 3, 198, 200, 250–74, 487
lex Iulia theatralis, 174, 177, 487
lex Manilia, 94, 112
lex Munatia Aemilia, 66, 69
lex Oppia, 170, 173–4, 177
lex Papia Poppaea, 102n, 200, 250, 269, 274
lex Pompeia, 91–2, 94, 96–7, 103n
lex Quinctia, 102n
lex Rufrena, 66, 483
lex Titia, 54n, 62–3, 92, 96, 483
lex Trebonia, 94–5
lex Valeria Aurelia, 129n
lex Valeria Cornelia, 108–9
lex Vatinia, 93n, 94
lex Voconia, 177, 261, 267
libertas as political idea at Rome, 54, 83, 88, 349
Licinius Crassus, M. (*cos.* 70 BC), 94, 143, 402
Licinius Crassus, M. (*cos.* 30 BC), 156
Licinius Macer, Roman annalist, 411
lictors, 66, 76, 100, 103–4, 179, 184, 237, 244
Liebeschuetz, J. H. W. G., 98
literary evidence, 22, 24–5
Livia Drusilla, second wife of Augustus,

12, 38–9, 165–94, 281, 287, 291, 292, 303, 350, 352–3, 394, 483, 484, 488, 489, 490
  deification of, 186, 188–9
  villa of at Prima Porta, 183, 303
Livy (T. Livius), historian, 53, 82, 84, 173–4, 306, 399–415
Locris, 475
Lollius, M. (*cos.* 21 BC), 159, 160n, 487
Luce, T. J., 306, 309, 399–415
Lucius Caesar, grandson/adopted son of Augustus, 5, 36n, 56, 58, 123, 125, 144, 148–9, 152, 163, 191, 284, 290, 487, 488
ludi, 102n, 119, 174, 285, 289–90, 293, 296–7, 304, 318, 348, 357, 387, 382
  ludi Augustales, 289–90, 293, 298
  ludi Compitales, 296–7
  ludi Megalenses (games of Cybele), 382
  ludi Saeculares, 102n, 119, 174, 304, 318, 348, 357, 387
Lugdunum, 148
Lusitania, Roman province, 81, 427–67
luxury, Roman views on, 177n, 182, 341, 343, 346
Lycian *koinon* (confederacy), 480

Macedonia, Roman province, 156, 157, 161, 209–10, 410–11, 420, 479
Macedonian League, 479
McFayden, D., 110, 116
Maecenas, C., 45, 86, 190, 247, 305, 358
magistrates
  of local municipalities, 174, 471
  of the Roman state, 63–6, 82
  see also aediles, censors, consuls, praetors, quaestors, tribunes of the plebs
manumission of slaves, 270, 487; *see also* freedmen
Marcellus, M. Claudius, Augustus' nephew and son-in-law, 12, 119, 403
  theatre of in Rome, 185, 293, 319, 392
Marius, C. (*cos.* 107, 104–100, 86 BC), 204–6, 209, 312n, 368, 406, 429–30
Marius Gratidianus, M., 312
marriage, 171, 187, 190, 250–74, 343, 351, 403, 484, 486
marriage laws, 253–6
Mars Ultor, cult of, 432; *see also* Rome, city of: Temple of Mars Ultor
Martial, Roman poet, 177–8n, 255, 353

Mashkin, Nicolai, 20
materfamilias, 178n, 182n
Mater Matuta, cult of, 181
matronae (matrons), 38–9, 75, 76, 167–76, 179–81, 183, 189, 191–4, 287, 350, 352
Mauretania, 366, 421
Mazzarino, S., 172
Medusa, 451–2
Menenius Agrippa, 58n, 408, 414
Meyer, Eduard, 15, 16, 490
Miletus, 469–70
Millar, Fergus, 21–2, 34–5, 60–89, 420, 492
mints
  at Rome, 48, 107, 312–13, 364, 366, 367
  in Roman Empire, 107, 140, 351, 363, 366, 428–32, 448
Moesia, Roman province, 4, 161, 210
Momigliano, Arnaldo, 16, 18–19
Mommsen, Theodor, 9, 14–17, 36, 76, 90–1, 93, 101n, 102n, 126, 409, 411–13, 470n, 490
monuments, Roman public, 310–33, 390–5
moral decline at Rome, 200–1
moral reform at Rome, 2–3, 88, 198–201, 306
mosquito nets, 343, 372
Münzer, Friedrich, 17, 21
Mummius, L. (*cos.* 146 BC), 311
Munatius Plancus, L. (*cos.* 42 BC), 66, 69, 318
Mussolini, Benito, 8, 18–19, 490
Mylasa, 73
Mytilene, 119, 469, 472

names and nomenclature, Roman system of, 40–59
Naples, 175
Naulochus, battle of, 138, 148, 284, 314, 323, 324, 363, 432
Neapolis *see* Naples
neo-Attic reliefs, 321–4
Nepos *see* Cornelius Nepos
Neptune, 13, 293, 326–9
Nero, Roman emperor, 129n, 215, 217, 223, 237, 369, 465, 466
Nicolaus of Damascus, biographer, 6, 8
Nicolet, Claude, 25, 37, 491
Nicopolis, 13–14, 139–40, 432, 476–7, 479

night-watch (*vigiles*) at Rome, 241–2, 244
nobiles (nobles), in Roman society, 41–3, 56–7, 219–20, 317–19
Nock, A. D., 277
Noricum, Roman province, 213, 246
novi homines (new men), 219–20
numen (divine power) of Augustus, 53n, 292–3, 298

oaths
  general, 189, 295n, 296
  magistrates', 80
  military (*sacramentum*), 211, 215
Octavia, sister of Augustus, 64, 170, 176–7, 178, 182n, 191, 316, 343, 351–2
Octavian *see* Augustus
Octavius, C. (father of Augustus), 1
oil-lamps, terracotta, 329–32
Olympia, 474
orientalism, discourses of at Rome, 334–80
Otho, Roman emperor, 466
ovations, 138, 148, 484
Ovid, Roman poet, 87–8, 144, 180, 306, 403

Palatine Hill in Rome, 189, 275–6, 282, 284, 286, 287, 308, 328, 382, 390–1, 393–7
palladion/palladium (statue of Pallas Athene), 323, 460–1
Pamphylia, Roman province *see* Galatia-Pamphylia
Pannonia, 120, 125, 163, 166, 216, 221
Parthia and Parthians, 4, 70, 85, 138, 143–8, 151, 155, 156n, 157–8, 160, 162n, 163–4, 212, 284, 288, 303, 362, 364, 365, 368, 402, 431
paterfamilias (head of the household), 184, 200, 295
pater patriae, title, 54, 87, 123, 126, 179, 402–3, 488
Patrae, Roman colony at, 475, 480
patricians, 41–2
patronage and patrons, 21, 41, 65, 179, 199, 206, 211–14, 217–18, 253, 256, 261–2, 264–8, 305, 345–6, 351
  gods as patrons, 363, 392
  of cities, 180n
Pausanias, travel-writer, 468–9, 475n
Pax *see* Peace
Peace (Pax), Roman goddess, 83, 140, 187; *see also* Ara Pacis Augustae
Pelham, H. F., 94, 105–6, 110
Penates (guardian gods of the household), 386–7
Perusia, siege of, 353–4, 484
petitions, 76
Petronius, P., 156
Philippi, battle of, 68, 69, 284, 399, 402, 432, 483
Phocis, 475
Phraataces, Parthian king, 144
Phraates IV, Parthian king, 144, 146, 157, 364, 368
Piganiol, A., 123
Pisa, 175
Pisidia, 420
Pliny the Younger, 251, 258, 266
Plutarch, biographer and essayist, 64, 259, 336, 354, 359, 408, 411
poisoning, 191–2, 344, 351
pomerium, 99, 100, 102–3, 106, 107, 110, 122, 124, 126, 128, 393,
Pompeii, 447
Pompeius Magnus, Cn. (*cos*. 79, 55, 52 BC), 34, 43, 47, 59, 81, 90–2, 94–5, 100, 104, 111–12, 147, 154, 158, 233, 243, 311, 346, 406–7, 469–71
Pompeius, Sex., 43–4, 46, 50, 52, 64, 139, 243, 361
Pomponius Atticus, T. *see* Atticus, T. Pomponius
pontifex maximus, 12, 46, 123, 126, 129, 289, 295–6, 413, 487
pontifices, Roman priestly college, 280
Pontus, Roman client kingdom, 470
portrait-sculpture, 13–14, 23, 316, 351, 366–7, 444, 447, 448, 456, 460, 462–4, 467
Postumius Regillensis, A., 407–8
Potamo of Mytilene, 469
praefectus annonae see prefect of the grain supply
praefectus praetorio see praetorian prefect
praefectus urbi see urban prefect
praetorian cohorts, 74, 98, 107n, 127, 203, 215, 240, 245, 252
praetorian guard *see* praetorian cohorts
praetorian prefect (*praefectus praetorio*), 245
praetors, 1, 49, 63, 64, 65, 66, 84, 95, 96n, 109, 112, 197, 237, 238, 241, 243–4, 261, 271, 273, 381, 403, 409, 411, 469

prefect of Egypt, 156, 245–6
prefect of the grain supply (*praefectus annonae*), 244–5, 247–8
prefect of the night-watch (*praefectus vigilum*), 242, 244–5, 247
prefect of vehicles (*praefectus vehiculorum*), 236
prefects of the treasury, 238
Premerstein, Anton von, 17, 97–8, 490
Prima Porta statue of Augustus, 24n, 145n, 303–4, 317, 368–70, 430
Primus, M. 57, 101n, 157, 486
princeps senatus, 221
proconsular *imperium*, 81, 90, 93, 99–100, 102–3, 106n, 121–2, 209, 218, 246, 477
proconsular provinces, 95–7, 116–25, 154, 162, 223
proconsuls, 1, 10, 45–9, 68, 80–1, 90–9, 103, 107, 111–28, 154, 156–7, 161–2, 219, 221, 232–3, 306, 392, 419, 471n, 486
procurators in the Roman provinces, 232–5
Propertius, Roman poet, 22n, 83, 143–4, 251, 305, 306n, 334, 342–4, 348, 349–50, 355, 358, 361, 372–3, 393
proscriptions, 62, 63, 65, 483
protests and riots, political, 252
provincial governors and governance, 1, 4–5, 10, 25, 45–9, 62, 68, 80–1, 85, 90–9, 103, 107, 109, 110–28, 153–8, 161–2, 209–10, 212, 215–16, 219–21, 223, 228, 231–5, 245–6, 264, 306, 392, 419, 423, 426, 428, 466, 468–81, 486, 497
Ptolemaic dynasty, 334–80
Ptolemy II Philadephus, 338
Ptolemy XII Auletes, 339
Ptolemy XIII, 339
Ptolemy XV Caesar *see* Caesarion
public provinces *see* proconsular provinces
Purcell, Nicholas, 38–9, 165–94

quaestors, 64, 233–4, 238, 246–7, 410, 411, 430
Quinctilius Varus, P. (*cos*. 13 BC), 4, 13, 126n, 141, 151, 163, 489
Quinta Claudia, 170–1
Quintilian, 76

Raaflaub, Kurt, 198–9, 203–28
Raetia, Roman province, 212–13, 246
recommendations, letters of, 73–4
Res Gestae of Augustus, 5–6, 9, 55, 84–5, 105, 118, 137–8, 141, 144–5, 211, 212, 237, 275–6, 288–9, 356–7, 361, 404, 420
revolts, military, 215–17, 223
Rhine, river, 12–13, 158, 159, 161–3, 166, 212, 246
Rhosus, 69, 72, 73–4
Rich, J. W., 37–8, 95–6, 98–9, 137–64
roads
  in Italy, 236–7, 288, 314
  in the Roman provinces, 436, 481
  see also curatores viarum and *cursus publicus*
Robert, Louis, 425
Robigo, cult of, 286
Roma and Augustus, cult of, 477
Rome, city of, 3, 238–45, 275–99
  Ara Fortunae Reducis (Altar of Fortune Returning), 288–90
  Ara Maxima of Hercules, 390
  Ara Numinis Augusti (Altar of the Divine Power of Augustus), 292
  Ara Pacis Augustae (Altar of Augustan Peace), 10–11, 12, 19, 138, 139n, 140, 145, 159, 186, 187, 291, 315, 317, 353, 487, 488, 490
  Ara Providentiae Augustae (Altar of Augustan Providence), 291
  arch commemorating Augustus' victory at Actium in the Forum Romanum, 138, 148, 282, 284, 288, 290, 362, 364
  arch commemorating Augustus' victory over Parthians, 138, 148, 284, 288, 290, 362, 364
  area Capitolina, 284
  Campus Martius, 138
  Capitol, 148, 182–3, 281, 347, 372, 390, 469
  Circus Flaminius, 293, 316
  Circus Maximus, 138, 174n, 408, 411
  curia Iulia see senate-house
  Esquiline, 182
  Forum Augustum, 138, 140, 148, 276, 284–5, 306, 309, 315–16, 323, 399–415, 448, 450–8
  Forum Bo(v)arium, 390
  Forum Holitorium, 284
  Forum Iulium, 446
  Forum Romanum, 24n, 64, 65, 74, 76, 77, 138, 170, 280, 282, 284, 288, 290, 314, 362, 364, 390, 446

horologium (sundial) in Campus
  Martius, 11–12, 138–9, 292, 317n
house of Augustus, 393–5
'house of Livia', 394
Lupercal on the Palatine, 286, 390–1,
  393–4
Macellum of Livia, 182
Mausoleum of Augustus, 5, 11–12,
  138, 291, 357, 404
Palatine hill, 189, 275–6, 282, 284,
  286, 287, 308, 328, 382, 390–1,
  393–7
Pantheon, 449
Porta Mugionia (or Porta Mucionis),
  390–1
Porticus ad Nationes, 138
Porticus of Livia, 182
Porticus of Octavia, 316
Porticus Vipsania, 138–9
Quirinal hill, 322
Regia, 280, 390–2
Rostra, 138, 282–3, 314, 383
scalae Caci (stairs of Cacus), 394
senate-house (*curia Iulia*), 138, 139,
  284, 314, 485
sundial in Campus Martius see
  horologium
Temple of Apollo on the Palatine, 183,
  275, 282, 284, 308, 316, 357–8,
  361–2, 393–4, 397
Temple of Apollo Sosianus *in circo*,
  293, 318–20, 392
Temple of Concordia, 181–2
Temple of Cybele on the Palatine, 382,
  394n
Temple of Divus Augustus, 181–2
Temple of Divus Iulius, 138, 282–4,
  290, 314, 316–17, 323–4, 446
Temple of Janus, 53, 67, 84, 139–40,
  145, 156, 162, 400n, 431, 485,
  486
Temple of Jupiter Feretrius, 281, 286–7
Temple of Jupiter Optimus Maximus
  on the Capitol, 284, 357
Temple of Jupiter Tonans, 282, 284
Temple of Mars Ultor in the Forum
  Augustum, 148, 282, 284, 399–402
Temple of Mars Ultor on the Capitol,
  148
Temple of Saturn, 318
Temple of Venus Genetrix, 343, 352,
  371, 446
Temple of Venus Victrix on the
  Capitol, 183
Temple of Victory on the Palatine, 308,
  393–5
Theatre of Marcellus, 185, 293, 319,
  392
Tiber, river, 229, 239–40, 286, 287,
  387, 402
water supply, 238–9
Rome, suburbs
  grove of the Dea Dia, 285–7
  Temple of Fortuna Muliebris, 180–1,
    287
  villa of Livia at Prima Porta, 183, 303
Romulus, 11, 54, 253, 285, 286–7, 309n,
  315, 381, 389, 393, 394–5, 397,
  402, 404, 456
roof-tiles, 324–6

sacrifices, 65, 281–2, 285–96, 381, 449
St-Bertrand-de-Comminges, 139
Salamis, sea-battle of, 323
Salassi, 159
Sallust, Roman historian, 350
Salmon, E. T., 20
Salvius Otho, M., Roman emperor,
  466
Samos, 180n, 186, 469
Sardinia, Roman province, 246
Sardis, 470
Scheid, John, 198, 201, 275–99
Scriptores Historiae Augustae, as source,
  171–3
sculptural workshops, 456–64
Secular Games see *ludi saeculares*
Secular Hymn see *carmen saeculare*
Seleucus of Rhosus, 69, 73–4
sella curulis, 92, 408
Sempronius Atratinus, L., 156–7
senate
  in the imperial period, 1, 6–7, 9–11,
    14, 15, 21, 36–7, 39, 43, 44, 53, 58,
    83–7, 95–8, 100–2, 106–7, 109n,
    114, 117–18, 122, 126–9, 141–2,
    147, 153–4, 158, 168, 197, 207–11,
    218–22, 229–30, 236, 239, 241–6,
    247–9, 284, 288, 291, 295, 298,
    309n, 310–11, 314, 347, 356, 483,
    485, 486
  in the Republican period, 45–7, 82–3,
    92, 206
  in the triumviral period, 44, 62–3,
    66–70, 74–5, 86
senatus consulta, 98, 111, 117, 121, 126,
  162, 172, 205, 239, 244, 274, 371,
  357, 489

senatus consultum de Pisone patre,
     111–16, 121, 291
Servius, grammarian, 360, 412
sewers, 438
sexuality, construction of at Rome,
     334–80
shield-roundels *see clipei*
Sibylline books, 284, 357, 382
Sibylline oracles, 341
Sicily, Roman province, 4, 44, 51, 80,
     116, 313n, 367–8, 420, 484, 486
slaves, 5, 64, 71, 169, 238–9, 241–2,
     261–2, 330, 343, 361, 368, 469
  public slaves (*servi publici*), 239, 241
Sosius, C. (*cos.* 32 BC), 66, 318–19
source criticism, 411–12
Spain, 140, 141, 149, 155, 156, 158,
     209, 212, 233, 403, 420, 427–67
Sparta, 474
spolia opima, 46, 80, 287, 306, 402, 405
Statilius Taurus, T. (*cos.* 26 BC), 65, 67,
     107n
statues, 13, 145n, 184–5, 281–2, 295,
     298, 303–4, 314, 316, 368–70, 402,
     444, 455–62, 469
Stein, Arthur, 17
stola, dress of Roman matron, 167, 445
Strabo, geographer, 99, 145–6, 155, 469
Straub, J., 172–3
Suetonius, biographer, 85–6, 142, 155,
     203, 229–30, 239, 248–9, 284
Sugambri, 159, 160n, 161
sulcus primigenius, 432
Sulla *see* Cornelius Sulla, L.
sumptuary legislation, 177
sundial (*horologium*), in Campus
     Martius, 11–12, 138–9, 292, 317n
supplications, 149, 212, 364
Surrentum, 175
Syme, Sir Ronald, 16–22, 33–4, 37,
     40–59, 60, 149–52, 277, 358, 490,
     491
Syria, Roman province, 68, 112, 116,
     155, 157, 158, 209, 216, 246, 420

Tacitus, Roman historian, 6, 57–8, 80,
     82, 84, 126, 189–90, 216, 250,
     270–1, 405
Tarn, W. W., 16, 17
taxation, 5, 76, 105, 170, 203, 233–4,
     253, 258, 421, 469, 472, 473, 480
temples, 53, 67, 84, 138–40, 145, 148,
     156, 162, 181–3, 275, 281, 282–4,
     286–7, 290, 293, 308, 314, 316–20,
     323–4, 343, 352, 357–8, 361–2,
     371, 382, 392, 393–5, 397,
     399–402, 431, 441–7, 485, 486
Terentius Varro, M., 140, 383
theatres, 9–10, 65, 174, 177–8, 185, 293,
     319, 392, 424, 438–40, 448, 449,
     460–2, 465
Theocritus, Hellenistic poet, 338
Theophanes of Mytilene, 469
Thessalonica, 476
Thessaly and Thessalians, 478–9
Thrace, 157, 161
Thyatira, 480
Tiber, 229, 239–40, 286, 287, 387, 402
Tiberius, stepson and son-in-law of
     Augustus, Roman emperor, 5, 55,
     56, 98, 105, 115, 121, 123, 125–9,
     148–9, 154–5, 158, 161, 163, 166,
     181–2, 184–5, 212–13, 216, 220–1,
     222–3, 240, 274, 281, 291, 292,
     294n, 396, 466, 475, 483, 487,
     488–9
Tigranes, king of Armenia, 158
Timgad, 447
Tiridates, king of Parthia, 157
togate statues, 456–60
trade, 476, 480–1
Trajan, Roman emperor, 81, 141, 252,
     258, 297
Tralles, 480
transmission of property, at Rome,
     253–68
treasury, military *see aerarium militare*
treasury of Saturn *see aerarium Saturni*
trials, 471
tribunes of the plebs, 66, 100–3, 112,
     176, 241, 383, 484
tribunician power, 10, 36, 54, 79, 84, 98,
     99–107, 117–19, 119–29, 130n,
     200, 487, 488, 492–3
tribunician sacrosanctity, 177–9
Trillmich, W., 423–5, 427–67
triumphal arches, 138, 148, 282, 284,
     288, 290, 314, 362, 364
triumphal monuments, 430
triumphs, 13–14, 46–7, 80, 107, 138,
     144, 148–9, 156–7, 166, 212, 277,
     282, 288, 314, 319, 327, 344, 355,
     357–8, 360, 362, 365, 371, 372,
     392–3, 403, 406–10, 413, 432
triumvirate, 50, 54, 60–78, 170
triumviri monetales (moneyers), 107, 313
triumviri r(ei) p(ublicae) c(onstituendae),
     50, 54, 60–78, 170

trophies, Roman military, 13, 139, 311, 313, 315, 319, 321–5, 366, 429–32, 461
Tullius Cicero, M. (*cos.* 63 BC) *see* Cicero
Tullius Cicero, M. (*cos.* 30 BC), 64, 66
tutela (legal guardianship), 97–8, 176–7, 253, 255, 352
Tweedsmuir, Lord *see* Buchan, John
Tyre, 68, 481

urban cohorts, 240
urban plebs, 243
urban prefects, 240

Valerius Antias, Roman annalist, 411–12
Valerius Maximus, 258–9, 264
Valerius Maximus, M', 408, 411, 413
Varro *see* Terentius Varro, M.
Varus *see* Quinctilius Varus, P.
Velitrae, 1, 408
Velleius Paterculus, Roman historian, 2n, 13, 22n, 58, 62, 83–4, 112, 125n, 138, 141, 188, 192, 197, 216, 233, 354, 359, 403
Venus, cult of, 11, 71, 139, 175, 303, 316, 363, 366, 402
Venus Genetrix, cult of, 317, 343, 352, 371, 446
Venus Victrix, cult of, 183, 317
Verginius Rufus, L. (*cos.* AD 63, 69, 97), 217, 223
Verrius Flaccus, M., 411–13
Vespasian, Roman emperor, 237, 447
Vesta, cult of, 181
Vestal Virgins, 169n, 174, 176–7, 275, 288, 294n, 407–9, 414
veteran soldiers, 72, 208–9, 211, 214, 258

Via Appia, 236
Via Flaminia, 237
Via Latina, 237
vici (urban neighbourhoods) of Rome, 241, 276, 296–7, 312–13
vicomagistri, 241, 247, 297
vicoministri, 297
Victory, Roman goddess, 139–40, 308, 314–17, 321–32, 363, 366
vigiles see night-watch
violence, political at Rome, 7, 21, 61, 79
Virgil, Roman poet, 74, 75–6, 334, 342–4
  Aeneid, 174, 343–4, 349, 355, 372, 384–9, 393
  Georgics, 357–8
Virtus, cult of, 367
Vitruvius, 53, 86–7
Vonones, king of Parthia, 146
voting tribes, at Rome, 312–13
vows for the well-being of the *princeps*, 294

Wallace-Hadrill, Andrew, 25–6, 250–74
water supply *see* Rome, water supply
wills, 254, 256–68, 272
Wiseman, T. P., 308, 381–98
Wissowa, G., 278
women in Rome and the ancient world, 165–94, 335
Wyke, M., 307–8, 334–80

Xiphilinus, 128

Zanker, Paul, 23–4, 37, 282, 284, 304–5, 307, 403–4, 423, 464

EU representative:
Easy Access System Europe
Mustamäe tee 50, 10621 Tallinn, Estonia
Gpsr.requests@easproject.com

www.ingramcontent.com/pod-product-compliance
Lightning Source LLC
Chambersburg PA
CBHW070005010526
44117CB00011B/1430